The Corporeal Turn

AN INTERDISCIPLINARY READER

Maxine Sheets-Johnstone

imprint-academic.com

Published in the UK by Imprint Academic
PO Box 200, Exeter EX5 5YX, UK

Published in the USA by Imprint Academic
Philosophy Documentation Center
PO Box 7147, Charlottesville, VA 22906-7147, USA

ISBN 9 781845 401535

A CIP catalogue record for this book is available from the
British Library and US Library of Congress

To my grandchildren
Dylan, Brendan, Joshua, Vassilya, Erin

May you never run out of questions
about yourself or the world
and never shy from the challenge of answering them.

Contents

Acknowledgements

I gratefully acknowledge the following editors and publishing houses for their kind permission to include articles or chapters that appeared in an earlier publication: Nancy Stark Smith, editor of Contact Quarterly; Tomasz Komendzinksi, editor of *Theoria et Historia Scientiarum*, Arnold Berleant, editor of *Contemporary Aesthetics*; John Benjamins Publishing; Springer Publishing; Blackwell Publishing.

CHAPTER I (1979): '*Can* the Body Ransom Us?' *Contact Quarterly*, vol. 4/nos. 3–4 (1979), pp. 14–20.

CHAPTER II (1981/1999): 'Thinking in Movement,' *Journal of Aesthetics and Art Criticism* 39/4 (1981), pp. 399–407; an expanded version of the article appears as Chapter 12 of *The Primacy of Movement* (Amsterdam: John Benjamins, 1999).

CHAPTER III (1986): 'Existential Fit and Evolutionary Continuities,' *Synthese* 66 (1986), pp. 219–48.

CHAPTER IV (1986/1990): 'On the Conceptual Origin of Death,' *Philosophy and Phenomenological Research* 47/1 (1986), pp. 31–58; with minor revisions, the article appears as Chapter 8 of *The Roots of Thinking* (Philadelphia: Temple University Press, 1990).

CHAPTER V (1992/1996): 'Taking Evolution Seriously: A Matter of Primate Intelligence,' *Etica & Animali* 8 (1996), pp. 115–30. In its original form, this essay was presented at the American Philosophical Association Pacific Division Meeting in San Francisco in March 1991 under the title 'Taking Evolution Seriously.' Under the same title, the essay was published in *American Philosophical Quarterly* (29/4 [October 1992], pp. 343–52). With a specific and fine focus on The Great Ape Project and on the essay's invited inclusion in a special issue of *Etica & Animali* devoted to The Great Ape Project, I rewrote portions of the original text or added to it, beginning with the addition of a subtitle.

CHAPTER VI (1996): 'Surface Sensitivity and the Density of Flesh,' invited catalogue essay for *In the Flesh*, art exhibition at the Aldrich Museum of

Contemporary Art, Ridgefield, Connecticut, 1996, pp. 26–40. The present essay is an expanded version of the catalogue original.

CHAPTER VII (1998/1999): 'Consciousness: A Natural History,' *Journal of Consciousness Studies* 5, No. 3 (1998), pp. 260–94; the article appears as Chapter 2, Part I of *The Primacy of Movement* (Amsterdam: John Benjamins, 1999).

CHAPTER VIII (1999): 'Emotions and Movement: A Beginning Empirical-Phenomenological Analysis of Their Relationship,' *Journal of Consciousness Studies* 6, No. 11–12 (1999), pp. 259–77.

CHAPTER IX (1999): 'Sensory–Kinetic Understandings of Language: An Inquiry into Origins, *Evolution of Communication* 3:2 (1999), pp. 149–83.

CHAPTER X (2003): 'Kinesthetic Memory,' *Theoria et Historia Scientiarum: An International Journal for Interdisciplinary Studies* (published by the Nicolas Copernicus University Press in Torun, Poland), special issue on 'Embodiment and Awareness,' ed. Shaun Gallagher and Natalie Depraz, VII/1 (2003), pp. 69–92.

CHAPTER XI (2004): 'On Bacteria, Corporeal Representation, Neandertals, and Martha Graham.' In *In the Beginning: Origins of Semiosis*, ed. Morana Alac and Patrizia Violi. Bologna, Italy: Brepols Turnhout, 2004, pp. 105–36.

CHAPTER XII (2005): '"Man Has Always Danced": Forays into an Art Largely Forgotten by Philosophers', *Contemporary Aesthetics* (electronic journal), vol. 2, no. 1, 2005.

CHAPTER XIII (2005): 'What Are We Naming?' In *Body Image and Body Schema*, ed. Helena De Preester and Veroniek Knockaert. Amsterdam/Philadelphia: John Benjamins Publishing, 2005, pp. 211–31. (This chapter was originally presented as the invited Keynote Address at a conference titled 'Body Schema and Body Image: (Neuro)phenomenological, (Neuro)psychoanalytical and Neuroscientific Perspectives,' held in Ghent, Belgium, in 2003.

Note:
'The Kinetic Basis of the Biological Disposition to Sense-Making: Further Steps toward an Evolutionary Semantics' (Chapter XIV) was given as a guest lecture at the Haskins Language Laboratory at Yale University in 2003; 'On the Challenge of Languaging Experience' (Chapter XV) was given as a guest lecture at the German–American Institute in Heidelberg, Germany in 2005.

Introduction

The Corporeal Turn spans a diversity of issues, questions, concepts, and relationships deriving from and centering on the body and bodily life. The essays range across topics in the humanities, the arts, and the sciences. The animate is their abiding thematic. Given the quintessential relationship of the animate to life itself, it is not surprising that conceptual and ideational links should exist among the essays, their diversity and official academic homes notwithstanding.

The purpose of *The Corporeal Turn* is to document in a single text the impressive array of investigations possible with respect to the body and bodily life, and to show that, whatever the specific topic being examined, it is a matter of fathoming and elucidating complex and subtle structures of animate meaning. The first thirteen essays were originally published as distinct articles at some point over the past twenty-six years. In light of this history, the book is clearly not seeking support for a revolutionary new movement. A corporeal turn has already been taken, and by a multitude of people beside the present author. The turn, however, is far from complete, and in more than one sense. The essays are not an up-to-the-minute review of a variety of perspectives on the body.[1] Indeed, with one exception—Chapter Six, which was written in conjunction with, and thus originally had references to, a specific art exhibition—the previously published essays have not been appreciably altered. They are rather, as indicated, a documentation of a diversity of perspectives on the body, all of which warrant assiduous and continuing examination, awakening continued curiosity and interest, and leading people across a variety of disciplines to investigate further. The corporeal turn is indeed envisioned as an ever-expanding, continuous, and open-ended spiral of inquiry in which deeper and deeper understandings are forged, understandings that in

---

1   Attention, however, should be called to two important and in many ways essential additions to Chapter XIII, "What Are We Naming?", the first detailed and supplemented with references in note # 1, the second detailed and supplemented with references in note #4.

each instance themselves call out for deeper and deeper inquiries. The two new essays are testimony to this open-ended spiral of inquiry.

No ideology attaches to this endeavor; that is, no set of beliefs or rules apply other than a belief in experience as the grounding source of knowledge and a dedicated examination of experience as the testing ground of one's knowledge. That such dedicated examination requires methodological acuity and thoroughness, and that such acuity and thoroughness themselves require training should go without saying, though it might be appropriate to note explicitly that cursory or expeditious observations and third-person observations on the order of naive verbal reports are inadequate to the methodological task. Dedicated examination of experience furthermore requires an openness to interdisciplinary investigations and this because experience is historically embedded, not only in the classic phenomenological sense of sedimentations that provide experience a context of past meanings and of horizons that provide it a situated framework in the living world, but in both the ontogenetic sense of developmental capacities and the phylogenetic sense of evolutionary capacities, both of which provide experience a background of natural life-sustaining possibilities and realizations.

The historical background of the corporeal turn itself constitutes an important dimension of its open-ended spiraling character. The humanities and human sciences were the spawning ground of two fundamental conceptual shifts in the twentieth century: the earlier linguistic turn and the later corporeal turn. In each instance, attention turned to something long taken for granted. With the corporeal turn, however, it was a matter not only of attending to something heretofore simply assumed and largely ignored, but of correcting something misrepresented for centuries. Through its Cartesian legacy, the body was consistently presented as mere material handmaiden of an all-powerful mind, a necessary but ultimately discountable aspect of cognition, intelligence, and even affectivity. I elsewhere characterized this misrepresentation as a 350-year-old wound, and later pointed out that the wound was actually being covered over — not healed — by the lexical band-aid of "embodiment". The 350-year-old wound is in fact still in need of healing, even as, ironically, it is being reopened and widened in this twenty-second century by reductionist thinking that collapses body into brain — *the* brain — thereby bypassing its living reality. The task of bringing presuppositions to light and of correcting past and present misrepresentations is formidable. The corporeal turn and the challenges it presents have thus hardly ended.

In bringing together diverse investigations undertaken in response to the challenges, *The Corporeal Turn* also seeks to validate a claim. I introduced the phrase "corporeal turn" in 1990 in *The Roots of Thinking*, describing the turn in terms similar to those above. But I claimed there too and in later writings as well that just as the linguistic turn produced extraordinary insights, so a corporeal turn would surely do no less. The essays gathered here attempt to validate that claim from quite distinct perspectives. They in fact encompass a triumvirate of perspectives — phenomenological, phylogenetic, and ontogenetic — upon what was once commonly called "the human condition". Though the specific concerns and immediate subject matter of each perspective is distinct, the aim of each is to elucidate origins. In this sense, the separate perspectives are thematically convergent. But they are also mutually illuminating. The importance of their convergent concern with origins is indeed substantively heightened by their shared (if not always explicitly acknowledged) foundational concern with the body. A veritable corporeal turn in fact necessarily spans all three perspectives because the body is the foundation — or, to borrow a phrase from Husserl, "the root soil" — of all three. As distinct disciplines, phenomenology, phylogeny, and ontogeny testify to rich and complex dimensions of bodily being. As linked interdisciplinary fields of study, they attest to the importance of exploring the living realities of corporeal life and of understanding in the deepest sense in each instance what it means to be the bodies we are. It bears repeating that the essays gathered here are far from exhausting the depth of these many meanings. What they demonstrate is the range and diversity of the corporeal turn as they progressively examine particular topics within its compass.

The essays are arranged in chronological order, a chapter ordering that serendipitously resulted in underscoring a spiral of inquiry in that a question constitutes the title of the first and last previously published essay. In view of the interdisciplinary character of the essays as well as the diversity of topics covered, a brief but sufficiently detailed synopsis of each chapter will be given. The synopses will attest to the basic conceptual affinities and relationships among the chapters. It might be helpful first, however, to cluster the essays under general topics. A reader might thereby gain a sense of the general themes and overall content of the book, and, if so inclined, begin his or her reading by selecting a topic of particular interest.[2]

---

2 I thank the two anonymous reviewers of this book, each of whom suggested in a different way the helpfulness of a topical introduction to the book. An ordering by general topics should aid the reader in navigating what might otherwise seem an overwhelmingly wide range of interdisciplinary studies. In what follows, I have in fact utilized the well-chosen topical headings suggested by one of the reviewers. The possible usefulness of a topical ordering notwithstanding, I should perhaps note explicitly that I have retained my original chronological sequencing to preserve and underscore the open-ended spiraling character of the corporeal turn.

Four chapters may be grouped under the heading of *Living Bodies*:

- Chapter I: *Can* the Body Ransom Us?
- Chapter III: Existential Fit and Evolutionary Continuities
- Chapter IV: On the Conceptual Origin of Death
- Chapter VI: Surface Sensitivity and the Density of Flesh

Two chapters may be grouped under the heading of *The Genesis of Consciousness*:

- Chapter V: Taking Evolution Seriously: A Matter of Primate Intelligence
- Chapter VII: Consciousness: A Natural History

Four chapters may be grouped under the heading of *The Primacy of Movement*:

- Chapter II: Thinking in Movement
- Chapter VIII: Emotions and Movement: An Empirical-Phenomenological Analysis of Their Relationship
- Chapter X: Kinesthetic Memory
- Chapter XII: "Man Has Always Danced": Forays into an Art Largely Forgotten by Philosophers

Five chapters may be grouped under the heading of an *Evolutionary and Phenomenological Semiotics*:

- Chapter IX: Sensory-Kinetic Understandings of Language: An Inquiry into Origins
- Chapter XI: On Bacteria, Corporeal Representation, Neandertals, and Martha Graham: Steps toward an Evolutionary Semantics
- Chapter XIII: What Are We Naming?
- Chapter XIV: The Kinetic Basis of the Biological Disposition to Sense-Making: Further Steps toward an Evolutionary Semantics
- Chapter XV: On the Challenge of Languaging Experience

The first chapter—"*Can* the Body Ransom Us?"—poses a question prompted by an article titled "The Mysterious New Novel" by literary critic Daniel Stern, who remarked that D. H. Lawrence knew that "when the world is too much with us, the body ransoms us." Lawrence's conviction is both profound and provocative. Which body is it that might ransom us? The one identified as a machine or as a technological marvel? The narrowly-conceived biological body of molecular parts and neurological happenings? "*Can* the Body Ransom Us" is a reflective essay that attempts to pinpoint *the primordial first-person body* that we initially are when we come into the world, the body that in the course of Western adult living often comes to be objectified, not just sexually pasted over with baubles, for example, but medically and politically de-humanized and thereby trivialized or forgotten. The essay asks what ransoming means, what it accomplishes, and why, if we can be ransomed from a world that is "too much with us", it is the body that can ransom us.

The first chapter puts the living body center stage. "Thinking in Movement", the second chapter, puts the full animate character of the living body on stage. The chapter opens with a phenomenological account of a paradigmatic instance of thinking in movement and proceeds to a consideration of two assumptions, each of which might impair an unbiased reading of the account: the Cartesian assumption that minds think and bodies "do", and the widespread assumption that there is no thinking outside of language or apart from some kind of symbolic system. Analysis of the paradigmatic experience shows that thinking and moving are not separate happenings but aspects of a *kinetic bodily logos* attuned to an evolving dynamic situation. It shows further that thinking in movement involves no symbolic counters but is tied to an on-going qualitatively experienced dynamic in which movement possibilities arise and dissolve. The analysis accords in fundamental ways with psychological studies showing that an infant's initial concepts are linked to dynamic events, to kinetic experiences of both its own movement and movement in its surrounding world. Drawing initially on child psychologist Lois Bloom's extensive studies of the transition from infancy to language, the chapter shows that studies of infants indirectly affirm that infants think in movement. It discusses psychologist Jerome Bruner's lengthy research and writings on infant/child development, his essential finding being that the principal interest of infants — an interest that carries over into language — centers on agentivity and action. It consults the clinical findings of psychiatrist Daniel N. Stern, specifically those identifying nonverbal behaviors that never become linguistically encoded but that have variable affective tones and that articulate intercorporeal intentions. Through such citings of the literature on infant and child development, the chapter shows that, rather than designating the period before language *pre-linguistic*, we should speak of the advent of language as the *post-kinetic*. The phenomenon of thinking in movement is then put in phylogenetic perspective. The chapter shows that instances of thinking in movement abound in the literature on nonhuman animal life, as when ethologists describe how killdeer move in distinctive ways to protect their young from harm, when field biologists describe the spatially and temporally complex food-supplying behaviors of sand wasps, and when laboratory biologists describe escape behaviors of creatures such as paramecium and fan worms. In each instance, as the chapter demonstrates, a natural kinetic intelligence, a kinetic bodily logos, is at work in each instance, an intelligence that cannot be written off either as mere instinct, i.e., as robotic, or as merely an adaptive mechanism. The intelligence or logos is an elemental biological character of life, a dimension of animate form that, however written between the lines, is confirmed in the writings of zoologists, primatologists, and ethologists. The implicit confirmation is not that animals think in terms of *behavior*, but that they think in terms of kinetically dynamic patterns: in terms of movement. From this vantage point, behaviors *evolve* only because behaviors are essentially complex dynamic patternings of movement, and movement being the mother tongue of all animate forms, thinking in movement is both a primary fact and a perpetual possibility of animate life.

As the title suggests, "Existential Fit and Evolutionary Continuities" examines the body from an integrated evolutionary-existential perspective. The chapter questions received wisdom in terms of the common existential distinction between a "physical" body and a "lived" body and finds that physical and lived bodies are in fact quintessentially coherent; animate forms that survive across evolutionary time are thus properly described *existentially fit*. The chapter shows how this coherency or fit is assumed in Merleau-Ponty's concept of *propriety* and how experiences of sheer physicality—lovemaking and dancing being taken as examples—belie received wisdom. It goes on to show in finer detail how tactility and movement, which is to say the tactile-kinesthetic body, are at the core of experiences of sheer physicality and how such experiences are not wholly unique to humans, hence how evolutionary continuities are apparent. In doing so, it stresses the importance of understanding the lives of living creatures in *sensory-kinetic* terms, which ultimately means in terms of a certain livability in the world, a certain domain of "I cans" which are the differential expression of a species' existential fit.

"On the Conceptual Origin of Death" turns finer attention to psychological understandings of the body and of what it means to be animate. It poses the question of how the concept of death could have arisen and shows how the emergence of the concept is contingent on the presence of a certain Other, an Other in the form of a physical body perceived and ultimately conceived *as such*. It begins with an inquiry as to why nonhuman animals do not have a concept of death and in turn considers both how language might mistakenly be taken as being essential to the concept and how a behaviorist explanation of the concept would mistakenly rest on the simple awareness of an inert, unresponsive body. What is in part requisite to an answer to the question are detailed descriptive accounts of nonhuman animals, both in their general everyday intercorporeal relations with others and in their specific encounter with a dead other, and a subsequent deciphering in sensory-kinetic terms the nature of their experiences. Among many other facets of corporeal life that are uncovered, this hermeneutics of nonhuman animate life discloses how, in the everyday visual spectacle of fellow creatures about them, nonhuman animals experience not physical objects but certain portentous physiognomies of one kind or another: threatening, caring, playful, fearful, and so on. A visual material body is not abstractively separated or separable from a living body; hence there is no physical body *as such*. The chapter moves from this hermeneutics to a Husserlian phenomenology, specifically, the phenomenology of the concept of a *punctuated existence*, an existence that is not simply that of a now inanimate Other but that is mine too, the concept being generated by an awareness that my life too is on the line, that I too will be transfigured by death into a purely visual body, a silent and unmoving physical form. Prominent in this analysis is the experience of an analogical apperception *manqué*: the other-in-death presents a stillness that fails to accord analogically with my own livingness. It is an Other with whom no commerce of any kind is now possible. The descriptive analytic traces out the temporalities implicit in this experience, singling out both a communal temporality that is now ended — what Husserl terms a "common time form" — and an individual temporality that defines my own life and death.

While the previous chapter demonstrates an evolutionary discontinuity between human and nonhuman animals in terms of the concept of death, "Taking Evolution Seriously: A Matter of Primate Intelligence" constitutes a rejoinder to those who would disavow or take issue with evolutionary continuities. The chapter sets forth a critique-in-reverse of anthropocentrism by tracing out the intimate relationship between criticisms of anthropomorphic descriptions of nonhuman animals and an anthropocentric privileging of humans. It opens with a critical look at standard philosophical practice in the philosophy of biology. In its focal concentration on molecular genetics, units of selection, and the like, standard philosophical practice neglects human evolution, overlooks the fact that human language and human rationality are themselves products of evolution, and not infrequently tends to set up an "Us" and "Them" division between humans and nonhumans, sometimes even proposing a difference in kind and not in degree. The essay shows how appreciations of the *historical* dimension of evolution is mandatory and how a selective reading of Darwin compromises such appreciations. It in turn poses the question of why Darwin's organic and evolutionary wholism is not taken seriously and goes on to explain how anthropocentrism rather than anthropomorphism is at the core of the problem. Interpreting nonhuman creaturely life in ways that consistently exalt the measure of humanness preserves the distinction of humans as special creations and deprecates not only evolutionary continuities between humans and nonhumans but organic continuities as well. As a result of this anthropocentric act, all capacities customarily

associated with *mind* are divorced from the body and regarded special creations along with their unique human possessors. Pursuing a Darwinian
course instead, the essay asks two seminal questions: can bodies evolve in
the absence of mental powers? and correlatively, can mental powers
evolve in the absence of bodies? It becomes clear in the course of answering these questions that anthropocentrists are lacking in objectivity. The
constructional activities of nonhuman animals, their newly initiated acts,
and their deceptive behaviors, for example, belie the notion that bodies
can evolve in the absence of mental powers or that mental powers can
evolve in the absence of bodies. To acknowledge as much is to acknowledge a historical process infinitely larger than one's own human self, and,
in effect, to acknowledge one's species-specific place in nature and the ties
that bind all living bodies in a common creaturehood. Recognizing ourselves and conceiving ourselves as *primates* is thus a matter of primate
intelligence.

"Surface Sensitivity and the Density of Flesh", originally an invited catalogue essay written for an art exhibition titled *In the Flesh*, examines the
relationship between animate flesh and the flesh of objects. It begins by
linking the sensuous aesthetics of skin with the sensuous density of flesh,
and then, by extension, linking the sensuous aesthetics of surface with the
sensuous density of artworks. By probing the meaning of surfaces and
skin — of "coverings" — and thereby coming to an appreciation of surface
sensitivity and tactility, the essay deepens a combined evolutionary-existential appreciation of living bodies. It takes seriously the fact that a diversity of life is first of all a diversity of *form*, form that is realized in virtue of a
membranous covering of some kind by which animate beings are separate
from their surrounding world and at the same time sensuously connected
and responsive to it. In focusing on form in this way, the chapter shows
how surface sensitivities mark not only the beginnings of life but the
beginnings of drawing as well: to draw is to animate a surface and thereby
bring it to life. The evolutionary and aesthetic significances of paleolithic
cave art demonstrate the intimate connections between animate flesh and
the flesh of objects and how these intimate connections attune us
affectively to the world. In particular, when humans lose sight of these
connections, they develop a thick skin and lose touch with the sensuous
density of their own flesh and that of others. They become not merely aesthetically blind but blind to the ways in which violations of flesh de-ani-
mate the animate, severing those bodily ties that bind them in a common
humanity and a common creaturehood.

Chapter Seven elucidates the animate along a particular evolutionary
line: a natural history of consciousness. The history in fact sets forth a more
finely detailed and extensive study of surface sensitivity and a density of

flesh. It lays out the natural history in terms of animate form, showing consistently that the question of "how consciousness arises in matter" is a misconceived question. It critically assesses reductively materialist renditions of consciousness and takes responsivity seriously as "a fundamental and almost universal characteristic" of life. It shows in turn how the common practice of using quote marks (e.g., an animal "knows") to differentiate among cognitive capacities in living organisms is without justification, and demonstrates at length how the Socratic imperative "know thyself" is a built-in biological matrix that has its evolutionary roots in proprioception. It specifies how the surface recognition sensitivity of protists and bacteria is essentially a tactile phenomenon definitive of a consciousness of something outside oneself, and how animate forms, from the earliest invertebrates onward, are structured in ways that are sensitive to movement, thus how, with respect to the animal kingdom, consciousness is fundamentally a corporeal consciousness resonant with tactile-kinetic sensitivities. Finally, it presents evidence showing that external organs of proprioception were internalized in the course of evolution eventuating in a kinesthetically-tethered corporeal consciousness, and further, how these internally-placed organs constitute an epistemological gateway, a gateway holding open the possibility of more complex affective and cognitive lives. The chapter thus demonstrates how, in truth, what Daniel Dennett calls "The Reality of Selves" has its roots not in words but in corporeal consciousness. Through all of its critical assessments, questionings, and analyses, the chapter shows how, by paying attention to corporeal matters of fact as they are articulated in the natural history of life, and by hewing to sensory-kinetic analyses of these corporeal matters of fact, one is led inexorably to understandings of consciousness that are rooted in animate form. It concludes by briefly identifying three implications, the first having to do with received wisdom concerning the chronological relationship of unconsciousness to consciousness; the second with present-day fixations on *the brain* to the exclusion of serious in-depth attention to natural history; the third with armchair pronouncements—upon consciousness and upon creatures such as lobsters and scallops—that issue from philosophical ivory towers and that lack an informed and requisite evolutionary backbone.

Chapter Eight, "Emotion and Movement: A Beginning Empirical-Phenomenological Analysis of Their Relationship", begins by presenting three methodologically distinct empirical studies of emotion, each of which carries forward Darwin's insights into the emotions, vindicates Roger Sperry's finding that the brain is an organ of and for movement, and testifies to the ties between affectivity and the tactile-kinesthetic body. The studies are methodologically as well as theoretically unique, the first being carried out by medical doctor and neuropsychiatrist Edmund Jacobson, who formulated a rigorous auto-sensory observation method, the second by psychiatrist Nina Bull, who formulated an hypnotic methodological approach, and the third by psychologist Joseph de Rivera, who formulated a geometric methodological approach through an analysis of kinetic forms of emotion. A phenomenological analysis of movement deepens these substantive empirical findings by showing how the dynamic character of movement gives rise to *kinetic qualia*. Analysis of the qualitative structure of movement shows in turn how motion and emotion are *dynamically congruent*. Three descriptive accounts of the experience of fear are presented — phenomenological, ethological, and literary — to demonstrate the dynamic congruency, the phenomenological one being of a person being pursued by an unknown assailant at night in a deserted area of a city, the ethological one being of a greylag goose observed by Konrad Lorenz, the literary one being of a character in a novel by William Faulkner. All three descriptive accounts of fear testify to the fact that emotions move us, and move us in ways quintessentially linked to our tactile-kinesthetic bodies. Five implications follow from the analysis, including the implication that movement is not equivalent to behavior, that experience is not physiological activity, and that a brain is not a body.

The ninth chapter focuses on an evolutionary semantics from the viewpoint of the origin of human language. "Sensory-Kinetic Understandings of Language: An Inquiry into Origins" shows how archetypal corporeal-kinetic forms and interanimate relations among animal species are rooted in species-specific tactile-kinesthetic invariants, and how these bodily invariants ground interanimate meanings. In the course of demonstrating archetypes and invariants, the chapter shows how often-used explanatory terms such as "schema" and "embodied image schemata" fall short of capturing the real-life qualitative movement dynamics that constitute communicative acts, whether a matter of nonhuman animal displays or of verbal language. The chapter specifies how the significance of these dynamics to the origin of language was recognized more than a hundred years ago by biologist Alfred Wallace and how the significance has been more recently attested to by linguist Mary LeCron Foster's research on primordial language. The chapter shows how the studies of both Wallace and Foster testify to a *kinetic semantics* in which movement and meaning are of a piece. The chapter furthermore shows how analogical thinking is modeled on the body and how *corporeal* rather than *prelinguistic* concepts structure animate meaning. Finally, the chapter shows how syntax in the most elementary sense is a kinetic phenomenon. It describes how kinetic syntactical relationships underlie nonhuman animal communications such as male-male baboon greetings, and how they underlie if/then relational concepts that develop in infancy such as "if I close my eyes, it gets dark". It thereby shows how the sequential ordering of human speech derives from everyday sequential patternings of movement in animate life. On the basis of its multiple investigations into language, the chapter concludes by underscoring the strong empirical validity of a sensory-kinetic approach to understandings of the origin of language.

Chapter Ten—"Kinesthetic Memory"—might be said to address the question of how we do what we do. It investigates the nature of habit and its basis in a kinetic dynamics. Central to its investigations are the writings of famed Russian neurologist Aleksandr Romanovich Luria, specifically those writings in which Luria uses the term *kinetic melody*—and *kinaesthetic melody*—to describe the successful accomplishment of some task or to explain how a complex sequential activity unfolds. Luria's writings elucidate both experiential and neurological dimensions of kinetic melodies, showing, for example, how they are tethered to kinaesthetic afference and to temporal understandings of movement, that is, understandings of how muscular innervations and denervations are temporally ordered in the performance of any skilled movement—what Luria more generally terms "complex sequential activity"—and how it is their ordering that makes skilled movement possible. Through related phenomenological analyses of movement, the chapter goes on to show how, in the course of our everyday lives, we kinetically instantiate what we already know kinesthetically. A critique of doctrines that occlude understandings of kinesthetic memory plays an equal role in the chapter's investigations and has several anchor points. The first has to do with a questioning of the term "motor"—as in the labels "motor behavior" and "motor control"; the second with an examination of Merleau-Ponty's notion of a motor intentionality; the third with an inquiry into the meaning and conceptual propriety of the terms "body image" and "body schema"; the fourth with a discussion of the conceptual liabilities and underpinnings of a pointillist conception of movement, a conception that has seemingly been embedded in Western thought since Descartes and is still very much alive today. The liabilities of a pointillist conception are highlighted at the end of the chapter by a comparison of Merleau-Ponty's and Merce Cunningham's account of how one learns a dance. The comparison shows that pointillist conceptions fail to capture the body-kinetic dynamics that animate movement presents and that Luria's kinetic/kinaesthetic melodies, in contrast, capture just that.

By examining the evolutionary record from the perspective of sense-making, in the double sense of making sense of the world and making sense in what one does and says, "On Bacteria, Corporeal Representation, Neandertals, and Martha Graham" testifies to a semiotic continuity linking the evolutionary history of signs to the evolutionary history of symbol-making. A Peircean semiotic system recognizes an interpretant within its logic of signs but falls short of an evolutionary semantics, in large measure because its central concern is ontological rather than epistemological; it focuses more on rule-bound semiotic relationships than on sense-making organisms themselves, particularly sense-making organisms as originators of meaning. After reviewing differences between a Peircean semiotics and a Husserlian semantics, and following an exemplification of the distinction in a critique of anthropologist Terrence Deacon's account of the origin of human language, the chapter shows how semiosis has a history in the life of living forms all the way back to bacteria, specifically, in the phenomenon of surface recognition sensitivity, a phenomenon in which meanings are tactilely mediated. The chapter proceeds to show how corporeal representation in the form of morphological features is the source of a visual semantics, markers of meaning whereby animals distinguish one another with respect to age, for example, and sex. It shows further how kinetic corporeal representation is yet another source of meaning within an evolutionary semantics, animals symbolizing the spatio-kinetic dynamics of their own kinetic/tactile-kinesthetic experiences, as in the classic instance of a honey-bee's *Tanzsprache*, in the tongue-flicking sexual gestures of female howler monkeys, and in the linguistic root forms of primordial language. Such forms of kinetic corporeal representation constitute a kinetic semantics in which the body functions as a semantic template, meanings being analogically articulated along the lines of the body. In such instances, meanings are symbolized. But analogical articulations along the lines of the body do not always result in symbolization, as the paleolithic production of stone tools shows. While paleoanthropologists consistently point out that stone tools replaced teeth and in turn often identify stone tools as symbols of teeth, stone tools are not symbols. The chapter specifies the advent of symbols and the relationship between analogical thinking and symbolization through reference to both Neandertals and Martha Graham. With respect to the former, it shows that one can hardly denigrate the semiotic abilities and acuity of *Homo neandertalis* on the basis of the species being big and brawny rather than tall and gracile like *Homo sapiens sapiens*, characterizing their tools, for example, in unflattering ways and their speech as being "simple" and "slow". With respect to the latter, it shows how Martha Graham's dance *Lamentation* eloquently exemplifies a created symbolic form, thus how a kinetic semantics not only constitutes a further form of sense-making at the heart of an evolutionary semantics, but opens a vast realm of symbolizing possibilities.

As its title indicates, Chapter Twelve focuses attention on dance and the fact that philosophers have had comparatively little to say of the art of dance. The fact is surprising given the range of people both inside and out-side of dance who have claimed that "man has always danced". The adage was particularly common in the 1930s, 1940s, and 1950s when modern dance was being born and introduced into educational systems. The aim of the chapter is to substantiate the claim by an inquiry into the origins of dance, its central concern hinging on the word *always*, any specific linkage to males deriving from that central concern. The chapter opens with a com-parison of painter and dancer in light of Merleau-Ponty's claim that in painting, the painter "takes his body with him" and "shows how things become things, how the world becomes world". It then documents the popularity of the claim that "man has always danced", citing dancers, dance educators, poets, and art historians, and in turn taking up psycholo-gist Havelock Ellis's evolutionary perspective on the adage. It follows through on Ellis's evolutionary perspective by documenting what Jane Goodall terms a male chimpanzee's "bipedal swagger" and what another primatologist terms a male chimpanzee's "short dance". The described male movement pattern lends support to Ellis's thesis that dance origi-nated in "love dances" and is the oldest art. On the basis of this phylogen-etic evidence, the chapter raises the question of the pan-culturality of dance: what it is about humans that generates dance across cultures? The chapter proceeds to show how bipedality, a qualitative kinetics, rhythm, and play enter into and affirm both evolutionary continuities and the pan-culturality of dance, and further, that the realization of dance as an art form is an extraordinary dimension of an evolutionary semantics, a kinetic semantics anchored in species-specific tactile-kinesthetic invariants. Through this kinetic semantics, dancers are able to capture and communi-cate ineffable qualia of life, precisely as exemplified in Graham's "Lamentation".

The thirteenth chapter, "What Are We Naming?", questions the termi-nological and conceptual propriety of the labels "body schema" and "body image" and specifies the correlative challenges the labels pose: the challenge of languaging experience and the challenge of being true to the truths of experience. What the terms and concepts ostensibly attempt to explain is "how we do what we do", that is, how we move about the world knowledgeably, effectively, and efficiently. The chapter points out how misconceptions of movement—the idea that we have "sensations" of movement, that movement is a change of position, that movement is sim-ply behavior—not only abound in academic literature as in the popular mind, but obfuscate the dynamic realities of movement, realities well doc-umented in ontogenetical studies and by dynamic systems theorists. The chapter proceeds to show in detail how and why "body schema" and "body image" are misleading terms, the former conjuring, for example, something static rather than dynamic and postural rather than kinetic, the latter conjuring, for example, something visual and imagined rather than tactilely and kinetically perceived. Reification and reductionism are part and parcel of the terminological and conceptual muddle and belie the kinetic melodies that inform our lives. The chapter shows that creating a structure to explain a function or creating a package by way of "embodied experience" to describe the felt spatio-temporal dynamics of animate life is to fall short of meeting the challenge of languaging experience and to be untrue to the truths of experience. Insofar as the aim of "body schema" is essentially to explain neurologically "how we do what we do", the more apt term and concept points toward neuromuscular sequencing, hence toward *corporeal-kinetic patterning*. Correlatively, insofar as the aim of "body image" is essentially to describe how we experience ourselves doing what we do, the more apt term and concept points toward bodily-felt meaning, hence toward *corporeal-kinetic intentionality*. In both instances, not just the spatial nature but the temporal nature of movement is recognized. Indeed, the moving nature of time and the fleeting nature of movement are given their due.

When we ask, "What Are We Naming?", we give voice both to the fact that language is not experience and to a question whose answer is — *mirabile dictu* — foundationally anchored in that same first-person body that has the power to ransom us when the world is too much with us. The previous synopses show that the chapters are all so anchored. It is thus not surprising that they should give ample evidence of the conceptual ties noted at the beginning of this Introduction: sensory-kinetic understandings, surface sensitivity, an evolutionary semantics, a kinetic semantics, "how we do what we do", movement patterns, corporeal concepts, a kinetic dynamics, body schema, body image, kinetic melody — all and more are recurrent sub-themes within the all-embracing theme of the animate. The two new chapters carry forward these conceptual ties that bind the whole at the same time that they extend the spirit as well as the spiral of inquiry in fresh and distinctive ways.

Chapter Fourteen, "The Kinetic Basis of the Biological Disposition to Sense-Making: Further Steps toward an Evolutionary Semantics" addresses the question of how interanimate meanings are forged. It centers attention not on the "sender" but on the "recipient" insofar as a sender can gesticulate or vocalize in seemingly endless new ways, ostensibly "making sense" in this novel way and that, but until the individual to whom the novel gesticulations and vocalizations are addressed ratifies their meaning, making sense of them in a sensibly responsive way, the gesticulations and vocalizations remain socially meaningless. The question of how interanimate meanings are forged thus becomes basically a question of how a recipient makes sense of sense-makings. Taking an initial evolutionary perspective on the question, and drawing on examples from primate life, the chapter shows how sense-making originates in species-specific kinetic understandings emanating from a common body of movement, hence from a common body of tactile-kinesthetic invariants. On the basis of this evolutionary analysis, the chapter proceeds to a consideration of ontogenetic sense-makings. In particular, it shows how experimental evidence demonstrating success in reading to be contingent on a child's awareness of phonemics, specifically on his or her ability to make that awareness "consciously available," is at bottom a matter of articulatory gestures; that is, success in reading is contingent on a range of experiences of movement, including an infant's awareness of itself as a sound-maker and hearer of speech sounds long before it begins to speak, much less read. As experimental and clinical studies of infants show, infants ratify in a kinetically responsive way the gestures and vocalizations of adults. They thereby enter into a commonly shared world structured in a kinetic dynamics. Movement indeed structures the learning of any language. Whatever the particular sense modality of shared meanings—tactile, aural, or visual—it is consistently tied to the common sensible that is movement. It is not surprising, then, that articulatory gestures that structure phonemic awareness undergird the developmental passage from an aural world of speech to a visual world of reading: visual figures awaken a lingual kinetic dynamics.

The final chapter, "On the Challenge of Languaging Experience" presents an in-depth case study of experience—the experience of inside(s)—in an attempt to demonstrate in livingly present ways the actual challenge that experience presents to language. It does so after having discussed and exemplified both the inadequacy of everyday language to capture the dynamics of experience and the waywardness of thinking that concepts are language-dependent, and after having highlighted—by way of William Shakespeare—how, by giving voice to insides in a language that is precisely *not* everyday language, one rises to the challenge of languaging experience. The case study examines the experience of insides from four distinct perspectives: that of infants; of paleolithic cave art; of breath, pneuma, and spiritus—all of which are connected with warmth and life; and of the shadow, as described by Jung in his psychoanalytic and as exposed by Shakespeare in his languaging of interiority. The perspectives show that the challenge of languaging experience lies in the intrinsically dynamic nature of emotions and movement, and that being true to the truths of experience hinges on a methodology proper to the task. Whether a matter of phenomenology or phenomenologically-informed descriptions, or of a literary imagination, the methodology requires stepping back from habitual and conventional languagings that objectify and name, and focusing attention instead and from the beginning on the dynamic nonlinguistic nature of experience itself.

A final introductory thought may be added that turns on the relationship of inquiry to interdisciplinary studies. In exploring fundamental realities of life itself, one finds more often than not that those realities exceed the bounds of a single discipline — whatever that discipline might be — and that to pursue those explorations is necessarily to open to wider and wider vistas in which it is not so much conclusive answers one seeks as comprehensive understandings adequate to the realities themselves.

Chapter I

Can the Body Ransom Us?

Daniel Stern, in an essay, "The Mysterious New Novel", stated that several contemporary writers "know something D.H. Lawrence knew: when the world is too much with us, the body ransoms us" (Stern, 1971, p. 29). In the eight years since the essay was published, it appears that more and more people have come upon that same knowledge. The body has come of age: not only is it permissible, one might even say that it is popular nowadays to be a body. Much time, energy, and money are being invested in it, all the way from T'ai Chi to massage parlors and then some. If redemption it be, transactions for ransoming are running apace.

Is the investment sound? And what kind of security is it buying? Why the body? *Can* it ransom us? Has it indeed the mysterious possibilities that Stern suggests?

In the past year, the body was star of its own television special, "The Incredible Machine." In the past year also, Time-Life Books offered a new publication in its Science Library series: *The Body*, which was billed as "The most amazing machine ever created." We were urged to "learn how it works ... what science has in store for its future."

Is this the body that might ransom us?

Hardly. But not because a certain popularity has eroded its erstwhile mysteries.

While the incredible machine has become less and less a mystery, the precision and details of its functioning and structure remain awesome: 20 billion cell divisions take place daily; 500 million red cells are gathered in one drop of blood. Can such phenomena fail to instill in us a sense of wonder? The mystery may be vanishing but its aura of fascination and bafflement is not dispelled.

Still, the machine is *out there*, a second-hand body in a third-person world. Incredible or not, it is something I can perceive only at a distance, something I can know only insofar as someone renders it for me.

The simile of a machine obviously reduces the body to the status of a mechanical object, devoid of intentionality, of affections, of autonomous power. The reduction invites us to regard or to care for our bodies in the same way we regard or care for our cars, toasters, outboard motor boats, and electric can openers. The ad for the Time-Life book in fact tempts us to discover "why [our] bones are such *superb shock absorbers*" (italics added). The analogy with cars is no doubt the strongest: our cars are gassed and oiled, washed, dried, and polished, diagnosed for malfunctions by specialists, taken to the shop for repair, put into garages for protection, allowed to cool off and rest after grueling use, and so on. Aside from perhaps more efficient and speedier servicing, the body's future as a machine must be new and better replacements of its parts, new and better treatment of its ills. The only significant difference between the body as a machine and the machine itself is that bodies are not and cannot be recalled by their maker—though who knows what the future will bring?

As a machine the body verges on being considered *the* technological *tour de force*, the ultimate creation in a long line of technological achievements, precisely as if it were the product of technology rather than evolution. The image is of a body detached or detachable from any living human presence. It is in fact reminiscent of one of Joyce's characters, a Mr. James Duffy who "lived at a little distance from his body, regarding his own acts with doubtful side-glances … [and who] had an odd autobiographical habit which led him to compose in his mind from time to time a short sentence about himself containing a subject in the third person and a predicate in the past tense" (Joyce, 1947, p. 119).

Even were we to amend the simile by qualifying it as a living machine moves us no further toward a body whose redemptive powers might deliver us. True, a living machine might be said to be capable of reproduction, regeneration of injured or lost parts, and other organic wonders in contrast to a mere machine which holds the promise of no such possibilities. But the problem with a living machine is basically no different from the problem of an inanimate one; both need a helmsman, a director, a master, a conductor. Even a viable ghost would do. Whether living or not, the machine plunges us down a Cartesian-inspired chasm where even given the soothing and temperate voice of a pilot, "Attention! This is your Captain … Attention! This is your Captain …" is always too remote to save us.

No. It is the simile of a machine that leads us astray, that makes of us Duffy-bodies removed from any immediate living presence to the world. A machine is a technological, not a biological entity. No matter what we conjure up in the way of a qualifying adjective or of a commander, the fit is always of a square knob in a round hole. Of course we might imagine a square knob in a round hole just as we might imagine a smiling robot selling shoes in a department store and frolicsome zombies trying them on. The technological and the biological can meet, but the one cannot be assimilated wholly to the other without losing its primary identity.

Is it the biological body, then, which might ransom us?

If we discard the simile of the machine and consider the body in its simple objective appearance, we come upon an unadorned de-metaphored living human body. No longer a mechanical wonder but a wondrous biological specimen, the body has clearly changed hands. The question is whether or not they are still second hands. The biological body breathes, blinks, locomotes, secretes, bends, twists, perspires, excretes: engaged in the process of living it is quite literally a busy body. But it is a body whose busyness lacks the reality of a first-person world. It is an observed rather than a living presence.

At the moment of birth a body is very much a living presence. It is alive and kicking, but not of course because we inspect it and say that it is. Neither our scrutiny of it nor our words about it cast any magical animating powers. But aliveness does not depend either upon *knowing* that one is alive. Think of the first representatives of organic life. Not only was no one around to validate their aliveness but they were not themselves aware of "being alive": they simply went around being it. The theory of evolution in fact assumes that first-person aliveness; it takes for granted the immediate actuality of lived and living presences. Without that first-person presence, no animal of whatever cellular dimensions would have survived or would survive today. If animals did not *feel* hunger, in whatever way particular animals feel hunger, or if they did not *feel* an urge to mate, in whatever manner particular animals feel an urge to mate, and so on, animals would long ago have perished. In effect, biology would be out of business.

On the other hand, if biology did not begin with the already accomplished fact of living presences, it could take no third-person stance in relation to those presences. There would be no identifiable domain of objects for it to classify, observe, study, compare, and the like. For example, the biological human body has two living feet on the ground but those feet, to remain biological, must be ones seen or touched from a distance. They are not the feet which ache after a long day of standing or the ones which spring into action in a game of tag. The biologist must assume their aliveness, past or present, in order to proceed with his/her study, but the biologist cannot take account of that immediate aliveness within the confines of a third-person objective world. For all biological intents and purposes, they are feet that have fallen asleep. In effect, though their evolution may be historically reconstructed, though they may be structurally dissected, functionally analyzed, or compared with other kinds of animal feet, no matter from which biological direction we approach them, they show no signs of being the feet which might carry us off from a world that is too much with us.

We obviously need to find a credible body, a body whose possibilities for ransoming us are believable. The likeliest candidate is the first-person body, the body that we know directly in the context or process of being alive, the body that we cannot take apart or put back together again, the body whose mysterious possibilities lie within our immediate grasp. That body is the one in which we came into the world prior to technology or science, that is, prior to science or technology telling us what we are made of, how we are put together, how that togetherness works, etc. The body that emerges alive and kicking is the primordial one. From the moment of birth that body is the center and origin of our being in the world. It is in fact our first world and reality. To find that body is not a matter of our being like children again or like infants, at least not necessarily. The first-person body is not a body that we outgrow or even can outgrow; it is only one we can choose to deny or to deprecate. It is a body not lacking biological reality but a body whose biological reality is neither separable from, nor a third-person dimension of its lived and living presence.

Can you smile without a face, wiggle without hips, pant without a chest? Can you go out for a game of tennis, make love, repair a roof, or plant a garden short of being in the flesh? Cheshire cats might be able to accomplish such feats and if any humans could they might undoubtedly find a place in the Guinness Book of Records. The first-person body is not a phantom presence but a concrete physical one, a physical presence that is not detachable from the first-person world in which it originally exists, not just at birth but throughout its existence. We know that physical presence as a separate domain or area of study and knowledge only insofar as we rupture the original primordial unity of the body. In any immediate experience that physically real presence is part and parcel of the feeling, the action, the intention. The smile does not exist apart from the face and neither does the face exist apart from the smile. There are not two things present; there is only one thing present. And it is not actually that "they" are inseparable, but that in the first-person world, "they" do not exist. Only in departing from that first-person world can we meet with a stray face—or a disembodied smile.

If it is the first-person body alone that can ransom us, then we need to reform the notion implicit in the question that that body is something distinct from us. If taken literally, the question would seem to be asking whether a certain object in the world were capable of redeeming us. A number of images bubble up, not the least of which is Super Body battling its way through to us, succeeding (against great odds!), and carrying us off piggyback toward a receding sun—or toward whatever direction the world is not. If we are in fact speaking of a second-hand body, short of science fiction fantasies or comic book spectaculars coming to life, ransoming hardly seems possible. How could *we* possibly exercise *that* body in such a way that it could ransom us? Clearly, only by reforming the notion do we have some basis for considering the redemptive possibilities of the body.

How, for example, are redemptive possibilities arrived at? Do they add up to something more than a self-indulgent retreat? Does the lived body ransom us simply by supplying us a fully equipped pre-packaged pleasure-dome, a ready-made hedonist's haven to which we can retire at any time? As pointed out earlier, transactions run all the way from T'ai Chi to massage parlors and then some. Clearly some people elect redemption primarily or wholly through sexuality, a sexuality that may be either broad or narrow in its redemptive possibilities. In contrast to what we might call paths of instant reawakening are paths of gradual enlightenment, disciplines of the body that make demands upon us before they yield up their restorative powers. These latter paths compel us to attend to our senses, to listen to our bodies. It is only in attending or listening that we have the possibility of awakening a body that, whether through habit, cultural impositions, or whatever, has been prematurely blocked off.

To re-enter the world of the living body is to recover a world of mysterious possibilities and to forego, at least for a time, a world of self-made empirical certainties. That world of possibilities exists because the living body is a source of mystery yet at the same time is utterly transparent; it is guileless, without pretensions, it hides nothing. The mysterious could not otherwise come to light. It is only our choices that black out its transparencies. The living body is a source of mystery because it is always a source of potential surpassing, that is, a source where novelty, no matter how seemingly trivial, is a perpetual possibility. Sometimes the novelty might be no more than a fleeting new awareness, as of space between fingers; other times it might be protracted as in discovering and yielding to the flow of air breathing one now inward, now outward. Whatever the new awareness, it is always fully saturating, an experience to which nothing can be added or subtracted by way of further enhancement. It delights or awes, excites or subdues us. It catches us off guard and comes unbidden. Though someone might direct our attention to new modes of awareness and we duly attend to the person's instructions, we must await the moment of insight; we cannot conjure it forth. We are not sorcerers but apprentices of the body's mysteries.

The redemptive possibilities of the body are mysterious not only because of their freshness and unexpectedness. They are mysterious also because there is no cause-effect sequence that might be said to underlie them. After experiencing one of these moments, one cannot say, "Because I did this, I discovered that", or, "Because I did this, that happened". Moments of illumination or insight that come in attending or listening to the body are not within our direct control. This becomes even clearer if we consider that the experiences are not necessarily repeatable, not in the sense that one does not cross the same river twice, in which case no experience would be repeatable, but in the sense that in doing the same thing as before, one may not arrive at the exact same new illumination. One may not come upon any new awareness. Or a totally new awareness might spring forth. There is, in short, no way in which the advent of the mysterious can be predicted or controlled. This is true even in relation to the most commonplace of sexual experiences. While it is possible to identify a cause-effect sequence in terms of gratification or climax, the mystery is not thereby nullified, or at least it need not be. It depends in which grammar our body is to be found: a first-person one or a third-person one. If the former, the experience, though implicitly known, is neither predictable— what will happen and when anything will happen are unknown—nor controllable. In effect, the mysterious is not elided on the basis of implicit knowledge but remains within the realm of possibility. Where knowledge is not implicit but orchestrating and conducting the experience, our body is a third-person body. Controlling the experience, we are no longer in the midst of experience but outside of it, following a self-observed pleasure as we would a clinical rendering, a second-hand thriller. Given these blighted conditions, the mysterious could hardly come to light.

Freshness, unexpectedness, fortuity, non-controllability, these are the ways in which mysterious possibilities are encoded. It is in these mysterious possibilities that the redemptive powers of the body are discovered. The world that is too much with us is forgotten. We enter a pristine world where the mysterious is not unraveled in facts about the body but in feeling and intuiting its transparencies. We enter a world that is uncharted and that, in spite of illuminations, remains so. It is a world wherein one illumination, though unrelated to others that succeed it, seems to beget them, where through revival, the senses long accustomed to habitual modes of perception begin spontaneously to see, hear, smell, feel things anew. It is not uncommon then that a spin-off of perceptual energies occurs, where, upon re-entering the world that has been too much with us, we begin to discriminate more finely, attend more closely, and experience more fully. We come back regenerated. It is in this sense that ransoming is a sound investment: it allows us to discover an equilibrium, for a time at least, an equilibrium in which the world is not too much with us but is with us in just the right amount.

While the investment may be sound, the security it buys is not assured. We are not the beneficiaries of an impregnable haven nor the recipients of long- or even short-term guarantees. How could something mysterious offer such security? Paths that revive the senses have no immediately practical function: they serve neither to protect us from the world nor to provide us sureties against its future. What they do offer us is quite literally resourcefulness: a fullness of ready energies, security in the form of sentient-kinetic resiliency. We spring forth again in the full measure of our aliveness. In actuality, we are buying back something we have always had but were too oblivious or too busy to realize. In realizing our resourcefulness we have the opportunity of recovering and reaffirming the center and origin of our being, of recapturing the vitality of its primal energies: we reawaken capacities perhaps long dormant for feeling, for moving, for acting; we revitalize potentialities and discover new ones; we unlearn the familiar; we bring to light the "unlived lines" of the body; we sustain and sharpen our appetite for being alive at the same time we discover a plenitude of possibilities in that aliveness.

Male or female, our bodies are no Cleopatras: age can wither them and custom stale their infinite variety. Senses, energies, perceptions, thinking, actions, all can grow dull with age or through habit. But mysterious possibilities do not of themselves fade away nor is their number determinate. The process of aging and the furrows of habit can diminish the possibilities of the first-person body only insofar as we choose to diminish them. Habit can blind us only if we choose habit. Age makes a difference but only a difference: mysterious possibilities have no axiological status unless we give them one. Only we can mark off the possibilities of our lives, discover or ignore the resourcefulness latent in being a first-person body.

That resourcefulness stretches in two directions. The world that is too much with us may be either one turning so fast we are dizzied by the myriad events we behold or one turning so slowly we are dulled by the unremitting sameness before us. Whichever the world that is too much with us, it binds us to its landscape. It is not that we cannot do anything about it directly. Of course we can vote, we can take an active stand on certain issues, we can confront others with alternate ideas, and so on. But all of these actions do not change the *feeling* that the world is too much with us; that the illnesses and problems we find there merely change names from day to day or that they are each day radically and jarringly different. The security to be found through the redemptive powers of the body is a counter to either unrelenting landscape.

The first-person body is no stranger to us; it is our first and only home and its address never changes. Moreover it is always *at* home. Where else could it go if its address never changes? If the world is too much with us in its churnings and turnings we have the possibility of making our way back and reaffirming a measure of permanence in the world. This does not mean sitting for hours on end gazing into our navels or peering intently over any other body part for that matter. At least not necessarily. It does mean attending and listening, whatever the path, and re-establishing contact with the ongoing ever-present source of our aliveness. Correlatively, if it is the monotonous self-same landscape that is too much with us, we have in that same first-person-body-resourcefulness the possibility of restoring a measure of change to the world. This does not mean leaping from one bed to the next, for example, honoring now this partner now that one in a kind of sybaritic square dance. Again, not necessarily. It does mean attending and listening, whatever the path, this time to discover the freshness and varieties of awareness potential in any of our experiences, to sense and move anew.

The security that ransoming buys is clearly a gamut of potential energies which allow us to balance, compensate, or otherwise equalize the pressures and burdens of a world that is too much with us. It is a kind of inner ballast that is always with us but which we much touch upon in some way in order that it stabilize us and keep us buoyantly afloat. Whether balancing us in one direction or the other, our resourcefulness puts us in touch with our aliveness and with the mysterious possibilities that aliveness engenders.

It would be incorrect, however, to think that in returning to that source and in discovering its mysterious possibilities that we cut all worldly strings. The first-person body is in and of the world, a felt lived world, and so are all paths leading to its revival. In turning away from the world, we are turning away from the urgencies, tensions, dullness, uncertainties, or whatever, that we chronically feel in face of it. The world that is too much with us and that we forget for a time is in other words a part of our first-person world. We could otherwise never feel that it is too much with us or speak of its being so. In the act of ransoming, we are acknowledging and focusing upon the singular core of that world, our own living presence, apart from its daily context of work, wars, family, traffic, meetings, accidents, shows, late news, and so on. We focus wholly upon the center and origin of our being alive and in the world: our first-person body. We do not abandon the world; we simply take a temporary leave of absence from that part of it that is too much with us.

It would otherwise make no sense to speak metaphorically of recoiling temporarily for the purpose of rebounding more vitally. The point of ransoming is to redeem us from a worldly captivity not by supplying us a final departure ticket but by issuing us a new admission one upon our return. Supposing we could cut all worldly strings in the process of being ransomed, our bodies could conceivably ransom us with a finality we might not have anticipated. We might be orbiting in some far-out sphere, mere spirits of our former selves, where it is true that the world that was too much with us would no longer be, but where we would no longer be either in any substantial felt sense. Poof! Moreover short of some masterful legerdemain, re-entry would be impossible: how would we go about reclaiming our body or even attach ourselves to a different one assuming either were handy? There are undoubtedly all kinds of mysterious possibilities, but the ones of which we are speaking are ones that people can and do come back to tell us about. They are ones that have to do precisely with our being in the world and with our choosing to follow paths that restore and revitalize our powers, that illuminate anew our immediate presence within and to the world.

On the other hand, attending and listening have to do with something more than putting a figurative ear to the body and gluing it there to the exclusion of the first-person world about us. Ransoming has to do with finding, affirming, even celebrating one's center, not with being self-centered. If ransoming meant nothing more than turning inward and crawling into the folds of our own interiority, the world that is too much with us would indeed fade away, but so also would the very pith of our aliveness: our immediate presence would lose all meaning, being no more than a series of soundings along a stark and isolated strand. Lacking a context of aliveness, we could hardly resonate as a living presence. Even the paths that revive the senses do not exist in a vacuum. They are found within the context of other people, at least in the beginning, and always in the context of a particular surround: a room, a studio, a beach, a park, a meadow, a backyard. Our immediate presence is always somewhere and the form and quality of our relationship to that somewhere is an integral part of our first-person world. In fact, redemption in part lies precisely in awakening ourselves to the spatiality of our being and attuning ourselves to its demands and possibilities.

If the first-person body ransoms us, it does so on its own ground: being in the world and in the flesh inseparably, a consummate unity of aliveness. Indeed, this is why there can be so many different paths; each first-person body lives at its own address. The ground of our aliveness is the same for all of us, yet at the same time unique to each one of us. What one might hear acutely from one perspective, another from that same perspective might find blurred or might even hear no sound at all. For that very reason, we cannot say that there is only one path to follow, that any one hearing is the only way to hear. We need not experience the same mysterious illuminations, we need not devote ourselves for equal amounts of time to our respective path or paths, we need not have the same background of experiences in order to achieve redemption. Each path invites us to discover in a different way the mysterious possibilities of the body.

Redemption is also the same yet different for all of us. For all of us redemption lies in our awakening to the world anew, in releasing the discoveries, energies, insights, and illuminations we find along the path into our everyday world so that that world takes on a fresh and different appearance to us and is no longer too much with us. But we do not come back into that world with the same resiliency and sensitivities or discover within it the same freshness or tranquility. We all hear with greater equanimity and joy the sounds of the world, but we each hear in our own way; we each find our own equilibrium.

That we should all have a propensity for the mysterious is not really so mysterious. We are on the contrary admirably suited to discover the hidden possibilities of our aliveness. Who else should discover them or how else should they be discovered? That we should also have the resources to regenerate ourselves and to spring forth anew is simply a measure of the scope and potency of that aliveness. Aliveness is not a condition of the body but its one and only mode of being, a mode that is neither static nor absolute, but a fluctuating continuum of affectivity and energy. We are describing not a mechanical or a biological body whose aliveness is something we know through tests and measurements, but a living body whose aliveness is something of which we are qualitatively aware. It is because we are qualitatively aware of our living bodies that we can feel and say that the world is too much with us: it threatens and jeopardizes our aliveness, it saps our vitality, and corrodes our sensitivity so that we are less keenly alive both to it and to our own immediate presence within it.

The aliveness of the living body might in fact be aptly characterized as *an aliveness to ...* As we grow weary of the world, we feel less and less disposed toward being alive to it, but alive to it we are to the degree we feel its weight upon us and to the degree we tolerate that weight without going mad. To go mad would also be a way out, a way of ransoming ourselves, but a much more difficult path and one in which we must end by surrendering a great part of our aliveness. Offered a choice between the two, we should certainly give the body a try first: our chances for recovery are greater and the cure is more pleasurable. In fact, it is not only more pleasurable, it is closer at hand. Redemption is as far away as we are from our own bodies.

References

Joyce, James. 1947. "A Painful Case", in *The Portable James Joyce* (New York: The Viking Press), pp. 118–29.

Stern, Daniel. 1971. "The Mysterious New Novel", in *Liberations: New Essays on the Humanities in Revolution*, ed. Ihab Hassan (Middletown, CT: Wesleyan University Press), pp. 22–37.

Chapter II

Thinking in Movement

And what is *thinking*? — Well, don't you ever think? Can't you observe yourself and see what is going on? It should be quite simple. You do not have to wait for it as for an astronomical event and then perhaps make your observation in a hurry. (Wittgenstein, 1963, p. 106)

As I was led to keep in my study during many months worms in pots filled with earth, I became interested in them, and wished to learn how far they acted consciously, and how much mental power they displayed... . [A]s chance does not determine the manner in which [they drag] objects [leaves or paper] ... into [their] burrows, and as the existence of specialized instincts for each particular case cannot be admitted, the first and most natural supposition is that worms try all methods until they at last succeed; but many appearances [i.e., observations] are opposed to such a supposition. One alternative alone is left, namely, that worms, although standing low in the scale of organization, possess some degree of intelligence. This will strike every one as very improbable; but it may be doubted whether we know enough about the nervous system of the lower animals to justify our natural distrust of such a conclusion. With respect to the small size of the cerebral ganglia, we should remember what a mass of inherited knowledge, with some power of adapting means to an end, is crowded into the minute brain of a worker ant. (Darwin, 1976 [1881], pp. 19–20, 58)

1. The Twofold Purpose

What I hope to do in this essay is elucidate both the experience and foundations of thinking in movement. The foundations include both our own human developmental background and that evolutionary ground of animate life of which we humans are a part. I begin with a descriptive account of what I take to be a paradigmatic experience of thinking in movement, the experience of moving in an improvisational dance. Thinking in movement is at the core of this experience, indeed, a *sine qua non* of the realization of its aesthetic form. In taking this experience as paradigmatic, I hope to show how its dynamically-tethered thematic typifies such thinking, not that all experiences of thinking in movement accord with it through and through. Forms of thinking in movement can differ considerably. Think-

ing in movement in infancy, for example, can have practical, self-instruc-
tional, or explorative ends in contrast to the aesthetic ones of
improvisational dance. So also with animate life generally. It is possible
thus to distinguish structures in one kind of experience of thinking in
movement that are not present in another. What a descriptive account of
the experience of thinking in movement in improvisational dance provides is a bare bones example of such thinking — a laying out of the qualitative nature of its essentially dynamically-tethered thematic — or in other
words, an example in which the qualia or cardinal structures of movement
and of thinking in movement are magnified.

2. Dance Improvisation: A Paradigm of Thinking in Movement

A dance improvisation is unique in the sense that no score is being fulfilled, no performance is being reproduced. The dancers who are improvising understand this uniqueness in the very manner in which they
approach the dance. They have agreed to follow the rules, as it were, of a
dance improvisation, rules that might very generally be summed up as:
dance the dance as it comes into being at this particular moment at this
particular place. More detailed and possibly restrictive rules might structure a dance improvisation, rules that specify, for example, a certain kind
of improvisation or certain sequences of movement: "contact improvisation only", for instance, or "fast group movement to alternate with slow,
large individual movement". Such rules notwithstanding, the aim of the
dancers is not to render something planned or choreographed in advance.
Whatever the framing rules might be that act as a constraint upon movement, the aim of the dancers is to form movement spontaneously. It is to
dance *this evening's dance*, whatever it might turn out to be. In view of the
uniqueness of *this evening's dance* — as of all *this evening's dances* — the common aesthetical question of ontological identity does not arise. In other
words, being the only one of its kind, *this evening's dance* is not measured
against or viewed with respect to other performances nor is it measured
against or viewed with respect to a score. The question of its ontological
status is thus not at issue. Unlike a set piece of choreography — Marius
Petipa's and Lev Ivanov's *Swan Lake*, Twyla Tharp's *Red, White, and Blues*,
Alvin Ailey's *Revelations*, for example — *this evening's dance* is a singular
performance. It is either in the process of being created — in the very process of being born — or it is not at all. If pressed for an artistic comparison,
one might say — though only in a quite broad and general sense — that a
dance improvisation is akin to a jazz jam session wherein a group of musi-
cians literally make music together. They bring something into being,
something which never before was, something which will never be again,

thus something that has no past or future performances but exists only in the here and now of its creation.

In view of its unique appearance, it is not surprising that a dance improvisation is commonly described as an unrehearsed and spontaneous form of dance. What is not commonly recognized, however, is that that description hinges on the more fundamental characteristic suggested above, namely, that in a dance improvisation, the process of creating is not the means of realizing *a* dance; it is *the* dance itself. A dance improvisation is the incarnation of creativity as process. Its future is thus open. Where it will go at any moment, what will happen next, no one knows; until the precise moment at which it ends, its integrity as an artwork is uncharted. It is in virtue of its perpetually open future, its being in the process of being created, that a dance improvisation is unrehearsed and spontaneous. Because no set artistic product exists in advance or in arrear, the dancers have nothing in particular to practice or perfect in advance, nothing in particular to remember in order to keep. Their dance improvisation is process through and through, a form which lives and breathes only in the moving flow of its creation, a flow experienced as an ongoing present. Indeed, to create a dance improvisation is to create an unbroken now—something akin to what Gertrude Stein called a "prolonged present" (1926, pp. 16–17) to what William James (borrowing from E.R. Clay) called "a specious present" (1950, vol. 1, p. 609) and to what Henri Bergson called "a live present" (1991, p. 137)—an ongoing flow of movement from an ever-changing kinetic world of possibilities.

How is such a dance possible? How can dancers create a dance on the spot? To unravel the nature of an ongoing present and discover its generative core requires a description of the creative process from the perspective of a dancer engaged in the process. In the course of giving this description, we will find that what is essential is a non-separation of thinking and doing, and that the very ground of this non-separation is the capacity, indeed, the very experience of the dancer, to be thinking in movement. To say that the dancer is thinking in movement does not mean that the dancer is thinking *by means of* movement or that her/his thoughts are *being transcribed into* movement. To think is first of all to be caught up in a flow of thought; thinking is itself, by its very nature, kinetic. It moves forward, backward, digressively, quickly, slowly, narrowly, suddenly, hesitantly, blindly, confusedly, penetratingly. What is distinctive about thinking in movement is that not only is the flow of thought kinetic, but the thought itself is. It is motional through and through, at once spatial, temporal, dynamic. The description that follows will attempt to capture this motional character.

I should perhaps emphasize in advance that the account is basically descriptive, not theoretical. As such, it is not an *argument* for a certain conception of dance improvisation. The purpose of the analysis is not to claim or document a theory about dance improvisation but to describe as accurately as possible, indeed, to capture, the essential character of a dance improvisation as it is experienced by a dancer to the end that the kind of thinking that lies at the core of its spontaneous creation is clearly elaborated. The account may in this sense certainly be elaborated further; it may be amended; and so on. It is offered as a phenomenological account. Precisely because its aim is to render the experience of the dancer justly, it leaves an objective language behind, the latter language more easily tying us to facts about the experience than leading us to a conception of its living quality or character. In other words, what is of interest is not that I flexed my knee, for example, or that I circumducted my arm, or that I saw another dancer out of the corner of my eye, but the experienced kinetic reality of these events. Moreover, as may be readily apparent, a first-person descriptive account is called for, an account of the experience of thinking in movement as it is lived first-hand. If in the course of the description phrases or terms appear to be precious or fanciful verbal excesses, their successive elaboration should clarify their meaning such that anyone interested in grasping the process of creating an improvisational dance is led to the heart of that experience and to an understanding of its inherent structure: thinking in movement.

To say that in improvising, I am in the process of creating the dance out of the possibilities which are mine at any moment of the dance is to say that I am exploring the world in movement; that is, at the same time that I am moving, I am taking into account the world as it exists for me here and now in this ongoing, ever-expanding present. As one might wonder about the world in words, I am wondering the world directly, in movement. I am actively exploring its possibilities and what I perceive in the course of that exploration is enfolded in the very process of my moving—a density or fluidity of other dancers about me, for example, or a sharpness and angularity in their movement. The density or fluidity, like the sharpness and angularity, are not first registered as a perception (still less as stimuli, and certainly not as sense-data), a perception to which I then respond in some manner by doing something. Qualities and presences are enfolded into my own ongoing presence and quality. They are absorbed by my movement, as when I become part of the swirl of dancers sweeping by me or am propelled outward, away from their tumultuous energies, or when I quicken to the sharpness of their movement and accentuate its angularity or break out of its jaggedness by a sudden turn and stillness. In just such ways, the global dynamic world I am perceiving, including the ongoing kinesthetically felt world of my own movement, is inseparable from the kinetic world in which I am moving. Sensing and moving do not come together from two separate regions of experience, fortuitously joining together by virtue of their happening in, or being part of, the same body. Perceptions are plaited into my here-now flow of movement just as my here-now flow of movement is plaited into my perceptions. Movement and perception are seamlessly interwoven; there is no "mind-doing" that is separate from a "body-doing". My movement is thus not the result of a mental process that exists prior to, and is distinguishable from, a physical process in which it eventuates, nor does my movement involve no thinking at all. To separate myself into a mind and a body would be to perform a radical surgery upon myself such that a vibrant kinetic reality is reduced to faint and impotent pulp, or excised altogether. In effect, the separation would deny what I experience myself to be: a mindful body, a body that is thinking in movement and that has the possibility of creating a dance on the spot.

The world that I and other dancers are together exploring is inseparable from the world we are together creating. Thus, it is not as if I am contemplating — or must contemplate — a world of possibilities in order to choose from among them a ripest course of action, given now this, now that present situation. My possibilities at any moment in the ongoing present are not explicit and neither is my choosing. The idea that thinking is separate from its expression — a thought in one's head, so to speak, existing always prior to its corporeal expression — is a denial of thinking in movement. Certainly it is possible that a thought might occur to me prior to its overt expression. For example, it is possible that in the course of improvising, I may have a kinetic image or inclination and thus experience a thought prior to moving. For instance, at the same time that I am moving, I might have an image of a leg extension or a fleeting image of a particular movement quality — perhaps a strong and abrupt upward movement of my arm. Similarly, at the same time that I am moving, I might have an inclination to run toward another dancer or toward a particular place on the stage. Such thoughts, while emerging within the experience of an ongoing present, do not interrupt the flow of movement which is the dance. I do not stop moving; I am not impeded in any way, brought to a standstill by the passing image or inclination and made to choose explicitly what I shall do. On the contrary, I might indeed extend my leg or thrust my arm upward or run toward another dancer or toward a particular place on the stage. The image or inclination is a kinetic form within a form, a motional thought that momentarily intrudes itself into, or superimposes itself upon, the ongoing process of thinking in movement. Insofar as thoughts *of* movement are thoughts within the global form — thinking in movement — they can be distinguished from the latter. Thoughts *of* movement are experienced as discrete events: I have an image of a certain leg extension, an image of a certain strong and abrupt movement of my arm, and so on. Within the context of improvisational dance, such thoughts arise autonomously; they are spin-offs of thinking in movement rather than the result of an ongoing process of thinking in images while moving or the result of any deliberative thinking, e.g., "what if I ... " or "shall I ... " or "if I were to ... " and so on. In the same way that my sensings and movings are not sequential happenings but integrally entwined facets of a dance that is a dynamic in-the-making, so I am not mentally exploring a world of possibilities first, and then later taking some action in consequence of them.

Thoughts *of* movement are not the only way in which discrete movements might find their way into the ongoing present of the dance I am creating. I might, for example, think my way into movement that, by certain cultural standards, is distinctly referential in one way or another. I might shrug my shoulders, for instance, or wave to a dancer leaving the stage, or push another dancer off balance, or fall into the arms of a nearby dancer. But this is only to say that, within the context of improvisational dance, thinking in movement is not limited to thinking in what one might call *dance* movement. Hence, the incorporation of movement and gestures from everyday life that have certain culturally recognized meanings is always possible. It should be added, however, that such gestures or movements do not necessarily make the dance symbolic nor necessarily make the particular movement symptomatic. To use the above examples in turn, the dance in which such a movement happens is not thereby a dance about resignation, a dance about partings, a dance about aggression, or a dance about love. While each of the movements might be read off as standing for something, for the dancer creating the dance, it is the dynamic patterning of movement, its subtleties and explosions, its range and rhythm, its power and intricacy that are foundational, not its referential value as such. Thus, in *this evening's dance*, a particular movement is not "about" something any more than a smile is about pleasure.

Any process of thinking in movement is tied to an evolving, changing situation. Hence, if one would speak at all of a systematic reasonableness of meaning, it would not be in terms of an externally imposed scheme of some kind but in terms of *a kinetic bodily logos*, a body that, in thinking in movement, "knows what to do". To be thinking in movement means that a mindful body is creating a particular dynamic as that very dynamic is kinetically unfolding. A kinetic intelligence is forging its way in the world, shaping and being shaped by the developing dynamic patterns in which it is living. Thus we see once again that possibilities at any moment do not stand out as so many recourses of action; possibilities are adumbrated in the immediacy of the evolving situation itself, a situation that moment by moment opens up a certain world and a certain kinetic way of being in that world. In improvisational dance, possibilities arise and dissolve for me in a fluid complex of relationships, qualities, and patternings without becoming thematic for me. We see once again too, then, that choices are not explicitly made. Rather, a certain way of moving calls forth a certain kinetic world and a certain kinetic world calls forth a certain way of moving. It is as much a matter of the fluid complex moving me as it is a matter of my moving it, and from either end of that phenomenal kinetic world, a bodily logos is clearly its core.

There is a thus a further way in which the actual moment by moment creation of the dance may be described as my thinking in movement. The movement that I actually create at any moment is not a *thing* that I do, an action that I take, a behavior in which I engage, but a passing moment within a dynamic process, a process that I cannot divide into beginnings and endings. There is a dissolution of my passing movements into my perpetually moving present and a dilation of my perpetually moving present into my continuing movements. The sequential, waving gesture I am now making with my arm, for example, is spilling over into a turning movement I am now making with my head, and the turning movement I am now making with my head is spilling over into a bending of my torso and a sideward leaping in a direction opposite to that of my turning head, and so on. I have indeed made each of these movements—I have wandered my way into them in the course of improvising—yet they are not detachable moments. They have no separate or separable existence for me. They are like the passing stages of a forward-rolling ongoing spiral that coils back on itself in the process of rolling forward. Even were the sequential, waving gesture I am now making with my arm to dissolve into stillness or end abruptly, I could not say when the gesture ended and when the stillness began, or that the stillness was not an ongoing creation of the dance. My thinking in movement is thus not an assemblage of discrete gestures happening one after the next, but an enfolding of all movement into a perpetually moving present. Thinking in movement is an experience in which all movements blend into an ongoing kinetic happening: a singular kinetic density evolves. This ongoing flow, this perpetually moving present, is nothing other than this moment in which my arm is sequentially waving, this moment in which my head is turning, this moment in which my torso is bending, and so on. My experience of an ongoing present exists only in virtue of an immediate moment, that is, the actual here-now creating of this gesture or movement. But this gesture or movement is itself an opening out of the dance, a *process* of moving. It has a spatio-temporal thickness or dynamic density about it. In this sense, the turning movement I am now making with my head capsulates the dance, as it were, gathering up in its momentum all that has gone before and all that might lie ahead. Each actual movement of the dance has such a dynamic density, a pregnancy of being that stretches out the present moment, transfiguring it from a mere passing phase of a movement into a kinetic fullness or plentitude that radiates outward in a boundless process of motion. The ongoing present I experience is thus indistinguishable from the actual movement I am here and now creating. Thinking in movement is a perpetual dissolution and dilation, even a mutability, of here-now movements and a moving present. In fact, I am creating the dance moment by moment in the possibilities of movement I discover in moving and in the possibilities of moving I discover in movement.

There is one further aspect to be touched on in this descriptive account of improvisational dance. We have seen that, in contrast to a quite particular reification of thinking and/or to a conception of thinking as an exclusively mental event, thinking in movement is a way of being in the world, of wondering or exploring the world, taking it up moment by moment and living it directly in movement, kinetically. Thinking in movement is thus clearly not the work of a symbol-making body, a body mediating its way through the world by means of a language, for example; it is the work of an existentially resonant body. An existentially resonant body creates a particular dynamic world with no intermediates. The world it creates is neither the given world nor an immutable or factitious world, but a protean world created moment by moment. It is a world experienced as an elongated or ongoing present, one in which there are no hereafters, no sooner-or-laters, no definitively expected end or places of arrival, and so on. Thus it is clear why the kind of dance created is not a dance that the dancer might acknowledge as being "about" something, unless that something were movement itself. To understand such a phenomenon is akin to understanding what Gertrude Stein meant when she said, "a rose is a rose is a rose". Clearly a rose is not about something. And neither is it a capricious jumble of petals. The same may be said of a dance improvisation. The kinetic intelligence that creates the dance informs the dance itself. No more than the body must a dance stand for or refer to something beyond itself in order for the phenomenon to be dance. In short, *to have meaning is not necessarily to refer and neither is it necessarily to have a verbal label.*

It would seem that if we are to fathom such strata of experience, we must turn toward the animate world, or find in our highly symbol-laden human one patches where such phenomena as thinking in movement come to light. Only in so doing might we discover that fundamental creativity founded upon a kinetic bodily logos, that is, upon a mindful body, a thinking body, a body that opens up into movement, a body that, in improvisational dance, breaks forth continuously into dance and into *this* dance — as a body might break forth continuously into painting and into *this* painting or into music and into *this* music — a body which moment by moment fulfills a kinetic destiny and so invests the world with meaning. When we reflect upon our experience of moving in just such ways and examine the experience from a phenomenological perspective, we readily discover thinking in movement. We are in turn propelled to rethink our notion of thinking — and in the process, to realize that insights gleaned from a descriptive account of improvisational dance have consequences for epistemology and evolutionary thought as well as for aesthetics.

Before proceeding straightaway to a consideration of such broader topics, it is helpful to consider two assumptions about thinking, assumptions that, the preceding descriptive account notwithstanding, might otherwise impede a clear and unprejudiced grasp of what it is to think in movement. The first assumption has to do with thinking itself and has several layers. To begin with, it is commonly assumed that thinking is tied to language and that it takes place only via language. It is furthermore commonly assumed that thinking and language are tied in an exclusive way to rationality. The basis for these assumptions seems itself to be an assumption: that thinking, language, and rationality form a holy though human triumvirate, a congealed sacred hallmark of preeminently *human* existence. To link thinking, language, and rationality in this manner, however, is to claim a necessary and inherent interdependence before examining the evidence from experience itself and prematurely to declare impossible something that may not be impossible at all, and perhaps, on the contrary, quite common, i.e., thinking in movement. Moreover to deny peremptorily the possibility of thinking in movement on the basis of the foregoing assumption(s) may readily involve a further assumption, namely, that thinking takes place only by means of something, in particular, a symbolic system of some sort — e.g., mathematical, linguistic, logical — a system having the capacity to mediate or carry thought referentially. As the previous description demonstrated, however, to affirm the possibility of thinking in movement is to make neither of these latter claims about movement; it is to regard movement neither as a vehicle for thinking nor as a symbolic system through which reference is made to something else. Indeed, steadfast and serious reflection on the phenomenon of improvisational dance shows that movement is neither a medium through which a dancer's thoughts emerge nor a kinetic system of counters for mediating his or her thoughts; movement constitutes the thoughts themselves. One might in this context paraphrase philosopher Maurice Merleau-Ponty's remarks upon language and say that, in order to understand what it means to think in movement, "*movement* must somehow cease to be a way of designating things or thoughts, and become the presence of that thought in the phenomenal world, and moreover, not its clothing but its token or its body" (Merleau-Ponty, 1962, p. 182). Similarly, one might paraphrase neurologist Kurt Goldstein's remarks upon language and say that,

> As soon as man uses *movement* to establish a living relation with his fellows, movement is no longer an instrument, *no longer a means; it is a manifestation, a revelation of intimate being and of the psychic link which unites us to the world and our fellow men (ibid.,* p. 196).

Whether a matter of binding thinking exclusively to language and rationality or a matter of tying it exclusively to a symbolic system of one kind or another, the first assumption is essentially based on a reification of thinking. It is thus based essentially on a substantive rather than processual metaphysical conception and understanding of thinking. It is important to emphasize that neither the reification nor the substantive conception of thinking are unfounded; they are only narrow. In other words, what the previous descriptive account of improvisational dance challenges is not *a* linkage between thinking and language or between thinking and rationality, nor *a* linkage between thinking and symbolic systems of thought, but the view that there are no other forms of thinking, that thinking is wholly dependent on, and to that extent limited to, symbolic structures of thought, hence that it is transactable only in terms of a hard currency like language, and furthermore that it proceeds in a strictly linear fashion, its progression being marked by a systematic reasonableness that develops on the basis of exact and particular connections between what are in essence bead-like thoughts arranged in propositional sequences and/or on the basis of specific syntactic rules demanded by the symbolic counters or currency utilized. What the descriptive account of improvisational dance suggests is that to reify thinking in this exclusively linguistic, or more broadly, symbolic, manner is to perpetuate a metaphysics that is at odds with experience, and in fact, not simply at odds with a particular kind of aesthetic experience, but with a fundamental form of experience. What it correlatively suggests is that such reification is axiologically unwarranted in that it exalts humankind at the expense of denying dimensions of human experience, i.e., dimensions of thinking which, though nonsymbolic, may nonetheless be designated rational and which, from both a developmental and evolutionary perspective, may in fact be evidenced across a broad spectrum of animate life.

The assumption rooted in a reification of thinking and a substantive metaphysics may be accompanied by a parallel assumption rooted in a Cartesian separation of mind and body. To assume that thinking is something only a mind does, and doing or moving are something only a body does is, in effect, to deny the possibility of thinking in movement. If thinking is furthermore assumed to be always separate from its expression—a thought in one's head always existing prior to its corporeal expression—then thinking must necessarily be transcribed—or, given a strictly linguistic conception of thinking, *transliterated*—into movement. When the mind formulates a thought, for example, the tongue and lips move to express it; when the mind thinks of going to the store, the body complies by walking or driving it there. The notion that thoughts must be corporeally transliterated, that they exist separately from and prior to their expression, has been justly criticized by philosophers such as Wittgenstein and Merleau-Ponty. "When I think in language", Wittgenstein points out, "there aren't 'meanings' going through my mind in addition to the verbal expressions" (1963, p. 107). Merleau-Ponty similarly points out that "speech is not the 'sign' of thought, if by this we understand a phenomenon which heralds another as smoke betrays fire.... Nor can we concede ... that it [speech] is the envelope and clothing of thought" (1962, pp. 181–2). Although in these examples it is a question of *language* and not of movement, the same critical insights into the phenomenon of *thinking* apply. What the descriptive account of improvisational dance challenges is not the possibility that thinking, or a single thought such as an image, never occurs prior to its overt expression in some form, that is, prior to a movement or an action of some kind. When one thinks in general terms about what one will say prior to expressing the thought verbally to others, verbal thinking clearly occurs prior to its active expression. What the descriptive account challenges is the notion that thinking always and necessarily takes place in this way, thus that the mind is always one thoughtful step ahead of the body, always there beforehand to mobilize it into action.

There is an aspect of this assumption that we would do well to clarify in some detail. Though typically so regarded, movement is hardly given its due when presumptively conceived merely as the medium of a body's everyday transactions with the world. Movement is, on the contrary, first and foremost the natural mode of being a body—a ready and perpetual kinetic susceptibility and effusion, as it were, of animate life. Serious reflection on this fact readily leads one to the realization that animate forms readily inhabit movement in the literal sense of living in it and that thinking in movement is foundational to being a body, as much an epistemological dimension of bodily life as a biological built-in that makes sense. One aspect of this naturally kinetic manner of being — this spontaneous thinking in, and opening up into movement — is implicit in Merleau-Ponty's remark that Cézanne's description of himself as "thinking in painting" is a process in which "vision becomes gesture" (1964e, p. 178). Merleau-Ponty's remark is clearly not intended to mean that movement follows perception, i.e., doing follows seeing, but that perception is interlaced with movement, and to the point, we might add, where it is impossible to separate out where perception begins and movement ends or where movement begins and perception ends. The one informs the other — inextricably, and all the more inextricably when it is a question not of *vision* becoming gesture, but of *movement* becoming movement. Consider, for example, the two basic ways in which thinking in movement may enter into the creation of a dance. One can readily distinguish between thinking in movement in and of itself and a kind of thinking in movement that is analogous to Cézanne's "thinking in painting". The distinction is in fact integral to an understanding of the difference between improvisational dance — what we might characterize as the creation of dance as artistic process — and non-improvisational dance — the creation of dance as artistic product. In creating the latter kind of dance, a choreographer obviously thinks in movement as she creates the dance, precisely in a way similar to the way in which Cézanne "thinks in painting". In broad terms, what Cézanne does with hand and brush, the choreographer does with other bodies. Moreover, like the painter, she also stands back from time to time and views the work in progress with an eye to judging its form — to changing the timing of a particular movement sequence perhaps, or of attenuating a particular gesture, or of cutting a whole passage because its dynamics are discordant. Thinking in movement is thus a compound process for a choreographer. One might characterize the difference between an improvisationally choreographed dance and a non-improvisationally choreographed one in terms of how the process of thinking in movement stands in relation to the actual making of the dance, i.e., in terms of whether the process of thinking in movement is at times "transcendental" to the dance or at all times "immanent" in the making of the dance, or in other words, whether thinking in movement is at times "thought about action" or consistently and throughout "thought in action".[1] The difference may furthermore be characterized as an out-

---

1 Harrison spells out the difference I am drawing between improvisational and non-improvisational dance in terms of "a creator who is 'transcendental' to his creation and [a creator who is] ... imminant (*sic*) in the process of his creation's coming to be" (1978, 34). I came

side/inside difference. Obviously, in improvisational dance, there is no critical or creative outside eye. Thinking in movement is all from the inside. The choreographed form evolves spontaneously from the ongoing process of thinking in movement. Non-improvisational dances are choreographed from the outside; hence, thinking in movement may at any time in the choreographic process be a critical thinking in movement at the same time that it is a creative thinking in movement. In formally judging a dance, or in changing its dynamics in any way, a choreographer is casting a critical thinking eye at the kinetic form she is in the process of creating. Viewing the dance with a moving eye that is consummately absorbed in the movement of moving bodies, she is caught up in a flow of kinetic thought, perceptually experiencing the dance as an unfolding kinetic drama, a dynamic form-in-the-making (Sheets-Johnstone, 1966). Thinking in movement in this choreographic way, she is not only turning "vision into gesture", but also gesture into vision; in the act of choreographing, she is transforming dance into movement—her "vision into gesture"—and movement into dance—"gesture into vision". In effect, while a further dimension of thinking in movement opens up in choreographing a dance from the outside, perceiving and moving are not thereby separable moments of the experience of thinking in movement. Whether choreographed from the inside or outside, in one non-stop choreographic swoop or over a period of time, the basic process of thinking in movement is patently central to the making of a dance. By having turned attention exclusively to improvisational dance, we have been able to flesh out this basic process undistracted by critical concerns, and show how this mode of thinking, by its very nature, is the work of a mindful body.

3. Thinking in Movement:
Our Human Developmental Background

In the context of showing how experimental psychological research on human infants coincides with the phenomenological notions of primal animation and of a kinetic attunement to the world, or how, in other words, movement is foundational—"primitive"—in both an epistemological and metaphysical sense, I elsewhere showed that an infant's first mode of thinking is in movement (Sheets-Johnstone, 1999). This insight into our original mode of thinking can be further elucidated and in fact substantively documented in ways that draw on developmental as well as

---

across his book after having written the original *Journal of Aesthetics and Art Criticism* article, but found his mode of distinguishing between "thought in action" and "thought about action"—the focus of his second chapter—richly topical. For a full phenomenological account of dance as a dynamic form-in-the-making, see Sheets-Johnstone, 1966.

experimental research on infants. Studies of language development that are concerned not merely with words, but with experience before language, are particularly instructive and relevant to this elucidation and documentation. Well-known infant-child psychologist Lois Bloom's first book, for example, a monograph titled *One Word at a Time*, was concerned in part to show that first single-word utterances are in fact "conceptual rather than linguistic" (Bloom, 1993, p. ix). The single-word utterance — "bye-bye", for instance, is pegged to someone's leaving the room; it is not a locutionary statement as such, or, as Bloom describes it, a "syntactic" one. Single words are initially paired with *happenings* of some kind or other — thus "down", as in getting down from a chair; objects are paired with certain perceived dynamics — thus "tick-tock", as with a clock. In her most recent book, *The Transition from Infancy to Language*, Bloom fleshes out this conceptual terrain in the process of reviewing the literature on infant development and in her related discussions of topics such as movement and change, general object knowledge, and object concepts. She does so not in great detail but to a sufficient degree to afford a general sense of what is there before language. In other words, she approaches a child's progressive mastery of language by beginning with the life of the child as an infant, in particular, with those "developing cognitive abilities in infancy that bring the infant to the threshold of language at the end of the first year" (1993, p. 35). It is of critical importance to emphasize that in doing so, Bloom does *not* address the relationship between movement and thinking, or use the terms nonlinguistic and linguistic, or in fact concern herself in any central sense with *thinking* — the central terms of her discourse are cognition and affect. It is of equally critical importance to emphasize that her account of the transition from infancy to language is nevertheless replete with references to movement that incontrovertibly support the notion that infants think in movement. The value of her account in the present context consists precisely in these dual facts. In what follows, the underlying thematic of *thinking in movement* will be brought to the surface.

One of Bloom's first references to movement unequivocally attests to its primacy in the life of an infant and to its cogency in the development of language. Bloom states that "The foundation for the semantic structure of language … is in the theories of objects, movement, and location that begin to be formed in the first year of life" (1993, p. 37). The ensuing discussion — in fact, the section that immediately follows — is devoted to "Movement and Change" (37). Though not stated outright in the discussion , it is clear that an infant's burgeoning idea of objects is tied not to a simple visual experience of them — to *looking* at them — but to noticing whether they change, how their appearance is different in different circumstances, whether they change in conjunction with what the infant itself does with them, including how it moves in relation to them, thus also including how, though it does not locomote itself, how the act of being carried about by others affects its relation to objects, and so on. We might note that such a "theory of objects" coincides basically with what both eighteenth-nineteenth century physiologist Hermann von Helmholtz and phenomenological philosopher Edmund Husserl affirm about the constitution of objects. Both von Helmholtz and Husserl describe how we learn about objects originally by moving in relation to them and by noticing their changing appearances in concert with our movements (see Sheets-Johnstone, 1999, Chapter IV, for examples and a discussion of their descriptions). Moreover this same kinetically-tethered "theory of objects" has further resonances. When Bloom, in a section on "Movement and Change", speaks of feeding bottles and blankets having "a dynamic quality" according to where the infant is in relation to them, how the infant moves or is moved by others relative to them, how they, as objects, move or do not move, and so on (p. 38), her words recall in an abbreviated way infant psychiatrist Daniel Stern's much more highly elaborated account of vitality affects. "A blanket", she says, for example,

> appears when the baby is put down to rest, and then it disappears when the baby is taken up for feeding and playing.... . [M]oreover, its movements are integrated with the baby's own twisting, turning, trying to rise up, and so forth (p. 38).

It is furthermore significant that Bloom first mentions in just this dynamic context the fact that "when [children] begin to say words, their earliest words express something about objects that move" (p. 38). As Bloom points out, this empirical finding about the centrality of movement to earliest words has in fact been made by many researchers (p. 272, note 10). Bloom herself goes on to make a most provocative comment. She states,

> Both conceptual categories and eventual linguistic categories build on an infant's nascent theories about objects, motion, space, and causality, and these theories originate in the early experiences that come about with movement and change in location.

Now by "conceptual categories" Bloom obviously means categories prior to language since she goes on to mention "eventual linguistic categories". In effect, though not named as such, Bloom implicitly acknowledges that infants have nonlinguistic concepts, concepts in advance of language, indeed that they have *theories* in advance of language since it is theories about "movement and change" originating in early experiences of movement and change that ultimately spawn "linguistic categories". Of further moment is that although psychologists disagree on how an infant arrives at a "theory of objects", and disagree as well as to the nature of that theory, they are in accord that "movement and invariance in the face of change" (p. 39) are central to an infant's theory of objects. In other words, movement is a foundational character of the world; even while some objects are static—like walls or pieces of furniture—there is movement in relation to them. What is crucial, then, is making sense of what is invariant amidst change. Indeed, as Bloom emphatically points out in reviewing a study by T.G.R. Bower, which showed that infants were less disturbed or did not even notice that an object changed but became quite "disturbed when the path in which it moved changed," "*Movement* [is] the critical factor: either the movement of the object or the path of movement or the infant's head movement while following the object" (p. 40). Clearly, *thinking in movement* is our primary way of making sense of the world. We see this truth enunciated again, clearly, in the conclusion drawn from experimental research, namely, that "infants as young as 2 to 4 months of age can track a moving object and anticipate its reappearance" (p. 40). Infants as young as two to four months of age are *thinking in movement*: to anticipate is first of all to think ahead, as in expecting something to happen; to expect the reappearance of an object that has been moving along a certain path and disappears at a certain point on that path is to *think in movement*. Moreover if an infant's perception of objects and "theory of objects" matures in conjunction with movement—its developing perception of objects being tied both to the movement of objects and to its own movement—then again, an infant is *thinking in movement* (see Ruff, 1980).

As Bloom implicitly shows, "physical knowledge" matures in conjunction with an infant's developing "theory of objects" (pp. 43–46). By physical knowledge is meant such properties as solidity, object permanence, and even such things as gravitational effects. Infant researchers have long remarked on the fact that infants are attracted to novelty; they habituate to what is regular or expected and pay particular attention to what is unusual. The latter phenomenon—"preferential looking", as Bloom at one point describes it (p. 43)—is regularly used as an empirical measure of an infant's perceptions, expectations, interests, and so on. Drawing in particular on a series of research studies of child psychologist Elizabeth Spelke and Renée Baillargeon that utilize just such a standard technique, Bloom describes how infants even as young as two and a half months have a sense of object continuity and solidity, and how those at six months have a beginning appreciation of gravity and inertia (pp. 43–4). In summing up these studies, she writes, "In all these experiments, infants demonstrated these abilities with respect to objects that *move*" (p. 44; italics in original).

Again, empirical research validates the claim that infants are *thinking in movement*. Indeed, the research itself all but articulates the truth. Precisely by *thinking in movement*, infants are gaining knowledge of "objects, motion, space, and causality" — and, we could add, of time. In progressively attaining to physical knowledge about the world in ways that are integrally tethered to movement, they are gaining knowledge about invariant and variant spatio-temporal and dynamic features of the world. We should perhaps emphasize once more that it is not Bloom's intention to present a case for movement or for thinking in movement. On the contrary, as initially suggested, the case is made by itself. We see this yet again when, after underscoring the importance of "objects that *move*", Bloom writes — a few lines later — that "A theory of objects clearly begins very early in infancy, and experiments have shown its beginnings in perceptions of objects that move in relation to a physical field" (p. 45).

When Bloom goes on to consider what she terms "relational" concepts, the basic developmental phenomenon of thinking in movement is implicitly elaborated in further ways. Relational concepts develop outside of language. They develop on the basis of observation. Bloom defines them by saying that "Children learn about relationships between objects by observing the effects of movement and actions done by themselves and other persons" (p. 50). It is instructive to note that Bloom's "relational concepts" are akin to what Stern describes as "consequential relationships" and to what Husserl describes as "if/then" relationships. All three are descriptive of the same basic phenomenon. An infant notices, for example, that slapping bath water causes a splash; closing one's mouth impedes the insertion of food into it; pulling on a blanket brings it closer; pushing against a bottle or a ball causes it to roll on the floor; being picked up has a certain feel to it and changes the way things in the surrounding world appear; and so on. Bloom's "relational" concepts — and their kin — are *not* language-dependent. Moreover they are not simply stepping stones integral to language development, thus essentially "pre-verbal" or "pre-linguistic" phenomena. On the contrary, they are the fundamental backbone of an infant's — and an adult's — knowledge of its surrounding world. They are the bedrock of our notion of objects, motion, space, causality — and time — just as Bloom points out. They derive from experiences in which and by which infants attain concepts of different objects and gain "physical knowledge" generally. Though just such concepts and knowledge are undeniably basic to an infant's ultimately having something to talk about, at least some of these concepts and some of this knowledge may in fact never even wend their way into language. In other words, they are not *necessarily* articulated or even articulable. What a blown-up balloon does, for example, when it is suddenly untied is hardly expressed by the word "deflates" or the words "splutters about". The actual dynamic kinetic event is not reducible to a word or even to a series of words. We all have knowledge of just such "physical" events just as we all have nonlinguistic concepts of their dynamics. We have this knowledge and these concepts because we have all been nurtured by an original capacity to think in movement, a capacity that does not diminish with age but merely becomes submerged or hidden by the capacity and practice of thinking in words.

Psychologist Jerome Bruner's focal emphasis upon narrative as the primary form of discourse and upon the central place of action in that discourse affirms this very insight. He writes that when young children "come to grasp the basic idea of reference necessary for any language use ... their principal linguistic interest centers on *human action and its outcomes*" (1990, p. 78). His point is clearly that narrative structure is, in the beginning, concerned with movement, in particular, with "agentivity" (p. 77). "Agent-and-action, action-and-object, agent-and-object, action-and-location, and possessor-and-possession", he says, "make up the major part of the semantic relations that appear in the first stage of speech" (p. 78). A particularly interesting experiment implicitly demonstrates the ready concern of infants with movement in the sense of "agentivity". In this experiment, luminous points are placed at eleven anatomical joints strategic to human walking—e.g., ankles, knees, elbows, and so on. When set in motion, the luminous points create the illusion of a person walking (or running or carrying or throwing or involved in other acts). Not only do adults readily see a person walking (or engaged in other acts: see, for example, Runeson and Frykholm, 1981, 1983), but three-month-old infants do also. When the eleven luminous points are randomly organized and set in motion in computer simulations, or when the moving point-figure is turned upside down and set in motion, a coherently moving shape is no longer perceived (Bertenthal and Pinto 1993; Bertenthal, Proffitt, Cutting, 1984).[2] Though some infant researchers have tied the experimental findings to the notion of infants having a "body schema"—a body schema "that permits not only the control of their own bodies but also the recognition of their fellow humans" (Mehler and Dupoux, 1994, p. 108)—no such hypothetical entity is actually necessary. Even as a fetus in utero, an infant has a sense of gravity, i.e., of the vertical; even as a fetus in utero, an infant has a sense of its joints, i.e., through kinesthesia. Though as an infant, it has never itself walked, it has seen others walking, and again,

---

2   See Runeson 1994 for an informative critique of computer-simulated point-light display experiments as against point-light display experiments of actual humans in action.

even as a fetus in utero, it has a tactile-kinesthetic sense of its own body as an articulable, essentially dynamic form. "Agentivity" specifies a dynamic concept of action coincident with this articulable, essentially dynamic form. "Agentivity" is thus intimately related to *primal animation*. Primal animation indeed is the epistemological ground on which *thinking in movement* develops, hence the ground on which the concept of "agentivity" develops, agentivity both with respect to one's own actions and the actions of others, as is evident in a three-month-old infant's recognition of a coherent moving form that in fact exists only sketchily as a luminous point-figure.

Aspects of this original mode of thinking warrant consideration with respect to their differences from linguistic thinking and with respect to the fact that in many cases, as the earlier balloon example suggests, what is thought in movement is opaque to language. With respect to differences between thinking in movement and thinking in words, attention might first be called to a coincidence highlighted in an earlier publication (Sheets-Johnstone, 1996). Both Husserl and Stern remark upon a certain lack of fit between language and experience, as evidenced by the disruptive character of language with respect to actual experience (Husserl), or by the elision of experience by language (Stern). Husserl writes,

> It is easy to see that even in (ordinary) human life, and first of all in every individual life from childhood up to maturity, the originally intuitive life which creates its originally self-evident structures through activities on the basis of sense-experience very quickly and in increasing measure falls victim to the *seduction of language*. Greater and greater segments of this life lapse into a kind of talking and reading that is dominated purely by association; and often enough, in respect to the validities arrived at in this way, it is disappointed by subsequent experience (1970b, p. 362; italics in original).

Stern observes that there is a "slippage between experience and words," noting that experiences of self having to do with a sense of coherence and continuity, for example, "fall into a category something like your heartbeat or regular breathing" (1985, p. 181). He goes on to say that

> periodically some transient sense of this experience is revealed, for some inexplicable reason or via psychopathology, with the breathtaking effect of sudden realization that your existential and verbal selves can be light years apart, *that the self is unavoidably divided by language* (p. 181; italics added).

In one sense, of course, Stern's observation straightaway validates a Lacanian psychoanalytic theory: language *is* Other, though not necessarily, of course, the Lacanian Other. In a quite different sense, however, Stern's notion of a self-divided-by-language is wholly contrary to Lacan's psychoanalytic and this because at its core, the self is, and has been, a quite different self, in precisely the way Stern has previously described, both clinically and experimentally. The core self is an *existential* self, a preeminently bodily presence that carries with it a sense of coherence, agency, affectivity, and continuity. In the descriptive terms Husserl uses many times over, the core self is fundamentally *animate* and *animated*. Thus both the "originally intuitive life" that Husserl describes and the core or existential self that Stern describes are anchored in a dynamics of aliveness that is not simply a state of being that is there before language, but an aliveness that language, when it does emerge, can and often does fail to capture. Indeed, such a linguistic feat, we might say, is not the mission of language; one word after another, while potentially itself a highly dynamic happening, is not equipped to render — at least in an everyday, non-poetic sense — the qualitatively dynamic metaphysics of aliveness — of breathing, for example, or of the synaesthetic experience of waves crashing relentlessly upon a shore. What moves and changes is always in excess of the word — or words — that tries to name it. Thinking in movement is different not in degree but in kind from thinking in words. Words are not sharper tools, more precise instruments by which to think about dynamics, by which to hone our sense of space, time, energy, causality, or "agentivity". When the definitive shift into language takes place, that is, when thinking in words comes to dominate thinking in movement, a foundationally rich and subtle mode of thinking is displaced and typically subdued, commonly to the point that it is no longer even recognized as a mode of thinking. Experience itself may be fundamentally transformed if the shift is so compelling and overpowering, and so ultimately transforming of the person, that any other form of thinking is categorically denied.

Earlier in his career, Stern wrote of certain infant behaviors as being "resistant" to language. He termed these nonverbal behaviors "intention movements" (1981, p. 47), following along the lines of ethological studies and attempting to show how the behaviors were biological built-ins in the service of communication. The nonverbal behaviors he singled out were "gaze, head orientation, upper and lower body orientation, spatial positioning, and assumption of posture and distance" (p. 45). He spoke of these nonverbal behaviors in the context of an infant's readiness or unreadiness to interact with others, viewing readiness and unreadiness not as an either/or condition of the infant, but as dynamic behavioral possibilities existing along a continuum. What is of moment is Stern's emphasis on the fact that these nonverbal communicative behaviors are neither transformed nor transformable into language; that is, while some infant nonverbal behaviors such as pointing or reaching for an object might be viewed as "'proto-linguistic' (or linguistic precursors) because they later become linguistically encoded" — as pointing, for example, becomes "gimme" (pp. 54–5) — some of their nonverbal behaviors such as averting their gaze or lowering their head "will never undergo an analogous [linguistic] transformation" (p. 55). In discussing the reasons for their resistance to linguistic encoding, Stern points out that a word naming a behavior has none of the effect of the actual behavior itself; language is thus not equal to the communicative power of these nonverbal behaviors. He points out further that the nonverbal behaviors are dimensional rather than categorical in character; they transmit or signal "gradient information" (pp. 57–58). Postures, gaze, upper and lower body orientation, and so on, have a variable affective tone according to *how* they are enacted; they signal a variable level of arousal, for example, according to *how* they are enacted. Though Stern does not speak of affective variability in such terms, there is no doubt but that the gradient character of the nonverbal behaviors is through and through a question of spatio-temporal dynamics: an infant can slowly or suddenly avert its gaze with respect to another person; it can turn its head away abruptly coincident with its sudden gaze aversion, thus intensifying its unreadiness to interact with someone; it can turn its upper torso minimally toward another person, let its head follow minimally, and then make brief eye contact with a person, thus tentatively showing a readiness to interact; and so on. Endless spatio-temporal intercorporeal dynamics are possible. In contrast to "a verbal message" (p. 58), the "gradient information" is precise in character. It is also transmitted with greater speed than a verbal message. In short, there is a richly subtle and complex nonverbal world that is there from the beginning of all of our lives, a dynamic world that is neither mediated by language nor a stepping stone to language, but that is literally significant in and of itself and remains literally significant in and of itself, a dynamic world articulating intercorporeal intentions that, although clearly affective in origin, are enmeshed in "agentivity", in expectations, in consequential relationships, and thereby in the phenomenon of thinking in movement (cf. Bull, 1951).[3]

When Stern in his later writings examines the impact of language, he consistently emphasizes and reiterates the differences between a nonverbal and verbal world. He again points out, for example, how "Language is slow", how "Words cannot handle global experiences well", how language in fact "breaks apart rich, complicated global experiences into rela-

---

3   Bull's theory is posturally, i.e., neuromuscularly, based. A certain preparatory motor attitude — what might be termed a certain corporeal readiness — is the requisite basis of a certain action or range of possible actions. Feelings "come into the picture" between the preparatory attitude and the action (1951, p. 4). A "motor attitude" is thus "the initiator of feeling as well as action" (1951, p. 5).

tively impoverished component parts", how language "is clumsy at noting gradations between its categories", how it "may split thought away from emotion", and how some experiences such as "looking into someone's eyes while he or she is looking into yours ... can simply never be captured in words; at best [such experiences] can be evoked by words". He states further that for the young child, language "creates a wide gulf between [a] familiar nonverbal world of experience and [a] new world of words", that the "schism is confusing and at times painful". In fact, "for the first time in [its] young life", a young child, "has to hold onto two different versions of the same event". He says that "Life will now ... be lived more in parallel", that "The simple wholeness of experience has been broken", but that "the verbal and the nonverbal constructions of experience will live together all the same" (1990, p. 114).

Now while the advent of language is radically intrusive on Stern's account and to that degree may appear incomprehensible if not radically wrong to many, his account is difficult to discount. To begin with, serious and extended study of a subject may well turn up findings that are radically incompatible with popular beliefs and attitudes. Indeed, Stern's account cannot be peremptorily dismissed precisely because it is informed by years of both clinical experience with infants and developmental research into infancy, a time of life, we might note, with which we are all familiar in varying degrees, but which most of us have never actually studied either close-up or longitudinally. At the very least, what Stern's professional findings call upon us to do is to suspend judgment, to listen carefully to what is being said, to reflect carefully upon it, and then, to the best of our own abilities and situation, test out what is being said in the light of our own observations of infants. The idea that infants are nothing until they speak, that there is no thinking outside language, that there is not even consciousness outside language – all such ideas are readily open to question when we turn in this suspended way "to the things themselves". More than this, insights are gained into language itself. When we go back to infancy and seriously attend both to Stern's account and to what is there in the form of living flesh before us, we can hardly miss the fact that *language is not experience and does not create experience*. We readily discover this fact because we can indeed hardly miss it: infants experience themselves and their surrounding world. They are animate forms in an animate world: they are reaching, kicking, smiling, pulling, turning, babbling, and more – and they consistently notice and respond to things that move. They are *sensibly* caught up in the primacy of something quite other than words. They are caught up in the primacy of movement and in thinking, not in words, but in movement.

When we listen and attend in this way, when we read descriptions of infant behaviors and interactions, when we observe infants, when we reflect back upon our own fundamental knowledge of ourselves and the world, we realize that our most basic human concepts are foundationally *corporeal concepts*; they derive from our own dynamic bodily lives. When we turn to any basic spatio-temporal or dynamic concept, the concept of distance, for example, and ask how we first *thought about* distance, in what terms we came to conceive of distance, or how we first came to have a concept of suddenness, in what terms we first experienced and thought about it, we realize straightaway that we did so nonverbally. These fundamental spatio-temporal concepts are not in the least language-dependent. They are first and foremost *corporeal concepts* (Sheets-Johnstone, 1990). As infants, we forged just such concepts. Although we have a word to designate them, there is nothing basically linguistic about them in the least. Corporeal concepts in each case derive from experience and in no way require language for their formulation. Moreover the idea that language is there implicitly as some kind of ultimate and proper conceptual form, a kind of conceptual destiny toward which we inexorably progress as toward what, in an evolutionary context, zoologist Stephen Jay Gould describes as the "*summum bonum* of bigger brains" (Gould, 1994, p. 27), is a notion at odds with corporeal matters of fact. Infancy is not a *pre*-linguistic or *proto*-linguistic state of mind.[4] It is not a *primitive* state of being, an antediluvian, prehistoric, barbarian time of life. Infancy is infancy, a period in our lives that affords all of us the crucial opportunity to experience the world and ourselves directly, as animate forms, and correlatively, to know the world and ourselves in their most basic terms: dynamically, kinetically. If anything, *language is post-kinetic*. Spatio-temporal-energic concepts come from experiences of movement, movement both in the form of self-movement and in the form of the movement of individuals and things in one's surrounding world. The experience of change is equally fundamental—as with the change from light to dark and dark to light, for example. We do not even need to witness a sunrise or sunset to appreciate such change; blinking suffices. Indeed, our own bodily changes, our own bodily processes, quantitative ones as in growth and development as well as qualitative ones as in feelings of hunger giving way to feelings of satiety—an experience that Stern describes for an infant as a "*hunger storm ... that passes*" (1990, pp. 31–5, 36–43)—are temporal processes. We live in and through the changes. As adults, we tend not to follow the temporal dynamics of change closely. We would not say, for example, that hunger

4   An analogy might be made to silent films, the value of which could hardly be captured by the designation "pre-linguistic".

"sweeps through [our] nervous system like a storm, disrupting whatever was going on before and temporarily disorganizing behavior and experience". Nor would we ordinarily say that our hunger then "establishes its own patterns of action and feelings, its own rhythms" (Stern, 1990, p. 32), making us breathe faster, for example, and more jaggedly. Yet as infants, hunger affected us in just such ways and when we were fed, sucking produced rhythms that overrode the fast and jagged breathing rhythm. When as adults we begin recognizing the fecundity and breadth of our spatio-temporal corporeal concepts, we wean ourselves in reverse: we back down the linguistic ladder from which we customarily see and appraise ourselves — and other creatures — a ladder whose ascension has been richly prepared for in earlier ways, but that appears to us now virtually untainted by them. We come back down to earth and recontact that original ground which gave us our first footings and which has never actually disappeared but has only been buried under a vainglorious and myopic view of language. Weaning ourselves away from the thought that all thought is language-dependent, and equally, from language-dependent thought, we wean ourselves away from a basically object- or substance-tethered metaphysics. In turn, we afford ourselves the possibility of grasping the momentous significance of movement and change, and of attaining to a metaphysics quintessentially attuned to the dynamic nature of an animate world and animate forms. A process metaphysics accurately describes the natural world, the living forms that inhabit it, and the natural contours of life itself. Thinking in movement is not only coincident with that metaphysics; it is the methodological point of departure for its formulation. Precisely as Heraclitus indicated: bodies *step* into *running* rivers.

4. Thinking in Movement: Our Phylogenetic Heritage

Killdeer are ground-nesting birds that protect their young in one of two ways depending upon the immediate danger. When approached by predators who will eat their young, they move away from the nest and flutter their wings as if injured; when cattle approach who might trample their young, they remain at the nest, spreading their wings in a conspicuous display, which action ordinarily deflects the cattle away from the nest (Griffin, 1984, p. 36), or lunge toward a cow's face "thereby startling it and causing it to veer away" (Ristau, 1996, p. 80).

Instances of thinking in movement abound in the literature on nonhuman animal life just as they abound in the literature on human infant life. That the killdeer's behaviors *are* examples of thinking in movement, and not merely blind, robotic behaviors adaptively favored by natural selection, is an issue that will be duly addressed. Of moment now are the distinctive movement dynamics created by the killdeer in each situation. As instances of *thinking in movement*, the dynamics are aptly fitted to the circumstance; each movement dynamic is in its own way a reasonable act in the service of kin-protection. Similarly, each movement dynamic has its own integrity as an act of kin-protection. To be effective, movement dynamics must be just so structured. Focusing attention on the movement dynamics of these protective acts highlights the extended and more complex spatio-temporal dynamics of predator-prey interactions,[5] where, as ethologist Donald Griffin points out,

> The stakes are extremely high. For the prey it is literally a matter of life and death. For the predator, success or failure in a particular effort is less crucial, but its survival and reproduction depend on succeeding reasonably often (1984, p. 73).

The prize being on the one hand to stay alive, and on the other, to have a good meal, prey and predator are at near corresponding risks. The drama that evolves between and through them is clearly played out in movement, a kinetic drama through and through. Precisely because it is a spontaneous dynamic interaction not orchestrated in advance, but played out from moment to moment, it is a drama that involves thinking. To claim that there is no thinking involved would in fact be absurd. It would be absurd to claim, for example, that predator's and prey's progression of movement is tied to a set of rules that algorithmically specify both the immediate moment and the global event, as if the animals involved were following a script, their every movement being orchestrated in advance. Moreover it would be equally absurd to claim that the thoughts the animals think exist separately from the movement the animals make, or in other words, that the animals' thoughts are successively transcribed into movement—as if one of two hungry female lions in tandem strategic pursuit of a zebra were first thinking in some way to herself, "Let's see, if I head off the zebra from this direction, perhaps Mary over there will move up on its right flank and ... ", the lioness then following through by bodying forth her thoughts in the flesh. All such claims overlook the obvious: predator and prey alike are thinking in movement, their progression of thought—their process of thinking in movement—being tied to the evolv-

---

5   It is of interest to call attention to the fact that hunting behavior is not studied in laboratories and could hardly be studied in laboratories. Predator-prey interactions are not amenable to experimental designs. They are spontaneous, real-life interactions that can be captured in nothing less than real-life situations. Recording animal behaviors in these situations—who does what, under what circumstances, and so on—gives a sense of the intensity of the drama, but only indirectly gives a sense of the phenomenon of thinking in movement that necessarily informs it. Consider, for example, the fact that a predator chasing a fast-running prey animal must aim its charge ahead of where the prey animal is and that when the prey animal changes directions, it must adjust its own directional charge accordingly.

ing, changing situation itself, the situation they themselves are dynamically creating moment by moment in their very movement. That
dynamically evolving situation develops its own logic, i.e., its own reasonableness and integrity, and it develops that logic on the basis of a *kinetic
bodily logos*, a natural kinetic intelligence that is there from the beginning in
both prey and predator and that evolves on the basis of experience. In
stalking, in chasing, in avoiding—in other words, in crouching, creeping,
sprinting, racing, suddenly changing directions, putting on speed, and so
on—prey and predator alike make their way in a kinetically intelligent
manner, a manner that is at once spontaneous and contextually appropriate. Agonistic situations in which pursuit and flight are dominant themes
demand just such a kinetic intelligence, an intelligence that is not a fixed
and static body of knowledge but a dynamically evolving intelligence that
grows and changes on the basis of past experience. The reproductive success of prey and predator alike depends on just such an intelligence.

The old division between instinctive and learned behavior is a spurious
one, as most biologists have come to realize, an oppositional way of thinking that does not accord with facts of life. In their classroom text *Biological
Science*, William Keeton and James Gould, for example, state that

> it is extremely unlikely that any behavior can be classified as strictly
> innate or strictly learned: even the most rigidly automatic behavior
> depends on the environmental conditions for which it evolved, while
> most learning, flexible as it seems, appears to be guided by innate
> mechanisms.

They conclude that "*Instincts* ... can be defined as the heritable, genetically
specified neural circuitry that organizes and guides behavior", and that
"behavior that is thereby produced can reasonably be said to be at least
partially innate" (Keeton and Gould, 1986, p. 554).[6] Instructive cases in
point that confirm this conception of behavior are paths and shelters. Animals that make paths for themselves are not automatons blindly following
a motor program, any more than are human animals who blaze trails or
build roads. As Keeton and Gould's remarks implicitly indicate, creatures—including human ones—build according to what is available
and/or at hand, according to what the contour of the land allows, according to what construction and/or destruction is in fact required if a path,

---

6   An egregious and lamentable error should be pointed out in Keeton's and Gould's text. In their
    introduction, they state, "To early 'mechanistic' philosophers like Aristotle and Descartes, life
    was wholly explicable in terms of the natural laws of chemistry and physics". A reading of *De
    Anima* should be required reading for all biologists, along with *The History of Animals, Parts of
    Animals, Movement of Animals, Progression of Animals,* and *Generation of Animals,* and also some
    excellent commentary texts, especially what is considered "the bible" with respect to
    Aristotle's biology: *Philosophical Issues in Aristotle's Biology,* edited by Allan Gotthelf and James
    G. Lennox.

trail, or road is to be successfully made, and so on. Moreover what starts out in a happenstance manner may be progressively improved. Griffin points out, for example, that a vole runway

> may have started as an incidental result of repeated walking over the same route, but its users soon work on it actively, nibbling away at the lower parts of some plants while leaving in place the blades of grass that lean over the runway.

In this way, they make the runway smooth, level, and "almost invisible from above" (Griffin, 1984, p. 96). The building of shelters correspondingly involves thinking in movement and tailoring one's building accordingly. The nest-building of weaverbirds provides an exceptional example; its nest incorporates not only an extraordinary number of possible stitches and fastenings, but ones requiring complex weavings. Ethologist W.H. Thorpe diagrams nine different styles, including a half hitch, an overhand knot, an alternately reversed winding, a series of interlocking loops, and a slip knot (Thorpe, 1974, p. 149). In the context of discussing instincts understood as genetically-determined behaviors, Thorpe emphasizes the fact that experience affects genetically-generated behavior. In other words, instincts are malleable; their particular realization depends upon an individual's past experience, for example, upon whether, in the course of an action, an individual is interrupted in its activities, upon what available resources provide, and so on (Thorpe, 1974, pp. 134–71). Griffin makes this very point with respect to nest-building behaviors when he states that however instinctive the behavior might be, "nest-building is anything but a stereotyped and fixed sequence of behavior patterns" (1984, pp. 107–8). In the context of discussing various aspects of nest-building, such as whether a bird repairs a damaged nest or abandons it and builds a new one, he remarks upon the flexibility and sensibleness of their choice, but states too, "This is not to say that birds never do foolish things in the course of nest building". He proceeds then to relate how blackbirds may become confused, starting to build "many nests in some artificial structure that has many similar-looking cavities". Their confusion, he says, appears to be about just where the nest should be located and ends in their not completing any nest. He goes on to say with respect to this behavior that

> we tend to infer a total lack of thinking when animals do something foolish and wasteful of effort. But we do not apply the same standard to members of our own species, and we never infer a total absence of thinking when people behave with comparable foolishness (1984, p. 109).

The point is an important one. To say animals think is not to say that they think infallibly, or as Griffin puts it, it is not to say that their thinking "always corresponds perfectly to external reality". Just like humans animals, nonhuman animals make mistakes. "[E]rror", however, as Griffin points out, "is not the same as absence of thought" (p. 109). By a similar token, instinctive behavior is not the same as absence of thought.

Intelligence in action is instinctive. *All* animals — humans included — could hardly survive much less reproduce if intelligence in action were not instinctive. In just this sense, a kinetic bodily logos is at the heart of thinking in movement. It is what makes such thinking spontaneous and contextually appropriate to the situation at hand. It is what ties thinking not to *behavior* but to *movement*, that is, to kinetic meanings, to spatio-temporal-energic patterns. Instinctive behaviors are malleable precisely because they are fundamentally kinetically dynamic patterns and not chunks of behaviorally labeled "doings". To think in movement is not to think in monolithic comportmental wholes: eating, mating, courting, defending, aggressing, threatening, and so on; it is to think in dynamic terms — in terms of speed, postural orientation, range of movement, force, direction, and so on. Behavioral variations exist precisely because *kinetically dynamic possibilities* exist. It is just such kinetically dynamic possibilities that distinguish one creature from another: one creature runs faster than another, is more agile over a rough terrain than another, is more awkward in climbing than another, is less easily aroused or startled than another, is quicker to withdraw than another, and so on. From this essentially kinetic vantage point, the malleability of what are called instinctive behaviors, indeed, their *evolution*, is a matter of movement. Instincts have their genesis in animation — primal animation. When circumstances change, ways of living change, and those changes in the most basic sense are a matter of movement possibilities. A kinetic bodily logos is not some kind of adaptive mechanism; it is a real-life dimension of animate forms. An intelligence in action is a built-in of animate life. Thinking in movement is the natural expression of this elemental biological character of life.

When ethologist Niko Tinbergen relates in some detail particular animal behavioral studies of colleagues over a twenty-five year period, his descriptions implicitly exemplify again and again a kinetic bodily logos and the phenomenon of thinking in movement. An especially impressive example concerns the seven-year study of a species of sand wasp (*Ammophila*) by G.P. Baerends ánd J. van Roon (at that time students of Tinbergen). The sand wasps in question live not on open land but in "knee-deep Heather" in a terrain that has "few outstanding landmarks"; what is more, they carry their "heavy prey [caterpillars] home walking over the ground below the Heather shrubs" (Tinbergen, 1968, pp. 104–5). In other words, in supplying caterpillars to their young buried in the ground, the female wasps walk the highly uneven ground below the heather; they cannot fly there. But this is not all. Each female wasp has two, three, and sometimes more nests at one time—what Tinbergen describes as a "telescoping of broods" (p. 112). This means, of course, that she must remember the location of more than one nest. Furthermore, after constructing each nest originally and laying an egg on the first caterpillar she places in it, she makes two more calls to each nest over a period of days, provisioning each one according to its needs. An interesting difference between these wasps and what was, at the time, a more highly studied species (*Philanthus*) concerns the former's building habits. Although *Ammophila* already build their nests in a highly overgrown and therefore visually difficult terrain, rather than leaving the sand they excavate in building the nest by the nest itself, thus giving a clue as to its location, they carry it away so that a sandpile does not distinguish the nest from its surrounds. To arrange the physiognomy of the landscape in such a way, that is, to create certain spatial relationships, is to think in movement. Moreover the building of the nest itself is a complicated process of thinking in movement: the female digs earth, pushes pebbles or bits of wood into the shaft that she makes, "works sand among the pebbles," "rakes sand," and so on (Tinbergen, 1968, p. 106). In the course of provisioning the larvae, for example, she clears sand away that has dropped into the opening as a result of her removing the pebbles to enter the nest, and she uses her head as a hammer against the pebbles so as to close the nest after a visit. What is more, when she first returns to the nest after initially building it and laying her egg atop a caterpillar, she does not bring anything the next time, but simply "calls", as Tinbergen puts it, to evaluate the needs of the larva. Only after doing so does she return with caterpillars—in the amount necessary to sustain the larva. In other words, what she does next—what is literally her next move: to find one, two, or three more caterpillars to bring back to the nest—is each time determined by what she finds on her inspection. As Tinbergen emphasizes many times over, "All the time she remembers where all the nests are and, roughly, in what stage they are" (1968, p. 114). Perhaps the purest and most sophisticated example of the wasp's thinking in movement concerns her ability to home in on the nest with the food. The wasp invariably climbs either a bush of heather or a young pine tree, and then,

> Arrived at the top after a laborious climb, she turn[s] in various directions, as if having a good look round. Then she [takes] a long jump, which [is] always in the direction of her nest. The weight of the caterpillar decide[s] how long this 'flight' [will] be.... The wasp then [begins] to walk, stumbling and plodding along over the rough ground.

Although starting out in the right direction, she might make a wrong turn or even go in loops. She will then again climb a heather bush or young pine, look around again, and again, make another jump—in the correct direction of the nest. Various studies clearly show that the wasp's movement is tethered to landmarks—landmarks such as tufts of grass or a clump of pebbles or pine cones—"the positions of which she has to learn" (p. 120).

Thinking in movement is not only the natural expression of a kinetic bodily logos; it is the natural noetic sequel of actual experiences of movement, both self-movement and the movement of others. As indicated earlier, experiences of movement are the generative source of concepts of agentivity, of if/then relationships, of spatio-temporal invariants. They generate expectations; they are replete with kinetic concepts having to do with energy, distance, speed, range of movement, direction—in short, with a complex of dynamic qualities inherent in the experience of movement itself. Consider, for example, the seemingly simple behavior of moving away from something noxious. As zoologist John Paul Scott observes,

> Escape depends on some power of movement. A paramecium quickly withdraws from an injury, and even the sluggish ameba slowly crawls away... . [T]hose forms which can move at all retreat or withdraw in some way. Even clams can disappear quite rapidly into their native mud, as anyone who tries to dig them out soon discovers. Snails, turtles, and other animals with hard shells often escape by simply withdrawing into their armor... . An opossum which is overpowered will go completely limp and apparently lifeless for several minutes, then suddenly bound to its feet and escape if it is no longer held. Similar reactions are seen in turkey buzzards (1963, pp. 70–1).

The tendency to place all such movement—or at least all such movement of "lower animals"—in the category of reflex behavior does less than full justice to the actual situation. An animal, even a so-called "lower animal", can, for example, hesitate before crawling away or withdrawing, just as it can hesitate before re-emerging after withdrawing. Consider the behavior of fan worms. As invertebrate zoologist Martin Wells observes, "Touch them, or pass a shadow across [their] filtering crown, and they vanish [i.e., 'duck very quickly'] down their tubes, only emerging, with great caution and very slowly, after a matter of several minutes" (Wells, 1968, p. 80). Now surely if a fan worm moves "with great caution and very slowly", however that caution and slowness might be actually measured objectively and quantified, then it can move with either a bit more or a bit less "great caution", and similarly, it can attenuate even further or accelerate just a bit its very slow movement. In short, it can vary its movement. In fact, it is reasonable to assume that the several minutes that elapse before a fan worm reappears, and its great caution and very slow movement in reappearing, are all variable according to the variability of the circumstances themselves. In some real-life situations, for example, should a touch or shadow appear again in the course of its cautious and very slow reappearing, a fan worm will again "duck very quickly", interrupting its slow and cautious re-emergence. Clearly, a kinetic intelligence is at work in the observed behavior of fan worms. There is nothing wayward at all in this understanding of animate life, wayward in the sense of putatively ignoring the concept of adaptation and of natural selection and proffering another, we might say, "mindful" explanation in its place. On the contrary, recognizing the phenomenon of a kinetic bodily logos — in essence, primal animation, surface recognition sensitivity, proprioception, kinesthesia, and the capacity to think in movement — is of the very quintessence of adaptation and selection. Animate forms that are born to move but that fail to be sensitive to their surrounds, that fail to be sensitive to their own bodies, and that in turn fail to think in movement do not survive. They are deficient in the very business of living. However circumscribed the range of their movement possibilities, however restricted their particular *Umwelt*, their lives depend on being responsive to a particular surrounding world as it is at this particular moment in this particular place. The world, after all, is not the same from one day to the next and neither is a creature's life. Moreover creatures are themselves spontaneous; they move motivated by their own dispositions to move. Even anemones, animals one thinks of as sedentary, are spontaneous, generating activity on their own, and not just in response to stimuli in their surrounding world (Wells, 1968, p. 40). Further still, individual behaviors can and do change as a result of experience. Again, even the behaviors of anemones can and do change as a result of experience (p. 42).

The focus on "lower animals" has been intentional. The tendency of many, perhaps all too many, humans is to order animate life hierarchically and to belittle what lies "below" — wherever that dividing mark might be drawn. In this respect, at least some humans readily accredit a kinetic bodily logos to "higher" animals, however indirectly. Abundant examples exist that validate the accreditation. Well-known primatologist Jane Goodall relates two incidents that, even in their brief description, straightaway illustrate and implicitly affirm a kinetic bodily logos in action. One of the related incidents concerns a chimpanzee who saves his much younger brother from severe treatment by an adult male. The younger brother's temper tantrum — the result of being hurled away by a female in estrus — was irking not only to the female but to the alpha male who was courting her. Hearing the tantrum, the older brother who had been feeding some distance away, came hurrying up to see what was going on. For a moment he stood surveying the scene then, realizing that Pax was in imminent danger of severe punishment, seized his still screaming kid brother by one wrist and dragged him hastily away! (1990, p. 199).

The other related incident concerns a group of six male chimpanzees and is equally if not more telling since it involves concerted intelligent action. The group of males came upon a female baboon carrying a small infant and feeding in a palm tree. All of the chimpanzees stood gazing up at the baboon, "their hair bristling." One of them slowly climbed a tree close to the one in which the baboon was feeding and to a height where he was level with her. Then two other males climbed two other trees so that one chimpanzee was "now stationed in each of the trees to which their victim could leap. The other three chimpanzees [waited] on the ground". The first chimpanzee suddenly leaped into the baboon's tree. The baboon made a huge leap into a tree in which another chimpanzee was stationed. That chimpanzee seized the baboon and pulled her infant away from her. All six chimpanzees subsequently shared the infant as a meal (1990, p. 128).

Each incident clearly indicates a kinetic intelligence at work, a spontaneously integrated and reasoned course of action. In neither case were the chimpanzees taught what to do, for example. Neither had they practiced, nor were they practicing, a "behavior". Rather, they were *kinetically attuned* to a particular situation at hand. Kinetic attunement is the work of a kinetic bodily logos, a logos that comes with a creature's being the animate form it is. From this perspective, the designations "higher" and "lower" are clearly inappropriate; each creature is what it is and is not another thing. It is quintessentially suited, and in multiple ways, to the life it lives. Not only is there an existential fit with respect to its physical and living body — what might roughly be described as a fit between its anatomical and animate form (Sheets-Johnstone, 1986) — but an existential fit obtains between the organism and its environing world, a fit that is kinetically expressed. Each species of animate form is kinetically suited to the life it lives by way of an intelligence that is of the very nature of the form itself, an intelligence that is plaited into its very tissues and expressed in the sensible ways in which it lives its life. In sum, a kinetic bodily logos is an instinctive disposition toward intelligent action. It is a disposition that is common to all animate forms of life.

We might note that it is incomprehensible how any so-called purely instinctive behavior could otherwise have gotten started. It would be absurd, for example, to think that the first living form was programmed to some *behavior* or other in advance of its leading any particular kind of life. To be viable, its instinctive behaviors would have to be effectively tethered to particular environing circumstances, which in fact could only be faced at the moment the form first encounters them. More than this, however, it is not *behavior* that first appears. In the beginning is not *behavior* any more than it is—or was—*words*. In the beginning is—and was—movement, sheer movement. What lives moves, and in moving, goes toward and away from things. It is in the process of spontaneously moving about that animate forms discover aspects of the world, and it is on the basis of this process of spontaneous movement and discovery that instincts are formed. Certain movements are instinctively ingrained because organisms *find satisfaction in their movement*. It is not too much to say that they realize that their movement works, *and that in consequence, they do again what they did* when in a similar situation, *and again do what they did* when in a similar situation, and so on. In short, instincts do not have their origin in *habits*. Instincts have their genesis in movement, in primal animation; they start kinetically. They have their origin in responsivity, in the fact that creatures are *responsive* and in the fact that their responses, however accidentally they might arise, do not take place in a vacuum and are certainly not blind, but are satisfying, or dangerous, or unproductive, or have any number of other possible consequences for the creatures themselves. What starts out in movement, in exploration or by chance, is kinetically taken up, repeated, even honed and fine-tuned in dynamic, spatio-temporal ways; or it is kinetically abandoned and a different kinetic exploration and strategy are tried. Instincts develop on the basis of movement and ways of moving. They are fundamentally forms of thinking in movement, and it is because they are fundamentally forms of thinking in movement that they are malleable.

If responsivity is a near universal characteristic of life, if perception is a preparation to respond, if the fundamental nature of organisms is not to be neural repositories of information, much less information-processing machines, but to be kinetically alive to, and in, their respective worlds, then it is readily understandable why thinking in movement is a built-in disposition of animate forms. The not uncommon tendency to carve at certain self-serving human joints and thereby make honorific and pejorative distinctions on the order of "this one thinks", "this one does not", generates and reinforces an arrogantly biased metaphysics and epistemology. A broader sense of the animate is not only needed but proper in that that broader sense accommodates facts of life as enumerated in any biology text: mealworms congregate, cats pounce; creatures move toward and away from things in their environment. Animation is a primary fact of life—and thinking itself, as noted earlier, is itself a form of animation:

moving forward, backward, quickly, slowly, narrowly, broadly, lightly, ponderously, it itself is kinetic.

5. Summation

A common kinetic thematic suffuses improvisational dance, human developmental life, and the lives of animate forms. In each case, a non-separation of thinking and doing is evident; so also is a non-separation of sensing and moving. In each case, qualities and presences are absorbed by a mindful body in the process of moving and thinking in movement; in each case, an evolving, changing world emerges. A finer dimension of this common thematic is furthermore evident. Through the dynamics their movements explore and articulate, dancers bring forth a particular — though not necessarily singular — qualitative world. *This evening's dance* may be gay and buoyant, for example, playful in its energies, zany in its interactions, and so on; or it may be intense and brooding, a world in which movements appear portentous and ominous, where relationships appear on edge and threatened; or it may be erratic in its swings from one dynamic contour to another, the whole united by a kinetic logic having its own unspoken integrity. Just so in the living world of animate forms, where playfulness, wariness, fitfulness, and so on, are all kinetic possibilities. Moving organisms indeed create kinetic melodies — to borrow Luria's evocative phrase (1973, p. 179) — by the very fact of their aliveness. These melodies are created because qualia are inherent in movement, inherent in the dynamically moving bodies of animate forms. They are the foundational kinetic units, the cardinal structures of movement and of thinking in movement. A dynamically attuned body that knows the world and makes its way within it kinetically is thoughtfully attuned to the variable qualia of both its own movement and the movement of things in its surrounding world — to forceful, swift, slow, straight, swerving, flaccid, tense, sudden, up, down, and much more.

Caught up in an adult world, we easily lose sight of movement and of our fundamental capacity to think in movement. Any time we care to turn our attention to it, however, there it is.

References

Bergson, Henri. 1991. *Matter and Memory*, trans. Nancy Margaret Paul and W. Scott Palmer (New York: Zone Books).

Bertenthal, Bennett I. and Pinto, Jeanine. 1993. "Complementary Processes in the Perception and Production of Human Movements". In *A Dynamic Systems Approach to Development: Applications*, ed. Linda B. Smith and Esther Thelen (Cambridge: Bradford Books/MIT Press), pp. 209–39.

Bertenthal, Bennett I., Proffitt, D.R., and Cutting, J.E. 1984. "Infant Sensitivity to Figural Coherence in Biomechanical Motions", *Journal of Experimental Child Psychology*, 37: 214–30.

Bloom, Lois. 1993. *The Transition from Infancy to Language: Acquiring the Power of Expression* (Cambridge: Cambridge University Press).

Bruner, Jerome. 1990. *Acts of Meaning*. Cambridge: Harvard University Press, 1990.

Bull, Nina. 1951. *The Attitude Theory of Emotion* (New York: Nervous and Mental Disease Monographs [Coolidge Foundation]).

Darwin, Charles. 1976 [1881]. *Darwin on Earthworms: The Formation of Vegetable Mould Through the Action of Worms with Observations on Their Habits* (Ontario, CA: Bookworm Publishing Co.).

Goodall, Jane. 1990. *Through a Window: My Thirty Years with the Chimpanzees of Gombe* (Boston: Houghton Mifflin Co.).

Griffin, Donald R. 1984. *Animal Thinking* (Cambridge: Harvard University Press).

Harrison, Andrew. 1978. *Making and Thinking: A Study of Intelligent Activities* (Indianapolis: Hackett Publishing Co.).

Husserl, Edmund. 1981. "The Origin of Geometry", trans. David Carr. In *Husserl: Shorter Works*, trans. P. McCormick and F. A. Elliston (Notre Dame: University of Notre Dame Press), pp. 251–70.

James, William. 1950. *The Principles of Psychology*, 2 vols. (New York: Dover).

Keeton, William T. and Gould, James L. 1986. *Biological Science*, 4th ed. (New York: W.W. Norton).

Luria, Aleksandr Romanovich. 1973. *The Working Brain: An Introduction to Neuropsychology*, trans. Basil Haigh (Harmondsworth: Penguin Books).

Mehler, Jacques and Dupoux, Emmanuel. 1994. *What Infants Know*, trans. Patsy Southgate (Cambridge: Blackwell).

Merleau-Ponty, Maurice. 1962. *Phenomenology of Perception*, trans. Colin Smith (London: Routledge & Kegan Paul).

Merleau-Ponty, Maurice. 1964. "Eye and Mind", trans. Carleton Dallery. In *The Primacy of Perception*, ed. James M. Edie. Evanston (Northwestern University Press), pp. 159–90.

Ristau, Carolyn A. 1996. "Aspects of the Cognitive Ethology of an Injury-Feigning Bird, The Piping Plover." In *Readings in Animal Cognition*, ed. Marc Bekoff and Dale Jamieson (Cambridge, MA: Bradford Books/MIT Press), pp. 79–89.

Ruff, Holly. 1980. "The Development of Perception and Recognition of Objects". *Child Development* 51: 981–92.

Runeson, Sverker and Frykholm, Gunilla. 1981. "Visual Perception of Lifted Weight", *Human Perception and Performance* 7/4: 733–40.

Runeson, Sverker and Frykholm, Gunilla. 1983. "Kinematic Specification of Dynamics as an Informational Basis for Person-and-Action Perception: Expectation, Gender Recognition, and Deceptive Intention", *Journal of Experimental Psychology* 112/4: 585–615.

Scott, John Paul. 1963. *Animal Behavior* (Garden City, NY: Natural History Library/Anchor Books).

Sheets-Johnstone, Maxine. 1966. *The Phenomenology of Dance* (Madison: University of Wisconsin Press) (Second editions: London: Dance Books Ltd. 1979; New York: Arno Press 1980.)

Sheets-Johnstone, Maxine. 1986. "Existential Fit and Evolutionary Continuities". *Synthese* 66: 219–48.

Sheets-Johnstone, Maxine. 1990. *The Roots of Thinking* (Philadelphia: Temple University Press).

Sheets-Johnstone, Maxine. 1996. "An Empirical-Phenomenological Critique of the Social Construction of Infancy", *Human Studies,* 19: 1–16.

Stein, Gertrude. 1926. *Composition as Explanation* (London: L. and Virginia Woolf [(Hogarth: Second Series]).

Stern, Daniel N. 1981. "The Development of Biologically Determined Signals of Readiness to Communicate, Which are Language 'Resistant'. In *Language Behavior in Infancy and Early Childhood,* ed., Rachel E. Stark (New York: Elsevier/North Holland), pp. 45–62.

Stern, Daniel N. 1985. *The Interpersonal World of the Infant: A View from Psychoanalysis and Developmental Psychology* (New York: Basic Books).

Stern, Daniel N. 1990. *Diary of a Baby* (New York: Basic Books).

Thorpe, W.H. 1974. *Animal Nature and Human Nature* (Garden City, NY: Anchor Press/Doubleday).

Tinbergen, Niko. 1968. *Curious Naturalists* (New York: Anchor Books).

Wells, Martin. 1968. *Lower Animals* (New York: McGraw-Hill).

Wittgenstein, Ludwig. 1963. *Philosophical Investigations*, trans. G.E.M. Anscombe (Oxford: Basil Blackwell).

Chapter III

Existential Fit and Evolutionary Continuities

Man himself could only appear when a very high level of organization had been attained. For hands and a big brain would not have made a fish human; they would only have made a fish impossible. (Howells, 1959, p. 341)

The reality of evolution is not only the connective tissue of the whole of biology; silently or not, it threads its way through all studies of animate being. Merleau-Ponty's existential analyses are particularly rich in this respect. They answer, to the question of human uniqueness and in so doing engender a certain view of evolutionary continuities. Here we will take up that answer and view in the form of both a critique and an elaboration of Merleau-Ponty's thought.

The essay is comprised of three sections. The first situates the question of human uniqueness in the context of scientific thought and pinpoints problems inherent in the Darwinian scientist's quest for human uniqueness. The second section is a critique of Merleau-Ponty's claims for human uniqueness. Those claims are implicitly and explicitly spelled out in his first work, *La Structure du Comportement* and they are also evident in his later writings, especially *Phenomenology of Perception* and "Eye and Mind". A rigorous review of these claims dramatizes the need for acknowledging the evolutionary dimensions of existence and the evolutionary problems attaching to analyses of human being-in-the-world. In this sense the critique sets the stage for the concrete elaboration of the radically different view of human uniqueness pithily if fleetingly suggested by Merleau-Ponty in "Eye and Mind". In quite general terms, the critique shows that, failing a direct acknowledgement of evolutionary dimensions of existence, existential claims regarding human uniqueness are left dangling: there is no viable framework in which to assess their truth. More importantly, the critique shows that existential accounts may themselves call out for completion: they may lack a coherent and developed evolutionary context of meaning. The third section attempts to provide this context but in such a way as to continue rather than oppose Merleau-Ponty's thought. Existential fit is a concept presaged in *The Structure of Behavior* in the heavily emphasized notion of "propriety" and its concrete expression is assumed in "Eye and Mind" in the passage where Merleau-Ponty capsulizes what it is, to be a human body. In brief, on the evolutionary side, an examination of existential fit shows clearly why human uniqueness is to be elaborated at the level of sensory-kinetic worlds, not at the level of features, attributes, organs, accomplishments, and the like. At the same time, on the existential side, it shows why a correction is to be made in the traditional existential understanding of the physical and lived bodies; namely, that in a foundational existential-evolutionary sense these bodies are not separate but all of a piece.

1. The Question of Human Uniqueness in View of an Evolutionary Biology

The *question* of human uniqueness is as old as the concept of Darwinian evolution. It would never have arisen if Darwin had not upset a human-centered applecart. The question has recently become more urgent. The discovery that nonhuman animals make and use tools was a critical factor: tool-making/tool-using was one of the four major factors identified by Darwin as being taxonomically distinctive of human evolution. Along with intelligence, upright posture, and reduced canines, tool-making/tool-using was taken to be an ultimate defining mark of *Homo sapiens*. Once tools proved inadequate to their taxonomic task, language, presumably taken as the quintessential expression of intelligence, was identified as the feature making humans unique. But controversy regarding this feature has been rife of late with such interdisciplinary leaders as Chomsky, Langer, Myers, and Washburn tugging on the one side (see, eg, Chomsky, 1967, Langer, 1972, pp. 210–4, 265–355, Myers, 1976, and Washburn, 1978) and Griffin, Savage-Rumbaugh *et al.*, Fouts, Premack and their respective contingent of chimpanzees tugging on the other (see, eg., Griffin, 1976, Savage-Rumbaugh *et al.*, 1978, Fouts, 1975, and Premack, 1976). As positive claims for uniqueness continue to run into critical cross-fire, the tugging has become more tenacious. Griffin in fact has noted,

> It seems that the more difficult the question under consideration and the less adequate the available evidence, the more definite become the generally accepted assertions about the differences between human language and animal communication (Griffin, 1976, pp. 45–6).

Actually Griffin gives a most thorough account and review of the controversy in terms of mental experience generally (*Ibid.*, see pp. 4–8 for
Griffin's definition of mental experience). A considerably briefer quasi-
historical account is given by Gould (1977, pp. 49–55) who discusses areas
in which battles for uniqueness have been waged. The concern to identify
and spell out a human/nonhuman discontinuity, that is, to pinpoint
human uniqueness, has not been and is not negligible. Although not fully
recognized as such the task is difficult precisely because an affirmation of
human uniqueness entails theoretical contradictions. These are palpably
evident in the fact that first, a vast amount of scientific research (which
incidentally may have completely other aims, e.g., NASA, medical science) is based upon the steadfast evolutionary assumption that insights
into nonhuman physiology and behavior bear directly upon human physiology and behavior. Second, studies in comparative anatomy have demonstrated unequivocal morphological continuities between human and
nonhuman animals; and third, genetic research has disclosed foundational ties between humans and nonhumans not only in molecular structures such as DNA but also by way of protein analyses which show
startingly close kinships between humans and nonhumans.

   In face of such evidence and the steadfast evolutionary assumption, any
affirmation of human uniqueness spelled out in terms of behavioral, morphological or genetic differences appears doomed. The hub of the problem
is of course that if the Darwinian evolutionary model is preferred over a
creationistic model, for example, then actual discontinuities — absolute,
brusque changes — are in some crucial, pivotal instances impossible to conceive. For example, the idea that one fine evolutionary day, quite out of the
blue, a creature began speaking. That creature would be specified as
human by definition but its parents would not be. There is thus a filial
problem which is more than semantic. When the notion of actual discontinuity is brought down to the level of paleological reality, that is, to an
actual scenario of the past, it appears incredible precisely because of the
sudden break it demands. Where, for further example, would the *idea* of
speaking have come from? Even Lucretius 2000 years ago scoffed at, the
notion that speech was one day invented by a creature out of the blue (*De
Rerum Natura* V).

   The problem then in part is that if humans may be specified as unique in
some way today, that uniqueness has a certain lineage, which is to say that
it has made its way through an evolutionary time warp. Whatever the
unique feature, in the beginning, it would have to have grown out of a
broadly typical primate mode of living to the degree that early hominids
were more closely related in their lifestyle to nonhuman primates than to

today's humans—at least a belief in Darwinian evolution would entail that scenario. At the same time it is apparent that while fossilized tools in conjunction with other fossilized evidence lead to certain paleoanthropological reconstructions, particular recreations of a *human* past, sticks chosen and modified for use in fetching termites, for example, do not fossilize. Thus what might at first appear unique to humans may well turn out to be a practice common to nonhumans. Furthermore, one cannot be sure that those or other nonhuman practices do not predate hominid ones.

On the other hand, the problem is partly due too to the fact that affirmations of human uniqueness have been vigorously challenged by innovative and ingeniously devised experimental programs which counter the positive claims by giving evidence of, and thus underscorary continuities. One might refer here in fact to a burgeoning industry run by insurgents with a fourth world population. Certainly it is difficult not to characterize the ongoing research with chimpanzees alluded to earlier as "language habilitation programs".

In sum, any feature or ability designated as being unique to humans cannot be discretely located in the evolutionary past, traced back to a beginning point in strictly hominid space-time, any more than a human being itself can be so located. At the same time, the feature or ability cannot be conclusively located in the present either: an Egyptian vulture which is observed to throw stones at ostrich eggs (Thorpe, 1974, p. 277) or a chimpanzee which learns Ameslan or other symbolic modes of communication, confute the erstwhile evidence for human uniqueness.

2a. Human Uniqueness in the Structure of Behavior: A Brief Exposition and Critique

Merleau-Ponty did not specifically address the twin questions of human uniqueness and evolutionary continuities, yet the questions are clearly a major undercurrent of concern in his writings, most notably in *The Structure of Behavior* where he writes, for example, "... one cannot speak of the body and of life in general, but only of the animal body and animal life, of the human body and of human life", and goes on to say that "man can never be an animal" (Merleau-Ponty, 1967, p. 181). But the concern is also incisively if fleetingly apparent too in *Phenomenology of Perception* as well as in "Eye and Mind". If the concern is initially surprising, it ceases to be so the moment one realizes that an existential inquiry into human being is, wittingly or-not, a one-sided account of human/nonhuman differences. That is, to describe the nature of human being-in-the-world is necessarily to situate it in the reality of animate being-in-the-world: a claim for human uniqueness is implicitly if one-sidedly spelled out and by the same token, so also is an answer to the larger question of evolutionary continuities.

In *The Structure of Behavior*, Merleau-Ponty attempts to show that organisms have particular behavioral *a prioris* which make them distinctive. Furthermore, by an examination of the behavioral *a prioris*[1] of nonhuman animals, especially nonhuman primates",[2] Merleau-Ponty aims to show that human *a prioris* are different *in kind*. Humans are unique in virtue of a "superior mode of structuration", a superior *form* of living in the world. The evidence on which his claim is based comes from experimental studies in animal psychology. On Merleau-Ponty's interpretation of the data, chimpanzee behavior is not regulated by the objective properties of a thing, in which case the thing — a box, a rod, a ring — would be perceived as being a such-and-such and as being amenable to such-and-such usages regardless of where or under what conditions it might be perceived. The chimpanzee "cannot recognize something in different perspectives as the same *thing*" (*ibid.*, p. 118). Because it does not perceive the essential nature of things or their relational possibilities — a box as a seat, for instance, and the same box as an instrument, e.g., for reaching food (*ibid.*, p. 114) — the chimpanzee lacks the ability to transform things in its world. Merleau-Ponty claims that the chimpanzee lacks both the possibility of transforming *its* behavior relative to an instrument and the possibility of transposing something in its environment in a way relative to its own behavior, as when it is the goal that must move in relation to the chimpanzee itself as a stationary part of the behavioral field. Lacking a multiplicity of perspectives upon the same object, the chimpanzee has no possibility of *free* or *cognitive* conduct: it is incapable of *symbolic behavior* (*ibid.*, pp. 120–2).[3] The chimpanzee is thus seen as locked into particular structures of behavior which preclude an "openness to truth" and an understanding of "the proper value of things" (*ibid.*, p. 122).

In the process of making this case for human uniqueness, Merleau-Ponty comes close at two points to suggesting that his interpretation of the

1   "Likewise one finds, immanent to the phenomenal organism, certain nuclei of signification, certain animal essences – the act of walking toward a goal, of taking, of eating bait, of jumping over or going around an obstacle – unities which reflexology ... does not succeed in engendering from elementary reactions, and which are therefore like an *a priori* of biological science" (Merleau-Ponty, 1967, p. 157).

2   Lest Merleau-Ponty be wrongly accused of ignorance concerning taxonomy, attention should be called to the fact that the English translation of *La Structure du Comportement* is egregiously at fault insofar as the distinction between apes and monkeys is not recognized: "*singe inferieur*" is incorrectly translated word for word — as "inferior monkey" — while "*singe*" is simply "monkey". Thus chimpanzees in the English translation are frequently referred to as "monkeys".

3   See also p. 162: "The animal organism constructs a stable milieu for itself corresponding to the *monotonous a prioris* of need and instinct..." (italics added).

tests is not really fair since the tests take the animal out of its natural behavioral framework (*ibid.*, p. 113); and that the observed chimpanzee behavior might be better likened to, and measured against the behavior of human children or "primitive" humans than against the behavior of human adults (*ibid.*, pp. 115–6). But these potentially significant and critical points are not actually taken up as such. On the contrary, they are pointedly used as evidence to show that the chimpanzee's world is a mechanical-static one which does not measure *up* to the geometric-physical one of humans, most specifically, of world-wise humans. Thus Merleau-Ponty does not consider the possibility that that judgement is skewed which assays intelligence in the chimpanzee on wholly human grounds. He does not consider, for example, that upright posture, while assumed and assumable by a chimpanzee, is not its dominant postural attitude and that this fact might lave something to do with its not stacking boxes in equilibrium (*ibid.*, p. 116): if in its common state a chimpanzee is never at a loss for balance, then verticality is not felt, that is, it is not lived through as a hazard or as something to be achieved. Merleau-Ponty's analysis is in this sense biased in respect to both his interpretation and his theoretical use of the data.

To appreciate the criticality of this bias one might suppose, for example, that some humans were taken captive (as opposed to being observed and studied in the wild) by some inquisitive, enterprising, knowledge-seeking gibbon researchers and asked to brachiate 100 feet in the air in the middle storey of a rainforest, to a "goal" (a hamburger?) hanging from a tree limb some quarter of a mile away. The question of communication aside—how do the humans know what the gibbons expect of them, how do they know, for instance, that there *is* a goal, much less where it is?—how would the humans fare according to the gibbons? Would the gibbons liken the humans' efforts to their young or to "primitive" gibbons?; or, since they think humans more intelligent than some other vertebrates, would they compare their efforts straight-away with adult gibbons? Would they justify the reasonableness of the task on the grounds that humans are capable of brachiating and brachiate on occasion (on playground rings and gymnastic equipment) in the same way that they, the gibbons themselves, are capable of walking upright and indeed do so on the forest floor? Would they furthermore think that it is no different for them to ask humans to make their way in a treetop world than for humans to ask chimpanzees to make their way in an upright one? Would they think the efforts of the humans clumsy, over-cautious, lacking judgement, indecisive, uncooperative? Would they characterize them as slow learners? Might they even think that given e.g., disinterested, uncooperative, cowering responses, humans are primarily emotional creatures incapable of those cognitive functions which would allow them to judge distances efficiently and intelligently or to perceive and weigh advantages of alternative routes with precision and dispatch, and so on? As farfetched as this scenario might at first appear, it is not altogether fictional. One well-known and respected anthropologist whose intelligence would not be doubted made himself the subject of his study and discovered that he was a failure at fishing for termites with a stick (Teleki, 1974).

Merleau-Ponty's claims suffer from another bias as well, but this one unavoidable and apparent now only in retrospect. This bias actually ameliorates to some extent the above criticism of his efforts to establish biological grounds for human uniqueness. Since all of the scientific studies he utilized were done prior to 1942 when *La Structure du Comportement* was first published in France, Merleau-Ponty necessarily relied on experimental studies of the 1930's and earlier. The kind and amount of literature available on nonhuman primates were thus severely restrictive by today's standards and so also was the nearly exclusive behavioristic bent of scientific literature on animals other than primates. Ethological research and field studies of animals in their natural habitats were hardly common at that time; projects devoted to an understanding of nonhuman animals in their own worlds were barely underway. Thus, had they been current and/or available at the time, studies showing the use of symbolic gestures by pygmy chimpanzees, for example (Savage-Rumbaugh *et al.*, 1977) — to say nothing of bee dances or the language habilitation programs mentioned earlier — would have readily stopped Merleau-Ponty from making a statement such as, "In animal behavior signs always remain signals and never become symbols" (Merleau-Ponty, 1967, p. 120). Moreover studies showing a chimpanzee's ability to differentiate invariant properties of things in its environment (Savage-Rumbaugh *et al.*, 1978) would have been equally fatal to his central thesis that chimpanzees lack all sense of things as such. In sum, in default of an extensive descriptive and experimental literature, Merleau-Ponty's analysis and judgements were themselves skewed: they were untempered by a wide and solidly based research knowledge of nonhuman animal behavior.

If viewed directly in terms of human uniqueness, a third criticism could be added to the first two. Not only was the data used to establish human uniqueness severely limited and invalidated by evidence available today, and not only was it interpreted and judged by standards extrinsic to itself, but some quite telling data appear missing altogether: while accounts are given of nonhuman animal, behavior, no similar accounts are given of human behavior. The distinguishing feature of humankind — consciousness or mentality — is not carved out but is taken as a *fait accompli* from the beginning[4] and in fact as a *fait accompli* exclusive in the biological world. In effect, human uniqueness is not grounded by Merleau-Ponty in an analysis of human realities themselves and that analysis taken in comparison with an analysis of nonhuman realities.[5] Human realities are in large measure taken for granted. Perceiving the same object in different guises, for example, is unanalyzed either as a general or as a developmental human phenomenon. A neutral reader of *The Structure of Behavior* might thus get the impression that Merleau-Ponty is biased to begin with in wanting to make the claim that humans are unique in kind rather than in degree. This impression is bolstered by clear indications in the text that Merleau-Ponty does not want to vouchsafe *intelligence* to nonhuman primates: "Is it not to this mode of organization that the term intelligence ought to be reserved?" he asks in respect to his unanalyzed but posited "superior mode of structuration" (Merleau-Ponty, 1967, p. 116); "Will it ever be completely?" he asks in respect to the function of a thing being grasped with more than partial precision, i.e., a box as directly instrumental rather than as a vague something-or-other which might have "something to do" with the behavioral field (*ibid.*, p. 115).

Yet Merleau-Ponty would seem to want to say also that humans and nonhumans differ in degree as well as in kind since nonhuman animal structures — the vital structures — are enfolded in human structures. But this claim is never actually made because the kind of evolutionary continuities essential to its realization never surface. Behavioral continuities exist for Merleau-Ponty only in the form of fundamental biological dimensions of life, that is, in the form of "properly vital categories — the sexual object, the alimentary object, the nest ..." (*ibid.*, p. 153). All organisms realize these biological necessities according to their "preferred behaviors." (*ibid.*, p. 146ff.) Evolutionary continuities are present therefore only in the sense that every living creature in one way or another finds food, eats, finds a mate, mates, perceives dangers, avoids them, and so on. There is no significant difference in degree here at all: eating is eating and sleeping is

---

4   One need literally read only the table of contents and opening sentence of the introduction to the book. There is no mention of "mentality" until arrival at "the human order."

5   There might otherwise be, by today's standards, no reason to speak of use objects and cultural objects as Merleau-Ponty does; that is, as exclusively human accomplishments. Not only do chimpanzees and orangutans make and use tools, but Beck has persuasively argued that the stone-throwing exhibited by certain gulls is strikingly similar to tool-using by chimpanzees. For an up-to-date discussion of the matter including the Benjamin B. Beck article, "Chimpocentrism: Bias in Cognitive Ethology", see *Journal of Human Evolution* 11 (1), (1982). Also to be noted is the fact that if culture is a matter of passing on certain traditions, the potato-washing ritual of Japanese macaques must be considered as must also the fashioning of sticks with which to fish for termites.

sleeping. That a chimpanzee eats more meat than a gorilla but less than a human, for example, might be of interest to an ecologist or to a vegetarian but is hardly a sufficient basis for maintaining there are evolutionary differences in degree. What would be necessary to the latter would be an account of how vital structures are in fact enfolded in human structures, that is, how certain nonhuman animal behaviors are encompassed within human behaviors or conversely, how human behaviors have their antecedents in nonhuman behaviors. When the opportunity arises to examine this relationship, Merleau-Ponty in fact turns his back on it, as we have seen in respect to intelligence.

What is peculiar is that Merleau-Ponty seems to promise a difference in degree from the very beginning of the book. In his first sentence he states, "Our goal is to understand the relations of consciousness and nature ..." (*ibid.*, p. 3). A page later he states that his method of reaching this goal is to start " 'from below' and by an analysis of the notion of behavior" (*ibid.*, p. 4). In effect, from the beginning, there is a higher and a lower order—eventually exposited in terms of a human *mentality* and a nonhuman animal *vitality*—which are to be conjoined in some way. Indeed, while Merleau-Ponty wants to show that the human order is a new unity by virtue of a reorganization of structures, he also wants to show that the human order is co-extensive with the lower physical and vital orders: he wants, in his own words, to show that the higher is "liberated" from the lower but at the same time is "founded" upon it (*ibid.*, p. 184). But as noted, the founding aspect in an evolutionary sense appears to be nothing more than the mere fact that humans, like nonhumans, eat, mate, and so on. It is the liberated aspect that is all-compelling. Indeed, in the transformation from vital to human order, the former is all but devoured. In attempting "to make more precise the relations of the properly human dialectic with the vital dialectic by using the example of the Freudian system" (*ibid.*, p. 177), for example, Merleau-Ponty speaks of some people who fail to live a human life; for instance, "prisoners of a parental complex ... [who] believe they 'are marrying' when in reality they are seeking a maternal protection" (*ibid.*, p. 179). He goes on to say, "This is because the reorganization, the new birth ... is accomplished in them in word and not in reality" (*ibid.*, p. 179–80). In contrast to such seemingly pseudo-humans,

> there are other men, capable of integrating into their existence, by unifying it, what in the preceding ones was only ideological pretext, and these *would be* truly men. With respect to them, the causal explanations of Freud would always be anecdotal; they would account only for the most external aspects of a true love just as, according to Freud himself, physiological explanations do not exhaust the content of a dream (*ibid.*, p. 180).

In brief, if the founding aspect is expressed or apparent at all in an evolutionary sense, it appears as a hindrance to living a human existence rather than as a positive, if surpassed, dimension of it.

2b. Beyond *The Structure of Behavior*

Merleau-Ponty did not continue to explore nonhuman animal behavior as the foundation for understanding consciousness but neither did he amend his original interpretations and judgements or rescind them as such in his later works. The question of human uniqueness might thus be thought to have been either conclusively answered or abandoned by Merleau-Ponty as he turned his attention to human reality itself and to a deeper and deeper penetration of the human body as phenomenal center of that reality. But as noted earlier, to describe the nature of human being-in-the-world is necessarily to situate it in the reality of animate being-in-the-world: a claim for human uniqueness is adumbrated if not spelled out directly. Thus, though his attention shifted to a more exclusive focus, the question of human uniqueness was still engendered and was necessarily pursued in his later work. At the same time, and no doubt because the question was only indirectly addressed, the original assumptions remained unexamined. That this is so is apparent in *Phenomenology of Perception*, for example, where Merleau-Ponty put forth the conception of rationality and certain behaviors going hand in hand, that is, human hand in human hand. Earlier in *The Structure of Behavior*, Merleau-Ponty wrote, "Man is not a rational animal" (*ibid.*, p. 181). What he meant was that man is not an animal to which rationality has been added. It is not a matter of a new ingredient but of a new unity—a reorganization of structures of behavior. Later, in *Phenomenology of Perception*, he wrote, "it is no mere coincidence that the rational being is also the one who holds himself upright or has a thumb which can be brought opposite to the fingers; the same manner of existing is, evident in both aspects" (Merleau-Ponty, 1962, p. 170). This statement is actually followed by a footnote referring to two pages of *The Structure of Behavior* which have to do with an organism's "preferred behaviors", behaviors which are expressed by a variety of *a prioris*: e.g., "certain constants of conduct, of sensible and motor thresholds, of affectivity, of temperature, of blood pressure ..." (Merleau-Ponty, 1967, p. 148). Now the problem at a strictly philosophical level is that if "the same manner of existing" is simply a matter of "preferred behaviors," then the opacities of the earlier work have clearly not been repaired but simply rechristened: the one-to-one correspondence between rationality and upright posture or between rationality and an opposable thumb is synonymous with "a superior mode of structuration". But if, as Merleau-Ponty state just a few pages later in *Phenomenology of Perception*,

> there is not ... a form of behaviour which does not owe something to purely biological being ... and cause forms of vital behaviour to deviate from their pre-ordained direction, through a sort of leakage (1962, p. 189),

then the leakages must be either peculiarly deleterious — as per the aforementioned pseudo-humans suffering Freudian maladies and in which case leakage paradoxically runs counter to the realization of a true humanity — or the term "leakage" appears to be a misnomer: a "preferred behavior" can hardly be said to constitute a "leak". To conceive upright posture or an opposable thumb, for example, as a spilling over of a biological form onto a human or cultural form is to confound evolutionary theory. Culture and humanity are an outgrowth of biological life not its foundational forerunners.

Furthermore, the philosophical problem is substantially compounded when "the same manner of existing" is examined biologically. An opposable thumb and upright posture are part of a great ape's heritage. Grooming, for example, could not take place if the thumb were not opposable to the fingers; twigs could not be stripped of leaves if a digital opposability were not present. The opposability of a human and nonhuman primate thumb is different in degree but not in kind. The same is true of upright posture. In fact, chimpanzees are capable of several different modes of bipedal walking and even baboons — Old World monkeys — walk bipedally at times (see, eg., Napier, 1968, also Kortlandt in Tuttle, 1975, p. 230). In the upright posture of humans and nonhumans there is again a difference in degree, not in kind. In consequence, one can ask, does upright posture or an opposable thumb belong to the human order or the vital order? Can two orders be clearly distinguished in these terms at all? A less conclusive but not- unsimilar situation is apparent in respect to rationality. If rationality can be seriously examined by a philosopher in relation to *bees* (Bennett, 1964) and if the negative findings from that examination can be seriously challenged by biologists (Griffin, 1976, pp. 44–5),[6] then the question of rational intelligence in the animate world cannot be an already settled one and neither, by the same token, can the question of human uniqueness.

How then is one to understand "the same manner of existing"? The evidence seems to point toward the possibility that "the same manner of existing" exists itself along a continuum. Indeed, arguments against that possibility collide with a Darwinian evolutionary world. Moreover if

---

6   Griffin was echoing the criticism voiced by J.L. Gould (1976).

humans are not animals to which rationality has been added, then perhaps nonhuman animals are not animals from which rationality has been subtracted. Given these perspectives, features such as upright posture or attributes such as rationality cannot be plucked out of a biological repertoire and made to dance on exclusively human feet. To understand "the same manner of existing," what is necessary to begin with is a broader and deeper understanding of nonhuman animal behavior. Armed with such evolutionary understandings, amendments and corrections may be made of Merleau-Ponty's thought as suggested above. But in fact it is possible not only to amend and correct Merleau-Ponty's thought; it is possible at the same time to *continue* it.

In the last published work before his death, Merleau-Ponty wrote,

> There is a human body when, between the seeing and the seen, between touching and the touched, between one eye and the other, between hand and hand, a blending of some sort takes place — when the spark is lit between sensing and sensibles, lighting the fire that will not stop burning until some accident of the body will undo what no accident would have sufficed to do ... (1964).

Surely there is an altogether different notion of human uniqueness expressed in these lines, lines which incidentally are repeated in less eloquent fashion in Merleau-Ponty's posthumous work, *The Visible and the Invisible*.[7] It is as if a blueprint were given whereby one could recognize a human not by its attributes or by its organs, for example, but by the peculiar subtleties of its experiences. The level of distinction has been deepened: it is no longer a question of behavior but of what one might call sensory-kinetic domains. Given this new and deeper insight it is possible to flesh out Merleau-Ponty's account of the uniqueness of human being-in-the-world from an enhanced existential-evolutionary perspective. Existential fit is the key to that perspective. In the first place, the concept of existential fit provides the framework for making some necessary corrections, e.g., of Merleau-Ponty's early formulations of the physical body which, coupled with a reading of the available experimental scientific literature of the day, led him to espouse an absolute evolutionary discontinuity between humans and nonhumans. Of equal if not greater significance, the concept allows an elaboration of his later writings in which, as indicated above, in complete but provocative glimpses of human uniqueness appear. In short, through an exposition of the concept of existential fit and descriptive accounts of its expression, an existen-

---

7   "There is a circle of the touched and the touching ... there is a circle of the visible and the seeing ... there is even an inscription of the touching in the visible, of seeing in the tangible—and the converse; there is finally a propagation of these exchanges to all the bodies of the same type and of the same style which I see and touch ...." (Merleau-Ponty, 1968, p. 143).

tial-evolutionary dimension of being is uncovered which provides the context for amending and fleshing out Merleau-Ponty's accounts of human being, for grounding their validity and integrity, and for coming to an original understanding which anchors human uniqueness in the heart of life—both human and nonhuman—as it is lived rather than in the abstracted realities of features, organs, or behaviors. At this level, one might say, behavior becomes style and the "outside spectator" becomes phenomenologist.[8]

3. Existential Fit

In existential studies, the physical and lived bodies are usually described as oppositional. The one belongs to a third person world, the other to a first person world; the one is there for others, the other is here for me. From what point of view is this opposition discovered and conceptualized? It is not the definitive conclusion of a phenomenology of the body—an insight discovered through a foundational and thoroughgoing description of human bodily life. It is discovered in the analysis of certain bodily experiences tempered by two already drawn dichotomies: that of the self and the social (or the public and the private) as in Sartre's "my body for me and by body for others", and especially that of the existential and the scientific, as in the early writings of Merleau-Ponty and the writings of many other existential philosophers. In brief, it is a description and conception of the body that is rooted in certain views and/or practices common to the Western world. From this perspective it is preeminently a cultural conception of bodily being. To balance the corporeal scale one needs to dig down below the surface of the cultural and consider the phenomenon of bodily being in existential-evolutionary perspective, a perspective in which the fundamental life theme of existential fit is everywhere apparent. A fish, for example, is a creature which lives the life of a fish. But it is not of course a question of fish alone: no creature in the world is a physical specimen upon which a certain mode of living is grafted and neither is it a certain mode of living upon which a certain enabling physicality is grafted. That a fish is a creature that lives the life of a fish is rooted not in causal or teleological accounts of behavior but in the quintessential coherency of physical and lived bodies—in existential fit.

Since the major concentration of this section will be on an experiential account of existential fit, it would be well to indicate briefly beforehand

---

8   Allusion is made here to the actual conceptual and methodological shifts in MerleauPonty's writings, from early concerns with behavior to progressive and later concerns with styles of being, and from his early mode of inquiry in the stance of an "objective spectator" (1967, p. 162), to his later phenomenologically oriented modes of inquiry.

something of what is involved in its methodological elucidation—and thus something of the conceptual shifts it entails—and something also of its character in evolutionary and existential terms.

The methodological significance of the hyphenated adjective, existential-evolutionary, can be capsulized in the simplest way perhaps by quoting from Merleau-Ponty's posthumous work, *The Visible and the Invisible*, and saying that here too, "reversibility … is the ultimate truth"(1968, p. 155). Insofar as what exists evolves and what evolves exists, what is requisite is a reading of existential inscriptions in evolutionary accounts of life and a reading of evolutionary inscriptions in existential accounts of life. What is to be understood then is not a physico-chemical or physiological body in relation to a lived body, but life itself—animate being—as an existential-evolutionary phenomenon. Here the physical body is placed not in the cultural perspective of the sciences but is taken *in situ*: a living form, in the context of its immediate relationships and natural history. In effect, whatever the infra-structures of life, they are illuminated by looking through and at the whole of living life itself—through existence at evolution and through evolution at existence.

The phenomenon of existential fit can be briefly summarized in evolutionary terms through two abbreviated examples, one at the level of the individual, the other at the species level. In the human abnormality known as progeria, there is a disjunction of the physical and lived bodies. What is old is young and what is young is old and both at the same time. The warping of the physical precludes a simple act of reaching while a life too little lived is spent in dying. In a word, the child is out of joint with life. There is a schism at the most primordial level of being. In contrast, existential fit shows itself in every facet of a normal creature's life. What is existentially fit is existentially viable. An intact readiness exists to take up the living of a life. A particular subject is not merely alive in the world but livable.

Yet it is not simply an individual livability but a particular *kind* of individual livability which is alive in the world. While individual livability has its origin in existential fit, so *kinds* of livability have their origin in its differential expression. Hence what is necessary is an understanding of sensory-kinetic domains. In other words, any particular domain of "I can's"[9] is the differential expression of existential fit. A prime example of this expression is transparent in the story of some lobe-finned fish, a story that is an accepted chapter in evolutionary history.[10] Eons ago, these fish

---

9   This phrase is Husserl's (*Ich kann*) but it is taken up repeatedly by Merleau-Ponty. See, for example, 1962, p. 137; 1964, p. 102; 1968, pp. 171, 225, 255.

10 While zoologists never express doubt that it was lobe-finned fish which made the transition from a water-living environment to a land-living one, there is not unanimity about the reason

explored beyond the perimeters of their customary aquatic world and made their way on land. In doing so, they altered the course of organic evolution. Now it was not a group of fins that marched onto the land any more than it was a group of genes that decided that it was in the best interests of all to go forth and multiply. The water-to-land transition is a question not of abstracted physical bodies but of possible modes of living in the world, that is, a question of a particular domain of I can's whose inscriptions lie equally within the physical and lived bodies. Thus the fish that made the transition were in fact these fins, these genes, and so on, but not as the sole ultimate realities of their being: they were living subjects of a particular world. By the same token, the fish were in fact a certain kind of livability alive in the world, but not in abstraction from any particular body. The water-to-land transition entailed an opening in a particular domain of I can's; it was bodied forth by particular creatures. In brief, land-living as a possible way of being in the world was not only the expression of a quintessential coherency of physical and lived bodies — of existential fit — but also a measure of its differential expression in the world of living beings.

There is one more summary indication to be given. The phenomenon of existential fit is to be situated in existential as well as evolutionary perspective. Actually it is less a matter of situating than of acknowledging insofar as existential fit is already present in certain accounts in veiled form to begin with. In *The Structure of Behavior*, Merleau-Ponty speaks of a species as elaborating stimuli in a manner "which is proper to it" (1967, p. 129); he speaks of stimuli intervening "according to what they signify and what they are worth for the typical activity of the species considered" (p. 130); he speaks of situation and reaction participating "in a structure in which the mode of activity proper to the organism is expressed" (p. 130); he speaks of "the conditions of life … [being] defined by the proper essence of the species" (p. 174). What is this *propriety*, this appositeness without which neither existence nor evolution would be possible? What is this *propriety* which is acknowledged but passed over in silence? This a priori manner of elaborating a stimulus, this mode of activity proper to the

---

for their exodus. Various scenarios are offered to explain their behavior, e.g., the fish were stuck in the mud by drought conditions; their usual food supply was exhausted and they had to seek out a new source; they were stranded by accident and simply ventured forth; and so on. However reasonable any one of these scenarios might appear, a nagging question remains: why did some lobe-finned fish make their way onto land? Drought conditions, new food sources and the like might seem to answer this question but of course they do not do so at all. Causes are transformable into reasons only by way of internalization in a living subject. What makes any particular behavior possible is the creature itself, that is, a certain coherency of form and style of living in the world.

organism, this stimulus intervening according to what it signifies and what it is worth for the typical activities of the species considered — all these proprieties are testimonials to existential fit. The character of being proper to a certain species, the character of species themselves in terms of proper essences, both are an affirmation of a quintessential coherency of physical and lived bodies. The physical and the lived are not two distinct evolutionary sequences meeting and happening in the same creature, analogous in a sense to the laboratory conjunction of two strands of DNA, one recombinant and one natural. What exists and evolves are not parts but wholes, not fragments of life, but life itself. What is lived then in an existential-evolutionary sense are different sensory-kinetic worlds: these fins, these eyes, this fur, these wings, these ears, these arms, these legs, and so on, are a certain opening onto the world; they bespeak certain sensory-kinetic powers and sensitivities. To understand existential fit in existential terms is to understand precisely what it means to say that each species is a certain kind of livability in the world, a certain *propriety* of being.

With these preliminary remarks, it is possible to turn to a reading of inscriptions firsthand: to describe existential fit in experiential terms, to see it from the inside as it were. To do this means to find experiences where the remarkable consonance of the physical and lived bodies is close to the surface, where, in fact, the lived body rises up as *wholly* physical; that is, where it is not simply a matter of the felt body in any given experience but a matter of the felt body being felt as a *consummately* physical presence. Let me begin by offering a few varied examples.

A young chimpanzee swings repeatedly between the same two resilient branches then drops down and begins somersaulting and frolicking on the ground (van Lawick-Goodall, 1974, p. 156).

In the crevice between two hills, two birds are soaring; they are riding a single upcurrent of air; it is taking them no place in particular (see, for example, Thorpe, 1963, p. 363).

I am walking in a hillside park and come to a densely-grassed knoll. I fling myself down on the greenery and roll to the bottom.

The essential quality of these experiences is *sheer* physicality. What is being lived here is wholly the physical, but not as a display of certain skills, for example. Moreover what might in other circumstances be horizonal to the experience is here transformed in being lived directly. In a word, movement is experienced for its own sake; its meaning is capsulized in its own wild splendor. There is, in effect, nothing beyond the sheer physicality of the kinetically lived body: movement is all-consuming.

Now sheer physicality is the genus of what Lingis has described in terms of voluptuosity (Lingis, 1978) and what Plugge has described in terms of onerousness (Plugge, 1970, pp. 293–311). These two seemingly disparate existential accounts may thus be seen to have a common ground: each describes a sheer sensuous density of being. This kind of experience is an affirmation of the fundamental coherency of the physical and lived bodies and indeed is rooted in that fundamental coherency. In the one kind of experience the physical body is exultantly celebrated; in the other it is suffered as an inescapable affliction. The two experiences appear to reflect two poles of possible experiences of the physical body lived as consummately physical, poles describable as radical pleasure and radical pain. What I would like to suggest is that there are indeed two basic forms of sheer physicality and that while voluptuosity and onerousness are exemplars of each of these two forms respectively, a different kind of analysis is needed to plumb the depths of a sheer sensuous density of being and the foundational coherency of the physical and lived bodies in which that experience is anchored. What I would like to undertake is just such a beginning analysis by examining briefly one of the two basic forms.

Let me begin by describing briefly two paradigmatic experiences; the possible experience of sheer physicality in making love and in dancing. Though spoken of in the same breath, the experience of dance and of sexuality are not necessarily equatable in the least. I am in fact choosing these two experiences to highlight the difference between the two fundamental modes in which sheer physicality as radical pleasure can be experienced, namely, kinetically or tactilely — a sensuous density of being in movement or a sensuous density of being in the flesh.

The paradigmatic dance experience is one of pure movement. It is a solo dance in which no story is being told and in which movement stands for nothing but itself. The dance is a purely kinetic happening; it is a dance in which I am moving for the pure joy of movement — its suspensions, its bursts of speed, its shifts in accent and amplitude. Yet it is not as if I am *doing* the movement; on the contrary, I ride it like a wave but in such a way that its contours and mine coincide completely. There is, in effect, a union of myself and the dance. It lives through me at the same time that I live and breathe in it. The density of the dance and the density of my being thus come together: we meet in the sheer physicality of movement which is both me and the dance. Movement here is thus not a simple sensation of my body present in such and such a way at a particular time but an all-enveloping dynamic which radiates to the tips of my being. In the same way, I reach to every corner of the movement, drawing out all the powers of its form. I am nothing more than the movement and the movement is nothing more than me. How indeed tell the dancer from the dance? We envelop one another; we cohabit the same space-time; our physicalities match; two purely sensuous densities come together that are woven of the same kinetic cloth; they are each of them cast of the same sheer physicality that is movement.

There is a structure of this dance experience that is not only quite striking but that has far-reaching significance in terms of existential fit and evolutionary continuities. It is a structure implied by, but not spelled out in the foregoing description. To experience the dance as the sheer physicality of movement is to experience a dilation of the present. The customary surge of time from past to future is halted. In its place a singular dimension is present, but it is exaggerated, engorged, as it were. Now dominates not only the moment but its typical horizons as well. Protentions and retentions are virtually nonexistent.[11] In effect, I am not moving toward a future nor out of a past; I am moving only in the present moment which is enlarged beyond measure. What I experience temporally is thus a density of now, a density that matches and is engendered by the sheer sensuous density of my being and the sheer sensuous density that is the dance. There is indeed a perfect accord between the movement I experience as sheer physicality and the thickened present in which the dance and I live; we are all part of the same temporality.

In lovemaking too, being is caught up in the sensuous density of now. It is the present moment that holds sway and is all-consuming; it is again a time in which the moment now is suddenly wild, overrunning its ground and pushing past and future to almost invisible horizons.[12] The essentially tactile sensuous character of lovemaking, however, makes it an experience quite different from a pure movement dance. In the act of making love what is of moment is not movement *per se* but the fleshly reality of being entwined on being. If movement at times enthralls, it is the touch of flesh on flesh which carries it to enthralldom. Its dynamics are felt on the common ground of a shared tactility. Thus, my movements are not experienced as kinetic figures but as tactile patterns upon the other. Similarly, the other's movements ride a tactile strand of flesh coiled on flesh; that is, they arouse me not because of their kinetic quality *per se* but because their

11 "Nonexistent" refers only to the fact that no aim attends, and no concrete recollections weight the immediate experience. It does not mean that there are no layers of meaning attaching to the experience in the form of habits (e.g., my capacity to move in these ways), memories (e.g., my knowledge of the dance), expectations (e.g., to dance the dance through to completion), and the like.

12 Again (see note 4 above), it is not a matter of there being nothing in the way of bodily remembrances and anticipations. It is simply that past and future do not intrude as such upon the immediate experience itself: I am not thinking of what happened a minute ago, for example, or of what will happen in the next several moments.

intensities and rhythms are tactilely revealed to me. In short, I feel the other's movement through my flesh and the livingness of my own movement through the flesh of the other. The *making* of love is indeed a *tactile* creation.

In the sheer physicality of flesh, two sensuous densities come together. The experience of touch is not then a mere surface phenomenon; it is not cutaneous stimulation. Making love is a tactile fathoming of the sensuous density of the other — just as it is a yea-saying of my own sensuous density. Moreover given that the experience is one in which the fleshly sensuousness of being is dilated, it is easy to understand why it is that in being stroked, licked or squeezed, for example, touching is not either experienced as a punctual phenomenon. It is not as if there is nothing in between the places touched. There is not even what might be called, correlative to the visual, a negative tactile space which is set over and against a positive one. The places actually touched bespeak and awaken a whole; they radiate to the outermost edge of being — as in a *frisson* of ecstasy — or they magnetize the whole of being as in a rush of orgasmic shudderings. In all the experiences of being touched and whatever their particular form, it is a question of concentric ripplings outward or inward, magnifications from, or concentrations in, an original tactile center which ignite the whole of being. All touchings are an immediate incandescence of my flesh. In like fashion, my act of touching the other is not experienced as a compendium of localized tactile sensations of my own flesh or that of the other. The places I touch are places of literal joining but they gather up a whole. My tactile feelings of the other and my feelings as tactual subject are not then punctual phenomena either, mere spatially locatable events analogous to a sensory homunculus in my cortex. Moreover in embracing the other, I embrace not a fragment but a sensuous density whose form is adumbrated in all the actual frontiers of flesh on flesh. The other exists for me not as a series of parts touched but as an infrangible whole whose boundaries are beyond my flesh yet which my flesh nevertheless encompasses and extols.

Now if the above abbreviated descriptive accounts of lovemaking and of dancing are paradigmatic examples of sheer physicality then it should be possible through them to illuminate what makes the experience of a sheer sensuous density of being possible and thus come to a deeper understanding of the fundamental coherency of the physical and lived bodies — of existential fit.

To begin with, to be lived as sheer physicality the physical body must be not simply sensible in and of itself but sensible to a radical degree. This radical prominence of the physical is grounded in a reversibility of experience at the moment of erstwhile "worldly" experience itself, that is, in the awakening of a wholly sensuous and self-revealing dimension of bodily being. The possibility thus depends upon the sensory-kinetic world of the subject which is to say that the physical body can be lived as radical pleasure only insofar as a self-reflexive sensory modality exists: the physical body can otherwise not be thrust to the foreground of experience—lived for its own sake. The brief examples given earlier, e.g., of a chimpanzee swinging repeatedly between the same resilient branches, then somersaulting and gamboling about on the ground, are descriptive of just such kinetically reversed experiences. They are cameos of the more fully described dance experience. In these kinetic experiences of sheer physicality, movement is lived for its own sake. It stops short of imprinting itself on the world, so to speak, but turns back upon the creature itself. It is not experienced as movement for something, but is wholly consuming in its own right. Movement is an experience of radical pleasure then precisely insofar as a subject can live it and it alone, that is, precisely insofar as a subject can transform the experience of *mere* movement or *horizontal* movement into a sheer kinetic density of being. The possibility of reversible kinetic meanings is thus engendered or not in the I can's of a living subject, I can's that signify a certain kind of livability in the world that is the differential expression of existential fit.

In a tactile experience of sheer physicality equally reversed meanings are present but in the language of the flesh. What is curious here, however, is that no indication of a radical tactility is to be found in accounts of non-human animals.[13] A sense of radical pleasure in the form of a wild splendor of flesh on flesh is missing. Touch as a self-reflexive modality appears to be a uniquely human character.

Yet hard and fast lines cannot be so swiftly drawn. Evolutionary continuities are just that: affinities cannot be ignored. On the one hand, for example, there is the fact that chimpanzees enjoy being tickled;[14] on the other hand, there is the fact that domestic and other humanly-accessible animals enjoy being stroked;[15] if a third hand were permitted, there is also

---

13   What is curious in face of this curiosity is the fact that when humans accuse each other of "acting bestial", of "being an animal", with respect to their sexual behavior, the accusation has no basis in fact: nonhuman sexual encounters are marked by an uncommonly unboisterous, non-sybaritic carnality.

14   See, for example, van Lawick Goodall, 1971, pp. 154–5; see also Montagu, 1971, p. 36: "In their passion for being tickled [chimpanzees] will draw the tickler's hand to their bodies."

15   Ashley Montagu writes, "Almost every animal enjoys being stroked or otherwise having its skin pleasurably stimulated" (*ibid*. p. 28). What is overlooked in this statement of course is the fact that stroking is a *human* occupation—or preoccupation, i.e., nonhuman animals do not stroke, humans do. What is overlooked then in fact makes the immediate point so far as evolutionary continuities are concerned: there are obvious evolutionary overlaps. But what is overlooked also makes the later point regarding the preeminently human character of a radical tactility.

the fact that in mammalian life, offspring are licked often and profusely by their mothers.[16] Although there are no ready cameos here of the more fully described experience of lovemaking, a radical pleasure of the flesh is nonetheless adumbrated in one way and another in these nonhuman tactile experiences.[17] All the same, there are distinctive human/nonhuman differences and it is precisely an elucidation of these differences that will throw into relief what it means to say that existential fit is an invariant differentially expressed across all of evolutionary history. To describe this invariant in broad terms is to answer the question, what makes the experience of a sheer physicality of movement possible to human/nonhuman creatures but a sheer physicality of the flesh possible to preeminently human ones? In finer terms, it is to answer the question, what is the meaning of existential fit in terms of the experience of a sheer sensuous density of being in the flesh—or alternatively, in relation to nonhuman primates, of not being in the flesh, since what is not experienced in mating rituals appears to be precisely the physical body as such. Let us pursue the matter briefly by way of the finer point first.

From an evolutionary perspective, the phenomenon of lovemaking cannot be explained as a cultural refinement or embellishment of mere animal mating or sexual intercourse. In fact, in lovemaking there is a superfluity of touchings and entwinings that no mere sexual dimorphism or cultural elaborations suffice to explain. The experience of a radical pleasure of the flesh can be understood only in the light of a body made for touching and being touched. Looked at in this light, it is first of all clearly a tactile openness that grounds the possibility of a radical tactility of the flesh: human bodies are exposed to touch: they are upright and they are naked. They are topologically accessible to touch and directly so. One might almost say they are vulnerable to touch; they are bodies whose skin is virtually unprotected and whose relatively tiny base of support is a stark contrast to a full three-dimensional tactile exposure to the world. But uprightness and nakedness bequeath them as well a power to touch. Most obviously, of course, arms can embrace, hands can fondle, fingers can probe, nails can scratch. But over and above this peripheral tactuality, a human body can stretch out, press, roll, or rub full length against another body. Moreover that extensive contact is again direct: a virtually uncovered skin is in

---

16   Ashley Montagu's book, *Touching,* offers the most complete overview and bibliography on this subject.

17   This adumbration might be characterized as a capacity for pleasure in being touched. There is in this sense an openness or proclivity toward a radical pleasure of the flesh in terms of a *sensitivity* to touch. What is missing is an equal openness or proclivity in terms of a *power* to touch. As suggested later in the text, being touched outstrips touching: a tactile but not a tactual subject is present.

immediate communion with the world. In effect, human bodies can be lived as a radical pleasure of the flesh precisely because they are tactual subjects steeped in tactility: all my I can's are indeed drenched in this humanness which I am—these arms, these legs, this torso, this head are what I live in lovemaking, not as so many parts but as both a freedom and a destiny I choose to fulfill. As an expression of existential fit, a radical pleasure of the flesh is thus continuous with a radical tactility and vice versa. A sensory-kinetic subject whose exposure and power to touch are extraordinary and a sheer physicality of the flesh go hand in hand.

If a radical being in the flesh is preeminently a human possibility it is because human flesh is above all a tactile affair and conversely, because tactility is beyond all an affair of the flesh. Touching and being touched offer the continual possibility of taking hold and enveloping one completely in an experience of radical pleasure. In contrast, tactility in nonhuman primates appears by and large to retain both a cutaneous and punctual character: it stops on the surface and is localized. Pleasure is possible but not yet a full-blown *radical* pleasure of the flesh. It is only where what is tactilely felt becomes an erotic awakening of one's own flesh and where correlatively, what is tactually felt heralds a similar erotic awakening that a radical pleasure of the flesh is possible. That touchings tend to remain on the surface and localized in nonhuman animals is thus to be seen in the context of a differential expression of existential fit. For example, mother-infant and physical peer play relationships aside, tactility in nonhuman primates remains predominantly in the service of the other senses. A world of soft things, smooth things, rough things, hard things, round things, warm things, small things, and so on, is not built up by them. They are not preeminently *tactual subjects:* they do not go about feeling the world directly as a mode of knowing it and making consummate sense of it. Moreover where touch itself has meaning in social contacts, it enters at the level of the symbolic rather than the sensuous. Thus, the pat on the hand, arm or buttocks that reassures; the tactile ministrations of grooming that unite and calm; the semblant tactile gestures of a male that request a female to turn or to adopt a certain position.[18] All such tactile social gestures are one-sided, fleeting, and/or static. In such contacts the tactile subject does not pass continuously over into the realm of the tactual and the tactual subject continuously over into the realm of the tactile.

---

18   It might be noted in this context that evolutionary continuities are again apparent and that humans are not so unique as they might think themselves to be so far as a face to face positioning in sexual encounters is concerned—see, for example,Bronowski, 1973, p. 401: "We are the only species that copulates face to face." On the contrary, pygmy chimpanzees—bonobos—mate at times in what is described in biological literature as a "ventro-ventral" copulating position. See Savage-Rumbaugh *et al.*, 1977, pp. 97–116.

Moreover the encounter itself is not an encounter of two animate beings committed to touch: a truly dyadic dimension is missing. Indeed, being touched outstrips touching: even in mother-infant relationships, stroking, petting, fondling and caressing are not evident. In short, touching and being touched are not intertwined but separated by a sensuous and interanimate abyss.

It thus becomes clear why neither uprightness nor nakedness would make nonhuman primates ardent lovers but would only make any particular kind of nonhuman primate impossible. In the same way that a bird neither flies because it has wings nor has wings because it flies, so humans neither make love because they are upright and naked nor are upright and naked because they make love. It is not a matter of possessions or attributes *per se* or the lack thereof, but of a certain coherence of physical and lived bodies. At the same time it becomes clear why one could not teach a nonhuman primate to make love. A chimpanzee might rehearse certain tactual gestures with another chimpanzee, for example, or conceivably, even with a human, but one could not teach the chimpanzee to *feel* a certain kind of sensuous transport, to feel that is, a sensuous density of being in the flesh. Lovemaking is not a matching of parts, a simple joining like the coupling of boxcars, nor is it a certain series of tactual gestures, the *doing* of certain acts. Lovemaking is a certain way of being a body in the world; it is a celebration of a certain I/World relationship; it is the having of a certain interanimate world. Being in the moment in the wild splendor of flesh on flesh is clearly the differential expression of existential fit.

At one existential-evolutionary level, tactility is a way of knowing the world and making sense of it directly. It is a way of inquiring into the nature of things directly by taking them up, handling them, feeling them. It is perhaps the primordial way an epistemological subject comes to grips with the world and grounds its reality. But there is also another tactile mode of knowing the world, that is, as radical pleasure. Knowing the world directly by touch may be reversed at times to reveal glimpses of this wild splendor, as some nonhuman as well as human experiences might indicate. The reversal is an opening onto the possibility of a radical tactility of the flesh, an erotic awakening of being in the flesh. This mode of knowing might be described as the domain of the pre-epistemological subject, but not in the sense of a temporal, developmental, or evolutionary priority. Knowing here is a matter of carnal knowing,[19] a knowing where

---

19   It might be of interest to note that the verb, "know", has the same linguistic root as the verb, "can". This would of course root the activity of knowing in the body and thus vindicate further the suggestion of a pre-epistemological subject. It might also have some rather provocative implications in respect to Husserl's original way of referring to bodily knowledge as "I can's".

subject and world come together in a sheer sensuous splendor of being. Hence carnal knowledge is knowledge of a pre-epistemological subject in the sense that the *hyle* carries its own meaning. The temporal structure of the experience of sheer physicality bears out this self-contained meaning. Going beyond the given or the moment now is minimal; any surpassings are ground rather than figure in the experience. Meanings begin and end in heightened bodily sensitivities, in effulgencies of feeling and being.

A pre-epistemological subject is equally evident in the experience of moving for movement's sake. Here too a sensory modality recoils on itself; movement is not a mode of knowing the world directly but a mode of radical pleasure. The pre-epistemological subject is thus not limited to, but subsumes the libidinal subject within its domain. It lives in heightened meanings of the body itself, reverberating in exultant, erotic, voluptuous, joyful, ecstatic, yea-saying, or life-rejoicing awakenings of its own kinetic or tactile being-in-the-world. What makes a sheer physicality of the flesh preeminently possible to humans is of course a body which exists as flesh, a body that nonhuman animals do not know in a full-blown way. They live the body as sheer physicality in movement, or more precisely, certain animal's I can's allow them to turn movement into a kinetic joyride. In such instances, it is not the body *tout court*, but the body-in-movement that is lived. In other words, the lived body rises up as wholly physical only as a body-in-movement. The experience of the physical body *as such*, i.e., as flesh, is thus an existential-evolutionary elaboration of lived physicality, the differential expression of existential fit. In light of this differentially lived physicality, perhaps what makes humans unique is not their language but their lovemaking. But then again, what makes their lovemaking unique is in part wrapped up in a tongue that also speaks. The moral would seem to be that human uniqueness does indeed lie not in certain accomplishments, attributes, organs, and so on, but in a rich and complex tactility that grounds all manner of human being-in-the-world.

A final postscript should be added and a final summation too regarding the seminal way in which Merleau-Ponty's later thought contributes to a fresh and fundamental understanding of human uniqueness. As to the former concluding point, the physical-lived levels at which existential fit has been described is one of three interlocking levels. A second dimension of existential fit is apparent at the level of I/World relationships. For example, the consummate experience of the physical body *as flesh* can be described in terms of differential I/World relationships insofar as radical pleasure here is an intersubjective phenomenon. More obviously and more generally, of course, this level can be described in terms of particular *Umwelts*. But if "the manifest fit between organisms and their environment is a major outcome of evolution" (Lewontin, 1978, p. 213), it is no less an existential dimension of all living forms. Furthermore, just as existential fit is expressed in the experiences of a pre-epistemological subject, so it is also expressed at the level of the epistemological subject. This third level is best captured in Merleau-Ponty's tantalizing statement partially quoted and discussed in the second section of this paper:

> Everything in man is a necessity. For example, it is no mere coinci-
> dence that the rational being is also the one who holds himself upright
> or has a thumb which can be brought opposite to the fingers; the same
> manner of existing is evident in both aspects.

To spell out this *necessarily* "same manner of existing" is to spell out a dif-ferential, i.e., human, expression of existential fit in epistemological expe-rience: how the physical body *as such*, that is, flesh, is intertwined with rationality.

Given these varied expressions, it becomes clear why existential fit is not a contingent but a fundamental fact of life and why, though unacknowl-edged as such, it is also fundamental to Merleau-Ponty's thought. If *propri-ety* is a *necessity*, for example, it is an existential-evolutionary necessity. Where there is no livability, there is neither existence nor evolution. More-over in the same way that Merleau-Ponty's concept of propriety in *The Structure of Behavior* is anchored in the reality of existential fit, so also is his concept of a uniquely human body. In his "There is a human body ..." statement in "Eye and Mind", what is *proper* to a human body is spelled out. In effect, where there is a *particular kind* of livability in the world, there is a particular domain of sensory-kinetic powers and sensitivities.[20]

In sum, after acknowledging and clearing away errors of interpretation of nonhuman animal behavior and after amending the theoretical formu-lations those erroneous interpretations supported by way of evolutionary relationships and claims of human uniqueness, a legacy of insights clearly remains. These insights are not markers *along* a path but markers *of* a path leading to new and fundamental understandings of evolutionary continu-ities and human uniqueness. They indicate that what distinguishes the human from the nonhuman in the most fundamental sense are lifestyles grasped and interpreted as different sensory-kinetic modes of living in the world. Insofar as what evolves are not biological items *per se*, that is, one by one attributes, organs, capabilities and the like, but groups of creatures liv-ing certain kinds of lives, claims of uniqueness would seem to be rightly

---

20 An appreciation of the evolutionary strain in Merleau-Ponty's thought might include reference to his use of biological concepts — e.g., chiasm, dehiscence — as essential anchors in his existential analyses. In fact, "chiasm" is *the* pivotal concept in Merleau-Ponty's account of reversibility, i.e., reversibility is grounded in "the blending of some sort [which] takes place ... between sensing and sensible."

founded in the sensory-kinetic realities which in fact constitute those kinds of lives. Such a theme runs like an undercurrent deep below the surface of Merleau-Ponty's writings after *The Structure of Behavior*. When that theme surfaces it does so with forceful resonance as in the "Eye and Mind" passage: "What no accident could suffice to do" is a measure of existential fit.

References

Beck, Benjamin B. 1982. "Chimpocentrism: Bias in Cognitive Ethology", *Journal of Human Evolution* 11 (1).

Bennett, Jonathan. 1964. *Rationality (London:* Routledge & Kegan Paul).

Bronowski, J. 1973. *The Ascent of Man,* (Boston: Little, Brown and Co.).

Chomsky, Noam . 1967. "The General Properties of Language", in Frederic L. Darley and Clark H. Millikan (eds.), *Brain Mechanisms Underlying Speech and Language* (New York: Grune and Stratton), pp. 73–88.

Fouts, Roger S. 1975. "Capacities for Language in Great Apes", in R.H. Tuttle (ed.), *Socioecology and Psychology of Primates* (The Hague, Mouton Publishers), pp. 371–90.

Gould, J. L. 1976. "The Dance-Language Controversy." *Quarterly Review of Biology.*

Gould, Stephen Jay. 1977. *Ever Since Darwin* (New York, W.W. Norton).

Griffin, Donald R. 1976. *The Question of Animal Awareness* (New York, The Rockefeller University Press).

Howells, William. 1959. *Mankind in the Making* (New York: Doubleday & Co.).

Kortlandt, A. 1975. In a discussion section of *Primate Functional Morphology and Evolution,* Russell H. Tuttle (ed.) (The Hague: Mouton).

Langer, Susanne K. 1972. *Mind: An Essay on Human Feeling,* vol. II (Baltimore:John Hopkins University Press).

Lewontin, Richard C. 1978. 'Adaptation', *Scientific American,* 239 (3).

Lingis, Alphonso. 1978. 'Intentional Libido, Impulsive Libido', paper presented at the Society for Phenomenology and Existential Philosophy.

Lucretius. *De Rerum Natura* V.

Merleau-Ponty, Maurice. 1962. *Phenomenology of Perception,* trans. Colin Smith (London: Routledge & Kegan Paul).

Merleau-Ponty, Maurice. 1964. 'Eye and Mind', in James M. Edie (ed.), *The Primacy of Perception* (Evanston: Northwestern University Press).

Merleau-Ponty, Maurice. 1967. *The Structure of Behavior,* transl. A.L. Fisher (Boston: Beacon Press).

Merleau-Ponty, Maurice. 1968. *The Visible and the Invisible,* ed. Claude Lefort, trans. Alphonso Lingis (Evanston: Northwestern University Press).

Montagu, Ashley. 1971. *Touching* (New York: Columbia University Press).

Myers, Ronald E. 1976. "Comparative Neurology of Vocalization and Speech: Proof of a Dichotomy", in S.R. Hamad, H.D. Steklis and J. Lancaster (eds.), *Origins and Evolution of Language and Speech,* Annals of the New York Academy of Sciences, vol. 280, pp. 745–57.

Napier, J.R. 1968. "A Classification of Primate Locomotor Behaviour", in S.L. Washburn and Phyllis C. Jay (eds.), *Perspectives on Human Evolution*, vol. I (New York: Holt, Rinehart and Winston), pp. 85–93.

Plugge, Herbert. 1970. 'Man and His Body', transl. Erling Eng, in Stuart F. Spicker (ed.), *The Philosophy of the Body* (Chicago: Quadrangle Books).

Premack, David. 1976. "Mechanisms of Intelligence: Preconditions for Language", in S.R. Hamad, H. D. Steklis and J. Lancaster (eds.), *Origins and Evolution of Language and Speech*, Annals of the New York Academy of Sciences, vol. 280, pp. 544–61.

Savage-Rumbaugh, E. Sue, Wilkerson, Beverley, and Bakeman, Roger. 1977. 'Spontaneous Gestural Communication Among Conspecifics in the Pygmy Chimpanzee *(Pan paniscus)'*, in G.H. Bourne (ed.), *Progress in Ape Research* (New York: Academic Press).

Savage-Rumbaugh, E. Sue, Duane M. Rumbaugh, and Sally Boysen. 1978. "Linguistically Mediated Tool Use and Exchange by Chimpanzees", *The Behavioral and Brain Sciences,* vol. I, No. 4, pp. 539–54.

Teleki, G. 1974. "Chimpanzee Subsistence Technology: Materials and Skills", *Journal of Human Evolution* 3, pp. 575–94.

Thorpe, W.H. 1963. *Learning and Instinct in Animals*, 2nd ed. (London: Methuen & Co.).

Thorpe, W. H. 1974. *Animal and Human Nature* (Garden City, N. Y.: Anchor), p. 277.

van Lawick-Goodall, Jane. 1974. *In the Shadow of Man* (New York: Dell Publishing Co.).

Washburn, Sherwood L. (with Elizabeth R. McCown). 1978. "Human Evolution and Social Science", in *Human Evolution: Biosocial Perspectives,* vol. IV (Menlo Park, The Benjamin/Cummings Publishing Co.), pp. 285–94.

Chapter IV

On the Conceptual Origin of Death

The human race is the only one that knows it must die, and it knows this only through its experience. A child brought up alone and trans-ported to a desert island would have no more idea of death than a cat or a plant. (Voltaire)

Introduction

Merleau-Ponty described the objective body as the "impoverished image" of the phenomenal body (Merlau-Ponty, 1962, p. 431). In an earlier work, Sartre drew a similar distinction when he described the body being-for-itself and the body-for-others as existing "on different and incom-municable levels" with one another (Sartre, 1956, p. 305). Many existential philosophers have gone on to extol these critical determinations and to incorporate the distinction in their work as a fundamental verity of human existence. Thus, Schrag, for example, has insisted on the necessity of consis-tently contrasting "the body as *concretely lived*" with "the body as *objectively known*" (Schrag, 1979, p. 156). On the other hand, Plugge, and more recently, Zaner, have spoken of the entwinement of the physical and lived bodies: "The bodily as physical", says Plugge, "also exists phenomenally within the frame of the bodily live" (Plugge, 1970, p. 296). Zaner uses the concept of the uncanny to describe the intrinsic entwinement peculiar to embodiment (Zaner, 1981, pp. 47–66). More recently still, Sheets-Johnstone has examined the physical and lived bodies from an existential-evolutionary perspective and described their quintessential coherence in terms of "existential fit" (Sheets-Johnstone, 1986, pp. 219–48). Together, these latter works suggest a reassessment is underway, modest in impact perhaps still at this point, but with substantial implications for a more just hermeneutics of the body, a more exact *Leibkorper phenomenologische*.[1]

An examination of death within the context of this apparently nascent reassessment might at first glance seem counter-productive. Death, after

---

[1]   Zaner's *Context of Self* (1981, p. 55) suggests just such a domain of study, see p. 55

all, commonly means not an entwinement but a separation: a cessation of the lived body and a slow decay of the physical one. But the initial impression misses the point: what *was* unitary—what was entwined or quintessentially coherent in the everyday flow of corporeal life—is in death sundered. An understanding of the conceptual origin of death thus rests upon an understanding of how a certain Other came into the world, an Other in the form of a physical body perceived and ultimately conceived *as such*.

Along with the above remarks which situate the paper within the context of phenomenology and existential philosophy, a few words should be said regarding methodology and methodological implications. To begin with, being an examination of the origin of the concept of death, the concern is not ontological but epistemological. How is it that we humans came to be aware of death? More precisely, since the concept of death did not originate with modern *Homo sapiens*—burial practices of Neandertals, for example, point toward an older genesis—how is it that our long-ago ancestors came to an awareness of death? To answer this question is to elucidate an existential-evolutionary history: it is to show in an existential-evolutionary sense the origin of the chiasmatic notions of animate and terminal existence. To this end both a hermeneutical and phenomenological analysis are needed: the former to root the investigation in evolutionary perspective, the latter to flesh out the complex structures of awareness discovered in the paleoanthropological hermeneutic.

The detective work at times necessary to the hermeneutic enterprise is in principle no different from that necessary to other similar existential studies: clues are gathered and interpreted. What might be deemed unique here is that in part a wholly different realm of clues is used. Existential significations will be extracted neither from pathological or medical findings nor from customary everyday ontic sources. In order to chart the origin of certain strikingly human awarenesses, what is needed are evolutionary clues, some of which are discoverable through a bracketed examination of given evolutionary behaviors; some of which are discoverable through an examination of the everyday worlds of nonhuman animals; and some of which are discoverable through an interpretation of certain behavioral practices in preliterate societies.

The gathering and using of such clues assume the essential correctness of evolutionary theory. More than this, they indicate that evolutionary theory is being taken *seriously*: it is not just organs and systems that evolved, but sensitivities and powers, awarenesses and behaviors. In other words, evolutionary changes are not partial or disembodied alterations—survival is not a matter of the mere *having* of a certain anatomical part—but organic variations of *whole, living* creatures; an evolutionary history is permeated through and through with existential significations. But furthermore, if evolutionary theory is to be taken seriously, it is clear that existential philosophy can no longer disregard the fact that humans did not suddenly descend from the treetops, neither as freedom (Sartre) nor as *Dasein* (Heidegger) nor as any other wholly isolated evolutionary being. Or, to put the point more emphatically, humans did not spring *undescended* into the evolutionary world. Whatever humans are — in an existential sense whatever ontological structures might be described as theirs and theirs alone — they are evolutionary creatures: ontological structures are necessarily ones that evolved and ones that, for all we know, are still evolving and will continue to evolve. While humans might admittedly be too short-sighted to appreciate that long-range bio-ontological relativity, they cannot be too shortsighted to acknowledge their evolutionary heritage short of espousing a creationist doctrine of human existence. Thus, if self-disclosedness is what makes *Dasein Dasein*, then the evolutionary origin of self-disclosedness is an issue. In default of evolutionary grounding, the concept of *Dasein* either collapses in the face of evolutionary theory or it sustains itself through a creationist doctrine. Neither of these alternatives is attractive. But neither need be taken. By extending the range of genetic phenomenology, that is, by employing a phenomenological hermeneutics with respect to paleoanthropological reconstructions, it is possible to ground *Dasein* in evolutionary time and in so doing, illuminate the onto-epistemological structures that constitute the opening of its Being-toward-Death.

Something similar can be said with respect to the being-for-itself which is human freedom. As with *Dasein*, the entrance of such a being onto the worldly scene necessitates a *deus ex machina* in the wings. Such backstage manoeuvering clearly undermines the credibility of the very being for whom it is being undertaken. What is crucial to the ontology is evolutionary grounding. As with the grounding of self-disclosedness, the grounding of being-for-itself is to be sought in a phenomenological hermeneutics which, in its application to paleoanthropology, is akin to genetic phenomenology: in both undertakings, it is a question of uncovering and elucidating *origins*.

1. Nonhuman Animal Death:
The Question of Language and Behaviorism

It might be thought that the reason nonhuman animals do not know death as such — that is, as a conceptually distinctive phenomenon — is that they have no verbal language; and correlatively, that we humans know death because we speak. Only through the having of such a language could the recognition of death be conceptually fixed. Thus, it might be said that the reason Olly and her daughter, Gilka, chimpanzees of the Gombe Stream area (van Lawick-Goodall, 1971, pp. 214–7), traipsed about with Olly's dead four-week-old new baby was that they had no verbal language by which they could conventionally identify the state of the baby as dead. Had they such a language, their behavior would conceivably have been different: Olly would not likely have carried the corpse along with her in the days following the infant's death, slinging it over her shoulder, letting it drop to the ground with a thud when she sat down, or dangling it from an arm or leg when she stood up; presumably neither would Gilka have tickled the corpse, played with it, or groomed it. Interpreted at face value, these behaviors suggest that although the infant was no longer behaving "properly", it was being treated as if it were still living: however carelessly, it was still being carried about by its mother; however unresponsive, it was still being groomed; and so on. The body as a lifeless specimen of flesh, a fly-ridden carcass, a physically present but non-moving being was not apparently recognized as such. Would the word *death* have sufficed to change all this?

On the other hand, if Olly's and Gilka's behaviors cannot be said to be indicative straight off of an awareness of death, they might perhaps be seen as an expression of loss. Consider, for example, the behavior of Humphrey toward Mr. McGregor after the latter had become paralyzed and eventually died (*ibid.*, pp. 218–24). Humphrey stayed with his old friend almost constantly. When Mr. McGregor was literally no longer present — after euthanasia, his body was secretly removed —

> it looked as if Humphrey did not realize he would never meet his old friend again. For nearly six months he kept returning to the place where Gregor had spent the last days of his life, and would sit up one tree or another staring around, waiting, listening. During this time he seldom joined the other chimps when they left together for a distant valley; he sometimes went a short way with such a group, but within a few hours he usually came back again and sat staring over the valley, waiting, surely to see old Gregor again … (*ibid.*, p. 224).

Was Humphrey wondering what had happened to his friend? Was he grieving his loss? Was he at a loss to explain his loss? Was he thinking his friend would return if only he waited long enough? Is Humphrey's wondering, or mourning, or confusion, or expectation dependent upon language? Certainly it would seem not. Certainly too it would seem that one cannot deny some such cognitive-affective experience as wondering, expecting, grieving, and the like, to Humphrey. Why otherwise would a social animal such as a chimpanzee spend six months away from its confreres, returning instead to the site where he last saw his friend and sit solitarily, staring over the valley? There is in fact something subtly familiar about Humphrey's behavior, else it would not be conjectured that "Humphrey did not realize he would never meet his old friend again", or that "Surely, he was waiting to see old Gregor again, listening for the deep, almost braying voice ... that was silenced forever" (*ibid.*).

The stunning non-comprehension of death which humans sometimes feel at the sudden loss of a loved one is apparent in the sudden cessation of the everyday world with its typical behaviors. The loss is a shock that loosens — even severs — ties to customary concerns and practices. Humphrey's behavior seems to recall such experiences; it seems woven of the same existential cloth. What, then, is lacking to Humphrey's experience of loss such that he might have a concept of death? The 'no-moreness' of loss, after all, appears similar to the 'no-moreness' of death: in both cases, an Other is no longer vitally present. From this perspective, Olly's and Gilka's behaviors might be seen as on a continuum with Humphrey's: Olly and Gilka, although not conceptually awakened as such, are confronted by the no-moreness of death, Humphrey, in a more humanly evocative way, by the no-moreness of loss. The problem, however, is that no matter how conceptually similar the experiences might appear, no mere conceptual leap can bridge the gap. The concept of death — whether verbal or nonverbal — is not fully derivable from an experience of loss. Such a concept would have too narrow a compass: the deeper and wider no-moreness peculiar to death would be missing. What is lacking to Humphrey for a concept of death — or to Olly and Gilka — is not a word that would anchor all their experiences of lifeless Others — a singular identifying verbal epithet that could be cast like a net over any experienced lifeless forms — or conceivably, even a singular *non*linguistic concept of lifeless being. While it could be said that the word *death* is used (or even that a certain nonlinguistic concept comes into play) whenever an individual becomes permanently inert and unresponsive — that is, whenever this sort of individual is met with, one knows one is in the presence of death — such a usage does not reflect the richer notion customarily associated with death. Death does not just *name* a certain state of affairs relative to another body — e.g., inert, unresponsive, even putrid, grotesquely colored, and so on — nor does it merely mean that such a state of affairs obtains. Conceptually, it connotes an awareness of terminality, of a punctuated existence which is inevitable and which is mine and the lot of all living creatures. Where does this awareness of punctuated existence come from? What are its conceptual origins? Clearly, the aspect of death which such an awareness grasps, and which such an awareness must once have grasped in an originary sense, cannot simply be pointed to, any more than it can be conceptually derived from and verbally fixated upon the experience of loss. Clearly, the origin of this awareness lies neither in a readily available nor ready-made language, but in a particular kind of awareness of bodily life, one in which, as illustrated by the previous examples, a body can be either present or absent in the death sense of no-moreness.[2]

If the above examination of nonhuman animal death calls into question the claim that short of language there are no concepts, it also forces the hand of any behaviorist who claims knowledge of death resolves itself into an awareness of inert, unresponsive bodies. If the question, how is it that our long-ago ancestors came to be aware of death?, is answerable at all, behavioristic perspectives need to be surpassed if not relinquished. In other words, one has to go beyond accounts of the Other's death, or perhaps more aptly still, one has to find in the Other's lifeless form the path leading to an awareness that one's own existence is on the line. Thus, before coming to designate the concept of punctuated existence in language, our hominid ancestors would have had to have had a complex of nonlinguistic notions of bodily life, and these notions, of course, on the basis of particular kinds of awarenesses of bodily life. Short of acknowledging such foundational awarenesses and notions, we are left with a problem akin to that characterized by Nagel in respect to the point of view of a bat, i.e., we, like our death-recognizing hominid ancestors, have a certain concept beyond the reach of substantiating facts. Thus, as Nagel points out, "We can be compelled to recognize the existence of ... facts without being able to state or comprehend them" (Nagel, 1974, p. 441). Certainly we know death when we see it and certainly, by definition, our death-recognizing ancestors knew death when they saw it. What we do not know in the least, and what they did not know either, is what death is like — in the Nagelian sense of the experiencing creature itself — even if it is *nothing*. How, then, could we or they possibly come to have a concept of it? If we believe nothing is there — indeed, if we know death to be the end of our possibilities — surely we must have some bodily sense for believing so, and surely that sense of the body must have precipitated our long-ago ancestors' originary notion of death. Otherwise, however inert, unresponsive, putrid, and grotesquely-colored the bodies (and however rich our verbal vocabularies), neither we nor our ancestors should have any reason to conceive of *death*, but only of inert, unresponsive, putrid, grotesquely-colored bodies.

---

2 Attention might be called here to a situation which our early ancestors might have experienced — perhaps not infrequently: some hunters might not return to the group's base camp, having suffered a fatal accident in the process of hunting.

2. Nonhuman Animals and Physical Bodies

What does it mean to say that for themselves, nonhuman animals do not have physical bodies as such? It means that by and large they do not appear to themselves, nor do their fellow creatures appear to them as analyzable and manipulable bodies. In the visual spectacle of themselves and creatures about them, what appears is not a mere physical object—an object of such and such parts, for instance, or of this or that degree of rotational possibility. What appears is a certain portentous physiognomy of some kind: threatening, caring, playful, fearful, curious, and so on. What appears, in short, is not a material body abstractively separated or separable from a living body. Consider, for example, the phenomenon of recognition in a penguin rookery. There is no reason to think penguins recognize their own mate and offspring among thousands of others in any way other than the way we humans, searching for a familiar face in the crowd, come finally to recognize an overall facial form or style of walking—to recognize a certain "pattern of wholeness (Scheler, 1954, p. 210).This pattern is not a matter of analysis but of physiognomic form: it is not an assemblage of discretely and serially distinguished physical features but a singular and immediate qualitative *Gestalt*.

Now the having of a physical body as such, that is, an analyzable and analyzed, manipulable and manipulated body, is what makes twentieth century biology and medical science possible. Short of a separation of *this* body from the living body, there would be no temperatures to be taken, no organs to be transplanted, no cells to be counted. There would be no body to *inspect*, to examine and to study to the end that one could deduce certain relationships, certain cause and effect sequences—such as that which might be seen to obtain, for instance, between a limp and a swollen ankle. Certainly this separation of physical and lived bodies has been described in many ways before. What has not surfaced, however, is precisely the fact that in nonhuman animal societies there is no such kind of inspection. Whatever bodily inspections are carried out in the infancy or adulthood of nonhuman animals, they do not appear to go beyond a qualitative noticing: what emerges from the inspections is not an abiding material thing in the world but a certain physiognomic form. How then does one get from not distinguishing a physical body *as such* to the distinguishing of one? To answer "through the having of a different kind of brain" is, of course, to opt for a reductionism which evades the question entirely: it is not a question of laboratory distinctions but of first-person sensory-kinetic worlds.

However bizarre it might appear at first glance to say that nonhuman animals do not have physical bodies as such, the truth of the statement is borne out in many ways—including the observation that even the more

intelligent of nonhuman animals—as twentieth century Westerners estimate chimpanzees, orangutans, and gorillas—do not have witch doctors,
shamans, or other kinds of medical practitioners among them. Medicine—in whatever form—can only be practiced on, or with reference to,
physical bodies. If physical bodies do not exist, no one can minister to
them clinically, no matter how hurt or in pain a creature might appear to
be. The licking of wounds is not the result of an examination and diagnosis
but the dispositional tactile response of a lived body in face of suffering—its own or another creature's. The human response of embracing and
stroking is an elaboration of that tactile consolation; it is a manual expression of a once-lingual gesture (Montagu, 1971, p. 37).

Further corroboration is had in considering what happens when a very
young nonhuman primate is wounded. Its mother appears to notice
changes in its behavior straightaway and may compensate for the youngster's inability to get about in the way it has in the past, but she does not
investigate the source of its difficulty; she does not look to see what is the
matter; she does not set about analyzing why it is the youngster is unable
to keep up with the group and thereby discover that its leg is broken or
otherwise injured in such a way as to make walking impossible. She does
not know what an injured leg looks like because she has never inspected in
an analytical sense a normal leg and come to know what *it* looks like. In a
word, the youngster's physical body *as such* does not exist for her any
more than a physical world *as such* exists for her. If nonhuman animals do
not have a medical practice—or a full-scale geology or astronomy—it is
not that they lack a language in the form of human speech or a culture by
human standards. It is because in an evolutionary-existential sense they
have no physical bodies as such. The having of a physical body and a physical world are a matter of apprehending physicality in a preeminently
material rather than physiognomic sense.

This is not at all to say that there are no instances or intimations of physical thinghood in a nonhuman world. To begin with, consider the following
account quoted by Portmann in his book, *Animals as Social Beings*
(Portmann, 1961, pp. 182–3):

> The position of a male with high social standing is abruptly shattered
> as soon as he loses his antlers. In the spring of 1951, in the Basel Zoo, I
> was able to watch the moment when a fallowbuck sank to a lower level
> (alpha, beta, gamma, here describe the levels in social rank). On April
> 18th, at 3:45 P.M. the herd of five males and eight females were beg-
> ging for food from the zoo visitors. Suddenly they were slightly star-
> tled by a playing child, so that some of them trotted off, including the
> alpha male. He happened to graze with the right side of his antlers the
> branch of a fir-tree lying in the enclosure. Immediately this half of the
> antlers fell clattering to the ground. Obviously upset, with tail raised,

he sniffed at the piece he had just lost. Almost at the same moment the beta buck realized what had happened, and attacked and pursued him vigorously. The other three yearling antler-less gamma bucks took scarcely any notice of the occurrence nor did the does. After about half an hour both the alpha and beta bucks had more or less calmed down and were again begging for food. But the former buck was not tolerated at the fence by his rival, and therefore kept right at the back of the enclosure... . Up to the evening the one-palmed animal carried out peculiar head movements, as were observed by Heck (1935) after the loss of antlers. On 23rd April the beta buck also had shed his first antlers. From this time on there was the same social ranking as had prevailed before the alpha animal shed his.

One would be hard-pressed to deny an inchoate sense of materiality to the fallowbucks, be it ever so colored over physiognomically. The literal piece of the deer that has fallen off is out there in the world, on its own, so to speak; but it is a thing the deer recognizes as some-*thing mine*. Marjorie Grene's comment on the report corroborates the notion of a rudimentary apprehension of a physical body as such in some nonhuman animals: "That the stag 'knows' about his antlers," she writes, "is confirmed by many other studies, notably, for example, those of Hediger on the psychology of animals both in captivity and in the wild" (Grene, 1974, p. 272).

As to a further instance of materiality, it can be said generally that tool-making and tool-using among nonhuman animals clearly demonstrate a use of things *as things*, that is, as material and not *merely* or *only* as sensuous objects, e.g., the use of leaves to wipe oneself after defecating (Jordan, 1982, p. 36; Lethmate, 1982, p. 53). But in addition to this tool-using behavior, as it is reported in the literature, there is also a more direct manipulation of things as things. Japanese macaques who wash their sweet potatoes in water to rid them of sand deposits before eating them are clearly manipulating things *as things* in their world. English tits who discovered they could puncture milk bottle tops and skim off the cream are also manipulating things as things. Curiosity fosters investigations and manipulations. Yet these discoveries of thinghood do not seem to generalize into a physical world as such, into a cosmology, so to speak. All are intimations of a material world, they do not found it. And indeed, they cannot found it. The point from which such a world could come into view is missing. One's own body itself must first come into view as a consistent and permanent physical reality. In the case of the deer, the visual body of the other might be said to have come into a partial such view, but the visual body which is one's own has not. What there is of that latter body lies not only detached on the ground but must seemingly be sniffed in order to be verified as one's own: it is not straightaway recognized. Of course the point could be made that so far as mammals are concerned, a quadruped cannot see its body as readily as an upright creature can. What is actually visible of its visual body comes into view naturally in a less immediate way. It is certainly true too that if *we* had antlers, upright posture would allow us no better visual vantage point upon them than the deer's. But the point could also be made that smell — a dominant sense in nonprimate and nonmarine mammals — is not a sense which can objectify things in the world as consistent and permanent realities 'out there'. The smell of "mine" is not only an ingested awareness, a quasi-tactile entity, it is a one-dimensional object: it has no parts. In contrast, the vision of "mine" is 'out there' and it remains 'out there', a complex, multi-dimensional object, and one which in turn can be analyzed and manipulated.

3. Death and the Visual Body

If it appears that the having of a physical body is linked to the having of a *visual* materiality, it is because the physical body as such and as we know it is above all a visual specimen. Certainly a physical body can be awakened and subsequently examined by touch, smell, movement, sound, and even taste — we can feel the downy texture of its skin, smell its sweat, kinesthetically reckon its joint mobility, listen to its heart, taste its tears — but its *inspection* is preeminently the work of two eyes, and this not on etymological grounds, but quite the reverse: because two hands, nostrils, ears, or a tongue cannot approximate to the corporeal wholeness and profusion of detail grasped by two eyes. In effect, what more natural way to have come to an awareness of the physical body than visually and what better way to have begun inspecting its physicality than by *looking* at it?

When one inquires into certain decisively hominid practices which single out a physical body, it becomes apparent that in the origin and evolution of these practices, visual meanings were indeed being asserted, meanings have to do with decidedly visual analyses and visual manipulations. Counting by the body and counting on the body — the latter practice observed in preliterate cultures and predating the exclusive use of the fingers to count (Lévy-Bruhl, 1966)[3] — and caring for the injured are paradigmatic instances of these two modes of visual meaning. What is remarkable is that counting by the body and caring for the injured seem to reach far back into hominid history. Let us consider briefly each practice in turn.

Milford Wolpoff, a paleoanthropologist, remarks of a break line in the femur of an East African australopithecine that "the fact that the break

---

3   It might also be pointed out that according to accepted linguistic theory, a one-two counting system predated the decimal system, i.e., predated the use of the fingers to count. (see Swadesh, 1971). It is possible that the original binary system was tied to the evolution of hominid upright posture. A hermeneutical account of this possibility was first presented by Sheets-Johnstone, 1984a; see also Sheets-Johnstone, 1990.

healed indicates that the individual was taken care of by others" (Wolpoff, 1980, p. 150).[4] Now of course by the notion "care by others", Wolpoff does not mean splinting or casting, but rather that in this Pliocene period of hominid evolution, members of a hominid group apparently protected and ministered to the needs of the injured. That this evolutionary picture of caring contrasts markedly with descriptions of the treatment of injured members in extant nonhuman primate societies is significant: whereas the usual method of paleoanthropologists is to draw analogies to the latter societies in rendering reconstructions of early hominid ones, only a dis-analogy can be drawn here. The dis-analogy is rooted in a difference in sensory-kinetic worlds; namely, the ascendancy of the visual body as a separate reality. In order to minister to an injured individual, it is first necessary to see concretely that something is wrong. It means not merely sensing that something is peculiar or amiss in the way that an individual is acting, but apprehending what that something is and ministering to the individual accordingly, e.g., bringing food, protecting against predators. The situation of the injured hominid is thus quite different from that of a paralyzed Mr. McGregor shunned by his confreres save for his friend Humphrey, who protected him from the aggressions of others, but who left him to fend for himself so far as food was concerned and who ceased to groom him. These latter omissions are not neglected social niceties; they are the measure of a certain sensory-kinetic domain of sensitivities and powers. The situation is equally dissimilar from that in which chimpanzees who, initially frightened by the queerness of a polio-stricken confrere, "rushed for reassurance to embrace and pat each other while staring at the unfortunate cripple." Eventually their fear subsided, "but, though they continued to stare at him from time to time, none of them went near him, and eventually he shuffled off, once more on his own" (van Lawick-Goodall, 1971, p. 221).

The dawning emergence of the visual body as physical object necessarily meant a dawning awareness of the everyday appearances of the body — the concrete everyday functioning of its 'members'; and correlatively, a dawning awareness that those everyday functional appearances could change — that the living powers of the individual could be altered. These dawning visual awarenesses were certainly not a matter of language but of the gradual materialization of physiognomic perceptions. What before might have been perceived as queer, e.g., moving in an abnormal manner, was gradually transformed into a perception of a visibly physical injury.

---

4   See also Poirier, 1977, on much later fossil remains (in the Shanidar cave in Iraq) which also show evidence that caring treatment by others was given.

As to numerical awareness, there are, as suggested earlier, two modes that warrant comment. To begin with, the practice of counting by the body is evidenced in tool-making — both in the earliest known bifacial Oldowan artifacts estimated at two and a half million years, and the later Acheulian axes. A rudimentary visual notion of 'how many' is apparent in each, a notion not necessarily verbalized at all but, on the contrary, one most likely to have been felt as enacted by the body. With respect to Acheulian axes, for example, Ashley Montagu writes,

> It is clear that each flake has been removed in order to produce the cutting edges and point of the tool with the minimum number of strokes ... If one examines this tool carefully, one may readily perceive that no more flakes have been removed than were minimally necessary to produce the desired result (Montagu, 1976, p. 271).

Montagu's observations strongly suggest that a numerical awareness was connected both with the tool itself as a visual object — it had a certain regular appearance in terms of its surfaces and consequent shape — and with bodily movements as tactile-kinesthetic realities — they too had a certain regular numerical as well as dynamic character. Given descriptively detailed accounts of the preeminently physiognomic nature of preliterate societies (Lévy-Bruhl, 1966) — and the standard paleoanthropological practice of drawing analogies to these societies — it is likely that the felt tactile-kinesthetic numerical character was perceived by early hominids as *transferred* to the visual object in its own right. A distinctive visual object — a tool — was, after all, being created before someone's very eyes. Thus there must have been an awareness of a distinctively physical object coming into existence: a certain visual form *qua* physical object must have been recognized as being achieved.

When accounts of enumeration in extant non-Western cultures are interpreted in terms of sensory-kinetic worlds, the situation appears remarkably similar. That is, with respect to counting on the body, visual meanings, while anchored in and solidified by tactile-kinesthetic gestures, are nonetheless visual meanings. While numbers are brought to life by touching particular parts of the body and in sequence, yet at the same time, the numerical awareness is clearly a visual phenomenon. It is the visual body perceived as a system of parts, a numerically divisible entity, which anchors the enumeration. Whatever the body parts tactiley enumerated — finger, nose, ear, forearm — and in whatever sequence, a visual corporeal standard grounds the practice. In fact the visual body is counted on as a physical object in both a literal and metaphorical sense — it is amenable to such an analysis and in turn is analyzed and manipulated as such. The practice of counting on the body is rooted in the dawning emergence of just such an object. Indeed, what else but a physical object in the form of the visual body could furnish the analytical and manipulational permanency and consistency necessary to the formation of a numerical standard?

If it is the visual body which came to be abstracted and distinguished from the lived body and to stand out from it as a distinctly physical entity, then the question is how this visual body came to be so dissociated. In concrete terms, how would our early ancestors have stumbled upon the visual body as a material thing in the world? The answer would seem to lie in an understanding of the aura of strangeness pervading a perceived difference in something heretofore familiar, a perceptual shift not unlike that of the chimpanzees' perceptions of change in the visual appearance of their polio-stricken confrere: thus, initially, an understanding of how fingers, seen in the familiar act of picking seeds or fruit, or a hand seen in the familiar act of gathering stones or of touching another's hand, or feet seen in the familiar distinct process of watching one's footing, or even particular parts of the body seen in the process of learning a new skill — how such everyday visual apparencies turned suddenly strange; and in a way unmatched by any other sensory modality, particularly the tactile-kinesthetic. A given movement coordination, for example, might have felt strange, but only because it was a new technique being learned — forging a tool for the first time perhaps, or trying to adhere to a set standard in forging it. Similarly, a feeling of dizziness or of pain might appear strange, but again, only in the sense of not being experience before, not in the sense of something familiar being suddenly experienced as *alien*. When perceived as strange in this latter sense, aspects of the visual body were no longer enfolded in the overall lived action; they were momentarily cut from their familiar moorings; the naturally forged coordination of the tactile-kinesthetic and the visual bodies was perceptually sundered. A radical separation was born.

Whatever the innumerable sudden glimpses and however drawn out the gradual insights, the visual body in time came to be seen as an outsider, a thing out there, a materiality, ultimately a full-fledged physical object in a world of full-fledged physical objects.[5] In fact it seems likely that whatever the particular cultural practices at any particular time and place in hominid history, the growing sense of the physicality of the body was consistently reflected in a proportionally growing sense of the physicality of the world: the material complexity of the one was no less and no more strange and wondrous than that of the other.

---

5 Full-fledged physical objects, so commonly experienced today in Western cultures, contrast strikingly with the participatory mode of experience which dominates in preliterate societies and which has been described in detail by Levy-Bruhl. See Lévy-Bruhl, 1966 and 1975 .

Perhaps it should be emphasized more strongly that the physicality of the body was not forged overnight nor was the visual body from some very early time onward seen only and wholly as a purely physical specimen. Accounts of physiognomic perception in preliterate societies clearly confute both notions as do our own everyday twentieth century Western lives in which our visual bodies are normally melded into the task at hand, i.e., the visual body is an element within the totality of the lived body — as in driving, playing tennis, hammering, washing dishes, writing, or playing the violin. The physicality of the visual body was a dawning awareness stretching over perhaps millions of years and in fact only since the rise of Western medicine and science has the visual body as physical specimen become, and in relatively hurried fashion (in the last second to midnight on the now proverbial cosmic time clock), a truly separable and separated reality — literally, *a thing*, an object analyzed and manipulated in its own right. Moreover, it is not that "once" perceived as such, the visual body was (or is) never seen as anything more than a material thing. The point is simply that "once" perceived as such, its perceptual and ultimately conceptual separation from the felt body marked a radical turning point in hominid history: it was the spawning ground of revolutionary new practices — caring for others and counting by and on the body; and it was the spawning ground of revolutionary new beliefs: the conceptual measure of death was made on a visually mattering body.

The question then is, how did death enter into a visually mattering world? If a human were isolated completely from birth onwards, with no living beings about, he or she would have no reason to conceive of death. Nothing in experience would lead to such a concept. By itself, a living body does not know death; nothing in its experiences of the world or of itself prepares it for such an eventuality. Whether caught up in the world at hand, or reflecting on its singular universe, there is seemingly nothing which would precipitate it toward such an awareness. An emerging awareness of the visual body as physical specimen would not in these circumstances adumbrate a notion of death either. While this body might be awakened in moments of casual inspection or through injury, these momentary insights would not suffice to conjure a sense of death: the mere perception of a physical body as such does not lead a creature to conceive of death. The conceptual origin of death lies in something more, that is, in a social world, or at least an interanimate one, and this because to meet with death is not only to be a physical body; it is also to be other than what one is now, other in a way similar to the way in which others are other for me: they are visual bodies unconnected to what I know directly as my own felt body. Clearly this originary sense of otherness needs amplification.

4. From a Paleoanthropological Hermeneutics to a Husserlian Phenomenology

The distinct move to a Husserlian phenomenology in this particular context demands a shift to a first-person account, for unlike the concept of a tool or of a verbal language, the concept of death does not refer to something palpably out there in the world in some way. Accordingly, a corporeal journey is required — from the preceding hermeneutics of the concept of death to the hermeneutics' foundational source in corporeal experience. The *I* that makes its appearance here is to be understood as a "phenomenologically reduced" *I*, that is, as the *I* of any reader who takes the journey him- or herself.

How were fellow creatures likely to appear to our long-ago hominid ancestors? An approximation to their viewpoint is had in part by bracketing: putting out of play twentieth-century cultural expectations, attitudes, assumptions, and beliefs. Interpreted in evolutionary contexts, insights from this bracketed world can be of seminal significance. Bracketed perceptions, in other words, are amenable to "primitive" interpretations insofar as everyday twentieth-century Western theses are temporarily suspended (Sheets-Johnstone, 1984b). Thus, when bracketed, others appear not as persons, or human beings, or males, or females, for example. They appear simply as visual forms, forms in-animation and of-ever-changing-physiognomies. There is no *inside* to these moving visual forms; there is only threat, entreaty, comfort, playfulness, and the like, that is, physiognomic aspects palpably present in their gestures and expressions, posturings and amblings. That I see *these* physiognomies is an aspect of their appearance which would require its own analysis, but that elucidation is not critical or at issue here. What is critical here is that, seen as sheer visual appearances, these forms have no interiors. Nothing that I see of these moving visual forms and changing physiognomies suggests an interior — an inner material depth. There is, in effect, not actually an *outside* which I see: there is only the moving visual form of ever-changing physiognomies.

Now were any one of these moving visual forms opened up and made visible to me by accident or injury of some kind, what I would see are entwined, moist, layered, reddish objects of various shapes: hard and soft things bearing no resemblance at all to the moving form I just saw with its ever-changing physiognomies. There is no reason for me to connect these appearances or to ponder their relationship: the moving visual form is one thing, these hard and soft things quite another. Hence I do not conceive of inside and outside *as such* at all, much less think that *I* have an inside like the one before me. On the contrary, I have twinges, pressures, pains, nodules of tension, and so on, not in so many words, of course, and not by a reflective nonlinguistic comparison either, but as *sheer somatic experiences*. In effect, I hardly begin to wonder what these tubules, bones, sinews, and fibers have to do with me.

In evolutionary contexts, these observations take on all the more weight since in their daily lives, our hominid ancestors must have seen moving visual forms and hard and soft things on many occasions without connecting them: as hunters they would have seen them regularly; yet not *as such*, that is, not as outsides and insides. What was eaten, for example, was more than likely to have been a matter of edibility, not spatial relationship. Yet on some occasions relative to their own kind, these hominids must also have seen moving visual forms and hard and soft things. At some time, then, the perception of hard and soft things must suddenly have been fraught with strangeness. This primordial experience of strangeness can be captured by a return to a bracketed world.

From a bracketed perspective, the moment I apprehend the two appearances of a visual Other to be appearances of the *same* spatio-temporal object, I am aware of an inside and outside as such. I am aware of the same visual form in two seemingly conflicting guises: one animated and affectively charged, the other inanimate and a pastiche of pulpy masses and rocklike solidities. The lack of connection appears strange, as strange as, or perhaps even stranger than the initial awareness of my own visual hand *qua* physical object. In the latter experience I can at least discover my felt hand and my visual hand to be connected in the singular experience of moving it and seeing it move. In the course of picking fruit, for example, or of watching my step, I have some sense of a felt-visual correspondence. In the experience of the other, however, there is no sense of a relationship at all, there is no perceived correspondence between the two realities; yet the two appearances are appearances of the same spatio-temporal object. Hence the stronger sense of strangeness. Here inside and outside are *queer*. There is something unaccountably peculiar in this juxtapositioning of inside and outside: they are strange bedfellows, so to speak, as strange as would be the juxtapositioning of my twinges and pressures with those tubules and bones, sinews and fibers. These awarenesses are not of course language-dependent — any more than are the awarenesses of a preverbal child who sees and understands that a round knob does not fit into the square opening in a chain of detachable beads with round and square knobs and holes. Unlike the chain of beads, however, there are no ultimate collateral matches to be found between inside and outside, or between twinges and tubules: the other's inside and outside simply do not match in any coherent way and my inside and the other's inside do not match in any coherent way either. The only things which match in a general way are our intact moving visual bodies with their ever-changing physiognomies: only outsides match.

Now when we remember that these thoughts are thoughts without words, that the experience is a sense of queerness, not its verbalization, then it is clear that I am caught up in the peculiarity of certain relationships — or far more precisely, certain nonrelationships. It is not a matter of explaining these nonrelationships, but only of sensing their queerness. When confronted with the natural death of the other — a phenomenon I of course do not yet know as such — the strangeness is heightened in the extreme and the complexity of the situation augmented. Here what I witness is a radical transfiguration of the moving visual form; its ever-changing physiognomies are gone; it is no longer gesturing, opening its mouth, squinting, running, or carrying things about. It is utterly still. The other that I knew is yet *another* other. Strangeness is compounded by change. However queer the earlier experiences, they were not radical and stark in the way this queerness is: this queerness is an utter change of being which is extraordinary. Commerce with *this* other is no longer possible: I cannot play with this other; I cannot be entreated, comforted, or threatened by it any longer. Its visual form is no longer the same.

Yet it *is* the same. Though unanimated and of an unchanging physiognomy — even as unmoving and unexpressive — the form I now perceive is distinctively but not wholly different from the moving visual form I not long ago perceived, wholly different, that is, in the way that the inside of another is different from the outside, or in the way that the inside of another is different from my inside. The two terms of this relationship — moving visual form and nonmoving visual form — are identical and not identical; the visual form is at the same time two forms and only one form. Described in this way, the experience is in fact conceptually similar to the experience of duality-unity that obtains in preliterate societies: a corpse is perceived to be both a single and dual object. It is a unitary phenomenon, but it is also dual insofar as it is adjoined at the same time and without felt contradiction whatsoever to its ghost. Here, of course, the phenomenon of death has been elaborated. A belief system for understanding and dealing with death is well beyond the originary experiences of strangeness and change. Yet the belief system clearly indicates, and in a most forceful way, the radical queerness attaching to the originary experience in its very attempt to explain it. In the originary experience, one is confronted by something that is all there, yet that is not all there: something is missing; and alternatively, something is missing, yet everything is all there. What the corpse/corpse-ghost concept does is to nullify the missing factor on the one hand and to attest to its missingness on the other. Extraordinary change is thus accommodated by having it both ways, so to speak.

Both the queerness of the Other and the transfiguration of the Other into yet Another describe stages in an awareness of fellow creatures apprehended simply as moving visual forms. Together with an awareness of one's own visual body *qua* physical object, these awarenesses can be seen to converge on the concept of death. Yet even with a burgeoning notion of the materiality of the visual body, even with the sensed queerness of insides and outsides of the Other, even with the Other's extraordinary transfiguration into Another, the concept of death is not yet attained. Only with the notion of *my* punctuated existence do the threads of the concept weave together; that is, the concept of death is ultimately rooted in a certain realization of *my* being. Death is 'out there', but it is also in me. In a strongly Sartrian sense of Otherness, death is plaited in my very being; in a strongly Heideggerian sense, it is my own. What must be shown is how the materiality of the visual body, the queerness of insides and outsides, and the sense of extraordinary change come together, and in such a way that there is a realization that, like the Other, I too will change radically and become a merely visual body.

To approximate most closely to this realization, we must differentiate between the experience of natural and of accidental death and follow through its methodological implications. In the lives of the early hominids, accidental deaths would likely have been commonplace. Whatever the fatal maimings and disembowelments, however, and whatever the sense of no-moreness, a concept of death as inevitable, as mine, and as the lot of all living creatures would not have been thereby grasped. On the contrary, there might well have been a vague sense that "barring such a fate, I will go on 'forever'." In other words, only with experiences of natural deaths might the concept of death have taken root. Only through such experiences might it have been realized that a certain nullifying fate was inevitable and mine. If this realization is put in the perspective of the Husserlian analytic of the constitution of Other Egos, a considerable clue is found as to how it might have come about, and this because prior to a realization of death, there must first have existed just such Others, i.e., Others-than-I constituted and understood on the basis of "my own animate organism."[6] Without these Others—without an interanimate world, as noted earlier—there would have been no ground upon which the concept of death could have arisen. Indeed, short of granting an innate idea of death, a possibility which is absurd in logical as well as evolutionary/genetical terms, there would be no concept of death at all. Put in

6   Husserl, 1973. The phrase is found throughout the Fifth Meditation.

Husserlian terms, in the experience of another's natural death, there would have been a dissolution of the primal instituting of the other as animate organism similar to my own, and a consequent breakdown of the passively generated pairing of I and Other. The Other would no longer have the same sense for me as animate organism that it previously had; similarity would no longer be apparent as before; the associative pairing of I/Other and the mutual transfer of meanings carried by the pairing would be annulled by overwhelming difference. Clearly, the Other could no longer continue "to prove itself as actually an animate organism, solely in its changing but incessantly *harmonious 'behavior'*" (Husserl, 1973, p. 114). Clearly, the Other would no longer be apperceived as an analogue of myself, an "intentional modification" (*ibid.*, p. 115) of my own animate organism. Clearly, the mutual transfer of sense vouchsafed by pairing would be nullified "with the consciousness of 'different'" (*ibid.*, p. 113). At the same time, however, and still holding to a Husserlian perspective, it is clear that with the experience of the-Other-in-death, all intersubjective significance is hardly lost. Although no longer having the same sense for me as animate organism, a residual sameness lingers in the appearance of the-Other-in-death; our bonds are tenuous but they are not completely dissolved. I experience the Other as a muted and distant Thereness, a Thereness that is now unfulfilled and unfulfillable, not simply because of the mutedness and distance, but because there is no longer the familiar crossing over to "such as I should be if I were There" (*ibid.*, p. 119). What is to be understood, then, is precisely how a lingering sameness, or residual pairing, founds an experience of an apperception *manqué*, that is, an aborted or failed making co-present of something that is not actually given in perception.

5. The Experience of the-Other-in-Death

In the appearance of the-Other-in-death, a no-moreness of similarity is set against a persistence of similarity. It is of course an initial sense of likeness that awakens both — the still resonating and the dilute similarity of self to Other. As Husserl points out,

> It is clear from the very beginning that only a similarity connecting, within my primordial sphere, that body over there with my body can serve as the motivational basis for the *'analogizing'* apprehension of that body as another animate organism (*ibid.*, p. 111).

In the Husserlian analytic, analogical apperception results in a grounding of the life processes of the Other in my own life processes, not as a reasoned out correspondence, a one-by-one recounting to myself of our similarities, as it were, but through a passively generated synthesis reaching beyond what is actually perceived, an intentionality that itself is grounded in the beforehand giveness of my own ongoing subjective life. Husserl speaks of this beforehand givenness as the primally institutive original: it is as I myself who is "always livingly present" (*ibid.*, p. 112) and it is this I myself who thereby sees apperceptively in the Other a similar flow of living presences. The flow is made co-present with what *is* given perceptually of the Other and in a single act. The question, then, is what happens to this pairing in the experience of the-Other-in-death where similarity fades but is not wholly extinguished?

In Husserlian terms, death is a nonorginary experience. It is appresentationally perceived in the form of Others who have changed radically and who are no more than merely visual bodies, i.e., they are no longer moving visual forms of ever-changing physiognomies. A methodological point derives from this insight and it turns on the fact that death is always so perceived: the perception could not be otherwise and still be a perception of *death*. Thus a descriptive account of the experience in twentieth-century terms is not tied to a particular way of seeing the world. Whatever the evolution in conceptualization, that is, in whatever direction our hominid ancestors might have eventually been led to explain and to understand death, their concept of, and beliefs about death would have had to have been grounded in nonoriginary experience. Let us, then, pursue the description in keeping with the Husserlian analytic.

What is apparent in death is a stillness, a radical behavioral change, a sleeplike demeanor from which the Other is unrouseable. What is present, in other words, is an Other I can no longer know, an Other whose being escapes me. In effect, this merely visual form, this impenetrable façade marks a cessation of community, a no-moreness of intersubjective life. As described earlier, I can no longer play with this Other, be entreated or threatened by this Other. But the no-moreness is double-edged: the Other's stillness is coincident with my stillness toward him: the Other's no-moreness of entreaty is as much mine as his. As Husserl points out, the transfer of meanings grounded in the passive generation of pairing is a *mutual* transfer (*ibid.*, p. 113). Not only this but

> every successful understanding of what occurs in others has the effect of opening up new associations and new possibilities of understanding; and conversely, since every pairing association is reciprocal, every such understanding uncovers my own psychic life in its similarity and difference, and by bringing new features into prominence, makes it fruitful for new associations (*ibid.*, p. 120).

Now the central problem is precisely one of understanding how a "successful understanding" of death was originally achieved. A "successful understanding of what occurs in others" in death was certainly not had by our early ancestors in straightaway fashion, much less simply in virtue of their being hominids. If substantial clues are to be found, they must be sought in an analysis of the close-up and not infrequent views of natural death our ancestors must have had. To describe such an experience through a bracketing of our own face-to-face view of death is to describe an awareness of utter separation: in this experience, the Other is closed off in his or her impenetrable solitary silence; but so also am I. In the suspension of a communal life, the other is alone; but so also am I. A reciprocality of meanings is singularly apparent in this utter separation. Let us begin by describing the former set of meanings first. What does the other's utter separation from me signify?

The cessation of community with the Other stirs an inchoate sense of ending amidst life, of an island of stillness in the midst of movement. On the other hand, in the aloneness of the Other from me there is a sudden end of sharing, an unexpected parting of ways. With the Other's solitary stillness there is no longer the possibility of a mutually-created togetherness of projects in the world. In fact, a radical transformation marks the solitary and impenetrable appearance of the Other: in place of the Other I once knew is *Another*, a stranger with whom no community is possible. In my face to face meeting of the-Other-in-death, I come up abruptly and continually against this *Another* whose presence I cannot fathom but whose presence separates me completely from the Other I once knew.

On the other hand, there is a sense of former encounters with this now still and solitary Other; there are images of commonly lived moments. No matter the radical transfiguration, the Other remains Other. A particular past creeps in and with it a sense of ongoing consistency enduring through change. Throughout the variety of recollections and images, a persistent sameness anchors a once-communal life. An aura of continuity impresses itself upon the kaleidoscope of remembrances and images, however fleeting or vague. The temporal sweep of our communal life begins to solidify; the island of stillness in the midst of movement is tied to a commonly lived past.

A further dimension is present beyond these dual significations of a once-communal life, one which both sustains and at the same time transcends the "common time form" (*ibid.*, p. 128) of our past. It is through this further dimension that Other and Another, past and present, recollections and ending, come together. In fact, only when the Other's present ceases to be strange — when the Other ceases to be Another or when endings are understood as continuous with the past — that awarenesses central to the concept of death arise. To grasp these awarenesses in an originary sense, we need to re-enter the descriptive analytic.

In my face-to-face meeting of the-Other-in-death, the awakened vestiges of the past give rise not only to an awareness of a communal life, they also gather together, as it were, and converge upon a single point: upon the unmoving visual body before me. Were it not for the impenetrability of that body these remembrances would enter into its stillness. Yet so much are these vestiges of the past vestiges of *that* body, they slip into its flesh; they fill out its form. I apperceive the Other as a density of being-in-the-past. The façadelike repose of the Other remains impenetrable but gives way to a growing temporal thickness. At this moment there is no longer an Other and an Another, recollections and ending, a past and a present. There is a continuity separable from, but enfolding our communal life. The very persistent sameness that called forth a past-and-now-ended communal life calls forth a temporal continuity that is not ours but that belongs wholly to the Other. The visual form that is the Other is apperceived as a change that exists in continuity with its own past. What appears in the aloneness of the Other is thus a heightened sense of individuality. No matter how still the figure, it has temporal girth; those vestiges of the past that have converged upon the Other and entered into its flesh have given it an historical density of its own. Thus, in the Other's utter separation from me I find ultimately not only a temporal continuity and ending of our communal life, but I also find an individual temporality that is ended.

6. The Experience of the Other-in-Death and Self-Understanding

In the ongoing encounter with and understanding of the-Other-in-death, new associations and new possibilities of understanding indeed open up: Other and Another, recollections and ending, past and present become joined; temporal solidifications point the way toward the realization of a common time form; a burgeoning awareness of an individual temporal continuity points the way toward a new composite understanding of change and sameness. How does this successful understanding of the Other reverberate within my own "psychic life"? If the notion of my own "temporality-toward-death" can arise only on the basis of an experience of the Other-in-death, not myself-in-death, then the concept of death is clearly born in a *reverse* analogical apperception: though I do not know in the least what it is like to be There in place of the Other, I know that it is ultimately and inevitably my fate to be There where the Other now is. How could this knowledge have come about? How could the Other's aloneness present me with such knowledge of myself, in particular when the Other is no longer "governing somatically" in a manner coincident with "my own organismal governing" (*ibid.*, pp. 119–20), that is, when I no longer can effectively associate my actions and responses, my conduct and general style of being in the world with the Other who is now before me? How, in Husserl's terms, is my understanding of the-Other-in-death a "reciprocal … understanding of my own psychic life in its similarity and difference"?

Precisely because the experience of death is never mine originally, and in turn, because the concept of death is rooted in a reverse analogical apperception, the apperception is an analogical apperception *manqué*. It is a matter, in other words, of my never quite achieving an apperception of myself in death, of my never successfully and completely making co-present something that is not actually there in any given perception of myself, something that, in fact, invariably eludes my grasp. To uncover the structures of this analogical apperception *manqué*, let us begin with my failed analogical apperception of the Other.

Whatever the Other's processes might be — even if they are nothing, and indeed, precisely if they are nothing — I cannot fill them in. Whatever the degree of residual pairing, it is insufficient to ground a fulfilled intentionality. No change in point of view — no different stance taken and no new profile gained — suffices to modify the suddenly truncated meanings in any way. I do not and cannot know what the Other's stillness means beyond its literal meanings of being still: an end of what was both a communal and an individual temporal form.

An attempted imaginal projection of myself There, in place of the Other, bears out this unfulfilled and unfulfillable intentionality. In any strivings toward meaning through an imaginal projection of myself toward the Other's Thereness, my lived body follows me; that is, in the course of imagining my being there, I find my felt body creeping into the image. On the one hand, in a spectated image, what I first take to be "myself over there" — eyes closed, still, a visual body, a facade, an outside — turns out to be not necessarily me at all. "My" body over there could in fact by *Any Body*: the visual body over there is an amorphous form lacking the precision of detail that would definitively identify it as mine. So long as it is unanimated, a merely visual body, an aura of arbitrariness hangs over it. Any attempts to make it my body result in subtle intrusions of my somatic body. In delineating the closed eyes as mine, for example, I find my actual eyes crossing over the threshold from the real to the imaginary, thus animating the "merely" visual form. The problem of course is that I cannot imagine myself as a merely visual form, a form without movement, a form devoid of even the slightest motions of breath. I cannot imagine myself, *that body over there*, as not breathing, for example, without actually holding my breath, or at the least, causing actual confusion in my normally regular

and usually unheeded breathing pattern. In short, I cannot imagine
myself-in-death in spectator fashion. By itself, the imaginal body's identity is obscure; with enforced ownership, it is no longer a *merely* visual
form.

On the other hand, neither can I imagine myself There in utter stillness
from the inside. It is impossible to silence my living body completely, both
in terms of movement and of feelings. Although I do not know that the
Other is not feeling anything, there are no indications that anything is
being felt at all, indications which would be harmonious with a past in
which analogical apperceptions of feeling *were* present. The Thereness that
is present now and that I aim at emulating imaginally is a queerness that
eludes me completely: I am to be There, utterly still as the Other is, *but also*
utterly emptied of movement and of feeling—a shell felt from the inside
and at the same time not felt at all since the shell covers nothing in the way
of a felt body. Such a Thereness is in fact, exactly as Husserl would
describe it, a kind of mock creature: "Precisely if there is something discordant about its behavior", Husserl writes, "the organism becomes experienced as a pseudo-organism" (*ibid.*, p. 114). No matter how strong the
concentrated aim, I cannot grasp myself imaginally as such a creature; I
cannot fulfill such an image. Here my living body is not an intruder but an
impediment. It blocks my every aim to be the Other's stillness imaginally
by an assertion of its livingness, its assertion of movement and of felt
presence.

The failed imaginal projections bring into striking focus the fact that the
merely visual body of the Other and my own visual body no longer mirror
each other in a fulfilled manner. Even though they remain structurally
coincident, our visual bodies are no longer mutually paired or pairable as
before. The basis of our former analogical pairing was precisely a *moving*
visual form; visual form *tout court*—structural coincidence alone—is a necessary but by itself insufficient condition for our continuingly fulfilled
associative pairing. This insight is borne out by Husserl's analysis of the
verificatory procedures vital to ongoing paired association. "The first
determinate content" that supports verification of the Other as *my* Other
has to do with movement, with bodily modes of engaging the world:
"Consistent confirmation," Husserl says, comes in "the understanding of
the members [i.e., structural organs of the body] as hands groping or functioning in pushing, as feet functioning in walking, as eyes functioning in
seeing, and so forth" (*ibid.*, p. 119). By themselves the Other's "members"
are *not* the first determinate content. In effect, the fundamental stratum
vital to a fulfilled pairing and to a mutual transfer of meaning is nowhere
evident in my encounter with the-Other-in-death. Where I fall short of the

Other in my failed imaginal projections, so the Other falls short of me in its failed appearance as a moving visual form. Both failures are confirmations of our utter separation. Both failures are in fact mirror images of each other and as such are descriptive of the nature of the analogical apperception *manqué*, an apperception bereft of its formerly coincident analogical structure.

There is a still deeper significance to be uncovered in the unyielding differences I find now between myself and the Other. While the Other is dumb, as it were, to my concernful gaze and gesturings, there is no longer either, and reciprocally, a sense of care or concern from the Other *toward me*. The Other's muteness is an emphatic cessation of what I have experienced until now: continuous and consistent pairing *with me*. No longer do I find myself mirrored in the Other; no longer does the Other's regard look back toward me. In place of a mirror, there is a void. With the cessation of community, there is an end of the Other as analogue of myself. While there is no longer the familiar "such as I would be if I were There," there is now an awakening sense of the isolatedness of my Hereness, a Hereness that is stranded, and that no imaginal projections can repair or reconcile. This awakening sense of solitude that comes back to me from the Other deepens proportionally in the burgeoning sense of my own Hereness, my own individuality and temporality. My own flow of experiences stand out in relief against the stillness of the Other. *I too* have a continuity separable from but enfolding our communal past; *I too* am a persistent sameness across a manifold of change; I *too* am a present in continuity with a past. At the same time, however, I am wholly distinct from this Other. Unlike the present of the Other, my present is a felt and moving present. In this most discordant and irreconcilable of differences, this utter incompatibility of presences, I find the sense of my livingness heightened. In this experience I find myself not just a certain *livingness*, but embarked upon a *life*: I am not just this contrasting presence here and now but a continuing continuity of being; I am not only a moving present in continuity with a past, but this ongoing flow of feelings and movement. I not only have temporal girth but a certain temporal open-endedness. I am at the center of a distinct temporal flow that is wholly mine. This inchoate sense of a life, *my life*, is decisive. I am at the conceptual threshold of death.

That threshold is crossed in a moment of insight. The concept of death is born when the sense of "I too" and the sense of distinctive contrast are heightened in equal measure. With the sense of "I too" I ultimately grasp *my* punctuated existence; with the sense of distinctive contrast, I grasp the inevitability of my death. The concept of death is thus as grounded in my experience of utter likeness to the Other I once knew as it is in my experience of utter contrast to the Other here before me. The felt similarities and felt differences reverberate with the existential dissonance of life and death, of *my* life and *my* death. A radical new understanding is born. This temporal stretch of being that I am is not just animate: it is a life, my life. And this life which is mine and which I am — *this more than just animate being* — is not a never-ending expanse of being but a punctuated one. In this moment I realize that it is precisely my possibility to be There where the Other is now, but *in time*. It is in this moment that I grasp both my living temporality and my ultimate end.

In my encounter with the-Other-in-death, pairing is faded; yet however mute and distant, it suffices to carry forward for me the double meanings of an analogical apperception *manqué*: my own livingness and my own death, my own moving and felt presence and my own ultimate end. It is thus not simply that the Other is unmoving, but that its stillness has created a vacuum in me; it is not simply that the Other is remote from me but that its separation has created a hollow in me. What comes back to me finally from the Other becomes a cleft in the very marrow of my being, an unlived and unlivable moment of my own history, a transfiguration of myself into a merely visual form I will never know.

7. Afterword

The ascendancy of the visual body *qua* physical object — a body wholly distinct from the lived body — marks critical turning points in the history of hominid life. No matter how culturally engrained and appropriated the concept today, there was a time when flesh and blood hominid creatures came to conceive of death — as they came to conceive of caring for the injured, of counting, of tool-making — even of language. These originary conceptions are sedimented in our own awarenesses and thinking; indeed they are the bedrock of current beliefs and practices. Hence, if an exact and rigorous philosophical understanding is to be had of what it is to be human, then the importance of "historical disclosure" (Husserl, 1981, p. 265) in the Husserlian sense of making these originary concepts explicit and bringing them to self-evidence cannot be denied. In fact, the foregoing analysis strongly suggests that a Heideggerian metaphysics needs grounding, at least in this instance, in a Husserlian epistemology. As Dan Magurshak pointed out several years ago in relation to Heidegger's metaphysics of death, "epistemological issues need resolution" (Magurshak, 1979, p. 116). It would seem that if the metaphysics is to gain concrete resonance, recourse must be had to a genetic phenomenology in the inclusive sense of a paleoanthropological hermeneutics. The analysis strongly suggests too that were Sartre's account of death and the Other a literally fleshed out thematic, one in which an epistemological hermeneutics of the body figured as prominently as an existential ontology, striking points of coincidence would be found. "If the Other did not exist," Sartre says, but without concrete elaboration, "[death] could not be revealed to us, nor could it be constituted as the metamorphosis of our being into a destiny"; death, Sartre writes, "transforms us into the outside" (Sartre, 1956, p. 545). In sum, it would appear that short of a paleoanthropological hermeneutics, an understanding of such seemingly simple yet unique human concepts as that of death will always remain shrouded; and correlatively, that given a paleoanthropological hermeneutics, understood as an extension of, or complement to, a Husserlian genetic phenomenology, the deepest of deep structures, those having to do with evolutionary-existential origins, will come gradually to light.

References

Grene, Marjorie. 1974. *The Understanding of Nature* (Dordrecht: D. Reidel).

Husserl, Edmund. 1973. *Cartesian Meditations*, trans. Dorion Cairns (The Hague: Nijhoff).

Husserl, Edmund. 1981. "The Origin of Geometry", *Husserl: Shorter Works*, ed. Peter McCormick and Frederick A. Elliston (Notre Dame: University of Notre Dame).

Jordan, Claudia. 1982. "Object Manipulation and Tool-use in Captive Pygmy Chimpanzees (*Pan paniscus*)," *Journal of Human Evolution*, 11.

Lethmate, Jürgen. 1982. "Tool-Using Skills of Orang-utans," *Journal of Human Evolution*, 11.

Lévy-Bruhl, Lucien. 1966. *How Natives Think*, trans. Lilian A. Clare (New York: Washington Square Press).

Lévy-Bruhl, Lucien. 1975. *The Notebooks on Primitive Mentality*, trans. P. Riviere (New York: Harper & Row).

Magurshak, Dan. 1979. "Heidegger and Edwards on *Sein-Zum-Tode*," *The Monist*, 62.

Merleau-Ponty, Maurice. 1962. *Phenomenology of Perception*, trans. Colin Smith (London: Routledge & Kegan Paul).

Montagu, Ashley. 1971. *Touching: The Human Significance of the Skin* (New York: Columbia).

Montagu, Ashley. 1976. "Toolmaking, Hunting, and the Origin of Language," *Origins and Evolution of Language and Speech* (Annals of the New York Academy of Sciences 280), pp. 266–274.

Nagel, Thomas. 1974. "What Is It Like to Be a Bat," *Philosophical Review*, 83: 435–450.

Plugge, Herbert. 1970. "Man and His Body", *The Philosophy of the Body*, ed. Stuart F. Spicker (Chicago: Quadrangle Books).

Poirier, Frank E. 1977. *Fossil Evidence*, 2nd ed. (St. Louis: C.V. Mosby).

Portmann, Adolph. 1961. *Animals as Social Beings*, trans. O. Coburn (London: Hutchinson).

Sartre, Jean-Paul. 1956. *Being and Nothingness*, trans. Hazel E. Barnes (New York: Philosophical Library).

Scheler, Max. 1954. *The Nature of Sympathy*, trans. P. Heath (New Haven: Yale University Press).

Schrag, Calvin O. 1979. "The Lived Body as a Phenomenological Datum," *Sport and the Body: A Philosophical Symposium*, ed. Ellen W. Gerber and William J. Morgan (Philadelphia: Lea & Febiger).

Sheets-Johnstone, Maxine. June 1984a. "On the Origin of Counting: A Re-Thinking of Upright Posture", paper presented at the American Association for the Advancement of Science, in San Francisco, CA.

Sheets-Johnstone, Maxine. March 1984b. "What Was It Like To Be Lucy?" paper presented at the American Philosophical Association, Long Beach, California.

Sheets-Johnstone, Maxine. 1986. "Existential Fit and Evolutionary Continuities," *Synthese* 66 (1986): 219-48.

Sheets-Johnstone, Maxine. 1990. *The Roots of Thinking* (Philadelphia: Temple University Press).

Swadesh, Morris. 1971. *The Origin and Diversification of Language* (Chicago: Aldine).

van Lawick-Goodall, Jane. 1971. *In the Shadow of Man* (New York: Delta).

Wolpoff, Milford H. 1980. *Paleoanthropology* (New York: Knopf).

Zaner, Richard M. 1981. *The Context of Self* (Athens, Ohio: Ohio University Press).

Chapter V

Taking Evolution Seriously

A Matter of Primate Intelligence

Except insofar as *theory* is concerned, philosophers tend to place evolution at an exclusively scientific address. In practice this means they divorce historical significances of evolution from their particular theoretical concerns—from axiomatic formulations derived from population genetics or molecular biology, for example—and subsequently ignore them. The overall effect of standard practice is not only to overlook the vast temporal span and diversity of life preceding the immediate human present, but to disregard the more intimately related science of paleoanthropology. Where, for example, do we read of primordial language, ancestral hominid tool-making, burial practices, or cave paintings in the context of philosophical investigations of human language, cognition, or art? Even in the philosophy of science, philosophers uniformly bypass paleoanthropology, most often in favor of either a neurophysiology whose centerfold features the brain and its circuitry, or an anorexic biology whose living flesh is so emaciated as to be virtually absent. Standard philosophic practice is well exemplified by Michael Ruse in his *The Philosophy of Biology*, a book devoted to showing that the theory of evolution is not dissimilar from theories in the physical sciences, and that the single discipline of population genetics (reducible ultimately to molecular biology) stands at the explanatory center of evolutionary theory. Ruse mentions the historical side of evolution but only to argue away its centrality to evolutionary theory. Linking paleontology to what is dead and long gone—to bare fossils and little more—he in fact calls evolution with its historical aspect intact an "old concept," and refers to "the supposedly *historical* nature of organic phenomena" (Ruse, 1973, pp. 213 and 211). For Ruse, as for many philosophers (cf. Rosenberg, 1985), molecular genetics alone offers a bona fide philosophical basis for examining and understanding evolutionary theory.

Standard philosophic practice is equally well exemplified by the ongoing, complex "unit of selection" controversy (see, for example, Sterelny and Kitcher, 1988; Kitcher *et al.*, 1990; Sober, 1990; Shanahan, 1990). The question of the level(s) at which selection acts and of whether there is a "true unit of selection" (Kitcher *et al.*, 1990, p. 159) is not without interest — either to biologists or to philosophers. Neither was the question of fitness which occupied centerstage several years back (e.g. Rosenberg, 1983; Sober, 1984). However, when such questions are taken as paradigmatic of *the* type of question of proper concern to philosophers of biology, then not only are concerns about concrete historical processes of evolution, including *human* evolution, nowhere in evidence, but the total absence of these historical concerns from philosophical discussion strongly suggests that they are not properly the province of philosophers at all but only of biologists. In other words, with respect to actual evolutionary processes that have taken place, the attitude of the philosopher of biology is, "there is no philosophy of biology to be done there." Even in philosophical contexts in which concerns with historical significances of evolution appear to be central, there is not uncommonly a noticeable gap. The Philosophy of Biology in Historical and Cultural Contexts course that was offered through the National Endowment for the Humanities to philosophers in the summer of 1989 is a case in point. Although ample attention was called to Darwin, the "Darwinian tradition," and "Darwinism" in the two hundred and twenty-five word course description, the historical side of evolution — the side that Darwin was at pains to explain — was nowhere alluded to. The irony was compounded by the fact that, though the intent was in part to develop "a new and humanistically richer philosophy of science," paleoanthropology was nowhere mentioned.

A further exemplification of standard philosophic practice centers on philosophers' interest in nonhuman animals, particularly but not exclusively in the context of philosophy of mind.[1] The intent in these philosophical enterprises is generally to shed light on the relationship between human and nonhuman intelligence. For example, the intent has recently been "to help cognitive ethologists to interpret their findings" (Bennett, 1988, p. 197), or to aid cognitively-oriented scientists by supplying them "a descriptive language and method that are neither anachronistically bound by behaviorist scruples nor prematurely committed to *particular* 'information-processing models'" (Dennett, 1983, p. 343). Standard philosophic practice is apparent in such enterprises when, in the drawing of comparisons or implications, philosophers fail to take evolution, particularly our own human evolution, into account. The result is a failure to realize that

---

1   Indeed, as this essay will go on to suggest, the repercussions of this particular mode of standard philosophic practice do not reverberate exclusively within the domain of philosophy of mind, but affect a number of subdisciplines including both ethics and metaphysics.

short of divine intervention, human rationality and human language are themselves products of evolution, and not in the sense of novel neural brain circuitry gradually (much less suddenly) appearing such that communally understood words began sprouting from the mouths of a few no doubt surprised-because-heretofore-verbally-mute hominids, but in the sense of actual living creatures *inventing* new modes of behavior. Jonathan Bennett, in his 1987 Presidential Address to the Eastern Division American Philosophical Association, noticeably ignores human evolution in just this way. To begin with, he states that his aim is to specify "[the] main differences there are between *Homo sapiens* and other known terrestrial species, or (for short) between man and beast." He elaborates this aim by saying that he thinks we humans all intuit the same difference—"I think we have the same *picture* of the difference, the same *sense* of what it is" (Bennett, 1988, p. 197)—and that his purpose is to try to "parlay" that picture or intuition into "an agreed description" (*ibid.*). By way of further elaboration, he says that the difference he is interested in descriptively pinpointing is a difference in kind and not in degree, and this on the basis of what we already think is there, that is, on the basis of "what we already know about us and about them." The problem of course is what "we" *do not* know about us and about them. As is clear from what has been said thus far of standard philosophic practice, Bennett ignores what philosophers generally tend to ignore; that is, he tends to discount as relevant knowledge the actual historical process of evolution and with it, our own hominid history, the study of our own human evolutionary past.[2] The

2   Daniel Dennett ignores the actual historical process of evolution to the extent that he takes *present-day human adult* intellectual abilities for granted—that is, he gives no indication of thinking of those abilities as having evolved—and that he aligns preverbal human children's intellectual abilities with those of nonhuman (presumably adult) animals. For example, although he points out that humans function at a lower intentional level than they might think, that like "vervet monkeys (and chimps and dolphins, and all other higher nonhuman animals) [humans] exhibit mixed and confusing symptoms of higher-order intentionality" — "[they are not] unproblematic exemplars of third- or fourth- or fifth-order intentional systems" (1983, p. 349)—he does not put the comparison in evolutionary perspective (or even intimate that it might have such a perspective). Rather, he puts the comparison in the perspective of another comparison: that between small children and monkeys. He states, "I expect the results of the effort at intentional interpretations of monkeys, like the results of intentional interpretations of small children, to be riddled with the sorts of gaps and foggy places that are inevitable in the interpretation of systems that are, after all, only imperfectly rational" (*ibid.*) A later commentary fleshes out the reason for an "imperfect rationality." In the context of discussing how we are to interpret "animal messages," Dennett states his disagreement with Wittgenstein—that "If a lion could talk, we could not understand him." But he also goes on to say that "I do think we'd find the lion had much less to say about its life than we could already say about it from our own observation. Compare the question: What is it like to be a human infant? My killjoy answer would be that it isn't like very much. How do I know? I don't "know," of course, but my even more killjoy answer is that on my view of consciousness, it arises when there is work for it to do, and the preeminent work of consciousness is dependent on sophisticated language-using activities" (*ibid.*, p. 384). Clearly, an imperfect rationality is

import of this neglect is sizable. One aspect of it will become readily apparent in what follows. Suffice to say here that without this historical dimension, those philosophical studies that aim at discovering relationships between human and nonhuman intelligence can never be anything more than a comparison between present-day humans and present-day chimpanzees (or gorillas, or orang-utans, or baboons, or lemurs, or langurs, or vervet monkeys, and so on — or pigeons and crows,[3] for that matter). They will never tell us anything in an *evolutionary*, i.e., substantively biological — including ethological — sense about "what makes us special" (Bennett, 1988, p. 197). They reduce simply to philosophical justifications for cherishing ourselves.

Standard philosophic practice is not uncommonly queer in an etymological sense, in the sense that what evolves are precisely organic wholes, and in the sense that understanding humanness was at least in the beginning what constituted the pursuit of philosophy. The counters identified in a molecular biology and/or formulated in an axiomatic system, for example, are not the stuff of *evolution* — the actual living process in virtue of which we are here today. That process is defined by all those sensing, moving creatures who found and made their niche in the world in myriad ways over eons of time — some of them successfully, many quite unsuccessfully — and it includes those creatures who constitute the subject matter of paleoanthropology and who, as relatives, should be dear to our human hearts. A concern with molecular regularities and with explanation — with evolutionary theory *qua theory* — need not devalue a concern with that historical process or the creatures who define it — with evolutionary theory *qua evolutionary* theory. More than this, the concern need not saw off the branches that support it. In default of an historical dimension, there could be other theories in biology — theories of spontaneous generation, of animal spirits, of a sentiment intérieur, and other formulations in the conceptual style of a pre-Darwinian biology, but there would be no

---

tied to a lesser consciousness, and a lesser consciousness to the lack of "sophisticated language-using activities." Forms of "imperfect rationality," however, were capable of fashioning stone tools and conceiving of death. There is no way of knowing conclusively of course just when verbal language evolved in the course of hominid evolution. On the other hand, there is a way of knowing when such practices as stone tool-making and burying the dead began, and these activities, as has been shown elsewhere (see Note 12), are not dependent on sophisticated language-using activities; they are rooted in the body. The very concept of a tool, like the complex concept of death, is a matter of corporeal matters of fact, thus of corporeal concepts. Taking evolution seriously holds the possibility of enlightening us about things we do not know.

3   For an incisive and at the same time thoroughly engaging commentary on the axiology implicit in academic nonhuman animal research studies, see (former primatologist) Thompson, 1976, pp. 221–30.

theory of *evolution*.[4] Furthermore, as emphasized, to ignore the historical aspects of evolution is to omit understandings of our ancestral kinfolk, thus to disregard significant dimensions of our own human evolution. Especially in light of their considerable accomplishments, our kinfolk matter. As with our own families, our biological Family tells us something about ourselves. When we examine our ancestral past, we learn something about who we are. Such an examination is what in a truly philosophical sense Darwinian evolutionary theory was originally all about.

Darwin wrote three major books on evolution: *The Origin of Species, The Descent of Man and Selection in Relation to Sex*, and *The Expression of the Emotions in Man and Animals*.[5] In the first of these consecutive formulations, Darwin considers physical characters and behavior; in the second he considers mental powers and moral qualities, and then proceeds to a study of sexual behavior; in the third he turns his attention to emotions. It is clear from these successive writings that Darwin is both an organic and evolutionary wholist. His initial concern with distinct aspects of animate form notwithstanding, he clearly regards animals not as piecemeal assemblages nor as reflex machines on the order of "protoplasmic record changers" (Rorty, 1979, pp. 186–90), but as, in eminent British biologist J.S. Haldane's phrase, "persistent wholes" (Haldane, 1931, p. 13); and he furthermore regards the attributes and capacities of *all* creatures to have evolved. In consequence, evolutionary continuities pertain not simply to atomistic parts or to physical bodies but to animals as living wholes. By the same measure, they pertain not to some creatures but to all creatures: evolutionary continuities are evident throughout the animal kingdom, including humans, and they are describable in physical, mental, moral, sexual, and emotional terms. Darwin's three books attest incontrovertibly to this conception.

Darwin's wholistic conception of evolutionary continuities is never mentioned in twentieth-century Western scientific or philosophic circles. It has never been openly challenged. It has never been methodically rebutted. It has simply been ignored. By twentieth-century Western standards, only *The Origin of Species* and the second half of *The Descent — Selection in Relation to Sex* — count as evolutionary theory. The rest is silence, but not necessarily because one knows not of what one might speak. On the contrary, an affirmation of evolutionary continuities beyond the merely physical is an obvious dimension of, for example, NASA programs utilizing

---

4   For a detailed discussion of how the concept of evolution was a uniquely Darwinian concept, see Sheets-Johnstone, 1982.

5   The latter book was to be the final section of *The Descent of Man*, but *The Descent* was already so long, Darwin decided to publish it separately.

nonhuman animals; medical and psychological studies of behavior in which nonhuman animals figure as subjects; language-learning programs featuring especially chimpanzees, but also including gorillas, orang-utans, and parrots; and more. The pressing question then is, why is there a selective reading of Darwin? Since *never explicitly discredited*, why is his organic and evolutionary wholism not taken seriously?

Behaviorism and logical positivism might go a long way in answering the question, but they are far from providing the whole answer. With respect to the neglect of "the descent of man", the whole answer would likely take in cultural relativism and the not unrelated structuralist emphasis on synchrony over diachrony since both doctrines, in eschewing in one way and another the notion of 'getting back', would see no philosophical significance in the descent itself and/or no cultural relevance of the descent to modern humans. Each of these avenues of response would be interesting to consider. The focus here, however, will be on a quite different answer, namely, anthropocentrism. Because it has not been previously exposed, because it sheds a basic and particularly penetrating light on the selective reading of Darwin and the decline of his organic and evolutionary wholism, and because, in turn, it accords "man" *carte blanche* powers over "beast" and thus ultimately has far-reaching ethical implications, the practice of anthropocentrism is of considerable interest and import. Detailed consideration will show that the central issue is not fundamentally that of attributing human characteristics to nonhuman animals, i.e., anthropomorphism, but of assuming humans as the center of the animate world such that, for example, any assessment of nonhuman mental powers must take as its standard of measurement a human mind.

The charge of anthropomorphism is normally a pejorative judgment rendered upon a person who purportedly interprets the behavior of nonhuman creatures in ways that wrongly humanize the behavior and that in turn credit the creatures with far more in the way of intelligence than the creatures actually deserve. Morgan's canon is rigorously adhered to by scientists as a bulwark against anthropomorphism. Morgan's canon dictates that no nonhuman animal behavior may be interpreted at a higher level if it can be explained at a lower level.[6] The canon is often equated to

---

6　Lloyd Morgan, a comparative psychologist of the late 1800s and early 1900s, has actually been misinterpreted. His 'canon,' as Michael T. Ghiselin points out, "could in fact be invoked on the other side ... A higher faculty could explain more behavioral facts than a lower one." The immediate point, however, is that what Morgan was enunciating was an evolutionary principle, not a principle of simplicity or parsimony. His canon was anchored in the evolutionary fact that lower forms of intelligence developed before higher ones, and are thus represented to a greater degree in the evolutionary world than the latter. It is not then a question of "logical simplicity, but of theoretical probability" (Ghiselin, 1983, p. 363). See Morgan, 1930.

parsimony, though Occam's notion of parsimony was tied to maintaining a spartan explanatory ontology, not to the formulation of what must be regarded self-serving explanatory protocols. What the charge of anthropocentrism pinpoints and calls into critical question is precisely the customary practice in virtue of which the charge of anthropomorphism is purportedly avoided in the first place. Most simply stated, it is the charge that *reading humanness out is an anthropocentric act*. By such an act, nonhuman creaturely life is interpreted in ways that consistently exalt the measure of humanness: humans become special creations. Man is indeed the measure of all things in such a world, *man* understood here not as independently-perceiving individuals but as self-privileging beings apportioning sub-mental credit from on high to the whole of nonhuman animate life.[7] Indeed, the act of reading out is an aggrandizing gesture by which the whole human species is plucked out—saved as it were—from its place in the evolutionary mainstream of life.[8] It is thus clear why to depreciate nonhuman animal behavior is a denial of evolutionary wholism. The same strict interpretive rule that applies to nonhuman animals—Morgan's canon—does not apply to humans. In consequence, humans can be as generous and self-flattering as they please toward themselves. They can declare, for example, that without exception all humans have an intelligence that in every instance is uniquely superior to that of nonhuman animals. Thus whatever the navigational abilities, tool-using/tool-making skills, distinctive cultural practices (see, for example, McGrew, 1994, specifically, ch. 4 and his discussion of "the grooming-hand-clasp" of chimpanzees), and other demonstrable modes of nonhuman animal intelligence might be, they are necessarily of a lower order, an order that is *discontinuous with* the navigational abilities, tool-using/tool-making skills, distinctive cultural practices, and so on, of modern humans. The charge of anthropocentrism calls into question the practice of protecting and privileging humankind in this way. It affirms the fact that it is as anthropocentric to deal humans all the cards as it is to deal nonhuman animals too many aces.

Clearly, so long as anthropomorphism is the perenially favored scapegoat, anthropocentrism goes unrecognized and unacknowledged as its parent form; anthropomorphism and its inverse are both forms of anthropocentrism. Anthropocentrism is thus primary and the charge of

---

7   It might be pointed out that, however unenlightened Protagoras's (reinterpreted) gender-biased claim might appear today, his sexist generalization cannot be criticized: males unequivocally command worldviews and practices in present-day Western society, including the present-day worldview and practice of reverse anthropocentrism.

8   In their article Cavalieri and Singer (1995) describe this aggrandizing gesture as an exclusionary form of humanism.

anthropocentrism can actually be made from either of two directions. Consider, for example, the conveniently ignored but seminal collateral question raised by the quest for objectivity and the linking of anthropomorphism with a lack of objectivity. In a recent article in *The Chronicle of Higher Education* titled "Scientists Rethink Anthropomorphism," writer Kim A. McDonald begins by describing the linkage:

> Long considered taboo among researchers studying animals, anthropomorphism violates a central tenet of science: that researchers should strive to be totally objective and dispassionate observers of nature. As a result, scientists who suggest that animals possess intentions, emotions, or other qualities assumed to be *uniquely* human are often viewed by colleagues as careless, gullible, or even irresponsible … . So despised is the practice that animal researchers can discredit others in their field by simply labeling their work anthropomorphic (McDonald, 1995, p. A8; italics added).

McDonald goes on to say that animal researchers such as Marc Bekhoff are now vindicating the practice of anthropomorphism on the grounds of its being "a valuable scientific tool" (*ibid.*). The conveniently ignored collateral question concerns the exoneration of *reverse* anthromorphism. In particular, why are anthropocentrists who privilege humans by reading humanness *out* not similarly scorified by their failure to be "totally objective and dispassionate observers of nature"? Surely human arrogance is a liability, and not "a valuable scientific tool." As a further example, consider that humans are merely one among ten million species and that, their numerical insignificance notwithstanding, they readily pronounce judgments on all remaining 9,999,999 species, and this even though, philosophically speaking, they have not been able to show convincingly much less conclusively that they are not dreaming or a part of someone else's dream (see Johnstone, 1991, for considerable progress toward the resolution of such obdurate epistemological chestnuts). Clearly, anthropocentrism has a much larger compass than commonly recognized, and an unrestrained one at that.

In the most basic sense, the dual liabilities of anthropocentrism should lead us to ponder seriously and at length the inescapability of our human perspective. But they should lead us at the same time to an immediate acknowledgment of the necessarily limited range of our understandings and of our correlative need to temper proclivities toward human arrogance and in turn, monitor critically our judgments of nonhuman creatures accordingly. Most specifically, they should lead us to the realization that, particularly with respect to judging the intelligence of nonhuman animals, it is far more reasonable—and in turn morally far wiser—to err on the side of generosity than on the side of miserliness. Evolutionary theory, with its emphasis on "persistent wholes," informs us of this reasonability and instructs us toward just such judgments. It implicitly demonstrates to us that organic wholism, like evolutionary wholism, falls by the wayside with reverse anthropomorphism. It implicitly attests that *reading humanness out* is substantively far more pernicious than reading humanness in. With reverse anthropomorphism, intelligence and cognitive acumen—in broad terms, all capacities customarily associated with *mind*—are divorced from the body and regarded special creations along with their unique human possessors.[9] In short, the belief implicit in this form of anthropocentrism is that unlike the human body the human mind never evolved. Presumably it arose *sui generis, deus ex machina*, or by interplanetary intervention—perhaps we are the artificial intelligence of creatures on Alpha Centauri. It is instructive to call attention to an apparently ill-recognized fact and curious practice connected with the belief. Philosophers—and other non-science people as well—who bring nonhuman animals into the human picture typically use them in a way quite unlike evolutionary scientists (see, for example, Margolis, 1978; Carruthers, 1989). Comparisons of humans to extant nonhumans, particularly primates, are made by primatologists, paleoanthropologists, and other evolutionary scientists *not* on behalf of specifying immediate relationships but far distant ones: the behavior of extant nonhuman primates serves as an analogical measuring stick for reckoning *ancestral* hominid behavior. This way of using data gathered on nonhuman animals, or this use of "the comparative method" (as evolutionary scientists term it), is quite different from the way in which philosophers are prone to using it, namely, either to substantiate or to deny a resemblance between 'us and them', 'here and now'. In short, unlike evolutionary scientists, philosophers do not consider primate or other nonhuman animal data in *evolutionary* perspective.[10] It is because of this that the much-prized treasure, human uniqueness, can be so effortlessly secured: so long as the method is misunderstood, the evolutionary significance of nonhuman animal behavioral studies is missed; so long as the evolutionary significance of these studies is missed, our own evolution is ignored; so long as our own evolution is ignored, our kinfolk are ignored, and so long as our kinfolk are ignored, a miserly anthropocentrism is easily installed and practiced with the result that an organic and evolutionary wholism continually gives ground to special creation.

9   Wilfrid Sellars's "Philosophy and the Scientific Image of Man" is a prime if extreme example. In this article, Sellars presents an unabashed argument for "Special Creation" (his phrase, his capitalizations). See Sellars, 1963, pp. 1–40.

10   Jonathan Bennett's assessment of rationality in honeybees is an excellent instance of this lack of an evolutionary perspective. See his *Rationality*, 1964.

It is with great interest one reads in Hume a lengthy footnote explaining both why humans differ among themselves with respect to reasoning powers, and why humans differ from nonhumans with respect to the same capacities. Hume's explanation is in principle strikingly similar to Darwin's explanation of differing capacities among individual creatures with respect to a differential mortality and reproduction, so much so that Hume's explanation appears to be not simply prescient but perhaps even a direct influence on Darwin. That Darwin read Hume has been noted by historians of science (e.g. Richards, 1987). But historians have not observed the remarkable correspondence between Darwin's and Hume's accounts of differing capacities. For both Darwin and Hume, the latter were a matter of individual, native dispositions, whether human or non-human. Hume writes of individual humans differing "in attention and memory and observation," for example, in the ability "to carry on a chain of consequences," and in "the forming of general maxims from particular observation" (Hume, 1977, p. 71). The same native differential abilities that explain "the great difference" among humans in their various capacities to reason, Hume states, explain the great difference in various reasoning capacities between humans and nonhumans. For his part, Darwin first of all affirms that

> [i]f no organic being excepting man had possessed any mental power, or if his powers had been of a wholly different nature from those of the lower animals, then we should never have been able to convince ourselves that our high faculties had been gradually developed. But it can be clearly shewn that there is no fundamental difference of this kind (Darwin, 1981, pp. 34–5).

He then proceeds to give evidence showing that

> man and the higher animals, especially the Primates, have the same senses, intuitions and sensations — similar passions, affections, and emotions ... they feel wonder and curiosity; they possess the same faculties of imitation, attention, memory, imagination, and reason, though in very different degrees (*ibid.*, pp. 46, 48).

In sum, for Darwin as for Hume, just as there is a difference in degree and not in kind in capacities among animals of the same species, so there is a difference in degree and not in kind between different species, i.e., between humans and nonhumans. In consequence, for neither Hume nor Darwin are there Rubicons to be crossed in accounting for human "minds." Put in evolutionary perspective, this means not only that "mental powers" (to use Darwin's phrase) evolved, but that they evolved as a dimension of animate life.

Careful readings of Darwin's three classic works on evolution reveal many times over an organic and evolutionary wholism in opposition to the idea of special creation. Special creation and the practice of anthropocentrism that in part upholds it are clearly inconsistent with evolutionary theory. Present-day philosophy of biology thus has another and quite different task from the one it presently addresses: to expose the inconsistency in all its guises and in consequence show how evolution is to be taken seriously, and *can* be taken seriously in the very doing of philosophy. The task in fact has far-reaching consequences for philosophy, beginning with a Cartesian metaphysics and ending with a justifiable human ethics insofar as wholistic themes support evolutionary continuities and evolutionary continuities raise certain questions both about the evolution of mind and, for example, about the human treatment of nonhuman animals. The task in this longer view might more rightly be designated an *intra-* disciplinary one in that it necessitates a broad philosophical perspective. It can be exemplified with respect to a Cartesian metaphysics, specifically the classic mind/body dichotomy, by two seminal question: Can bodies evolve in the absence of mental powers?; and correlatively, can mental powers evolve in the absence of bodies? Suggestions follow as to the kind of evidence to be considered if just and sound answers are to be had.

Of prime importance with respect to the first question are situations in which a creature is engaged in some constructional activity, constructional in the sense of the creature's devising from moment to moment in the light of a particular and immediate play of events. Thus, beavers building dams or lionesses hunting zebras — in fact hunting and hunted animals generally — must take into account the particular moment by moment situation as it develops. There are no tapes on which all the right moves are recorded such that no matter what the exigency, a neurological program exists. Constructional activity clearly calls into serious question the idea that bodies have evolved or can evolve in the absence of mental powers.[11]

---

11 A reviewer of this article believed that there was a logical problem created by my using hunting as an example of how bodies cannot evolve in the absence of mental powers since hunting is an example of how bodies *do* require mental powers. Whether there is a logical problem or not turns to my mind on whether our concern is with evolutionary forms of life as we know them or whether our concern is with other *possible* forms of life. My concern is with actual evolutionary processes. Hence whether bodies do *or can* evolve in the absence of mental powers concerns actual living forms, i.e., cases in point. My claim is that given the nature of *constructional activity* as described in the text, that is, given the necessity of a discriminating, moment-by-moment, finely-attuned perceptual system to predator and prey alike, it is implausible to think that the particular bodies concerned could carry out predation or escape in the absence of mental powers. The question of bodies evolving in the absence of mental powers, then, is akin to a thought experiment on the basis of empirical matters of fact, to wit, is the life a particular predator (such as a lioness) or prey (such as a zebra) lives such that it could do without mental powers? My answer here, as with the constructional activities of beavers, is "no".

What must furthermore be considered is the fact that animals are from time to time initiating agents. They begin practicing new strategies, for example, or they implement new behaviors such that an entire group of creatures begins behaving in new ways. Not only is there now classic evidence of initiating agents in primate groups studied by Japanese primatologists (see Kawai, 1965, and Itani and Nishimura, 1973), but many of our own kinfolk were initiating agents. Consistent bipedality was a new practice; tool-making was a new practice; burying the dead was a new practice; speaking was a new practice; counting was a new practice; cave-painting was a new practice. Present-day humans can look back as far as three and a half million years and find new practices. All of the practices attest to new concepts, as detailed research has shown.[12] All of the practices were initiated by hominids. The point of signal importance is that *while all humans are hominids, not all hominids are humans.* As represented by the subspecies *Homo sapiens sapiens*, humans arose only some 40,000 years ago.[13] On the basis of paleoanthropological evidence to date, we can thus conclude that with one exception, *the above-mentioned practices were initiated by nonhuman primates.* Recognition of the evidence thus mandates a recognition of mental powers outside an elitist human circle and provides powerful grounds for affirming that nonhuman living bodies, simply on the basis of their nonhumanness, cannot reasonably be regarded as lacking mental powers.

Evidence of animals as initiating agents is equally significant to a just and credible answer to the corollary question, can mental powers evolve in the absence of bodies? Short of a body, one can only wonder where the felt motivations, felt curiosities, and active explorations might be that sustain any thoughtful endeavor such as burying an individual, chipping away at one stone with another, or hammering away at something to see

12   See Sheets-Johnstone, 1990. Four of the eight paleoanthropological case studies in this book were published earlier: "On the Conceptual Origin of Death", *Philosophy and Phenomenological Research* 47 (September 1986): 31–58; "On the Origin of Language", *North Dakota Quarterly* 51 (Spring 1983): 22–51; "Hominid Bipedality and Sexual Selection Theory", *Evolutionary Theory* 9 (July, 1989): 57–70; "On the Origin of Counting", first presented at the American Association for the Advancement of Science meeting, San Francisco, 1984, subsequently requested for inclusion in *The Life of Symbols*, ed. by M. LeCron Foster (anthropological linguist) and J. Botscharow (physical anthropologist) (Boulder: Westview Press, 1990).

13   The time-span, 40,000 years, might be debated depending on how current questioning of the relationship between *Homo sapiens sapiens* and Neanderthal hominids is ultimately resolved, i.e., are modern-day humans descendants of Neanderthals or did modern humans interbreed with and then replace Neanderthals? See Bower, 1989, p. 229 for a discussion of the recent controversy. See Brace and Montagu, 1965, for a detailed and lucid discussion of the original and developing controversy over Neanderthals.

what is inside.[14] It is not a question of *brains* — not only because it is "persistent wholes", not brains, that evolve — but because it is not brains that are motivated, curious, or explorative; it is creatures who are. The nonsensical, even comic, consequences of thinking otherwise are well exemplified by the biologist who affirmed that "Nonhuman primates have brains capable of cooperative hunting" (Harding, 1975. p. 255),[15] as if when summoned by hunger, it is brains that roll forth in concert to do battle on the savannah. From a Darwinian perspective, it is difficult to deny that the evolution of mental powers is tied to living bodies engaged in the real world of procuring food, escaping danger, finding new resources, exploring a new terrain, making choices in the pursuit of a mate, deterring rivals — in short, engaged in the demanding, challenging, complex, practical business of making a living.

A just assessment of whether bodies can evolve in the absence of mental powers would also have to take into account nonhuman animal behaviors that fall outside formally devised protocols. Two primate psychologists interested in tactically deceptive behavior have collected "anecdotal" data from a wide range of primatologists whose formal writings omit reference to any such data. By way of example, one of the contributing primatologists tells of a female gorilla who, in the lead with four others behind her in a relatively straight line, was travelling between feeding sites along a narrow trail. In the words of the primatologist,

> S [the female] looks up into *Hypericum* tree and spies a nearly obscured clump of *Loranthus* vine. Without looking at those behind her, she sits down by the side of the trail and begins to self-groom intently until the others have passed her and all are out of sight.... . Only then did S stop 'self-grooming' to rapidly climb into the tree, break off the vine clump and descend with it to the trail to hastily feed on it before running to catch up with the group (Whiten and Byrne, 1988, p. 237).[16]

The utilization of such anecdotal data within animal behavioral studies is in general sanctioned only by cognitively-oriented scientists and philoso-

---

14   Lest it be thought that such activities are reserved to primates alone, it should be noted that English tits began an entirely new practice — pecking open the waxboard lids of delivered milk bottles. The first-recorded instance of this activity was in 1921. Since then, the thirst-quenching practice spread both across species and geographically, from its original sighting in Southampton to Wales, Scotland, Ireland, Sweden, Denmark, and Holland. See Fisher and Hinde (1972), "The Opening of Milk Bottles by Birds", and "Further Observations on the Opening of Milk Bottles by Birds".

15   A *façon de parler*, it should be emphasized, is not dismissible as *merely* a way of speaking. *Façons de parler* are *façons de penser*, which means they have sturdily-positioned conceptual bases. See Lakoff and Johnson, 1980.

16   The example comes from Diane Fossey. Following the example, Whiten and Byrne note that "Similar examples in chimpanzees were offered by Ploog, Menzel, van Lawick-Goodall, and de Waal" (1998, p. 237).

phers;[17] it is not sanctioned by behaviorists even though to omit anecdotal data is to leave gaps in the record, thus to be less than objective by giving only a partial report—indeed, to give a "subjectively-biased" account of animal behavior. By comparison, no physicist or astronomer who found an anomaly would ignore it on the basis of its being "anecdotal." Neither would students of human behavior overlook such a ploy as that of the female gorilla in their investigations and reported observations of human actions. Indeed, in the human instance, the ploy would undoubtedly be classified as "ingenious." One need only recall Oliver North's cover-up to find what constituted for many Americans just such an "ingenious" example of tactical deception.

However brief the above suggestions, they show that evolutionary biology has much to contribute to the philosophical discussion and resolution of certain metaphysical questions and intimately related ethical issues. In broader terms, they show that Darwin's twin themes of organic and evolutionary wholism clearly challenge us, both to expose inconsistencies in the evolutionary records we keep and to keep those cleared-up records in sight as we ourselves do philosophy. To be so challenged is of course to acknowledge being part of a historical process infinitely larger than ourselves. The acknowledgment of that history, like the acknowledgment of the earth's revolution around the sun or the acknowledgment of our own death—the acknowledgment of any natural spatio-temporal system of change—is in fact not only rational, but perhaps the necessary first step in understanding what it means to be rational, not to say in living up to the star billing we give ourselves as rational animals. In her interpretive essay on Aristotle's concept of *pneuma* and his concept of soul and body in *De Motu Animalium*, Martha Nussbaum was led to remark on the fact that "an essential part of [Aristotle's] search for the best account of animal physiology was an examination of the goal-directed motions of the heavenly spheres" (Nussbaum, 1978, p. 163). In other words, for Aristotle, animal motion and heavenly motion were essentially related and were to be studied and understood together. Nussbaum's conclusion is that Aristotle's view affirmed that "no being can be exhaustively studied without an account of his placement in the whole of nature" (*ibid.*, p. 164)—a 2,300

17 With respect to cognitively-oriented philosophers, see, for example, Daniel C. Dennett, "Intentional Systems." See also Dennett's commentary (titled "Why Creative Intelligence Is Hard To Find") on Whiten and Byrne, 1988, p. 253. It might be noted that what is frequently overlooked in the skirmish between behaviorist and cognitivist is the fact that in the course of making a living, creatures behave in clever, off-beat ways that promote their well-being. And not only primates. One highly esteemed field study documented the fact that a female lioness, after a kill, pretended as if nothing had happened so that she would not have to share her bounty with anyone else. See Schaller, 1972, p. 268.

year-old view that coincides significantly with Darwin's organic and evolutionary wholism.[18]

To achieve that view, what we perhaps need most basically, that is, to begin with, is not a different conception of nonhuman animals—a different conception that is as vital as Cavalieri and Singer (1995) have shown it to be—but a different conception of ourselves. Indeed, a different conception of ourselves is primary in the sense that *to conceive ourselves as primates* leads us in both directions at once: to an acknowledgement of our own species-specific historical placement in "the whole of nature" and at the same time to an acknowledgment of those readily demonstrable ties that so intimately bind *we primates* in a common creaturehood.[19] With this re-conceptualized evolutionary view of ourselves, our spontaneous disposition to read humanness *in*—anthropomorphism—is precisely what we should expect to find in ourselves. Given our common genealogical heritage, we primates are cut of the same cloth. To trace out the ties that bind us in a common creaturehood does not mean that distinctions—our species-specific differences—are ignored or effaced. It means only that primate patterns of thinking, feeling, and behaving, being in fundamental ways of an evolutionary piece, are brought to light and given their due.

References

Bennett, Jonathan. 1964. *Rationality* (London: Routledge & Kegan Paul).
    September 1988. "Thoughtful Brutes", Presidential Address, Eastern Division American Philosophical Association, *Proceedings and Addresses of the APA*, 62/1.
Brace, C.L. and M.F. Ashley Montagu. 1965. *Man's Evolution* (New York: Macmillan).
Carruthers, Peter. May 1989. "Brute Experience", *Journal of Philosophy*, 86/5, pp. 258–69.
Cavalieri, Paola and Peter Singer. 1995. "The Great Ape Project", *Ape, Man, Apeman: Changing Views Since 1600*, eds. Raymond Corbey and Bert Theunissen (Leiden: Leiden University Press), pp. 367–76.
Darwin, Charles. 1981. *The Descent of Man, and Selection in Relation to Sex* (Princeton: Princeton University Press).
Dennett, Daniel. 1983. "Intentional Systems in Cognitive Ethology: The 'Panglossian Paradigm' Defended", *Behavioral and Brain Sciences*, 6, pp. 343–390.
Fisher, James and R.A. Hinde. 1972. "The Opening of Milk Bottles by Birds", and "Further Observations on the Opening of Milk Bottles by Birds", both in *The*

18 It might be noted that were Aristotle suddenly alive today, he would undoubtedly be busy revising his original biological treatises, studying animate life with as much zeal and thoroughness as originally, but enlightened now by the concept of phylogeny and its evidential foundations. Perhaps his *contemporary* interest in animate life would be philosophically infectious, as his ancient interest has not been.

19 For an example of how a conceptualization of ourselves as primates sheds light on our human behavior, see Sheets-Johnstone, 1994, in particular, chapters 1 and 2: "Optics of Power and the Power of Optics" and "An Evolutionary Genealogy."

Function and Evolution of Behavior, ed. P.H. Klopfer and J. P. Hailman (Reading, Mass.: Addison-Wesley), pp. 366–373 and 373–378, respectively.

Ghiselin, Michel T. 1983. "Lloyd Morgan's Canon in Evolutionary Context", a response to Daniel C. Dennett's "Intentional Systems in Cognitive Ethology: The 'Panglossian Paradigm' Defended", *Behavioral and Brain Sciences* 6, pp. 362–3.

Haldane, J.S. 1931. *The Philosophical Basis of Biology* (New York: Doubleday, Doran and Co.).

Harding, Robert S.O. 1975. "Meat-Eating and Hunting in Baboons", in *Socioecology and Psychology of Primates*, ed. R.H. Tuttle (The Hague: Mouton), pp. 245–257.

Hume, David. 1977. *An Enquiry Concerning Human Understanding*, ed. Eric Steinberg (Indianapolis: Hackett.)

Itani, J. and A. Nishimura. 1973. "The Study of Infrahuman Culture in Japan", in *Precultural Primate Behavior*, ed. E. Menzel (Karger: Basel), pp. 26 –50.

Johnstone, Albert A. 1991. *Rationalized Epistemology* (Albany: State University of New York Press).

Kawai, M. 1965. "Newly-acquired pre-cultural behavior of the natural troop of Japanese monkeys on Koshima islet", *Primates*, 6, pp. 1–30.

Kitcher, Philip, Kim Sterelny and C. Kenneth Waters. 1990. "The Illusory Riches of Sober's Monism", *Journal of Philosophy*, 87/3, pp. 158–61.

Klopfer, P. H. and J. P. Hailman, eds. 1972. *The Function and Evolution of Behavior* (Reading, Massachusetts: Addison-Wesley).

Lakoff, George and Mark Johnson. 1980. *Metaphors We Live By* (Chicago: University of Chicago).

Margolis, Joseph. 1978. *Persons and Minds* (Boston: D. Reidel).

McDonald, Kim A. 1995. "Scientists Rethink Anthropomorphism", *The Chronicle of Higher Education*, XLI/24 (24 February 1995), pp. A8, A9, A14.

McGrew, W.C. 1994. *Chimpanzee Material Culture: Implications for Human Evolution* (Cambridge: Cambridge University Press).

Morgan, Lloyd. 1930. *The Animal Mind* (New York: Longmans, Green and Co.).

Nussbaum, Martha. 1978. *Aristotle's De Motu Animalium* (Princeton: Princeton University Press).

Richards, Robert J. 1987. *Darwin and the Emergence of Evolutionary Theories of Mind and Behavior* (Chicago: University of Chicago Press).

Rorty, Richard. 1979. *Philosophy and the Mirror of Nature* (Princeton: Princeton University Press).

Rosenberg, Alexander. 1985. *The Structure of Biological Science* (New York: Cambridge University Press).

Rosenberg, Alexander. 1983. "Fitness", *Journal of Philosophy*, 80/8, pp. 457–73.

Ruse, Michael. 1973. *The Philosophy of Biology* (London: Hutchinson University Library, 1973).

Schaller, George. 1972. *The Serengeti Lion* (Chicago: University of Chicago Press).

Sellars, Wilfrid. 1963. "Philosophy and the Scientific Image of Man", *Science, Perception and Reality* (London: Routledge & Kegan Paul), pp. 1–40.

Shanahan, Timothy. 1990. "Evolution, Phenotypic Selection, and the Units of Selection", *Philosophy of Science* 57, pp. 210–25.

Sheets-Johnstone, Maxine. 1982. "Why Lamarck Did Not Discover the Principle of Natural Selection", *Journal of the History of Biology*, 15, pp. 443–65.

Sheets-Johnstone, Maxine. 1990. *The Roots of Thinking* (Philadelphia: Temple University Press).

Sheets-Johnstone, Maxine. 1994. *The Roots of Power: Animate Form and Gendered Bodies*(Chicago: Open Court Publishing).

Sober, Elliott. 1984. "Fact, Fiction, and Fitness", *Journal of Philosophy*, 80/7, pp. 372–83.

Sober, Elliott. 1990. "The Poverty of Pluralism: A Reply to Sterelny and Kitcher", *Journal of Philosophy*, 87/3, pp. 151–8

Sterelny, Kim and Philip Kitcher. 1988. "The Return of the Gene", *Journal of Philosophy*, 85/7, pp. 339–61.

Thompson, Nicholas S. 1976. "My Descent from the Monkey", *Perspectives in Ethology*, vol. 2, ed. P.P.G. Bateson and Peter H. Klopfer (New York: Plenum Press), pp. 221–30.

Whiten, A. and R.W. Byrne. 1988. "Tactical Deception in Primates", *Behavioral and Brain Sciences*, 11 , pp. 233–73.

Chapter VI

Surface Sensitivity and the Density of Flesh

In her prospectus for an art exhibition titled *In the Flesh*, Curator Jill Snyder identified a number of themes pertaining to flesh—containment, protection, exposure, disguise, pain, pleasure. All of these themes, she said, "allude to the role of skin in the evolution of human consciousness" (Snyder, 1995).

What I want to do in this essay is to articulate a fundamental dimension of this role to the end that a beginning natural philosophy of flesh emerges. By tracing out the role of "coverings" from their very beginnings in organismic life to pervasive present-day Western habits of the flesh, I want to put in historical, aesthetic, and cultural perspectives the profound allusions linking the sensuous surface of skin with the sensuous density of flesh. In a word, I want to sketch out an in-depth morphology, its evolutionary realities, its aesthetic beginnings and elaborations, and its present-day cultural transmogrifications.

1

In the beginning was the membrane, an enclosing tissue separating both one organism from another and organisms from the medium and environing world in which they lived. These first forms of life were bacteria and blue-green algae. Stephen Jay Gould has remarked that, as it was in the beginning, is, and always will be, this is The Age of Bacteria (Gould, 1994, p. 8). The stability of bacteria over some 3.5 billion years testifies to their indestructibility. Membranes are undeniably life-enhancing. But morphologically, they are something more. Membranes are contour-defining; they set off a certain spatial individuality. Indeed, in the beginning was not simply a membrane but *form*. The diversity of life is first of all a diversity of *form*.

How are we to understand the emergence of flesh within the emergence of a diversity of form? A natural history of flesh begins with surface sensitivity. This sensate faculty is not a matter of what physiologists and other body scientists call "cutaneous stimulation." Rather, surface sensitivity is a matter of animate sensitivity, a sensitivity that by turns may express itself in curiosity, explorations, recoilings, quiverings, affections, hastenings, hesitancies, accelerations, avoidances, persistence, and much more. Surface sensitivities resonate dynamically precisely because they are alive with meaning. They describe what I have elsewhere termed a *tactile-kinesthetic* engagement with the world (Sheets-Johnstone, 1990 and 1994).

From his fine and painstaking observations of animate life, Aristotle was led to observe that "without touch it is impossible for an animal to be" (Aristotle 435b 17–18). Along with movement, tactility is the premier faculty of living things. Other senses may be destroyed in one way or another, yet the animal still lives. With the death of the tangible, however, comes the death of the animal itself. In fact, tactility is the mark of *soul*. In *De Anima* — Aristotle's treatise *On the Soul* — Aristotle affirms that "[E]very body that has soul in it must ... be capable of touch" (435a14). This is because all soulful bodies have certain soulful — or "psychic" — powers beginning with the nutritive, and touch, Aristotle says, "is the sense for food" (414b7). Thus plants are soulful bodies; they take in water, nutrients, sunlight. Additional powers of the soul — or psyche — come into play with animate life: appetitive powers — desires, wishes, passions — sensory powers, locomotive powers, and thinking powers. Appetitive and sensory powers in particular go hand in hand; desires and wishes are linked to pleasures and pains, and pleasures and pains are sensate phenomena. A desire for something would be meaningless apart from the possibility of its sensory satisfaction. Here again, Aristotle tells us, touch is distinctive among the senses. The distinctiveness in this instance in fact causes him trouble in providing a uniform explanation of perception. The power to see, to hear, and to smell is realized indirectly; that is, a medium of some kind — e.g., air, water — intercedes in each case between object of sense and organ of sense. Touch alone (including taste, insofar as it is a form of touch) puts an animal in direct sensory contact with the things it appetitively seeks. Aristotle solves the problem of non-uniformity by designating flesh as the medium of touch, a medium that is affected along with the organ of touch which lies "farther inward" — i.e., the organ of touch is the heart (422b23). By conceiving flesh to be the medium of touch rather than acknowledging it as the organ of touch, and by conceiving the organ of touch to be affected *along with* rather than *by* the medium, as with the other senses, Aristotle balances the realities of experience with the need for explanatory order: he "saves the appearances". Indeed, in the act or fact of touching, nothing mediates between animal and object — between knower and known. His manoeuverings on behalf of uniformity aside, Aristotle is thus quite right: the immediacy of touch is an inescapable aspect of animate sensitivity, a fundamental mode of knowing the world. Like all other animals, we are always in touch with *something*, however far from focal attention that tactilely-felt something might be — the inside of our shoe, for example, or the shirt on our back, or the chair on which we sit, or the pencil with which we write.

There is a telling moment in the radically objectivating march of twentieth-century Western science that demonstrates how easily and summarily the resonant immediacy of touch — surface sensitivity — can be compromised. In a book commemorating the centennial of Darwin's *The Origin of Species*, a twentieth-century biologist urged correction of Darwin's description of a cat rubbing itself against someone's leg (Barnett, 1959). Darwin had described the cat as being "in an affectionate frame of mind" (Darwin, 1965, p. 59). As might be apparent from earlier remarks attempting to distinguish surface sensitivity from its scientific mufflings, his critic insisted that the correct description of the cat's act of rubbing was "cutaneous stimulation". Clearly, Darwin's critic wanted to restrict descriptions of the animate to a certain twentieth-century Western way of looking at organisms and of explaining them, and to a corresponding vocabulary. But the felt import of tactility is only impoverished by such descriptions. What plays on the animate reverberates with the life it touches; surface sensitivity is not a mere cutaneous event. As Aristotle indicates with respect to touch, surface sensitivity is an animate power, a mark of soul. Moreover Darwin's critic erred in a further important way in his attempted emendation. Because living things are never without "cutaneous stimulation" of one kind or another, it makes no sense to describe particular tactile acts such as rubbing "cutaneous stimulation." In such terms, no distinctions are possible. Life by membranous definition is a non-stop parade of "cutaneous stimulations". It is more exacting, not to say, truthful, to say that living things are never without surface sensitivities; and equally more exacting and truthful to say that because they are never without surface sensitivities, they are always potentially at the threshold of the world, sensitive to its nuances and portents.

In sum, surface sensitivity is consistently there, present, in the flesh — in animate form. We have merely to attend, and there it is. It is because it is consistently there, present, in the flesh, that "the *flesh* of objects", as Jean-Paul Sartre first emphatically described the fundamental palpable experience we have of things, is correlatively there, or potentially so (Sartre, 1956, p. 392). But to experience the *"flesh* of objects", the quintessential palpability of things — everyday things such as our clothing, the air, the wind that Sartre specifically called our attention to — we have to attend finely and without haste. We have to open ourselves to the sensuous link connecting our flesh with theirs; we have to allow our own flesh to be awakened by theirs. But in fact this awakening is already incipiently there in everyday ways, often practical ones, when tactile values come to fore and inform our experience of the visual. We see the sharpness of a knife, the smoothness of a velvet shirt, the straight edge of a ruler, the seriate contour of a leaf, the thickness of a book. Clearly, there is a natural disposition to link our flesh with the flesh of objects. Our very experience of *seeing* is spontaneously permeated with *tactile* qualities. We are indeed potentially open to "the flesh of the world", as Merleau-Ponty came later to describe and expand upon Sartre's "flesh of objects" (Merleau-Ponty, 1968), but we ourselves must actualize it by giving it our rapt attention.

2

The import of tactility in the evolution of life is plainly evident in the complex surface features of animate forms. From the simple formally delineating membranes of unicellular organisms such as bacteria to the stiff cellulose walls, pseudopods, or shells defining the contours of different protozoa, to the epithelial cells of creatures like sponges, to the exoskeletal plates, hairs, and cuticular tissue of invertebrates, to the skin, scales, and fur of vertebrates, Nature testifies amply both to the import of a boundary — something that in a physical sense separates one organism from another and organisms from the world in which they live — and to the import of surface itself. Exquisitely diverse and complex tactile structures are the fundamental mode by which organisms actively meet the world.

The earth, after all, is full of bumps and the air is full of currents. But precisely, creatures are consummately attuned in particular morphological ways to their particular worlds or *Umwelts*, as biologist Jakob von Uexküll termed the physiognomically distinctive worlds that different creatures inhabit. Ernst Cassirer aptly paraphrased von Uexküll's notion of creaturely worlds when he wrote that "Every organism ... has a world of its own because it has an experience of its own" (Cassirer, 1970, p. 25). Cassirer's paraphrase can itself be glossed in two notable ways. First, every organism is formally distinct: it is a particular kind of body or animate form. It is precisely because every organism is formally distinct, a particular kind of body or animate form, that "it has an experience of its own" and "a world of its own". Indeed, only on such *corporeal* grounds can there be a physiognomic fit of experience and world: a certain kind of world is congenial to a certain kind of body and a certain kind of body is congenial to a certain kind of world. Each animate form thus has its niche — or fails to survive. Yet however different its world from that of others, one creature's attunement to *its* world is fundamentally the same as every other creature's attunement to *its* world. This is because attunement lies fundamentally by way of surface sensitivities. Given not merely the appetitive-locomotive nature of animate life but the rich and ever-changing physiognomy of the world, one might well ask, how could it be otherwise?

Surface sensitivity is the way creatures have made their way from the very beginning: knowing the world through touch and movement — through proprioception, which literally means "one's own taking in". Through proprioception, creatures sense themselves moving, touching, and at the same time sense themselves in contact with objects. External proprioceptors are surface organs that are tactilely sensitive to deformations: slit sensilla of spiders compress; so also do campaniform structures on insect bodies and limbs; hairs on the faces of locusts bend in singular ways; so also do the cuticular articulated peg organs that are situated around the joints of lobsters. Contacts create pressures, and pressures, however minimal, create deformations — surface phenomena. Bodies are squeezed by things, bent by things, rustled by things. They are formally deformed in highly varied ways by what they meet. In a very real sense, they *give in* to the world and in giving in, recognize what in the world they are touching. It is thus their very formal deformations that are at the heart of their knowledge.

A creature's tactilely-won knowledge does not begin and end with its discernment of what in the world it is touching. Formal deformations are at the heart of its knowledge of itself as well as of its knowledge of the world. In particular, through bodily deformations, a creature is proprioceptively aware of itself in the act of touching something — as being jostled or pushed by something, for example. Moreover, by these very tactile deformations — and quite apart from any direct sense of movement that comes from internal sensory organs in muscles, joints, and tendons — it is aware of itself as moving, as being still, or as being in a certain corporeal position. Such knowledge is possible because deformations occur both as a result of external circumstances *and* as the result of body movement itself. When an organism bends its leg, for example, it brings two surfaces in contact with each other — in mutual deformation. In effect, in the same way that creatures *give in* to the world, so they *give in* to their own movement. Their very form reverberates in distinctively deforming ways—by stretching, folding, flattening, thickening. External coverings are literally *re-markable* in this sense; they are over and over again marked both by movement and by external circumstances. They compress, bend, expand, vibrate, and so on. And they are furthermore remarkable in the preeminent sense of being full of import: the unique and intricate surfaces of animate forms are consistently alive with meaning. In undeniably superficial but profound ways, a creature knows both itself and the world.

3

Insofar as we humans are awakened and pride ourselves on being awakened by aesthetic surfaces, we might readily question whether the unique and intricate surfaces of aesthetic forms that are alive with meaning and the unique and intricate surfaces of animate forms that are alive with meaning are not related in some way. The question is of moment precisely in the context of an evolutionary appreciation of *form*. In particular, when addressed to the aesthetic forms lining the walls of paleolithic caves, the question points us toward original understandings of surface and density that have strong implications for an in-depth morphology. This is first of all because in considering paleolithic cave art, we find ourselves connected with a distant past in which sense of surface and density of meaning are most simply but perfectly married. The marriage is indeed immediately apparent in the very fact of there being *drawings* on the walls of *caves*, and correlatively, in the very experience of *drawings* on the walls of *caves*. In other words, the mere physicality of the scene is tangible evidence of the marriage: in the fact as in the experience, surface and depth are consummately joined. The question furthermore points us toward original understandings of surface and density because paleolithic cave drawings clearly draw upon our natural attunement to the world; they play upon and articulate in a crystallized and undistracted way the complex world of our surface sensitivities—sensitivities that allow us not only to be struck by a configuration of line fragments or hand prints, for example, or to apprehend subtle and varying surface textures of the cave walls themselves, but to experience *being inside*. In so doing, they lead us to the realization of the import of our evolutionary heritage. Reflection upon our attunement to these ancient forms indeed readily provokes us to take account of our beginnings. The fact of the drawings and our experience of them call upon us to make sense of ourselves in a deep historical sense, not just culturally in the twentieth century, or even as far back as the Renaissance, the Middle Ages, or Ancient Greece, but all the way back to the earliest creative joining of surface and density. In this sense, these ancient aesthetic forms lead us to the possibility of discovering first-hand how our own surface sensitivities and flesh make possible an apprehension of the flesh of objects. They invite us to ponder how we could possibly come to know the flesh of objects except through our own tactilely sensitive surfaces, or how we could possibly arrive at meanings that resonate deeply within us except by way of the palpable.

A brief descriptive account of the original conjoining of surface and density in paleolithic cave art will bring these basic self-questionings and understandings directly to the fore.

Aesthetic surfaces are remarkable because they are markable to begin with. The drawing of a line animates a surface; it brings a flat and precisely *un*-remarkable expanse to life. What the drawing of a pictorial line leaves in its wake is a *linear form*. The form may be open or closed — an arc or a circle, for example; it may describe a contour or demarcate a boundary. In either case, an original surface is transformed into something wonderful, something that, simply in virtue of *line* becomes animated. The first tactile-kinesthetic acts of "scribing" a contour and of "marking" a closed boundary thus had — and still have — formidable transforming powers: where there was once an unanimated surface, a mere expanse, there is now *form*; where before there was no concept of drawing, no concept of engaging a surface in both a tactile and kinesthetic sense, there are now both contour- and shape-defining lines. With such form-creating lines comes the possibility of depiction, that is, the possibility of graphically portraying the complex forms of things actually seen. Such a possibility hinges on a sense of how line, in addition to animating a surface, can capture the distinctive bodily character of things, thus on a tactile-kinesthetic sense of *containment*, and of *insides* and *outsides*. The depiction of animate forms on the walls of caves — bison, mammoth, horses, and so on — attests to this sense. Paleolithic cave art attests to the discovery of *drawing* and its power to capture the form of a thing by formally delineating its contours or boundaries, whether the curve of a spine or the full outline of a figure. It attests to the discovery of surface and depth, the surfaces and depth of the cave itself, certainly, but more basically still, the surface sensitivities and density of flesh that are its foundation.

With the momentous beginning discovery of drawing came the possibility of discovering qualitative aspects of line such as roughness, evenness, softness, jaggedness and myriad number of other qualities we come to know by having touched the world and having been touched by it. Thus, a surface that in the beginning is tactilely transformed by the drawing of lines may later come to engender tactile values beyond those related to contour and shape. The act of drawing may thus become a qualitatively more complex tactile-kinesthetic act, and the drawn object correlatively a qualitatively more complex form. Moreover, aesthetic surfaces themselves may come to be manipulated; that is, they may come to be transformed in more elaborate ways than by the drawing of lines. Aesthetic surfaces — wood, hide, leaves, paper, canvas, tissue, tape, wax, cloth, and so on — may be crumpled, twisted, hammered, chiseled, squeezed, bent, folded, stretched, and more. Like the surfaces of animate forms, they may be *formally deformed*. Their integrity is not compromised by this process of deformation; on the contrary, it is aesthetically magnified, and this because rather than being destroyed or damaged by the process, the tactile aesthetic potential of the worked surface is in each case actualized or brought to light — indeed, in a way similar to the way in which the integrity of animate forms are magnified and kinetic aesthetic potentials actualized in the formal deformations of a running or dancing body. In fact, the basic formal similarity between aesthetic forms and animate forms extends even further. Like the surfaces of animate forms, aesthetic surfaces reverberate with a history, a history both of what has touched them and how they have been touched. In each instance, surface sensitivities reverberate in depth.

If the above verbal descriptions have made sense, then it is of less moment whether one has actually experienced paleolithic cave art in the flesh or seen only representations of paleolithic cave drawings or simply imagined drawings on the walls of caves, than whether one has reflected upon the source of one's sense-making and discovered its origin. Whether perceived directly or indirectly, whether imagined or grasped through verbal description, what allows the sense of the drawings to resonate within us is our own bodily life, our own tactile-kinesthetic experiences of knowing the world and making sense of it. We know from our own tactile-kinesthetic experiences that line animates a surface, that the drawing of contours may lead to the drawing of boundaries, that the limning of a certain shape may evolve into the limning of an inside and an outside, and so on. Further still, we know from our own bodily experiences that all such formal developments begin with the sensitivity of a surface and its capacity to be deformed — by the layering of paint, by chiseling, twisting, squeezing, and any number of other tactile-kinetic modes of engaging a surface. In short, there is no doubt but that we understand the tactile-kinesthetic process of drawing on the walls of caves, of manipulating aesthetic surfaces, and so on, on the basis of our own bodily life. It is important to emphasize that we understand formal deformations and, in a more extended sense, the relationship between our own flesh and the flesh of the world not in so many words nor in ways that we have necessarily made explicit to ourselves. We understand them because we are animate

forms to begin with. We understand them corporeally. Our heritage as animate forms is rooted in just such tactile-kinesthetic understandings. It is
these understandings — obviously, *nonlinguistic* understandings — that are
the foundation of our surface sensitivities to the flesh of objects and of our
capacity to grasp a density of meaning in our experiences of aesthetic
form.

Aesthetic forms heighten nonlinguistic understandings, amplifying
what is already incipiently there. As noted earlier, aesthetic forms articulate in a crystallized and undistracted way the fundamentally physiognomic world of our senses. The challenge they present is precisely one of
turning from our daily, often overwhelmingly verbal, commerce with the
world and of opening ourselves to non-linguistic in-depth morphologies.
Our capacity to open ourselves in this way mirrors our capacity to open
ourselves to the flesh of another and to the flesh of objects in our everyday
lives — not only to our clothing, the air, and the wind, as Sartre indicated,
but to equally mundane items such as tables, chairs, plates, cabbages,
trees, stones. When we fathom another person or creature, or when we
experience the form of things in our everyday world, when we fathom
ancient paintings on the walls of caves, or any aesthetic form for that matter — in other words, when we experience a form in depth rather than as
some recognizable but vague thing over which our gaze passes — we let
our own surface sensitivities come to the fore. In so doing, we open ourselves to being touched and moved by what is there. In turn, we open ourselves to fathoming the density of another living being or thing. We allow
a certain form to carry us from our own surface sensitivities to a density of
flesh. We open ourselves to new possibilities of attunement.

4

However varied and finely differentiated, the external proprioceptive
organs of animate forms are all attuned to the same end: surface sensitivity
through deformation. In a very real sense, vertebrate skin is no different: it
stretches, compresses, and folds in response to external circumstances and
to body movement. But there is something peculiar about the skin of a
human vertebrate — or primate: its ideational connection or association
with sex.

Desmond Morris's book, *The Naked Ape*, appeared in 1967. It created a
popular stir — it was a "sensational worldwide bestseller", according to its
jacket cover — and little wonder since, inside its cover it asked, "Mirror,
mirror on the wall, who's the sexiest primate of them all? Don't look now,
reader, but it's you." Conceptual risks perhaps attend any kind of exposure, but exposing the comparative nakedness of humans amidst the

furredness of other primates can create especially mistaken impressions. Primary among these are both a misconception of skin as mere surface phenomenon and a misconception of humans as semantically foreclosed by their unique epidermal status among primates. The misconceptions are in each case fostered by an inverse neglect: what is overlooked in the first misconception is what is conceptually seized upon in the second, and what is overlooked in the second misconception is conceptually seized upon in the first. What is wanting on the one side is an evolutionary perspective, a history of animate form in which the quintessential epistemo-teleological significance of surface sensitivities is clearly acknowledged and set forth. What is wanting on the other side is an awakened sense of how cultures rework — distort, exaggerate, suppress, or elaborate — what is evolutionarily given, thereby establishing highly specific cultural attitudes, beliefs, and practices — for example, the cultural idea that nakedness, hence naked skin, is equivalent to sexiness. One possible result of these respective blindspots is a misunderstanding of what is or might be celebrated as human uniqueness, if indeed, at this tag-end of an exploitative and wantonly violent twentieth century, humans can reasonably think themselves unique in any honorific sense at all. The misunderstanding turns on a superlative: "the sexiest". What the superlative affirms on the basis of nakedness is something quite other than a dimension within an in-depth morphology. It bypasses completely evolutionary understandings of external proprioceptive organs. It thereby precludes basic understandings of human surface sensitivities. In particular, rather than comprehending the pleasures of sex within an in-depth morphology of skin, that is, rather than embracing human sexuality within the domain of a natural history of flesh, a naked ape gazes upon itself in a mirror, and, on the basis of its nakedness, sees itself the sexiest primate of all. In effect, surface sensitivities are summarily displaced by a mere surface phenomenon.

In preceding sections, I have attempted to draw out the intimate connections between animate flesh and the flesh of objects by distilling the fundamental significance of surface sensitivity within both an evolutionary and an aesthetic perspective. I would like now to do something similar but more briefly within a cultural perspective by considering critical aspects of our own (Western) cultural reworkings of skin. Elaborating on the idea of attunement, I want to show how human surface sensitivities, while given with the human bodies we are, are not on that account automatically robust and vibrant. On the contrary, human surface sensitivities must be cultivated, attended to, respected, cared for — in a way precisely similar to the way in which aesthetic surface sensitivities must be cultivated, attended to, respected, cared for. These sensitivities may otherwise remain dormant, in a state of suspended animation. Indeed, they may be more than this. While potentially there, present, in our own flesh any time we care to attend to them, and correlatively, potentially there, present, in the flesh of objects any time we turn attentively to them, surface sensitivities may in fact be purposely ignored, studiously blotted out of experience, resolutely excluded as a possibility, and thus nullified. To bring to the fore an appreciation of the culturally contingent nature of human—and aesthetic—surface sensitivity is to bring to the fore a cultural understanding of flesh commensurate with our times, that is, an understanding of the cultural meanings and values of surface sensitivity in our own Western culture. While dominant meanings will be set forth below, appreciation and understanding hinge ultimately on progressive self-exposure. They require that we examine attentively and without haste the varied and complex meanings we have each of us cultivated of our own skin and flesh in the context of our cultural groomings.

5

In this great age of relativism that substantively helps to fuel present-day postmodern Western culture, we are encouraged to nourish along our differences and nourish them we do. We fractionate into finer and finer groups by which we label ourselves in distinctive ways from everyone else. In a quite unremarkable way, however, we are concomitantly—and perniciously—nourished by the same attitudes to establish and maintain blinders. We are, in other words, impelled toward the belief that there are no ties that bind us to each other or to the world. When we look out at each other, we perceive difference; when we look out on the everyday world, we perceive anything but its flesh. Ready signs of this cultivated detachment hardly need itemizing. They range from ethnic cleansings and religious fanaticisms to racial tensions and terrorist militias; from the degradation of nonhuman animals to the depletion of ozone. It is not hyperbole to describe the tag end of twentieth century human life as a time when humans are out to save their own skin and to destroy the skin of others; nor as a time when humans have lost touch with their fundamental attunement with the world.

Violations of flesh are a de-animation of the animate. Violations of human flesh are featured in near mandatory "murder-news-of-the-day" reports in the United States, in reminders of recent past events in Bosnia or of the Holocaust in Europe, or in accounts of some altogether new barbarous human-on-human acts. Violations of the flesh of "objects"—"objects" such as gorillas, coral reefs, and elephants—and violations of the flesh of

the world — the decimation of rain forests, for example — are not reported
with the same vigilance, but the savage deeds are no less on human hands.
In a word, twentieth century cultural reworkings of skin are tied to the
slaughtering not only of our own flesh but the flesh of the world. The connection is precisely by way of a loss of surface sensitivity. In lieu of surface
sensitivity, we pedestal sexiness and process information. Indeed, we
think of ourselves as computational systems. In just such ways, surface
sensitivity is culturally muffled and suppressed. We ourselves become a
mere surface, indeed, a veritable *screen* across which changing scenes pass
but without touching us. We become hardened to distress, toughened to
violence; we develop a thick skin. In effect, we lose touch with the density
of flesh, our own, that of others, and of the world.

There is another way in which twentieth century Western culture has
critically reworked surface sensitivities. Where skin is differentially valued and in turn selectively treated and mistreated, so also is flesh. When
we fail to appreciate the surface sensitivity of others as being equal to our
own, we blot out the possibility of recognizing them as kindred others,
which is why we can be inured and indifferent to violations of their flesh.
When we valorize our own skin above all others, whatever color our own
skin happens to be, we fail to perceive, much less conceive, of those fundamental ties that bind us in a common humanity and in a common
creaturehood. In failing to appreciate the surface sensitivity of others, we
have in fact already lost touch with our own surface sensitivity. An exclusive valorization of our own skin comes at a price. We renounce our natural history. We put on blinders and cultivate our differences. We save our
own skin — but as a mere surface phenomenon.

Skin holds us together; flesh binds us together. Skin holds us together
and grounds our knowledge of ourselves and of the world; flesh binds us
together and grounds the possibility of an enlightened and reciprocating
humanity that, celebrating the diversity of life, celebrates also its commonalities, and that taking from the flesh of the earth, takes care also to protect
and preserve it. Through an awakening of our own flesh, we open ourselves to a profound understanding of what it means to be animate — what
D.H. Lawrence once described as being "alive and in the flesh and part of
the living incarnate cosmos." The source of this profound understanding
is not tucked away in our brains but inheres in the morphological structures and sensuous densities of our own bodies.

Present-day cultural meanings of skin and valuings of flesh clearly challenge us. They challenge us in a far more critical sense, in a much more
immediate and everyday way, and certainly on a much broader scale than
aesthetic surfaces challenge us. Yet the challenge is basically similar: to

open ourselves to an in-depth morphology. The opening is risky. We are vulnerable to new feelings, new ideas, new others. We risk misunderstandings, perplexities, a lack of control, uncertainty. We risk the security of our tough skin and habits of the flesh. We risk the loss of our own pre-eminence. What we risk gaining in meeting the challenge and in progressively awakening to in-depth morphologies are understandings and appreciations of form: not only understandings and appreciations of the animate forms we are, but of the animate forms we are not; not only understandings and appreciations of the forms immediately surrounding us in our everyday world, but of those more distant or altogether foreign ones we know only through our knowledge of the earth. What we risk gaining as well is that deeper sense of form itself that comes in the course of reflection and that consistently turns us back to tactile-kinesthetic foundations, to the miraculous power of surface sensitivities and a density of flesh, and to the equally miraculous power of the flesh of objects and of the world, and that furthermore has the possibility of turning us forward, toward the awesome task of awakening cultural meanings and values consistent with those formidable foundations and formal powers.

References

Barnett, Samuel A. 1959. "The 'expression of the emotions' ", in *A Century of Darwin*, ed. Samuel A. Barnett (Cambridge: Harvard University Press), pp. 206–30.

Cassirer, Ernst. 1970. *An Essay on Man* (New York: Bantam Books).

Darwin, Charles. 1965 [1872]. *The Expression of the Emotions* (Chicago: University of Chicago Press).

Gould, Stephen Jay. June 1994. "The Power of This View of Life", *Natural History* 103/6, pp. 6–8.

Merleau-Ponty, Maurice. 1968. *The Visible and the Invisible*, ed. Claude Lefort, trans. Alphonso Lingis (Evanston: Northwestern University Press).

Morris, Desmond. 1967. *The Naked Ape* (New York: Dell Publishing).

Sartre, Jean-Paul. 1956. *Being and Nothingness*, trans. Hazel E. Barnes (New York: Philosophical Library).

Sheets-Johnstone, Maxine. 1990. *The Roots of Thinking* (Philadelphia: Temple University Press).

Sheets-Johnstone, Maxine. 1994. *The Roots of Power: Animate Form and Gendered Bodies* (Chicago: Open Court Publishing).

Snyder, Jill. August 1995. *In the Flesh* (Prospectus), unpaginated.

Chapter VII

Consciousness: A Natural History

[W]e always start at the sensory end and try to come out at the motor side. I very much agree with the late von Holst when he suggests that we start at the other end and work our why (sic) back toward sensation. . . . It requires some different way of looking.

H.L. Teuber[1]

If any person thinks the examination of the rest of the animal kingdom an unworthy task, he must hold in like disesteem the study of man.

Aristotle (*Parts of Animals*, 645a26–7)

1. Introduction

Thomas Nagel, in a review of John Searle's (1992) book, *The Rediscovery of the Mind*, states that "we do not really understand the claim that mental states are states of the brain". He follows this statement more finely with the remark that, "We are still unable to form a conception of *how* consciousness arises in matter" (Nagel, 1993, p. 40). The missing conception is, of course, really a missing answer:

How *does* consciousness arise in matter?

Nagel implicitly raises the question at the culmination of a discussion of what he categorizes as Searle's first arguments against materialists. He lays out these arguments after summarizing Searle's view of how various theories of mind have attempted to reduce the mental to the physical and of how they all fail to take consciousness into account. Without an account of consciousness, according to Searle, none of the theories can rightfully claim to be a theory of mind. Quoting Searle, Nagel points out that "The crucial question is not 'Under what conditions would we *attribute* mental states to other people?' but rather, 'What is it that people *actually have*

---

1   Teuber (1966), pp. 440f. He is discussing D.M. MacKay's paper "Cerebral Organization and the Conscious Control of Action", the theme of which is "the controlling function of the brain in voluntary agency".

when they have mental states?'" (p. 38). Nagel's agreement with Searle that "the subjective' is precisely the crucial question to address is exemplified in his recognizably-worded statement that `Facts about your external behavior or the electrical activity or functional organization of your brain may be closely connected with your conscious experiences, but they are not facts about *what it's like* for you to hear a police siren" (p. 39, italics added). The question of `*how* consciousness arises in matter' thus appears absolutely central for both Nagel and Searle.

In this paper I outline basic reasons for thinking the question spurious. This critical work will allow me to pinpoint troublesome issues within the context of definitions of life and in turn address the properly constructive task of this essay: to demonstrate how genuine understandings of consciousness demand close and serious study of evolution as a history of animate form. I should note that this demonstration will omit a consideration of botany, though plant life is indisputably part of an evolutionary history of animate form. The omission has nothing to do with importance, but with keeping a manageable focus on the question of consciousness; and it has nothing to do either with a trivialization of the ways in which plants are animate, but with an intentional narrowing of the complexity of an already complex subject. As will be shown in the concluding section, the demonstration has sizable implications for cognitivists generally and for philosophers in particular, notably: (1) a need to re-think the common assumption that unconsciousness historically preceded consciousness; (2) a need to delve as deeply and seriously into natural history as into brains and their computational analogues; (3) a critical stance toward arm-chair judgments about consciousness and a correlative turn toward corporeal matters of fact.

2. Reasons For Critically Questioning the Question

To begin with, while the question seems to phrase the difficult point in exacting terms, it in fact assumes certain metaphysical distinctions in advance of identifying them, showing them to be the case, and/or justifying them theoretically. To that degree, the question either undermines or precludes any answer that might be proposed.[2] The assumed metaphysical distinctions are actually three in number. Two of them have a relationship to a particular history, the relationship in each case depending upon the interpretational latitude given to the word "arises". In the most general sense, the question assumes a historical distinction between the organic and the inorganic, i.e. an arising of the former from the latter.

---

2   Whether it undermines or precludes depends upon the degree to which the assumptions are recognized and acknowledged.

Thus, in a broad sense, the question assumes a certain placement of consciousness with respect to cosmic history. At closer range, the question assumes a historical distinction between "higher" and "lower" forms of life, i.e. a time at which "higher" capacities arose. In a broad sense, it thus assumes a certain placement of consciousness with respect to the evolution of life, most especially, human life. In still finer perspective, the question assumes a distinction between mind and body, i.e. an arising (development, emergence, issuance) of the mental from the physical. In a broad sense, it thus assumes a certain placement of consciousness with respect to (merely) corporeal being. The first two distinctions are plainly historical; the third distinction has no particular historical character, though some people—for example, philosopher Daniel Dennett—accord it one in ontogenetic terms. Writing of human infants, Dennett says that "[consciousness] arises when there is work for it to do, and the preeminent work of consciousness is dependent on sophisticated language-using activities" (Dennett, 1983, p. 384). To acquire a bona fide historical character rather than being assigned one on the basis of an unsubstantiated ontogenesis, the third distinction would have to address the question of the origin of consciousness within the context of the two earlier distinctions, since it is only in the context of those distinctions that the third distinction actually comes to prominence. In effect, an answer to the question of "*how* consciousness arises in matter" does not reduce to saying how a certain physical or neurological maturity drives consciousness; it must specify how consciousness comes to be in the context of a progressively finer natural history, one that takes into account the actual lives of individual living forms as they are understood within cosmic and animate evolutionary histories. To answer the question in this way, however, necessitates a revision in the question itself, precisely because the historical character of the first two distinctions demands it. In particular,

consciousness does not arise in *matter*;
it arises in organic forms, forms that are *animate*.

What is required is thus an exact rendering of how consciousness is grounded in animate form. How does consciousness come to be in the natural history of living creatures and to inhere in the animate?[3]

---

3   A reviewer wrote that "giving an explanation of 'how' if one cannot identify 'what' seems difficult, since the object of the inquiry is not specified". In practice, where the study of consciousness is concerned, the distinction between "how" (consciousness arises) and "what" (consciousness is) is far less straightforward than this remark implies.
      As may be apparent from the discussion thus far, a perusal of current literature on consciousness shows no consideration of the distinction, and thus no apparent inclination on the part of writers to be concerned with it or to think that *what* must be clarified before a

Approaching the question of consciousness from an historical perspective is certainly not unique. Neurobiologist Gerald Edelman has emphasized repeatedly the necessity of genetic understandings, genetic not in the sense of genes, but in the sense of origins. As he insists, "There must be ways to put the mind back into nature *that are concordant with how it got there in the first place*" (Edelman, 1992, p. 15, italics added). His approach is to consider morphology and history at all levels: not just at the level of the embryological development of brains, but continuing through to the level of actual life, thus to the level of movement and of experiences of moving, and to a consideration of the effects of these experiences on morphology. Through an attentiveness to an experiential history and its morphological moorings and effects, Edelman conjoins typically separated aspects of creaturely life. He discovers cells, anatomy, and morphologically structured mappings within the brain as undergoing "continuous electrical and chemical change, driving and being driven by animal movement'. He furthermore finds animal movement itself to be `conditioned by animal shape and pattern, leading to behavior" (p. 15). Though he does not term it such, *animate form* is clearly central to his investigations.

Whether or not one is persuaded by Edelman's theory of the origin of consciousness, his focal emphasis upon the need for a proper history of consciousness cannot be dismissed. It articulates from an explicitly evolutionary vantage point the implicit but unexamined historical claims of Nagel and Searle. The essentially evolutionary convergence is not surprising given Searle's insistence on "biological naturalism"[4] and Nagel's famous inquiry about a bat (Nagel, 1974); each evinces overtones of a natural history of the animate. Conversely, when Edelman (1992) writes, "[I]t is not enough to say that the mind is embodied; one must say how" (p. 15), he

consideration of *how.* Indeed, writers on consciousness launch their inquiries straightaway, even sometimes specifying in the beginning what consciousness is in terms that beg the question of saying just what it is — e.g., "we can say that a mental state is conscious if it has a *qualitative feel.* . . . The problem of explaining these phenomenal qualities is just the problem of explaining consciousness" (Chalmers, 1996, p. 4). The muddle strongly suggests that clarification of the distinction requires an acknowledgment of what is called "the hermeneutic circle". In classic terms, one already understands that which one is on the way to interpreting; and conversely, one has already interpreted that which one has already understood. In more scientific terms, one already knows *the what* that one is about to investigate; and conversely, one has already investigated *the what* that one already knows. In short, a researcher could hardly investigate anything if there were not already a known delimited subject at hand, a subject that the researcher already knows at least to the extent that s/he wants to investigate it. Moreover the process of investigation is itself a hermeneutic circle: as what is investigated becomes known in more exacting ways, that new knowledge becomes the basis for further investigation. In just this way, *what* consciousness is may be continually elucidated in the process of elucidating *how* it arises. The present paper progressively does just that: it answers the *what* question in the course of specifying *how consciousness arises in animate form.*

4   "Mental events and processes are as much part of our *biological natural history* as digestion, mitosis, meiosis, or enzyme secretion" (Searle, 1992, p. 1, italics added).

is giving voice to a *how* as pressingly and provocatively "subjective" (e.g. 'each consciousness depends on its unique history and embodiment', p. 139) as that of Searle and Nagel, but a *how* explicitly tethered to the evolution of life.

Philosophers of mind commonly pursue the same *how* question as Searle and Nagel but many, if not most, take quite other paths and enter at a decisively earlier point. Daniel Dennett and Paul Churchland are notable in this respect and warrant special attention. Both endeavour to offer a historical perspective by placing consciousness first of all in cosmic time. Their respective attempts are not protracted by any means — they do not reflect at any length upon the cosmic beginnings of life — and neither speaks explicitly of *the organic* and *the inorganic*. In what is nonetheless a clearly cosmological answer to the *how* question, both advert straight off to the advent of replicators and of the process of self-replication. Churchland's opening sentence of the first section ("Neuroanatomy: The Evolutionary Background") of a chapter titled "Neuroscience" reads: "Near the surface of the earth's oceans, between three and four billion years ago, the sun-driven process of purely chemical evolution produced some *self-replicating* molecular structures" (Churchland, 1984, p. 121, italics in original).[5] Dennett's opening sentences of the second section ("Early Days") of a chapter titled "The Evolution of Consciousness" reads: "In the beginning, there were no reasons; there were only causes ... The explanation for this is simple. There was nothing that had interests. But after millennia there happened to emerge simple *replicators*" (Dennett, 1991, p. 173, italics in original). Clearly, in both cases there is an attempt to separate out the inchoate creaturely from the "purely chemical", thus to specify the cosmic beginnings of life and thereby the nature of the cross-over from the inorganic to the organic.

Dennett's and Churchland's modest nod in the direction of a natural history is short-lived, as such nods generally tend to be among cognitivist philosophers. Their respective "findings" from studies of the beginnings of life on earth are neither carried forward in a consideration of the evolution of animate forms nor examined in the light of a diversity of intact, actually living bodies. Their respective allusions to self- replication suffice

5   It is of interest to point out that Churchland's idea of a natural evolutionary course of events, a kind of biological determinism with respect to life and intelligence, conflicts with prominent ideas and experimental findings in biology. Churchland states that "[G]iven energy enough, and time, the phenomena of both life *and* intelligence are to be expected as among the natural products of planetary evolution." Stephen Jay Gould is a strong proponent of the view that evolution is a thoroughly contingent, non-repeatable historical process (see, e.g., Gould, 1989; 1995). See also McDonald, 1995. The article summarizes microbiologist-zoologist Richard E. Lenski's intricate experiments and their results, which show the play of chance in the course of evolution and the unrepeatability of natural history.

to locate the origin of a natural history of consciousness. In finer terms, self-replication offers for them a fully satisfactory answer to the historical question of *"how* consciousness arises in matter" because self-replication is where it all began and where it all began is where it still is: consciousness is a matter of matter. The molecular explanation of consciousness is succinctly exemplified in Churchland's *Matter and Consciousness.* Whatever Churchland says of the self- replicating beginnings of life at the end of his book is predictably cued in advance by what he has stated at the beginning of his book about human life:

> [T]he important point about the standard evolutionary story is that the human species and all of its features are the wholly physical outcome of a purely physical process ... We are notable only in that our nervous system is more complex and powerful than those of our fellow creatures ... We are creatures of matter. And we should learn to live with that fact (Churchland, 1984, p. 21).

The problem comes not in living with that fact but in living hermetically with that fact. Living hermetically with that fact comes at the expense of a viable natural history, for the fact passes over fundamental understandings of animate corporeal life. These omissions in understanding emerge in a striking way in the metaphysical relationship Churchland proposes between the organic and inorganic (though again, not specifically using these broadly cosmic terms). He insists that "living systems" differ from "nonliving systems" "only by degrees": "There is no metaphysical gap to be bridged" — or as he says a paragraph later with respect to "the same lesson" (i.e. difference "only by degrees") applying to intelligence: "No metaphysical discontinuities emerge here" (p. 153). This, perhaps at first surprising, viewpoint on the organic and inorganic is not *shown* to be true by Churchland, not even through his "lessons" in how to forge definitions of life that will be opaque to discontinuities, such as claiming that "the glowing teardrop of a candle flame ... may just barely meet the conditions of the definition [of life] proposed", i.e. life is "any semiclosed physical system that exploits the order it already possesses, and the energy flux through it, in such a way as to maintain and/or increase its internal order". In brief, Churchland's viewpoint is *of necessity* true in virtue of Churchland theory: if human consciousness is mere matter — relatively "more complex and powerful" matter (p. 21), but mere matter nevertheless through and through — then the organic can differ from the inorganic "only by degrees". Metaphysical distinctions are blurred by fiat as only they can be in such a theory.

At least one consequence of the blurring should be singled out in order to demonstrate the questionable propriety of claiming that "No metaphysical discontinuities emerge here". A continuous metaphysics creates a problem for distinguishing in traditional western ways between life and death. However rationally doubtful, on the smudgy face of things, quasi-eternal life ("quasi" insofar as eternal life is apparently punctuated from time to time but not wholly discontinued) suddenly emerges as a viable metaphysical future possibility — if only materialist philosophers can deliver up their stone, aided, of course, by deliveries on promises by western materialist science. Of course, the notion of cosmically differing "only by degrees" is in a metaphysically twisted and thoroughly ironic way also supportive of eastern notions such as reincarnation and of so-called "primitive" notions of life after death, notions exemplified by non-western burial practices in which dead persons are interred along with items they will need in their ongoing journeys. With respect to these latter notions, however, it is rather some form of the mental that is primary; matter is simply contingent stuff for the instantiation of spirit. What differs "only by degrees" is thus not fundamentally matter at all but a principle of life — *spiritus, pneuma*, or whatever else might be conceived to constitute invincible and inexhaustible animating vapours.

The consequences and ramifications of holding a "no-gap-here" metaphysical theory about the organic and inorganic aside, the major question is how — and to what extent — such a theory actually clarifies consciousness. In particular, however much information Churchland gives us, whether about self-replication, "energy flux" (pp. 152–4), neurophysiology, or any other material aspects of living systems — and whether in direct terms or in terms of computational networks — and whatever the progressively refined definitions he gives us of life, we never seem to arrive at an elucidation of consciousness. The reductive equation of consciousness to matter is not *in fact* shown. The reductionist programme is at best a matter of correlation; that is, when there is consciousness, there is a certain kind of electrical activity ongoing in a brain; when there is not consciousness, there is not that certain kind of electrical activity ongoing in the brain, but electrical activity of another kind, or no electrical activity at all. No actual identity has ever been shown to exist between a thought, an awareness, a concept, an intention, a meaning, or any other kind of "mental" happening and a particular constellation of material happenings, i.e. neural events in a brain. As physiologist Benjamin Libet has observed, "One can only describe relationships between subjective phenomena and neural events, not how one gets from one to the other" (Libet, 1985, p. 568). The reduction of the mental to the physical — or the identification of the former with the latter — is thus evidentially ungrounded. In effect, without collateral substantiating facts, it is impossible to cash in reductionist- or identity-theory.

Impediments other than the metaphysical ones discussed above similarly plague accounts of "how consciousness arises in matter". Primary among these is the claim that consciousness is a brain activity exclusive to humans, hence that short of a *human* brain, there is no consciousness, or at least no consciousness worthy of the name. This thesis impedes an understanding of consciousness in a number of ways. Most importantly, it hazards a conceptual break with evolutionary theory. Not that new capacities and/or new modes of living cannot emerge that are discontinuous with previous capacities or modes in the manner specified by punctuated equilibrium theory, but that a disposition to set humans categorically apart from the rest of nature — whether on the basis of language, art, or whatever — goes unexamined and unchecked. Indeed, with such a thesis, one form or another of creationism can easily hold sway. This is because the core concept of evolution in a historical sense — *descent with modification*, to use Darwin's exact phrase — is ignored. Humans may in turn be conceived as special creations, even "Special Creations", as one well-known philosopher affirms (Sellars, 1963, p. 6). A fundamental problem with the view may be stated in the form of a historical truth: while all humans are hominids, not all hominids are human. In particular, with the notion that consciousness is exclusive to *human* brains, aspects of *hominid* evolution become virtually impossible to understand — the beginnings of stone toolmaking, for example, by members of the species *Homo habilis* some two and a half million years ago and the development of progressively more complex tool-making techniques by other nonhuman hominid species over the span of those same two and a half million years.[6] Furthermore, nonhuman animal social behaviours, especially those of our nearest extant primate relatives that have unequivocal affinities with our own social behaviours, become virtually impossible to accredit — patting another individual to reassure, for example, or hiding something from another. Grounds vanish for delimiting these social phenomena as behaviours in the first place, which in turn makes grounds for behavioural categorization, much less grounds for warranted human interpretation and assured comprehension of these nonhuman animals, nonexistent. If consciousness is something only human brains produce, then no matter how much a nonhuman brain, even a *hominid* nonhuman brain, might resemble a human one anatomically, creatures that are not human are not conscious but merely robotic pieces of matter. Hence, however much their practices in tool-making or their social interactions might evidence continuities with

---

6   The burial practices of nonhuman hominids also become virtually impossible to understand since such practices entail a concept of death. See Sheets-Johnstone (1990), chapter 8, "On the Conceptual Origin of Death".

our own, there are no "mental" connections linking us together. In short, to espouse the notion that consciousness is an exclusively human capacity means that human mental powers are evolutionarily discontinuous with those of other creatures whose behaviours are actually the point of origin of many fundamental human ones and even basically resemble human behaviours. Discontinuity in this instance thus means not an espousal of punctuated equilibrium but an espousal of the view that, however close any particular lineal relationships might be, the connection is purely physical.

It is important to consider this kind of privileging because for all its inconsistencies with evolutionary thought, it is not that disfavoured a view. Dennett's conception of consciousness, for example, strongly exemplifies and even urges just this privileging of humankind. Unequivocally tethering his view of consciousness to the having of language, Dennett is loath to find consciousness in any creature that does not speak. He claims specifically that "languageless creature[s]" such as bats and lobsters are severely hampered in having no "center of narrative gravity", and thus have a "dramatically truncated" consciousness "compared to ours". After making this claim, he asks — himself as much as the reader — "Isn't this an awfully anthropocentric prejudice?" He goes about answering the question in an even bolder and more radically separatist way, for he immediately counterposes to himself the question, "[W]hat about deaf-mutes? Aren't they conscious?" His answer: "Of course they are — but let's not jump to extravagant conclusions about their consciousness, out of misguided sympathy." Dennett's criterion is austere and unwavering. No matter a human pedigree, as with bats and lobsters, unless there is language, there is a decidedly impoverished consciousness, if any at all. Dennett concludes that "Many people are afraid to see consciousness explained" because they fear "we will lose our moral bearings"; that is, we might get into bad habits, "treating animals as if they were wind-up toys, babies and deaf-mutes as if they were teddy bears, and — just to add insult to injury — robots as if they were real people" (Dennett, 1991, pp. 447–48).

We are a long way from a natural history of consciousness. Given the ultra- exclusive defining terms Dennett insists on, it is no surprise that that history is hard to come by. By radically privileging language, Dennett pulls the evolutionary rug out from under us.[7] Whatever modest nods

---

7   He continues to do so in his later writings (1995; 1996). Not only does his consistent use of quotation marks (e.g. "Clever experiments by psychologists and ethologists suggest other ways in which animals can try out actions 'in their heads'" [1996, p. 91]) to make distinctions between "us and them" alert us to the hazards of making simple comparisons among extant creatures over the benefits of examining natural history (cf. Sheets-Johnstone, 1992; 1994 [chapter 2]; 1996); but his consistent assessment of nonhuman animals in terms of tasks not common to the behavioural repertoire of the species (e.g. 1996, pp. 133, 157) alerts us to the

made in the direction of an evolutionary history at the beginning of his quest to `explain consciousness', he does not follow through. A consideration of language itself in the terms he conceives it shows his lack of follow-through unequivocally. If, as Dennett explains, human language explains consciousness, then consciousness arose in the form of human language. The question Dennett does not ask himself is how human language itself arose.[8] Clearly, he *should* ask the question. Indeed, he should ask not only how human language could even have been conceived short of an already existing consciousness but how human language in the beginning could even have been standardized short of already intact consciousnesses.[9] Dennett does not seem remotely aware of such questions, much less aware of their needing answers — which is why only linguistic creationism can explain a Dennettian consciousness.

In sum, we cannot arrive at an understanding of "how mind got there in the first place" by espousing biological naturalism but neglecting natural history, by wondering what it is like to be a body other than the one one is but neglecting penetrating studies of other animate forms, by championing a metaphysical theory that shackles inquiry before it even begins, by giving selective definitions of life, by privileging human brains, or by explaining consciousness in narrative terms. In none of these instances do we arrive at an elucidation of consciousness as a dimension of the *animate*. Until such an elucidation is given, a viable answer to the question of "how mind got there in the first place" will be consistently baffled.

3. Life and Its Definitions:
A Question of Animation and Justification

It is instructive at this point to examine definitions of life more closely — both to exemplify the import of the animate and to highlight in a proper manner the troublesome textual use of quotation marks as a means of apportioning mental credit and distinguishing among mental attributes. Biological texts often devote some pages to definitions of life. Among the constituents of those definitions is self-replication. Order and energy —

---

hazard of making self-serving prescriptions (e.g. "[W]e must not *assume* that [nonhuman animals think]",1996, p. 160) over the benefits of examining the presumptions underlying those prescriptions, including the assumption-laden claim that "[T]hose who deplore Artificial Intelligence are also those who deplore evolutionary accounts of human mentality" (1995, p. 370).

8   Even in his latest book, he takes the invention of language completely for granted: "There is no step more uplifting, more explosive, more momentous in the history of mind design than the invention of language. When *Homo sapiens* became the beneficiary of this invention ..." (Dennett, 1996, p. 147).

9   For a discussion of these matters in detail, see Sheets-Johnstone (1990), chapter 6, "On the Origin of Language".

features Churchland too comes to incorporate in his progressive definitions of life—are also named. Responsivity is specified as a further prime
constituent. As one text notes: "Plant seedlings bend toward the light;
mealworms congregate in dampness; cats pounce on small moving
objects; even certain bacteria move toward or away from particular chemicals. . . [T]he capacity to respond is a fundamental and almost universal
characteristic of life" (Curtis, 1975, p. 28). Oddly enough, this "fundamental and almost universal" dimension of life does not typically figure in definitions of life (living systems, consciousness) offered by cognitivists
generally, nor philosophers of mind in particular, especially those in
either category who are wedded to information-processing, computational models. Yet responsivity—bending, congregating, pouncing, moving toward or away, in short, *animation*—commonly appears an integral
part of phenomena such as cognition, hence part and parcel of consciousness. If queried on the matter, cognitivists and philosophers might
respond—in a manner consistent with pervasive present-day western
thought—that it depends on what is doing the bending, congregating,
pouncing, or moving toward or away, whether the terms "cognitive" or
"conscious" apply, that is, whether the terms are proper ascriptions or not.
This answer unfortunately skirts the critical point at issue: justifying the
cognitive distinctions one makes diacritically. The point is neatly exemplified by Churchland precisely because his account of consciousness, i.e.
eliminative materialism, conceptually precludes diacritical practice to
begin with. If the distinction between the organic and the inorganic is
blurred, then of course distinctions among the organic are also blurred—
just as Churchland in fact says they are blurred with respect to intelligence: there are differences "only by degrees". But the blurring between
organic forms is necessarily finer than the blurring between the organic
and the inorganic since organic forms are comparatively more closely
related to each other than they are to the inorganic. In effect, to be consistent with Churchland theory, common textual practice should be altered.
Quotation marks typically surrounding cognitive functions as they are
ascribed to what are termed "lower" forms should be erased. A difference
"only by degrees" does not justify them.

To counter that a difference "only by degrees" does not entail that we
cannot justly distinguish between degrees of consciousness (cognitive
abilities, intelligence) within the organic—that we cannot justly make distinctions on the basis of *who is doing the pouncing*, for example—is a claim
difficult to uphold. Proper justification is lacking in the form of wholly
objective supporting facts. This is because what basically matters is not
who is doing the pouncing; what matters is the ability to provide a wholly

unprejudiced rationale for common textual practice. Indeed, the original charge can still be pressed because a fundamental mandate exists; namely, specification of the exact degree(s) at which quotation marks are appropriate. *This mandate exists regardless of what metaphysical theory one espouses.* It is as necessary to Searle's account of consciousness, for example, as to computational cognitivists' accounts. But as might be evident, the mandate poses an insuperable problem. Whatever might be claimed to constitute a criterion for distinguishing among degrees of consciousness (intelligence, cognitive abilities) is not a matter of fact but a matter of human judgment. While cranial capacities, neuron counts, dendritic branchings, and body size, for example, certainly constitute matters of fact, these matters of fact do not *in themselves* specify anything whatsoever in the way of a standard. One need only recall what Darwin wrote on the basis of his study of Hymenoptera:[*] "It is certain that there may be extraordinary mental activity with an extremely small absolute mass of nervous matter" (Darwin [1871/1981], p. 145).[10] In short, the mandate to show appropriateness appears doomed from the start. Specification — whatever its theoretical context — turns out to be as completely arbitrary as it is absolutely mandatory; a wholly objective supporting base is nowhere to be found. Indeed, in its arbitrariness, specification can only be labelled "subjective"; a standard completely impervious to human bias cannot possibly be identified. In consequence, a cancelling of all quotation marks appears warranted — though as indicated not necessarily on the grounds of Churchland theory at all. The following description of a bacterium moving "toward or away from particular chemicals" is an especially interesting as well as exemplary candidate in this respect.

> Processing in a bacterium may be thought of as a sort of molecular polling: ... the positive "votes" cast by receptors in response, say, to increasing concentrations of a sugar are matched against the negative votes produced by increasing concentrations of noxious compounds. On the basis of this continuous voting process, the bacterium "knows" whether the environment, on the whole, is getting better or worse. The results of this analysis appear to be communicated by electrical signals to the response centers. The final stage, the response, consists of a brief change in the direction of rotation of the several stiff, helical flagella that propel the bacterium. The result is that the bacterium founders briefly and then strikes out in a new direction, once again sampling to see whether the environment is improving or deteriorating (Keeton & Gould, 1986, p. 452).

[*] For a glossary of biological terms see the end of this chapter.

10 Darwin goes on to say: `[T]hus the wonderfully diversified instincts, mental powers, and affections of ants are generally known, yet their cerebral ganglia are not so large as the quarter of a small pin's head. Under this latter point of view, the brain of an ant is one of the most marvellous atoms of matter in the world, perhaps more marvellous than the brain of man.'

In addition to being an exemplary candidate for diacritical erasure, the descriptive passage demonstrates in an intimately related way why responsivity—the "fundamental and almost universal characteristic of life"—is of critical import. Sampling, foundering, and striking out in a new direction are precisely a matter of animation and animation is precisely in some sense cognitive or mindful—as in assessing propitious and noxious aspects of the environment. Cognitive aspects of organic animation—in this instance, cognitive aspects of a bacterium's animation—cannot thus reasonably be considered mere figurative aspects. More generally, cognitive capacities cannot reasonably be reserved only for what are commonly termed "higher-order" organisms.[11]

The unjustifiable use of diacritical markings to distinguish cognitively among organisms leads to a series of interlinked demands: a cessation of reliance on what is in fact a conceptually lazy, inapt, and/or obfuscating textual practice; a corollary recognition of the import of animation; a consequent investigation of the animate in terms of its natural history; a delineation of what it means cognitively to be animate. In a quite provocative sense, one might say that Churchland's blurring of metaphysical lines itself leads to such a series of interlinked demands. His overarching metaphysical blurring on behalf of an unrelenting materialism—whether one finds the latter credible or not—forces an examination and justification of common textual practice and typical western thinking regarding so-called "higher" and "lower" forms of life. It clearly calls our attention to a fundamental question about where and on what grounds cognitive lines are diacritically drawn in order to distinguish among capacities of various forms of organic life. All the same, it is important to emphasize that in answering to the fourfold demand, we are not charged with the task of *understanding matter*, that is, of making appropriate distinctions in material complexity by taking neuron counts and the like. On the contrary, we are charged with the task of *understanding the animate*, precisely as the bacterium example demonstrates. Accordingly, the quest begins from the other side. We take the phenomena themselves as a point of departure, not theory, and earnestly inquire into what we observe to be living realities. Denying distinctions thus becomes in this instance and in a heuristic sense epistemologically salutary rather than metaphysically catastrophic.

Searle's intense concern with preserving distinctions between kinds of intentionality by maintaining diacritical markings is decidedly topical in this context. After giving examples of what he terms "metaphorical attributions of intentionality", and insisting on the necessity of distinguishing

11 For an even more impressive indication of a bacterium's cognitive capacities, see Losick and Kaiser (1997).

between "intrinsic intentionality" and "as-if intentionality", he states rather hyperbolically that "If you deny the distinction [between the two] it turns out that everything in the universe has intentionality" (Searle, 1990, p. 587). Because he is concerned not just with the animate world but with carburetors, computers, and such, his broad claim is perhaps less rash than it might at first appear. Understood specifically in terms of present concerns, his point is that when language is used as in the bacterium passage quoted above, intentionality must be read as describing an "as-if" intentionality — not the real "intrinsic" thing. To accede to Searle's line of reasoning and broad warning, however, is precisely to miss the epistemological challenge, and indeed to forego examining what might lead to foundational[12] understandings within "biological naturalism". In this latter respect, it is of course also to miss the challenge of a descriptive metaphysics that would adequately comprehend natural history and on that account offer fundamental understandings of the animate world that are informed by evolutionary thought. While the penalty of blurring distinctions can certainly be confusion, it does not necessarily "turn out" that one reaches "absurdity" if one blurs them, as Searle claims (*ibid.*). If the phenomena themselves are taken as a point of departure, it in fact turns out neither that "everything in the universe [is] mental" nor that everything in the universe is material. It turns out only that everything in the *animate* universe needs to be considered as what it is — *animate* — and that in consequence we need to take seriously the historical perspective of evolutionary thought: by examining the lives of living creatures, by determining the corporeal matters of fact that sustain those lives, and by tracing out in an evolutionary sense how consciousness arises in animate form. Only by doing so are we likely to get our conceptual bearings, justify new textual practice, if any, and in the end come to sound understandings of the complexities as well as provenience of consciousness.

4. Corporeal Consciousness: A Matter of Knowing

"Know thyself" is a Socratic imperative. It may also be said to be a built-in biological one in a special and fundamental sense. It is important to set this biological imperative explicitly in the mainstream of general cognitivist trends in current western thought and American philosophy of mind. In so doing, we can show in unequivocal terms how the imperative offers a more exacting evolutionary understanding of consciousness. We can furthermore expose, and in equally unequivocal terms, what is typically omitted in the way of empirical evidence in contemporary theories of con-

---

12 "Foundational" is a perfectly good English word, as in the sentence, "Evolutionary understandings are foundational to understandings of what consciousness is all about."

sciousness. Accordingly, a longer but proportionally richer and more informative route will be taken to its exposition. We might call this route "The Liabilities of a Paradigmatic Cognitivist Account of the Socratic Imperative". The account is based on descriptive remarks Dennett makes about "The Reality of Selves" in the process of explaining consciousness.

Energetically affirming that "every agent has to know which thing in the world it is!" Dennett (1991, p. 427) begins by specifying what this knowing entails. He considers first "simpler organisms" for whom "there is really nothing much to self-knowledge beyond the rudimentary biological wisdom enshrined in such maxims as When Hungry, Don't Eat Yourself! and When There's a Pain, It's Yours!" In this context, he says of a lobster that "[It] might well eat another lobster's claws, but the prospect of eating one of its own claws is conveniently unthinkable to it." He goes on to say that "Its options are limited, and when it 'thinks of' moving a claw, its 'thinker' is directly and appropriately wired to the very claw it thinks of moving."

The situation is different, Dennett says, when it comes to controlling "the sorts of sophisticated activities human bodies engage in", because "there are more options, and hence more sources of confusion" (*ibid.*). He states that "the body's control system (housed in the brain) has to be able to recognize a wide variety of different sorts of inputs as informing it about itself, and when quandaries arise or scepticism sets in, the only reliable (but not foolproof) way of sorting out and properly assigning this information is to run little experiments: do something and look to see what moves" (pp. 427–28). The experimental approach is the same, Dennett says, whether a matter of "external signs of our own bodily movement" or "internal states, tendencies, decisions, strengths and weaknesses": "Do something and look to see what moves." With respect to internal knowledge, he adds that "An advanced agent must build up practices for keeping track of both its bodily and 'mental' circumstances" (p. 428).

Dennett's descriptive passages of course readily offer themselves as candidates for erasure no less than passages in biology, not on cosmic historical grounds — Dennett's materialism does not appear to run so far as to blur the distinction between the organic and the inorganic — but on evolutionary and mind/body ones: Dennett marks `mental' phenomena diacritically both in order to make distinctions between "higher" and "lower" forms of life and in order to maintain a thoroughly materialized consciousness. In short, his theory of consciousness demands that he temper the meaning of "the mental" at both metaphysical levels. What his diacritical markings actually allow is having his material cake and eating it too. However loose his vocabulary (e.g. a *thinking* lobster), and however much it strays from purely materialist theory (e.g. *mental* as well as bodily circumstances), it is diacritically reined in to accord with the theoretical distinctions he wants to maintain and the materialist doctrine he wants to uphold.

What makes both the entailments and elaboration of Dennett's energetic affirmation such a compelling and richly informative point of departure for examining the bio-Socratic imperative is precisely what they overlook in theory, method, and fact. It is as if proprioception in general and kinesthesia in particular[13] did not exist; whatever the talk of movement with respect to humans, for example, it is as if the *sense of movement* were nonexistent. Thus, one has to *look* and *see* what is moving.[14] In such an account, the kinesthetic is more than overridden by the visual; it is not even on the books. Were one to examine Dennett's theory of human agency with respect to infants, one would straightaway discover its error. Were one to examine his theory with respect to blind people, one would do the same. In a word, and *contra* Dennett, we humans learn "which thing we are" by moving and listening to our own movement. We sense our own bodies. Indeed, we humans, along with many other primates, must *learn* to move ourselves. We do so not by *looking* and *seeing* what we're moving; we do so by attending to our bodily feelings of movement, which include a bodily felt sense of the direction of our movement, its speed, its range, its tension, and so on. Our bodily feelings of movement have a certain dynamic. We feel, for example, the swiftness or slowness of our movement, its constrictedness or openness, its tensional tightness or looseness, and more. In short,

we perceive the *qualia* of our own movement;
our bodily feelings of movement have a certain *qualitative* character.

It is instructive to recall Sherrington's experiential account of proprioception in this context. However inadvertently he excludes kinetic qualia from his account, Sherrington explicitly if briefly affirms it in the course of specifying and describing the nature of our experiential awareness of movement. Underscoring first of all the fact that we have no awareness of neural events, e.g., of nerve fibres "register[ing] the tension at

---

13   Proprioception refers generally to a sense of movement and position. It thus includes an awareness of movement and position through tactility as well as kinesthesia, that is, through surface as well as internal events, including also a sense of gravitational orientation through vestibular sensory organs. Kinesthesia refers specifically to a sense of movement through muscular effort.

14   Lest it be thought that Dennett is idiosyncratic in his procedure, consider the nineteenth-century German philosopher J.J. Engel's criticism of British philosopher David Hume's account of the derivation of the concept of force: "He ought to use his muscles, but instead he uses his eyes; he ought to grasp and struggle, and instead he is content to watch" (Quoted by Scheerer, 1987, p. 176).

thousands of points they sample in the muscles, tendons, and ligaments of [a] limb", he says "I perceive no trace of all this [neural activity]". With respect to the limb, he states that "I am simply aware of where the limb is, and when it moves". In this context, he also points out that we are not even aware that the limb "possess[es] muscles or tendons" (Sherrington, 1953, p. 248). He goes on to emphasize the lack of this kind of anatomical aware-ness in actual experience when he describes the experience of moving the limb "to pick up a paper from the table": "I have no awareness of the mus-cles as such at all" (*ibid.*, pp. 248–49).[15] The lack of direct experiential awareness of "muscles as such", however, does not impede an experien-tial awareness of the movement. As Sherrington affirms, though "I have no awareness of the muscles as such at all, ... I execute the movement rightly and without difficulty. It starts *smoothly* as though I had been aware precisely of how tense and how long each muscle and how tense each tendon was, and, thus aware, took them as my starting point for shortening or paying out as may be, each one further" (italics added). Interestingly enough, he then points out that if he had moved "*clumsily*", it would not do much good "*to look at my limb*" (p. 249, italics added). As he himself says, *looking* provides him no more than an *additional* sense of where his limb is. In effect, with respect to one's own body, he affirms that vision is not a primary but a supplemental spatial sense. Sherrington con-cludes his experiential account of movement by characterizing "[t]he proprioceptive percept of the limb" as "a mental product", a product "derived from elements which are not experienced as such and yet are mental in the sense that the mind uses them in producing the percept" (*ibid.*). Insofar as "[s]uch mental products are an intimate accompaniment of our motor acts", he says that "[w]e may suppose therefore there obtains something like them in our animal kith and kin as accompaniment of their intentional motor acts" (*ibid.*).

---

15   It should be noted that Sherrington uses the word *tension* in a purely neuromuscular sense when he says, in tandem with his statement that "I have no awareness of the muscles as such at all," that "I have no awareness of tension in the muscles" (p. 249). Tension *is* absent in the specified neuromuscular sense, but it is *not* absent in an experiential sense. Sherrington could hardly go on to describe his awareness of his movement as *smooth* if he did not move with a certain tensional quality coincident with smoothness: a certain kinetic tension is integral to smooth movement. That kinetic tension is not a constituent of jagged movement, for example, or of myriad other movements between the two extremes of smooth and jagged. It would thus be an epistemological mistake to think Sherrington's disavowal of an awareness of discrete muscle tensions a disavowal of a direct experiential awareness of the tensional qualities of movement. This would be to conflate neuroscience with experience. On the other hand, it would also be an epistemological mistake to think Sherrington's characterization of proprioception as a "mental product" correct since the *smoothness* Sherrington experiences is not only there, directly evident in his movement; the *smoothness* is created by his movement and exists in virtue of his movement.

Now clearly, if we carefully examine Sherrington's account and reflect both on what he is implicitly affirming and at the same time on what he is inadvertently excluding, we find an open avowal of kinetic qualia. An awareness of *smoothness* is first of all an awareness of something over and above an awareness of *where* a limb is and of *when* it is moving. It is an awareness of *how* a body part or the body as a whole is moving; *how* precisely *not* in the neurophysiological sense Sherrington himself details as impossible, but *how* in the same experiential sense as *where* and *when*. Moreover *smoothness* is not "a mental product", any more than jerky or swift or hesitant or expansive or collapsing or intense or constricted or weak or abrupt are "mental products".[16] Neither is weight "a mental product", the weight one perceives in the felt heaviness or heft of one's body or body parts in moving; neither is mass "a mental product", the mass one perceives in the felt three-dimensionality or volume of one's body and in its felt smallness or largeness. In short, *qualia* are integral to bodily life. They are there in any movement we make. They are differentially there in the bodily life of animate forms. They are not a "mental product", but the product of animation. They are created by movement itself. Accordingly, any time one cares to attend to the felt sense of one's movement, one perceives qualia.

When we learn to move ourselves, we learn to distinguish just such kinetic bodily feelings as smoothness and clumsiness, swiftness and slowness, brusqueness and gentleness, not in so many words, but in so many bodily-felt distinctions. Short of learning to move ourselves and being

---

16   One might claim that terms such as swift and weak describe movement directly, while terms such as "hesitant" describe an affective state derivative from movement. The claim is a provocative one, bearing out the etymology of the word "emotion". The term "expansive", for example, describes a generous, open person, one who is affectively sympathetic toward others, a usage clearly tied to movement, i.e. to an expansive — open, generous — spatiality of the body in moving. Observations of infant psychologist and psychiatrist Daniel Stern support the idea of a coincidence, if not a derivation, of affect from movement. In particular, Stern describes what he calls "vitality affects": "qualities [of experience] that do not fit into our existing lexicon or taxonomy of affects [but that] are better captured by dynamic, kinetic terms, such as 'surging', 'fading away', 'fleeting', 'explosive', 'crescendo', 'decrescendo', 'bursting', 'drawn out', and so on" (Stern, 1985, p. 54). Affects may well be "better captured by dynamic, kinetic terms" than special feeling terms because they have their origin in the tactile-kinesthetic body. From this perspective, complexity of affect may be tied to complexity of movement. If this is so, then the evolution of affect might be studied from the viewpoint of the richness and variability of tactile-kinesthetic bodies, and not just from the viewpoint of a social world. A passing remark of anthropologists Sherwood Washburn and Shirley Strum is suggestive in this respect. In their discussion of the evolution of speech, they write that "Attempting to teach a monkey to make more sounds is like trying to teach it to have more emotions" (Washburn and Strum, 1972, p. 475). If the emphasis is on the making of sounds and not on the sounds themselves, then a relationship between species-specific possibilities of movement and species-specific possibilities of affect is clearly adumbrated. In turn, however superficial and abbreviated the suggestion, one may well ask, is kinetic complexity the basis of affective complexity?

attentive in this way to the qualia of our movement, we could hardly be effective agents — any more than a creature who `does something and then looks to see what moves' could be an effective agent. In neither case is there an agent in the true sense of being in command of — or as phenomenological philosopher Edmund Husserl would say, of "holding sway in" — one's own body. An agent who holds sway is a bona fide agent precisely insofar as she/he is aware of her/his own movement, aware not only of initiating it, but aware of its spatio-temporal and energy dynamics, which is to say of its rich and variable qualia.[17] With respect to Dennett's injunctions, were they taken literally to the letter, his agent — so-called — would suffer not only from having to have in sight at all times all parts of his/her body in order to see where they were and what they were doing. His agent, being oblivious of qualia, could in no way build up practices in the manner Dennett suggests, for the build up of such practices depends upon kinesthesia and kinesthetic memory, i.e. upon an awareness of the spatio-temporal and energy dynamics of one's movement. An agent devoid of kinesthesia in fact belongs to no known natural species. Agents — those having the power to act — necessarily have a kinesthetic sense of their own movement.

When Dennett considers "simpler organisms" such as lobsters, the perceptual situation is no different from what it is with humans. Kinesthesia, or its counterpart, is nowhere acknowledged as a feature of these "lower" creatures. The idea that these creatures have a sense of their own body and body movement is alien to the theory of a thoroughly materialized consciousness as well as an alien thought in itself. Whoever `the thinker' might be in Dennett's zoology — a lobster "thinker", a bat "thinker", a lion "thinker" — it appears to get what it wants, if it gets it at all, simply in virtue of its impeccable motor wiring, nothing more. "The thinker" in other words appears not to have — or need — any proprioceptive connections to its body; its body, in fact, is on Dennett's account no more than a "directly and appropriately wired" mechanical contrivance for getting about in the world. Yet we should ask what it means to say that a lobster will eat another's claws but that *conveniently*, as Dennett puts it, it finds eating one of its own claws unthinkable. Does it mean that there is actually a rule "Don't eat your own claws!" wired into the lobster's neurological circuitry? But it is patently unparsimonious to think that there is such a rule and just as patently absurd to think that every creature comes prepared with an owner's manual, as it were, a rulebook replete with what Dennett calls "maxims". Such a maxim, for example, would be only one of an

---

17 It might be noted that the degrees-of-freedom problem is intimately related to the fact that movement creates rich and variable qualia.

indefinitely great number of maxims that a lobster (or, in analogous terms, any other "simpler organism") could be said to carry around in the neural machinery that counts as its "Headquarters" (Dennett, 1991):[18] "Don't try to go on land!" "Don't try to eat a squid!" "Shovel in new sand grains after molting!" "The large claw is for crushing!" "The small claw is for seizing and tearing!" And so on. What makes eating its own claws "conveniently unthinkable" is clearly something other than a rule of conduct. The putative evolutionary sense of convenience that Dennett invokes is misguided. "Convenience" is not a matter of an opportune adaptation but of an astoundingly varied and intricately detailed biological faculty that allows a creature to know its own body and its own body in movement.

Dennett is not alone either in his omission of the kinesthetic or in his privileging of the visual. Typically, kinesthesia never makes an appearance in discussions of "the senses" — the *five* senses. Any cursory glance at indices of relevant books in biology, psychology, and philosophy discloses either a radically abbreviated treatment of kinesthesia in comparison to vision (and audition), or a complete lack of treatment altogether. One might say with good reason that the mind/body problem is written into the very texts themselves. Moreover the topic of body movement, if making an appearance at all, typically comes on the scene only marginally in these books. The way it does so is through reduction to *the* brain and its efferent pathways. In both typical instances, we come up painfully short of a sense of movement. In one respect it is not surprising that kinesthesia is omitted or slighted and that we believe ourselves to have only five senses. As adults, we have long since forgotten how we learned to move ourselves — in a very real sense, how we learned our bodies. Only if now, as adults, we pay kinesthetic attention — for example, to what it feels like, or rather, *does not feel like* when our arm falls asleep — might we begin to realize how fundamental kinesthesia is. It is fundamental not only to our knowledge of "which thing in the world we are"; it is fundamental both to our ability to make our way in the world — to move knowledgeably in it — and to our knowledge of the world itself. Though we may have forgotten what we first learned of the world through movement and touch, there is no doubt but that we came to know it first by moving and touching our way through it, in a word, through our tactile-kinesthetic bodies.[19]

---

18   For example, p. 106: "The brain is Headquarters, the place where the ultimate observer is."

19   For a detailed account of the tactile-kinesthetic body, see Sheets-Johnstone (1990). In an ontogenetic sense, the priority of movement and tactility is not surprising. The sequence of development of embryonic neural tissue underscores their significance.In particular, there is early beginning development (the fourth week of life) of the semicircular ear canals which, through vestibular sensations, provide a sense of balance or imbalance, and (at the fetal stage) of receptors in the muscles which, through kinesthetic sensations, provide a sense of position

The astoundingly varied and intricately detailed biological faculty that allows knowing one's own body and body movement and that in the most basic sense allows knowing the world is a dimension of consciousness. Inversely, consciousness is a dimension of living forms that move themselves, that are *animate*, and that, in their animation, are in multiple and complex ways engaged in the world. The earlier description of a bacterium's cognitive capacities is relevant precisely in this context. What the description points to is a chemically-mediated *tactile* discrimination of bodies apart from or outside of the body one is. Given its stereognostic sensitivity, a bacterium's discriminative ability might justifiably be termed a "meta-corporeal" consciousness, a consciousness of something beyond itself. Clearly, the essentially tactile ability to discriminate bodies other than oneself is not the same as a proprioceptive ability to discriminate aspects of oneself as an animate form, though just as clearly tactility is a vital dimension of that proprioceptive ability. Proprioceptively-endowed creatures are not only always in touch with something outside themselves; they tactilely compress and deform themselves bodily in the process of moving. When a creature bends its leg, for example, it brings two surfaces in contact with each other — in mutual deformation. Tactility thus enters into the essentially kinetic cognitional abilities by which a creature discriminates aspects of itself as an animate form. In the most fundamental sense, these kinetic cognitional abilities constitute a *corporeal consciousness*, a consciousness that, as I shall try now to show at some length, is an astoundingly varied and intricately detailed biological faculty. The purpose of the demonstration is to link understandings of consciousness to corporeal matters of fact and thereby to an evolutionary history. In other words, with a recognition of this biological faculty, and with attendant understandings of its rootedness in corporeal matters of fact, we can begin to grasp the possibility of a true evolutionary history of consciousness. It bears emphasizing that *we do this by direct consideration of the topic at issue: consciousness*, and not by appeal to constituents in definitions of life — to self-replication, organization, and so on. The notion of consciousness as fundamentally a corporeal phenomenon in fact already suggests a radical revision of the common evolutionary characterization

and movement. Though rudimentary, the sensory system for balance is in place by the beginning of the fourth month. By the beginning of the fourth month too, reflexive behaviour appears, which means that the movement of the fetus is coordinated in response to stimulation. The comparatively early development of neural tissue related to movement is of particular interest in conjunction with physiological studies suggesting that neural development of the motor cortex is stimulated by the body movements of the fetus itself. In other words, form does not develop solely on its own. Movement influences morphology. Myelination studies also show that motor neurons myelinate early and that acoustic-vestibular neurons myelinate next. For a discussion of prenatal development and behaviour, see Robeck (1978) and Windle (1971).

of consciousness both as "a higher-order" function i.e. a function having nothing to do with bodies, and as a "higher-order" function exclusive to "higher" forms of life, i.e. a preeminently human endowment. Similarly, it already suggests a radical revision of the materialist's characterization of consciousness as identical with neurological brain events. The key to the reconceptualization of consciousness and to the evolutionary import of that reconceptualization is the realization that bodies in the form of living creatures are not mere physical things but animate forms.

Consciousness is thus not in *matter*;
it is a dimension of living forms,
in particular, a dimension of living forms that move.

Transposed to this context, Searle's "biological naturalism" — his biological naturalization of consciousness—properly begins with movement. It would show how consciousness is rooted in animate form. Indeed, it would show concretely how, in the evolution of animate forms, consciousness emerged not as a "higher-level" or "intrinsic" stalk that one day sprouted out of a neural blue, but as a dimension that itself evolved along with living, moving creatures themselves.

What is necessary to the task of reconceptualization is a sense of the evolutionary history of proprioception, including a sense of the history of its derivation. It should be clearly evident that a sense of this history does not entail a concern with the evolution of the neural circuitry of proprioception in general, an assessment of the neurology of proprioception in mammals in particular, nor of the neurology of proprioception in humans in singularly fine detail. It entails a concern with the proprioceptive lives of living creatures, invertebrate and vertebrate, insofar as they have been studied and recorded by naturalists, zoologists, and biologists, and insofar as one can discern within such studies what is at times left unsaid with respect to an awareness of movement. However neglected or understated, proprioception is a corporeal matter of fact. Its roots are embedded in the kinetic possibilities of the earliest forms of life. Thus a sense of its evolutionary history means coincidently a concern with organisms such as bacteria and protozoa. In short, understandings of the evolution of proprioception lead precisely to understandings of the provenience of consciousness. With these understandings come a vocabulary consistent with corporeal matters of fact and conceptual clarifications by which one can formulate a standard for linguistic practice that is neither arbitrary nor superficial—a mere diacritical band-aid — but a standard warranted by the evidence from natural history.

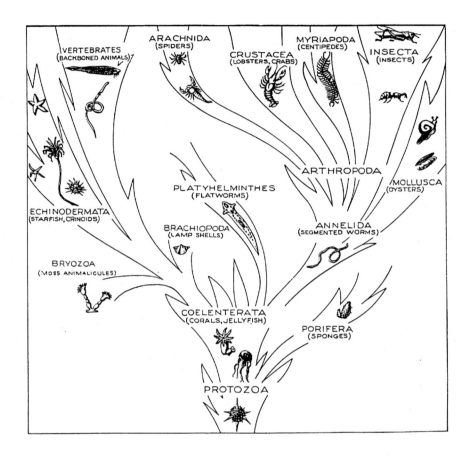

Figure 1

A simplified family tree of the animal kingdom, to show the probably
relationships of the vertebrates. (After Romer, *Man and the Vertebrates*,
University of Chicago Press. Reproduced by permission.)

5. To the Things Themselves: Corporeal Matters of Fact[20]

Animate forms are built in ways that are sensitive to movement. Their sensitivity can be doubly reflected; they can be sensitive to dynamic modifications in the surrounding world and to dynamic modifications of their own body. They can, in other words, be sensitive to the movement of things in their environment, including the very medium in which they live, and to the movement of their own bodies. A moment's serious reflection on the matter discloses a major reason why this sensitivity to movement is both basic and paramount: no matter what the particular world (*Umwelt*) (von Uexküll, 1928).[21] in which an animal lives, it is not an unchanging world. Hence, whatever the animal, its movement cannot be absolutely programmed such that, for example, at all times its particular speed and direction of movement, its every impulse and stirring, its every pause and stillness, run automatically on something akin to a lifetime tape.[22] Consider, for example, an earthworm, its body pressed against the earth as it crawls along, or a beetle walking along the ground. In each case, the immediate environment is tangibly inconsistent; it has topological and textural irregularities—bumps here, smoothness there, moisture here, hardness there, and so on. Both earthworm and beetle must adjust kinetically to what they find in the immediate moment. A prominent invertebrate researcher makes this very point: "Information regarding the absolute disposition of the body is imperative in order that minor adjustments of muscular activity may be made to cope with irregularities in the surface" (Laverack, 1976, pp. 4–5). Clearly, the world is less than consistent in its conformations and any animal that survives must literally or figuratively bend to its demands. Consider further the very fluid or changing medium in which some animals live. Air and water move, and that movement in the form of currents or winds—currents and winds that themselves shift from gentle to moderate to turbulent—agitates, deforms, or otherwise impinges on the animal's body. In effect, such movement influences how

20 Evolutionary studies of proprioception are no longer fashionable. Indeed, attention should be called at the beginning of this descriptive analysis to the fact that contemporary study of proprioception lags so far behind studies of vision and audition that it is barely perceptible in the literature. Moreover most of the journal literature is devoted to proprioceptive injuries to the knee, to knee surgery, and to topics related to the loss of proprioception. Of the 27 articles on proprioception published in scientific journals in 1994 and the first six months of 1995, 14 of them were devoted to such topics. Accordingly, where evolutionary references are pertinent or seem necessary, I use earlier writings, the most comprehensive text being the 686-page volume *Structure and Function of Proprioceptors in the Invertebrates*, edited by P.J. Mill (1976).

21 Cf. Ernst Cassirer's concise explanation of why there are *Umwelts*: "Every organism ... has a world of its own because it has an experience of its own" (Cassirer, 1970, p. 25).

22 As, for example, philosopher Peter Carruthers indicates when he writes that "brutes" have only "nonconscious experiences", and so experience "nothing" (Carruthers, 1989, pp. 268, 259).

the animal moves from moment to moment; it influences what the animal can do and what it actually does. A locust is proprioceptively sensitive in just this way to air currents. Its face is covered with hairs that respond to the movement of air across their surface: "Each hair responds maximally to wind from a specific direction, with the optimal direction being determined by the angle of curvature of the hair shaft" (pp. 5 f.). Sensitivity to its facial hair displacements facilitates the locust's control of lift during flight and is informative of orientation in flying. The intricateness of a spider's external proprioceptive system offers equally impressive testimony to the importance of proprioception. Spiders also have hairs on their body that, when bent, inform them, for example, of the disposition of their body relative to their web (p. 27). Far more numerous than their hairs, however, are other surface sensory organs called slit sensilla. These are single or complex proprioceptive organs, the complex ones — lyriform organs — being located on their appendages, pedipalps, and walking legs. A spider's slit sensilla are functionally analogous to an insect's campaniform sensilla (see, e.g. Wright, 1976, pp. 353 f.); both are sensitive to deformation, i.e. cuticular stress through compression. To give an idea of the singular importance of such proprioceptors, consider that the hunting spider *Cupiennius salei* has over 3000 slit organs on its walking legs (*ibid.*; see also Laverack, 1976, pp. 24 f.). Given the quantity of such organs, it is no wonder that "the quantity of proprioceptive information ... from an appendage at a particular time (e.g. during walking) may be considerable" (Wright, 1976, p. 354).

The above corporeal matters of fact can be put within the purview of a more explicit evolutionary history of animate form by a proportionately broader consideration of invertebrates. Broader consideration of these forms of animate life provides an especially edifying evolutionary viewpoint insofar as ninety per cent of animal species are invertebrates — creatures ranging from sponges and coral to lobster, scallops, mites, centipedes, segmented worms, spiders and hosts of other animals, although most are insects, of which the largest category comprises species of beetles.[23] Fuller consideration will furthermore bring to the fore the immediacy of most creatures' lives with respect to their surrounds. Indeed, it would be erroneous to judge invertebrates by human standards, especially fully-clothed western ones, for external proprioception functions far more as a form of movement detection for them than for humans.

An invertebrate may be soft- or hard-bodied. Hard-bodied invertebrates are so called because they have articulable body parts attached to an

---

23   There are approximately 800,000 species of insects of which approximately 275,000 are species of beetles.

exoskeleton. As suggested by the above examples, hard-bodied inverte-brates have external sensilla of various kinds: hairs, exoskeletal plates, epidermal organs, cilia, spines, pegs, slits, and so on. It is these external sensory organs that make possible an awareness of surface events in the double sense noted above: an awareness of the terrain on which and/or the environment through which the animal is moving and an awareness of bodily deformations or stresses occurring coincident with moving on the terrain and/or through the environment. To appreciate in a beginning way the difference in proprioceptive sensitivity between hard- and soft-bodied invertebrates, compare, for example, a beetle and a polyp. A beetle that is walking on the ground has tactile contacts that allow an awareness of the ground's irregularities — bumps, stones, holes, and so on — and tactile contact with the air — breezes, vibrations, and so on — as well as an awareness of itself as topologically deformed or agitated by these contacts. Proprioception is thus distinctively informative of both body and surrounds. A sedentary hydrozoan polyp has tentacles bearing cilia that are sensitive to vibrations in the surrounding water. When vibrations occur, the polyp bends its tentacles toward their source, thus toward food particles such as barnacle nauplii. English marine biologist, D.A. Dorsett states, "The response is reflexive rather than proprioceptive in that it [the polyp] is not responding to movements generated by or imposed upon the animal itself" (Dorsett, 1976, p. 447). What Dorsett means is that the response is characterized as reflexive because the bending movement is neither generated by the polyp — it is generated by the vibrations — nor imposed upon the polyp — it is not the result of actual surface to surface contact, i.e. contact of animal body with solid object. His point is more broadly made in the context of an analysis by M.S. Laverack, another Eng-lish marine biologist, who distinguishes among four basic modes of exter-nal proprioception in invertebrates (Laverack, 1976, pp. 3–4). The simplest mode is through distortion of the body, whether through muscle contrac-tion or passive deformation: external proprioceptors are in either case affected. The second mode is tethered to the fact that animals move rela-tive to space; in effect, contact of the surface of an animal's moving body with a solid object results in proprioception concerning its movement and position relative to the object. The third mode is also tethered to the fact that animals move relative to space; it is a reiteration of the second mode of proprioceptive stimulation but with reference to a substrate rather than to a solid object. The fourth mode derives from the circumstance in which movement of one body part tactilely stimulates another body part through contact of external sensors of one kind or another, e.g., hairs, such contact providing information regarding movement and position of the two body parts. To say that the polyp's bending movement is reflexive is thus to say both that the polyp is not stimulated to move by bodily deformation or stress (the first mode)[24] nor is it stimulated to move because a surface of its body has come into contact with a solid object (the second mode). That the polyp is sedentary means, of course, that it does not budge from its base; hence, the third mode of stimulation is not a possibility. Neither is the fourth mode since the movement of the tentacles does not proprioceptively stimulate another body part.

Polyps belong to a class of animals called coelenterates, "primitive aquatic animals" (Keeton and Gould, 1986, p. 161). It might be tempting to generalize about proprioception in coelenterates—and perhaps in other soft-bodied invertebrates such as annelids and molluscs as well—on the basis of the above example and discussion, but given the diversity of coelenterate forms of life, it would be a mistake to write off proprioception altogether in such creatures. Different proprioceptive capacities—or counterparts thereof—are highly suggested by the movement of creatures within the same class and even within the same phylum. The somersaulting hydra, for example, is an exception to what might otherwise be considered "the sedentary hydrozoan polyp rule" with respect to the third possible mode of external proprioception; fighting sea anemones (anthozoans rather than hydrozoans) are sensitive to the touch of an alien form of anemone, thus sensitive in ways consistent with the second possible mode of external proprioception; in moving from one place to another on a rock —one inch per hour—a fighting sea anemone changes contact with a substrate, thus, like the somersaulting hydra, it too is open to proprioception through its own movement in space; an anemone belonging to the genus *Actinostola*—a "swimming anemone" — though normally sessile, not only moves to distance itself from chemical substances emitted by starfish but writhes and somersaults in the process (McConnaughey, 1978, pp. 270–72). Clearly, there is a diversity of possible proprioceptive acuities commensurate with the diversity of life itself. In spite of the fact that proprioception is less evident in soft-bodied invertebrates and is difficult to document (Dorsett, 1976, p. 479), marine biologists readily affirm a range of proprioceptive possibilities in soft-bodied invertebrates. Laverack, for example, states that "Proprioceptive units in the flexible body wall of soft-bodied animals are probably legion, [although] … few have been shown either anatomically or physiologically" (Laverack, 1976, p. 11); Dorsett states

---

24   If one considers that tentacle cilia are passively deformed by vibrations in the surrounding water, then of course a polyp's bending response *is* proprioceptive, not reflexive. See further in the text itself Laverack's remark about cilia as the beginning of specialized sense organ structure.

with respect to soft-bodied invertebrates generally that "abundant opportunities for true proprioception occur" (Dorsett, 1976, p. 479). Their affirmation in the face of comparatively slim evidence warrants a moment's
reflection as does the related conceptually challenging notion of "true
proprioception".

The best evidence for proprioception in soft-bodied invertebrates comes
from studies of gastropods (molluscs). In their complex feeding behaviour, a number of species protract and retract a buccal mass in coincidence
with whose retraction, a radula rasps against the substrate, taking up bits
of plant or animal tissue in the process. The behaviour is modulated by
proprioception according to load. Given the difference in animate form
between a gastropod and a sedentary hydrozoan polyp—which difference
of course means a difference in movement possibilities, thus a difference
in behavioural possibilities[25]—it is not surprising to find proprioceptive
capacities readily evident in the one and not in the other. It is precisely in
this context of recognizing differences in animate form that the significance of both the affirmation and the idea of "true proprioception"
becomes apparent: What would dispose marine biologists to affirm
"proprioceptive units" in the face of slim evidence if not an intuitive sense
of the central importance of proprioception to animate life in general, and
in particular, of its necessity in carrying through observed complex
life-enhancing behaviours such as those of certain gastropod species
described above? What if not this intuitive sense generates the idea of such
a phenomenon as `true proprioception', thus the idea that there are lesser
forms of the same, forms one might historically call proto-proprioception?
Consider the following remark that validates just such *evolutionary*
notions: "[I]n passing from the coelenterates to the annelids and molluscs,
we are looking at some of the earliest stages in the evolution and organization of the nervous system and must ask ourselves at what stage does a
true proprioceptive sense arise" (Dorsett, 1976, p. 443). The question is
indeed provocative: at what stage *does* "a true proprioceptive sense arise"?
Does it arise with molluscs, for example? Or can it be said to have arisen
with some of the presumably earlier evolving coelenterates? On the other
hand, what is "true proprioception"? And can a "stage" be pinpointed as
its inception?; that is, is it possible to say with respect to any particular
group of creatures and with respect to any particular evolutionary period,

---

25 For an excellent discussion of morphology in relation to movement and of the evolution of
arthropods from annelids with respect to that relationship, see Manton (1953). The eminent
biologist J.B.S. Haldane spoke laudingly of Manton's work, saying "Manton has done for a
phylum what comparative ethologists have done for small vertebrate groups such as the
Anatidae." He described her as a "pioneer" with respect to her phylogenetic focus on
movement (Haldane, 1953, pp. xvi, xvii).

"true proprioception starts here"? In view of the diversity of creaturely life, one might rather say that `true proprioception' arises for each creature according to the animate form it is, and that if "true proprioception" does not arise, the form does not arise either because it is not kinetically viable. In other words, one might want to say that the origin of proprioception is not an historical event as such; it is an event tied to the evolution of *animate* forms. Indeed, the evolution of formal diversity speaks to the evolution of a diversity of proprioceptive capacities because it speaks of the same phenomenon: the evolution of forms of life as forms of animation.

On the basis of the above corporeal matters of fact, we can in fact begin to distill a sense of the evolution of proprioception,

> from a meta-corporeal consciousness to a corporeal consciousness through the evolution of external sensors.

As all of the above examples suggest, the undoubtedly multiple beginnings of proprioception are in each instance tied to *surface recognition sensitivity*. Not only are the cilia of polyps tactilely sensitive to movement, but the surface sensitivity of cilia themselves, organelles that are present in groups of creatures from protozoa (unicellular eukaryotic organisms such as paramecia and amoebas) to mammals, attests to the significance of an original tactile faculty subserving movement and the recognition of something outside of one's own body. Laverack's remark about cilia is in fact highly suggestive in this respect. He writes that "If the cilium may be taken as at least a simple starting point for sense organ structure we may look for receptors even amongst the protozoa. Sensitivity towards physico-chemical events is well known, but specialized receptors much less so" (Laverack, 1976, p. 17). His remark may be glossed in the following way: the evolution of sense organs at the most primitive eukaryotic level heralds a new kind of sensitivity, one mediated by specialized sense organs, i.e. cilia, rather than by physico-chemical events, but still serving the same basic function: movement and the recognition of something outside one's own body. While this surface sensitivity is spoken of in terms of "mechanoreception" (*ibid.*), it is clearly, and indeed, from the viewpoint of living organisms, more appropriately specified as a form of *tactile*-reception. The protozoan ciliate species *Stentor*, for example, uses its cilia to sweep away noxious particles and the *Stentor* itself bends away from the tactile disturbance.[26] Tactility in the service of movement and of recogniz-

---

26   Cf. Curtis (1975) p. 311: After bending away from a noxious stimulus, and if "the offensive stimulus persists, the *Stentor* will reverse its cilia and try to sweep the particles away. If bending and sweeping are not successful, it contracts and waits. Once it has contracted, it does not bend or sweep again, but it may reach out to sample the water several times before it finally swims away. The length of time it tolerates the noxious stimulus apparently depends on

ing something outside one's own body similarly describes the cilia-mediated tentacle movement of a sedentary hydrozoan polyp toward a food source. From the viewpoint of cilia as the beginning of specialized sense organ structure, a polyp's movement is not reflexive but proprioceptive.[27] More broadly, the notion of `true proprioception' is definitively recast. It is not a historical attainment; it is a function of animate form.

Specified in animate terms, living forms disclose even broader evolutionary continuities. A bacterium that goes about sampling the environment, as described earlier, shows a related sensitivity. The bacterium—a prokaryotic organism, that is, a single-celled organism without a nucleus and without membrane-enclosed organelles—is environmentally sensitive not to shape or to movement but to the chemical composition of its environment (but see also below on a further mode of bacterial sensitivity). Its sensitivity is all the same similarly mediated by touch, it similarly subserves movement, and it is similarly meta-corporeal. Hence, in both prokaryotic and early unicellular and multicellular eukaryotic forms of life, tactility determines what a particular organism does: a bacterium's surface sensitivity and a ciliated protozoan's and cilia-mediated polyp's sensitivity are founded on contact with something in the environment, a meta-corporeal phenomenon or meta-corporeal event which excites the organism to move in some way. An evolutionary pattern thus begins to emerge with respect to *surface recognition sensitivity*. The pattern is evident in prokaryotic organisms, which are tactilely sensitive to their physico-chemical environment and which move dynamically commensurate with that sensitivity, i.e. sampling, foundering, changing direction; eukaryotic forms of life emerge, which are tactilely sensitive to the environment through specialized sense organs and which move in ways coincident with that sensitivity, protozoan ciliates responding to noxious elements in the environment by bending or sweeping movements, for example, the cilia of sedentary polyps responding to vibrations in the surrounding medium and exciting the polyp to bend a tentacle toward food, mobile forms such as annelids and molluscs moving in strikingly more intricate and varied ways on the basis of more complex external organs sensitive to deformation and stress. In sum, the pattern is a *dynamic* one. Whatever the form of surface sensitivity in prokaryotic and early unicellular and multicellular eukaryotic forms of life, it is ultimately in the service of movement: toward or away from chemicals in the environment, toward sources of food, away from noxious elements or alien creatures, and so on.

whether or not its site had previously proved a good feeding area. Thus, even ciliates show some flexibility in behavior."

27   See footnote 24 above.

A surface sensitivity subserving movement becomes apparent the moment one looks to corporeal matters of fact, analyses them in sensory-kinetic terms, realizes the centrality and significance of movement to creaturely life, and begins thinking in terms of a natural history of *animate forms*. It clearly suggests the basis on which proprioception arises and is clearly suggestive too of its crucial significance. A commonly cited definition of proprioceptors justly acknowledges a prime aspect of this significance: "Sense organs capable of registering continuously deformation (changes in length) and stress (tensions, decompressions) in the body, which can arise from the animal's own movements or may be due to its weight or other external mechanical forces" (Lissman [1950], p. 35; quoted in Mill, 1976, p. xvi).[28] In a word, proprioceptive sensitivity is *continuous*. Not only is a creature's surface in contact continuously with other surfaces in the environment, whether it is moving or whether it is still, but its own conformations continuously change in the course of moving. Continuous sensitivity is thus doubly indicative of how a moving creature profits from such organs: it is sensitive both to the changing world in which it finds itself and to its own movement and changing bodily form. Moving creatures—animate forms—are, in fact, topological entities, changing shape as they move and moving as they change shape. Proprioception implicitly articulates this truth. Deeper and more detailed study shows it to articulate a further factual truth; namely, that animal movement, however centrally programmed, cannot be considered to be wholly devoid of proprioception.[29]

To understand this further factual truth, we need first to note that understandings of consciousness on the basis of animate form are conceptually revisionary in many respects, perhaps not least in calling into question the practice of bestowing consciousness in miserly and self-serving

---

28 Lissman amends Sir Charles Sherrington's original 1906 coinage and definition of the term "proprioceptors"—sensory organs stimulated by "actions of the body itself"—in that, as Lissman states, Sherrington's definition "does not appear quite adequate, because, clearly, there are few types of sense organs which cannot be stimulated by actions of the body itself" (p. 35).

29 "[P]roprioceptive information plays a vital part in the control of movements and orientation." It is of interest to note in this context the remarks of zoologist M.J. Wells with respect to the question of the relationship between proprioception and learning: "Because it is normally impossible to eliminate all the proprioceptors and never be quite certain that one has succeeded in eliminating all other sensory cues, it is rarely possible to be certain that an animal is using proprioceptive information when it learns. ... One must examine cases where animals learn in circumstances that, *prima facie*, imply that they are taking into account information derived from within their own joints and/or muscles and/or organs of balance and explore these cases rather carefully to see what alternative explanations are possible. It should be emphasized that the object of this exercise is not to establish whether particular sorts of animal can possibly learn from proprioceptive inputs in *any* circumstances (since that question is unanswerable), but rather whether they normally appear to do so" (in Mill, 1976, pp. 567 f.).

fashion. The practice flies in the face of corporeal matters of fact, precisely as those detailed above. To those facts may be added the following: Any creature *that moves itself*, i.e. that is not sessile, senses itself moving; by the same token, it senses when it is still. Distinguishing movement from still-ness, motion from rest, is indeed a fundamental natural discrimination of living creatures that is vital to survival. The lack of constancy of the every-day world demands such discrimination. As emphasized earlier, what-ever the particular *Umwelt* might be for any particular moving creature, that world is not consistent: weather fluctuates; terrains are irregular; sur-rounds change with growth and decay; the movements and habits of other creatures alter the environment; different creatures themselves appear and disappear each day; sequences of events shift: what occurred progres-sively yesterday is not what occurs progressively today; and so on. Clearly, no undeviating world presents itself day in and day out for any creature; *Umwelts* repeat themselves neither spatially nor temporally nor dynamically. By the same token, creaturely movement is not the same from one day to the next, "the same" in the sense of an undeviating replica-tion of some master program. Certainly a creature's basic behaviours do not normally change, but they are nonetheless context- dependent in a spatial, temporal, and dynamic sense. A creature does not pursue some-thing that is not actually there for it, for example. What a creature does, that is, how and when it *moves*, is determined at each moment by the situa-tion in which it finds itself. The new and challenging mathematical science of cognition dynamics underscores these very points in its emphasis on "*real*-time". Cognition from a dynamic standpoint is processual, not a static series of representations. It takes place "in the *real* time of ongoing change in the environment, the body, and the nervous system". With respect to these three factors, dynamic analyses show the structure of cog-nition to be "*mutually and simultaneously influencing change*" (van Gelder and Port, 1995, p. 3).[30] Accordingly, however rote its basic behaviours might be with respect to its day to day living in the world,[31] a creature is necessarily sensitive in a proprioceptive sense to the present moment; it begins crawling, undulating, flying, stepping, elongating, contracting, or whatever, in the context of a present circumstance. It is *kinetically spontane-ous*. Elucidation of this further truth about the nature of animate form will show in the most concrete way how animate form is the generative source of

---

30   See also Beer (1995), Giunti (1995), and Schöner (no date).

31   We might note that it is only specified behaviours that are chosen for observation and recording, not behaviours outside a set protocol to begin with. Thus the conveniently discardable file called "anecdotal behaviour". See, for example, the consternation with which some researchers greet the idea of "tactical deception in primates" as put forth by primatologists Whiten and Byrne (1988).

consciousness—and how consciousness cannot reasonably be claimed to be the privileged faculty of humans.

6. From Corporeal Matters of Fact To Corporeal Consciousness

A creature's corporeal consciousness is first and foremost a consciousness attuned to the movement and rest of its own body. When a creature moves, it breaks forth from whatever resting position it was in; it *initiates* movement, and in ways appropriate to the situation in which it finds itself. The inherent kinetic spontaneity of animate forms lies fundamentally in this fact.[32] Kinetic spontaneity may be analysed in terms of kinesthetic motivations, a species-specific range of movement possibilities, a repertoire of what might be termed "I cans", and—by way of proprioception and, more particularly, of kinesthesia—a sense of agency. As might be apparent, these dimensions of spontaneity are keenly inter-related. A creature's initiation of movement is coincident with its kinesthetic motivations, its dispositions to do this or that—turn, pause, crouch, freeze, run, or constrict; its kinesthetic motivations fall within the range of its species-specific movement possibilities—an ant is not disposed to pounce any more than a cat is disposed to crawl; these possibilities are the basis of its particular repertoire of "I cans", a repertoire that may not only change over the lifetime of the animal as it ages, but that may be selectively distinguished insofar as the animal can run faster, for example, or conceal itself more effectively than other members of its group; as enacted, any item within its repertoire of "I cans" is undergirded proprioceptively (kinesthetically) by a sense of agency. A creature's corporeal consciousness is structurally a composite of these four kinetic dimensions of spontaneity. It is a composite not in a studied analytical comparative sense—e.g., "I, a horse, cannot fly like a bird"—and certainly *not* in the sense of demanding linguistic formulation, but in an existentially kinetic sense, in the sense of being *animate*. In effect, creatures know themselves—"they know which thing in the world they are"—in ways that are fundamentally and quintessentially consistent with the bodies they are. They know themselves in these ways not by *looking*, i.e. not by way of what is visible to them of their visual bodies, but proprioceptively, or more finely, kinesthetically, i.e. in ways

---

32 Kinetic spontaneity describes fundamental dimensions of *animation*. The term is not tied in any way to a centralist doctrine. Hence, the term should not be confused with the older notions of "innervation sensations", "willing", "volition", or "effort", or in any other way confused with the classic efferent side of the efferent/afferent divide. (For a thoroughgoing criticism of the idea that there is "a consciousness of the motor discharge [from the brain]", see James, 1950, p. 494).

specific to movement alone, sensing their bodies as animate forms in movement and at rest.

This form of creaturely knowing can be spelled out along evolutionary lines, indeed, along the lines of descent with modification. The evolutionary pattern sketched above emphasized the basic phenomenon of surface recognition sensitivity — beginning with bacteria and proceeding to ciliated protozoa, to sedentary invertebrates, and to molluscs and annelids. This beginning sketch can be amplified. Creatures such as lobsters and spiders are creatures with an articulable skeleton, hence they have not only external sensors but internal ones as well, particularly around their jointed appendages. Generally termed chordotonal organs in invertebrates, these internal proprioceptors are sensitive directly to stresses within the body itself. On the basis of organic analogues and structural homologies, biologists believe these internal proprioceptors to have derived from external sensory organs, that is, to be the result of a migration of certain formerly external proprioceptive bodily structures. Such structural migrations are, of course, not unknown in evolution. A quite commonly cited homology concerns three reptilian jaw units that over time came to form the auditory ossicles of the mammalian middle ear: the stapes, malleus, and incus. Using a different example, Laverack makes this very comparison between invertebrate and vertebrate organ derivations or homologies. After noting that "Evolutionary trends in several groups [of invertebrates] show a gradual removal of proprioceptors from the surface to a deep or internal placement", he points out that this derivation, while apparent in some invertebrates, "is demonstrable in vertebrates", giving as example "the change in position of the acoustico-lateralis system in fish and amphibia" (Laverack, 1976, p. 19). Laverack in fact gives various examples of analogous proprioceptive organs in invertebrates: for example, the exoskeletal plates of a hermit crab are analogous to limb proprioceptors in other invertebrates (p. 10). He later gives a specific example of a possible invertebrate proprioceptive homology or derivation: "[T]he chordotonal organs of decapod Crustacea [e.g., lobsters] may have originated . . . from groups of hairs, very similar to hair plates of insects, of which the individual sensilla have shortened, lost their contact with the surface, and finally been incorporated in a connective tissue strand or sheet. The remaining vestiges of hairs are evident as scolopidia [the complex cellular unit of a chordotonal organ]." Further, with respect to the similarity of decapod chordotonal organs to insect hair plates, he adverts to research that, on anatomical and ontogenetic grounds and in consideration of the process of molting, suggests that "the cuticular sheath of sensory hairs and campaniform sensilla [in insects] are homologous to the extracellular cap or tube of scolopidia" (p. 21).

If the thesis is correct that external proprioceptors were modified and internalized over time, then a singularly significant consequence obtains: internally-mediated proprioception, however variously accomplished in terms of anatomical structures, remains nonetheless epistemologically consistent in its results, *viz*, a directly movement-sensitive corporeal consciousness.[33] Such a proprioceptive consciousness is kinesthetically rather than tactilely rooted. Corporeal consciousness thus evolved from its beginnings in tactility into kinesthesia, into a direct sensitivity to movement through internally mediated systems of corporeal awareness. In effect, through all the intricate and changing pathways of descent with modification, *know thyself* has remained a consistent biological built-in; a kinetic corporeal consciousness informs a diversity of animate forms.

The thesis that internal proprioceptors evolved from external proprioceptive organs may be expanded and in a challenging and perhaps unexpected direction. Laverack writes that external sensors have two major disadvantages: "(1) A lack of discrimination between stimulation generated by movement of the body and that generated by external tactile events. (2) A vulnerability to wear and damage. A superficial placement is bound to expose hairs and pegs to abrasion and other accidents" (p. 46).[34] He states that these disadvantages "may have placed adaptive significance upon the subsequent development of parallel, internal proprioceptors". His perspective on the disadvantages of external sensors and the adaptive significance of internal ones has certain unexpected affinities with the perspective of molecular biochemist R.M. Macnab who, writing on sensory reception in bacteria, conjoins within a single perspective two otherwise opposed viewpoints on "the sensory apparatus of a unicellular prokaryote" (Macnab, 1982, p. 98). Macnab discusses the sensitivity of a bacterium to surface events or environmental phenomena on the one hand, and to its own kinetic potential or energy level on the other, thus actually calling into question an account of bacterial knowing as only meta-corporeal. Being sensitive to its own kinetic potential, a bacterium can be said to have a rudimentary corporeal consciousness, rudimentary

---

33   Cf. Laverack, 1976, p. 48: "If the thesis that many internal receptors may derive from external receptors, (sic) is valid, then it would be anticipated that the properties of all mechanoreceptors will be similar. Variety may be expected as a result largely of anatomical rather than physiological attributes."

34   We might clarify the first disadvantage by noting that tactility is a reflexive sense, that is, one in which what is touching and what is touched coincide — or blend. Hence, the sense of touch can indeed be ambiguous, precisely as Laverack points out in general rather than sensory-specific terms.

not in the sense of being less than functional — incomplete or underdeveloped, for example — but in the sense of there being no proprioceptive organ other than the organism — the bacterium — itself. Indeed, the source of a bacterium's motility is PMF — "proton motive force, [or] proton electrochemical potential" (p. 78) — and it is described as both the "motor" and "the true sensory input" (p. 77); "the motor is an autonomous PMF sensing system" (p. 98). Clearly, movement and the potential for movement are at the heart of a rudimentary corporeal consciousness. The specific contrast in viewpoints that Macnab reconciles bears this out. The contrast concerns a "sensing of the physiological consequences of an environmental parameter [such as light, oxygen, and so on]" and a "sensing of the parameter itself" (p. 77). In other words, a bacterium can either sense itself with respect to the environment or sense the environment. Macnab points out that "Even in the rudimentary behavioural system of bacteria, both capabilities are present" (p. 77) — a remark of considerable interest to anyone concerned to provide a bona fide evolutionary account of consciousness. He later specifies explicitly the advantages and disadvantages of each kind of sensibility: in physiological sensing, "the signal can be thought of as: 'For reasons unspecified, your current direction of travel has already resulted in your PMF ... falling dangerously low'"; in environmental sensing, "[the signal can be thought of] as: 'Based on the following specific information — increasing aspartate in your external environment — your current direction of travel may offer enhanced opportunities for growth'." In the first instance, the freely moving bacterium relies on a sense of its own energy to determine the benefits of continuing travel in its present direction. If it senses its energic potential running low, it is not getting what it needs from its immediate environment and moves elsewhere. In this instance, the freely moving bacterium is monitoring its environment *internally* through an electrochemical sensitivity to the effect of the environment on its kinetic potential. In the second instance, the freely moving bacterium relies on specific sensing abilities, i.e. external chemoreceptors for amino acids and sugars, in order to determine whether the path it is following is likely to continue being propitious or not. Macnab points out the value and liability of each mode of sensing in what are actually exacting epistemological terms:

> The physiological consequence of sensory information [i.e. physiologically-derived sensory information] has the advantage that the information is certain, but the disadvantage that it is late; the anticipatory sensory information has the advantage that it is early, but the disadvantage that it is uncertain, because the physiological consequence is presumed, and may in fact never occur (p. 100).

The certainty of a bacterium's internally-generated information — as of an animal's internal proprioception — is clearly of moment. As the earlier definition of proprioception implied, continuous sensitivity to one's own bodily condition means knowing with exactitude the nature of that condition — whether one's kinetic potential, one's postural conformation, or the spatio-temporal dynamics of one's movement. An *internally* structured corporeal consciousness is from this viewpoint both kinesthetically indubitable and kinesthetically unambiguous. For a bacterium, this mode of consciousness translates into knowledge that is similarly indubitable and unambiguous. The adaptive significance of a continuous bodily sensitivity in the form of an internally structured corporeal consciousness of movement or of movement potential can thus hardly be minimized. It is the generative source of a creature's immediate kinetic spontaneity. A creature's initiation of movement, including the initiation of a change of direction, is always from a particular corporeal here and now — positionally, energetically, situationally, and so on. Given its particular corporeal here and now, certain species-specific kinetic possibilities exist for it — here and now; other species-specific kinetic possibilities may emerge only when another, different corporeal here and now obtains, the different corporeal here and now that comes with growth, for example, thus with a changed animate form. Similar possibilities and constraints hold with respect to a creature's repertoire of "I cans": given its own particular strengths and liabilities, it has certain corporeal possibilities and not others — here and now. Even a bacterium cannot automatically upgrade its PMF just because the environment is right. For example, while aspartate might be present in its environment, the bacterium's aspartate transport system may be defective. The bacterium may thus be unable to take advantage of the amino acid, precisely as Macnab suggests with respect to physiological consequences being presumed (Macnab, 1982, p. 100).[35] Finally, indubitable and unambiguous knowledge is basic to a creature's sense of agency. Lacking an internally structured corporeal consciousness that is both peculiar to the animate form it is and

---

35   A tangential but critical point might be made with respect to the twofold sensitivities of a bacterium, the one sensitivity being described as immediate, the other as anticipatory, the one informative of the bacterium's present energic state but not of the environmental cause of that state, the other informative of particular aspects of the bacterium's environment but not of what its consequences will be. A caveat might be in order with respect to what amounts to an equipotential weighting of a corporeal consciousness and meta-corporeal consciousness. A bacter-ium can be conceived profitably attuned to the future only with a certain reserve. If the bacterium has both capabilities, then its sensitivity to its own body is paramount. If there is no guarantee that present environmental munificence will continue and even grow, there is no guarantee either that the bacterium itself will continue and even prosper. If its sensitivity to its own energic level becomes deficient for any reason, it could conceivably exhaust itself in the midst of plenty or in the pursuit of more.

epistemologically resonant at each moment, a creature could hardly initiate movement — change direction, increase speed, pause, reach out with an
appendage, turn itself around, avoid an obstacle or predator, explore, flee,
or move purposefully in innumerable other ways — *or stop* — all such
movement or cessation of movement being consistent both with the situation in which it finds itself and with its own immediate spatio-temporal
corporeality.

Clearly, the corporeal path by which we can trace the evolution of consciousness can be richly elaborated in terms of the inherent kinetic spontaneity of animate forms. Such elaboration decisively challenges the
putative evolutionary notion of an agent as something that `does some-
thing and then looks to see what moves'. Attention to corporeal matters of
fact demonstrates that a bona fide evolutionary account of consciousness
begins with surface recognition sensitivity. It thereby acknowledges a
meta-corporeal consciousness. It furthermore takes into account the emergence of a diversity of animate forms, showing how surface recognition
sensitivity, while mediated by touch, is actually in the service of movement for creatures all the way from bacteria to protists to invertebrate
forms to vertebrate ones. It strongly suggests how a form of corporeal consciousness is present in bacteria.[36] Indeed, it shows how a bacterium, being
an animate form of life, is something first of all that *moves* and is capable of
moving on its own power rather than being always impelled to move from
without; it shows further how it is something that feeds, that grows, that
changes direction, that, in effect, can stop doing what it is doing and begin
doing something else. A bona fide evolutionary account shows how, with
the evolution of varied and complex external sensors, a different form of
corporeal consciousness is present, and how, with the evolution of internal sensors from external ones, a still different form of corporeal consciousness is present. It shows how each of these forms of corporeal
consciousness is coincident with the evolution of varied and complex animate forms themselves, and equally, how each form of proprioception that
evolved, from the most rudimentary to the most complex of kinesthetic
systems, is coincident with particular forms of life. It shows all this by
paying attention to corporeal matters of fact and by presenting concrete
sensory-kinetic analyses.

There is a final point to be made. For an invertebrate or vertebrate, an
internally structured corporeal consciousness is not directly vulnerable to
environmental wear and tear and in this sense is protected. As Laverack's
second remark suggests, a creature with internal proprioceptors is not at

---

36 See also Losick's and Kaiser's (1997) account of how "[b]acteria converse with one another and
with plants and animals" (p. 68).

the direct mercy of the surrounding world. For a bacterium, such protection is not of course of moment; being unicellular, it has no sensory or internal organs as such. Some soft-bodied invertebrates such as annelid worms have hydrostatic skeletons, muscles lengthening and shortening the body against semi-fluid body contents that do not compress so that volume remains constant while segments of the animal increase and decrease in diameter. Although internal proprioception has been suggested via studies of stretch response, and although some annelids have very tough outer cuticles which *inter alia* would offer protection for internal proprioceptors, a strong case cannot reasonably be made for protection or the need for protection in the sense Laverack suggests, i.e. the evolution of internal proprioception as a means of protecting sensory organs from environmental wear and tear. The decisive turning point for proprioceptive protection is clearly evidenced in the evolution of an articulable skeleton. Arthropods and vertebrates are notable in this respect. Though their evolutionary lineages are distinct, species within each phylum are similar in having a skeletal structure and in being extremely mobile forms.[37] Although their respective skeletal structure is differently placed, the attaching muscular structure is in each case internal and functions in a similar manner; when a muscle contracts, skeletal joints close, pulling two body segments toward each other. A direct and continuous sensitivity to movement thus appears to have evolved in two distinct but highly mobile forms of life and with the same advantage: an internally-mediated corporeal consciousness of movement that is not dependent on external stimuli, hence on tactility, but that is internally mediated. This kind of corporeal consciousness is not only relatively protected as well as continuous in comparison to an externally-mediated corporeal consciousness. Being internal, its possibilities for elaboration are quite different. In particular, what is being sensed in the case of an internally-mediated corporeal consciousness has the possibility of opening up, of expanding into a richly variable and complex domain of awarenesses. The possibility of such a domain is adumbrated in the question "What is it like to be a bat?" Indeed, the question "What is it like to be a bat?" presumes the existence of an internally-mediated corporeal consciousness that has already opened up into a range of kinetically tied and internally felt phenomena and acts. In other words, it presupposes a range of experiences that a bat has of itself as an animate form.

---

37 Cf. Fields (1976), who explicitly draws a parallel between crustaceans and vertebrates with respect to the need for precise control of a multi-jointed, highly mobile body in changing circumstances — e.g., variable load, muscle fatigue, and the like. In particular, Fields draws attention to the fact that the muscle receptor organ of crustaceans is similar to the muscle spindle of vertebrates.

Proprioception is in this sense an *epistemological gateway,*
one that, by descent with modification,
may clearly be elaborated both affectively and cognitively.

In just these ways, corporeal consciousness shows itself to have the possibility of expanding into a sense of self. The evolution of proprioception foundationally explains this possible expansion. "The Reality of Selves" has its roots in corporeal consciousness.

7. Implications

Three implications in particular warrant mention. First, the natural history of consciousness described above demands a re-thinking of the common assumption that historically — particularly with reference to the evolution of nonhuman animals — unconsciousness preceded consciousness. Corporeal matters of fact show this assumption to be unfounded. It has never in fact been shown that nonhuman animals do not think, or choose, or even deliberate with respect to movement,[38] or that they do not have a sense of speed, space, effort, and so on. On the contrary, if the above sensory-kinetic analysis of consciousness is correct, then the evolution of such corporeal capacities and awarenesses is coincident with the evolution of animate forms. Corporeal awareness is a built-in of animate life; as stated in the beginning, *know thyself* is incontrovertibly a fundamental biological built-in.

Second, there is in present-day western society a tendency to be mesmerized by brains, so mesmerized that the larger creaturely world of which humans are a part is forgotten, egregiously slighted, or arrogantly distorted. Cognitivist programmes of research in science and philosophy are at the forefront of this mesmerization. Should researchers in these disciplines find that the subject of nonhuman animals is in general not congenial to their interests, or that the foregoing evolutionary analysis of consciousness is in particular not exciting in the way that computerized study of their own brains is exciting, it may well be because they have lost touch with their own natural history. Indeed, compared with Aristotle's studious forays into the world of animals — human and nonhuman — cognitivists' knowledge of animals appears in many cases painfully limited. One is easily led to think, at least with respect to some of the creatures they write about — lobsters and scallops, for example — that their only encounter with them has been on a plate. Yet serious study of animate forms is required for understandings of consciousness. Included in this requisite study is a study of hominids themselves and for the following

---

38 "Animals may constantly be seen to pause, deliberate, and resolve" (Darwin, 1871/1981, p. 46).

reason: any evolutionary understanding of human consciousness — any "naturalistic study of consciousness" (Flanagan, 1984, p. 307) — must acknowledge a historical fact recorded previously, namely, that while all humans are hominids, not all hominids are human. Accordingly, any evolutionary rendition of human consciousness must take into serious account artifactual evidence attesting incontrovertably to the intellectual acumen of nonhuman animals. Such an account can hardly be rendered in computational brain-state terms. It can, however, be rendered and in fact has been rendered in sensory-kinetic terms demonstrating a corporeal consciousness (cf. Sheets-Johnstone, 1990).

The third implication is related to the second. We can hardly hope to understand consciousness if we make authoritative and self-serving evolutionary armchair pronouncements such as "Consciousness did not have to evolve. … Consciousness is not essential to highly evolved intelligent life. … However, from the fact that consciousness is inessential to highly evolved intelligent life, it does not follow that it is inessential to our particular type of intelligent life" (Flanagan, 1992, p. 129; the first sentence appears in his 1984, p. 344); or, if in the course of explaining how it is possible "that some living things are conscious" (Flanagan, 1984, p. 307; 1992, p. 1), we make claims about creatures whom we have not bothered to study but about whom we feel entitled to make judgments. To affirm, for example, that scallops "are conscious of nothing", that they "get out of the way of potential predators without experiencing them as such, and when they fail to do so, they get eaten alive without (quite possibly) experiencing pain" (Flanagan, 1984, p. 344 f.; 1992, p. 132), is to leap the bounds of rigorous scholarship into a maze of unwarranted assumptions, mistaking human ignorance for human knowledge. As a matter of fact, a well-known introductory biology text shows a picture of a scallop "sensing an approaching starfish", and "leap[ing] to safety". The same book, commenting on the complexity of a scallop's eyes, elsewhere notes that although the lens of its eyes "cannot focus on images", it detects "light and dark and movement" (Curtis, 1975, pp. 29, 387).

Evolutionary understandings of consciousness on the basis of animate form are clearly a radical departure from materialist conceptions that, basically identifying consciousness and matter, eschew serious inquiry into the nature of animate life. It is thus not surprising that in offering their reductive programmes, materialists offer a metaphysics in advance of an epistemology and a natural history that support it. Their metaphysics is in advance of a supportive epistemology in that both experience and meticulous study belie theory. Proprioception in general and kinesthesia in particular advert to a knowing subject, a subject that, at minimum, knows when it is moving and knows when it is not. Consciousness can therefore be judged neither `inessential' nor essentially linguistic, a "center of narrative gravity". Consultation of and reflection upon corporeal matters of fact testify to a corporeal consciousness that is epistemic in nature and that can be ignored only at the peril of a degenerate epistemology. Their metaphysics is in advance of a supportive natural history in that it ignores close knowledge of the literature on nonhuman animals, including, as suggested above, those nonhuman animals that were the direct hominid ancestors of modern-day humans. An evolutionary backbone is thus essentially lacking to their metaphysics, which is why it must be propped up by molecular definitions of life and why the life the metaphysics describes, being mere ongoing states of a brain, offers a portrait of life as if life were a series of stills. In sum, serious inquiry into the *nature* of consciousness perforce must take into account its natural history.

GLOSSARY

Although many terms used in the text are defined in the text, a listing is given here for convenience and added reference. (Note: Biological classification is in terms of kingdom, phylum, class, order, family, genus, species.)

Amoeba: A genus of protozoan organisms distinguished by their pseudopodia.

Annelida: a phylum of invertebrate animals that includes earthworms and marine worms, all of which have segmented bodies. (From Latin *anellus*, ring.)

Anthozoa: a class of coelenterates that includes sea anemones and corals. (From Greek *anthos*, flower + *zoion*, animal.)

Arthropoda: a phylum of hard-bodied invertebrate animals — the largest phylum in the animal kingdom — that includes lobsters, spiders, ants, and centipedes, all of which have an external skeleton and thus articulable body parts. (From Greek *arthro*, joint + *podos*, footed.)

buccal: pertaining to the cavity of the mouth.

campaniform sensilla: bell-shaped proprioceptive organs in insects that are sensitive to deformation.

chordotonal organs: internal proprioceptive organs of invertebrates.

cilium (pl. cilia): a hairlike structure that protrudes from the surface of a cell and is commonly found in rows; it has a characteristic 9+2 internal structure, i.e. nine pairs of microtubules surrounding two microtubules at the center.

Coelenterata: a phylum of invertebrate animals that includes polyps, jellyfish, sea anemones, and corals. (From Greek *koilos*, hollow + *enteron*, intestine.)

Crustacea: a class of arthropods that includes barnacles, prawns, crab, water fleas, and crayfish. (From Latin *crusta*, the shell or hard surface of a body.)

decapod Crustacea: crustaceans such as lobsters and crab having five pairs of legs and belonging to the order Decapoda.

eukaryote: a cell that has an outer membrane that separates it from its environment and both a membrane-bound nucleus and membrane-bound organelles. (From Greek *eu*, good + *karyon*, nut, kernel.)

flagellum (pl. flagella): a hairlike structure that protrudes from the surface of a cell and that is instrumental in locomotion and feeding; it is longer than, but has an internal structure similar to, a cilium.

Gastropoda: A class of mollusks that comprises the largest number of species of mollusks (80,000). The class includes whelks, snails, limpets, conches, and abalones, which have either a univalve shell or no shell at all, and which are more mobile than bivalve mollusks such as the scallop. (From Greek *gastro*, stomach + *podos*, footed.)

Hydrozoa: a class of coelenterates which includes polyps and jellyfish and of which the polyp is the dominant form. (From Greek *hydor*, water + *zoion*, animal.)

Hymenoptera: an order of insects that includes bees, ants, and wasps. (From Greek *hymen*, membrane + *pteron*, wing.)

Mollusca: a phylum of soft-bodied invertebrate animals that includes snails, slugs, oysters, mussels, scallops, octopuses, and squid. (From Latin *molluscus*, soft.)

nauplius (pl. nauplii): a larval form of crustacean.

Paramecium: a genus of protozoan organisms distinguished by their cilia-mediated movement.

polyp: a coelenterate animal that is usually sessile and that has a vase-shaped or cylindrical body, the mouth of which is surrounded by tentacles.

prokaryote: a cell that has an outer membrane that separates it from its environment. (From Latin *pro*, before + Greek *karyon*, nut kernel.)

Protista: a kingdom of eukaryotic, unicellular organisms.

Protozoa: a phylum of organisms within the kingdom Protista. The animals are characteristically one-celled organisms that are invisible to the naked eye. They are classified according to their form of locomotion: movement by means of flagella, of cilia, or of pseudopodia. Some protozoa — the sporozoans — are nonmotile forms. (From Greek *protos*, first + *zoion*, animal.)

radula: a feeding organ by which gastropods rasp or scrape off bits of plant or animal tissue. (From Latin *radere*, to scrape.)

scolopidia: complex peg- or spike-like structures comprising the cellular units of chordotonal organs in invertebrates.

sensilla: external proprioceptive organs such as hairs, pegs, slits, and plates.

sessile: stationary, attached to a substrate, not freely moving. (From Latin *sedere*, to sit.)

Stentor: a genus of protozoan organisms distinguished by their cilia-mediated movement.

References

Beer, Randall D. (1995), "Computational and dynamical languages for autonomous agents", in *Mind as Motion: Explorations in the Dynamics of Cognition*, ed. Timothy van Gelder and Robert F. Port (Cambridge, MA: Bradford / MIT Press).

Carruthers, Peter (1989), "Brute experience", *The Journal of Philosophy*, **86** (5), pp. 258–69.

Cassirer, Ernst (1970), *An Essay on Man* (New York: Bantam Books).

Chalmers, David J. (1996), *The Conscious Mind* (New York: Oxford University Press).

Churchland, Paul M. (1984), *Matter and Consciousness* (Cambridge, MA: Bradford / MIT Press).

Curtis, Helena (1975), *Biology* 2nd ed. (New York: Worth Publishers).

Darwin, Charles (1871/1981), *The Descent of Man and Selection in Relation to Sex* (Princeton: Princeton University Press).

Dennett, Daniel C. (1983), "Intentional systems in cognitive ethology: the 'panglossian paradigm' defended", *Behavioral and Brain Sciences*, **6**, pp. 343–90.

Dennett, Daniel C. (1991), *Consciousness Explained* (Boston, MA: Little, Brown and Co.).

Dennett, Daniel C. (1995), *Darwin's Dangerous Idea* (New York: Simon and Schuster).

Dennett, Daniel C. (1996), *Kinds of Minds* (New York: Basic Books).

Dorsett, D.A. (1976), "The structure and function of proprioceptors in soft-bodied invertebrates", in Mill (1976).

Edelman, Gerald (1992), *Bright Air, Brilliant Fire* (New York: Basic Books).

Fields, H.L. (1976), "Crustacean Abdominal and Thoracic Muscle Receptor Organs", in *Structure and Function of Proprioceptors in the Invertebrates*, ed. P. J. Mill (London: Chapman and Hall).

Flanagan, Owen (1984), *The Science of the Mind*, 2nd ed. (Cambridge, MA: MIT Press).

Flanagan, Owen (1992), *Consciousness Reconsidered* (Cambridge, MA: Bradford / MIT Press).

van Gelder, Timothy and Port, Robert F. (1995), "It's about time: an overview of the dynamical approach to cognition", in *Mind as Motion: Explorations in the Dynamics of Cognition* (Cambridge, MA: Bradford / MIT Press).

Giunti, Marco (1995), "Dynamical models of cognition", in *Mind as Motion: Explorations in the Dynamics of Cognition* (Cambridge, MA: Bradford / MIT Press).

Gould, Stephen Jay (1989), *Wonderful Life* (New York: W. W. Norton & Co.).

Gould, Stephen Jay (1995), "Spin doctoring Darwin", *Natural History*, **104**, pp. 6–9, 70 f.

James, William (1950), *Principles of Psychology*, Vol. 2 ((New York: Dover Publications).

Keeton, William T. & Gould, James L. (1986), *Biological Science*, 4th ed. (New York: W.W. Norton and Company).

Haldane, J.B.S. (1953), "Foreword", *Evolution*, pp. xvi, xvii.

Laverack, M.S. (1976), "External proprioceptors", in Mill (1976).

Libet, Benjamin (1985), "Subjective antedating of a sensory experience and mind-brain theories: Reply to Honderich (1984)", *Journal of Theoretical Biology*, **114**, pp. 563–70.

Lissman, H.W. (1950), "Proprioceptors", in *Physiological Mechanisms in Animal Behaviour (Symposia of the Society for Experimental Biology*, vol. IV) (New York: Academic Press, Inc.).

Losick, Richard and Kaiser, Dale (1997), "Why and how bacteria communicate", *Scientific American* **276** (2: February), pp. 68–73.

McConnaughey, Bayard H. (1978), *Introduction to Marine Biology* (St. Louis: C.V. Mosby).

McDonald, Kim A. (1995), "Replaying 'Life's Tape'", *The Chronicle of Higher Education* (August 11, 1995).

Macnab, R.M. (1982), "Sensory reception in bacteria", in *Prokaryotic and Eukaryotic Flagella (Symposia of the Society for Experimental Biology 35)* (Cambridge: Cambridge University Press).

Manton, S.M. (1953), "Locomotory habits and the evolution of the larger arthropodan groups", in *Evolution (Symposia of the Society for Experimental Biology), No. VII* (New York: Academic Press).

Mill, P.J. (ed. 1976), *Structure and Function of Proprioceptors in the Invertebrates* (London: Chapman and Hall).

Nagel, Thomas (1974), "What is it like to be a bat?", *Philosophical Review*, **83**, pp. 435–50.

Nagel, Thomas (1993), "The mind wins!" *New York Review of Books* (March 4, 1993), pp. 37–41.

Robeck, Mildred C. (1978), *Infants and Children* (New York: McGraw-Hill Book Co.).

Scheerer, Eckart (1987), "Muscle sense and innervation feelings: a chapter in the history of perception and action", in *Perspectives on Perception and Action*, ed. Herbert Heuer and Andries F. Sanders (Hillsdale, NJ: Lawrence Erlbaum Associates).

Schöner, G. (no date), "What can we learn from dynamic models of rhythmic behavior in animals and humans?" in *Prerational Intelligence: Adaptive Behavior and Intelligent Systems Without Symbols and Logic* (unpaginated), book ms under review by Kluwer Academic.

Searle, John R. (1990), "Consciousness, explanatory inversion, and cognitive science", *Behavioral and Brain Sciences*, **13**, pp. 585–642.

Searle, John R. (1992), *The Rediscovery of the Mind* (Cambridge, MA: Bradford / MIT Press).

Sellars, Wilfrid (1963), *Science, Perception and Reality* (London: Routledge & Kegan Paul).

Sheets-Johnstone, Maxine (1990), *The Roots of Thinking* (Philadelphia: Temple University Press).

Sheets-Johnstone, Maxine (1992), "Taking evolution seriously", *American Philosophical Quarterly*, **29**, pp. 343–52.

Sheets-Johnstone, Maxine (1994), *The Roots of Power: Animate Form and Gendered Bodies* (Chicago: Open Court Publishing).

Sheets-Johnstone, Maxine (1996), "Taking evolution seriously: A matter of primate intelligence", *Etica & Animali*, **8**, pp. 115–30.

Sherrington, Charles (1953), *Man on His Nature*, 2nd ed. (New York: Doubleday).

Smithers, Tim (2000), "On behaviour as dissipative structures in agent-environment system interaction spaces", in *Prerational Intelligence: Adaptive Behavior and Intelligent Systems Without Symbols and Logic*, vol. 2, ed. Helge Ritter, Holk Cruse and Jeffrey Dean (Dordrecht: Kluwer), pp. 243–58.

Stern, Daniel N. (1985), *The Interpersonal World of the Infant* (New York: Basic Books).

Teuber, H.L. (1966), "Discussion of D.M. MacKay's 'Cerebral organization and the conscious control of action'", in *Brain and Conscious Experience*, ed. John C. Eccles (New York: Springer-Verlag).

von Uexküll, Johannes (1928), *Theoretische Biologie* 2nd ed. (Berlin: J. Springer).

Washburn, Sherwood L. and Strum, Shirley C. (1972), "Concluding comments", in *Perspectives on Human Evolution*, Vol. 2 (New York: Holt, Rinehart and Winston).

Whiten, A. and Byrne, R.W. (1988), "Tactical deception in primates", *Behavioral and Brain Sciences*, **11**, pp. 233–73.

Windle, William F. (1971), *Physiology of the Fetus* (Springfield, IL: Charles C. Thomas).

Wright, B.R. (1976), "Limb and wing receptors in insects, chelicerates and myriapods", in Mill (1976).

Chapter VIII

Emotion and Movement

A Beginning Empirical-Phenomenological Analysis of their Relationship

1. Introduction

In his discussion of time and of "how many ways we speak of the 'now'", Aristotle unwittingly highlights in a striking way the nature of a qualitative dynamics. He says that "'now' is the link of time" referenced in expressions such as "at some time", "lately", "just now", "long ago", and "suddenly" (*Physics* 222b27–29.) Something radically different is conveyed by the last example: "suddenly" has a decisively dynamic aspect wholly distinct from the other terms or phrases. Aristotle says simply that "'Suddenly' refers to what has departed from its former condition in a time imperceptible because of its smallness" (*Physics* 222b15–16). He is obviously taking "suddenly" as a quantitative term parallel to the other quantitative terms. But "suddenly" is basically something both more and other than an interval of time "imperceptible because of its smallness." It is a *qualitatively* experienced temporality, just as rushed, prolonged, and creeping are *qualitatively* experienced temporalities. In brief, the distinctive dynamic that defines "suddenly" derives from felt experience. It is fundamentally not a quantitative term but an experienced kinetic quale. As such, it has a certain affective aura: "suddenly" may describe an earthquake, a fall, an ardent kiss, an urge or inspiration, or one of multiple other possible experiences, each of which has a certain affective resonance. What is kinetic is affective, or potentially affective; by the same qualitative measure, what is affective is kinetic, or potentially kinetic.

Recognition of the everyday qualitative character of *suddenly* opens up an intricate and challenging domain of experience emblematic of the intimate bond between emotions and movement. In what follows, I offer a beginning sketch of the relationship, concentrating first on empirical research that preceded the rise of cognitivist science with its prominencing

of an information-processing brain (Bruner, 1990) and its correlative dislo-
cation of movement.[1] I summarize three empirical studies of emotion[2] that
carry forward the work of Darwin, and that vindicate in different ways the
work of physiological psychologist Roger Sperry on perception and his
principle thesis that the brain is an organ of and for movement (Sperry,
1952).[3] The summaries make evident the theoretics that bind the studies
together and reveal the tactile-kinesthetic body that is in each case their
foundation. I turn then to a summary phenomenological analysis of movement, showing how the dynamic character of movement gives rise to
kinetic qualia. The analysis exemplifies how empirical studies may be
epistemologically deepened through phenomenology, in this instance
through a phenomenological elucidation of the fundamentally qualitative
structure of movement, a structure that grounds the relationship between
movement and emotion in a qualitative dynamics and formal dynamic
congruency. In virtue of that congruency, motion and emotion — kinetic
and affective bodies — are of a dynamic piece.[4] Methodological consequences follow from this exposition. So also do implications for
cognitivism, which range from the observation that movement is not
behavior and that the term "embodied" is a lexical band-aid covering a
three-hundred-fifty-year-old wound, to the observation that animate

1   With its frequent experiential ascriptions to brains — e.g., "If you see the back of a person's
     head, the brain infers that there is a face on the front of it" (Crick and Koch, 1992: 153) — the
     prominencing exacerbates our already precarious status as lumbering robots.

2   A reviewer of this essay stated that "the three investigators the author selects ... have not really
     produced the types of rigorous studies that most scientists would currently deem to be of
     sufficient quality to constitute essential and unambiguous empirical progress in the area." It is
     important to point out that the research of the three investigators has not been critically shown
     to be lacking in rigor, to be of inferior quality, and so on, but has only been ignored, and this
     most probably because the research is not currently popular: it deals with *experience*, not with
     behavior, and it deals with intact living humans, not with brains. In this respect, it should be
     noted on the one hand that the positive value of an empirical study holds until specifically
     shown to be indefensible — e.g., the study is invalidated on procedural grounds, it is shown to
     be unreliable because unreplicatable, and so on; and on the other hand that science progresses
     as much by discovery in arrears — e.g., Mendel, Wegner — as by discovery in advance. In
     evidential support of both hands, we may readily look to Karl Pribram's commanding citations
     of Nina Bull's research (e.g., in Pribram, 1980, pp. 246, 256) and to Manfred Clynes's positive
     citation of the same (in Clynes, 1980, p. 281).

3   Sperry's later groundbreaking experimental research involving brain commissurotomies
     eclipsed his earlier groundbreaking experimental research on perception and movement. To
     be noted in this context is that however much present-day textbooks veer off into a
     preeminently information-processing view of brains, in their sections on movement, some of
     them contradict the view and clearly support Sperry's thesis, e.g., "The brain is the organ that
     moves the muscles. It does many other things, but all of them are secondary to making our
     bodies move" (Carlson, 1992, p. 214).

4   The dynamic congruency is elegant in a way analogous to the way in which mathematical
     formulations and scientific explanations are said to be elegant. At the level of animate forms
     themselves, the congruency of affective and kinetic bodies is similarly elegant.

forms are not machines and that a kinetic, qualitative (meta)physics follows naturally from the study of animation and animate form.

2. Empirical Studies of Emotion

The first research that warrants our attention is the lifelong experimental work, empirical methodology, and related clinical practice of Edmund Jacobson. A close friend of Karl Lashley, Jacobson was a medical doctor and neuropsychiatrist with a doctorate in psychology.[5] Jacobson developed and honed a form of introspection, a practice he called "auto-sensory observation", which he taught to his patients, enabling them to monitor and ultimately dissipate excessive, unproductive bodily tensions, and in consequence to decrease felt anxieties and other debilitating feelings. In this way, they were able to take personal responsibility for their problems (Jacobson 1929, 1967, 1970). Jacobson's technique of self-observation was learned and taught by other physicians and psychiatrists, and by other persons as well. During World War II, for example, his technique was taught to U.S. Navy Air Cadets—15,300 men—who suffered "[a]nxiety states accompanied by fatigue, restlessness and insomnia, including what were called *breakdowns*" (Jacobson, 1967, p. 171).

The self-observational technique that Jacobson developed centers on a tactile-kinesthetic awareness of the tension level of one's specific and overall bodily musculature. Jacobson validated the technique by electroneuromyometry, i.e., the measurement of neuromuscular action potentials. He is in fact credited with being "the first to record the action potentials in the muscles and to show that they vary in a predictable way with mental activity and especially with feelings of tension" (Fishbein in Jacobson, 1967, p. viii). A basic principle of the theory emanating from his experimental findings and clinical practice is quite simple: neuromuscular tension is emotionally laden; "neuromuscular acts participate in mental activities ... including emotions" (Jacobson, 1970, p. 34). It is notable that Jacobson pointedly contrasts his theory with the traditional view of the brain, the view "that all mental activity occurs in the brain alone; that the brain does our thinking, e.g., as the alimentary tract does our digestion", or, as he later says, with the view of those who regard neuromuscular activity "as the tail wagged by the dog" (*ibid.*, p. 32). He calls our attention as well to the error of those who, hearing of the practice of "auto-sensory

---

5   For information on his background, see Jacobson, 1970, pp. xi–xxi. In a paper on the electrophysiology of mental activities, Jacobson mentions "[a] rather amusing comment" made by Lashley: "Lashley told me with a chuckle that when he and Watson would spend an evening together, working out principles of behaviorism, much of the time would be devoted to introspection" (Jacobson, 1973, p. 14; see also Jacobson, 1967, p. 16). Because of its omission of introspection, Jacobson regarded behaviorism "only half a science" (*ibid.*, p. 17).

observation" equate it to "suggestion" by the instructor (*ibid.*). A number of Jacobson's findings are of particular interest, such as "[T]he trained observer (not the tyro) identifies and locates signals of neuromuscular activity as integral parts of the mental act [of "attention, imagination, recall, phantasy, emotion, or any other mental phenomena"]. He does not discern two acts, one so-called "mental" and the other "neuromuscular", but one act only" (*ibid.*, p. 35); and "objective and subjective data indicate conclusively that when the trained observer relaxes the neuromuscular elements apparently specific in any mental activity, the mental activity as such disappears accordingly" (*ibid.*).[6] In sum, Jacobson's fundamental experimental finding—and hence the significance of auto-sensory observation—is that what happens in a brain does not happen apart from muscular innervations. "Those who would do homage to the brain with its ten billion cell-amplifiers can well continue to do so", Jacobson says, but they must also not overlook empirical evidence: that "muscles and brain proceed together in one effort-circuit, active or relaxed" (*ibid.*, pp. 36, 34).

Empirical evidence of a singular muscle-brain "effort-circuit" confirms the basic premise implicit in Darwin's *The Expression of the Emotions in Man and Animals*: movement and emotion proceed hand in hand. The fundamental concordance between the two phenomena lies in the fact that bodily movement is expressive. What Darwin sought to explain in his book was the origin of the concordance on the basis of serviceable habits, the principle of antithesis, and the phenomenon of "nerve-force"; that is, certain movements arise because they are of benefit to the animal, or because they are called forth in opposition to innate kinetic practices, or because of a spontaneity or excess of "nerve-force." Throughout the book, what Darwin basically describes is *movement*. For example, with respect to joy and vivid pleasure, he writes that "there is a strong tendency to various purposeless movements" (Darwin, 1965 [1872], p. 76), and several sentences later remarks,

> Now with animals of all kinds, the acquirement of almost all their pleasures, with the exception of those of warmth and rest, are associated with active movements, as in the hunting or search for food, and in their courtship. Moreover, the mere exertion of the muscles after long rest or confinement is in itself a pleasure, as we ourselves feel, and as we see in the play of young animals. Therefore on this latter princi-

---

6   To assure clarity, I add the following annotation: Jacobson does not say *all* mental activity disappears; he says that "the mental activity as such disappears." The *as such* qualifies the particular mental activity that disappears, i.e., the mental activity ongoing before the onset of relaxation. With all due attention to Jacobson's emphasis upon the necessity of developing capacities in auto-sensory observation and differential relaxation—of being a trained observer, not a tyro—readers might nevertheless try consulting their own experience to corroborate the disappearance of a specific mental activity upon neuromuscular relaxation.

ple alone [the principle of the action of the nervous system] we might
perhaps expect, that vivid pleasure would be apt to show itself conversely [that is, in contrast with long rest and confinement] in
muscular movements (p. 77).

The implicit premise is furthermore explicitly and succinctly attested to in
his remark concerning the variable relationship of movement and emotion: "I need hardly premise that movements or changes in any part of the
body ... may all equally well serve for expression" (*ibid.*, p. 28). In short,
the *expression* of emotion in man and animals is a kinetic phenomenon, a
neuromuscular dynamic that, as we will presently see, has a certain spatiality, temporality, intensity, and manner of execution. This complex
kinetic structure is essentially demonstrated in movement notation analyses by ethologists who thereby capture the dynamics of animal behavior.
The ethological studies of mammalian pre-copulatory interactions
(Golani, 1976) and of the dynamics of wolves fighting (Moran, Fentress,
Golani, 1981) are classics in this respect.

The import of Jacobson's work to Darwin's evolutionary studies of emotion, and to movement-oriented ethological studies as well, lies in the
strong empirical data it presents showing that emotions are grounded in a
neuromuscular dynamic. The dynamic is delineated along further empirical lines in the experimental research of psychiatrist Nina Bull. Bull's work
shows that emotions are shaped by motor attitudes, that "a basic
neuromuscular sequence is essential to the production of affect" (Bull,
1951, p. 79).[7] It demonstrates, and in a striking way, that there is a *generative* as well as *expressive* relationship between movement and emotion. Her
work is in this respect a significant amplification of Darwin's. A summary
account follows.

In a first group of experimental studies showing how a preparatory postural attitude is vital to the feeling of emotion, subjects were hypnotized,
then told "[that] a word denoting a certain emotion would be uttered, that
they would then experience this emotion, that they would show this in
outward behavior in a natural manner", and that they would afterward be
asked to describe what happened (*ibid.*, p. 78). Six emotions were investigated in this manner: fear, anger, disgust, depression, joy, triumph. The

7   Ginsburg and Harrington (1996), in their review of research on bodily states and emotions,
     thoroughly misrepresent Bull's monograph and the experimental work that it details when
     they characterize her view of feeling as a "pause" between "'motor attitude' and instrumental
     action" (p. 249). Bull is at pains to describe emotions as a *process*, and a process that includes
     thinking. Toward the end of her first chapter, with respect to one aspect of that process,
     "attitude-affect," the aspect with which she is particularly concerned, she states that while it
     may seem to be a *state* or a "static quality," attitude-affect is actually "a moving series of
     neuromuscular events, a process which, for want of any better name, we must continue to call
     emotion" (Bull, 1951, p. 13).

subjects' reports validate Bull's thesis that a certain neuromuscular attitude is necessary to, and coincident with, each particular emotion. With
respect to fear, for example, one subject reported "First my jaws tightened,
and then my legs and feet ... my toes bunched up until it hurt .... and ...
well, I was just afraid of something" (*ibid.*, p. 59). With respect to anger,
"subjects mentioned wanting to throw, pound, tear, smash and hit" — and
what restrained them was "always the same, *clenching the hands*" or making some similar restraining movement (*ibid.*, p. 65).[8] It is important to
emphasize that the preparatory postural attitude is in all instances a spontaneously arrived at attitude; what subjects are reporting in each case is
how they were moved. In the succeeding set of experimental studies, hypnotized subjects were read a particular description from one of their own
experiential reports, the description beginning with phrases such as "Your
jaws are tightening" (fear), or "You feel heavy all over" (depression), or
"There is a feeling of relaxation and lightness in your whole body" (joy), or
"You can feel your chest expanding" (triumph), and so on. Following this
initial descriptive reading, the subject was told "You are now locked in
this physical position. There will be no changes in your body — no new
bodily sensations — until I specifically unlock you." The experimenter then
told the subject, "When I count to five I shall utter a word denoting a certain emotion. When you hear the word you will feel this emotion — feel it
naturally — and will be able to tell us about it afterward" (*ibid.*, pp. 79–80).
The emotion the experimenter named was antithetical to the one coincident with the position in which the subject was locked. What the experiment showed is that subjects were unable to have any other feeling than
the one into which they were locked. In other words, they were unable to
feel the designated contrasting emotion, and this because any change in
affect required a change in postural set or bodily attitude. As one subject
said, "I reached for joy — but couldn't get it — so tense"; and as another
said, "I feel light — can't feel depression" (*ibid.*, pp. 84, 85).

8   Of particular significance is Bull's attention to kinetic detail in the form of identifying
conflicting motor attitudes. In anger, there is "a primary compulsion toward aggression or
attack, and a secondary powerful restraint, or holding back, which was always muscular and
attitudinal" (1951, pp. 62–3). Equally divergent but different attitudes are found in fear and in
disgust. Bull speaks of "[t]he jointed character" of disgust (p. 48), the one distinct reaction
being a felt nausea and a preparation for vomiting and the other a turning away or avertive
attitude of the body. Thus, one reaction was "predominantly visceral and the other
predominantly skeletal" (p. 48). Proportions were different in each case so that the overall
experience varied, but "[the] two reactions [were] so closely interwoven as to be apparently
inseparable" (pp. 48–9). Again, in fear, "two separate incompatible reactions [were] going on at
once, but in this case the conflict was between posture and movement within the same
muscular system," both reactions being skeletal rather than skeletal and visceral in nature. The
"*desire to get away* [was] opposed by the *inability to move*" (p. 58).

From a methodological viewpoint, what makes Bulls' study of particular interest is that it utilizes hypnosis to access the experience of emotions. Introspective reports so obtained do not require time-intensive observational training as, for example, Jacobson's introspective auto-sensory observational studies do. Most important, however, are two facts: first, experiences of emotion reported by hypnotized subjects are near indisputable, i.e., there is no reasonable basis for challenging their authenticity; second, experiences so obtained are readily and incontrovertibly detailed as preeminently experiences of the tactile-kinesthetic body. The avertive pattern of disgust, for example, is described by one subject as "I tried to back away — pushed back on the chair — straight back. All the muscles seemed to push straight back. I could feel that rather strong"; the dual character of fear is described by another subject as "I wanted to turn away in the beginning ... I couldn't ... I was too afraid to move ... [my legs were] made of lead ... I couldn't move my hands either. It was as if they were nailed to the chair"; the expansive and powerful character of triumph is described by another subject as "I had an urge to stand on my toes in order to look down on people at a more acute angle" (*ibid.*, pp. 53, 58, 73). With respect to the evidential preeminence of the tactile-kinesthetic body, and to the origin of emotion in a qualitatively felt neuromuscular dynamics,[9] Bull's comment about the subjects' general lack of distinction between bodily feelings and the feeling of an emotion is significant. Although she also remarks that subjects "seemed always aware of a difference", she concludes by saying that "[t]his important matter requires further investigation, and no exact definition of emotional feeling or affect, as distinct from organic sensation, will be attempted at the present time" (*ibid.*, p. 47). In effect, she leaves the question of the relationship between bodily feelings and emotional feelings mid-air. Yet if having a feeling in an emotional sense depends on a certain postural set, a certain tactile-kinesthetic attitude and thus a certain tactile-kinesthetic feel,[10] and if one must get out of

9   Emotions obviously originate in more than a qualitatively felt neuromuscular dynamics. They originate situationally, in the context of other people, particular environments, constricting or enabling circumstances, and so on, each of these variables having its own distinctive cognitive as well as affective dimensions. The focus here is on an invariant subtending these variables, or on what, from an analytic perspective, may be identified as a necessary condition of emotion in the form of corporeal tonicities.

10 Usual counterexamples offered to this line of reasoning concern paraplegics and paralyzed persons. What is not customarily recognized, however, is that persons so afflicted were once not so afflicted. As experimental subjects, there is no doubt but that their testimony is conditioned by previous experience: they know what it is like to feel anger, fear, and so on, in a full bodily felt sense. (It is telling that most people do not realize — or they commonly forget — that Helen Keller was not blind and deaf from birth, but became blind and deaf when she was 19 months old. Fundamental experiences and learnings in the first months and years of life can be neither ignored nor discounted.) It is furthermore apparent from the empirical

this tactile-kinesthetic attitude and feel in order to have a different emotion, then clearly, definitions and distinctions are less important than the recognition and descriptive analysis of a basic corporeal matter of fact: *affective feelings and tactile-kinesthetic feelings are experientially intertwined.* That subjects generally do not distinguish between the two feelings is testimony to the fact that they are regularly experienced holistically, not as piece-meal parts that become progressively apparent, and not as causally sequenced phenomena, but integrally. It thus suggests that bodily feelings and feelings of emotion are divisible only reflectively, after the experience. Further, as the experimental evidence shows, affective feelings are consistently true to tactile-kinesthetic dynamics; the two sets of feelings are mutually congruent. Their congruency defines the character or nature of their intertwinement. The summary phenomenological analysis of movement that will presently follow lays the groundwork for elucidating the foundational dynamics undergirding the congruency.

Now a postural attitude is defined by Bull as a readiness to do something, a corporeal readiness to act in some way or other, and it is this postural attitude that is the generative source of emotion (Cf. Varela 1999, pp. 132–3 on "ontological readiness" and "readiness potential"; Sheets-Johnstone, 1999, Chapter 9, on "readiness toward meaning").[11] The postural attitude is thus coincident with what might be designated the onset of emotion: *with a felt urge to do something* — approach something, strike something, touch something, run from something, and so on. Emotion, then, is not *identical* to kicking, embracing, running away, and so on, but is, from the beginning by way of the postural attitude, the motivational-affective source of such actions.[12] As such it might be conceived within Bull's analy-

studies cited in the present text that some kind of preparation is necessary to obtaining veridical reports on the tactile-kinesthetic body, and this because adults, especially Western ones, are notoriously afflicted with Cartesian disease. In other words, adults need to be trained to attend to their bodies and to be meticulous observers. This applies to all persons involved in introspecting tactile-kinesthetic experience.

11   Specific attention should be called to the fact that the postural readiness to act is a *spontaneous* bodily happening, not a voluntary cultivated one. Attention too should be called to the fact that *readiness* is a phenomenon in dire need of recognition and study by cognitivists and researchers generally in the area of cognition and semantics. Readiness is obviously related to attention — one of the "mental powers" itemized by Darwin (Darwin, 1981 [1871]), and to receptivity, a fundamental dimension of experience analyzed by Husserl (1973b) in terms of *turning toward*. Implicit in both Darwin's and Husserl's accounts is a recognition of living bodies, i.e., readiness is a phenomenon that is anchored in living bodies and being so anchored, is a phenomenon that necessarily requires the study and understanding of animate form.

12   The movements of grief and of joy are not actions but precisely movements. In effect, there is no less a distinctive postural readiness to the having of these and other such emotions. The body folds heavily inward in grief, for example, in contrast to its expansive lightness in joy. Hence, "preparation for action" may in some instances be a certain postural readiness and corporeal tonicity tied not to action but to a purely qualitative kinetics or kinetic form — a way of being a body.

sis as the necessary substrate or foundation of action. An observation by Darwin succinctly illustrates this point. Darwin writes that "[W]hen we start at any sudden sound or sight, almost all the muscles of the body are involuntarily and momentarily thrown into strong action, for the sake of guarding ourselves against or jumping away from the danger, which we habitually associate with anything unexpected" (Darwin, 1965, p. 284). The action itself, that is, the "guarding ourselves against" or "jumping away from" is not the feeling nor does it generate the feeling; the guarding or the jumping are its expression. By the same token, the "strong action" of the postural attitude—"all the muscles of the body are involuntarily and momentarily thrown into strong action"—is what makes the guarding or jumping possible. Without the readiness to act in a certain way, without certain *corporeal tonicities*, a certain feeling would not, and indeed, could not be felt, and a certain action would not, and indeed, could not be taken, since the postural dynamics of the body are what make the feeling and the action possible.

Psychologist Joseph de Rivera's "'geometry of emotions" (Dahl in de Rivera, 1977, p. 4) provides further documentation of the essential relationship between emotion and movement, and in ways that both corroborate and extend Bull's experimental studies. His "geometry" or structural theory of emotions rests on two fundamental observations: when we experience emotion, "we experience ourselves ... as *being moved*" (*ibid.*, p. 11, italics in original; see also, among others,[13] Sartre, 1948, p. 15: "[T]he phenomenologist will interrogate emotion ... He will ask it not only what it is but what it has to teach us about a being, one of whose characteristics is exactly that he is capable of *being moved*" [italics added]); and when we examine our experience, we discover "different movements of the emotions" and in turn can specify "the nature of the movement that each [emotion] manifests" (de Rivera, 1977, pp. 35, 38). De Rivera elaborates the first observation when he writes that "the paradox of emotional experience" is that "we are passively being moved rather than acting and yet this movement seems to be coming from *within* us" (*ibid.*, p. 12). He does not inquire specifically into the provenience of this *coming from within*; he does not trace its roots to Jacobson's felt bodily tensions, to Bull's felt neuromuscular dynamics, or to what I have identified phenomenologically as the tactile-kinesthetic body, but it is clear that he recognizes this *generative* source of emotions even as he focuses on what he defines as the transformative nature of emotion (they transform our relation to the world [*ibid.*, p. 35]), and even as he fuses, or perhaps better, prematurely fuses and thus confuses "the movement of emotions" and emotional transfor-

13   See below in this text: emotions "happen" to us (Ekman, Davidson, Friesen, 1990).

mations. His recognition of a tactile-kinesthetic dynamics — of the coming
from within as a postural attitude that engenders an urge to move in certain ways — is evident in the corporeal illustration he gives of the four basic
differential movements of emotion. The illustration implicitly specifies,
and in concrete kinetic terms, the coming from within. Presented in the
chapter "The Movements of the Emotions," the illustration names four
fundamental kinetic relations — what we might designate four basic *kinetic
forms* — that can obtain between subject and object and that are instanced in
the feelings of anger, fear, affection, and desire. De Rivera's illustration of
the differences between and among these forms is firmly anchored in common, everyday bodily movement experiences and warrants full quotation:

> It is intriguing that the distinction between these four basic relations
> [of anger, fear, affection, and desire, which he delineates in terms of
> moving against or away from an object in the first two instances and in
> terms of moving toward an object in the second two instances] may be
> captured by different bodily movements of extension and contraction.
> If the arms are held out in a circle so that the finger tips almost touch,
> they may either be brought toward the body (a movement of contrac-
> tion) or moved out in an extension. The entire trunk may follow these
> movements. [So also, we might add, may one's legs, and thus one's
> whole body.] Now if the palms are facing in, the extension movement
> corresponds to a moving toward the other — a giving — as in tender-
> ness, while the contraction movement suggests a movement toward
> the self — a getting — as in longing. If the palms are rotated out, the
> extension movement corresponds to the thrusting against of anger,
> while the contraction intimates the withdrawal away of fear ... If one
> allows oneself to become involved in the movement and imagines an
> object, one may experience the corresponding emotion (*ibid.*, p. 40).

On the basis of these "four basic emotional movements" (*ibid.*, p. 41), de
Rivera elaborates a complex structure of emotions that includes consideration of a subject's emotions toward him/herself (emotions such as shame
and pride), of emotions as fluid or fixed, of movement from one emotion to
another, and so on. The point of moment here is not the complex interrelated structure that de Rivera progressively builds, but the basic kinetic
structure underlying the whole: *all emotions resolve themselves into
extensional or contractive movement*, movement that goes either toward or
against or away from an object, including the object that is oneself. The
simple self-demonstration that de Rivera describes aptly captures this
basic kinetic structure and with it, the quintessential kinetic dynamics of
emotion. It does so through a recognition of the spatiality inherent in the
generative kinetic form of emotions: we are moved to move toward or
against or away; we are moved basically to extend or to contract ourselves.
The correspondence between the spatiality of these basic movements and
the spatiality expressed in statements of Bull's subjects is transparent: they

say not only that "I reached for joy—but couldn't get it—so tense", but "My chest was expanded and held out"; "I wanted to pound the table or throw something, but I clasped my hand instead"; "I tried to back away—pushed back on the chair—straight back. All the muscles seemed to push straight back" (Bull, 1951, pp. 143, 146, 53); and so on. The spatial dimension of movement is thematic and palpably evident in these statements. But spatiality is only one dimension of movement; temporality, intensity, and the projectional character of movement are basic dimensions as well. The global phenomenon of movement is compounded of dynamically interrelated elements that together constitute the fundamental dynamic congruency of emotion and motion. Indeed, emotions are from this perspective *possible kinetic forms of the tactile-kinesthetic body*. This is the direction in which all of the empirical research points. A phenomenological analysis of movement will elucidate the dynamic structure underlying these possible kinetic forms.

3. The Phenomenology of Movement: A Summary Account

When we bracket our natural attitude toward movement,[14] which includes suspending the object-tethered, dynamically empty, and in turn epistemologically and metaphysically skewed definition of movement as "a change of position",[15] and turn our attention to a phenomenological analysis of the *experience* of movement, we find a complex of four basic qualities: tensional, linear, amplitudinal, and projectional (Sheets-Johnstone, 1966 [1979/1980], 1999). These qualities, separable only analytically, inhere in the global experience of any movement, including most prominently our experience of self-movement. Any time we care to notice them, there they are. We shall take an everyday experience of moving ourselves—walking—as a "transcendental clue" (Husserl, 1973a; see also Sheets-Johnstone, 1999), that is, as a point of departure for a summary phenomenological analysis of movement.

Walking is a dynamic phenomenon whose varying qualities are easily and plainly observable by us: we walk in a determined manner, with firm, unswerving, measured steps; we walk in a jaunty manner with light, cambering, exaggerated steps; we walk in a disturbed manner with tense, erratic steps that go off now in this direction, now in that, and that are now tightly-concentrated, now dispersed; we walk in a regular walking-to-

---

14   For a detailed account of bracketing (the phenomenological *epoché*), see Sheets-Johnstone 1999, Chapter 4: Husserl and Von Helmholtz—and the Possibility of a Trans-Disciplinary Communal Task.

15   What changes position are objects in motion, not movement. Movement is thus not equivalent to objects in motion (see Sheets-Johnstone 1979, 1999).

get-some-place manner with easy, flowing, striding steps. Tensional, linear, amplitudinal, and projectional qualities of movement are present in
each instance and in each instance define a particular dynamic.[16] With the
recognition of these qualities comes a beginning appreciation of their complexity and of their seemingly limitless interrelationships — and an appreciation as well of the fiction and vacuity of defining movement as "a
change of position" much less of conceiving it as output. As the examples
of walking indicate, movement is a variable phenomenon because it is an
inherently complex dynamic phenomenon. Motor physiologists have long
recognized this fact in what they term "the degrees of freedom problem"
(Bernstein, 1984). The problem is aptly designated phenomenologically
"the kinesthetic motivation problem" (Sheets-Johnstone, 1999): we can
raise our arm from the wrist, from the elbow, from the shoulder, for example, with different possible tensions and amplitudes, different possible
speeds, in different possible directions, and so on. Regarded in the
phenomenological attitude, movement is both a variable-because-com-
plex and complex-because-variable dynamic happening, an experience
which, as indicated, is there any time we care to notice it.[17]

By the very nature of its spatio-temporal-energic dynamic, bodily movement is a *formal* happening. Even a sneeze has a certain formal dynamic in
which certain suddennesses and suspensions of movement are felt aspects
of the experience. Form is the result of the qualities of movement and of
the way in which they modulate and play out dynamically. In a very general sense, tensional quality has to do with our felt effort in moving; linear
quality with both the felt linear contour of our moving body and the linear
paths we describe in the process of moving, thus, with the directional
aspect of our movement; amplitudinal quality with both the felt expan-

---

16 Languaging the dynamics of movement is a challenging task, perhaps more so than
    languaging any other phenomenon one investigates phenomenologically. Pinpointing the
    exact character of a kinetic experience is not a truth-in-packaging matter; the process of moving
    is not reducible to a set of ingredients. The challenge derives in part from an object-tethered
    English language that easily misses or falls short of the temporal, spatial, and energic
    qualitative dynamics of movement.

17 A reviewer called my attention to a paper by Georgieff and Jeannerod in connection with his
    concern that "it is not obvious that kinesthesia ALONE could be responsible for awareness of
    movement as self-initiated." The paper by Georgieff and Jeannerod (http://www.isc.cnrs.fr/
    wp/wpjea9805.htm) in part concludes that "normal subjects appear to be unable to
    consciously monitor the signals generated by their own movement" (p. 4). The experiment on
    which the conclusion is based, however, assumes a key element that needs to be investigated
    and taken into account, namely, attention (cf. Darwin 1981 [1871]). What one attends to is what
    one is conscious of: if one's attention is visually tethered to a visual desired result (and given
    "the well known dominance of visual information over information from other modalities," a
    point that Georgieff and Jeannerod themselves make http://www.isc.cnrs.fr/wp/
    wpjea9805.htm, p. 4), kinesthetic awareness will be proportionately lessened. The conclusion,
    in effect, is vitiated by oversight of a key "mental power" (Darwin 1981 [1871], pp. 44–5).

siveness or contractiveness of our moving body and the spatial extensiveness or constrictedness of our movement, thus, with the magnitude of our movement; projectional quality with the manner in which we release force or energy — in a sustained manner, for example, in an explosive manner, in a ballistic manner, in a punctuated manner, and so on. Linear and amplitudinal qualities obviously constitute spatial aspects of movement; temporal aspects of movement are a complex of projectional and tensional qualities. It is of singular moment to note that movement *creates* the qualities it embodies and that we experience. In effect, movement does not simply takes place *in* space and *in* time. We qualitatively create a certain spatial character by the very nature of our movement — a large open space or a tight resistant space, for example, a spatial difference readily suggestive of the distinctive spatialities of joy and fear. Analogous relationships hold with respect to the created temporal character of movement — a hurried and staccato flow of movement, for example, or a leisurely and relatively unpunctuated flow, temporal differences readily suggestive of the distinctive temporalities of agitation and calmness. In sum, particular energies, spatialities, and temporalities come into play with self-movement and together articulate a particular qualitative dynamic.

4. The Dynamic Congruency

As the examples of walking show, the formal dynamics of movement are articulated in and through the qualities of movement as they are created in the act of moving. The challenge now is to demonstrate concretely how dynamic kinetic forms are congruent with dynamic forms of feeling — how motion and emotion, each formally distinctive experiences, are of a dynamic piece. Because it is a common and well-researched emotion, I will use *fear* to illustrate the dynamic congruency.

Phenomenologically, it is sufficient to imagine oneself fearing (Husserl, 1983, Section 4) — as in being pursued by an unknown assailant at night in a deserted area of a city[18] — in order to begin studying the kinetic dynamics of fear. A beginning phenomenological account of the kinetic experience might run as follows:

> An intense and unceasing whole-body tension drives the body forward. It is quite unlike the tension one feels in a jogging run, for instance, or in a run to greet someone. There is a hardness to the whole body that congeals it into a singularly tight mass; the driving speed of

18   Obviously, this is only one possible example. A complete phenomenological analysis requires "free variations" (Husserl, 1977, 1973a), or in other words, consideration of multiple experiences of fear in order to identify invariants. A complete analysis would thus entail, for example, consideration of instances in which one is paralyzed with fear as well as mobilized by it.

the movement condenses airborne and impact moments into a singular continuum of motion. The head-on movement is at times erratic; there are sudden changes of direction. With these changes the legs move suddenly apart, momentarily widening the base of support and bending at the knee, so that the whole body is lowered. The movement is each time abrupt. It breaks the otherwise unrelenting and propulsive speed of movement. The body may suddenly swerve, dodge, twist, duck, or crouch, and the head may swivel about before the forward plunging run with its acutely concentrated and unbroken energies continues.

Compare this brief phenomenological description of fear to the description of Martina's fear on experiencing a change in accustomed habit. Ethologist Konrad Lorenz writes:

> One evening I forgot to let Martina [a greylag goose] in ... and when I finally remembered ... I ran to the front door, and as I opened it she thrust herself hurriedly and anxiously through, ran between my legs into the hall and ... to the stairs ... [A]rriving at the fifth step, she suddenly stopped ... and spread her wings as for flight. Then she uttered a warning cry and very nearly took off. Now she hesitated a moment, turned around, ran hurriedly down the five steps and set forth resolutely ... (Lorenz, 1967, pp. 65, 66–7)

Compare it to the fear of Temple in novelist William Faulkner's *Sanctuary*:

> She surged and plunged, grinding the woman's hand against the door jamb until she was free. She sprang from the porch and ran towards the barn and into the hallway and climbed the ladder and scrambled through the trap and to her feet again, running towards the pile of rotting hay. Then suddenly she ran upside-down in a rushing interval; she could see her legs running in space, and she struck lightly and solidly on her back and lay still ... (1953, pp. 75–6).

Descriptions of the dynamics of fear illustrate in each instance how the four basic qualities of movement inhere in an ongoing kinetic dynamic and how that dynamic is through and through congruent with the dynamics of fear: its felt urgency, clutchedness, stops and starts, desire for escape, sense of sudden impending disaster coming from everywhere and nowhere, and so on. In short, movement qualities can be described (and both more finely and more extensively than in the brief sketches above); and *fear* movement can in turn be distinctively detailed, and in different species as well as different instances. This is essentially because movement is movement—it is analytically the same in all instances—and because fear moves us—living creatures, animate forms—as all emotions move us: to move in ways coincident with its felt dynamics. Dynamics vary because fear itself varies: the clutchedness of fear may predominate over the desire for escape; urgency may be extreme at one moment or in one situation and far less pressing in another; and so on. Moreover each particular experience unfolds in a particular way, articulating a particular overall formal dynamic that begins in a certain way from a certain here-now other emotion,[19] that waxes and wanes, or is attenuated, heightened, reinforced, compounded, intensified, or unexpectedly calmed. Whatever the particular instance, when fear "happens" to us (Ekman, Davidson, and Friesen, 1990), i.e., when it moves us, we move in ways qualitatively congruent with the way(s) in which we are moved to move; spatial, temporal, and energic qualities of our movement carry us forward in an ongoing kinetic form that is dynamically congruent with the form of our ongoing feelings. Unified by a single dynamics, the two modes of experience happen at once; simultaneity of affect and movement is made possible by a shared dynamics.

It is evident, then, that a particular kinetic form of an emotion is not identical with the emotion but is dynamically congruent with it. Because there is a *formal* congruency, one can separate out the emotion — the felt affective aspect and the postural attitude that generates it, or allows it to generate — from the kinetic form that expresses it. An emotion may thus be corporeally experienced, on the one hand, even though it is not carried forth into movement, and it may be mimed, on the other hand, but not actually experienced.[20] In other words, one can inhibit the movement dynamics toward which one feels inclined — opening one's arms, moving quickly forward, and hugging; or throwing one's arms upward, wheeling about, and pacing; and equally, one can go through the motions of emotion — opening one's arms, moving quickly forward, and hugging; or throwing one's arms upward, wheeling about, and pacing — without experiencing the emotion itself.[21] The dual possibilities testify unmistakably to the dynamic congruency of emotion and motion. Corporeal tonicities are congruent with specific emotions from the beginning, as Bull's research shows. Whether and how one gives kinetic form to these tonicities is a matter of choice.[22] The two options appear to have different origins. With

---

19   Limited space precludes showing how emotion is continuous rather than a set of neatly packaged states that descend on us individually every so often.

20   One can precipitate autonomic nervous system activity, however, merely by "putting on a face." See Levenson, Ekman, Friesen, 1990; Ekman, Levenson, Friesen, 1983

21   The striking power of movement in dance to present us with the semblance of emotion (Langer, 1953) through the choreographic formalization of a kinetic dynamics is testimonial to the latter possibility (see also Sheets-Johnstone 1966 [1979/1980]). Martha Graham's *Lamentation* is a classic example.

22   Whether and how one moves (or, in highly simplified third-person behavioral terms, whether and how a person acts, e.g., aggressively, friendly, or disgustedly, for example, and what actions a person performs, e.g., pounding, patting, or turning away) are possibilities over and above the corporeal tonicities themselves in that whether and how one moves are both volitional. However much one is moved to move, and however much one is a creature of habit, one can elect to move — angrily or compassionately, for example — or not to move, e.g., to be

respect to inhibition, one ordinarily learns in childhood that to avoid certain unwanted consequences, self-restraint is desirable. However, precisely in these circumstances, one may learn to simulate — to go through the motions of — what parents or other adults deem proper. While inhibition is actively learned, that is, a child is taught to restrain him/herself from e.g., hitting, no one teaches a child to dissemble or simulate, e.g., to move compliantly when she/he feels like hitting. A child learns this from her/his own experience and intuitively practices the art of movement deception.[23] The dual possibilities not only testify to dynamic congruence; they underscore the fact that what is affective is kinetic or potentially kinetic, and that what is kinetic is affective or potentially affective. Restraining movement and simulating emotion attest to each fact respectively.

5. Methodological Significance of a Whole-Body Dynamics

The kinetic dynamics of emotion may be studied objectively through the use of a movement notation system. The possibility is not entirely new (see review of nonverbal behavior studies in Rosenfeld, 1982), but its methodological significance for empirical studies of emotion has not been recognized, in large measure because the fundamental congruity of emotion and motion has been neither acknowledged nor examined. To elucidate the significance, consider first some well-known empirical data.

Fear "is the dominant component of anxiety"; it measures the highest tensional mean of all emotional situations; it "brings about a tensing and tightening of muscles and other motor mechanisms, and in terror the individual may 'freeze' and become immobile" (Izard, 1977, pp. 378, 366, 365). Psychologist Carroll Izard amplifies these basic empirical findings, stating that "Intense fear is the most dangerous of all emotion conditions" and that "The innate releasors or natural clues for fear include being alone, strangeness, height, sudden approach, sudden change of stimuli, and pain" (p. 382).[24] The data bear out and broaden Jacobson's studies of anxi-

---

indifferent, or uninvolved, which kinetically means turning away in some manner, averting one's eyes, and so on. One is, in short, always responsible for one's movement (behavior).

23 See von Helmholtz (1971 [1870]) and Husserl (1980) on intuition and its distinction from reasoned processes of thought.

24 Todd (1937, p. 274): "The terrified cat at the top of the elm, his muscular strength greatly enhanced by his adrenalin secretion, stops digesting because of his more pressing needs. Rescue him, and he curls up in his corner and is soon fast asleep, recovering his equilibrium. Man, however, being the only animal that can be afraid all the time, prolongs his conflicts even after the danger is past. Proust died of introspection long before he died of pneumonia, burned out by the chemistry of seven volumes of "Remembrance of Things Past." See also Averill (1996, p. 218): "[F]ear: no animal has as many as man, not only of concrete, earthly dangers, but also of a whole pantheon of spirits and imaginary evils as well."

ety. With respect to felt bodily experiences of fear, however, they fall far short of what Bull's subjects offer. While facial expression is described, and extensively so, the body is not, except to say that "The person feels a high degree of tension and a moderate degree of impulsiveness" (p. 383).

Bodily movements coincident with emotion are different from both facial expression and autonomic nervous system activity, these phenomena being the prime focus of empirical studies of emotion. Studies of the former present emotion in the form of visual stills and deduced facial muscle involvement; studies of the latter measure physiological responses.[25] Neither focus on the *whole-body experience* of emotion, which means neither focus on the felt experience of being moved and moving. This is *not* to minimize the far-reaching epistemological value and significance of studies of facial expression or of autonomic nervous system activity vis à vis emotions. It is rather to call attention to the near complete lack of attendance to the felt bodily experience of emotion as in Bull's studies, to the felt kinetic unfolding or bodily process of emotion as adumbrated in de Rivera's "movement of emotion", and to the twin formal dynamics of being moved and moving as evident both in the above descriptive accounts and in diverse literatures generally.[26] In fact, by itself, our immediate and untroubled comprehension of descriptions of emotion — descriptions regularly given in primatological studies, ethological studies, and in all manner of literature on humans — calls attention to the foundational grounding of emotion in motion, which is to say in the experience of our own kinetic/tactile-kinesthetic bodies. How else explain our untutored understanding of a tightly tensed running body that suddenly stops, turns, swivels, then pitches on, or of a goose's "hurried" and "anxious" stop-and-start movements, or of a character's "surging", "plunging", "grinding", "springing", "scrambling" movements? We know immediately — in our muscles and bones — what it is to be pursued, to experience sudden and disruptive change, to be trapped; we know in a bodily felt

25   With respect to physiological studies, it is worthwhile pointing out that various researchers localize emotions in the (primitive) brain, especially the limbic system, and that the practice of localization is not without criticism. After considering various localization scenarios, Averill (1996, p. 221) comments that "As Von Holst and Saint-Paul (1960) have emphasized, questions of 'how' and 'why' are too frequently turned into the seemingly more simple problem of 'where'." He goes on to remark, "The recent past has been a period of great neuroanatomical progress, made possible by advances in electronic recording and stimulating devices; unfortunately there is little sign of corresponding progress in the conceptualization of psychophysiological relationships. The macroscopic phrenology of Gall and Spurzheim may be dead, but a kind of microscopic phrenology is alive and well in many a neurophysiological laboratory."

26   The lack is occasionally recognized: e.g., Ginsburg and Harrington (1996, p. 245): "There is a relative dearth of systematic research on the relationships between (sic) emotions and movements and postures."

sense what it is to be—in a word—fearful. Indeed, we recognize fear in these purely kinetic descriptions in the same way that experimental subjects recognize fear on being shown composite photographs of faces with widely opened eyes, raised and pulled together brows, and drawn-back lips, and who furthermore recognize their own facial expression of fear on being asked to make these composite gestures themselves (Ekman, Levenson, Friesen, 1983; Levenson, Ekman, and Friesen, 1990). *We recognize the kinetics of fear on the basis of our own kinetic/tactile-kinesthetic bodily experiences of fear.* Primatologist Jane Goodall documents this fact straightaway and more broadly when, in describing a variety of intraspecific whole-body emotional comportments in a chimpanzee society, she states, "We make these judgements [about how a chimpanzee is feeling] because the similarity of so much of a chimpanzee's behaviour to our own permits us to empathize" (Goodall, 1990, p. 17).

To omit attention to a *whole-body* dynamics is to reduce the dynamics of emotion—and more particularly, the dynamic form of an emotion as it unfolds—to a single expressive moment or to isolated internal bodily happenings. It is to de-temporalize what is by nature temporal or processual. Correlatively, it is to skew the evolutionary significance of emotion, which is basically not to communicate, but *to motivate action.* Sperry's principal finding—that the brain is an organ of and for movement—is central to this evolutionary understanding. Not only is the social significance of emotion, i.e., the value of letting others know how one feels and of knowing how others feel, contingent on being social animals, a comparatively late evolutionary development, but knowledge of the feelings of others is itself tied to movement. "Fearful behavior"—a "display" of emotion or what primatologist Stuart Altmann more generally and rightfully terms "comsigns" (Altmann, 1967; see also Sheets-Johnstone, 1990)—is articulated in bodily movement. Being articulated in bodily movement, it has a distinctive kinetic form recognizable by others. Indeed, like all communicative emotional behaviors, "fear behavior" *originates in movement*, movement that is communal in the sense of being performed or performable by conspecifics, movement that thus falls within the "I cans" or movement possibilities of the species and on that basis is immediately meaningful to all—*a comsign.* In short, emotional behaviors are fundamentally kinetic bodily happenings that originate in experiences of being moved to move and that evolve kinetically. Their communicative value is an evolutionary outgrowth of what is already there: motivations (from Latin *movere*, to move) are felt dispositions or urges to move in certain ways—to strike or to back away, or to peer, stalk, touch, snatch, or squeeze. To say that the social derives from what is evolutionarily given is to say that it derives from species-specific kinetic/tactile-kinesthetic bodies (Sheets-Johnstone, 1994; see also Ekman, 1994; Ekman and Davidson, 1994).

In sum, emotions are prime motivators: animate creatures "behave" because they feel themselves moved to move. Short of this motivation, the social significance of emotion would be nil. What would be the value of knowing another's feelings or of another knowing one's own if in each instance the knowledge was kinetically and affectively sterile, generating nothing in the way of interest, curiosity, flight, excitement, amicability, fear, agitation, and so on?[27]

Movement notation systems allow empirical study of a whole-body kinetic process in ways that would provide insight into the *differential dynamics of emotions*. In Labananalysis and Labanotation especially, both the *what* and the *how* of movement is notated, thus not merely a flexing of the knee or a twisting of the torso (Labananalysis), for example, but the manner in which the knee is flexed or the torso is twisted (Labanotation or Effort/Shape). In effect, one could specify both the qualitative dynamics of movement and the formal dynamics of emotion as they are simultaneously played out. One could thereby demonstrate empirically the dynamic congruency of movement and emotion in real-life. It bears noting that through the use of movement notation systems, dynamic congruency can be elucidated in species-specific ways that draw our attention to kinetic domains (Sheets-Johnstone 1983, 1999), thus to similarities and differences among and between species. Moreover dynamic congruency can be elucidated in culture-specific ways, allowing one to distinguish what is evolutionarily given from what is culturally transformed — exaggerated, suppressed, neglected, or distorted (Sheets-Johnstone, 1994). Insofar as one can find only what one's methodology allows one to find and to know only what one's methodology allows one to know, the value of movement notation systems to the empirical study of emotion is self-evident: the systems offer a methodology proper to *dynamical* studies of emotion, emotion as it is actually experienced in the throes, trials, and pleasures of everyday life. In this respect, they offer the possibility of a complete empirical science of emotion, a science that, not incidentally, is capable of addressing evolutionary and cultural questions on the basis of detailed pan-species and pan-human empirical evidence.

6. Implications for Cognitivism

Emotions move us, and in moving us are quintessentially linked to kinetic/tactile-kinesthetic bodies. Preceding sections have shown that

---

27 Limited space precludes showing that interest, curiosity, excitement, and other such feelings are no less emotions than fear and anger.

they are clearly tied to animation and to kinetic possibilities of animate life. Broad but conceptually fundamental implications follow from this beginning analysis. The characterization of living organisms as information processors or algorithmic machines and in turn as things whose various mechanisms can be thoroughly explained by studies of brains and behavior, i.e., *in exclusion of experience, which means in exclusion of phenomenological and empirically-focused investigations and analyses of experience*, skews an understanding of animate life. Calling attention to this experientially deficient understanding, the foregoing analysis has the following implications for cognitivism:

(1) Movement is not behavior; experience is not physiological activity;[28] and a brain is not a body. What emerges and evolves — ontogenetically and phylogenetically — is not behavior but movement, movement that is neatly partitioned and classified as behavior by observers, but that is in its own right the basic phenomenon to be profitably studied; what is of moment to living creatures is not physiology per se but real-life bodily happenings that resonate tactilely and kinesthetically, which is to say experientially; what feels and is moved to move is not a brain but a living organism.

(2) A movement-deficient understanding of emotion is an impoverished understanding of emotion. Being whole-body phenomena, emotions require a methodology capable of capturing kinetic form. When serious attention is turned to kinetic form and to the qualitative complexities of movement, emotions are properly recognized as dynamic forms of feeling, kinesthesia is properly recognized a dimension of cognition, cognition is properly recognized a dimension of animation, and animation is no longer regarded mere output but the proper point of departure for the study of life.

(3) Movement notation systems provide real-life as opposed to computational or engineering conceptions and mappings of animal movement. Modeled movement is no match for a real-life kinetics, which alone can provide detailed understandings of the spatio-temporal-energic dimensions of movement itself and of the dynamics of kinetic relationships and contexts.

---

28   A standard text, *Understanding the Scientific Bases of Human Movement*, inadvertently makes this distinction in such a striking way in a chapter titled "The Proprioceptors and Their Associated Reflexes" that it warrants citation. The text states that "Voluntary movement requires a foundation of automatic responses which assure a proper combination of mobility and stability of body parts," and that "Fortunately, neural control of muscles ... is mostly involuntary" (Gowitzke and Milner, 1988, p. 256). The emphasis on the neural intricacies of coordinated movement is well taken as is the emphasis on the integrated action of individual muscles. However, the authors go on to state that "The voluntary contribution to movement is almost entirely limited to initiation, regulation of speed, force, range, and direction, and termination of the movement" (*ibid.*). The "limited contribution" is in fact sizable, so much so that investigation of the rich and complex spatio-temporal-energic structures inherent in the experience of movement can hardly be ignored.

(4) The penchant to talk about and to explain ourselves and/or aspects of ourselves as embodied — as in "embodied connectionism" (Bechtel, 1997), and even as in "embodied mind" (Varela, Thompson, and Rosch, 1991; Lakoff and Johnson, 1999), "embodied schema" (Johnson, 1987), "embodied agents", "embodied actions" (Varela, 1999), and "phenomenological embodiment" (Lakoff and Johnson, 1999) — evokes not simply the possibility of a disembodied relationship and of near or outright tautologies as in "embodied agents", "embodied actions", and "the embodied mind is part of the living body" (Lakoff and Johnson, 1999, p. 565), but the spectre of Cartesianism. In this sense, the term *embodied* is a lexical band-aid covering a three-hundred-fifty-year-old wound generated and kept suppurating by a schizoid metaphysics. It evades the arduous and (by human lifetime standards) infinite task of clarifying and elucidating the nature of living nature from the ground up. Animate forms are the starting point of biological evolution. They are where life begins. They are where animation begins. They are where concepts begin. They are where emotions are rooted, not in something that might be termed "mental life" (e.g., Canabac, 1998, p. 184: "emotion is a mental feeling"), a "mental" that is or might be embodied in some form or other, but in animate forms to begin with. *Embodiment* deflects our attention from the task of understanding animate forms by conceptual default, by conveniently packaging beforehand something already labeled "the mental" or "mind" and something already labeled "the physical" or "body" without explaining — to paraphrase Edelman (1992, p. 15) — "how 'the package' got there in the first place" (cf. Sheets-Johnstone 1998, 1999).

5) Machines are sessile systems/devices anchored in one place as animate creatures are precisely *not* anchored. Robots are not forms of life to whom emotions happen but remote-control puppets to which signals are sent; they are not *moved* to move, but are *programmed* to move. Zombies are even more remote, being mere intellectual figments plumped with sound and fury but signifying nothing pertinent to understandings of animate life. In this respect, the hard problem is to forego thought experiments and to listen assiduously to our bodies, and to observe phenomenologically and empirically what is going on. The hard problem is to give animate form and the qualitative character of life their due. More broadly, the hard problem is to see ourselves and all forms of life as intact organisms, living bodies, rather than as brains or machines. We come into the world moving; moving and feeling moved to move are what are gone when we die. Surely when we lament or fear our own death, we do not lament or fear that we will have no more information to process. We lament or fear that we will no longer be *animate* beings but merely material stuff — *lifeless, unmoved,*

and unmoving. Nature is "a principle of motion", as Aristotle recognized, and kinetic form is its natural expression.

References

Altmann, Stuart. 1967. 'The structure of primate social communication,' in *Social Communication Among Primates*, ed. Stuart A. Altmann (Chicago: University of Chicago Press).

Aristotle *Physics*, trans. R.P. Hardie and R.K. Gaye, in *The Complete Works of Aristotle*, ed. Jonathan Barnes (Princeton: Princeton University Press).

Averill, James R. 1996. 'An analysis of psychophysiological symbolism and its influence on theories of emotion,' in *The Emotions*, ed. R. Harré and W.G. Parrott (London: Sage Publications).

Bechtel, William. 1997. 'Embodied connectionism,' in *The Future of the Cognitive Revolution*, ed. David Martel Johnson and Christina E. Erneling (New York: Oxford University Press).

Bernstein, Nicolas. 1984. *Human Motor Actions: Bernstein Reassessed*, ed. H.T.A. Whiting (New York: Elsevier Science Publishing Co).

Bruner, Jerome. 1990. *Acts of Meaning* (Cambridge, MA: Harvard University Press).

Bull, Nina. 1951. *The Attitude Theory of Emotion* (New York: Nervous and Mental Disease Monographs [Coolidge Foundation]).

Cabanac, Michel. 1999. 'Emotion and phylogeny', *Journal of Consciousness Studies*, 6 (6–7), pp. 176–190.

Carlson, Neil R. 1992. *Foundations of Physiological Psychology* (Boston, MA: Allyn and Bacon).

Clynes, Manfred. 1980. 'The communication of emotion: Theory of sentics', in *Emotion: Theory, Research, and Experience, vol. I, Theories of Emotion*, ed. R. Plutchik and H. Kellerman (New York: Academic Press).

Crick, Francis and Koch, Christof. 1992. 'The problem of consciousness', *Scientific American* 267/3: pp. 153–159.

Dahl, Hartvig. 1977. 'Considerations for a theory of emotions', in de Rivera (1977).

Darwin, Charles. 1965 [1872]. *The Expression of the Emotions in Man and Animals* (Chicago: University of Chicago Press).

Darwin, Charles. 1981 [1871]. *The Descent of Man and Selection in Relation to Sex* (Princeton: Princeton University Press).

de Rivera, Joseph. 1977. *A Structural Theory of the Emotions* (New York: International Universities Press).

Edelman, Gerald. 1992. *Bright Air, Brilliant Fire* (New York: Basic Books).

Ekman, Paul. 1994. 'Strong evidence for universals in facial expressions: A reply to Russell's mistaken critique', *Psychological Bulletin*, 115 (2), pp. 268–87.

Ekman, Paul and Davidson, Richard J. Ed. 1994. *The Nature of Emotion: Fundamental Questions*, (New York: Oxford University Press).

Ekman, Paul, Davidson, R.J. and Friesen, W.V. 1990. 'The Duchenne Smile: Emotional expression and brain physiology II', *Journal of Personality and Social Psychology*, 58 (2), pp. 342–53.

Ekman, Paul, Levenson, R.W. and Friesen, W.V. 1983. 'Autonomic nervous system activity distinguishes among emotions', *Science*, 221, pp. 1208–10.

Faulkner, William. 1953. *Sanctuary* (Harmondsworth: Penguin Books).

Georgieff, Nicolas and Jeannerod, Marc. 1998. 'Beyond consciousness of external reality. A "Who" system for consciousness of action and self consciousness', http://www.isc.cnrs.fr/wp/wpjea9805.htm: 1–10.

Ginsburg, G.P. and Harrington, Melanie E. 1996. 'Bodily states and context in situated lines of action', in *The Emotions*, ed. R. Harré and W. G. Parrott (London: Sage Publications).

Golani, Ilan. 1976. 'Homeostatic motor processes in mammalian interactions: A choreography of display,' in *Perspectives in Ethology*, vol. 2, ed. P.P.G. Bateson and Peter H. Klopfer (New York: Plenum Publishing).

Goodall, Jane. 1990. *Through a Window: My Thirty Years wih the Chimpanzees of Gombe* (Boston, MA: Houghton Mifflin).

Gowitzke, Barbara and Morris Milner. 1988. *Understanding the Scientific Bases of Human Movement* (Baltimore: Williams & Wilkins).

Husserl, Edmund. 1973a. *Cartesian Meditations*, tr. Dorion Cairns (The Hague: Martinus Nijhoff).

Husserl, Edmund. 1973b. *Experience and Judgment*, ed. Ludwig Landgrebe, tr. James S. Churchill and Karl Ameriks (Evanston, IL: Northwestern University Press).

Husserl, Edmund. 1977. *Phenomenological Psychology*, tr. John Scanlon (The Hague: Martinus Nijhoff).

Husserl, Edmund. 1980. *Ideas Pertaining to a Pure Phenomenology and to a Phenomenological Philosophy*, Third Book (*Ideas III*): *Phenomenology and the Foundations of the Sciences*, tr. Ted E. Klein and William E. Pohl (The Hague: Martinus Nijhoff).

Husserl, Edmund. 1983. *Ideas Pertaining to a Pure Phenomenology and to a Phenomenological Philosophy*, First Book (*Ideas I*), tr. F. Kersten (The Hague: Martinus Nijhoff).

Izard, Carroll E. 1977. *Human Emotions* (New York: Plenum Press).

Jacobson, Edmund. 1929. *Progressive Relaxation* (Chicago: University of Chicago Press).

Jacobson, Edmund. 1967. *Biology of Emotions* (Springfield, IL: Charles C).

Jacobson, Edmund. 1970. *Modern Treatment of Tense Patients* (Springfield, IL: Charles C. Thomas).

Jacobson, Edmund. 1973. 'Electrophysiology of mental activities and introduction to the psychological process of thinking', in *Psychophysiology of Thinking*, ed. F.J. McGuigan and R.A. Schoonover (New York: Academic Press).

Johnson, Mark. 1987. *The Body in the Mind* (Chicago: University of Chicago Press).

Kelso, J.A. Scott. 1995. *Dynamic Patterns: The Self-Organization of Brain and Behavior* (Cambridge, MA: Bradford Books/MIT Press).

Langer, Susanne K. 1953. *Feeling and Form* (New York: Charles Scribner's Sons).

Lakoff, George and Johnson, Mark. 1999. *Philosophy in the Flesh* (New York: Basic Books).

Levenson, Robert W., Ekman, Paul and Friesen, W.V. 1990. 'Voluntary facial action generates emotion-specific autonomic nervous system activity', *Psychophysiology*, 27 (4), pp. 363–84.

Lorenz, Konrad. 1967. *On Aggression*, tr. Marjorie Kerr Wilson (New York: Bantam Books).

Moran, Greg, Fentress, John C. and Golani, Ilan. 1981. 'A description of relational patterns of movement during 'ritualized fighting' in wolves', *Animal Behavior*, 29, pp. 1146–65.

Pribram, Karl H. 1980. 'The biology of emotions and other feelings', in *Emotion: Theory, Research, and Experience, vol. I, Theories of Emotion*, ed. R. Plutchik and H. Kellerman (New York: Academic Press).

Rosenfeld, Howard M. 1982. 'Measurement of body motion and orientation', in *Handbook of Methods in Nonverbal Behavior Research*, ed. K.R. Scherer and P. Ekman (Cambridge: Cambridge University Press).

Sartre, Jean-Paul. 1948. *The Emotions: Outline of a Theory*, trans. B. Frechtman (New York: Philosophical Library).

Sheets-Johnstone, Maxine. 1966 [1979/1980]. *The Phenomenology of Dance* (Madison, WI: University of Wisconsin Press; 2nd editions: London: Dance Books Ltd.; New York: Arno Press).

Sheets-Johnstone, Maxine. 1979. 'On movement and objects in motion: The phenomenology of the visible in dance', *Journal of Aesthetic Education*, 13 (2), pp. 33–46.

Sheets-Johnstone, Maxine. 1983. 'Evolutionary residues and uniquenesses in human movement', *Evolutionary Theory*, 6, pp. 205–9.

Sheets-Johnstone, Maxine. 1990. *The Roots of Thinking* (Philadelphia, PA: Temple University Press).

Sheets-Johnstone, Maxine. 1994. *The Roots of Power: Animate Form and Gendered Bodies* (Chicago, IL: Open Court Publishing).

Sheets-Johnstone, Maxine. 1998. 'Consciousness: A natural history,' *Journal of Consciousness Studies*, 5 (3), pp. 260–94.

Sheets-Johnstone, Maxine. 1999. *The Primacy of Movement* (Amsterdam: John Benjamins Publishing).

Sperry, Roger W. 1952. 'Neurology and the mind/brain problem', *American Scientist*, 40, pp. 291–312.

Todd, Mabel Elsworth. 1937. *The Thinking Body* (New York: Dance Horizons).

Varela, Francisco J. 1999. 'Present-time consciousness', *Journal of Consciousness Studies*, 6 (2–3), pp. 111–40.

Varela, Francisco J., Evan Thompson and Eleanor Rosch. 1991. *The Embodied Mind* (Cambridge, MA: MIT Press).

von Helmholtz, Hermann. 1971 [1870]. 'The origin and meaning of geometric axioms (I)', in *Selected Writings of Hermann von Helmholtz*, ed. and trans. R. Kahl (Middletown, CT: Wesleyan University Press).

Chapter IX

Sensory-Kinetic Understandings of Language

An Inquiry Into Origins

1. Introduction

A sensory-kinetic approach to the origin of language sheds light on the foundations of both semantics and syntax. Elucidated from the perspective of mobile, sentient bodies, semantics and syntax are in fact automatically illuminated because they are no longer regarded abstract objects of formal investigation but substantive aspects of experience. As such, they are open to a phenomenologically-informed analysis. A basic biological fact — responsivity — coincides with this approach and analysis. Responsivity is a prime constituent in definitions of life: "[T]he capacity to respond is a fundamental and almost universal characteristic of life" (Curtis, 1975, p. 28). By its very nature, the capacity to respond signifies both sentience and mobility. It is thus doubly significant to an inquiry into the origin of language. It indicates that living forms are *animate* forms, and that animate forms are *primed for meaning*. It is not surprising, then, that responsivity is linked to sensory-kinetic understandings of semantics and syntax, and that, correlatively, a sensory-kinetic approach to the origin of language, an approach that takes experience as its guide, outlines elements within a phenomenologically-informed analysis of responsivity.

2. Archetypal Corporeal-Kinetic Forms and Relations

Animate forms discover and respond to meanings in the world about them. Social animals in addition create interanimate meanings and articulate them in various ways. Animate forms furthermore live in a world that varies from day to day, a world that, all the same, has certain sequential regularities, not only in the form of day and night, but in the form of if/then, consequential relationships, for example, and commonly performed social exchanges. Moving themselves in function of a dynamically changing but ordered world, animate forms that prosper and survive are attuned to the unfolding regularities of their particular *Umwelt*, including the unfolding regularities that constitute their daily interactions with others. Given these basic facts of animate life, we can begin to appreciate how semantics and syntax enter naturally into the experiential lives of animate forms.

A displayed-to animal acquiesces to meaning. For example, it desists in doing what it is doing; or it approaches the displayer; or it reciprocates by a display of its own; and so on. How is this readiness toward meaning possible and how does it come to be? Archetypal corporeal-kinetic forms and relations undergird any language. Archetypal corporeal-kinetic forms and relations are implicit in linguist Ronald Langacker's delineation of archetypal semantic roles (e.g., agent, instrument, patient: Langacker, 1991, p. 285) and in Sheets-Johnstone's phenomenological analyses of fundamental human concepts (Sheets-Johnstone, 1990, 1994). In addition, archetypes figure prominently and powerfully in Jung's psychoanalytic (Jung, 1980). Archetypal corporeal-kinetic forms and relations are a more exact descriptive specification of nonlinguistic experience than "image schemata" (Neisser 1976) or "embodied image schemata" (Johnson, 1987; Johnson and Lakoff 1999). They are already corporeally patterned entities; a body does not need to be added nor does movement. By definition, an animate body is already present in archetypal corporeal-kinetic forms and relations. Image schemata, in contrast, need to be specifically packaged corporeally — to be *embodied* — in order not to remain embedded in a purely mental sphere. While image schemata fall nicely within the purview of present-day cognitive studies, allowing ready access to minds and brains alike (e.g., image schemata "are structures of our embodied understanding"; image schemata "organize our mental representations", Johnson, 1987, pp. 103, 23–4, respectively), allowing even an espousal of mind/brain unity, they are thoroughly hypothetical entities, posited things like cognitive maps and feature analyzers. They are not empirically demonstrable entities. Archetypal corporeal-kinetic forms and relations are. They are found directly in bodily experience and can be empirically described as the paradigmatic forms and relations they are (Sheets-Johnstone, 1994). Langacker's descriptive statement regarding semantic archetypes is apposite in this respect. He writes that "[Semantic role] archetypes reflect our experience as mobile and sentient creatures and as manipulators of physical objects" (Langacker, 1991, pp. 284–5). Clearly, animate forms, forms which, moving intelligently and in responsively intelligent ways in the world about them, are primed for meaning and those meanings are rooted in archetypal corporeal-kinetic forms and relations.

The greater explanatory power of bodily archetypes over image schemata warrants more detailed attention. Human archetypal corporeal-kinetic forms and relations include all those forms and relations commonly discussed under the label "embodied image schemata": *containment, journey, near-far, part-whole, balance, orientation, verticality, force,* for example (Johnson 1987). As indicated, from an archetypal viewpoint, these forms are already "embodied", and furthermore, they are already conceptual: they anchor fundamental corporeal concepts, nonlinguistic concepts. An infant closing and opening its hand over an object is at the same time forging a nonlinguistic, i.e., corporeal, concept that we might designate as *in, inside, being inside,* or more generally, as *insideness* (see, for example, T.G.R. Bower, 1974; Piaget, 1967; see also Sheets-Johnstone, 1990 for a phenomenological analysis of this concept and its ontogenetical and evolutionary significances). It is of conceptual and not just of linguistic interest to note that the preposition *in* is the first locative state and locative act to appear in a child's acquisition of verbal language (Clark, 1973, 1979; Cook, 1978; see also Grieve, Hoogenraad, and Murray, 1977); being in or inside something, and placing in or inside something, constitute prime and ongoing experiences in infant and early childhood life and are the basis of the corporeal concept of *insideness*. Archetypal forms and relations are thus not *pre*conceptual entities as embodied image schemata are consistently described (Johnson, 1987, e.g., pp. 1, 13, 14, 15, 22, 40, 42), but are the substantive conceptual backbone of language when it appears. Neither are archetypal forms and relations vague mental means whereby we forge concepts, something on the order of Platonic conjurations having no direct cognitive reality. Archetypal corporeal-kinetic forms and relations are conceptual by their very nature. We might even say that, rather than there being embodied image schemata that specify "*pre*conceptual structures of our experience" (*ibid.*, p. xxxvii; italics added), the situation is quite the reverse. Archetypal corporeal-kinetic forms and relations *embody* concepts, precisely in the sense in which we say that someone is the *embodiment* of courage, or that someone *embodies* the qualities we value. They are conceptual instantiations of such concepts as *insideness, thickness, thinness, animate being, power, verticality, force,* and so on (Sheets-Johnstone, 1990, 1994; see also Sheets-Johnstone, 1999a). They are structured in and by *corporeal concepts.*[1]

---

1   Phenomenological analyses show that fundamental human concepts derive from bodily experience. Thickness and thinness, for example, are concepts integral to early hominid stone tool-making and derive from the experience of one's teeth—precisely the items which

In sum, archetypal corporeal-kinetic forms and relations are already rooted in the body and are already experiential. For this very reason, they point us in the direction of a veritable phenomenology. Carrying out this phenomenology enables us to recognize the bodily source of concepts directly (Sheets-Johnstone, 1990, 1994, 1999a) and to recognize as well the basis on which we make our way in the world: not *pre*conceptually by schemata, but through movement of our tactile-kinesthetic bodies and through our related, developmentally achieved corporeal concepts. Carrying out the phenomenology, however, poses a challenge. Bona fide phenomenological insights into archetypal forms and relations challenge us to exact descriptive renderings of corporeal concepts and in so doing challenge us *to language experience*; that is, they challenge us to describe what is experientially present in terms that elucidate precisely the essential nature of the archetypal corporeal-kinetic form or relation in question. The challenge is thus both to trace fundamental corporeal-kinetic archetypes back to their often manifold originary bodily sources in experience—as, for example, to an infant closing and opening its hand, its mouth, and its eyes, or to an early hominid stone tool-maker running his tongue along the biting and grinding edges of his teeth[2]—and to present a thorough descriptive analysis of those experiences, elucidating them along precise lines of the body and of movement. The latter task is notably distinct from exemplifying "embodied image schemata" in language. The latter exercise, though it identifies experientially embodied sources and analyzes them in painstaking and edifying detail, identifies those embodied sources preeminently in terms of the metaphoric usage of words. It does not take us back to originary corporeal-kinetic experiences and to rigorous and detailed analyses of those experiences. In effect, it does not take us back to nonlinguistic corporeal origins. Archetypal corporeal-kinetic forms and relations do. They specify and articulate an ontogenetical-evolutionary perspective. Resting on species-specific tactile-kinesthetic invariants, they lead us back to the identification of these invariants. In other words, species-specific tactile-kinesthetic invariants give rise to archetypal corporeal-kinetic forms and relations, what primatologist Stuart Altmann terms "comsigns" (Altmann, 1967, pp. 335–6). Though Altmann does not gloss the word as such, it is clear that *com*signs are both

---

anthropologists and archaeologists uniformly link to the initial production of stone tools, i.e., "stone tools replaced teeth", but just as uniformly fail to analyze conceptually (see Sheets-Johnstone 1990, Chapter 2, "The Hermeneutics of Tool-Making: Corporeal and Topological Concepts"); animate being is a concept phenomenologically described in relation to the origin of the concept of death (Sheets-Johnstone 1990); power is a concept articulated in certain intercorporeal positionings, in making a spectacle of oneself, in inflating oneself, etc., and is described within an evolutionary genealogy of power in Sheets-Johnstone 1994.

2   See note 1.

common signs and communicative signs; that is, they are gestural acts, corporeal-kinetic forms and relations, which are common to all members of a particular group or species as a whole — all members can and do perform the gestural acts or are able to do so at some point in their lives[3] — and which are communicative signs within a particular group or species as a whole — the corporeal-kinetic forms and relations articulate the same basic meaning for all. Just because these gestural acts occur outside of verbal language does not mean that they are *pre*conceptual. On the contrary, and as we will presently see in greater detail, they are richly conceptual: gestural acts are semantically-laden acts and semantically-laden acts are necessarily concept-laden.

The following descriptive account of an embodied image schemata exemplifies how tactile-kinesthetic bodies, corporeal concepts, and bodily origins generally, can be and are bypassed, and at the same time how they are each in need of our attention. Johnson describes the embodied image schema *containment* as follows:

> Our encounter with containment and boundedness is one of the most pervasive features of our bodily experience. We are intimately aware of our bodies as three-dimensional containers into which we put certain things (food, water, air) and out of which other things emerge (food and water wastes, air, blood, etc.). From the beginning, we experience constant physical containment in our surroundings (those things that envelop us). We move in and out of rooms, clothes, vehicles, and numerous kinds of bounded spaces. We manipulate objects, placing them in containers (cups, boxes, cans, bags, etc.). In each of these cases there are repeatable spatial and temporal organizations. In other words, there are typical schemata for physical containment (Johnson, 1987, p. 21).

Johnson's discussion of *containment* then turns to a specification of "*in-out* orientation":

> If we look for common structure in our many experiences of being in something, or for locating something *within* another thing, we find recurring organization of structures: the experiential basis for *in-out* orientation is that of spatial boundedness. The most experientially salient sense of boundedness seems to be that of three-dimensional containment (i.e., being limited or held within some three-dimensional enclosure, such as a womb, a crib, or a room) (*ibid.*, pp. 21-2).

---

3   That female primates, early hominid ones in particular, while capable of assuming an erect posture, are not capable of penile erection or display — or of intromission as Altmann specifically points out (Altmann, 1967, p. 336) — does not mean that they do not have direct and highly discriminatory tactile-kinesthetic or visual experiences of these male behaviors, hence that the behaviors are not comsigns.

As briefly indicated above, "insideness" — *in, inside, being inside* — is a fundamental corporeal human concept.[4] *Containment* is a conceptual derivative: something is *contained* if and only if it is *found in* or *put inside* something else. *Insideness* is the archetypal relation grounding the relation of containment, thus the experiential foundation for the "embodied image schemata" *containment*. Johnson's account of containment appears to recognize insideness by way of the "three-dimensional container" that is our body, but his account becomes circular because the archetypal experience of *insideness* goes unrecognized. In his account, our experience of containment derives from "*in-out* orientation", which orientation derives experientially from spatial boundedness, which boundedness derives experientially (or "seems", as Johnson puts it, to derive experientially) from "three-dimensional containment". In effect, the embodied image schema *containment* derives from three-dimensional containment schemata.

Further problems with the account warrant attention. Containment is parasitic on experiences Johnson alludes to but does not describe in his subsequent analysis of "*in-out* orientation." These experiences — "held within some enclosure (such as a womb, a crib, a room)" — in fact have no *out* component to them at all except through the added notion of "spatial boundedness"; they are experiences focally oriented to an unexplicated form of *insideness*. Second, while the concept of three-dimensionality figures centrally in both the original description of containment and the subsequent specification of in-out orientation, three-dimensionality subsumes spatial coordinates having nothing to do with *insides*. Three-dimensionality stipulates an up-down or sagittal coordinate, a side-side or frontal coordinate, and a forward-back or transverse coordinate. It does not specify *insideness* — or an "*in-out* orientation", for that matter. Insideness is a fourth bodily dimension, a dimension traced out in the experience of volume, one's own bodily volume, as in a headache that surges *inside*.

In sum, because the starting point for descriptive analyses of embodied image schemata is verbal language, bodily experience enters only after linguistic fact, and then primarily only as it exemplifies linguistic metaphoric practices. While language is shown to refer back to the body in intricate and meaningful ways, the body is not recognized as being already conceptually alive, indeed, as being already attuned in fundamental and essential

---

4   The concept may even be a fundamental chimpanzee concept. Chimpanzees have a propensity to put themselves or objects inside chalk circles when given the cultural paraphernalia of Western humans (Premack, 1975). Moreover their use of human-made tools in ways involving a concept of *in, inside,* and *being inside* is exemplary (Savage-Rumbaugh, Rumbaugh, and Boysen, 1978).

ways to the world and to the nature of its own corporeal-kinetic realities.[5]
That nonlinguistic body is not properly deemed *prelinguistic*; on the contrary, the acquisition of verbal language is *post-kinetic* and should properly
be considered such (Sheets-Johnstone, 1999a). Until the foundational
kinetic dimension of human life (in fact, *all* life) is acknowledged, there is
no point of entry for nonlinguistic corporeal concepts in analyses of
"embodied image schemata", hence no recognition of archetypal corporeal-kinetic forms and relations. An elucidation of corporeal concepts
begins with bodily experience directly, which is to say with kinetic/tac-
tile-kinesthetic bodies, the source of corporeal-kinetic archetypes. Finally,
a basic challenge, as indicated above, is to language experience, specifically to language bodily experience. That challenge can be considerable. In
the beginning, it may well seem that "for all this, names are lacking".[6]

3. Bisociation and Apperception

Two sensory modalities are always involved in the production and comprehension of human languages, and the primary modality is always
kinetic. In other words, whether uttering words or performing signs, one
is making articulatory gestures. These dynamic kinetic figurations are the
foundation of language, the basis upon which language was first invented,
the basis upon which it is both produced and comprehended. The foundation is secured by species-specific possibilities and invariants. In particular, whatever the specific language, its articulatory gestures rest on
species-specific tactile-kinesthetic possibilities and invariants. Movement
is indeed our mother tongue (Sheets-Johnstone, 1999a).

Many theoretical and practical biases preclude and have precluded
appreciation of our mother tongue: the lack of a script by which we can
read it, as we can read words on a page; its fleetingness in contrast to the
substantiality of the printed word, thus a difficulty in pinning it down
with authority; and so on. But a deeper, hidden bias may well be the leading source of its non-appreciation. This deeper bias stems from the fact
that in verbal language — common everyday speech — dynamic kinetic fig-

5   These corporeal-kinetic realities can be spelled out in terms of the five characteristics of
     ownness that Husserl enumerates on the way to spelling out the basis of intersubjectivity:
     fields of sensation, I cans, I govern, self-reflexivity, and psychophysical unity. As I have
     elsewhere shown, these foundational experiences of oneself are all rooted in the
     kinetic/tactile-kinesthetic body. See Husserl, 1973, pp. 97–8; Sheets-Johnstone, 1999b.

6   Having no successive temporal parts in the form of befores, nows, and afters, Husserl found
     with respect to an adequate descriptive account of the temporally constitutive flux of
     transcendental subjectivity (constituting consciousness) that "For all this, names are lacking"
     (Husserl 1966, p. 100). Being fundamentally co-articulated and a streaming present, something
     similar may be said of body movement and kinesthetic consciousness respectively, thus of
     corporeal-kinetic experience. See Sheets-Johnstone, 1999a.

urations are nowhere in sight. In other words, articulatory gestures are unseen by the person spoken to, the person who, from an evolutionary perspective, is the displayed-to individual. Moreover in everyday verbal communication, both speaker and person spoken to are normally unaware of articulatory gestures, and furthermore, normally unaware at any later point of being unaware of them. The comprehension of speech is in consequence easily consigned to the head, i.e., it is conceived to be a product of mind, or more specifically of the brain, as we shall see. In effect, the understanding of speech—its comprehension—is not tied to *movement* but relegated to something "mental". Coincident with this view is the view of language as a purely mental phenomenon whose sensuous ties are arbitrary because the sensuous basis of language is itself arbitrary: the word "dog" has nothing to do with the four-legged creature that barks. A non-recognition and non-appreciation of our mother tongue follows readily from these views.

Yet what makes communication possible is precisely our mother tongue: species-specific kinetic/tactile-kinesthetic possibilities and invariants not only make possible the interchangeability of displayer and displayed-to individual; species-specific kinetic/tactile-kinesthetic possibilities and invariants are the foundation of our capacity to apperceive what is not present. Through speech apperception, a hearer of speech sounds makes co-present the articulatory gestures producing the sounds. Making these gestures co-present is neither an imaginative act nor a reasoned out one. It is, as philosopher Ronald de Sousa implicitly suggests in reviewing the extensive research studies of speech psychologist Alvin Liberman and colleagues, the result of a process tied to articulation: "Our phonetic perception is crucially conditioned by our own capacity to produce speech, though the process involves neither inference, nor argument from analogy, nor imaginative effort" (de Sousa, 1987, p. 155). In brief, and as I have elsewhere shown at length (Sheets-Johnstone, 1999a; see also Sheets-Johnstone, 1990), our capacity to link the perception of speech with the production of speech involves not an active intellectual doing of some kind, a kind of doing that we typically associate with thinking or reasoning, but *sense-making*, a sense-making that may be traced back to tactile-kinesthetic awarenesses and passive syntheses developing in normal experiential fashion in the course of infancy and early childhood. Without these awarenesses and this synthesizing activity, not only are gestural possibilities and invariants impossible, speech itself is impossible. In other words, until and unless infants and young children are aware of themselves first as sound-makers—in babbling and cooing, in gurgling, in tapping and smacking their lips together, and so on—and then as *articulators* of meaningful sound—in saying "mama" or "dada", for example—they can hardly become effective speakers and hearers.[7]

Because a tactile-kinesthetic awareness of vocal tract dynamics is not common in adult life, it is quite easy to relegate understandings of speech to the brain, and in particular to a hypothetical brain entity: "an internal, innately specified vocal-tract synthesizer … that incorporates complete information about the anatomical and physiological characteristics of the vocal tract and also about the articulatory and acoustic consequences of linguistically significant gestures" (Liberman and Mattingly, 1985, p. 26). Rather than conjure up such an entity, however, we can acknowledge *articulators* themselves—real-life individuals who discover themselves to begin with as sound-makers and go on to learn the articulatory possibilities and invariants of their mouths, tongues, and larynx by making sounds with or from them—and thus acknowledge both the articulatory gestures that make verbal speech possible and the tactile-kinesthetic possibilities and invariants on which the articulatory gestures rest. Such acknowledgements open the door not only to deeper understandings of language but to all-encompassing understandings, and this because tactile-kinesthetic possibilities and invariants are, as indicated, the foundation of language. They are the foundation of both verbal language (see Sheets-Johnstone, 1999a, chapter 9) and of sign languages, gestural systems of thought whose modalities are bisociated in a single act of vision and movement.

The basic modal difference between sign and verbal languages is not a difference of 'visual and auditory channels', as is commonly thought. It is more fundamentally a difference in the nature of the bisociation of the modalities involved. Because the bisociation of modalities in sign languages is totally visible, sign languages are not and cannot be associated in typical fashion with "the mental." Skeptical assessments of sign languages as languages, not to say their derision, are tied to this divergency, that is, to the fact that in sign languages, the gestural system of thought is present to perception; articulatory gestures are not *apperceived* but *perceived*. The bisociation of the two sensory modalities—vision and movement—is a singular event; nothing is hidden away, hence nothing is made co-present. What troubles and perhaps even unnerves some researchers is precisely this fact. Since there is nothing hidden away "in the head" as in verbal

7   Liberman and Mattingly (1985, p. 25) indirectly affirm a child's "tacit" appreciation of articulatory gestures. In the absence of original *awarenesses* of oneself as a sound-maker, however, and then as a maker of *this* sound, and *this* sound, and *this* sound, and so on, an infant's mastery of spoken language could hardly be attained. The specific passage in question is as follows: "Until and unless the child (tacitly) appreciates the gestural source of the sounds, he can hardly be expected to perceive, or ever learn to perceive, a phonetic structure." The passage is discussed at length in Sheets-Johnstone, 1999a, pp. 374–81.

language, or rather, hidden away in the head as it is thought to be hidden away in the head in verbal language, there is nothing mental about sign languages. In effect, sign languages can hardly be true languages. At the bottom of this judgment is a robust mind-body dualism heartily sustained by an enduring received ignorance that trivializes and underestimates the conceptual import of movement.

It should be noted that the motor theory of speech perception was criticized early on as "a curious hypothesis" (Neisser, 1976, pp. 157–8), but on partially false grounds since the theory originally did not rest on explicit imitation, as Neisser directly implies when he states that "we can only perceive speech by making small movements of our own tongues and other speech organs in tandem with those of the speaker" (ibid., p. 158). The original theory rested on "covert mimicry" or internal imitation (Liberman and Mattingly, 1985, p. 23). (In their revised cognitivist-computational version of the motor theory, Liberman and Mattingly state that the perception of phonetic structure rests on a "tacit" appreciation of the gestural source of speech [ibid., p. 25].) Neisser's criticism of the motor theory of speech perception stems from the false belief that it requires "that we perceive articulatory gestures" (Neisser, 1976, p. 158). Yet Neisser himself avers that "To perceive speech, we must pick up information that specifies articulatory gestures" (ibid., p. 161). The point, of course, is that we do not perceive articulatory gestures; we *apperceive* them by making co-present what is unperceived—in a way similar to the way in which we simultaneously apperceive that which is occluded when we perceive a book lying on a table or to the way in which we simultaneously apperceive what a person has in mind when she puts on her coat and walks toward the door, but in a way dissimilar from both of these examples in the fact that speech apperception rests on species-specific tactile-kinesthetic possibilities and invariants.[8] Accordingly, what we "pick up" is not "information that specifies articulatory gestures", but a common kinetic dynamic, a dynamic that we do not in fact "pick up" at all but grasp apperceptively on the basis of a common body and a common body of knowledge about that body. This phenomenological reading and analysis of the motor theory of speech perception rests on corporeal matters of fact. Instead of turning toward corporeal matters of fact, i.e., a species-specific tactile-kinesthetic body and common kinetic dynamics, Neisser argues for "schemata", the "schemata of speech perception", that themselves develop on the basis of schemata with which, he says, we are already "probably born", i.e., "schemata sensi-

---

8   Coarticulation does not contravene tactile-kinesthetic invariants. On the contrary, invariants are tied to coarticulated speech, and even as invariant, they range across a gamut of possible intonations, accents, and so on, depending upon context, individual experience, and so on.

tive to expressions of emotion and intention" (*ibid.*, p. 161). Clearly, the terms "schema" and "schemata" conjure something internal, something decidedly "mental." Especially in view of present-day neuroscience, they serve to suggest a "mechanism" in the brain, or as Neisser himself states, "a momentary state of the perceiver's nervous system" (*ibid.*, p. 181). With its linkage to bodily experiences, Johnson's definition of schemata comes much closer to the body; schemata are "embodied patterns of meaning-fully organized experience" (Johnson, 1987, p. 19). A proper designation of these patterns, however, would specify them not as "embodied", as we have seen, but as archetypal corporeal-kinetic forms and relations from the very beginning.

4. An Evolutionary Semantics

Nonhuman interanimate life is consistently described in terms of display. An evolutionary semantics begins with this biological phenomenon. Displays are structured in archetypal corporeal-kinetic forms and relations engendering species-specific meanings. Their relational significations are clearly evident in the fact that they are a specifically directed form of communication; they are addressed to a particular individual or to particular individuals. The specific form they take is contingent upon the displayer, as the following general description of an aggressive threat display enacted by olive baboons shows:

> At its lowest intensity, a simple lifting of the eyebrows reveals white eyelids, signaling that the sender is aware of what is going on and is not happy about it ... [As a drawing in the text shows], an adult male is intent on letting those around him know how he feels; he is much more upset. He has added an open-mouth threat to the eyelid signal, reveal-ing impressive canines. His hair is also beginning to stand on end, making him seem even more formidable. As the threat heightens in intensity, more sounds and ground slapping will be added (Strum, 1987, p. 270).

Jane Goodall's list of threat display possibilities among Gombe Stream chimpanzees demonstrates the variety of forms an aggressive threat dis-play may take or incorporate: glaring, head tipping, arm raising, hitting away ("the back of the hand directed toward the threatened animal"), flapping ("downward slapping movement of the hand in the direction of the threatened individual"), branching (shaking a branch or twig toward another individual), stamping and slapping, throwing sticks and other objects, bidpedal arm waving and running (toward another individual), bipedal swagger, quadrupedal hunch (Goodall, 1972, pp. 44–7).

Displays are more complex than signals (Bramblett, 1976). As is appar-ent from Strum's description and Goodall's list, their complexity allows a range of meaning. With respect to threat displays, meaning can range from light annoyance to wrath, for example, and, in addition, can be accentuated, reinforced through supplementary and less subtle bodily movements, expansive or more forceful bodily movements, sounds, and so on. Both Strum's descriptive account and Goodall's list implicitly testify not only to the fact that displays are meaningful but more generally to the fact that where meaning is represented, it is represented corporeally — kinetically, posturally, directionally, auditorily through sound-making, visually through staring or glaring. Archetypal corporeal-kinetic forms and relations are the symbolic counters of species-specific corporeal meanings. It should be noted that species-specificity does not contravene archetypal overlap among species. On the contrary, evolutionary continuities are amply apparent. Glaring, throwing, sound-making, slapping or hitting, for example, are aggressive threat displays that are hardly corporeally unique to olive baboons or to chimpanzees. Also to be noted is the phenomenon that ethologists term "ritualization": when certain kinetic features of a display "in the course of phylogeny [lose] their original function and become purely 'symbolic' ceremonies", they are ritualized in ways parallel to the ways in which human cultural rites are ritualized (Lorenz, 1967, pp. 54–5). Although Lorenz encloses the term *symbolic* in quotes, there is no reason to imply that such symbolization is not true symbolization. An olive baboon's open-mouth canine display, for example, symbolizes just what its name specifies: an aggressive threat. A threat is in fact by its very nature symbolic. It is symbolic of what is to come if …Hence, to threaten is necessarily to engage in symbolic activity of some sort: to raise one's fists, to draw oneself up or inflate oneself, thereby increasing one's size and by extension one's appearance of power, and so on. It is important to note in this context, and equally to emphasize, that a distancing of original function does not obliterate iconicity and that in turn, from the viewpoint of an evolutionary semantics, the roots of symbolization lie not in arbitrary counters but in iconic ones; *iconicity is not the opposite of symbolization but its foundation.* The work of anthropological linguist Mary LeCron Foster bears out this relationship. So also do writings on speech by Alfred R. Wallace. We will examine the research findings of both Foster and Wallace presently. The immediate concern is to specify further the import of display within an evolutionary semantics.

Being directed toward another individual or individuals, displays clearly articulate intercorporeal meanings. If we inquire as to the basis of these intercorporeal meanings, we are led once again to an appreciation of species-specific kinetic/tactile-kinesthetic bodies and to species-specific kinetic/tactile-kinesthetic possibilities and invariants — or, to use

Altmann's general term, to comsigns. What is represented kinetically, posturally, directionally, visually, or auditorily is in each case related to the addressed individual's own body of possible tactile-kinesthetic experiences. Intercorporeal meanings are thus etched along the lines of kinetic/tactile-kinesthetic bodies. On the one side, through the body and bodily movement, meanings are corporeally represented; on the other side, through intercorporeal attunement, meanings are affirmed. A common sentient-kinetic body is thus the foundation of a common body of significations that are solidified in archetypal corporeal-kinetic forms and relations.

An evolutionary semantics that traces out these forms and relations presents an evolutionary genealogy. The genealogy shows how species-specific and species-overlapping corporeally represented meanings are played out intercorporeally, as in displays of power, for example, where one individual positions himself higher than another or in front of another, or where an individual makes a visual spectacle of himself by brandishing something, for instance, or by throwing something, or by making boisterous movements and gestures, and so on (Sheets-Johnstone, 1994).[9] What evolutionary genealogies show is that animate forms signify in bodily meaningful ways according to the bodies they are. But again, it is the displayed-to individual, through its responsivity or lack of responsivity, that authenticates meaning, that underwrites or certifies the display in the species'—or group's—semantic repertoire. The displayed-to individual, in acquiescing to meaning, instantiates the display as an archetypal corporeal-kinetic form and relation. It is significant that, in the course of discussing the manual communication system of a deaf child who devised his own "homesign" system, Morford, Singleton, and Goldin-Meadow make this very point. They remark that, insofar as the child "used his homesign for communicative purposes, [h]e has, in a sense, tested his gestures to see if they convey the information he intends" (Morford, Singleton, and Goldin-Meadow, 1995, p. 315). In sum, natural selection of an intercorporeal semantics, an affective-cognitive semantics, turns on the displayed-to individual whose responsivity is rooted in those species-specific kinetic/tactile-kinesthetic possibilities and invariants that are the basis of its interchangeability with the displayer.[10]

---

9 It is important to emphasize that evolutionary genealogies attest to evolutionary continuities as well as discontinuities. In other words, similar bodily morphologies predispose toward overlapping kinetic dispositions.

10 "Mirror neurons" recently discovered by researchers in neuroscience (Rizzolatti and Gallese, 1997, Gallese et al, 1996, Gallese, in press) offer empirical support of another kind to the kinetic/tactile-kinesthetic roots of semantics described in this paper. On the basis of initial findings that motor neurons in the premotor cortex fire on the visual presentation of certain

Viewed from a phenomenologically-informed perspective, ethological and primatological studies show furthermore that archetypal corpo-real-kinetic forms and relations are physiognomic: they have a distinctive sensory-kinetic character, precisely as Strum's descriptive account of aggressive threat displays in olive baboons shows. It is their distinctive physiognomic character that makes them distinctively meaningful, i.e., the gesture *as meant* is corporeally codified.[11] In the most basic sense, what makes semantic codification possible is the fact that movement creates its own space, time, and force. Although it is common to think of movement as taking place *in* time and *in* space — and in fact common to think of move-ment merely as a change of position — movement is a *created dynamic phe-nomenon*. It is because it creates its own time, space, and force that it can be shaped in the first place, i.e., articulated in some bodily fashion, and that its shapings — its specific spatio-temporal-energic articulations — can lead to affective-cognitive gestural systems, in effect, to gestural systems of communication. What is decisive to an understanding of such systems, and in particular to an understanding of the original shaping of such sys-tems, is a dynamic rather than mechanical conception of movement. The inherently dynamic nature of movement is the source of changing physi-

objects (and not only when these objects are actually acted upon, i.e., grasped, held, and so on, but when they are merely seen), these researchers went on to show that certain neurons in the same premotor area fire whether someone else grasps the object or whether one grasps the object oneself. They termed these neurons "mirror neurons": "Whenever we are looking at someone performing an action, there is a concurrent activation of the motor circuits that are recruited when we ourselves perform that action" (Rizzolatti and Gallese, 1997, p. 225). The researchers claim that mirror neurons specify a relationship between agent and object such that visually presented objects attain meaning only by way of action.

It is one thing, however, to correlate the recognition of objects and the actions of persons with the firing of certain neural cells and to posit a motor system "vocabulary" of action on that basis (Gallese, in press). It is quite another thing to anchor the recognition and action reductively in the neural activity — e.g., "While mirror neurons data do not say who is reading the neural activity, the data discussed ... suggest that it is not occasional that the motor system, which gives meaning to objects, is also responsible of (sic) the interpretation of motor events, and, by inference, provide knowledge on (sic) the existence of their agents" (Rizzolatti and Gallese, 1997, p. 226). In other words, it is a kinesthetically-attuned subject who, through its own self-movement, forges meanings in the world and thereby comes to make living sense of it. A bona fide explanation of the initial neural visual/kinetic correspondence and of the subsequent mirror neuron correspondence can thus ultimately be had only by way of a subject kinesthetically aware of its own movement — a sense-making subject of whatever species. With all due respect for Gallese's "cognitive archaeology" (Gallese, in press, ms., p. 15), it is not neurons but intact living creatures who interact with objects and who thereby come to know them, recognizing them in terms of their own possible movement in relation to them.

11   The object *as meant* is the epistemological object, i.e., the object as it is cognitively and affectively experienced. The phrase is from Husserl. His original example of the object as meant is well-known in part because it was initially misunderstood and criticized. Husserl originally wrote that " The tree simpliciter can burn up, be resolved into its chemical elements, etc. But the sense — the sense *of this* perception, something belonging necessarily to its essence — cannot burn up; it has no chemical elements, no forces, no real properties" (Husserl, 1983, Chapter Three, #89: p. 216; see also Husserl, 1970, p. 242).

ognomies, which can be analyzed in terms of a qualitatively structured evolutionary semantics.

The qualitative nature of movement, notably the movement of *animate forms*, makes possible systems of formal values that define in each instance a qualitative kinetics. A specific visual dynamic—for example, the "[c]autious walk of a low-ranking female rhesus" (captioned drawing in Rowell, 1972, p. 88)—is portentous in virtue of certain formal values which give it a distinctive physiognomy: a lowered, crouched body, whose line of focus is clearly watchful to what is ahead, inches its way warily forward. In the same way that this specific visual dynamic has a certain qualitative flow in virtue of its created spatial, temporal, and energic character, so any movement whatsoever creates a certain qualitative kinetics through *its* formal values and thereby, potentially, depending upon the observer or displayed-to individual, a certain kinetically articulated meaning. Formal kinetic values are verbally condensed in terms like "sudden", "attenuated", "smooth", "jagged", "large", "small", "weak", "strong", "angular", "rounded", and so on. Such terms pinpoint different formal qualities of movement: its tensional quality or degree of forcefulness; its linear quality—the linear design of the body and the linear pattern described by the body's movement; its amplitudinal quality—the congealed-to-expansive carriage of the body and the congealed-to-expansive range of the body's movement; its manner of execution, that is, the way in which force is released—abruptly, ballistically, in a sustained manner, and so on. While the formal qualities of movement never exist separately, verbal condensations tend to cover over their always composite spatio-temporal-energic character, the terms "sudden" and "smooth", for example, seeming to have no spatial character, the terms "large", and "weak", seeming to have no temporal character, the terms "jagged" and "rounded" seeming to have no energic character. Affective descriptive terms such as "cautious", "excited", "aggressive", "fitful", "uneasy", and so on, tend to condense from the other direction; that is, without calling attention to any particular formal quality, they impart the sense of an overall spatio-temporal-energic dynamic. A certain whole-body dynamic is evoked, precisely in the sense in which Lieberman speaks of "a whole body gestural system" with respect to communication among chimpanzees (Lieberman, 1983). The semantic import of a qualitative kinetics is thus abundantly clear: the dynamic nature of movement is the foundation of archetypal forms and relations, specifically those archetypal forms and relations that are emblematic of affective-cognitive displays in nonhuman animal life, that are observed by humans precisely as affective-cognitive displays or as semantically-laden "behaviors"—e.g., a "cautious walk"—and that constituted the kinetically articulated semantics at the origin of human articulatory gestures.

When we frame the inquiry "how did human languages originate?" in terms not of adaptations but of living bodies, we are necessarily confronted with the creation of meaning, a creation that did not arise *de novo* but that was grounded in an already present semantic repertoire, itself grounded in archetypal corporeal-kinetic forms and relations that, as suggested, follow along biological Family lines, i.e., for hominids, along primatological lines. Accordingly, we should take not only gestural systems of communication seriously; we should take movement seriously, all the more so in view of the fact that in the bisociation of modalities, the kinetic modality is always primary: it is the source of meaning. This foundational confluence of movement and meaning is spelled out in concrete linguistic terms by Foster in her detailed reconstruction of primordial language and by Wallace in his observationally-tethered "mouth-gestures" thesis.

Wallace's 1895 article on "The Expressiveness of Speech" appears to be a little-known, or at least little-cited, article on the origin of language. The article's sub-title "Or, Mouth-Gesture as a Factor in the Origin of Language" is indicative of its provocative nature. Wallace presents evidence for thinking that the origin of language lies not only in gestures of the mouth, but in breath and in acts of breathing associated with the making of certain sounds (see also Wallace, 1881). What Wallace thereby provides is a *natural* basis (Wallace, 1895, e.g., pp. 529, 530, 543) for his theory about "mouth-gesture as a factor in the origin of language." In a sense, the *natural* basis extends further since his "great principle of speech-expression" (*ibid.*, p. 529) is based both on his own experience of speaking and on first-hand observations:

> During my long residence among many savage or barbarous people I first observed some of these mouth-gestures, and have been thereby led to detect a mode of natural expression by words which is, I believe, to a large extent new, and which opens up a much wider range of expressiveness in speech than has hitherto been possible, giving us a clue to the natural meaning of whole classes of words which are usually supposed to be purely conventional (*ibid.*).

Wallace then points out that "My attention was first directed to this subject by noticing that, when Malays were talking together, they often indicated direction by pouting out their lips. They would do this either silently, referring to something already spoken or understood, but more frequently when saying *disána* (there) or *ítu* (that), thus avoiding any further explanation of what was meant" (*ibid.*). He mentions how earlier scholars "christened" the "interjectional and imitative origin of language" the

"'Bow-wow and Pooh-pooh theory'" and how they treated it with "extreme contempt." He says that it is no doubt true that if one sticks to simple classes of words—"Ah! and Ugh!", for example, or to the imitation of animal or human sounds: mewing, whinnying, sneezing, snoring, and so on—that one can see the limitations of the theory. But Wallace states that these interjections and imitations are "merely the beginning and rudiment of a much wider subject, and [that the Bow-wow and Pooh-pooh theory] gives us no adequate conception of the range and interest of the great principle of speech-expression, as exhibited both in the varied forms of indirect imitation, but more especially by what may be termed speech or mouth-gesture" (*ibid.*).

As noted above, Wallace's account of the origin of language is movement- and breath-tethered. Admittedly constrained for the most part to exemplifying his great principle through English alone, Wallace at the same time strongly emphasizes the fact that for "primitive man", language was not conventional as it is today; thus, he affirms that confining his examples for the most part to English is not a liability. "Primitive man", he states, "had, as it were, to "struggle hard to make himself understood, and would, therefore, make use of every possible indication of meaning afforded by the positions and motions of mouth, lips, or breath, in pronouncing each word; and he would lay stress upon and exaggerate these indications, not slur them over as we do" (*ibid.*, p. 530). In his analyses proper, Wallace shows how in their very articulation certain words suggest motion away from the person speaking, as in the word *go*, and how other words imply motion toward the speaker, as in the word *come* (*ibid.*); he observes an outward breath in the pronunciation of certain pronouns ("*thou, you, he, they*") and an inward or self-directed breath in the pronunciation of other pronouns ("*I, me, we, us*") (*ibid.*, p. 531); he discusses how vowel sounds express outwardness ("*ah, o,* and *u*") and nearness to self ("*e* and *i*") (*ibid.*, p. 532); he points out how breathing may be the expressive aspect of speech, "the motion of the lips being very slight" (*ibid.*), and how certain words are "mouth words" (*ibid.*, pp. 532–3). He furthermore observes and shows how there is a distinctive difference between abrupt and continuous sounds—how some words end abruptly while others "admit of being dwelt upon and drawn out" (*ibid.*, p. 534)—and how these differences are consonant with the word's meaning in each instance. In sum, it is apparent first of all that Wallace is an extraordinarily keen observer of movement who, on the basis of his self-observations and observations of others, presents what can be called a physiognomy of sound that is rooted in movement and breath. He shows specifically how this physiognomy is tied to meaning. Second, from the viewpoint of an evolutionary semantics, his conception of mouth-gestures coincides with a conception of display in that it too justly recognizes the semantic import of kinetic/tactile-kinesthetic bodies and their kinetic/tactile-kinesthetic possibilities and invariants. Third, the focus on "mouth-gesture" — or more broadly on articulatory gestures — ties lingual meaning iconically to the body. However much present-day verbal languages are characterized by an arbitrary linkage of sound and meaning, and however much present-day researchers stress this arbitrary linkage, at the dawn of human language, meaning was iconically linked to gesture. Analogical thinking originally structured human language; the body was a semantic template (Sheets-Johnstone, 1990, 1999a). Foster's research on the symbolic structure of primordial language exemplifies in fine detail the centrality of iconicity. She makes it both palpably and kinetically evident.

Foster's work over the past several decades (e.g., Foster, 1978, 1982, 1990, 1992, 1994a, 1996) may in fact be seen as a detailed elaboration and emendation of Wallace's thesis.[12] Her thesis, in brief, is that the symbolic structure of primordial (verbal) language has its origin in root or elementary articulatory gestures, gestures such as closing the lips to make the sound *m*. These root gestures — what Foster terms "phememes", but which may also be termed archetypal kinetic forms — are pan-human possibilities. Foster's investigations, which extend over an impressive range and diversity of human languages, attest to the fact that these root articulatory forms have fundamental meanings. All reconstructed root forms of the sound *m*, for example, refer to bilateral relationships that are spatio-kinetically analogous to the act of bringing the lips together: "the fingers or hands in taking or grasping", for instance, or "two opposed surfaces in tapering, pressing together, holding together, crushing, or resting against" (Foster, 1978, p. 110). In primordial verbal language, the sound *m* thus referred to a particular motional-relational complex. It might have referred to resting against nest materials as in sleeping or against the earth as in standing, or to pressing together as in copulating, or to crushing as in chewing food, or to pounding one thing with another. In effect, what the linguistic reconstruction of the symbolic structure of primordial verbal language shows is that articulatory gestures were of primary semantic significance, which is to say that the felt, moving body, the tactile-kinesthetic body, was the focal point of symbolization.

---

12 The statement should perhaps be explicitly qualified as a personal observation since Foster's research is not actually based on Wallace's papers. Her work has proceeded strictly from her background as a linguist and she was in fact unaware of Wallace's writings until recently (pers. comm.).

Foster's research findings, which began with her discovery of root forms and her reconstruction of the symbolic structure of primordial verbal language on the basis of these root forms, are forthcoming in *Unraveling Babel*, a work-in-progress. Though technical in places, her Precis of this work is instructive and warrants full citation:

> Global cross-family language comparison with reconstructive reliance on the regularity of language-specific sound changes, reveals a universally shared, monogenetic, primordial stock of thousands of one- to six-consonant roots derived from combinations of phonological gestures (phememes) that originally served as facsimiles of spatial-relational configurations. While pheneme losses and fusions modified meanings and reorganized phonological inventories over the intervening millennia, all historic phonemes can be shown to derive from eleven semantically simulative, consonantal phememes: four voiceless oral stops — *p (outward), *t (juxtaposed), *c (oblique) *k (vertical); two laryngeal consonants — *≈ (interrupted), and *h (prolonged); five resonant continuants, including two semivowels — *m (bracketed), *n (interposed), *l (lax), *w (curvate), *y (lineal), plus a single, semantically neutral, epenthetic, central vowel, *a. Diverse methods of realizing consonantal combinations created historical Babel that the present study acts to unravel.
>
> Evolutionary understanding of linguistic prehistory requires no postulation of major genetic mutations, only a gradual conversion of signaled categorizations of happenings, as warning of presence of a predator becomes reference to predator as member of a category, or as vocal signaling of food-sighting becomes symbolic reference to the category of food sighted. Analysis of the recovered monogenetic lexicon illuminates evolutionary cognitive development, with progressive expansion of semantic differentiations, discovery of successive isoglosses marking phonological changes, and of semantic reorganizations on a deep, Whorfian level. That the roots of language are found to be categorically abstract rather than event-specific demonstrates that language did not begin as naming, as is commonly supposed, but instead converted early, abstractly categorical signaling to abstract relational reference: first perhaps as a mimetic transfer from whole- to part-body analogues, much as abstract whole-body analogues are displayed as spatial visual representations in the bee-dance: for bees a complex, representational signal rather than a symbol,[13] but suggesting an evolutionary means of hominoid, analogical spatial-relational progression from signal to symbol.

In sum, Foster's research shows at a more linguistically sophisticated level than Wallace's how, at the origin of verbal language, fundamental meanings were tied to fundamental movements of the mouth, tongue and vocal tract and further, how, contrary to popular belief, primordial verbal

---

13 For an analysis and justification of the claim that the dances of bees are rightly considered symbolic forms and not "representational signals", see Sheets-Johnstone 1990, Chapter 6 ("On the Origin of Language").

language did not name objects but specified motional-relational complexes. This kinetically articulated semantics and kinetic-spatial conception of the origin of verbal language coincide with the semantics of display in that they too justly recognize archetypal corporeal-kinetic forms and relations.

A final dimension of an evolutionary semantics warrants more detailed attention, namely, analogical thinking. In an earlier work I presented eight paleoanthropological case studies ranging from the origin of stone tool-making and the origin of language to the origin of the concept of death and the origin of paleolithic cave art (Sheets-Johnstone, 1990). These studies showed how, in each instance, corporeal concepts were the foundation of analogical thinking, and how analogical thinking generated the invention or discovery in question.[14] They showed, in other words, how thinking was modelled on the body or how the body was in each case a semantic template. It is significant that, although not acknowledged as such, Langacker's semantic archetypes — space, time, energy, substance — are archetypes deriving from the body; the archetypes specify foundational dimensions of movement and moving bodies, *animate forms*. This derivation follows from the fact that archetypes are, as Langacker affirms, "grounded in everyday experience and fundamental to our conception of the world" (Langacker, 1991, p. 13). Insofar as his billiard-ball model of the world with its noun and verb categories is an archetype of "our experience as mobile and sentient creatures and as manipulators of physical objects" (*ibid.*, p. 285), it is not surprising that his "cognitive semantics" all but names the body as its progenitor, as when he states that "The very foundation of cognitive semantics ... recognizes that certain recurrent and sharply differentiated aspects of our experience emerge as archetypes, which we normally use to structure our conceptions insofar as possible" (*ibid.*, p. 294). Furthermore, when he refers to his billiard-ball model of the world as an "archetypal folk model" and states that "it exerts a powerful influence on both everyday and scientific thought, and no doubt reflects fundamental aspects of cognitive organization" (*ibid.*, p. 13), he is affirming that the basic semantic elements of the model are precisely those of basic grammatical relations: objects and their interactions, thus

14 Nonlinguistic corporeal concepts preceded the invention of verbal language. Whenever that language was invented — before, coincident with, or after the invention of stone tool-making, for example, or before, coincident with, or after the practice of burying the dead, or before, coincident with, or after the practice of painting on the walls of caves — its invention necessarily rested on conceptual foundations that were already present. There would otherwise be no ground on which to conceive the possibility of verbal language or to stumble upon the possibility of its invention.

"space, time, material substance, and energy" (*ibid.*, p. 283), are at the core of both.

Corporeal concepts deriving from our bodily experience with the world structure our perceptions of the world because it is through our bodies that we come to know the world and to make sense of it. When Langacker writes that "I do not believe that semantic roles [e.g., agent, instrument, patient, mover] are first and foremost linguistic constructs, but are rather pre-linguistic conceptions grounded in everyday experience" (*ibid.*, pp. 284–5), he all but recognizes corporeal concepts. What precludes recognition is wrapped up in the term "pre-linguistic." Movement is not *pre-linguistic*. Verbal language is, on the contrary and as noted earlier, most properly conceived as *post-kinetic*. The same misconceived "prelinguistic" notion of life-before-language precludes psychologist Jerome Bruner from recognizing corporeal concepts. Bruner speaks specifically of "prelinguistic practices" rather than "pre-linguistic conceptions", and straightforwardly disavows any possibility of "linguistic forms 'grow[ing] out of' the prelinguistic practices" (Bruner, 1990, p. 75). Yet on the basis of his extensive research on infants and young children, he states that *agentivity* (*ibid.*, p. 77) is the center of a young child's linguistic interest: "Once young children come to grasp the basic idea of reference necessary for any language use ... their principal linguistic interest centers on *human action and its outcomes* ... Agent-and-action, action-and-object, agent-and-object, action-and-location, and possessor-and-possession make up the major part of the semantic relations that appear in the first stage of speech" (*ibid.*, p. 78).[15] Apart from the last-mentioned relation, we may rightfully ask, where else might the central interest in agentivity and action come except from a life already lived in movement? In short, corporeal concepts structure fundamental linguistic concepts. They similarly structured linguistic concepts at the dawn of language. From both an ontogenetical and evolutionary viewpoint, corporeal concepts ground what eventually for humans becomes linguistic. Indeed, corporeal concepts are the essential without which language cannot arise and could not ever have arisen. There would be nothing to hold language together, no body of thought which would anchor it. Language is not experience; it is the means by which we describe experience — or try to describe experience, for "the gap between the experiential and the linguistic is not easily bridged" (Sheets-Johnstone, 1999a, p. 148). Langacker's archetypal analysis directly complements this assessment: "Since language is the means by

---

15   It is notable that narrative, a central theme in Bruner's work, testifies to the idea of agent and action. So also does the popular, folk concept of a story; like narrative, it presupposes the concept of characters who act and who experience their own actions.

which we describe our experience, it is natural that such archetypes ["recurrent and sharply differentiated aspects of our experience"] should be seized upon as the prototypical values of basic linguistic constructs" (Langacker, 1991, pp. 294–5). With respect to corporeal concepts, one might ask what "recurrent and sharply differentiated aspects of experi-ence" would have been more meaningful than bodily experiences for those earlier hominids who invented language?; and what "recurrent and sharply differentiated aspects of our experience" are more meaningful than our bodily experiences in infancy — and onward?

In sum, analogical thinking structured the invention of language and analogical thinking is first and foremost modelled on the body. The body is the semantic standard, the source of corporeal concepts, the model for thinking; it is indeed the basis for metaphor, which is essentially a form of *analogical thinking*. If one is genuinely concerned with the question of how language originated, one must start with living bodies, animate forms, rather than with mutations or brains. Human language, after all, is a living art of communication that was invented; it did not arise "full-blown from the mouths of hominids like the goddess Athena arose full-blown from the head of Zeus" (Sheets-Johnstone, 1990, p. 118). Moreover if no one would claim that paleolithic cave art was the result of a mutation or a brain event, or that stone tool-making was the result of a mutation or brain event, why would one make such a claim with respect to language?

5. Syntax

The question of how linguistic syntax arose, i.e., how syntactical relations arose with the origin of human language, demands serious thought. The word *syntax* comes from ancient Greek *syn* + *tassein* to put in order. Simple reflection shows that something has already to be there in order "to put in order", that is, parts have already to be present before they can be arranged into a coherent whole or constituents have already to be present before they can be related to one another, or, *a conception* of systematized parts or *a conception* of relational constituents has already to be present. Accordingly, in order for there to be syntax either near or at the dawn of human language, then respectively, either words would have had to exist and await syntactical ordering, or the concept of systematized parts or relational constituents would have already existed such that the concept of a linguistic syntax was ready-made, so to speak. From the perspective of an evolutionary semantics, the latter alternative is evidentially sound and thereby the more compelling: syntactical relations are embedded in a kinetic semantics. Hence, a concept of syntax — a nonlinguistic concept—was already present prior to the invention of human language.[16] In effect, the concept and fact of syntax in human languages derives from the concept and fact of syntax in the already existing syntactical kinetic lives and relations of animate forms.

Syntax in the most elementary sense is embedded in movement: if I do (or do not do) this, then this happens. There is an order in which things occur which is contingent upon movement. Furthermore, meanings resulting from relations between events and dynamic happenings are contingent on movement. As infant psychiatrist/clinical psychologist Daniel Stern points out, when he gives an example of an infant's discovery of "consequential relationships" (Stern, 1985, p. 80): if I close my eyes, it gets dark.[17] In short, the concept of syntax derives ultimately from animate movement because it is embedded in animate movement. In addition to being embedded in expectations about what will occur, kinetically generated and kinetically understood syntactical relations are both a built-in of displays in which one set of actions follows from another, or is expected to follow, and a built-in of social interactions in which individuals perform a series of movements that together constitute a particular intercorporeal meaning. The concept of syntax is thus tied most basically to animate life and to a kinetic semantics. Living forms move in sequentially patterned meaningful ways and sense themselves and others moving in sequentially patterned meaningful ways. The concept of syntax is tied to these dual sense-makings: moving in patterned ways such as to make sense and perceiving movement—putting dynamic events together—in such a way as to make sense. In sum, syntax in human languages derives from the fundamentally kinetic nature of animate life itself and its kinetic semantics.

Whether in the form of display sequences or of more complex species-specific social interactions, animate movement is an ongoing, unfolding dynamic: an individual, by moving, communicates something, accomplishes something, or makes something happen. Another individual or other individuals respond by moving—or not moving—and thereby they too communicate something, accomplish something, or make something happen. In effect, since animate movement has meaning and consequences with respect to the movement of other creatures—and of things in the world—syntax is not uncommonly a collectively-created aspect of animate life: the response to a display, for example, may itself be a display that, by its relation to the initial display, elaborates the latter's meaning as

16   For that matter, a number of nonlinguistic corporeal concepts would have had to have been present, e.g., the concept of oneself as a sound-maker as discussed earlier (see also Sheets-Johnstone, 1990).

17   Stern describes consequential relationships in the context of describing invariants within the experience of self-agency.

in primate presenting and mounting. It is of particular interest to note in this context that archaeologists and anthropologists who attempt to link early hominid stone tool-making with verbal language often try to show that the cognitive abilities underlying the origin of stone tool-making are similar to the cognitive abilities underlying the origin of verbal language and that these abilities are encapsulated in "'the tendency to see reality symbolically'" (Kitahara-Frisch, 1980, p. 218). Thus, stone tool-making, like language, is a "symbolizing activity" or "symbolic behavior" and stone tools, like words, are symbols (Stringer and Gamble, 1993). A prime problem with these attempts (see Sheets-Johnstone, 1999a) is the precipitous leap to symbolization. Rather than being rooted in the lifeworld, human languages are rooted in an abstract realm called "the mental". Kinetic sense-making—making meaning through movement and making sense of movement—is nowhere recognized. Movement is in fact largely ignored. The idea that it is integral to the origin of human language no less than to the origin of stone tool-making indeed rarely surfaces.

Displays and species-specific social interactions are archetypal corporeal-kinetic forms and relations that, from the viewpoint of an evolutionary semantics, constitute the most fundamental syntactical as well as semantic units. Syntax is originarily not a static arrangement of parts but a dynamic ordering of movements or gestures.[18] This evolutionary understanding of syntax is consistent with the fact that meaning in its most elementary form is structured sequentially in and through the moving body, or, to put the point in socio-communicative terms, it is sequentially structured intercorporeally, in and through kinetic intercorporeal relationships. We grasp these relationships in observing the movement of animate forms and in the experience of articulatory gestures. This evolutionary understanding of syntax is complementary to Langacker's notion of syntax as a structure within cognitive semantics:

---

18 In their insightful and thought-provoking article, "The Evolution of Human Speech: The Role of Enhanced Breathing Control", MacLarnon and Hewitt mention how in nonhuman primate vocalizations, "the sequence of note production definitely can be important in conveying meaning." They cite as example Mitani and Marler's study of gibbons and Seyfarth and Cheney's study of monkeys. They go on to state that "However, most authors agree that nonhuman vocalizations contain nothing approaching human syntactical constructions, the encoding systems enabling rapid and highly flexible information transfer" (MacLarnon and Hewitt, 1999, pp. 357–8). Their point is that physiological and morphological differences are as significant as cognitive ones. My point is that whatever the differences, syntax is still plainly evident and can hardly be dismissed on the grounds that it does not approach "human syntactical constructions." By similar reasoning, one could dismiss human gymnasts on the grounds that they do not approach gibbon kinetic dexterity in brachiating. From the viewpoint of an evolutionary semantics, syntax is fundamentally a kinetic phenomenon evident in nonhuman as well as human animal communications. Its specifically verbal realization does not compromise its kinetic foundations.

In contrast to the generative dogma that grammar (or at least syntax) represents an 'autonomous component' distinct from both semantics and lexicon, it [cognitive grammar] maintains that lexicon, morphology, and syntax form a continuum of meaningful structures whose segregation into discrete components is necessarily artifactual. It claims, moreover, that this entire range of phenomena can be fully and optimally analyzed as residing in configurations of symbolic structures that conform to the content requirement (Langacker, 1991, p. 3).

To exemplify the dynamic nature of syntax and its status within a symbolic structure, consider the following account of a male-male wild olive baboon greeting:

A typical greeting begins with one male walking upright rapidly toward another with a straight-legged, rolling stride. The approaching male looks directly at his intended partner while making friendly gestures, such as smacking his lips, flattening his ears back, and narrowing his eyes. Often, the second male maintains eye contact and smacks his lips in return. In that case, the animals get up close and personal. They often begin with a quick hug or nuzzle. One then presents his hindquarters; the other grasps them, mounts the reversed partner, and touches his scrotum or gently pulls his penis. Sometimes participants exchange active and passive roles during a single greeting. After a completed greeting, which usually lasts no more than a few seconds, both males walk away using the stiff-legged gait characteristic of the approach. (B. Bower, 2000, pp. 280–1).[19]

A syntactical relationship obtains among the many kinetic forms within the total kinetic form labeled "male-male greeting"; that is, a specific — and "typical" — corporeal-kinetic order of dynamic events unfolds between the opening stiff-legged approach and the closing stiff-legged departure. Some of these intermediate movements are found in other communicative exchanges: smacking the lips, flattening the ears, presenting, mounting. Thus elements of the total form may appear in other intercorporeal exchanges. Moreover the total form may be incomplete in that one male may abruptly pull away from the other before the whole greeting has been kinetically articulated (Smuts and Watanabe, 1990; Watanabe and Smuts, 1999). Customary syntax may thus, as in human languages, be abruptly interrupted, an incomplete greeting, like an incomplete sentence, left dangling mid-air. On the other hand, a *customary* syntax is *customarily* observed: one male does not saunter up to another, for example, and then touch his scrotum or gently pull his penis. A particular sequence of move-

---

19 It is curious that, though concise as befits a scientific report on the research of others, Bower's description includes an inaccurate kinetic ascription. He writes that the baboons "often begin with a quick hug or nuzzle." Watanabe and Smuts — the researchers themselves (Watanabe and Smuts, 1990, p. 152; 1999, p. 102) — write that "face-to-body nuzzling" occurs less frequently than presenting, grasping the hindquarters of the other, mounting, touching the scrotum, and pulling the penis, and that "embracing" "rarely" occurs.

ments and a particular style of moving (the stiff-legged gait, the gentle pull) obtains within which certain movements may be included or omitted and within which a reversal of roles may take place.[20]

Other situations attest to a similar syntactical ordering of movements and to a similar elemental syntactical flexibility. In an attack-threat situation, for example, a baboon will stare in the direction of his opponent, possibly jerk his head up and down, flatten his ears, and raise his eyebrows, showing a white spot above the lids. He may intensify the threat by yawning, thus making evident formidable canines that Watanabe and Smuts (1999, p. 103) describe as "two-inch-long razor sharp canines [that] easily rank among the most lethal weapons on the African savanna." A variety of other body movements may accompany or follow these facial expressions: forward and backward scraping movements of the hand along the ground, a jerking of the body and/or the head forward and back, rearing on the hindlegs, and so on (Hall and DeVore, 1972, pp. 162–3, 169–70). The sequence of gestures is thus mutable; an attack may in fact commence immediately without any previous threat gestures being made, in which instance, of course, there are no syntactical relationships.

In the communicative behaviors of nonhuman animals that are termed displays, a particular meaning or complex of meanings is made evident through a particular kinetic performance or series of performances. In species-specific social interactions generally, a particular meaning or complex of meanings is similarly engendered in particular kinetic performances or series of performances.[21] Interanimate expectations attend both forms of

20   Sequentiality is not necessarily the defining aspect of syntax. Noun declensions in Latin, for example, specify syntactical relationships which are not sequentially ordered in a particular way within a sentence. It is pertinent to point out too that a kinetic syntax obtains only in the context of an interanimate semantics, that is, only in the context of an animal addressing its movement specifically to another. Were a baboon to stare off in the distance and flatten its ears as it ambles off in the direction of the stare, its gestures would not bear a syntactical relationship to each other. Its gestures would not constitute *articulatory* gestures.

21   It is instructive to note (though beyond the bounds of this paper to examine) a relationship between syntax and ritual, thus a possible relationship between the evolution of syntax and the evolution of ritual. Ritual involves performing a certain series of actions in a certain way and thereby has a syntactical structure. Ritual may thus be examined in the context of a kinetic semantics. The studies of anthropologist John Watanabe and psychologist Barbara Smuts offer an interesting point of departure for this examination. They have analyzed the male-male wild olive baboon greeting in terms of ritual following the theoretical analyses of ritual by anthropologist Roy Rappaport. Rappaport's analyses were based on his field studies of ritual pig feasting and warfare of the Tsembaga Maring of highland New Guinea. Watanabe and Smuts describe ritual as consisting "of more or less invariant sequences of acts and utterances that the participants themselves do not invent but to which they must conform, and that "in order to have a ritual at all, participants must actually perform these sequences rather than simply invoke or acknowledge them" (Watanabe and Smuts, 1999, p. 100). Interestingly enough, they quote Rappaport's comment that "The invariance of ritual, *which antedates the development of language*, is the foundation of convention ..." (*ibid.*, p. 101; italics added). Without doubt, *language* here refers to verbal language and as such implicitly underscores the point that

communication. A displaying individual or social participant expects certain things to happen in virtue of what he or she does; so also with the displayed-to individual or social participant who responds—or does not respond: he/she also expects certain things to happen in virtue of what he or she does. As indicated above, syntactical kinetic relations are a constituent part of expectations in the form of if/then relationships (Husserl, e.g., 1989, p. 63; 1970, pp. 161–2), "consequential relationships" (Stern, 1985). If an individual is stared at by another and then in addition sees the white spots above that individual's eyes, for instance, and if he/she furthermore sees that individual opening its mouth in a great yawn, then he/she may expect consequences to follow if he/she does not desist in doing whatever he/she is doing. In the context of interanimate life, if/then relationships are precisely consequential relationships that are contingent on movement and are saturated in expectations on both sides; individuals expect certain circumstances to follow from a particular gesture or movement or ongoing series of movements.

Displays and species-specific social interactions aside, if/then relationships are discovered and learned in the course of individual explorations such as those of an infant—or adult—when it notices what happens if it moves forward, for instance, or if it reaches out toward something and touches it. Though not specified as such, these essentially kinetic syntactical relationships have been described by infant-child psychologist Lois Bloom in the course of her extensive investigations of a child's transition to language. Though not acknowledged as such, movement is at the core of what she terms "relational concepts". She states that

> [C]hildren show us, in many ways, that they know something about the ways persons relate to objects and objects relate to each other long before they use the words that express such relationships. Their earliest relational concepts are not learned through language (Bloom, 1993, p. 50).

Bloom does not delve deeply into the question of how relational concepts are learned, but the centrality of movement lies just below the surface of her discussion. She states that "Children learn about relationships between objects by observing the effects of movement and actions done by themselves and other persons ... When objects move, the movement has a source—frequently a person who acts to cause the movement—and an effect—either on the object itself or on another object ... Certain movements the child makes produce specific effects, such as rolling over,

verbal language has its roots in a kinetic semantics. Watanabe and Smuts's interest, it might be noted, is in the evolution of cooperation and their purpose is to show how behavioral invariance sustains trust; that is, how "mutually enacted invariance can become iconic representations (sic) of interindividual reliability, certainty, and perhaps even truth" (p. 101).

splashing, eating, and throwing" (*ibid.*). After giving other examples, she concludes that "Infants learn to detect and recognize the regularities among a movement, its origin, and its effect" (*ibid.*, p. 51). Clearly, relational concepts are embedded in the experience of movement, one's own movement, the movement of others, and the movement of things, and they are anchored in syntactical kinetic relations. The concept of syntax in human languages is rooted in these relations, which are themselves rooted in a kinetic semantics.

6. A Sensory-Kinetic Approach to the Origin of Human Language

The above ontogenetic view of syntax complements the phylogenetic view exemplified earlier in the discussion of displays and species-specific social interactions. Both views show—and show unequivocally—that verbal language is *post-kinetic*. In the beginning, and in ontogeny as in phylogeny, syntax is a bodily created dynamic ordering of events within a kinetic semantics. From this perspective, meaning, concepts, and the various organizational structures of verbal language issue fundamentally not from abstract mental entities—"idealized cognitive models" (Lakoff, 1987, p. 68), for example—but directly from the body. Once corporeal concepts and a kinetic semantics are recognized and recognized as in no way inferior to their linguistic relatives—but on the contrary, in the most fundamental sense, recognized as their progenitors—there is no reason for recourse to abstract models and schema as grounding phenomena; the models and schema are cognitive offshoots or conceptual derivatives of corporeal-kinetic realities.

The resistance to acknowledging concepts outside of verbal language is a hindrance to the recognition of corporeal-kinetic realities and is a *human* and an *adultist* conceit.[22] A sensory-kinetic approach to the origin of lan-

---

22 With respect to a resistance to nonlinguistic concepts generally, consider, for example, that we all have a concept of what a balloon does when it is blown up and released. The word "splutters" hardly captures the movement dynamics of the released balloon, its quick changes in direction, for example, its unpredictable range of movement, its sudden collapse, and so on. No words adequately capture the sensed dynamics. We have a *corporeal concept* of the movement dynamics of the released balloon.

With respect to the resistance being a human conceit, consider that nonhuman animals such as wolves, dolphins, whales, ravens, weaverbirds, chimpanzees, gorillas, lions, tigers, dogs, and undoubtedly untold other species including reptilians and fish could hardly survive in the absence of corporeal concepts, of themselves, of the animate beings, including predators, i.e., species other than their own, with whom they come in contact or interact, and of objects in their environment such as stones, seaweed, or possible roosting niches.

With respect to the resistance being an adultist conceit, consider that when movement such as grasping an object is investigated at an adult level (e.g., Jeannerod, 1994), the investigation typically takes movement for granted such that a rich and proper understanding of the

guage exposes the conceit by showing how movement is our mother tongue, the spawning ground of corporeal concepts, and our original and abiding source of meaning. In broader terms, a sensory-kinetic approach shows that common bodies give rise to common bodies of meaning through movement. As we have seen, living bodies — animate forms — are natural sources of meaning. The movement of animate forms naturally *displays itself* to others, indeed, regularly and readily displays itself to those about them, communicating annoyance as in aggressive threat displays, or fearfulness, friendliness, playfulness, curiosity, and so on. This kinetic source of meaning links each of us to the interanimate world that is our particular *Umwelt*. It is our matchpoint with the world, the springboard of our responsivity. We are all kinetically attuned to each other and to a world of dynamically shifting physiognomies that portend something meaningful. As linguistically displayed-to animals in particular, humans are readily and keenly movement-sensitive. They visually perceive and kinetically apperceive the articulatory gestures of others in sign and verbal languages respectively; they recognize the kinetic/tactile-kinesthetic *comsigns* of their species and of their particular culture. As with other animate forms, movement is their mother tongue and their matchpoint with the world.

A sensory-kinetic approach to the origin of human language has positive implications for understanding the place of sign language in evolutionary history, not in the sense of giving a competitive edge to gestural language — as if there were a contest between linguistic forms — but in the sense of giving a *conceptual* edge. A sensory-kinetic approach reveals and elucidates a kinetic semantics that can be fleshed out along evolutionary lines. These lines clearly indicate evolutionary continuities. Evolutionary theory requires us to take these continuities seriously, not only with respect to morphology but with respect to cognition and emotion. Primatologist Emil Menzel long ago emphasized how chimpanzees communicate through bodily comportment, orientation, and movement

---

experience of movement and of its conceptual infrastructure are bypassed. Grasping an object is an *achievement* for an infant, not a ready-made. Human knowledge of the world and human competencies are built up. They are built up not through representations in a brain, but through first-person experience, through actual movement toward and around objects, movement in immediate tactile contact with objects, and so on. Representations are hypothetical entities once-removed from actual experience. Moreover human knowledge and competencies are built up not by *planning* movement as per common adultist accounts but by *moving*: an infant *moves* and experiences its own movement. In learning to move itself, an infant does not "look to see what moves" (as per Dennett, 1991, p. 428), but kinesthetically feels its own movement. However covered over by adultist renditions, movement is our beginning and abiding matchpoint with the world and our way of making sense of it. (For further discussion see Sheets-Johnstone, 1999a, particularly Chapter V, "On Learning to Move Oneself: A Constructive Phenomenology").

(Menzel, 1976), which is the context in which Lieberman, referring to Menzel's work, spoke of "a whole body gestural system". At whatever point in hominid evolutionary history human language originated and evolved, it grew out of just such a primate system of communication enhanced by consistent bipedalism,[23] which is to say out of an already existent kinetic semantics that involved the whole body and that was pre-eminently visual. The conceptual edge given to sign language stems from this semantics; it stems from movement, the immeasurable possibilities of movement, and from the fact that movement and meaning are naturally intertwined. With their subtle bodily inflections, condensations, elaborations, exaggerations, temporal compressions, indexical loci, and so on,[24] present-day sign languages exemplify this conceptual edge. They attest to corporeal concepts and to thinking in movement,[25] perhaps even to the point of being immensely sophisticated, culturally inundated relics of a hominid past.

Ontogenetical research implicitly validates a sensory-kinetic approach to the origin of language and strongly supports our taking developmental facts of life into equal consideration. These facts similarly reveal and elucidate a kinetic semantics. A kinetic semantics grounds Langacker's billiard-ball model of how we think about the world (Langacker, 1991, p. 13), and presumably think about it from the very beginning of our lives as infants. *Bodily movement* is at the heart of this model. There would be no physical objects as such without bodily movement in virtue of which we explore the world and come to recognize objects as such—by going around them, turning them over, drawing closer to them, approaching them from a different direction, and so on (Husserl, e.g., 1970, pp. 106, 217). This semantics is furthermore supported by the research studies of Foster and Wallace which show that verbal language is rooted in semantically rich corporeal-kinetic possibilities and invariants. The conceptual foundations of verbal language are thus to be found by way of the body. The body is a semantic template; thinking is modelled analogically along

---

23   Primates are bipedal in a variety of circumstances. See, for example, Pilbeam, 1972, Goodall, 1976, and Schultz, 1950. For a comparative estimate of the difference in bipedality between hominid and nonhominid primates, see Pilbeam 1986. Australopithecines are estimated to have been 55 percent bipedal and their ancestors to have been 10 percent bipedal.

24   A particular dimension of the "and so on" should perhaps be specified since it reinforces the claim that sign language derives from a primate "whole body gestural system." Armstrong, Stokoe, and Wilcox (1995, p. 84) point out that "being a language, and so more complexly organized than other gesture systems, a primary sign language also incorporates nonmanual actions as well; e.g., facial expressions, head movement, trunk movement, and changes of stance."

25   For an aesthetic, ontogenetic, and phylogenetic analysis of thinking in movement, see Sheets-Johnstone, 1999a.

the moving lines of the body (Sheets-Johnstone, 1990). Individuals can kinetically address each other in particular ways because they are sentiently alive to their own moving body and to the moving bodies of others, thus to the tactile-kinesthetic possibilities and invariants inherent in an intercorporeal kinetic semantics. As Armstrong, Stokoe, and Wilcox (1995, p. 4) so pithily state, "language comes from the body".

References

Altmann, Stuart A. 1967. "The Structure of Primate Social Communication", in *Social Communication among Primates*, ed. Stuart A. Altmann. Chicago: University of Chicago Press, pp. 325 62.

Armstrong, David F., William C. Stokoe, and Sherman E. Wilcox. 1995. *Gesture and the Nature of Language*. Cambridge: Cambridge University Press.

Bloom, Lois. 1993. *The Transition from Infancy to Language*. Cambridge: Cambridge University Press.

Bower, Bruce. 2000. "Cries and Greetings." *Science News* 157, no. 18 (April 29, 2000): 280–2.

Bower, T. G. R. 1974. *Development in Infancy*. San Francisco: W. H. Freeman.

Bramblett, Claud A. 1976. *Patterns of Primate Behavior*. Palo Alto, CA: Mayfield Publishing.

Bruner, Jerome. 1990. *Acts of Meaning*. Cambridge, MA: Harvard University Press.

Clark, Eve V. 1979. "Building a Vocabulary: Words for Objects, Actions and Relations", in *Language Acquisition*, ed. Paul Fletcher and Michael Garman. Cambridge: Cambridge University Press, pp. 149–60.

Clark, Eve V. 1973. "Non-Linguistic Strategies and the Acquisition of Word Meanings." *Cognition* 2: 161–82.

Cook, Nancy. 1978. "In, On and Under Revisited Again", in *Papers and Reports on Child Language Development* 15. Stanford, CA: Stanford University Press, pp. 38–45.

Curtis, Helena. 1975. *Biology*, 2nd ed. New York: Worth Publishers.

Dennett, Daniel. 1991. *Consciousness Explained*. Boston: Little, Brown and Company.

de Sousa, Ronald. 1987. *The Rationality of Emotion*. Cambridge, MA: MIT Press.

Foster, Mary LeCron. 1978. "The Symbolic Structure of Primordial Language", in *Human Evolution: Biosocial Perspectives*, ed. S. L. Washburn and E.R. McCown. Menlo Park, CA: Benjamin/Cummings Publishing, pp. 77–121.

Foster, Mary LeCron. 1982. "Meaning as Metaphor I." *Quaderni di Semantica* 3, no. 1: 95–102.

Foster, Mary LeCron. 1990. "Symbolic Origins and Transitions in the Palaeolithic." In in *The Emergence of Modern Humans: An Archaeological Perspective*. Edinburgh: Edinburgh University Press, pp. 517–39.

Foster, Mary LeCron. 1992. "Body Process in the Evolution of Language", in *Giving the Body Its Due*, ed. Maxine Sheets-Johnstone. Albany, NY: State University of New York Press, pp. 208–30.

Foster, Mary LeCron. 1994. "Symbolism: The Foundation of Culture", in *The Companion Encyclopedia of Anthropology*, ed. Tim Ingold. New York: Routledge, pp. 366–95.

Foster, Mary LeCron. 1996. "Reconstruction of the Evolution of Human Spoken Language", in *Handbook of Symbolic Evolution*, ed. Andrew Lock and Charles Peters. Oxford: Oxford University Press, pp. 747–72.

Foster, Mary LeCron. Precis of *Unraveling Babel*, work-in-progress.

Gallese, Vittorio. In press. ""The Acting Subject: Towards the Neural Basis of Social Cognition", in *Neural Correlates of Consciousness*, ed. T. Metzinger. Cambridge, MA: MIT Press.

Gallese, Vittorio, Luciano Fadiga, Leonardo Fogassi, and Giacomo Rizzolatti. 1996. "Action Recognition in the Premotor Cortex." *Brain* 19: 593–609.

Goodall, Jane van Lawick. 1972. "A Preliminary Report on Expressive Movements and Communication in The Gombe Stream Chimpanzees", in *Primate Patterns*, ed. Phyllis Dolhinow. New York: Holt, Rinehart and Winston, pp. 25–84.

Goodall, Jane van Lawick. 1976. "Free-Living Chimpanzees" and "Chimpanzee Locomotor Play", in *Play — Its Role in Development and Evolution*, ed. Jerome Bruner, Alison Jolly, and Kathy Sylva. New York: Basic Books, pp. 156–60.

Grieve, Robert, Robert Hoogenraad, and Diarmid Murray. 1977. "On the Young Child's Use of Lexis and Syntax in Understanding Locative Instructions." *Cognition* 5: 235–50.

Hall, K. R. L. and Irven DeVore. 1972. "Baboon Social Behavior", in *Primate Patterns*, ed. Phyllis Dolhinow. New York: Holt, Rinehart and Winston, pp. 125–80.

Husserl, Edmund. 1966. *The Phenomenology of Internal Time Consciousness*, trans. James S. Churchill. Bloomington, IN: Indiana University Press.

Husserl, Edmund. 1970. *The Crisis of European Sciences and Transcendental Phenomenology*, trans. David Carr. Evanston, IL: Northwestern University Press.

Husserl, Edmund. 1973. *Cartesian Meditations*, trans. Dorion Cairns. The Hague: Martinus Nijhoff.

Husserl, Edmund. 1983. *Ideas Pertaining to a Pure Phenomenology and to a Phenomenological Philosophy. (Ideas I)*, trans. F. Kersten. The Hague: Martinus Nijhoff.

Husserl, Edmund. 1989. *Ideas Pertaining to a Pure Phenomenology and to a Phenomenological Philosophy. (Ideas II)*, trans. R. Rojcewicz and A. Schuwer. Dordrecht: Kluwer Academic Publishers.

Jeannerod, M. 1994. "The Representing Brain: Neural Correlates of Motor Intention and Imagery." *Behavioral and Brain Sciences* 17: 187–245.

Johnson, Mark. 1987. *The Body in the Mind*. Chicago: University of Chicago Press.

Jung, Carl G. 1980. *The Archetypes and the Collective Unconscious*. Bollingen Series XX. Princeton: Princeton University Press.

Kitahara-Frisch, Jean. 1980. "Symbolizing Technology as a Key to Human Evolution", in *Symbol as Sense*, ed. Mary LeCron Foster and Stanley H. Brandes. New York: Academic Press, pp. 211–23.

Lakoff, George. 1987. *Women, Fire, and Dangerous Things*. Chicago: University of Chicago Press.

Lakoff, George and Mark Johnson. 1999. *Philosophy in the Flesh: The Embodied Mind and Its Challenge to Western Thought*. New York: Basic Books.

Langacker, Ronald W. 1991. *Foundations of Cognitive Grammar*, vol. II. Stanford, CA: Stanford University Press.

Liberman, Alvin M. and Ignatius G. Mattingly. 1985. "The Motor Theory of Speech Perception Revised." *Cognition* 21, no. 1: 1–36.

Lieberman, Philip. 1983. "On the Nature and Evolution of the Biological Bases of Language", in *Glossogenetics*, ed. E. de Grolier. New York: Harwood, pp. 91–114.

Lorenz, Konrad. 1967. *On Aggression*, trans. Marjorie Kerr Wilson. New York: Bantam Books.

MacLarnon, Ann M. and Gwen P. Hewitt. 1999. "The Evolution of Human Speech: The Role of Enhanced Breathing Control." *American Journal of Physical Anthropology* 109: 341–63.

Menzel, Emil. 1976. "Discussion", in *Origins and Evolution of Language and Speech*, ed. Stevan R. Harnad, Horst D. Steklis, and Jane B. Lancaster. *Annals of the New York Academy of Sciences* 280: pp. 167–9.

Morford, Jill P., Jenny L. Singleton, and Susan Goldin-Meadow. 1995. "The Genesis of Language: How Much Time Is Needed to Generate Arbitrary Symbols in a Sign System?" In *Language, Gesture, and Space*, ed. Karen Emmorey and Judy S. Reilly. Hillsdale, NJ: Lawrence Erlbaum Associates, pp. 313–32.

Neisser, Ulric. 1976. *Cognition and Reality*. San Francisco: W. H. Freeman and Co.

Piaget, Jean. 1967. *La naissance de l'intelligence chez l'enfant*.Neuchatel: Delachaux et Niestlé.

Pilbeam, David R. 1972. *The Ascent of Man*. New York: Macmillan.
        1986. "Distinguished Lecture: Hominoid Evolution and Hominoid Origins." *American Anthropologist*, n.s. 88: 295–312.

Premack, David. 1975. "Symbols Inside and Outside of Language", in *The Role of Speech in Language*, ed. James F. Kavanaugh and James E. Cutting. Cambridge, MA: MIT Press, pp. 45–61.

Rizzolatti, Giacomo and Vittorio Gallese. 1997. "From Action to Meaning", in *Les neurosciences et la philosophie de l'action*, ed. Jean-Luc Petit. Paris: Librairie Philosophique.

Rowell, Thelma. 1972. *The Social Behaviour of Monkeys*. Harmondsworth, Middlesex, England: Penguin Books.

Savage-Rumbaugh, Sue, Duane Rumbaugh, and Sally Boysen. 1978. "Linguistically Mediated Tool Use and Exchange by Chimpanzees (*Pan troglodytes*)." *Behavioral and Brain Sciences* 4: 539–54.

Schultz, A. H. 1950. "The Physical Distinctions of Man." *Proceedings of the American Philosophical Society* 94: 428–49.

Sheets-Johnstone, Maxine. 1990. *The Roots of Thinking*. Philadelphia: Temple University Press.

Sheets-Johnstone, Maxine. 1994. *The Roots of Power: Animate Form and Gendered Bodies*. Chicago: Open Court Publishing.

Sheets-Johnstone, Maxine. 1999a. *The Primacy of Movement*. Amsterdam/ Philadelphia: John Benjamins.

Sheets-Johnstone, Maxine. 1999b. "Re-Thinking Husserl's Fifth Meditation", *Philosophy Today* 43 (Supplement): 99–106.

Smuts, Barbara B. and John M. Watanabe. 1990. "Social Relationships and Ritualized Greetings in Adult Male Baboons (*Papio cynocephalus anubis*)." *International Journal of Primatology*, 11, no. 2: 147–72.

Stern, Daniel N. 1985. *The Interpersonal world of the Infant*. New York: Basic Books.

Stringer, Christopher and Clive Gamble. 1993. *In Search of the Neanderthals: Solving the Puzzle of Human Origins*. London: Thames and Hudson.

Strum, Shirley C. 1987. *Almost Human: A Journey into the World of Baboons*. New York: W. W. Norton.

Wallace, Alfred R. 1881. "Anthropology." *Nature* 204: 242–4.

    1895. "The Expressiveness of Speech, or, Mouth-Gesture as a Factor in the Origin of Language." *Fortnightly Review* 64: 528–43.

Watanabe, John M. and Barbara B. Smuts. 1999. "Explaining Religion without Explaining It Away: Trust, Truth, and the Evolution of Cooperation in Roy A. Rappaport's 'The Obvious Aspects of Ritual'." *American Anthropologist* 101, no. 1: 98–112.

Chapter X

Kinesthetic Memory

Introduction

This essay attempts to elucidate the nature of kinesthetic memory, demonstrate its centrality to everyday human movement, and thereby promote fresh cognitive and phenomenological understandings of movement in everyday life. Prominent topics in this undertaking include kinesthesia, dynamics, and habit. The endeavor has both a critical and constructive dimension. The constructive dimension is anchored in Luria's seminal notion of a kinetic melody and in related phenomenological analyses of movement. The dual anchorage stems from the general fact that kinesthetic memory is based on kinesthetic experience, hence on the bodily felt dynamics of movement, and on the particular fact that any movement creates a distinctive kinetic dynamics in virtue of its spatio-temporal-energic qualities. The critical dimension focuses on constructs that commonly anchor discussions of movement but bypass the reality of a kinetic dynamics, notably, Merleau-Ponty's "motor intentionality", and the notions of a body schema and body image. The pointillist conception of movement and the Western metaphysics that undergird these constructs is examined in the concluding section of the paper.

1. Luria's Kinetic- and Kinesthetically-Informed Neuropsychology

Russian neuropsychologist Aleksandr Romanovich Luria is regarded "a founding father of neuropsychology" (Goldberg 1990), lauded for his insights and meticulous clinical research (e.g., Teuber 1966, 1980; Pribram 1966, 1980). He describes movement pathologies as disturbed kinetic melodies; everyday movement no longer flows forth in effortless ways, or indeed, is no longer even a possibility for patients with brain lesions. In *The Working Brain*, Luria describes how kinetic melodies are constituted, using writing as an example. "In the initial stages", he observes, *writing* depends on memorizing the graphic form of every letter. It takes place through a chain of isolated motor impulses, each of which is responsible for the performance of only one element of the graphic structure; with practice, this structure of the process is radically altered and writing is converted into a single 'kinetic melody,' no longer requiring the memorizing of the visual form of each isolated letter or individual motor impulses for making every stroke (Luria, 1973, p. 32).

He later specifies how voluntary movement is a "complex functional system", fulfilled in "the perfect performance of a movement" on the basis of four fundamental conditions: (1) "*kinaesthetic afferentation*," (2) a system of "*spatial coordinates*" centered on "the visual and vestibular systems and the system of cutaneous kinaesthetic sensation", (3) a "*chain of consecutive movements*, each element of which must be denervated after its completion so as to allow the next element to take its place", and (4) a "motor task" which at more complex levels of conscious action "are dictated by *intentions*" (*ibid.*, pp. 35-37). At the neurological level, voluntary movement is thus the orchestrated result of "completely different brain systems" (*ibid.*, p. 37) that work together in such a way that a kinetic melody unfolds.

Of singular significance is Luria's recognition that voluntary movement is not just a spatial phenomenon but a *temporal* phenomenon. Luria in fact distinguishes between the temporal and spatial distribution of motor impulses in terms of the premotor and postcentral cortical zones, respectively, noting specifically that the premotor zones of the brain "are responsible for the "*conversion of individual motor impulses into consecutive kinetic melodies*" (*ibid.*, p. 179). Earlier, he pointedly emphasizes that "Movement is always a process with a *temporal course*" that "requires a continuous *chain of interchanging impulses*" (*ibid.*, p. 176). In this context, he reiterates in more general terms his descriptive account of the origin of kinetic melodies: "In the initial stages of formation of any movement this chain must consist of a series of isolated impulses; with the development of motor skills the individual impulses are synthesized and combined into *integral kinaesthetic structures* or *kinetic melodies* when a single impulse is sufficient to activate a complete *dynamic stereotype* of automatically interchanging elements" (*ibid.*, p. 176). He later specifies that the construction and performance of any complex movement depend on:

1. an intact frontal lobe, or what he designates an intentional "brain zone";

2. kinesthesia, or what he designates an "*integrity of its [the movement's] kinaesthetic afferentation*";

3. a temporal organization, or what he designates a "constant regulation of *muscle tone* ... and a sufficiently rapid and smooth *changeover*

from one system of motor innervations to another, with the formation of complete *kinaesthetic melodies* in the final stages of development of skilled movement" (*ibid.*, pp. 251–3).

With respect to the latter requirement, Luria emphasizes the necessity of the second requirement — kinesthetic afference — citing physiologist Nicolas Bernstein's detailed studies of movement and its fundamental "degrees of freedom" (Bernstein, 1984, 1996)). As he points out, the degrees of freedom in human movement and the constantly changing tone of the muscles "explain why it is that, in the performance of a voluntary movement or action, although the motor task preserves its regulatory role, the highest responsibility is transferred *from efferent to afferent impulses*" (Luria, 1973, p. 249). Kinesthesia is thus of maximal significance; successful voluntary movement and the formation of "a complete dynamic stereotype" depend on it.

Though not explicitly specified in this way, kinetic melodies are inscribed in the body. They are *"integral kinaesthetic structures"* (Luria, 1973, p. 176) and are thus essentially, i.e., in a living, experiential sense, not brain events but corporeally resonant ones, in-the-flesh dynamic patterns of movement that are *initiated* — and run off. The most basic of kinetic melodies, ones that might be called fundamental melodies of life — if not fundamental melodies *for* life — are forged in the course of infancy and childhood, some of them beginning in pre-natal life (Luria, 1980, p. 192). In each instance, they are kept alive by kinesthetic memory; their inscription in the body is by way of kinesthetic memory, which is to say by way of distinctive movement dynamics. Thus, in normal everyday adult life, a kinetic dynamics unfolds that is at once familiar and yet quintessentially tailored kinetically to the particular situation at hand: a familiar but distinctive kinetic dynamics unfolds in articulatory gestures as we speak, in repetitive downward swoops of our arm as we hammer, in subtle, varying shifts of direction and bendings of our body as we move quickly forward along a crowded sidewalk. The familiarity of these dynamics is grounded in invariants, invariants of speech, of hammering, of weaving a path around obstacles. Their tailoring is grounded in the particular situational vagaries found in the present experience: feeling ill at ease speaking to this particular person, hammering with this new hammer, weaving our way on this icy sidewalk.

Kinetic melodies that are inscribed in our bodies are dynamic patterns of movement. They constitute that basic, vast, and potentially ever-expandable repertoire of "I cans" (Husserl, 1970, 1973, 1980, 1989) permeating human life: walking, speaking, reaching, hugging, throwing, carrying, opening, closing, brushing, running, wiping, leaping, pulling, pushing. The basic kinetic repertoire is indeed virtually limitless, being constrained only by age, inclination — and pathology. Its sequential complexity and intricacy are similarly virtually limitless, not only with respect to everyday "I cans" such as writing and tying knots, for example, but with respect to dancing, diving, skiing, performing surgical procedures, administering medical courses of action, learning artistic modes of applying paint and of sculpting a piece of wood, and so on. In each instance, knowledgeability is not simply a know-*how*, a lesser form of knowledge that is "merely physical." Kinetic melodies are saturated in cognitive and affective acuities that both anchor invariants and color and individualize the manner in which any particular melody runs off.

Luria's concept of kinetic melodies is an experientially-based concept rooted in the kinetic dynamics of life as normally lived. "Kinetic melody" thus describes *an experienced kinetic event*: writing one's name fluently, reciting the months of the year, solving an arithmetical problem (Luria, e.g., 1966, p. 226; see also below). What is ruptured by tumors, hemorrhages, or brain lesions ruptures a normally *dynamic* life, a life of meaningful movement and of ease in movement. When Luria at one point characterizes a wounded patient as suffering an "*adynamia* of psychological processes" (*ibid.*, pp. 224-26), he quotes the patient's own reflections on his wound, reflections that show clearly that the patient's psychological *adynamia* is played out kinetically. The patient withdrew for weeks into idleness — "[I] just lay idly in bed" — and social indifference, not writing or speaking but "behav[ing] as if I were alone, or by myself, and with nothing to care about" (Luria, 1966, p. 225). "My comrades", he remarks, "even took me for a deaf-mute" (*ibid.*, p. 224). In the most fundamental sense, his adynamia is corporeally represented (for more on corporeal representation, see Sheets-Johnstone 1990). It is in fact significant that his adynamia begins to lift only with a resumption of movement: "Only after six weeks, when I began to do exercises, did I write my first letter" (*ibid.*, p. 225). It is as if he needed to reawaken himself *kinetically* — to his tactile-kinesthetic body and to *kinesthetically felt dynamics* — before he could rekindle the "kinetic melody" of writing.

Smooth kinetic melodies nevertheless proved beyond this patient. In particular, he was not able to carry out serially coordinated movement. In Luria's words, "The formation of a skilled movement in the form of a smooth 'kinetic melody' met with insuperable difficulties" (*ibid.*, p. 231). What is more, arithmetical calculations, which were formerly within his province, were no longer so. Luria notes that "Despite the differences between these [arithmetical] disturbances and the disturbances of skilled movements described above, they have one common feature: In both cases we are dealing with a disturbance of the smooth, automatized performance of complex operations" (*ibid.*, p. 256). In short, what was beyond this patient was *complex sequential activity*, including not only arithmetical calculations but coherent narrative speech. The effects of the lesion were thus spread out over a variety of activities — -"complex, smooth *skilled movements*", "*intellectual operations*", coherent narrative speech (*ibid.*, p. 290) — but all were rooted in a common thematic: complex sequential activity. It bears emphasizing that Luria's concern with complex sequential activity, hence with the *temporality* of movement, pervades his detailed neurological studies, and that, in consequence, animate movement is recognized not merely as a spatial phenomenon — movement with respect to a particular situation — but as a spatio-*temporal* one.

Luria's descriptive accounts of disturbances in kinetic melodies and of their linkage to pathologies in *brain zones* (Luria, 1973) constitute the basis for fundamental neurological understandings of human movement, that is, understandings of how pathologies impede or obliterate dynamic patterns of movement that are the bedrock of everyday human life activities. Given the acuity of his observations, his extraordinarily comprehensive clinical and experimental studies, and his central concern with movement, it is curious that his work is not mentioned in present-day studies of movement, if not by cognitivists, then by dynamic systems theorists. Although the latter's perspective is broader — ecological kinetics of organism-environment relations — and their aim narrower or reductive — mathematical formulations of movement or "law-based" principles (Kugler and Turvey, 1987, e.g., p. 6) — and although kinesthesia is totally eclipsed by "information" and an experiencing subject virtually discounted (cf. Wilberg, 1983), there is nonetheless a basic kinship. Dynamic systems theorist J.A. Scott Kelso's "dynamic patterns", for example, in spite of being analyzed in radically different terms (Kelso, 1995), are descriptively riveted on movement in the same way Luria's kinetic melodies are; both centralize attention not on objects in motion but on movement itself, and, in particular, on coordinated movement. Moreover Luria would agree with dynamic systems theorists Peter Kugler and Michael Turvey that movement is not "a complex *thing* put together from simpler things" like a reflex (Kugler and Turvey, 1987, p. 405); it is heterarchically, not hierarchically, organized. Luria's dynamic understanding of neurology and neuropsychology are in fact a model exemplification of how investigations of movement can be anchored in what many dynamic systems theorists term "real-time" phenomena (van Gelder and Port, 1995, Thelen and Smith, 1994) rather than exclusively in studies of *the* brain, in the kinetic artificialities of movement laboratories, or in computer modeling.

A critical commonality is notable as well, however. Neither Luria nor dynamic system theorists recognize the fact that movement creates its own distinctive temporal-spatial-energic qualities, and that this formative process results in the creation of a distinctive dynamics — precisely as "kinetic melody" and "dynamic pattern" so aptly suggest but do not specify. The dynamics are not only behaviorally observable; they are experienced by the self-moving body creating them and thereby potentially the basis of kinesthetic memory. In effect, through self-movement, there is always potentially a form to remember, a form not of sensations as such, but of a movement dynamic.

2. Kinesthetic Memory

Animation is of the nature of life. Being animate beings, we move, and in moving articulate a kinetic dynamics. We do so as adults in virtue of kinesthetic memory, and, to begin with, in virtue of our having learned our bodies and learned to move ourselves (Sheets-Johnstone, 1999). Because dynamic patterns of movement have distinctive spatial, temporal, and energic qualities,[1] they each have a distinctive spatio-temporal-energic dynamic form that is potentially invariant, depending upon whether we practice the pattern, and through repetition, learn it. Kinetic dynamics are thus of the essence of kinesthetic memory in precisely the way they are of the essence of kinetic melodies. Melody and memory are in fact dynamic images of one another — as Luria indicates when he identifies kinetic melodies as *"integral kinaesthetic structures."* In effect, being dynamically patterned, kinesthetic memories are not vague, abstract kinetic phantoms but are inscribed in the body as specific bodily dynamics, dynamics that, as enacted, are at once familiar and tailored distinctively to the particular situation at hand. Familiarity and distinctive tailoring were briefly specified earlier in the examples of speaking, hammering, and weaving one's way along a crowded sidewalk. A more detailed example will bring finer dimensions of both aspects to light.

Writing one's name is commonly thought of as an act rather than as a coordinated series of movements. Yet a coordinated series of movements defines more accurately "the act" of writing one's name. More specifically still, to write one's name is to move through a dynamic series of coordinated movements that is kinesthetically felt *both* as dynamic and as dynamically familiar. What makes the series familiar are invariant dynamic features common to all instances of writing one's name: greater

---

1   The qualities of movement — tensional, linear, amplitudinal, and projectional — are analyzed in detail in Sheets-Johnstone, 1966 [1979/1980]. The qualitative nature of movement is discussed in detail in Sheets-Johnstone, 1999.

and lesser moments of force occur at certain moments in the flow, moments where one accentuates a letter or part of a letter, for example; changes in direction take place smoothly or abruptly at certain places, and in a jagged or rounded manner; pauses occur at certain moments in the writing, perhaps with a felt sense of suspension as when one dots an *i* or crosses a *t*; the beginning of the signature and its end are clearly marked in some way. In short, in the writing of one's name, a distinctive spatio-temporal-energic dynamic plays itself out, and with it, a certain dynamic is experienced that is both familiar and unique. The uniqueness of the dynamics is first and foremost a kinesthetic uniqueness, not a visual uniqueness. In fact, it is fundamentally the kinetic and kinesthetically-felt dynamics that make the signature both visually unique and visually familiar.

At the same time, however, one's signature is tailored to present particularities: the writing implement one is using, for example, the surface on which one is writing, and the importance of the signature are variables capable of generating variations on a theme, as when, for example, one is writing one's name on a blackboard, or writing with a pen that is running dry, or signing a document such as a marriage license or a will. The dynamics of writing one's name—the ease, rhythm, size of one's movements, and so on—vary in proportion to the particularities of the immediate situation. A basically invariant and familiar dynamics adjusts itself to the situation at hand.

One can readily see how the dynamic series of coordinated movements unfolds as a kinetic melody: *once initiated*, the movement flows on by itself. Assuming one has learned to write one's name, and barring pathological disturbances, one does not need to oversee the drawing of each letter, for example, as one did when learning to write; one does not get lost somewhere in the process, as one might if suffering from a brain lesion. A coordinated series of movements whose dynamics are engrained in kinesthetic memory is run off and recognized kinesthetically. As it runs off, it is unified by retentions and protentions (Husserl, 1964) until the series and its familiar and unique dynamics come to an end. When Luria speaks of the *automatization* of movement, it is important to point out that he is describing the way in which a single impulse is sufficient to activate a kinetic melody, and not asserting that one is unaware of writing one's name, that one is unconscious of doing so, or that one can nod off while the process continues by itself. Furthermore, it is not merely that beginning a kinetic melody is sufficient to generate its entire performance; it is that the movement that flows forth effortlessly in a coherent dynamic does so because we know and remember the flow in a corporeally felt sense: *we kinetically instantiate what we know kinesthetically.* What is automatic is, in effect, kinesthetic memory. The melody runs off by itself because a familiar dynamics is awakened in kinesthetic memory and generated by it.

The point warrants further clarification, notably because the initial impulse is significant beyond the fact that it generates a kinetic dynamics on the basis of kinesthetic memory. The initial impulse is volitional. Unless we suffer from dementia or some similar malady, we do not find ourselves out of the blue brushing our teeth, for example, or walking on a street ten blocks from home. We initiate brushing and walking. We initiate them by initiating a certain kinetic dynamics that includes a certain bodily orientation, a certain environmental setting, a certain interaction with certain implements or items — a toothbrush or shoes, for example — and so on. Similarly, we do not suddenly find ourselves *not* brushing our teeth anymore but eating breakfast, or *not* walking anymore but sitting on a park bench. We are kinesthetically aware of a certain kinetic dynamics coming to an end. In short, our tactile-kinesthetic body is always present, and present along a gamut of possible awarenesses from marginal to maximal. Any time we wish to pay *closer* attention to it, there it is.

The relationship between voluntary action and kinesthesia has important implications with regard to attention, familiarity, and something "going wrong." The relationship is put in ironically sharp relief in a commonly used textbook, *Scientific Bases of Human Movement.* In a chapter titled "The Proprioceptors and Their Associated Reflexes", Gowitzke and Milner (1988, p. 193) write that "The voluntary contribution to movement is almost entirely limited to initiation, regulation of speed, force, range, and direction, and termination of the movement." Kinetic "limitations" are in fact sizable freedoms, precisely as Bernstein originally demonstrated by way of *degrees of freedom* in his studies of human movement and as any attempt by any normal person to duplicate a movement sequence with pinpoint exactitude readily indicates. Initiation, termination, speed, force, range, and direction of movement may in fact be "regulated", the last four "limitations" in particular specifying in an abbreviated and incomplete way spatio-temporal-energic qualities of movement, qualities we can voluntarily change in myriad ways virtually any time we wish and in so doing, change the dynamics of any movement we perform. We can, for example, change resolute movements into hesitant ones by changing the force, range, and speed of our movement. We might thereby radically alter the way in which we customarily write our name, brush our teeth, or walk — and thereby nullify a familiar dynamic.

Turning attention to our own movement in continuation of an initial volitional impulse, we attend to a kinetic melody in progress: as noted, any time we care to pay closer attention to our tactile-kinesthetic body, there it is. Turning attention elsewhere but continuing on with the melody, we marginalize tactile-kinesthetic sensitivities but are not totally unaware of ourselves in the process of moving. Thus, to say that we are aware of ourselves moving only when something goes wrong is misguided. Noticing that something is wrong necessarily assumes the familiar dynamic feel of that same or similar something going right. Indeed, we can be aware that something goes wrong only if we already know what commonly goes right. To insist otherwise is illogical.

Now to acknowledge that we can be aware that something is amiss only if we already know a familiar kinetic dynamics is to acknowledge that we can be aware of something going wrong only on the basis of kinesthetic memory. *Kinesthetic memory is the foundation of familiar kinetic dynamics.* It is thus not without reason that Luria at one point speaks of *"kinaesthetic* melodies" (Luria, 1973, p. 253; italics added). Kinesthetic memory is structured along the lines of "kinaesthetic melodies", and *familiar* "kinaesthetic melodies" are inscribed in kinesthetic memory.

3. The Term "Motor"

Motor skills are not properly "motor" phenomena, and the term "motor" is in fact wayward. The skills are kinetic, and they are learned through sensory-kinetic experience. Moreover complex concepts are generated in the course of sensory-kinetic learnings, concepts having to do with the dynamics created by self-movement, i.e., with spatio-temporal-energic qualities of movement.[2] "Motor" skills do not generate such concepts because no sentient moving person is present who is moving skillfully or learning to move skillfully: the erstwhile sentient moving person has been reduced to an operative motor.

The above broad criticisms of a "motor" vocabulary to describe organic movement need tempering in recognition of researchers not misled by the term, researchers who, being implicitly or explicitly aware of how a purely motor vocabulary effaces living subjects, justly take a sentient moving person into account.[3] Luria, for example, does not compromise the reality of sentient moving persons in his neurological investigations of "motor" tasks and "motor programmes" (Luria, 1973). His non-mechanization of self-movement stems from his dual conception of science, a conception

---

2   What the textbook names as voluntary aspects of movement—"speed, force, range, and direction"—are created qualities of self-movement; measurements of these aspects constitute third-person assessments.

3   As Merleau-Ponty might say, such researchers, unlike others, do not simply "manipulate things and give up living in them" (Merleau-Ponty, 1964, p. 159).

neuropsychologist Oliver Sacks eloquently eulogizes in his foreword to Luria's *The Man with a Shattered World* and a conception Luria himself eloquently puts forth in *The Making of Mind*. In essence, Luria distinguishes between classical and romantic science, the former being geared to a reductionist perspective, computer simulations, "mathematical schemas", and the like (Luria, 1979, p. 176); the latter being geared to observation and description—"phenomenological description" (*ibid.*, p. 177)—that is neither "superficial" nor "incomplete" (*ibid.*), but that traces out relationships among things and events in such a way that multiple perspectives are gained and "we come to the essence of the object, to an understanding of its qualities and the rules of its existence" (*ibid.*, p. 178). Given Luria's equal esteem for both sciences, it is not surprising that kinetic/kinesthetic melodies figure centrally in his neurological investigations: they are vital to a veridical account of neurological normalities and pathologies. His combined classical and romantic neuroscience contrasts markedly with the austere landscape of today's cognitive neuroscience where kinetic/kinesthetic melodies figure as alien, flimsy bodies lacking sturdy credentials and localization.

Unlike analyses of "motor behavior", analyses of kinetic/kinesthetic melodies open the way to commonly overlooked aspects of movement, in part, just those "limited" aspects of movement designated "voluntary." In opening toward these foundational aspects of self-movement, analyses of kinetic melodies readily defuse typically mechanical concepts underpinning motor analyses in the same way that they defuse typically mechanical understandings of automatization. This is because kinetic/kinesthetic melodies are descriptive of the dynamic phenomena themselves, not a mechanical reduction of them. More concretely, they pinpoint the nature of self-movement in a living sense; they *language kinetic experience*.[4] The term *motor* is no match for this experientially descriptive language. The term, after all, names a mechanical device, a man-made machine, and is not a term whose genesis lies in observations of living organisms. Darwin, whose round-the-world observations of life would authorize use of the term were it accurate, does not use it. In fact, the term has no evolutionary foundations. It is not difficult to appreciate why: "motor" does not describe the dynamics of living bodies but purportedly specifies something inside, something hidden from view, a "driving force" that gets the larger object in which it inheres moving in some way, *its* movement providing energies for the object to move or to do work. We can thus appreciate why neither dynamics nor volition are of topical, not to say strategic,

---

4   For more on the concept and challenge of *languaging experience*, see Sheets-Johnstone, 1999, 2002.

"motor" concern: a real-life kinetics and kinesthesia are nowhere to be found. Kelso documents this lack from a dynamic systems perspective when, in writing of "traditional approaches" to motor learning, he concludes that "The organism, to put it bluntly, is treated like a machine whose task is to associate inputs and outputs" (Kelso, 1995, p. 160).[5]

In sum, to continue to refer to sentient moving bodies in terms of motor behavior, motor memory, and so on, without balancing the ledger to include dynamic and voluntary aspects of movement, is to continue to think of animate forms as mechanical things that are capable neither of generating kinetic melodies nor of voluntarily initiating movement or of voluntarily shaping it by changing its dynamics. The point is of critical importance not only in light of the manner in which movement is commonly studied in today's scientific world, but in light of the manner in which uncritical usage skews understandings to the point that kinetic melodies are occluded even as they appear to be recognized. Merleau-Ponty's "motor intentionality" is a classic instance. It warrants extended discussion because it furnishes insights into veridical understandings of movement, kinesthetic memory, and habit.

4. Merleau-Ponty's "Motor Intentionality"

Merleau-Ponty's motor intentionality verges on Luria's kinetic melodies not only in offering an explanation of pathological disturbances, but in emphasizing the importance of the first instant of a movement: "being the active initiative, [the first movement] institutes the link between a here and a yonder, a now and a future which the remainder of the instants will merely develop" (Merleau-Ponty, 1962, p. 140). Because Merleau-Ponty does not examine *the experience* of movement, however, he never arrives at its dynamic kinetic structure. Moreover because he does not recognize kinesthetic experience, he does not recognize kinesthetic memory and the

5   The opening statement of a review of a recent neuroscience book on "motor learning" testifies to the preoccupation with something "inside": "Motor learning can be defined as a set of neural processes associated with practice that lead to changes in performance and capabilities" (Flash, 2001, p. 1612). The book — *The Acquisition of Motor Behavior in Vertebrates* — is amply instructive in this regard: brain structures and neural networks are the focal concerns; eye-blink conditioning is a major topic (e.g., "Eyeblink conditioning is recognized as a form of motor learning" [Hallett, Pascual-Leone, and Topka, 1995, p. 291]); ablation studies constitute a major form of investigation; verbal communication, communication that obviously requires sequential articulatory movement, is not recognized as "procedural" knowledge — knowledge that "refers to sequential behavior and usually relates to motor performance" — but is naively categorized as "declarative" knowledge — knowledge that "refers to facts and includes all information about which we think and that we communicate verbally" (*ibid.*, p. 289). Knowledge about "sequential tasks" lags behind knowledge about conditioned response. In fact, knowledge about living movement — kinetic melodies — is far in arrears of knowledge about laboratory-induced movement.

kinetically/kinesthetically forged sense of familiarity that is the basis of habit. He appears to believe that to recognize kinesthetic experience is to fall into the empiricists' trap of "a mosaic of 'extensive sensations'" (ibid., p. 143n) and that the truth of movement lies rather in the fact that the body "is a system which is open on to the world, and correlative with it" (ibid.). In brief, he appears to believe that to admit kinesthetic experience into his account would tether him to a subject in exclusion of a world. In effect, though he speaks specifically of "a kinetic melody" (ibid., p. 134), of the "melodic character" of a gesture (ibid., p. 105), of how a patient's move- ments have lost their "melodic flow" (ibid., p. 116), and of how the same patient fails to grasp a story "as a melodic whole" (ibid., p. 132), the experi- ential nature and history of the melody, and its dynamic character elude him. What structures kinetic melodies is in the end "ambiguated"[6] rather than phenomenologically analyzed. The 'motor' of "motor intentionality" is, in other words, hidden from view, as in classical science, located in "autonomous" and "anonymous" "functions" (ibid., e.g., pp. 84, 86, 160), or equivalently, inheres in a "prepersonal I who provides the basis for the phenomenon of movement" (ibid., p. 276, note 1). There is neither a tac- tile-kinesthetic body nor kinesthetic memory in these functions or prepersonal I, nor a kinetic history, a history not only of learning the kinetic melody of a new movement sequence, but of learning one's body and learning to move oneself to begin with (Sheets-Johnstone, 1999), self-directed learnings that each and every human initiates and carries out from birth. The essential familiarity of habit—its kinetic dynamics—has in turn no experiential foundations.

Yet *habit* is of central moment to Merleau-Ponty's "motor intentionality". Because "a movement is learned when the body has understood it" (Merleau-Ponty, 1962, p. 139)[7] and because it is the under- standing, competent body and not the learning or practicing body that defines Merleau-Ponty's "motor intentionality", motor intentionality is easily conceived to be fundamentally the work of a "habit body", *a body that already knows*. Indeed, it becomes ironically clear how and why a habit body holds a privileged position in Merleau-Ponty's account of move- ment. A habit body already knows how to move, and its movement is already all of a piece: a habit body is both already "expressive" and a

6   Johnstone (2001) uses the term "disambiguator" to designate a notational device that distinguishes two different meanings of an otherwise ambiguous sentence. I am borrowing and converting his term.

7   Cf. Bergson, whose writings were well-known to Merleau-Ponty and who, speaking specifically of how repetition "teaches" the body in the course of learning a new coordination, stated, "A movement is learned when the body has been made to understand it" (Bergson [1896] 1990, p. 112).

readily "expressive" storehouse of "kinetic melodies" (*ibid.*, p. 146). Accordingly, there is no need to dwell on *just how the body comes to be a habit body or what kinesthetically structures its understandings.* In a "prepersonal" kinesthetic-less world, habit has no experiential precursors and no need of such. The body "which is open on to the world and correlative with it" is a ready-made. Thus, when Merleau-Ponty defines habit as "knowledge in the hands, which is forthcoming … when bodily effort is made" (*ibid.*, p. 144), he passes over a tactilely and kinesthetically resonant body that is the source of knowledge "in the hands", a body that has *learned* its way in the world from the beginning by moving, gaining knowledge "in the hands" and elsewhere in the process. He thereby misses *the familiar kinetic dynamics that fundamentally constitutes habit,* in this instance, the habit that is there in person "in the hands." Moreover although he points out with respect to movement of one's body that "[t]he synthesis of both time and space is a task that always has to be performed afresh", thus indicating that the habit body is flexible, adjusting itself to the kinetic demands of the moment, the task "that always has to be performed afresh" never makes an appeal to kinetic knowledge or to kinesthetic memory. On the contrary, Merleau-Ponty affirms that "Our bodily experience of movement is not a particular case of knowledge [but] provides us with a way of access to the world and the object, with a 'praktognosia'" (*ibid.*, p. 140). Clearly, the very stuff of habits — their foundational kinesthetic familiarity, a familiarity renewed by way of kinesthetic memory each time they are reactivated — is nowhere recognized.

Merleau-Ponty's *habit body* is not only without kinesthesia but is also preeminently an adult body without a history, a body that thereby rings false neurologically as well as existentially. In both a neurological and existential sense, kinesthesia and kinesthetic memory are essential to progressive developmental achievements and capacities, and to the formation of habits on the basis of those achievements and capacities. Adultist views of oneself in the world, perhaps particularly ontologically-oriented "phenomenological" views,[8] ignore the complex nature of infancy and its intricate developmental history, a history without which one could not attain adult habits, let alone adultist views of oneself in the world. While Merleau-Ponty's "motor intentionality" and habit body rightly prominence the body, they ignore a previous and ongoing lifetime of kinesthetic learning and memory at the same time that they presuppose it at every step.

In sum, so strong is Merleau-Ponty's driving thematic of an indissoluble body-world relationship that it overrules an investigation of movement

---

8   One could cite Heidegger as well.

and in consequence effectively squelches a phenomenological account of self-movement, i.e., of kinesthetic experience. While it is true that Merleau-Ponty avoids the representations of the intellectuals and the "extensive sensations" of the empiricists by tying subject and object — body and world — together through a "motor intentionality" that "cease[s] to draw a distinction between the body as a mechanism in itself and consciousness as being for itself" (*ibid.*, p. 139), the move is not without hazard. Kinetic melodies demand kinetic explanations. Merleau-Ponty can speak of "melodic flows" devoid of kinesthesia and kinesthetic memory only by explaining the body's ready access to the world as "autonomous" and "anonymous" functions of a prepersonal *I*, in essence, as "motor" functions defined by classical science. But we must note that he also specifies another "motor" phenomenon, one that appears to be a subrogate for kinesthesia, namely, the body image (*schéma corporel*).[9]

5. Body Image

Merleau-Ponty is not the only person to invoke a body image to explain corporeal-kinetic phenomena, but his writings on the subject are a good place to begin since he takes up the term from its original coinage in neurology, and since his "existential analysis" (*ibid.*, p. 136) of it readily demonstrates how kinesthesia and kinesthetic memory may be trivialized or passed over altogether. He begins by considering the original definition of body image — in his words, "a *compendium* of our bodily experience" (*ibid.*, p. 98) — and goes on to improve on it, defining body image rather as "a total awareness of my posture in the intersensory world" (*ibid.*, p. 100). But he improves on this definition too, enlarging it, citing the fact that "Psychologists often say that the body image is *dynamic*" (*ibid.*). He makes "total postural awareness" *dynamic* by making it a bodily "attitude" rather than a bodily "form": "Brought down to a precise sense, this term means that my body appears to me as an attitude directed towards a certain existing or possible task" (*ibid.*). He discusses this bodily attitude essentially in terms of space, specifically, "a *spatiality of situation*" (*ibid.*). One looks in vain, however, in the examples he subsequently gives and in the discussions that follow, for a veritable *dynamic*: "the situation of the body in face of its tasks" (*ibid.*) nowhere spells out a *dynamic* beyond the rather commonplace fact that the body moves in face of its tasks.

Merleau-Ponty's re-definition of the body image as "a spatiality of situation" coincides with the self-description of the patient whose case study

---

9   See Gallagher (1986, 1995) for discussions of the confusion of body image and body schema.

constitutes the basis for his reformulation of the term. The patient—Schneider—is capable of kinetic melodies only in concrete situations, where specific objects calling for specific movements are present—for example, scissors, leather, needle, and thread—and not in abstract situations where he is requested to perform certain movements—for example, pointing to a part of his body. Of the former movements, Schneider states that "I experience the movements as being a result of the situation, of the sequence of events themselves; myself and my movements are, so to speak, merely a link in the whole process and I am scarcely aware of any voluntary initiative ... It all happens independently of me" (ibid., p. 105). The statement is a conceptual blueprint of the "third term" — existence—that Merleau-Ponty wishes to instantiate between the rationalists' representations—"the psychic"—and the empiricists' sensations—"the physiological" (ibid., p. 122n). With respect to kinesthesia and kinesthetic memory, the self-description is crucially telling: movement is simply "a result of the situation"; and the moving subject is "scarcely aware of any voluntary initiative." It is no wonder, then, that in Merleau-Ponty's correlative autonomous, anonymous, prepersonal body-world nexus, kinesthesia and kinesthetic memory are replaced by a body image whose dynamics consist simply in the fact that the body moves.[10] Being a power that projects the body into the world, the body image creates an "'intentional arc'" (ibid., p. 136) that existentially links it to the world. In the patient's case, the arc is truncated and otherwise damaged. To paraphrase Merleau-Ponty, the arc no longer "projects round about Schneider his past, his future, his human setting, his physical, ideological, and moral situation; it no longer brings about the unity of his senses, of intelligence, of sensibility and motility" (ibid.).

Body image and intentional arcs notwithstanding, Merleau-Ponty remarks pointedly on the extraordinary way in which Schneider uses movement to get his bearings with respect to a task he is asked to do or to an object he is asked to recognize. "If a part of his body is touched and he is asked to locate the point of contact, he first of all sets his whole body in motion and thus narrows down the problem of location, then he comes still nearer by moving the limb in question" (ibid., p. 107); "If the subject's arm is extended horizontally, he cannot describe its position until he has performed a set of pendular movements which convey to him the arm position in relation to the trunk" (ibid.); "The patient himself neither seeks nor finds his movement, but moves his body about until the movement

---

10 Ostensibly, Merleau-Ponty has reduced normal, everyday movement to its most elementary level, but that level in fact fails to account for the dynamics of movement—the basis of habit—and the ontogenetical realities of infant life.

comes" (*ibid.*, p. 110). Later, as if in summation of these facts, Merleau-Ponty comments that "concrete movements, which are preserved by the patient as are those imitative movements, whereby he compensates for his paucity of visual data, arise from kinaesthetic or tactile sense, *which incidentally was remarkably exploited by Schneider*" (*ibid.*, p. 113, italics added). In short, it is through moving, through "active movements" (*ibid.*, p. 107), that Schneider tries to find his way, follow an order, respond to a request, and so on. Merleau-Ponty thus appears to recognize kinesthesia, but only in the pathological instance when no kinetic melody is forthcoming, or more generally, "only when something goes wrong." Kinesthesia might thus seem to be something like the proverbial tree falling in the forest: unless we sense it, it does not exist. Indeed, Merleau-Ponty's solution is to relegate "consciousness of movement" to an amorphous *background*:

> [F]or the normal person every movement is, indissolubly, movement and consciousness of movement. This can be expressed by saying that for the normal person every movement has a *background* ... *The background to the movement is not a representation associated or linked externally with the movement itself, but is immanent in the movement inspiring and sustaining it at every moment (ibid., p. 110).*

The term "background" is both an expeditious and ambiguous way of reckoning with "consciousness of movement": it effectively nullifies kinesthetic experience and kinesthetic memory, and thereby makes "consciousness of movement" literally, logically, and experientially unintelligible. By invoking a "background", Merleau-Ponty recognizes what must be recognized — "consciousness of movement" — but cuts short its actual experience, nature, and significance. Certainly we are not ordinarily attentive kinesthetically in a *focal* way when brushing our teeth or weaving our way quickly through a crowd; we are concentrated on the task at hand. Our kinesthetic awareness of ourselves *is* in the "background". But being in the background does not mean that it is altogether outside awareness. It is not only that any time we care to pay *focal* attention to our "consciousness of movement", there it is, but that *the familiarity of our movement in the form of a certain kinetic dynamics undergirds our brushing, weaving, and so on, and is marginally or pre-reflectively in our awareness even as we focally attend to what we will have for breakfast as we brush or to the appointment to which we are rushing as we weave.* A kinetic dynamics is sensuously present at the lower end of the continuum that describes the intensity — or focal to marginal — gradient of consciousness. In fact, if as Merleau-Ponty writes, the background "is immanent in the movement inspiring and sustaining it at every moment", then a certain kinetic dynamics is undeniably underway that is familiar as well as self-propelling, a dynamics that is not there only if we notice it *focally*, but a dynamic that is present as a familiar, ongoing, and particular kinesthetic melody. How otherwise might one legitimately speak of a "consciousness of movement"?

In sum, a veritable kinetic dynamics is not reducible to a "[bodily] attitude directed towards a certain existing or possible task." Merleau-Ponty's reformulated body image falls short of fulfilling its dynamic promise. A veritable kinetic dynamics is kinesthetically felt, which is to say it is experienced in the flow of movement itself, and with a sense of familiarity (supposing the movement is not novel) generated through kinesthetic memory.

6. Body Image and Body Schema

The term body image is actually misleading since it conjures up not only something preeminently *visual*, but something not actually perceived, i.e., something *imaginary*. Philosopher Shaun Gallagher and neurophysiologist Jonathan Cole try to correct these false impressions by specifying body image in exacting terms and by distinguishing it from body schema (see also Gallagher, 1986, 1995). In their joint article on a "deafferented subject" — a man who lost virtually all kinesthetic awareness — they attempt to document just what is missing in the way of a body image and body schema, and how the subject — referred to as IW — compensates for the loss and learns to move anew. In the process, and unlike Merleau-Ponty, Gallagher and Cole do not trivialize or pass over kinesthesia. On the contrary, using the broader term "proprioception", they specify both a neurological informational system and a system of experiential awareness. They thereby distinguish body image from body schema: body image is "a complex set of intentional states" that includes perceptual experience, conceptual understandings, and emotional attitudes; body schema is "a system of motor capacities, abilities, and habits that enable movement and the maintenance of posture", a system that operates "preconsciously" and "subpersonally" (Gallagher and Cole, 1998, p. 132). They implicitly vindicate Luria's neurological diagnostic and his emphasis on the quintessential significance of kinesthetic afferents to intention or "will" when they state, "At the earliest stage of his illness IW had no control over his movements and was unable to put intention into action. There was, one might say, a disconnection of will from the specifics of movement" (*ibid.*, p. 135). The implicit vindication, however, is short-lived: neither body schema nor body image approximate to the neurological and experiential dynamics of a kinetic melody.

To begin with, a body schema has no basis in experience. It is at best an explanatory convenience, a hypothetical entity in the brain (or central nervous system as a whole) that is conjured to do the work of putting movement together, furnishing a kinetic blueprint for neurological eyes only, as it were. In contrast, a kinetic melody describes both what is constructed neurologically in the course of learning—a distinctive temporal course of innervations and denervations, as in learning to walk, to brush one's teeth, to make an abdominal incision, to do the tarantella—and what is experienced—a distinctive dynamic flow of movement. A kinetic melody is not a *thing* in the brain (or in the central nervous system) but a particular neurological and experiential dynamic. Each melody is in fact a *neuromuscular dynamic* whose innervations and denervations, together with the constantly changing muscle tone they generate, constitute a particular temporal organization. Kinetic melodies thus straddle two worlds; unlike a body schema, they describe inherently dynamic patterns that are at once neurological and experiential.

A body image suffers from the same lack of experiential grounding and dynamic resonance as a body schema. The identification of "the perception of movement" with body image (Gallagher and Cole, 1998, p. 134) not uncommonly reduces to a *positional* awareness of the body—e.g., "I can tell you where my legs are even with my eyes closed"; "Proprioceptive awareness is a felt experience of bodily position that helps to constitute the perceptual aspect of the body image" (*ibid.*, p. 137). While the perception of movement certainly includes positional awarenesses, it is quintessentially a *dynamic* awareness, and to overlook the kinetic/kinesthetic dynamics that are its source is to distort the account of "the perception of movement."

The problem with the body image might be judged to be basically a methodological problem: beginning with a construct instead of experience. Unless one begins with and hews to experience, the very thing one wants to explain eludes one, in this instance, the experience of an unfolding dynamics, the perception of one's own body in motion. The first question is properly not "How is such an experience possible?", but "What is the nature of kinetic experience?" In turn, the first task is not to come up with an explanatory entity but with a descriptive account of the phenomenon in question.[11] Methodology is thus of critical importance. Turning toward "the thing itself"—*self-movement*—one realizes that a body image is not up to the task set for it. The phenomenology of self-movement cannot be deduced from pathology. Certainly one may infer the normal from the pathological, but inference is not phenomenology.

---

11 One might cite neurophysiologist Kurt Goldstein (1939) as well as Husserl: "[I]t is the first task of biology to *describe carefully all living beings as they actually are*" (p. 6); *What do the phenomena . . . teach us about the 'essence' (the intrinsic nature) of an organism?*" (p. 7).

The importance of hewing to experience may be highlighted by noting a correspondence between Schneider and IW: IW too "exploits" movement to trigger movement. He exploits it not by actively initiating movement as Schneider does, but through his ready ideational access to earlier experiences of normal movement. IW already knows fundamental kinetic melodies; he knows "how they go", so to speak, and even how they are supposed to go. Thus, when Gallagher and Cole write that "IW's success in recovering useful movement function has depended primarily on his finite mental concentration, and to a much lessor (sic) degree on reaccessing or relearning motor programs which are, so far, poorly understood" (*ibid.*, p. 138), they neglect to consider that IW knows the movement he intends or "wills": he has a kinetic memory of what it is to reach, to grasp, to sit, to stand. He knows these movements in his bones, even though he can no longer move these bones except by visual initiation and monitoring. Thus, although he cannot call forth kinetic melodies from kinesthetic memory, he can structure his present visually guided movement on the basis of his kinetic knowledge of them. In fact, short of this dynamic memory of movement, he would not even know how to begin moving. To appreciate this, one need only consider what it would be like *to be born* as a "deafferented subject." IW's visual re-creation of movement does not begin from scratch but from a previous body of knowledge of such mundane kinetic melodies as walking, buttoning, and picking up an egg.

In sum, kinetic melodies describe the reality of movement in neurological and experiential ways that neither body schema nor body image can approximate. They do so because they explicitly recognize a bodily-kinetic dynamic. More explicitly still, they recognize a vast range of bodily-kinetic dynamics "in face of the world", each melody being distinctly analyzable as a dynamic pattern of movement. Body image and body schema are no match for this bodily-kinetic dynamic. Indeed, they are recalcitrant to Gallagher and Cole's noble clarifying efforts and should be jettisoned in favor of a veridical phenomenology of self-movement, one that recognizes the foundationally dynamic character of movement from the start.

7. The Pointillist Conception of Movement: Its Conceptual Underpinnings and Liabilities

Motion, Descartes stated, "[is] the transfer of one piece of matter, or one body, from the vicinity of the other bodies which are in immediate contact with it, and which are regarded as being at rest, to the vicinity of other bodies" (Descartes [1644] 1985, p. 233). With respect to a body in face of its task — sitting down, lifting a suitcase, cutting a swath of grass — point A and point B are typically the points of interest. They mark the place of departure and arrival of a moving body, and thereby the beginning and end of its task. The points say nothing of the dynamics of movement. They describe a basically static spatial world intermittently interrupted by bodies changing position.

The spatial concordance of body and world described by Merleau-Ponty is rooted in a pointillist conception of movement: individuals move from point A to point B, following along the lines of an intentional arc. In privileging *position*, the conception neglects to account for and virtually effaces movement itself. The neglect and virtual effacement are straightaway evident in Merleau-Ponty's concluding analysis of Schneider: "[T]he normal subject has his body not only as a system of present positions, but besides, and thereby, as an open system of an infinite number of equivalent positions directed to other ends. What we have called the body image is precisely this system of equivalents, this immediately given invariant whereby the different motor tasks are instantaneously transferable." (Merleau-Ponty, 1962, p. 141).[12] Movement — what putatively should make the body image *dynamic* — is nowhere in evidence because in fact there is no dynamic, but only a pointillist conception of "motricité."

The pointillist conception is similarly exemplified in the earlier quotations from Gallagher and Cole: knowing where one's legs are when one's eyes are closed, for example. The conception clearly leads one erroneously to believe that movement is simply a change of position, and in turn to conceive a kinesthetic awareness of movement to be an awareness of changed positions. The conception is actually spatially deficient in its non-recognition of the spatial qualities of movement and correlative kinesthetic awarenesses. In fact, however persuasive the notion of "a spatiality of situation" — "know[ing] indubitably where my pipe is" (Merleau-Ponty, 1962, p. 100) — its explanatory referents — body image and body schema — effectively suppress the essential insight that *movement creates its own space, time, and force, and thereby the dynamics that are movement itself.* If movement did not create its own space, time, and force, there would be no such thing as habit: no specific kinetic dynamic would exist to repeat, to practice, to learn. Equally, there would be nothing to remember, hence, no kinesthetic memory.

---

12   The temporality of movement is of notable significance in this context. As Luria points out, voluntary movement demands not only kinesthetic afference but an ever-changing series of innervations and denervations. What he terms the "dynamic stereotype" is habit, a basically invariant but still kinetically variable phenomenon: "*the invariant motor task is fulfilled not by a constant, fixed set, but by a varying set of movements which, however, lead to the constant, invariant effect.*" (1973, p. 248). Transferability is thus grounded not in a body image but in dynamic sedimentations constituting a familiar dynamics anchored in kinesthetic memory.

The pointillist conception of movement that body schema and body image implicitly support emanates from a bias of Western thought that anchors reality in the spatiality of things to the exclusion of their temporality, i.e., their impermanence, their flow, their temporal dynamics. A Western predilection for mechanics over dynamics, for mass — *things* — over flow — *dynamics* (e.g., Yates, 1987; Kelso, 1995) — testifies to this bias. Traditional views of motor behavior, motor memory, motor control, motor habits, and so on, exemplify a further dimension of the bias in their Cartesian reduction of movement to objects in motion, quantifiable *things* tied to positions in space and moments in time, and either by nature not kinesthetically attuned or by manner of study not recognized as being kinesthetically attuned. Not only is it easier to explain conditioned eye-blinking (see note 5) by way of objects in motion than to describe dynamic processes like piano-playing by way of kinesthesia and kinesthetic memory, but it is less perilous ontologically: like mechanisms, objects in motion are spatially-localized, stable entities that anchor functions. Correlatively, distinct units in the brain dedicated to short-term storage and long-term storage, and opposing species of memory — e.g., fact, declarative, and representational as against skill, procedural, and dispositional, respectively (Goethals and Soloman, 1989, p. 5]) — specify solid, well-defined memory repositories and categories as the kinetic dynamics of kinesthetic memory do not. Clearly, a motorized mechanics-over-dynamics goes hand in hand with a conception of movement that eschews the temporal in favor of the spatial.

Being temporal by nature, kinesthetic memories, like kinetic melodies, subsume not only rhythmicities within their compass, but temporally unfolding postural and orientational relations, kinetic protentions and retentions, and so on. Kinesthetic memory is thus not a pointillist system of remembered *sensations*, but a remembered spatio-temporal-energic dynamics. Indeed, kinesthetic memory is not memory of sensations of one's body, but of perceptions of the dynamics of self-movement. The point warrants elaboration.

Kinetic melodies are subtended by kinetic harmonies. Everyday movement involves the whole body; coordinated movement is the result of global kinetic orchestrations. Kinetic melodies are thus grounded in a *kinetic harmonics* that is the whole moving body. In turn, the experience of movement is not a matter of localized and discrete bodily sensations, but of a felt harmonious whole where particular areas may be tonally dominant, as when one kicks a ball, moves a fork to one's mouth, or stands up. Discrete, localized bodily sensations — sensations *as such* — are not dynamic awarenesses but preeminently positional ones like itchings and ticklings. Neurophysiologists Jonathan Cole and Jacques Paillard's (1995, p. 256) perspicuous but kinetically unelaborated distinction between "topokinetic" movement (e.g., pointing to a place on the body where one was touched) and "morphokinetic" movement (e.g., drawing figure eights in the air in front of one) adumbrates the difference between positional and dynamic awarenesses of movement. To be topokinetically attuned—to attend to or remember positional sensations *as such*—is to reduce movement to an object in motion in the manner of Descartes and thereby forego the sense of a dynamic kinetic harmonics. (It is significant that Cole and Paillard describe the *gestural language* of deafferented subjects as a "morphokinetic melody", while otherwise explaining the subjects' movement in terms of body image and body schema [*ibid.*, p. 259].) The kinesthetic memory of walking— *not a visual image but a morphokinetic recollection*—subsumes a kinetic harmonics; the memory is not a memory of positions but of a whole body dynamic, which is based not on bodily sensations—localized, positional happenings—but on the perception of movement. In short, kinesthetic memories are constituted through and through by dynamic, not sensational, sedimentations. There is in fact no position that the body is *in* in walking.[13]

The liabilities of a pointillist conception of movement point toward a challenging methodological question: what justifies starting with pathology, i.e., the loss of kinetic melodies? If the purpose is to understand everyday self-movement, why not start with a magnification of such movement rather than with its diminishment? Why, for example, not begin with dance, and ask whether motor theories, body schemas, and body images are up to the task of explaining how such intricate and complicated ongoing movement is learned and remembered. Merleau-Ponty spoke of dancing as a "motor habit" and said that "forming the habit of dancing is discovering, by analysis, the formula of the movement in question" (Merleau-Ponty, 1962, pp. 146, 142, respectively). Of his dance "Untitled Solo", Merce Cunningham wrote,

> A large gamut of movements, separate for each of the three dances, was devised, movements for the arms, the legs, the head and the torso which were separate and essentially tensile in character, and off the normal or tranquil body-balance. The separate movements were arranged in continuity by random means, allowing for the superimposition (addition) of one or more, each having its own rhythm and time-length. But each succeeded in becoming continuous if I could wear it long enough, like a suit of clothes (Cunningham, undated, unpaginated).

---

13   — any more than there is a position that the wind is *in* in blowing, or that a wave is *in* in rolling forward.

Untitled Solo is hardly a motor habit and learning it was hardly learning "by analysis, the formula of the movement." Through practice, the dance became a kinesthetically crystallized whole, etched in kinesthetic memory and articulated by way of kinesthetic memory. Were one to take Cunningham's description as a transcendental clue to coordinated movement, one might say that if one "wears movement long enough", it can become a kinetic dynamic that spins continuously out of one's body like the web of a web-spinning spider.

Beginning with extraordinary rather than diminished kinetic capacities means beginning with "the thing itself" and gaining direct knowledge about the inherent dynamics of movement.[14] While in one sense extraordinary movement is at the other extreme of pathological movement, the idea of a linking continuum is methodologically misleading, for precisely by beginning with the extraordinary, one begins with the neurological and experiential reality of a kinetic melody and a kinetic harmonics, and goes from there to foundational dynamic understandings. A methodological focus on the extraordinary has the power to bring these dynamic understandings to light because it magnifies rather than constricts subtleties and complexities inherent in kinesthetic experience and kinesthetic memory.

References

Bergson, H. 1991. *Matter and Memory*, trans. N. M. Paul. New York: Zone Books.

Bernstein, N. 1984. *Human Motor Actions: Bernstein Reassessed*, ed. H.T. A. Whiting. Amsterdam: North-Holland.

Bernstein, N. 1996. *Dexterity and Its Development*, ed. M.L. Latash, M.T. Turvey; trans. M.L. Latash. Mahwah, NJ: Lawrence Erlbaum Associates.

Cole, J. and J. Paillard. 1995. "Living without touch and peripheral information about body position and movement: studies with deafferented subjects." In *The Body and the Self*, ed. J.L. Bermúdez, A. Marcel, N. Eilan. Cambridge: Bradford/MIT Press, 245–66.

Cunningham, M. undated. *Changes: Notes on Choreography*, ed. F. Starr. New York: Something Else Press.

Descartes, René. 1985 [1644]. *Principles of Philosophy. The Philosophical Writings of Descartes*, vol. 1, trans. J. Cottingham, R. Stoothoff, D. Murdoch. Cambridge: Cambridge University Press.

Flash, T. 1997. "Motor Learning." *Science* 275: 1612.

Gallagher, S. 1986. "Body image and body schema: a conceptual clarification." *Journal of Mind and Behavior* 7: 541 54.

---

14 Such knowledge depends on a qualified observer. If cognitive science is to make use of experiential reports, it should insure that reportees are trained if not in phenomenological methodology, then in "auto-sensory observation" (Jacobson 1967, 1970). IW's report of "a 'crude' sense of effort" (Gallagher and Cole 1998, p. 137) is tantalizing in this respect. What is this "crude" sense?

Gallagher, S. 1995. "Body schema and intentionality." In *The Body and the Self*, ed. J. L. Bermúdez, A. Marcel, N. Eilan. Cambridge: Bradford/MIT Press, 225–44.

Gallagher, S. and J. Cole. 1998. "Body image and body schema in a deafferented subject." In *Body and Flesh*, ed. D. Welton. Oxford: Blackwell, 131–47.

Goethals, G. R. and P. R. Soloman. 1989. "Interdisciplinary perspectives on the study of memory." In *Memory: Interdisciplinary Approaches*, ed. P. R. Soloman, G. R. Goethals, C. M. Kelley, B. R. Stephens. New York: Springer-Verlag.

Goldberg, E. 1990. "Tribute to A. R. Luria." In *Contemporary Neuropsychology and the Legacy of Luria*, ed. E. Goldberg. Hillsdale, NJ: Lawrence Erlbaum, 1–9.

Goldstein, K. 1939. *The Organism: A Holistic Approach to Biology Derived from Pathological Data in Man*. New York: American Book Company.

Gowitzke, B.A. and M. Milner. 1988. *Scientific Bases of Human Movement*. 3rd ed. Baltimore: Williams and Wilkins.

Hallett, M., A. Pascual-Leone, H. Topka. 1996. "Adaptation and Skill Learning: Evidence for Different Neural Substrates." In *The Acquisition of Motor Behavior in Vertebrates*, ed. J.R. Bloedel, T.J. Ebner, S.P. Wise. Cambridge: Bradford Book/MIT Press.

Husserl, E. 1964. *The Phenomenology of Internal Time Consciousness*, trans. J.S. Churchill. Bloomington, IN: Indiana University Press.

Husserl, E. 1970. *The Crisis of the Euroepean Sciences and Transcendental Phenomenology*, trans. D. Carr. Evanston, IL: Northwestern University Press.

Husserl, E. 1973. *Cartesian Meditations*, trans. Dorion Cairns. The Hague: Martinus Nijhoff.

Husserl, E. 1980. *Ideas Pertaining to a Pure Phenomenology and to a Phenomenological Philosophy: Book 3 (Ideas III)*, trans. T.E. Klein and W.E. Pohl. The Hague: Martinus Nijhoff.

Husserl, E. 1989. *Ideas Pertaining to a Pure Phenomenology and to a Phenomenological Philosophy: Book 2 (Ideas II)*, trans. R. Rojcewicz and A. Schuwer. Boston: Kluwer Academic.

Jacobson, E. 1967. *Biology of Emotions*. Springfield, IL: Charles C. Thomas.

Jacobson, E. 1970. *Modern Treatment of Tense Patients*. Springfield, IL: Charles C. Thomas.

Johnstone. A. 2001. The Liar Syndrome. Unpublished paper.

Kelso, J. A. S. 1995. *Dynamic Patterns*. Cambridge: Bradford Book/MIT Press.

Kugler, P. N. and M. T. Turvey. 1987. *Information, Natural Law, and the Self-Assembly of Rhythmic Movement*. Hillsdale, NJ: Lawrence Erlbaum.

Luria, A. R. 1966. *Human Brain and Psychological Processes*, trans. Basil Haigh. New York: Harper & Row.

Luria, A.R. 1973. *The Working Brain*, trans. Basil Haigh. Harmondsworth, Middlesex, England: Penguin Books.

Luria, A.R. 1979. *The Making of Mind*, ed. Michael Cole and Sheila Cole. Cambridge: Harvard University Press.

Luria, A.R. 1980. *Higher Cortical Functions in Man*, 2nd ed. trans. Basil Haigh. New York: Basic Books.

Merleau-Ponty, M. 1962. *Phenomenology of Perception*, trans. Colin Smith. London: Routledge & Kegan Paul.

Merleau-Ponty, M. 1964. "Eye and mind." In *The Primacy of Perception*, ed. J. M. Edie. Evanston: Northwestern University Press, 159–90.

Pribram, K. 1966. "Preface" to A. R. Luria's *Human Brain and Psychological Processes*, New York: Harper & Row, xiii–xv.

Pribram, K. 1980. "Preface" to A. R. Luria's *Higher Cortical Functions in Man*, 2nd ed. New York: Basic Books, xv–xvi.

Sacks, Oliver. 1972. "Foreword" to A. Luria's *The Man with a Shattered World*, trans. Lynn Solotaroff. Cambridge: Harvard University Press.

Sheets-Johnstone, Maxine. 1966 [1979/1980]. *The Phenomenology of Dance*. Madison, WI: University of Wisconsin Press; 2nd editions: London: Dance Books Ltd.; New York: Arno Press.

Sheets-Johnstone, M. 1990. *The Roots of Thinking*. Philadelphia: Temple University Press.

Sheets-Johnstone, M. 1999. *The Primacy of Movement*. Amsterdam/Philadelphia: John Benjamins.

Sheets-Johnstone, M. 2002. "Descripive foundations." *Interdisciplinary Studies in Literature and Environment* 9/1: 165–179.

Teuber, H-L. 1966. "Preface" to A.R. Luria's *Human Brain and Psychological Processes*. New York: Harper & Row, vii–xi.

Teuber, H-L. 1980. "Preface" to A.R. Luria's *Higher Cortical Functions in Man*, 2nd ed. New York: Basic Books, xi–xiv.

Thelen, E. and L.B. Smith. 1994. *A Dynamic Systems Approach to the development of Cognition and Action*. Cambridge: Bradford/MIT Press.

van Gelder, T. and R.F. Port. 1995. "It's about time: an overview of the dynamical approach to cognition." In *Mind as Motion: Explorations in the Dynamics of Cognition*, ed. T. Van Gelder and R.F. Port. Cambridge: MIT Press, 1–43.

Wilberg, R.B. 1983. "Memory for movement." In *Memory and Control of Action*, ed. R.A. Magill. Amsterdam: North-Holland, 39–46.

Yates, F.E. 1987. "Foreword" to P.N. Kugler and M.T. Turvey's *Information, Natural Law, and the Self-Assembly of Self-Movement*. Hillsdale, NJ: Lawrence Erlbaum.

Chapter XI

On Bacteria, Corporeal Representation, Neandertals, and Martha Graham

Steps Toward an Evolutionary Semantics

1. Introduction

The purpose of this introduction is threefold: to specify the particular evolutionary approach taken in this essay, to clarify thereby what it means to answer the question of the origin of semiosis from the viewpoint of intact, whole-bodied living creatures — in effect, from the viewpoint of species-specific modes of signification — and to show how this approach is vital to semiotic understandings in ways beyond an approach anchored in a Peircean semiotics. By taking these preliminary steps, I hope to situate the main text of the essay within present-day perspectives on the origin of semiosis.

Living creatures are animate forms geared in bodily meaningful ways to the world about them. They are geared according to the body they are. In the most basic sense, this is what natural selection is all about: those creatures who are most congenially attuned to the particular world in which they find themselves — those who are able actively to make sense of that world in continuously life-enhancing ways — are the creatures who survive and reproduce. But animate forms may also be exploratory and creative; that is, they may create meanings as well as find them ready-made in an already existing world. They may thus affect the course of their evolution by new behaviors that maximize survival and reproductive capacities. Thus, to account for the origins of semiosis, one must account for "signs of meaning in the universe" — to use biologist Jesper Hoffmeyer's apt phrase (Hoffmeyer 1996) — not only as those meanings are found embedded in myriad ways in the world, but as those meanings are newly minted by animate forms themselves in the course of their evolution.

Spelled out in this way, the origin of semiosis demands a broader and deeper base than that offered by philosopher Charles Peirce's system of signs (for an introduction, see Peirce, 1991, 1992). It demands this enriched perspective because a consideration of animate forms requires a point of departure different from a logic of signs; it requires a beginning in evolutionary history and the construction of an evolutionary semantics. The starting point from this perspective is not "the sign" but sense-making organisms themselves, in terms of both the bodily ways in which the world is meaningful to them and the he bodily ways in which they go about making sense of the world. In each instance, sense-making is tied to animate forms in species-specific ways. It is thus tied to certain bodily conformations, markings, and colorations, certain kinetic dispositions and potentialities, certain sensory capacities and characteristic movement patterns, and so on (Sheets-Johnstone, 1999).

To approach the question of the origin of semiosis in this way is to set the answer within a *bona fide* epistemological framework. Though certainly pertaining and appealing at times to epistemological understandings, Peirce's referential categories have a basically ontological rather than epistemological status: categories rather than experience are the bottom Peircean line. His categorial grid sets the referential or representational record straight, so to speak, and does so according to law-like, ordered semiotic relationships. But the record is set straight at the price of deeper questions of meaning, notably, the living ways in which meanings are experienced and created across evolutionary time. What a phenomenological methodology and perspective allow is a forthright epistemological approach, and this because methodology and perspective are rooted in experience and in analyses of experience. Though characterizing his system early on as a phenomenology,[1] Pierce's system in large measure passes over an experiencing subject in favor of the semiotically known. A Husserlian phenomenology (Husserl, e.g., 1980, 1983, 1989), in contrast, requires an account not just of the known — in quite general phenomenological terms, the object *as meant* (e.g., Husserl, 1973, pp. 36–7); in Peircean terms, *the sign* as a triadic function — but of the knower, the epistemological subject. It thus elucidates not only so-called contents of consciousness — what it properly recognizes as *objects* of consciousness and a Peircean semiotics recognizes as and icon, index, or symbol, or as either quality, relation, or synthesis, or finally and more remotely, as either Firstness, Secondness, or Thirdness, (see e.g., Peirce, 1991, pp. 180–5) — but acts and structures of consciousness itself. A concern with the subject of

---

1   For an excellent article comparing Peirce's and Husserl's phenomenology, see Spiegelberg, 1956

experience directs us naturally to these acts and structures. It does so in the present instance by directing our attention to both the ways in which, and the means whereby, living subjects — animate forms of life — constitute meaning. Animate organisms make sense of their environment at the very least. Within the kingdom Animalia, most make sense of other creatures, at minimum those that are edible and those that are harmful. In some instances, they make sense of their own bodies prior to and/or coincident with these sense-makings (Sheets-Johnstone, 1999a). An appreciation of the ways in which and the means whereby meanings are constituted leads to an understanding of how sense-making itself has evolved in the course of evolution and of the diverse ways in which it is fundamental to life.

Though the constitutional facet of Husserlian phenomenology will not be of direct concern in this essay,[2] the constitution of meaning is important to recognize. One aspect of its importance is capsulated in primatologist Thelma Rowell's statement that "Once an intention movement has acquired meaning, or predictive value, *and this is a matter of the evolution of the receiver rather than the animal making the movements*, it may presumably come under selection pressure as a signal" (Rowell, 1972, p. 94; italics added). The question of how a displayed-to animal comes to validate a movement or gesture of another as meaningful, how it acquiesces to meaning and thus officially instantiates a particular meaning in the repertoire of the species, is a constitutional question fundamental to the origin of semiosis. It is indeed a basic question within the larger framework of an evolutionary semantics (Sheets-Johnstone, 1990, 1999a,b). Of interest in this regard is how questions about origin cut across disciplines. How things come to have the meaning and value they do is a foundational question in phenomenology (Husserl, 1970, 1973) and one quintessentially pertinent to understandings of the origin of semiosis in the sense that Rowell's statement indicates.[3] As formatively realized over the course of

2   The constitution of meaning is a complex phenomenon. Even to exemplify the phenomenon briefly would require showing how in the case of humans, for example, objects, others, and one's own body are not given fully and completely in one fell semantic swoop, but are built up and continue to be built up in the course of life experiences (Husserl, 1973, 1977, 1983, 1989); it would require showing through a phenomenological reading of animal behavioral studies how the same is true for other animals such as chimpanzees, and not altogether true of animals such as mice, and far less true of animals such as slugs, for example; it would require showing through the same kind of reading how other animals such as anemones make sense of their environment, and to some degree of other creatures such as starfish; and so on. In a word, it would require extensive investigations and analyses beyond the scope of this paper.

3   Husserl's essay "The Origin of Geometry" (1970) shows in a particularly exacting way how a genetic Husserlian phenomenology is concerned with the origin and constitution of meaning and how the methodology is thus particularly suited to a search for origins. (To avoid possible misunderstanding, it should perhaps be noted explicitly that Husserl's term "genetic" has nothing to do with genes; it specifies origins, as does the common English word *genesis*, which

evolution, sense-making has involved the constitution of new inter-animate meanings on the basis of new corporeal acts, dispositions, discoveries, developments, and so on. Because in all such instances it is a question of meaning and not reference (or information, for that matter), understandings of the origins of sense-making necessarily require understandings of the living organisms that define natural history, in particular, understandings of the diverse ways in which they both move about in and experience the world.

A final clarification warrants attention. In this essay I draw a distinction between signs and symbols based on progressively more complex forms of responsivity and "agentivity" (to borrow a term from psychologist Jerome Bruner [Bruner, 1990, p. 77]). An evolutionary semantics begins with living subjects — animate forms — not only in the Peircean sense of interpretants and in philosopher Susanne Langer's sense of active subjects who, in a manner akin to the semantically responsive displayed-to animal that Rowell pinpoints, *constructively* respond to the world (Langer, 1948), but subjects who, as indicated, themselves actively create meanings, subjects who are creative agents of semantic novelty and change. The acknowledgment of creative as well as responsive subjects necessarily points us in the direction of an evolutionary semantics rather than to an origin of semiosis and this because fundamentally distinct ways of meaning evolved with species-specific forms of life. There is, in other words, not an origin of semiosis but origins of semiosis; as this essay will show, different forms of semiosis evolved coincident with the evolution of a diversity of animate forms. This biological fact of life is true in a particularly strong sense with respect to symbol-making, for symbolization by definition is a creative act: to symbolize means to make one thing stand for another — conceptually, yes, as Langer (1948) would argue,[4] but conceptually not to

derives etymologically from the Greek word *genesis*, which itself derives from *gignesthai*, meaning to be born: *OED*.)

4   Langer's thesis, simply stated, is that signs signify: they are indicators that prompt action; symbols do not indicate but represent: they are "instruments of thought" that lead one to conceive of something not immediately present. It is this aspect — *conception* — that essentially distinguishes signs from symbols.

I follow Langer's distinction only in part because a clean separation between sign and symbol is not wholly viable. In particular, a clean separation does not jibe with experience — any more than an air-tight separation of "humans" from "animals" via language (Langer, 1948, 1972) jibes with research studies showing the ability of some chimpanzees to learn a symbolic language (Premack, 1975; Savage-Rumbaugh, 1994). Sight of one's national flag, for example, prompts action of some kind — a salute, a hand over the heart, or at the very least, consummate attention. A national flag may also lose its symbolic status, becoming simply a piece of material, no longer standing for something to be honored and thus no longer eliciting ritual action. The smell or sight of smoke, commonly taken as a *sign* of fire — a natural sign — exemplifies the non-viability of the distinction from the other end. The smell or sight can lead one not to action but to conceive of the town hall burning, for example, and in fact can evoke an the exclusion of bodily gestures and acts, or more precisely, to the exclusion of a *kinetic semantics*. We can exemplify the import of creative subjects briefly but clearly by a consideration of anthropologist Terrence Deacon's account of the origin of human language.

Deacon attempts to show continuity from sign to symbol through a Peircean grid: the passage from indexicals to symbols is the result of "unlearning" indexical associations as such, i.e., the one-to-one correspondence between signs and their objects, and seeing them instead as functional units within a single system of symbolic reference, what Deacon terms token-token relationships (Deacon, 1997, e.g., pp. 87, 92–3). The problem is that if "[s]ymbols are learned by first establishing ... indexical associations" (*ibid.*, p. 404), then the challenge of accounting for the origin of symbols remains. In broader terms, one cannot account for the origin of human language without accounting for the origin of words, and as Deacon himself seems to recognize, until words are "available" — "Probably not until *Homo erectus* were the equivalents of words available" (*ibid.*, p. 407) — words are not available. Indeed, they are not available until they are invented, and they are not invented until they are created by individuals who are aware of themselves both as sound-makers and as potential creators of sound (Sheets-Johnstone, 1990, 1999a).[5]

image of the town hall burning. Smoke may thus on Langer's definition shift from sign to symbol and slip over concretely into symbolic thinking. In short, a possible slippage is apparent from symbol to sign and from sign to symbol, which testifies to a less clean separation than that which Langer proposes. What leads us to conceive may well also lead us to act and what leads us to act may well also lead us to conceive. Conception and action are indeed most often experientially intertwined and separable only in analysis.

Langer's thesis, however, through its emphasis on conception and action (or more precisely, on conception and *act*; see Langer 1967), consistently presences a subject, a living intact organism, and this presencing, coupled with her analysis of discursive and non-discursive symbols and her notion of semblance with respect to the latter kinds of symbols, gives her thesis special evolutionary import — in spite of its strong and rigorous insistence on evolutionary discontinuities.

5   Vocalizations are inherently prosodic. Their pitch, timbre, intensity, length, rhythm, and so on, makes them distinctive. These prosodic elements might well have been the source of discovery of oneself as a creator of sound. A number of Deacon's comments supports just such a linkage.

Deacon speaks of prosodic elements as a "system of indices" that "probably had the longest co-evolutionary relationship with language." In particular, he states that prosodic elements "are used both to direct attention to what the speaker deems to be more salient elements and to communicate correlated emotional tone" (1997, p. 364). He conjectures that this system, "a parallel channel to speech" was probably "recruited from ancestral call functions", and that the various prosodic features "are most often produced without conscious intention" but reflect the "arousal level, emotional states, and attention" of the speaker (*ibid.*, p. 418). Earlier, he has said that "many aspects of this speech melody have been shown to have features in common with the innate vocalizations of primates" (*ibid.*, p. 313), noting in particular that there is a correlation "of changing pitch, volume, and rate of production with the level of arousal"; that a change "in the quality of vocalization" is "an indication of type of interaction (hostile, submissive, etc.)"; and that rhythm or "overall phrasing" is correlated with "breath control" (*ibid.*, p. 314).

This very problem threads its way through Deacon's account of language-learning by chimpanzees. However insightful and compelling his account, Deacon cannot properly make the analogy from chimpanzees to early humans precisely because in the latter instance, the invention — the *creation* — of linguistic symbols must be accounted for. Talk about teaching[6] and learning[7] "symbolic relationships" as in chimpanzee language-learning is not enough. Again, until words are available, words are not available. Thus, however clear the case with respect to Kanzi and other chimpanzees for whom the learning of indexical associations was "kept up until the complete system of combinatorial relationships between the symbols was discovered" (*ibid.*, p. 402), the same case cannot be made for early hominids for whom there was no ready-made symbolic system, i.e., verbal language, and hence no ready made symbolic "combinatorial relationships" to be rehearsed over and over again to the point that a symbolic system of reference "was discovered."

A further point warrants mention. All the selection pressures in the world will not invent language. Neither will any particular kind of brain. What is wanted are living subjects. At some point, it is necessary to bring to the fore intact, whole-bodied organisms, animate forms, the actual creatures who themselves created verbal language by creating symbols that were not simply referential tokens but semantically rich sounds. Deacon's account of the origin of symbolic reference does not extend this far,[8] and the basic problem goes unacknowledged to the end. Even so, Deacon appears marginally aware of the problem when, toward the end of his book, he makes two startling and confounding statements. He declares that, "The origins of the first symbolic communication have nothing intrinsically to do with language per se" (*ibid.*, pp. 408–9) and that "The

---

Though all these features are "most often produced without conscious intention" *in present-day human speech*, there are good reasons to think that at the dawn of verbal language, an initial and growing awareness of oneself as a creator of sound was linked to just these already existing prosodic features of vocalization: to intensitites, timbre, rhythm, length — to the shortness, shrillness, softness, regularity, cadencing, and so on, of any particular vocalization — and to the way in which these already existing prosodic features not only combine to produce meaning but are latent with meaning. In other words, the first creators of verbal symbols, becoming initially aware of the prosodic features inherent in their vocalizations and of how these features are cognitively charged, became aware of the qualitative possibilities of sound and of their own possibilities for creating meaningful sounds.

6   "How could a social environment have arisen spontaneously, which possessed the necessary supports for overcoming the immensely difficult and complicated task of teaching symbolic relationships to individuals whose brains were not only unprepared but resistant to learning them?" (Deacon, 1997, p. 402).

7   "Symbols refer to relationships among indices, and are learned by first establishing these indexical associations" (Deacon 1997, p. 404).

8   Or rather, one might say that it extends quite sketchily this far in the form of a "story" (Deacon, 1997, pp. 407–8).

argument I have presented is only an argument for the conditions which required symbolic reference in the first place" (p. 409), the conditions being basically the need for a marriage agreement which would cement a male provisioning and female reproductive arrangement. The second statement regarding the narrowness of his argument comes as a double surprise to the reader since *the origin of symbolic reference, not its original conditions*, has been at the forefront from the beginning, and since missing, but at the heart of the conditions he spells out, are living subjects. The first statement is doubly puzzling because, on the one hand, symbolic communication has been at the forefront from the beginning and because, on the other hand, language in its social, communicative function has been the only linguistic function of concern. In sum, Deacon's "symbolic species" falls short of explaining the origin of symbols because it falls short of explaining the invention of something semantically new. Without living subjects, there are no originating agents of semantic novelty and change.[9]

2. On Bacteria

Stephen Jay Gould has observed that

> If we must characterize a whole by a representative part, we certainly should honor life's constant mode. We live now in the 'Age of Bacteria'. Our planet has always been in the 'Age of Bacteria', ever since the

---

[9]   It is of interest in this respect to note Borchert and Zihlman's thesis (1990) that there is a difference between explaining the origin of language and the evolution of language. In explaining the latter, they too, like Deacon, draw on Baldwin's notion of organic selection and Waddington's notion of genetic assimilation in their thesis that phenotypic change preceded genetypic change. Moreover they consult the same chimpanzee studies that Deacon consults, notably studies of Sherman and Austin and of Kanzi (Savage-Rumbaugh et al 1978; Savage-Rumbaugh and Sevcik, 1984), but instead of concluding finally that a marriage agreement between consenting adults — the males in order to guarantee access to a female, the females in order to be adequately provisioned — was the precipitating cause of linguistic symbolization, Borchert and Zhilman find developmental phenomena to be precipitating events: "language evolved through changes in ontogeny" (p. 21). More specifically, they suggest that "the transition to vocal tool-using initially occurred not primarily because natural selection favored adults who were shomehow more competent with symbols, but because it favored *infants* who were more successful at using vocalizations to manipulate their mothers' behavior" (p. 34). ("Manipulate" is an unfortunate word choice that suggests fraudulent management of another; "solicit" would have been a better choice since soliciting the mother's attention is what appears of moment with respect to protection, affection, care, nourishment, and so on, precisely as Borchert and Zihlman go on immediately to specify: "Vocal symbolic tool-using [vocal symbolizations] may have increased infants' protection from predators and may have ensured them a reliable supply of food, water, warmth, affection, social interaction and cognitive stimulation" [*ibid.*].)

It should be noted too that in support of their thesis, Borchert and Zihlman call attention to the "Gestural Complex" (Borchert and Zihlman, 1990, p. 25 ff.) that emerged on the part of Sherman, Austin, and Kanzi, namely, the spontaneous use of pointing, and of showing, giving, and requesting objects in conjunction with their language-learning, a gestural complex that, they point out, is evident in language-learning in human infants and young children.

first fossils — bacteria, of course — were entombed in rocks more than three and a half billion years ago (1996, p. 176).

Semiosis has a history in the life of living forms all the way back to bacteria. Accordingly, I begin with a description of the way in which bacteria move in recognition of their surrounds, namely, through surface recognition sensitivity, a fundamental biological capacity. Consider the following description taken from a standard biology text:

> Processing in a bacterium may be thought of as a sort of molecular polling ... the positive 'votes' cast by receptors in response, say, to increasing concentrations of a sugar are matched against the negative votes produced by increasing concentrations of noxious compounds. On the basis of this continuous voting process, the bacterium 'knows' whether the environment, on the whole, is getting better or worse. The results of this analysis appear to be communicated by electrical signals to the response centers. The final stage, the response, consists of a brief change in the direction of rotation of the several stiff, helical flagella that propel the bacterium. The result is that the bacterium founders briefly and then strikes out in a new direction, once again sampling to see whether the environment is improving or deteriorating (Keeton and Gould, 1986, p. 452).[10]

Surface recognition sensitivity is a more precise way of characterizing what the text identifies as responsivity.[11] Surface recognition sensitivity is in the service of movement, movement toward and away from things in the environment. The sensitivity is essentially a *tactile* sensitivity; bacteria sample the environment through direct contact, by literally bumping into it, finding either propitious or noxious molecules in the process. While surface recognition sensitivity is commonly spoken of by scientists in terms of "mechanoreception" (Laverack, 1976, p. 17), as if the organisms in question were machines, from the viewpoint of living forms, the sensitivity is more appropriately specified as a form of *tactile*-reception. The protozoan ciliate species *Stentor*, for example, uses its cilia to sweep away noxious particles and the *Stentor* itself bends away from the tactile disturbance (Curtis, 1975, p. 311). Tactility in the service of movement, of recognizing something outside one's own body and moving accordingly, similarly describes the cilia-mediated tentacle movement of a sedentary hydrozoan polyp toward a food source. At the most fundamental level, organisms recognize particular features in their environment by touching

10 Another biological text describes the responsivity of a bacterium more exactly in terms of movement: "When the concentration of chemicals in the water is uniform, the cell [the bacterium] tumbles often, changing direction every time. By contrast, when the cell is moving along a gradient, there are fewer tumbles, so the cell continues longer in the same direction" (Curtis and Barnes, 1989, p. 131).

11 Responsivity is consistently identified in biological texts as "a fundamental and almost universal characteristic of life" (Curtis, 1975, p. 28).

them, and in touching them, pursue a certain course of action. To state the same biological truth from the opposite, Peircean-colored perspective, we can say that the world is replete with signs that signify for particular organisms depending on their surface sensitivities.

When biologist Jakob von Uexküll (1957) spoke of objects in an organism's *Umwelt* having particular functional tones — of an object being perceived as something to eat, for example, or something to shun, or something to climb, and so on — he implicitly acknowledged just such a relationship, what we may term a *kinetic semiotics*, the tone being created and established through a creature's possible movement in relation to the object. The basic dimension of a kinetic semiotics is surface recognition sensitivity. I might note that in acknowledging this signifying relationship between organism and surrounding world, von Uexküll gave a near Husserlian or phenomenological account of an object in that an object's functional tone is a dimension of *the object as meant* (Husserl, 1973, pp. 36–7), the object in terms of what it signifies to the perceiver.

3. Morphological Corporeal Representation

From a compound semiotic-evolutionary perspective, surface recognition sensitivity is related to corporeal representation,[12] *morphological* corporeal representation, or the formal means whereby one animal recognizes another as being of a certain age, as being male or female, and so on. Bodily conformations, patternings, and colorations signify. Biologist Adolf Portmann wrote of this morphological semiotics, though not terming it such. He described the way in which animals such as wild pigs and plovers recognize one another's age and social status by its external patternings and colorings (Portmann, 1967, pp. 152, 156, 158, 159). He spoke explicitly of *form production* in this context, exemplifying across a vast range of species how an individual's coloring, shape, conformations, and/or patternings are visually meaningful. In all such instances, Portmann affirmed, "form production may be termed *sematic*, since it has a striking, signal-like effect" (1967, p. 115). By the term *sematic* — not to be confused with *semantic* — Portmann means precisely a sign, not a symbol, function.[13]

It is important to emphasize that these built-in meanings of animate form derive not from what a particular animal does but directly from its morphology — its shape, conformations, patternings, and colorings as

12   For the original introduction and specification of this term, see Sheets-Johnstone, 1990.
13   Note, however, that in the discussion of Portmann which follows, I convert Portmann's term *sematic*, which is tied to signs, to *semantic*, which is tied to meaning, hence to living organisms, animate forms.

these formal features change or remain constant over time. It is thus understandable not only why Portmann conceived and subtitled his study "a study of the *appearance* of animals"—shape, conformations, patternings, and colorings are striking *visual* phenomena—but further, why his delineation of the inherently meaningful appearance of animate forms may be defined as morphological corporeal representation, and further, why morphological corporeal representation may be related to surface recognition sensitivity. The latter phenomenon specifies a tactile recognition of features and objects of the environment, as illustrated not only by bacteria and the protozoan ciliate *Stentor*, as we have seen, but by a locust's sensitivity to air currents, for example, and a spider's sensitivity to an object landing on its web; in these instances too, tactility is the primary sensory modality, a modality in the service of movement. Morphological corporeal representation specifies a different primary sensory modality, a modality also in the service of movement, but movement in relation to conspecifics. Concisely stated, surface recognition sensitivity is tied to tactility and to environmental features and objects; morphological corporeal representation is tied to vision and to other living creatures. In the one instance, the semiotic articulates a tactile organism-environment relationship; in the other instance, the semiotic articulates a visual organism-organism relationship.

Especially in the context of a morphological semiotics, it warrants mention that inquiries and studies of organic form[14] have all but disappeared. The pervasive concern in present-day Western science is not with morphology but with brains, and furthermore, not with meaning but with information. Bruner (1990), in tracing the rise of cognitivist science, has written eloquently of this displacement of meaning. Even without his narrative, however, one can easily appreciate how, with the shift to information, the epistemological terrain shifted: a concern with semantics gave way to a concern with mechanisms. Accounts of living creatures as living creatures—animate forms—and accounts of life as it is lived by living creatures—forms of life—become grist for mechanistic mills. Since a descriptive literature was no longer of value in itself nor directly relevant to an understanding of life, semiosis—the process of reading the environment and the process of reading other organisms—virtually disappears as a topic of concern within mainstream cognitivist science.

When descriptive studies such as those of von Uexküll and Portmann are excised, however, so also is a critical dimension of biological research, namely, research into origins. George Wald, Nobel prize-winning physiologist in 1967, remarked that there are three fundamental questions in

---

14   For an especially probing and informative example, see Sinnot (1963).

biology: where does it come from? how does it work? what is its survival value? Contemporary cognitivist studies in Western science and philosophy are tethered almost exclusively to the second and third questions, thus on delineating causal relationships and specifying adaptive value. In these endeavors, explanation reigns supreme; description is minimal. To work back to origins and to trace the history of a biological phenomenon, however, requires studious, detailed descriptions, precisely as Darwin's observational record of his travels aboard the *Beagle* so decisively shows. Short of these studious and detailed observations, the entire field of biology would collapse; the observations are the backbone of evolutionary theory and evolutionary theory is the glue that holds the whole of biology together.

Study of the origins of semiosis from an evolutionary perspective necessarily involves the study of organic form, for organic form is a source of meaning. Indeed, a study of the origin of semiosis should eventuate in a descriptive account of how it is that organisms first came to read each other in meaningful ways. Morphological corporeal representation is an initial step toward this end. The term "reading", I might mention, is only partially used in a metaphoric sense. The etymology of *read* includes both the sense "to discern" and the sense "to discover the meaning or significance [of something]." Surface recognition sensitivity and morphological corporeal representation are both semiotic markers in this respect, markers that, we might explicitly note, are not extinct any more than bacteria or wild pigs are extinct.

4. Kinetic Corporeal Representation

The semiotic significance of tactility and vision is apparent in a further form of corporeal representation, one that is kinetic rather than morphological and symbolic rather than sematic. In this kinetic form of representation, animate bodies symbolize the spatio-kinetic dynamics of their own kinetic/tactile-kinesthetic experiences — or neuro-muscular corollaries thereof. The honey bee dance is a classic instance. The distance and direction of a sugar source, knowledge of which is conveyed by a dancing bee through her movement, is rooted in the dancing bee's tactile-kinesthetic experience of flying to the sugar source. Whether humanlike tactile-kinesthetic experience is characteristic of the bee or not is beside the point. There is a spatio-kinetic similarity between the actual flight of the bee and the dance by which she represents her flight. The similarity is one in which kinetic experience is iconically linked to spatio-kinetic correlates. This is true not only with respect to the bee's bodily orientation to the sun in her actual flight and her correlative orientation to gravity in her symbolic rendition of the flight, but with respect to other behaviors that strikingly point up the role of tactile-kinesthetic elements further. For example, if the flight is experimentally made more arduous, the dance reflects the greater effort; if the sugar concentration is high — basically a tactile datum — the vigorousness of the dance is greater. An iconic relationship clearly exists between tactile-kinesthetically experienced meanings and tactile-kinetically represented meanings. The spatio-kinesthetic dynamics of actual corporeal activity serve as a semantic template for the spatio-kinetic dynamics that constitute the dance.

We see a similar form of kinetic representation in the tongue-flicking behavior of female howler monkeys. As described by C.R. Carpenter, whose world-renown field studies seventy years ago established the basis for much of the subsequent work in nonhuman primate social behavior, the tongue-flicking behavior leaves no doubt but that tactile-kinesthetic analogues function symbolically. Carpenter (1963, pp. 49–50) describes the behavior as follows:

> When approaching a male, [the female] will form an oval opening with her lips and her protruding tongue will rapidly oscillate in and out and up and down. It is clear to an observer ... that the function of this gesture is to invite copulation ... In a real sense the act is symbolic of sexual desire and readiness for copulation in the female and it stimulates appropriate responses in the male.

Tongue and mouth are *in this instance*[15] sexual analogues of male and female genitalia respectively. They are sexual analogues in the behavior of other primates as well. The tongue-smacking of some monkey species, especially *Macaca nemestrina* (Pigtailed macaque) in mating situations, is equally indicative of the genital/oral relationship (van Hooff 1969), for example, and in present-day hominids there is evidence of genital symbolization in the sexual tongue-flicking behavior of the !Ko Bushmen (Eibl-Eibesfeldt, 1974). Even a ram, in his attempts to interest a ewe in being mounted, flicks his tongue in and out of his mouth as he thrusts his head forward, sidles up to, and nudges a ewe — as any sheep farmer will attest.

15   I underscore "in this instance" (and include those further instances that follow in the text) in order to offset any misreading. In the oral version of this essay, I was mistakenly criticized by Philip Lieberman for making a hard and fast analogy between tongue and penis, and mouth and vagina. I was then, and am now, making no such analogy. Other analogical uses of the mouth, for example, include the mouth-opening of an infant in conjunction with its attempt to open a matchbox (Piaget, 1968). Why the infant opens its mouth is inexplicable apart from a certain corporeal conceptual relevance obtaining between the opening of its mouth and the opening of the matchbox. The conceptual relevance is implicitly noted by Piaget, but only by accident, as it were, since the spatial tactile-kinesthetic analogy between the two movements (or "behaviors") is neither identified nor examined by him (see Sheets-Johnstone, 1990, p. 337). The essential point is that thinking is fundamentally modeled on the body; bodies are sources of meaning and constitute semantic templates.

In sum, where interanimate meanings are represented, animate bodies represent them corporeally. In both their form and their movement, animate bodies are potential semantic templates. This is why a psychology, aesthetics, archaeology, and linguistics of symbolizing behaviors is possible—why pears and mountains can be interpreted to represent female breasts and umbrellas and tree trunks can represent penises, as in Sigmund Freud's psychology of dreams (Freud, 1938, 1953); why traditional works of art can be understood as symbols, their dynamic forms being logically congruent to the dynamic form of human feeling, as in Langer's analysis of aesthetic form (Langer, 1953); why archaeological artifacts in their design features can be interpreted as representations of female and male genitalia as in archaeologist André Leroi-Gourhan's analysis of paleolithic cave art (Leroi-Gourhan, 1971); and why the articulatory gestures of primordial language can be shown to be tactile-kinesthetic analogues of their referents, as in anthropological linguist Mary LeCron Foster's analysis of the symbolic structure of primordial language (Foster, 1978, 1994a, 1994b, 1996). In view of the commonly privileged status of human language, I will use the latter example—primordial language—to specify further the symbolic nature of kinetic corporeal representation, showing how, as with the honey bee dance, the articulatory gestures of primordial language were not arbitrary gestures but iconic counterparts of their referent.

5. Kinetic Corporeal Representation and the Origin of Language

Foster's global reconstruction of linguistic root forms demonstrates that primordial language was rooted in tactile-kinesthetic experience, an articulatory gesture being in each instance iconic with respect to its referent. For example, all root forms with *m* refer to some kind of bilateral relationship—"the fingers or hands in taking or grasping", or "two opposed surfaces in tapering, pressing together, holding together, crushing, or resting against" (Foster, 1978, p. 110). The bilateral relationship is in each case isomorphic with the bilateral articulatory gesture that produces the sound *m*. Moreover as the examples suggest, and as Foster points out, meanings in primordial language tend to focus on "motional-relational complexes" rather than on discrete objects (Foster, 1978; 1996). In just the same way, the honey bee dance represents not an objectified geographical location, or even an object *per se*, but *how far* and *in what direction* a sugar source is in relation to "home". In other words, primordial language was not a matter of *naming*, but a matter of indicating spatial relationships and bodily movement in relation to space. *Kinetic corporeal representation* indicates as much: it articulates a dynamic rather than static semantics; it is an analogi-cally rather than arbitrarily formulated semantics; and it is a relational rather than object-tethered semantics.

There are further commonalities with the honey bee dance that warrant consideration. Representation in primordial language as well as in the honey bee dance is *meta*corporeal. The iconic articulatory gestures are in each instance a spatio/tactile-kinesthetic transcription of worldly experi-ence or activity. That is, they specify something out in the world apart from the body yet iconically related to corporeal kinetic experience. This is of course immediately apparent in the case of the honey bee dance. But it is also apparent in the case of primordial language. The bilateral relationships *resting against, pressing together*, or *crushing*, for example, are primordial perceptual meanings anchored in what might aptly be termed *primordial bodily experiences*: *resting against* nest materials in sleeping or the earth in standing, for example; *pressing together* in copulating or in producing the sound *m*; *crushing* in chewing food or pounding one thing with another. In effect, root forms of language were anchored in correlative "root" bodily experiences. Where the bees' dance and primordial language differ is in both mode of articulation and mode of communication. In a honey bee's dance, articulation is of the whole body and what is communicated is transmitted in a whole-body tactile-kinetic manner from dancer to poten-tial recruit (in what linguist Philip Lieberman in a primatological context terms a "whole body gestural system"; see Lieberman, 1983). In primor-dial language, articulation is of the supralaryngeal parts of the body and what is communicated is transmitted not tactilely, through intimate body-to-body contact of articulatory parts, but aurally, through a *second* sensory medium. Communication is in the one instance directly by way of the tactile-kinetic gestures themselves, and in the other instance, by way of the sounds the gestures create.

In each instance, however, articulatory gestures constitute meanings. What is interesting in this regard is that studies of human speech show that speech perception is actually speech *apperception*. The listener makes co-present with aural perception something that is not actually given in the perception, namely, the articulatory gestures that make the sound: "The listener responds as though he is interpreting the acoustic signal in terms of the articulatory gestures that a speaker would employ to generate the word" (Lieberman, 1975, p. 535; see psychologists Alvin Lieberman and Ignatius Mattingly [1985] for a detailed and more recent account of the research on which Lieberman's statement is based). There is thus a *tac-tile-kinesthetic decoding of speech*. From this perspective, the ultimate differ-ence in mode of sensory communication between the honey bee dance and primordial and present-day human language is the difference between *actual tactile-kinetic* experience and *apperceived tactile-kinesthetic* experience, that is, between a recruit's actual tactile-kinetic experience of a dancing bee's movement and a listener's apperceived tactile-kinesthetic experience of a speaker's speech.

Now short of species-specific tactile-kinesthetic invariants, there could be no such intercorporeal communication. The honey bee dance, primordial language, the tongue and mouth movements of a female howler monkey, and all other forms of kinetic corporeal representation would in each instance be meaningless to the animal to whom the semantically-laden kinetics was addressed. This is precisely the import of primatologist Stuart Altmann's concept of *comsigns* (Altmann, 1967). What the term *comsign* pinpoints is the fact that most primate signals are part of the repertoire of *all* members of the species or particular group in question, at the very least for some period in each animal's life. What is true of primates is in this instance also true of bees. Potential recruits are potential dancers because tactile-kinesthetic invariants anchor interchangeability.

Before going on to show the relationship of tactile-kinesthetic invariants and iconicity to analogical thinking, I would like to interpose a question alluded to earlier: how are new interanimate meanings minted? In particular, how is it that one individual knows what another individual means when the latter individual does something the former individual has not seen before? This question arises when we think seriously about the fact that it is the perceiving rather than acting individual who solidifies meaning. An individual can, after all, gesticulate or make all kinds of sounds for that matter, but unless and until the individual on the perceiving end responds, and responds in a way coincident with the intended meaning of the gestures or sounds, the intended meaning goes unrecognized. The passage from Rowell cited earlier makes this very point: unless and until the receiver certifies meaning, the gestures or sounds will not enter the communicative repertoire of the species or group in question. In Altmann's terms, the gestures or sounds will not become a comsign. The question of how a displayed-to animal comes to validate the movements or gestures of another as meaningful is thus of critical importance. A particularly graphic example will serve to highlight the possible complexity of a new interanimate meaning. The example comes from a book titled *Primate Cognition*.

> [T]he initiation of play often takes place in chimpanzees by one juvenile raising its arm aboce its head and then descending on another, play-hitting in the process. This then becomes ritualized ontogenetically into an "arm-raise" gesture in which the initiator simply raises its arm and, rather than actually following through with the hitting, stays

back and waits for the other to initiate the play, monitoring its response all the while ... If the desired response is not forthcoming, sometimes the gesture will be repeated, but quite often another ges- ture will be used. In other situations a juvenile was observed to actu- ally alternate its gaze between the recipient of the gestural signal and one of its own body parts; for example, one individual learned to initi- ate play by presenting a limp leg to another individual as it passed by (an invitation to grab it an so initiate a game of chase), looking back and forth between the recipient and its leg in the process (Tomasello and Call, 1997, p. 244).

The gesturing chimpanzee clearly intends a meaning, but why should the presentation of a limp leg and a direct gaze at a passing individual con- stitute an invitation to play chase? From the point of view of validated meaning, the question is more properly formulated in terms of the addressed individual, i.e., in terms of *how* the gestures come to be per- ceived as meaningful, and it is answerable precisely in terms of the fact that *validated* meanings are rooted in species-specific kinetic capacities, dispositions, and possibilities. An addressed individual comes to validate meaning on the basis of a fundamental kinetic/semantic relationship that is not arbitrary but iconic, a relationship based on a formal similarity between movement and meaning. In the present instance, the relationship is compound and might be glossed as "legs are to chasing as eye contact is to inviting". What grounds the compound relationship is a common body and a common body of movement linking to two individuals. In effect, an answer to the question "how?" rests on a acknowledgement of the corpo- real underpinnings of comsigns. In the most fundamental sense, one body understands another body to the degree it not only resembles that body, but moves and gestures, or has the possibility of moving and gesturing, in ways similar to the ways in which that body moves and gestures; a body that, accordingly, has perceptual experiences that consistently combine certain tactile-kinesthetic/affective feelings with certain contextually situ- ated kinetic-visual or kinetic-auditory of kinetic-tactile awarenesses. Meaning is thus in the most fundamental sense corporeally structured; it is articulated along the lines of species-specific bodies.

At minimum, tactile-kinesthetic invariants predispose organisms toward iconicity since the most easily formulated, consistently utilizable, and readily understood signals are those that are structured in bodily movements and experiences shared by all members of the species—like the pressing together of lips to produce the sound *m*. It is important to emphasize, however, that the foundational disposition toward iconicity, as toward corporeal representation itself, is not necessarily a conscious disposition, nor are any of the associated kinetics consciously planned and executed. At the most basic level, tactile-kinesthetic symbols are structured not in reflective acts — such as "I think I'll make up a symbol" — but in prereflective corporeal experience; that is, they are the spontaneous product of certain species-specific bodily experiences. What Freud said of the dreamer is thus likely true of the symbolizing animal: "The dreamer's knowledge of symbolism is unconscious" (Freud, 1963, p. 148). But while the symbolizing animal is, like the dreamer, unconscious of its symbolizing behavior *as such, unlike the dreamer*, it is not unaware of its behavior. It is conscious of its own actions; it experiences its own body; it experiences its own appetites, desires, and proclivities toward movement and meaning. Its thinking is tied to these experiences, which are essentially kinetic experiences. A disposition toward iconicity is thus a disposition toward analogical thinking. To say that analogical thinking is at the root of kinetic corporeal representation is in turn to identify a process of thinking in which what is thought is thought along the lines of the body. Analogical thinking is foundationally a process of thinking not in words but in movement. Analogical thinking as a *reflective* act is an elaboration of this basic dispositional capacity.

In sum, tactile-kinetic symbols are spontaneously formed analogues of tactile-synesthetic experience. They are anchored in the tactile-kinesthetic perceptual lives of the creatures and species concerned. That they are structured in prereflective rather than reflective acts is substantiated not only by studies of speech perception and by the honey bee dance but by Carpenter's untroubled interpretation of a female howler's tongue-flicking gesture: "It is clear to an observer who has seen this series of events", Carpenter writes, "that the function of this gesture is to invite copulation" (Carpenter, 1963, p. 49). Carpenter was not puzzled by the behavior nor did he have to analyze it painstakingly either to determine its meaning or to justify that meaning to his readers. On the contrary, his brief verbal description suffices to convey immediately to the reader the same unequivocal meaning the actual behavior embodied for him in the flesh. Correlatively, our ready understanding of his description is a validation of our own basic and well-nurtured capacity to think analogically along the lines of our bodies and, in turn, to think in movement (Sheets-Johnstone, 1990, 1994, 1999a,b). No one taught us to think in these ways. We think quite naturally along the lines of our bodies and in movement. By this very token, we can understand why a male howler monkey understands the behavior of a tongue-flicking female howler monkey: he too knows without instruction of any kind "that the function of the gesture is to invite copulation." Were this not so, the gesture would hardly "stimulate appropriate responses in the male".

That primordial language was structured analogically along the lines of the body should give pause for thought. Received wisdom urges us to think that language is made up of vocal sounds that are arbitrarily formed and arbitrarily linked to objects in the world, and that naming things and naming them by way of arbitrary sounds is the crowning mark of humans. However brief, the foregoing evolutionary perspective—from precambrian semiosis to morphological and kinetic corporeal representation—challenges the wisdom of that view. More than that, it challenges the empirical evidence—or in truth, lack of evidence—for that view. Indeed, taking a cue from Gould and Lewontin's critique of adaptationist stories, with its cautionary emphasis against taking present-day utility of a trait or behavior as reason for its origin, we may similarly issue a cautionary note against taking the arbitrary counters of present-day human languages as the defining feature present at the origin of human language. Foster's comprehensive studies of languages worldwide point us in an exactly opposite direction and present us with a formidable array of evidence supporting the conclusion that the symbolic structure of primordial language was through and through analogical; particular meanings followed along the lines of the bodily dynamics constituted by particular articulations of the supralaryngeal tract.[16]

6. Neandertals

We can contrast the evidence for and the rigor of these findings—and in fact the whole of the foregoing evolutionary perspective concerning the origin of signs and the origin of symbols—with anthropologist Christopher Stringer's and archaeologist Clive Gamble's thesis that symbols "arose with the flick of a switch", notably with the advent of *Homo sapiens sapiens* (Stringer and Gamble, 1993, p. 203).[17] Their thesis is stated in the context of their investigation of Neandertals, specifically, in the context of their answer to the question of whether Neandertals are close kin or distant relatives. Their bias against Neandertals precludes not only a just evaluation of Neandertals; it precludes their own ability to think clearly and cogently both about symbols and how symbols arose. Their claim that symbols arose with the advent of modern humans is buttressed by the claim that the campsites of modern humans *were symbols*, that the tools of modern humans *were symbols*, and so on, and that such "symbolic behavior", as they term it, is antithetical to mere survival behavior, the behavior

16 See Sheets Johnstone 1999b for a presentation and discussion of the fascinating and apparently little-known findings of Alfred R. Wallace on this very topic.
17 For both a detailed and broader discussion of the controversy over Neandertals, together with its assumptions and implications regarding minds and bodies, see Sheets-Johnstone, 1999a.

that they say characterizes Neandertals.[18] They state that "arranging symbolic behavior according to symbolic codes" defines the onset and nature of symbolism, and that "Symbolism involves making mental substitutions and appreciating associations between people, objects and contexts" (*ibid.*).

Now to begin with, to speak of campsites and tools as "symbols" generates conceptual muddles. What is a campsite a symbol of? The answer is nowhere to be found in Stringer and Gamble's account. The same may be said for tools crafted by modern humans; how they function as symbols is nowhere elucidated. When put to the test — *cashed in for real currency* — the words making up their claims fail to deliver. This is because campsites themselves are not symbols nor are items such as tools that are found within them, nor are what Stringer and Gamble designate "patterns of settlement" or "new habitats". These constructions achieve symbolic status only on the basis of *being currently read as symbols*; that is, they are symbols only from the interpretive perspective of Stringer and Gamble — and others — who read them as *symbols* of intelligence. Pits used for the storage of fuel at a campsite, for example, or stacked mammoth bones that form a hut (Stringer and Gamble, 1993, p. 204), are not symbolic of anything. They refer to something beyond themselves only in the sense of referring to what Stringer and Gamble (and others) specify as "intelligence". Pits and huts may indisputably be regarded ingenious constructions, extraordinarily clever utilizations of the environment, and so on, but such positive regard does not make them symbols nor can it confer symbolic status upon the behavior of their makers. When Stringer and Gamble write that "architecture now embodies cultural, symbolic behaviour and not purely expedient survival behaviour" (*ibid.*), they are confusing their own judgments with that which they are judging. Their attributions are conceptually muddled because they are projections of their evaluations and not descriptive

---

18 The advent of symbolizing behavior — not symbolic behavior, as it is sometimes erroneously termed (e.g., Stringer and Gamble 1993; see Sheets-Johnstone, 1999a for further clarification) — is the result of analogical thinking that eventuates in the creation of a symbol of some kind. To distinguish between symbolizing behavior and symbolic behavior, consider the following brief examples.

If one joins a march to protest the decimation of rain forests, one's marching might be termed *symbolic* in that what one is doing by marching is symbolic of one's values: the march makes active reference to those values or brings those values to the fore. In contrast, the tongue-flicking movements of a female howler monkey, the dancing of a bee to inform conspecifics of a sugar source, the utterances of a speaker of primordial language, and the choreographing of a dance such as *Lamentation* are not *symbolic* behaviors. If they merit the designation "behavior" at all (they are more properly and most exactly specified in terms of movement, i.e., of kinetic form), they may be designated *symbolizing* behaviors; that is, they result in the creation of a symbol or symbols. The fashioning of stone tools is neither a symbolic behavior nor a symbolizing behavior: the acts involved in fashioning a stone tool neither stand for something apart from themselves nor does the completed act of production — the tool — result in a symbol.

of the things themselves. Their denigrating judgment of Neandertal language is indeed a classic case in point. After remarking that Neandertals "no doubt spoke, albeit simply and probably slowly" they write that "Neanderthals lacked complex spoken language because they did not need it" (1993, p. 217). Such judgments not only fail to elucidate the individuals we call Neandertals and to tell us anything about symbols and the origin and nature of human speech; they fail to be rational judgments in that no evidence is provided to substantiate them.

A crucially significant aspect of symbolizing activity can only remain hidden in these circumstances, namely, the variable relationship between analogical thinking and symbolization. Symbolization is fundamentally a form of analogical thinking, and analogical thinking is fundamentally structured in corporeal representation, representation that may or may not result in symbolization. In other words, analogical thinking does not *necessarily* eventuate in the production of symbols. Analogical thinking is basically a form of thinking that generates understandings on the basis of bodily experience, and these understandings may or may not eventuate in the production of symbols. Stone tools in fact provide an excellent example of how analogical thinking may *not* eventuate in the production of symbols.

That stone tools are an instance of analogical thinking is consistently attested to by anthropologists and archaeologists who, writing of the origin of stone tools, regularly state that stone tools replaced teeth; that is, like teeth, stone tools crush, tear, scrape, pierce, and so on.[19] That stone tools were functionally fashioned in the image of teeth, however, does not make them symbols of teeth; it makes them only analogues of teeth. But they are corporeal analogues in a further sense as well. The further analogy is implicitly adumbrated by anthropologist Paul Mellars in his article, "Technological Changes across the Middle-Upper Palaeolithic Transition: Economic, Social and Cognitive Perspectives." Mellars notes that "over large areas of Europe, the major changes in both the anatomy of the human populations, and the technology of the associated archaeological asemblages, can be shown to have occurred over at least broadly the same range of time—i.e., broadly between c. 40 000 and 30 000 BP" (Mellars, 1989, p. 338; note: "BP" means "years before the present"). The idea that morphology and technology are linked is in fact strongly suggested to any perceptive and non-Cartesian-thinking reader who compares two illustrations that Mellars includes in his article, one of European Neandertal (French Mousterian) tools, one of European modern human (Châtelperronian/Early

---

19 For a fully detailed account of how stone tools are analogues of teeth, see Sheets-Johnstone 1990, Chapter I.

Perigordian) tools. The former tools are squat, bulky, indeed, *robust* tools; the latter are lithe, elongate, indeed, *gracile* tools. With respect to bodily form, the former tools were created more in the image of a body's bulk than in the image of its bodily contours; the latter tools more in the image of a body's linear contours than in the image of its bulk. An analogical corporeal-lithic relationship is palpable in each instance.

Yet the archaeological situation is more complex than Mellars's illustrations of Western European artifacts indicate and would have us believe. Neandertals and modern humans, for example, produced essentially the same lithic technology in the Levantine Mousterian (Near East area, approximately 40 000 to 200 000 BP), Neandertals actually producing a preponderance of blade tools—spear points—in comparison with those produced by modern humans (John Shea personal communication, 2000; see Shea, 1997, 1998 on Levantine spear point use by Neandertals).[20] Yet such evidence does not countermand a corporeal-lithic relationship. The corporeal-lithic analogy specifies a *basic* formal correspondence between body and tool. When stone tools are made, they are geared to do a certain kind of work. The work they do is contingent on ecological circumstances, including kind of prey available in a particular site, for example. But it is in the most fundamental sense geared to the kinetic dispositions and movement possibilities of the body making the tool, and it is in this fundamental sense that tools are crafted along the lines of the body. The tools one makes and wields are, in other words, tools congenial to the body one is: tools that fit one's grip (however large or small, powerful or weak, for example), that fit one's style of moving (however fleet or heavy, long or short in endurance, for example), that fit one's range of movement (however flexible or constrained, ample or small, for example) and so on. In short, what one conceives and elaborates in the way of a tool is patterned on the kinetic possibilities and dynamics of the animate form one is. Thus, given the extraordinary thickness of bone in Neandertals and given the extraordinary physical powers of Neandertals that were called on daily for their survival—"Tremendous strength, endurance, and fortitude exceeding those of any modern human life-style were required on a daily basis" (Trinkaus and Shipman, 1993, p. 381)—it is likely that Neandertal spear points were in the service of close-up engagement with prey. In other words, Neandertals did not throw their spears but thrust and pierced with them. Anthropologist John Shea has in fact remarked that the overall

---

20 I am grateful to anthropologist John Shea for calling my attention to Mellars's Eurocentric perspective on Neandertals and modern humans, to the more complex facts of Levantine Mousterian tools, to his own innovative research strategies, and to the present-day controversy in which Mellars is involved with other anthropologists concerning the European Neandertal toolkit.

shape of Neandertal spear points "is more congruent with this kind of hunting tactic [thrusting] than it is with habitual long-distance throwing" (Shea, personal communication, 2000).

In the most fundamental sense, then, the body functions analogically as a semantic template. Archaeologists and paleoanthropologists tend to skip over the analogical relationship between body and tool and in doing so not only regularly skip over analogical thinking and the formidable question of the origin and nature of symbols, but regularly miss seeing the foundational connection between body and mind that would shed light on the origin and nature of symbols. To explain the difference between Upper and Middle Paleolithic tool-makers (modern humans and Neandertals), for example, Mellars vaguely speculates that modern humans "imposed form" on their stone tools and thus arrived at "symbolism and symbolically defined behaviour" or "symbolic meaning" (Mellars, 1989, pp. 358–60). The idea that thinking has something to do with the body — or the body with the mind — never surfaces in his account. In consequence, analogical thinking never surfaces nor does an awareness of the variable relationship between analogical thinking and symbolization.

7. Martha Graham's *Lamentation*: Analogical Thinking and Symbolization

To put the relationship between analogical thinking and symbolization in concrete present-day perspective, and to understand in finer terms why stone tools are the product of analogical thinking but are not thereby symbols, let us consider a contemporary instance of symbolization, a dance titled *Lamentation* that Martha Graham choreographed.

A figure is sheathed in a tube of jersey that reveals only feet, hands, and face. The upper open part of the jersey forms a triangle, with the apex at the head, and the base stretching from elbow to elbow; the lower open part stretches across the ankles. The figure is seated on a low platform and performs the dance almost in its entirety in that seated position. As the figure moves — twists, turns, extends obliquely, recoils, and so on — the jersey sculpts the moving torsions in conflicting lines that at times seem to pull the figure apart. The dance has been described as "a moving sculpture of grief" (Mazo, 1977, p. 194). The bodily drama of grief is etched kinetically into the moving fabric as it is visibly animated by every move of the moving body within. Drawing lines that do not simply mirror the anguished lines of a living body in grief but magnify its contorted pains, the ensheathing jersey follows every twinge and wrenching of the body, bringing grief *as it is experienced — lived —* to visible form. In effect, the covering turns the body inside out: what we see is a shifting qualitative landscape of grief as it is lived from within. The smallest movement spreads itself over the whole, and not languidly like a ripple in a pond, but severely, burdensomely, drawing all parts of the ensheathing fabric with it, no dimension remaining apart. The head turns away, for example, and its turning reverberates in contorting lines; the foot arches and its arching reverberates in a tautness that stretches upward to the knee and beyond; the body bends over, hands clasped, arms hanging heavily between the legs and moving ponderously from one side to the other, the entire form reverberating in a brooding oppression. Whatever the movement, it reverberates dynamically and throughout.

What we see is thus not a story about grief, a tale of lamentation, but its felt form. The movement dynamics echo the bodily pangs of grief — the keening, wailing cries of a body that grieves, the felt spasms and warpings of a body in pain. Yet there is no actual lamentation. How is this possible?

The movement dynamics of the moving form are congruent with the affective dynamics of sorrow, of deep mourning. The formula, so to speak, for symbolizing feelings through movement is palpable in the movement of the sheathed animate form we see before us. What Langer terms a "logical congruity" between forms of human feeling and aesthetic form is in actuality a *dynamic congruity* (Sheets-Johnstone, 1999c). There is no mistaking the solo dance *Lamentation*, for example, with the title figure's dance in *Afternoon of a Faun* or with the dance of the Sugar Plum fairy in *The Nutcracker*. What we see before us is a movement dynamics that is congruent with a form of human feeling that we either have lived through ourselves in everyday life or have empathically witnessed someone else living through. A recognizable bodily dynamics is amplified, all its grievings and moanings made visible, all its mournful feelings blown up in the full proportion of their felt, lived through reality.

Because dynamics themselves are not uncommonly complex phenomena, symbolizing the dynamics of a complex phenomenon may result in a complex mode of symbolization, more complex than the modes of iconic corporeal symbolization discussed earlier. The dynamic congruity epitomized by the dance *Lamentation* exemplifies this complexity. Its dynamics are a *qualitative* dynamics, an intricate tapestry of shifting intensities and energies that are spatially and temporally elaborated such that the dance symbolizes as a whole and is indeed a seamless whole that has no component symbolizing parts, as the honey bee dance, for example, has component symbolizing parts, direction being symbolized apart from distance, for instance. Formal congruency in Graham's *Lamentation* rests on an ongoing qualitative dynamic; formal congruency in the honey bee dance rests on discrete spatio-kinetic relationships — what might in quite broad terms be called discrete geometric corporeal/world relationships. Human feelings are complex qualitative phenomena whose forms could hardly be captured by discrete symbolizing geometries; in contrast, *direction* specifies a particular kinetic-spatial relationship that could hardly be captured by ongoing qualitative dynamics. Nonetheless, *similarity of form*—analogy—structures both modes of symbolization; it is the basis of both the congruency of Graham's qualitative dynamics and of a honey bee's kinetic-spatial geometries. Indeed, formal congruency rooted in analogy between symbol and thing symbolized underlies the symbolic structure of a speaker's utterance in primordial language, and of a female howler monkey's tongue-flicking movements, no less than a honey bee's dance and the dance *Lamentation*. Moreover there are or may be aspects of the one mode of symbolization within the other. For example, while the shifting postures of the grieving figure in *Lamentation* do not at any moment symbolize anything by themselves, the bearing of the body at any moment, its spatial attitude, is an integral aspect of the feeling symbolized. Correlatively, a bee that symbolizes the richness of a sugar source by the vigorousness of her movement approximates to the greater complexity of a qualitative dynamics, just as a speaker of primordial language might have approximated to it when, in making the sound *m*, he or she pressed his/her lips together with deliberate effort and intensity to signify crushing as distinct from resting against.[21]

In just this context, a distinction may be explicitly drawn between that which is symbolic and that which is not. The distinction, mentioned in passing in the earlier discussion of Neandertal stone tool-making, lies in a further dimension of symbolization, a dimension in fact of all modes of symbolization whether a formal congruity undergirds them or not, that is, whether symbolization is the result of an iconic or of an arbitrary relationship. All symbols are created entities that refer to something apart from themselves. Cultural anthropologist Raymond Firth recognizes the referential nature of symbols when he writes that the essence of symbolism lies "in the recognition of one thing as standing for (re-presenting) another" (Firth, 1973, p. 15). Langer does the same when she writes that symbols "let us develop a characteristic attitude toward objects *in absentia*, which is called 'thinking of' or 'referring to' what is not here" (Langer, 1948, p. 37). The defining referential aspect is succinctly specified in philosopher Albert Johnstone in his statement that a relation is a symbolizing one "if

---

21 A bee, who through her movement symbolized obstacles to be avoided along a certain directional path, would give a qualitatively nuanced sense of the way to the sugar source. To the degree that a spatio-kinetic or geometrically-rooted symbol approximates to a qualitative dynamics, it necessarily becomes a more complex phenomenon.

and only if it is a four-term relation of standing for, where in the eyes of a symbolizer something, the symbol, stands for some other thing, the symbolized, within the context of a particular activity" (Johnstone, 1984, p. 167). As functionally fashioned in the image of teeth, stone tools are an instance of analogical thinking, but symbolization requires something further than analogical thinking. It requires a referent, precisely as the tongue-flicking movements of a female howler monkey, the movements of a dancing bee, the articulatory gestures of a speaker of primordial language, and the movement dynamics of *Lamentation* demonstrate. In other words, although stone tools replaced teeth, they do not *refer* to teeth; they do not in fact refer to anything at all. Indeed, as one anthropologist observed, "Stone tools that are regarded as symbolic are generally *not* functional as powerful instruments" (anthropologist John Lukacs, personal communication). That stone tools replaced teeth and in this sense were fashioned along the lines of the body, however, is a significant fact from the perspective of the evolution of symbols, for *the body is both at the origin of analogical thinking and the foundation on which symbolizing activity and symbols originate and evolve.* The implication is that a greater attention to bodies might lead us to deeper evolutionary understandings of the nature of thinking and of how symbolic thinking arose.

In sum, the evolutionary history of signs and the evolutionary history of symbol-making form a continuous thread from the perspective of intact, whole-bodied living creatures — animate forms. Were we to trace this thread along all its corporeal lines, we would trace out the evolution of an evolutionary semantics, a semantics correlative to the evolution of animate forms, that is, correlative to the diversity of life as it has evolved from bacteria onward. The barest outlines of this semantics show that what begins in tactility, tactility in the service of movement, evolves into a visual morphology that enters into the behavioral ordering of social relationships, and that what begins in movement, in kinetic patternings or representations of experience, opens the way to a vast and boundless world of possible symbols. Living organisms — animate forms — are at the heart of this evolutionary semantics.

References

Altmann, Stuart A. 1967. "The Structure of Primate Social Communication." In *Social Communication among Primates*, ed. Stuart A. Altmann. Chicago: University of Chicago Press, pp. 325–62.

Borchert, Catherine M. and Adrienne L. Zihlman. 1990. "The Ontogeny and Phylogeny of Symbolizing." In *The Life of Symbols*, ed. Mary LeCron Foster and Lucy Jayne Botscharow. Boulder, CO: Westview Press, pp. 15–44.

Bruner, Jerome. 1990. *Acts of Meaning*. Cambridge, MA: Harvard University Press.

Carpenter, C.R. 1963. "Societies of Monkeys and Apes." In *Primate Social Behavior*, ed. C.H. Southwick. New York: Van Nostrand Reinhold, pp. 17–51.

Curtis, Helena. 1975. *Biology* (2nd ed.). New York: Worth Publishers.

Curtis, Helena and N. Sue Barnes. 1989. *Biology, Part I: Biology of Cells*, 5th ed. New York: Worth Publishers.

Deacon, Terrence W. 1997. *The Symbolic Species: The Co-Evolution of Language and the Brain*. New York: W. w. Norton.

Dolhinow, Phyllis J. 1972. "The North Indian Langur." In *Primate Patterns*, ed. P.J. Dolhinow. New York: Holt, Rinehart, and Winston, pp. 85–124.

Eibl-Eibesfeldt, Irenäus. 1974. "The Myth of the Aggression-Free Hunter and Gatherer Society." In *Primate Aggression, Territoriality, and Xenophobia*, ed. R. Holloway. New York: Academic Press, pp. 435–57.

Firth, Raymond. 1973. *Symbols: Public and Private*. Ithaca: Cornell University Press.

Foster, Mary LeCron. 1978. "The Symbolic Structure of Primordial Language." In *Human Evolution: Biosocial Perspectives*, ed. Sherwood L. Washburn and Elizabeth R. McCown (Menlo Park, CA: Benjamin/Cummings, pp. 77–121.

Foster, Mary LeCron. 1994a. "Symbolism: The Foundation of Culture." In *The Companion Encyclopedia of Anthropology*, ed. Tim Ingold. New York: Routledge, pp. 366–95.

Foster, Mary LeCron. 1994b. "Language as Analogic Strategy: Suggestions for Evolutionary Research." In *Studies in Language Origins*, vol. 3, ed. L.H. Rolfe, A. Jonker, and J. Wint. Amsterdam: John Benjamins, pp. 179–204.

Foster, Mary LeCron. 1996. "Reconstruction of the Evolution of Human Spoken Language." In *Handbook of Symbolic Evolution*, ed. Andrew Lock and Charles Peters. Oxford: Oxford University Press, pp. 747–72.

Freud, Sigmund. 1938. *The Basic Writings of Sigmund Freud*. New York: Basic Books.

Freud, Sigmund. 1953. *Complete Psychological Works of Sigmund Freud*, vols. 4 and 5, ed. and trans. James Strachey. London: Hogarth Press.

Freud, Sigmund. 1963. *A General Introduction to Psychoanalysis*. New York: Liveright.

Gould, Stephen Jay. 1996. *Full House*. New York: Harmony Books.

Hoffmeyer, Jesper. 1996. *Signs of Meaning in the Universe*, trans. Barbara J. Haveland. Bloomington: Indiana University Press.

Husserl, Edmund. 1970. "The Origin of Geometry." In *The Crisis of European Sciences and Transcendental Phenomenology*, trans. David Carr. Evanston, IL: Northwestern University Press, pp. 353–78.

Husserl, Edmund. 1973. *Cartesian Meditations*, trans. Dorion Cairns. The Hague: Martinus Nijhoff.

Husserl, Edmund. 1977. *Phenomenological Psychology*, trans. John Scanlon. The Hague: Martinus Nijhoff.

Husserl, Edmund. 1980. *Ideas Pertaining to a Pure Phenomenology and to a Phenomenological Philosophy, Book 3 (Ideas III)*, ed. Ted E. Klein and William E. Pohl. The Hague: Martinus Nijhoff.

Husserl, Edmund. 1983. *Ideas Pertaining to a Pure Phenomenology and to a Phenomenological Philosophy: Book 1 (Ideas I)*, trans. F. Kersten. The Hague: Martinus Nijhoff.

Husserl, Edmund. 1989. *Ideas Pertaining to a Pure Phenomenology and to a Phenomenological Philosophy: Book 2 (Ideas II)*, trans. R. Rojcewicz and A. Schuwer. Boston: Kluwer Academic.

Johnstone, Albert A. 1984. "Languages and Non-Languages of Dance." In *Illuminating Dance: Philosophical Explorations*. ed. M. Sheets-Johnstone. Lewisburg, PA: Bucknell University Press, pp. 167–87.

Keeton, William T. and James L. Gould. 1986. *Biological Science* (4th ed.). New York: W. W. Norton & Co.

Langer, Susanne K. 1948. *Philosophy in a New Key*. New York: New American Library.

Langer, Susanne K. 1953. *Feeling and Form*. New York: Scribner's Sons.

Langer, Susanne K. 1967. *Mind: An Essay on Human Feeling*, vol. 1. Baltimore: Johns Hopkins Press.

Langer, Susanne K. 1972. *Mind: An Essay on Human Feeling*, vol. 2. Baltimore: Johns Hopkins University Press.

Laverack, M.S. 1976. "External Proprioceptors." In *Structure and Function of Proprioceptors in the Invertebrates*, ed. P.J. Mill. London: Chapman and Hall, pp. 1–63.

Leroi-Gourhan, André. 1971. *Préhistoire l'art occidental*. Paris: Mazenod.

Liberman, Alvin M. and Ignatius G. Mattingly. 1985. "The Motor Theory of Speech Perception Revised." *Cognition* 21 (1): 1–36.

Liberman, A.M., F.S. Cooper, D.P. Shankweiler, and M. Studdert-Kennedy. 1967. "Perception of the Speech Code." *Psychological Review* 74: 431–61.

Lieberman, Philip. 1975. "On the Evolution of Language: A Unified View." In *Primate Functional Morphology and Evolution*, ed. R.H. Tuttle. The Hague: Mouton Publishers, pp. 501–40.

Lieberman, Philip. 1983. "On the Nature and Evolution of the Biological Bases of Language." In *Glossogenetics*, ed. E. de Grolier. New York: Harwood Academic Publishing, pp. 91–114.

Mazo, Joseph H. 1977. *Prime Movers*. New York: William Morrow and Co.

Mellars, Paul. 1989. "Technological Changes across the Middle-Upper Palaeolithic Transition: Economic, Social and Cognitive Perspectives." In *The Human Revolution*, ed. P. Mellars and C. Stringer. Princeton: Princeton University Press, pp. 338–65.

Peirce, Charles S. 1991. *Peirce on Signs*, ed. James Hoopes. Chapel Hill: University of North Carolina Press.

Peirce, Charles S. 1992. *The Essential Peirce*, vol. I, ed. Nathan Houser and Christian Kloesel. Bloomington: Indiana University Press.

Piaget, Jean. 1968. *La naissance de l'intelligence chez l'enfant*, 6th ed. Neuchatel: Delachaux et Niestlé.

Portmann, Adolph. 1967. *Animal Forms and Patterns*, trans. Hella Czech. New York: Schocken Books.

Premack, David. 1975. "Language in Chimpanzees?" *Science* 172: 808–22.

Rowell, Thelma. 1972. *The Social Behaviour of Monkeys*. Harmondsworth, England: Penguin Books.

Savage-Rumbaugh, Sue and Roger Lewin. 1994. *Kanzi: The Ape at the Brink of the Human Mind*. New York: John Wiley & Sons.

Savage-Rumbaugh, E. Sue and R.A. Sevcik. 1984. "Levels of Communicative Competency in the Chimpanzee: Pre-Representational and Representational." In *Behavioral Evolution and Integrative Levels*, ed. G. Greenberg and E. Tobach. Hillsdale, NJ: Lawrence Erlbaum, pp. 197–220.

Savage-Rumbaugh, E. Sue, Duane M. Rumbaugh, Sally Boysen. 1978. "Linguistically Mediated Tool Use and Exchange by Chimpanzees (*Pan troglodytes*). *The Behavioral and Brain Sciences* 4: 539–54.

Shea, John J. 1997. "Middle Paleolithic Spear Point Technology." In *Projectile Technology*, ed. Heidi Knecht. New York: Plenum Press, pp. 79–106.

Shea, John J. 1998. "Neandertal and Early Modern Human Behavioral Variability: A Regional-Scale Approach to Lithic Evidence for Hunting in the Levantine Mousterian." *Current Anthropology* 39, Supplement, June: S45–S78.

Sheets-Johnstone, Maxine. 1990. *The Roots of Thinking*. Philadelphia: Temple University Press.

Sheets-Johnstone, Maxine. 1994. *The Roots of Power: Animate Form and Gendered Bodies*. Chicago: Open Court Publishing.

Sheets-Johnstone, Maxine. 1999a. *The Primacy of Movement*. Amsterdam: John Benjamins.

Sheets-Johnstone, Maxine. 1999b. "Sensory-kinetic understandings of language: An inquiry into origins," *Evolution of Communication* 3/2: 149–183.

Sheets-Johnstone, Maxine. 1999c. "Emotion and movement: A beginning empirical-phenomenological analysis of their relationship," *Journal of Consciousness Studies* 6/11–12: 259–277.

Sinnott, Edmund. 1963. *The Problem of Organic Form*. New Haven: Yale University Press.

Spiegelberg, Herbert. 1956. "Husserl's and Peirce's Phenomenologies: Coincidence or Interaction." *Philosophy and Phenomenological Research* 17: 164–85.

Stringer, Christopher and Clive Gamble. 1993. *In Search of Neanderthals: Solving the Puzzle of Human Origins*. London. Thames and Hudson.

Tomasello, Michael and Josep Call. 1997. *Primate Cognition*. Oxford: Oxford University Press.

Trinkaus, Erik and Pat Shipman. 1993. *The Neandertals: Changing the Image of Mankind*. New York: Alfred A. Knopf.

van Hooff, J.A.R.A.M. 1969. "The Facial Displays of the Catarrhine Monkeys and Apes." In *Primate Ethology*, ed. D. Morris. Garden City, NY: Doubleday Anchor, pp. 9–88.

von Uexküll, Jakob. 1957. "A Stroll through the Worlds of Animals and Men", trans. Claire H. Schiller. In *Instinctive Behavior*, ed. Claire H. Schiller. New York: International Universities Press, pp. 5–80.

Chapter XII

'Man Has Always Danced'
Forays into an Art Largely Forgotten by Philosophers

[T]he first true art … is Dance (Susanne Langer).

Men, everywhere, dance. There are no human societies in which they do not (Charles Olson).

1. Introduction

If the statement 'man has always danced' were true, philosophers ought to have found a good deal more to say about dance than the little they have said. Indeed, dance is commonly a forgotten art in aesthetics (see e.g. Dickie and Sclafani, 1977; Beardsley, 1982; Kivy, 1997; Hanfling, 1992);[1] or if recognized is minimally treated in relation to other arts (e.g. Feagin and Maynard, 1997; Sparshott, 1963; but see also Sparshott, 1995), or is read off other arts such as sculpture and explained in terms of them (e.g. Aldrich, 1963). Music, painting, poetry and literature in general are the arts consistently at the forefront of philosophic attention. Were substantive reasons sought for philosophers' virtual abstinence of concern or regard for dance, appeal might be made to individual proclivities or to current modes of scientific explanation. But it is of no avail to cite variation among males, for example, as a reason, i.e., some males dance, some do not; some are aesthetically attracted to dance, some are not; and so on, as if natural selection were operative, putatively explaining why some males, and in fact a particular breed of male, namely he who is drawn to aesthetic philosophy, prefers not to recognize the art of dance much less consider that 'man has always danced'. It would be equally futile to claim that genetic determinism is at play, i.e., that with the exception of sports (in the biological sense of the abnormal), males are for some albeit as yet undetermined adaptational reason innately doomed to ignore or neglect dance. One might on

---

[1] But see also, in contrast, Arnold Berleant's provocative analysis of dance as performance in his book on the arts, *Art and Engagement* (1991).

the contrary invoke adaptation in a positive sense: male philosophers who concern themselves with dance are better adapted to being a body and in turn have potentially deeper evolutionary understandings of themselves that reach all the way from what it is to be animate, and in particular, an animate form that dances and makes dances, to the nature of the evanescent art that is dance, the art that, as Merce Cunningham perspicuously observes "gives you nothing back, no manuscripts to store away, no paintings to show on walls and maybe hang in museums, no poems to be printed and sold, nothing but that single fleeting moment when you feel alive", an art that in consequence "is not for unsteady souls" (Cunningham, 1968).

Philosophers hardly seem "unsteady souls." All the same, bodies not uncommonly seem either to frighten away philosophers or fail to offer themselves up as the stuff of aesthetic reflection, a moving body being enigmatic at best or formulaic at worst. Consider, for example, Merleau-Ponty's judgment that "dancing is a motor habit" and that one forms the habit of dancing by discovering analytically "the formula of the movement in question" (Merleau-Ponty, 1962, pp. 146, 142). Especially in light of his aesthetic judgment of painting—in agreement with Valéry, who first observed the conjunction—that "the painter 'takes his body with him'", and his assertion that in painting, the painter "show[s] how the things become things, how the world becomes world" (Merleau-Ponty, 1964, pp. 162, 181),[2] Merleau-Ponty's aesthetic judgment of dance is surprisingly ill-informed and appears utterly lacking an experiential base. Although the painter "takes his body with him", Merleau-Ponty does not reduce the painter's painting to a "motor habit." On the contrary, he affirms that his painting is capable of enlightening us about the way "the things" and "the world" come to be what they are.

A dancer obviously takes his body with him. If his dance is simply a motor habit, however, then unlike the painter, taking his body with him counts for nought aesthetically or epistemologically. In turn, the question of what he correlatively shows in his dance can never arise, for a motor habit is precisely formulaic, a kinetic performance that runs off in rote manner. In such a performance, the dancer is not present in any lived, dynamic sense, and, if the dancer is not present in any lived, dynamic sense, then the dance can hardly be. Moreover Merleau-Ponty's motor habit conception of dance misses a crucial elemental aesthetic distinction, the distinction between a dancer's moving through a form and the form

s/he [margin annotation]

---

2 See also *ibid.*, p. 166: "The painter's gaze asks them [light, lighting, shadows, reflections, color, all the objects of his quest] what they do to suddenly cause something to be and to be *this* thing, what they do to compose this worldly talisman and to make us see the visible."

moving through him. The aesthetic criticality of the form moving through the dancer is highlighted in the rhetorical question Yeats asks in his poem "Among School Children": "How can we know the dancer from the dance?" When the form does not move through the dancer, it does not come to life but remains something apart from the dancer, something the dancer precisely *moves through* or *does*, a certain set of moves he performs, whether in rote manner or self-consciously. In effect, whatever the particular motor habit might be, it is powerless to show anything of comparable aesthetic or epistemological import—how bodies become expressively resonant bodies, for example, how the animation of moving bodies is always dynamically structured, or how, in dance, dynamic structuring and meaning are of a piece.

Because both painter and dancer take their bodies with them, the correlative question of what the dancer shows remains potentially an intriguing question. If painting truly enlightens us about how things become things and world becomes world, then dance should enlighten us in correlative ways about movement and the animate world, and the idea that 'man has always danced' should lead us to insightful observations about those ways. Indeed, if man has not always painted but always danced, it should be of particular concern to philosophers of art to question the meaning of that enduring practice and its genealogy, or in other words, to know something of dance and its origins.[3]

2. Testimonials to the Antiquity of Dance

In the mid-1920s when modern dance was beginning to flourish and to get an accredited foot in the academic door as a full-fledged discipline, the statement "man has always danced" was invoked in one form or another and continued to be invoked in one way or another for many years. "Man has composed dances throughout the ages, from the earliest prehistoric era to the present time", declared Doris Humphrey, one of the foremost of American dance pioneers (Humphrey, 1959, p. 16).[4] "Primitive life is exultant", wrote Margaret H'Doubler, the foremost academic pioneer of dance. "Early man communicated his belief in the gods and the experiences of his own daily life by stamping, clapping, swaying, shouting,

3 One might add, "All the more so", since, in general, philosophers are and have been male from the very beginning of philosophy.

4 Arnold Berleant (pers. comm.) suggested my identifying Humphrey's quotation and many of the quotations that follow as rhetorical and speculative. While acknowledging his intent, I would like rather not to diminish the claims, but rather to show in this essay that, however rhetorical or given to hyperbole, they can be substantiated, and that in taking them seriously, one has the possibility of discovering what intuitively drives them in a foundational sense, i.e., in a sense that underlies the grandeur of dance.

grunting, and crying, with noise as well as with motion ... He had no other escape for his pent-up feelings than the movements of his own body. So he danced"(H'Doubler, 1940, pp. 5–6). "Dancing has existed at all times", German dance pioneer Mary Wigman declared, "and among all people and races" (Wigman, 1974 [1933], p. 149). Dance historian Selma Jeanne Cohen opened her book on dance as a theater art with the statement, "We cannot know precisely when man began to dance, but we may surmise that it was sometime in the dawn of prehistory" (Cohen, 1974, p. 1). In the context of her research on "Ritual in the Celtic World: The Dance of the Ancient Druids", dance historian Anne L. Herman commented more generally, "It appears that dancing is as old as man himself" (Herman, 1979, p. 202).

Dance educators, dancers, and dance historians were not the only ones to write that "man has always danced." Poets did—and do—as the above epigraph from Charles Olson shows and as Paul Valéry's explorative and perspicuous writings on dance show. In his essay "Philosophy of the Dance", Valéry perceptively remarks, for example, that "[Dance] is a fundamental art, as is suggested if not demonstrated by its universality, its immemorial antiquity ... the ideas and reflections it has engendered at all times. For the dance is an art derived from life itself, since it is nothing more nor less than the action of the whole human body; but an action transposed into a world, into a kind of *space-time*, which is no longer quite the same as that of everyday life" (Valéry, 1964, pp. 197-98).

Among philosophers, the comparatively lone voice of Susanne Langer is notable, the epigraph above encapsulating her valuation of dance as an historically privileged art. Elaborating on that valuation, and citing Curt Sachs, a noted historian of dance, as an authority, she states, "At the dawn of civilization, dance had already reached a degree of perfection that no other art or science could match" (Langer, 1957, p. 11).

Given such testimonials to the antiquity of dance from a variety of sources, it becomes more and more puzzling that dance languishes as a phenomenon worthy of philosophical study.[5] Moreover as some of the quotations show, recognizing dance's "immemorial antiquity" gives it an edge that prominences it socio-historically—and thus culturally—not only in the life of man but among most if not all other arts. Sachs's claim, "The dance is the mother of the arts ... The creator and the thing created, the artist and the work are still one and the same thing" (Sachs, 1963, p. 3), testifies to the latter prominencing. So also does psychologist Havelock Ellis's penetrating article on dance written precisely at the time dance was beginning to be recognized and incorporated within public school physi-

---

5   The general statement 'man has always danced' appears not to give 'man' respectability, though in the eyes of dancers, it surely gives dance respectability.

cal education classes in the United States and developed as an academic discipline of its own.[6] At the beginning of his article, Ellis claims that "Dancing and building are the two primary and essential arts. The art of dancing stands at the source of all the arts that express themselves first in the human person ... There is no primary art outside these two arts, for their origin is far earlier than man himself; and dancing came first" (Ellis, 1976, p. 5; reprint of Ellis, 1929, p. 34). In a later section of the article, we subsequently learn the reason Ellis claims their origin is "far earlier than man himself": their origin has evolutionary roots. Ellis in fact already intimates as much when, in a footnote appended to the statement "dancing came first", he suggests that the two arts may have a common "impulse", citing in support of his suggestion an article by Edmund Selous that appeared in a 1901 issue of *Zoologist* in which Selous suggests "that the nest may first have arisen as an accidental result of the ecstatic sexual dance of birds" (*ibid.*).

Ellis's perspective is provocative as an entrée into deepened understandings of the claim 'man has always danced', particularly since it is based on a perspicuous knowledge of Darwin's theory of evolution, which rests not only on the realities of natural selection but of sexual selection. Our initial foray into the idea that "man has always danced" will accordingly take Ellis's evolutionarily-grounded understandings of dance as a point of departure. In so doing, it will give fitting place to evolutionary continuities, that is, to foundational concerns to which studies of cultural differences might turn for proper historical perspective and anchorage. From the vantage point of evolutionary continuities, it will furthermore be possible to identify aspects of a common humanity that ground the immemorial antiquity of dance and thus offer support to the claim that 'man has always danced'. In what follows, then, it is not the word "man" that is central but the word "always". However interesting it might be to concentrate attention on the former term and critically assay its use as a sexually- or gender-biased term, more elemental or foundational matters concern us. In short, the immemorial historical phenomenon itself is the focal point of interest. Any linkage of 'man' in particular to dance will derive from that focal point.

3. Evolutionary Considerations

In the later section of Ellis's essay alluded to above, Ellis writes, "Dancing is not only intimately associated with religion [a topic he has addressed in the previous section], it has an equally intimate association with love.

---

6   On the educational history of dance, see Chapman, 1974.

Here, indeed, the relationship is even more primitive, for it is far older than man …Among insects and among birds it may be said that dancing is often an essential part of love. In courtship the male dances, sometimes in rivalry with other males, in order to charm the female" (*ibid.*, 1976 p. 10; 1929, p. 43).

It is undoubtedly on the basis of Darwin's observation that birds "present in their secondary sexual characters the closest analogy with insects", among which characters are male pugnacity, special weapons for fighting, special visual ornamentations, and specialized organs for "producing vocal and instrumental music" (Darwin, 1981 [1871], vol. 1, p. 422) that Ellis proposes an evolutionary correspondence of primitive human dance to the love-dances of insects as well as birds.[7] In a summary way, his statement aptly pinpoints the general nature of sexual selection: males battle among themselves to court and win females. His further account as to why "Among the mammals most nearly related to man … dancing is but little developed" is of interest. He observes, "[B]ut it must be remembered that the anthropoid apes are offshoots only from the stock that produced Man, his cousins and not his ancestors" (*ibid.*). With these words, he attenuates the judgment of "a close observer of the apes … [who] has pointed out that the 'spasmodic jerking of the chimpanzee's feeble legs', pounding the partition of his cage, is the crude motion out of which 'the heavenly alchemy of evolution has created the divine movements of Pavlova'" (*ibid.*), and goes on to remark, "It is the more primitive love-dance of insects and birds that seems to reappear among savages in various parts of the world… and in a conventionalised and symbolised form it is still danced in civilisation to-day" (*ibid.*, pp. 43–4). In this context, and following closely upon Darwin's descriptive accounts, he speaks of how the male, "By his beauty, his energy, his skill … must win the female, so impressing the image of himself on her imagination that finally her desire is aroused to overcome her reticence. That is the task of the male throughout nature, and in innumerable species besides Man it has been found that the school in which the task may best be learnt is the dancing-school" (*ibid.*, p. 11).

From an 80-year-later vantage point and with respect to "a close observer of the apes", we can of course readily consult myriad primatological texts which first of all inform us about the movement differences between caged and wild-living animals, texts we may in turn pursue to learn about the actual kinetic dispositions and capacities of

---

7   It is notable—and of moment with respect to Section 4 of this essay—that Darwin does not mention dance in his discussion of insects. In fact, he states that "the law of battle" —male-male competition for females—"does not prevail nearly so widely with insects as with the higher animals" (*ibid.*, p. 418).

nonhuman primates such as chimpanzees. The relevance of these consultations aside for the moment, it is obvious that Ellis is thoroughly familiar
with Darwin's two-volume, 828-page treatise on sexual selection (Darwin,
1981 [1871], vols. 1, 2), a treatise based on observations across the animal
kingdom — from molluscs, annelids, and crustaceans, to insects, fish,
amphibians, reptiles, and mammals, including man. Indeed, in the section
of his essay showing how dance is "far older than man", Ellis elaborates
specifically on what Darwin describes as "Love-Antics and Dances" of
male birds (*ibid.*, vol. 2, pp. 68–71), and later more generally describes as
male "love-dances" (*ibid.*, p. 233).

In the course of his elaborations, Ellis points out that with humans, it is
not only males who dance to compete for the love of females, but females
who compete for the love of males, "each striving in a storm of rivalry to
arouse and attract the desire of the other" (Ellis, 1976, pp. 11-12; 1929
p. 45). He goes on to marvel at how "every part of the wonderful human
body has been brought into the play of the dance" and how "men and
women of races spread all over the world have shown a marvellous skill
and patience in imparting rhythm and measure to the most unlikely, the
most rebellious regions of the body." He points out in his conclusion how,
at the end of the 1700s, "The grave traveller Peyron ... growing eloquent
over the languorous and flexible movements of the dance, the bewitching
attitude, the voluptuous curves of the arms, declares that, when one sees a
beautiful Spanish woman dance, one is inclined to fling all philosophy to
the winds" (*ibid.*, 1976 p. 13; 1929 p. 48). But he notes too in this context
how some church people have viewed dance as lascivious, commenting:
"There we have the rock against which the primitive dance of sexual selection suffers shipwreck as civilisation advances" (*ibid.*).

A remarkable feature of Ellis's brief but theoretically sound evolutionary account of dance is its implicit recognition of movement. In particular,
and again, following along the lines of Darwin's finely detailed descriptions of animal movement,[8] Ellis's reading does not reduce sexual selection to human or nonhuman animal *behavior*, not only a common tendency
in present-day evolutionary biology and psychology but an all-embracing
present-day academic predilection. A "behavioral stance"(cf. Dennett,
1987), as we might term it, occludes movement. The distinction between
behavior and movement is indeed significant to any investigations and
understandings of dance, as observationally crucial as it is conceptually
crucial. If one does not perceive movement, after all, one can hardly perceive dance. Precisely in this context, some might question whether non-

8   For a study of the similarity in the descriptive foundations of evolutionary biology, literature,
     and phenomenology, see Sheets-Johnstone, 2002b.

human animals are "really dancing", or alternatively, whether Darwin and Ellis are simply making metaphorical assertions about what they, respectively, observe and read. The question requires returning to the phenomenon in question and observing it, if not first-hand, then at least in descriptive flesh.

Consider, to begin with, Jane Goodall's description of a movement sequence that is part of a male chimpanzee's kinetic repertoire, a sequence that he performs in conjunction with his "sexual signalling behavior" or "courtship display", as present-day biologists commonly term "love-antics and dances": "THE BIPEDAL SWAGGER is typically a male posture and occurs only rarely in females. The chimpanzee stands upright and sways rhythmically from foot to foot, his shoulders slightly hunched and his arms held out and away from the body, usually to the side. He may swagger in one spot or he may move forward in this manner. This posture occurs most commonly as a courtship display, but it also occurs when one male threatens another of similar social status" (Goodall, 1968, p. 276).

Primatologist C.R. Rogers amplifies the description when he writes, "Soliciting by the normal male [chimpanzee] is highly stylized and involves squatting with knees spread wide to display an erect penis; most wildborn males accompany this by slapping the ground with open palms. If a female does not present to him, he may after several seconds rise to an erect posture and execute a short dance in some respect similar to a threat display. He will then frequently alternate from one pattern to the other if not interrupted by a sexually-presenting female (Rogers, 1973, p. 188).

What Rogers identifies as a "short dance", particularly in its similarity to threat display, appears to be what Goodall identifies as *bipedal swagger*, a movement sequence that Goodall too specifies as an aggressive as well as courtship display. Though commonly categorized and understood in behavioral terms, i.e., duly packaged and labeled, what is actually being described is *movement*. Just such description allows a *kinetic semantics* to come into view. In particular, whether the rhythmic swaying and other movements are executed in the context of threat or courtship, the "short dance" is meaningful. Only a chimpanzee could of course answer the question of whether the short dance is meaningful by convention or inherently meaningful, but a human observer or reader can readily point out, for example, that with respect to courtship, the positional stance of the male, i.e., with arms akimbo as he is swaying from side to side and as he swaggers forward, continuously presents an unobstructed view of his erect penis; slapping the ground with open palms resounds and calls the attention of others to the sound-maker; an upright posture and a bipedal gait are extraordinary in the sense of being outside a chimpanzee's more common posture and form of locomotion and hence draw attention, particularly in terms of an increase in size, and this over and above the fact that movement naturally calls attention to itself in the animate world. The movement sequence in effect appears inherently meaningful as a courtship display; its dynamic form, as Susanne Langer would say, is logically congruent with its import (Langer, 1953).

Most significantly too, the kinetic dynamics are semantically self-sufficient: no verbal forms assist in these meanings, though movement-produced sound certainly may. For both chimpanzee and human observer, a particular kinetic dynamics unfolds that is in and of itself meaningful.[9] However intuitive, Rogers's categorization of the patterned dynamics as "a short dance" is thus apt and fitting. On the same intuitively-grasped kinetic-semantic grounds, Darwin may have termed the sexually-inviting movement patterns of birds "love dances": the love-dance of the white-throat (*Sylvia cinerea*) male, for example, who "flutters with a fitful and fantastic motion, singing all the while, and then drops to its perch"; the love-dance of the male Indian bustard (*Otiss bengalensis*), who "rises perpendicularly into the air with a hurried flapping of his wings, raising his crest and puffing out the feathers of his neck and breast, and then drops to the ground ... [repeating] this manoeuvre several times successively" (Darwin, 1981, vol. 2, pp. 68–9). In each instance, a dynamically-patterned movement sequence — a "love-dance" — is semantically laden and self-sufficient, its dynamic character being meaningful to both performing male and observing females.[10]

Given a recognition and understanding of sexual selection and the above examples of sexual signalling behaviors, one might readily justify the claim that "man has always danced." Yet curiously enough, in biology, "sexual signalling behavior" begins with sticklebacks and other fish and ends with chimpanzees and other pongids: the question is never raised as to how newly bipedal hominids "signalled" their sexual longings. In turn, the idea never surfaces that bipedal male hominids possibly continued the kinetic semantics of their male primate cousins, particularly since the possibility of bipedal female hominids continuing the kinetic semantics of *their* female primate cousins, i.e., turning and presenting their hind quarters or "sexual skin" to the male (see Wickler's classic studies, e.g. Wickler, 1969), disappeared with hominid bipedality and an anteriorly situated

9   The same immediately meaningful kinetic semantics is strikingly apparent in primatologist C.R. Carpenter's description of the display behavior of female howler monkeys in estrus. See Carpenter, 1963, pp. 49-50. For further examples and a discussion of immediately meaningful kinetic semantics, see Sheets-Johnstone, 1990, ch. 5.

10   For analyses and discussions of newly minted meanings and an evolutionary semantics, see Sheets-Johnstone, 2002a and Sheets-Johnstone, 2003b.

vulva.[11] This visual/morphological relationship and state of affairs sub-stantiate evolutionary continuities and add weight to Ellis's claim. Dance may well have its roots in the love-dances of males, as he indicates, but in the slightly revised sense warranted by present-day enhanced knowledge of primates: dance germinated less from the "love-dances" of male avians than from the "love-dances" of our closest evolutionary male relative.

Yet we may still ask, what propelled man to move beyond love-dances (and, as per Ellis and others, beyond religious uses of dance)[12] toward dance proper? It is not, after all, just evolutionary continuities that point toward a foundational origin of dance; the pan-culturality of dance does also. Moreover the pan-culturality not only similarly supports the claim that "man has always danced" but indicates that there is something in the nature of man himself that disposes him toward dance irrespective of any particular village or culture in which he dwells or into which he is born. What are the conditions of this pan-culturality? What is it about humans and the experience of humans that generates dance across cultures?

4. Deepening Evolutionary Considerations

To ask such questions is to center attention on the evolutionary phenome-non of "man himself" insofar as "man himself" is the origin of a new evo-lutionary genus (*Homo*). It is notable that the most prominent feature of the genus, as evidenced in all evolving species of hominids, is the move toward consistent bipedality. The feature is of special moment here because the epithet 'dance' appears to be invoked primarily with respect to bipedally moving creatures—precisely as in the courtship movement patterns of birds and of male chimpanzees. Bipedality in fact appears to be an intuitive *sine qua non* of the appellation 'dance'. Not that bees do not dance or that waves do not dance, but that these and other such exceptions notwithstanding for the present—the *Tanzsprache* and dancing waves will surface pointedly if briefly in what follows—a prime condition of dancing in the vernacular human sense gravitates toward the having of two and only two feet. Indeed, one might say that empirically it centers on two and only two feet, exactly as in the bipedal swagger: "The chimpanzee stands upright and sways rhythmically from foot to foot."

---

11 For a discussion of this shift in visual/morphological relationship, see Sheets-Johnstone, 1989, pp. 57–70; and Sheets-Johnstone, 1990, Chapters 4 and 7.

12 One might in fact theorize, and with good reasons, that religious dances were a cultural elaboration of love dances. If males danced to please females and win their favor, then they might equally dance to please the gods. If the gods looked upon them with favor, the gods might give man what he wanted or desired. Man, after all, has no control over nature in the form of rain, sunshine, flooding, germination of crops, and so on, nor of course, his own death. Hence, dancing to win favor among the gods might not only have offset any sense of oneself as a tiny speck in a vast cosmos, but appease the gods and protect one from harm.

What is it about dance that makes two and only two feet intuitively and even empirically requisite if not imperative? If we reflect upon the nature of bipedally moving bodies, we readily see that such bodies have greater movement possibilities than quadrupedal, sextupedal, or octopedal ones. To begin with, they have freely moving or potentially freely moving parts: wings and arms are not weight-encumbered, for example, and can move independently of the base of support, as in fluttering and stretching; upright torsos are not positionally constrained and can similarly move independently of the base of support, as in tilting forward or leaning to the side. While specific morphologies certainly constrain movement in distinctive ways for all moving bodies, bipedal or not, bipedality clearly engenders a greater range of movement possibilities. Non-weight-supporting parts have in fact sizable movement possibilities: torsos can twist and bend; heads can swivel and fall in any direction; arms can swing and throw; and so on. Moreover a single base of support suffices at times, not simply as it might in shifting weight from one foot to the other, but in wheeling about on one leg, for example, or in stamping and kicking. Certainly quadrupedal animals have a variety of gaits including those with air-borne moments — galloping, running, cantering, and so on — but any and all gaits are constrained anatomically by the need to support a horizontally-elongated torso, i.e., a spinal column that is not freely moving but directly tethered to its quadrupedal supporting structure. The horizontally-elongated torso of mammals that is set directly over its base of support rather than supported through muscle power over a sprawling base as in reptiles is in fact in the service of speed and length of stride (Romer and Parsons, 1977, p. 198).

Bipedality clearly maximizes movement possibilities and is in this sense integral to the art of dance. Moreover in maximizing possibilities, it simultaneously opens a palette of qualitative possibilities, a freedom of movement aptly labeled by noted Russian physiologist Nicolas Bernstein "degrees of freedom".[13] From an aesthetic point of view, degrees of freedom are a springboard to the creative dynamics that constitute the art of dance; that is, they emanate not just from anatomy but from the qualitative structure of movement. In other words, they have to do not only with the *what* of movement, i.e., what is moving and from what specific bodily source it is initiated — for example, whether in a leg lift, the movement is initiated from the knee, the ankle, or the hip joint — but with the *how* of movement, i.e., the qualitative nature of the lift. A summary phenomenological analysis of movement (for an extended analysis, see Sheets-Johnstone, 1966 [1979/1980] and 1999b) will exemplify the basic qualita-

13   See an assortment of Bernstein's writings in Whiting, 1984.

tive structure of movement and thereby illustrate the intricacy and breadth of the *how* of any movement, in essence penetrating to aesthetically relevant degrees of freedom in human movement.

To begin with, any movement creates its own space, time, and force. It thereby creates a unique dynamic, whether a matter of a dancer's movement or the movement of a spluttering balloon. But as Valéry indicated without elaborating the point, the space-time that the dancer creates is different. In dance, Valéry observed, action of the whole human body is "transposed … into a kind of *space-time*, which is no longer quite the same as everyday life." Indeed, everyday space-time is a matter of heres and theres, nows and thens, locations and punctualities that are objectively tethered in the sense of objects in space and objectives in time. In other words, movement in everyday life is precisely perceived as being *in* space and *in* time. Being perceived *in* space and *in* time, it is caught up in everyday space-time realities that commonly occlude its own qualitative realities, and this because it commonly has ends other than a realization of the pure dynamics of movement itself. In contrast, the creation of any dance is the creation of a spatio-temporal-energic dynamic that not only is anchored in movement itself but is thoroughly unique, that flows forth with its own particular surges and fadings, expansions and contractions, intensities, attenuations, and so on. Hence, though as noted, all movement creates its own space-time-force whether a matter of animate or inanimate movement, the dynamics that movement creates in dance constitute from beginning to end movement's full significance.

If we inquire more closely into the unique spatio-temporal-energic dynamics, we see that they are the result of the qualitative structure of movement; that is, any movement has a certain tensional, linear, areal, and projectional quality. In effect, its dynamics can be analyzed in terms of qualia endemic to it. A leg lift, for example, might be forceful (tensional quality), straight-legged and forwardly directed (linear design of the body and linear pattern of the movement), barely elevated above the floor (areal design of the body and areal pattern of the movement), and abrupt (projectional quality). Alternatively — and antithetically put to indicate the continuum between extremes and/or the range of possible variations — the lift might be weak, bent-legged and diagonally directed, elevated high off the floor, and sustained. Furthermore, the lift might be weak, bent-legged and diagonally directed, elevated high off the floor, and abrupt — or be performed in a manifold number of other qualitative combinations. Further still, of course, the specific qualitative structure of the lift might be ineffable. Language, after all, is not experience and can at times fail to provide us a ready means of transliteration (for a further discussion of the fact that language is not experience, see Sheets-Johnstone, 1999b, and 2002b; see also Stern, 1985, pp. 181–2, and 1990). Indeed, in a fully literal sense, we may find that—to borrow an observation of Husserl (on the nature of the temporally constitutive flux of consciousness)—"For all this, names are lacking" (Husserl, 1964, p. 100), in effect be at a loss for words.[14] However ineffable the qualities might be,[15] however, we experience them. Tensional, linear, areal, and projectional qualities are the qualitative stuff of movement and inhere in the whole of any movement itself, each quality, whatever its specific character, contributing to the overall quality of the movement: the how of its surgings, fadings, expansions, contractions, intensities, attenuations, and so on.

Now if man has always danced, he was necessarily, from the beginning, attuned to the qualitative dynamics of movement. How else would he come to the experience of movement itself that is the bedrock of dance? An evolving kinetic dynamics arose with the advent of consistent bipedality, a dynamics whose intricacies and richness co-evolved with man himself. An important feature of this richness and intricacy warrants mention and concerns the projectional character of movement, specifically, the possibility of ballistic movement (for a discussion of ballistic movement from an evolutionary perspective, see Sheets-Johnstone, 1983). Humans, like chimpanzees, can move in a sustained manner, swaying from one foot to the other, for example. Similarly they can both slap the ground abruptly. But humans have a far broader range of ballistic movement. They can swing their torsos and legs, throw overhand, kick forcefully from a standing position, and so on. In fact, a multitude of ballistic movement possibilities exists, possibilities that are contingent precisely on upright bipedally-supported hominid bodies. Such possibilities are easily recognizable but challenging to describe for they are often, and especially in dance, intricate dynamic forms that commonly have no name, though skipping and jumping, kicking and throwing are basic and familiar forms. In ballistic movement, an initial thrust of energy sends the movement on its way, the amount of force and the velocity of the movement first increasing then decreasing as the initial energy and its gathering momentum are spent. Direction and distance as well as velocity are engendered in the initial

---

14   Infant psychiatrist Daniel Stern makes a related observation in introducing the new descriptive term "vitality affects": "It is necessary", he says, "because many qualities of feeling that occur do not fit into our existing lexicon or taxonomy of affects" (Stern, 1985, p. 54).

15   One could, of course, make up a word, but making up a word misses the point: qualitative aspects are not easily packaged, being not only fleeting and evanescent but having complex, subtle, and intricate shadings. One cannot make up a word for something one cannot package. The degrees of freedom problem in human movement attests to the linguistic impasse at the same time it attests to the qualitative realities of actual experience.

thrust.[16] The qualitative complexity of the patterns derives in part from the fact that ballistic movement is possible to the *whole* moving body — as in a broad jump, for example, or in a sideward torso throw that propels a diagonally or horizontally tilted upper body in a circular arc, weight being transferred from one leg to the other in the process. In short, ballistic movement dramatically augments possibilities within the qualitative spectrum of animate movement in addition to sizably increasing the kinetic repertoire that bipedality specifically facilitates.

In dynamic systems terms, one might say that with the advent of human bipedality, movement became an enhanced attractor in that, while moving oneself was a natural propensity in a straightforwardly biological sense, i.e. for securing food, escaping predators, cementing or disrupting social relationships, mating, and so on, it was also a natural propensity in an aesthetic sense, i.e., enjoyed for its own sake, hence recognized as meaningful in itself. In this latter sense, self-movement is close to play and to rhythmic patterning. Indeed, if bipedality is at the foundation of dance, the primary condition of its possibility, then play and rhythmic patterning were already embedded within it as evolutionarily derived features; that is, they were already substantive kinetic facets of animate life. Let us look briefly at each in turn, beginning with rhythm and again use Ellis's broad perspective as a point of departure.

"From the vital function of dancing in love, and its sacred function in religion", Ellis observes, to dancing as an art, a profession, an amusement, may seem, at first glance, a sudden leap" (Ellis, 1976, p. 13; 1929, p. 48). Indeed it does. Ellis provides linkage in essence by proposing the aesthetics of dance a spinoff of the primary joy of courtship and the profession of dance a spin-off of religious ceremonies requiring trained performers. A paragraph later, however, he straightforwardly declares, "In our modern world professional dancing as an art has become altogether divorced from religion, and even, in any biological sense, from love; it is scarcely even possible, so far as Western civilisation is concerned, to trace back the tradition to either source" (*ibid.*, 1976, p. 14; 1929, p. 48). With no historical tracings in view, he suggests there are Classical and Egyptian "tendencies" in the tradition of dance as it developed in Europe, and centers attention explicitly on rhythm, a phenomenon he has in fact invoked a number of times at the very beginning of his essay, e.g., "The joyous beat of the feet of children, the cosmic play of philosophers' thoughts rise and fall according to the same laws of rhythm." He in fact states explicitly,

---

16 Motor physiologists use the term "ballistic" to refer to the kinds of movement in which there is no feedback in the period between initiation of movement and completion. The idea is of a movement which, from the moment of initiation, is self-propelling, as in a ballistic missile.

> The significance of dancing ... lies in the fact that it is simply an inti-
> mate concrete appeal of a general rhythm, that general rhythm which
> marks, not life only, but the universe, if one may still be allowed so to
> name the sum of the cosmic influences that reach us ... It need surprise
> us not at all that rhythm .... should mark all the physical and spiritual
> manifestations life (*ibid.*, 1976, pp. 5–6; 1929, p. 35).

Ellis's advertences to rhythm justly illustrate the readiness with which
rhythm is invoked in conjunction with attempts to explain the origin of the
art of dance. Sachs, for example, specifies the foundational significance of
rhythm to dance when he writes,

> Rhythmical patterns of movement, the plastic sense of space, the vivid
> representation of a world seen and imagined — these things man cre-
> ates in his own body in the dance before he uses substance and stone
> and word to give expression to his inner experiences (Sachs, 1963, p. 3).

Later, in the process of trying to define dance, he states, "[I]t is almost
impossible to define the dance more narrowly than as 'rhythmic motion',
even though such a definition "does not exclude other rhythmic movements, such as running, rowing, turning a handle, working a treadle." In
recognition of these other rhythmic movements, he settles for what he calls
a "negative [definitional] approach": dance is "all rhythmical motion not
related to the work motif" (*ibid.*, pp. 5–6).

Dancers and dance critics similarly accentuate the elemental rhythmic
nature of dance. "I was born by the sea", declares Isadora Duncan, "my
first idea of movement of the dance ... certainly came from the rhythm of
the waves" (Duncan, 1979, p. 9). "[D]ancing is a simple rhythmic swinging, or ebb and flow", writes Mary Wigman, "in which even the minutest
gesture is part of this flow, and which is carried along the unending tide of
movement" (Wigman, 1974, p. 150). Dance critic Edwin Denby, echoing
the fall-and-recovery movement thesis of Doris Humphrey states, "In
dancing one keeps taking a step and recovering one's balance. The risk is a
part of the rhythm" (Denby, 1976, p. 115).[17] Critic and historian Lincoln
Kirstein writes, "Even before there was definite, separated accompaniment, primitive people could not help being conscious of the sound of
their feet tapping the earth. Dancers, in themselves, created a percussive
accompaniment, and it was but a short step from clapping palms together,
or on their thighs or bellies, to the slapping on an animal's skin, stretched
between squatting knees or over a frame" (Kirstein, 1969, p. 3).

In short, rhythm is regularly invoked as an integral element of dance if
not its defining feature. Why would this be if not for the fact that rhythm is
inherent in the movement of living bodies, inherent in their kinetic ways of

---

17 Though having nothing to do with risk, one could say that Martha Graham's "contraction and
release" technique is similarly founded on rhythm.

going about making a living for themselves, including their ways of making sound, as in the stridulations of crickets and the articulatory gestures that give rise to the prosodic elements of human speech?[18] Rhythm is a built-in of animate life. It is first and foremost the result of qualities inherent in movement, specifically its tensional and projectional qualities. (We might note that Sachs implicitly recognizes that rhythmic qualities of movement are distinct from spatial qualities of movement when he affirms constituents in the primal art of dance, as in his initial statement quoted above. Rhythmic qualities of painting and sculpture in fact derive from a sense of movement.) Tensional and projectional qualities are combined in complex and manifold ways in such simple pan-human movements as skipping and pounding, in such expressive pan-human bodily movements as laughing and crying, and of course in the basic pan-human everyday phenomena of breathing and walking. The rhythm of all such movements is qualitatively inflected by the intensity or degree of force of the movement — its tensional quality — and the manner in which force is released — its projectional quality — both of which qualities may shift and change in intricate ways in the course of any movement sequence, in each instance giving rise to a particular rhythmic pattern. A basic binary character, for example, defines both breathing and walking: first in, then out; first this side, then this side, the one ordinarily an involuntary kinetic phenomenon, the other a voluntary kinetic phenomenon. Whether involuntary or voluntary, however, the basic rhythmic character is always qualitatively inflected, as in lifting and carrying something heavy, for example, or walking hesitantly in the dark. In each instance, by paying attention to its respective kinetic dynamics, one experiences the distinctive rhythmic nature of the basic binary movement pattern with all its peculiar changes and variations. In dance, rhythm calls attention to itself naturally because it is part of the directly experienced kinetic dynamics that constitutes dance. While it is a qualitative aspect of all animate movement, it comes prominently to the fore in elemental ways in dance because a dance is movement from beginning to end.

Play is similarly an evolutionary dimension of animate life, though a dimension not as broadly evident across the animal kingdom as rhythm. In particular, play is typical of young mammals, particularly social ones,

---

18 It is of interest in this regard to note Darwin's observation that "The perception, if not the enjoyment, of musical cadences and of rhythm is probably common to all animals, and no doubt depends on the common physiological nature of their nervous systems" (Darwin, 1981, vol. 2, p. 333). Citing von Helmholtz on the physiological aspects of music, he points out that "Even Crustaceans, which are not capable of producing any voluntary sound, possess certain auditory hairs, which have been seen to vibrate when the proper musical notes are struck" (*ibid.*).

and even some avians. It is above all a kinetic happening in which the sheer exuberance of movement dominates and in which a certain freedom of movement obtains. Consider the following account of young antelopes by A.S. Einarsen, a wildlife specialist:

> Coming cautiously one day over a rimrock at Spanish Lake, I saw a group of seven antelope kids with their mothers on the hard shore-edge of the receding lake. The mothers were contentedly resting in the warm June sun, apparently at ease and unaware of my approach. The kids were having a great time in a quite highly organized game. Rushing away across the flat rim of the lake shore, as though started by a lifting of a barrier on a race track, they ran neck and neck, swung in a wide arc and then thundered back, their tiny hooves beating in unison as they soared rather than ran, their bodies parallel to the earth. Upon nearing the starting point they drew up to a stiff-legged stop at their mothers' sides, gazed with dreamy eyes around the immediate vicinity, then wheeled away on another flight, with apparently enough power and enthusiasm to drive them to the summit of the Rocky Mountains 1,000 miles away (Einarsen, 1948, p. 122).

Ethologist John Byers comments that Einarsen's description of prong-horn antelope play emphasizes "what all ungulate young do when they play. They run" (Byers, 1984, p. 43). More broadly, ethologist Robert Fagen, whose volume on play is considered a landmark volume, notes that "The best-known locomotor-rotational movements [a form of play] are leaping, rolling, headshaking, body-twisting, neck flexion, rearing, and kicking" (Fagen, 1981, p. 48). He remarks that "Common usage gives these lay movements special status by employing unique terms: gambol, caper, romp, scamper, frolic, rollick, frisk, jink, cavort, ragrowster, *gambader* (French), and *balgen* and *tollen* (German)" (*ibid.*).

Consider further the study of rough-and-tumble play in children. Taking the descriptive term 'rough and tumble play' from the Harlows who used it in their study of social deprivation in monkeys, ethologist N.G. Blurton Jones found this kind of play not only typical of young children but distinguished by "seven movement patterns which tend to occur at the same time as each other and not to occur with other movements", such as those involved when a child paints, for example, or works with clay (Blurton Jones, 1969, p. 450). The distinctive movements are: running, chasing and fleeing; wrestling; jumping up and down with both feet together; beating at each other with an open hand without actually hitting; beating at each other with an object but not hitting; laughing. Falling too "seems to be a regular part of this behaviour", Blurton Jones remarks, and "if there is anything soft to land on children spend much time throwing themselves and each other on to it" (*ibid.*).

The seven movements may justly be called *the kinetic markers* of rough-and-tumble play.[19] Sheer exuberance and freedom of movement aptly describe the character of the markers, their dynamic spontaneity. In fact, sheer exuberance and freedom of movement describe not only the character of dynamic spontaneity in rough-and-tumble play, but the character of dynamic spontaneity in early play in general. Where movement is an end in itself, dynamic spontaneity obtains, precisely as in the spectacular run of the young pronghorn antelopes. Moreover sheer exuberance and freedom of movement describe the qualitative character of dancing waves. Their dynamics are unpredictable. Indeed, the waves appear to move capriciously, as if bent on a momentary whim to do this or that, their movement exuding a spontaneity akin to dance.

Freedom of movement is of course morphologically constrained in animate life. Any animal—including any human one—is the body it is and is not another body: humans cannot fly; trout cannot crawl; worms cannot sit. Species-specific degrees of freedom condition an animal's actual play with movement and its creative movement possibilities. Kinetic possibilities of play and creativity are accordingly bodily bound. From this morphological vantage point and with specific reference to humans, play is the discovery of one's kinetic possibilities and mastery of the challenges they present in terms of both learning one's body and learning to move oneself (see Sheets-Johnstone, 1999b, ch. 5, and 2003a). Dance is a continuation of play precisely in the sense of learning one's body and learning to move oneself. It is grounded in the mastery of these early challenges and in the creative mining of a progressively larger and larger range of kinetic possibilities in terms of their formal dynamics. Put in evolutionary perspective, the creative enterprise that is dance has kinetic roots in early animal play that itself evolved with the evolving freedom of movement associated with primate bipedality and with consistent hominid bipedality in particular. The kinetic markers of rough-and-tumble play exemplify these roots both in individual terms, i.e., in movements such as running and jumping, for example, and in relational terms, i.e., in those movement patterns in which individuals move in concert with others such as chasing and fleeing, beating but not hitting. Subtle timings, spacings, and controls are apparent in these latter patterns of movement, timings, spacings, and controls that obviously play a fundamental role in learning to dance.

---

19 Just such movements would seem to have influenced both earlier adultist definitions of play as purposeless, irrational activity, and later functionalist explanations of play as motor training and practice for adult behavior. In other words, the significance of play is either nil or tethered to the future. See Sheets-Johnstone, 2003a.

On this account, dance is older than man, in his bones as it were, in the form of an evolving empowering morphology and qualitative kinetics. The realization of dance as an art form is an extraordinary dimension in the broad history of an evolutionary semantics, a kinetic semantics that exists across the kingdom Animalia (for more on an evolutionary semantics, see Sheets-Johnstone, 1999a. Kinetic semantics are anchored in tactile-kinesthetic invariants, what primate anthropologist Stuart Altmann at a behavioral level labeled "comsigns", i.e., behaviors common to all members of the species or group (Altmann, 1976). When properly analyzed in terms of movement, comsigns are clearly shown to rest on species-specific tactile-kinesthetic invariants: the "common signs" are precisely movement patterns that any member of the species or group can or could conceivably perform.[20] In effect, sender and receiver are interchangeable (Hockett, 1960). The *Tanzsprache* is a paradigmatic instance of interchangeability, a patterning of movement in the history of an evolutionary kinetic semantics and grounded like all such patterns in tactile-kinesthetic invariants.[21]

From the perspective of an evolutionary semantics, the statement "man has always danced" is an empirically-supported affirmation of evolutionary continuities that anchor the pan-cultural reality of dance, and equally, an empirically-supported affirmation of the extraordinary range of movement possibilities of the genus *Homo* and the realization of these possibilities in the pan-cultural phenomenon of dance. From the perspective of an evolutionary semantics, one might in fact answer the intriguing question posed earlier of 'what the dancer shows'. What the dancer shows is the extraordinary power of movement to capture and communicate ineffable qualia of life, memorializing ever anew that "single fleeting moment when you feel alive", and celebrating — to paraphrase James Joyce — the ineluctable modality of animate movement.[22]

---

20   A clarification is in order with respect to comsigns and a common body of experience. Along with their male counterparts, some female primates are capable of assuming an erect posture, but no females are capable of penile erection or display — or of intromission as Altmann specifically points out. That they are incapable, however, does not mean that they do not have direct and highly discriminatory tactile-kinetic or visual experiences of these male behaviors, hence that the behaviors are not comsigns. For a discussion of the relevance of tactile-kinesthetic invariants to comsigns, see Sheets-Johnstone, 1990, especially pp. 126–9, and ch. 15.

21   Interchangeability aside, we might note that the apian dancer is not moving for movement sake, but for communicative purposes that inform others of the whereabouts, the distance to, and the richness of a sugar source. The specific spatial pattern she creates is symbolically structured and that structure is anchored in tactile-kinesthetic invariants. For an analysis and discussion of the *Tanzsprache*, specifically with reference to primordial language, see Sheets-Johnstone, 1990, ch. 5.

22   "INELUCTABLE MODALITY OF THE VISIBLE: AT LEAST THAT IF NO more, thought through my eyes", Joyce, 1934, p. 38.

References

Aldrich, Virgil C. 1963. *Philosophy of Art*, Foundations of Philosophy Series, Elizabeth and Monroe Beardsley, eds. Englewood Cliffs, NJ: Prentice-Hall.

Altmann, Stuart A. 1967. "The Structure of Primate Social Communication", in *Social Communication among Primates*, ed. Stuart A. Altmann. Chicago: University of Chicago Press, pp. 325–62.

Beardsley, Monroe. 1982. *The Aesthetic Point of View*. Ithaca: Cornell University Press.

Berleant, Arnold. 1991. *Art and Engagement*. Philadelphia: Temple University Press.

Blurton Jones, N.G. 1969. "An Ethological Study of Some Aspects of Social Behaviour of Children in Nursery School", in *Primate Ethology*, ed. D. Morris. Garden City, NY: Doubleday & Co., pp. 437–63.

Byers, John. 1984. "Play in Ungulates", in *Play in Animals and Humans*, ed. P.K. Smith. Oxford: Basil Blackwel, pp. 43–65.

Carpenter, C.R. 1963. "Societies of Monkeys and Apes", in *Primate Social Behavior*, ed. Charles H. Southwick. New York: Van Nostrand Reinhold, pp. 24–51

Chapman, Sara. 1974. *Movement Education in the United States*. Philadelphia: Movement Education Publications.

Cohen, Selma Jeanne. 1974. *Dance as a Theatre Art*. New York: Dodd, Mead & Co.

Cunningham, Merce. 1968. *Changes: Notes on Choreography*, ed. Frances Starr. New York: Something Else Press, unpaginated.

Darwin, Charles. 1981 [1871]. *The Descent of Man and Selection in Relation to Sex* , 2 vols. Princeton: Princeton University Press, vol. 1.

Denby, Edwin. 1976. "Forms in Motion and in Thought", *Salmagundi*, 33–4, pp. 115–32.

Dennett, Daniel. 1987. *The Intentional Stance*. Cambridge, MA: Bradford Books/MIT Press.

Dickie, George and Richard J. Sclafani, eds., 1977. *Aesthetics: A Critical Anthology*. New York: St. Martin's Press.

Duncan, Isadora. 1979. "Excerpts from Her Writings", in *The Vision of Modern Dance*, ed. Jean Morrison Brown. Princeton: Princeton Book Co, pp. 7–11.

Einarsen, A.S. 1948. *The Pronghorn Antelope and Its Management.* Washington DC: The Wildlife Management Institute.

Ellis, Havelock. 1976. "The Art of Dancing", *Salmagundi* 33–34, pp. 5–22; reprint of "The Art of Dancing", in Ellis, Havelock. 1929. *The Dance of Life*. Boston: Houghton Mifflin Company), pp. 34–63.

Fagen, Robert. 1981. *Animal Play Behavior*. New York: Oxford University Press.

Feagin, Susan L. and Patrick Maynard. 1997. *Aesthetics*. Oxford: Oxford University Press.

Goodall, Jane van Lawick. 1968. "The Behaviour of Free-Living Chimpanzees in the Gombe Stream Reserve", *Animal Behaviour Monographs*, vol. 1, part 3, pp. 165–311.

Hanfling, Oswald, ed. 1992. *Philosophical Aesthetics: An Introduction*. Oxford: Basil Blackwell.

H'Doubler, Margaret. 1940. *Dance: A Creative Art Experience*. New York: Appleton-Century-Crofts.

Herman, Anne L. 1979. "Ritual in the Celtic World: The Dance of the Ancient Druids", *Dance Research Annual* X, pp. 201–12.

Hockett, Charles F. 1960. "The Origin of Speech", *Scientific American* 203, pp. 89–96.

Humphrey, Doris. 1959. *The Art of Making Dances*, ed. Barbara Pollack. New York: Grove Press.

Husserl, Edmund. 1964. *Phenomenology of Internal Time Consciousness*, ed. M. Heidegger, trans. James S. Churchill. Bloomington: Indiana University Press.

Joyce, James. 1934. *Ulysses*. New York: Modern Library.

Kirstein, Lincoln. 1969 [1935]. *Dance: A Short History of Classic theatrical Dancing.* New York: Dance Horizons.

Kivy, Peter. 1997. *Philosophies of Arts: An Essay in Differences.* Cambridge: Cambridge University Press.

Langer, Susanne. 1953. *Feeling and Form.* New York: Charles Scribner's Sons.

Langer, Susanne. 1957. *Problems of Art.* New York: Charles Scribner's Sons.

Merleau-Ponty, Maurice. 1962. *Phenomenology of Perception*, trans. Colin Smith. New York: Routledge & Kegan Paul.

Merleau-Ponty, Maurice. 1964. "Eye and Mind", trans. Carleton Dallery, in *The Primacy of Perception.* Evanston IL: Northwestern University Press, pp. 159–90.

Rogers, C.M. 1973. "Implications of a Primate Early Rearing Experiment for the Concept of Culture", in *Precultural Primate Behavior*, ed. Emil W. Menzel. Basel: Karger, pp. 185–91.

Romer, Alfred Sherwood and Thomas S. Parsons. 1977. *The Vertebrate Body.* Philadelphia: W.B. Saunders Co.

Sachs, Curt. 1963. *World History of the Dance*, trans. Bessie Schöenberg. New York: W.W. Norton & Co.

Sheets-Johnstone, Maxine. 1966. *The Phenomenology of Dance.* Madison: University of Wisconsin Press; second editions: London: Dance Books Ltd. 1979; New York: Arno Press, 1980.

Sheets-Johnstone, Maxine. 1983. "Evolutionary Residues and Uniquenesses in Human Movement", *Evolutionary Theory* 6, pp. 205–9.

Sheets-Johnstone, Maxine. 1989. "Hominid Bipedality and Sexual Selection Theory", *Evolutionary Theory* 9, pp. 57–70.

Sheets-Johnstone, Maxine. 1990. *The Roots of Thinking.* Philadelphia: Temple University Press.

Sheets-Johnstone, Maxine. 1999a. "Sensory-Kinetic Understandings of Language: An Inquiry into Origins", *Evolution of Communication* 3, 2, pp. 149–83.

Sheets-Johnstone, Maxine. 1999b. *The Primacy of Movement.* Amsterdam/ Philadelphia: John Benjamins Publishers.

Sheets-Johnstone, Maxine. 2002a. "Biological Foundations of Meaning: Further Steps toward an Evolutionary Semantics", guest lecture, Niels Bohr Institute, Copenhagen, Denmark.

Sheets-Johnstone, Maxine. 2002b. "Descriptive Foundations", Keynote Address, Association for the Study of Literature and the Environment Conference, Flagstaff, AZ, March 2002; published in *Interdisciplinary Studies in Literature and the Environment*, 9, 1 (Winter 2002), 165–79, and in *Irish Pages*, 2, 1 (Spring/Summer 2003), 17–30.

Sheets-Johnstone, Maxine. 2003a. "Child's Play", *Human Studies* 26, pp. 409–30.

Sheets-Johnstone, Maxine. 2003b. "The Kinetic Basis of the Biological Disposition to Sense-Making: Further Steps toward an Evolutionary Semantics", guest lecture, Haskins Laboratories, Yale University.

Sparshott, F.E. 1963. *The Structure of Aesthetics*. Toronto: University of Toronto Press.

Sparshott, F.E. 1995. *A Measured Pace: Toward a Philosophical Understanding of the Arts of Dance*. Toronto: University of Toronto Press.

Stern, Daniel. 1985. *The Interpersonal World of the Infant*. New York: Basic Books.

Stern, Daniel. 1990. *Diary of a Baby*. New York: Basic Books.

Valéry, Paul. 1964. *Aesthetics*, trans. Ralph Manheim, Bollingen Series XLV.13. New York: Pantheon Books.

Whiting, H.T.A., ed. 1984. *Human Motor Actions: Bernstein Reassessed*. Amsterdam: Elsevier Science Publishers.

Wickler, Wolfgang. 1969. "Socio-sexual Signals and Their Intra-specific Imitation among Primates", in *Primate Ethology*, ed. D. Morris. Garden City, NY: Doubleday & Co, pp. 89–189.

Wigman, Mary. 1974 [1933]. "The Philosophy of Modern Dance", in *Dance as a Theatre Art*, ed. Selma Jeanne Cohen. New York: Dodd, Mead & Co., pp. 149–53.

Chapter XIII

What Are We Naming?

Introduction

As my title indicates, I would like to pose a question concerning body image and body schema. The question revolves about the terms 'body image' and 'body schema', and the concepts 'body image' and 'body schema'. The challenge of *languaging experience* broadly identifies the terminological issue; the challenge of *being true to the truths of experience* broadly identifies the conceptual issue. I approach the interrelated challenges by way of a basic claim that grounds the inquiry. Spelling out this claim and its empirical foundations will set the stage for addressing the title question directly, and in turn allow me to specify inherent weaknesses in the terms 'body image' and 'body schema' and to recommend their replacement by terms that do empirical and conceptual justice to the phenomena in question.

A prefatory remark is apposite. I would like to single out and acknowledge the clarifying and ever-broadening researches and writings of Shaun Gallagher on body image and body schema (e.g., Gallagher, 1986, 1995, 2000; Gallagher and Cole, 1995). In a sense, my title might be taken as unnecessarily repeating the fine work already done by Professor Gallagher. My concern, however, is neither to recount his analyses nor to refine and extend them along further lines. It is rather to step back and ask quite pointedly: Just what are people, specifically people in present-day research, trying to understand and to explain by using the terms? What are they trying to capture by invoking a body image or body schema?[1]

---

1   One of the anonymous reviewers of this book, citing Gallagher and Cole's 1995 article, stated that my critique of body schema and body image was "inaccurate" and in fact recommended that "What Are We Naming?" be dropped from the book. In order to dispel any such possible future misunderstandings of the essay, I would like to underscore its constructive aim, give a brief sketch of its background history, and add new references.

    As noted in the introductory material to this book, "What Are We Naming?" was originally my invited keynote address at an international conference titled "Body Image/Body Schema: (Neuro)phenomenological, (Neuro)psychoanalytical, and Neuroscientific Perspectives." The

The basic claim that subtends my response to the question begins quite simply. In the most fundamental sense, when people use the terms body image and body schema, they are trying to answer the question, How do we do what we do? That is, in the most fundamental sense, they are trying to understand or to explain how it is we come to move knowledgeably, effectively, and efficiently in the world, or alternatively, to understand or to explain how it is we do *not* move knowledgeably, effectively, and efficiently in the world, questions that, I might point out, need answering not only with respect to deficiencies, i.e., pathologies, but with respect to proficiencies, i.e., masteries and learnings that originate in our common infancy and ontogenetic history, and progress to diverse individual achievements arrived at through processes of self-cultivation. In broader terms, their efforts might be said to aim at understanding and explaining how it is that not only human animals, but animals in general, come to move knowledgeably, effectively, and efficiently in the world. It should be added immediately that this animate capacity does not exist in a one-individual vacuum. It necessarily involves others; it is an intercorporeal as

conference was held at Ghent University in Belgium in March-April 2003. Conference presentations were subsequently published by John Benjamins in 2005 in a book titled *Body Image and Body Schema* (De Preester and Knockaert, 2005). Both Shaun Gallagher and Jonathan Cole gave papers at the conference and contributed to the book.

Gallagher's book article, "Dynamic Models of Body Schematic Processes", is of specific interest in the present context. The article differs from his conference presentation precisely in addressing the "more recent criticism that has been developed in both phenomenological (Sheets-Johnstone 2003) and neuroscientific (Jeannerod 2002) perspectives ... [B]oth of these recent critiques complain that the notion of the body schema is too static to be of use in recently developed dynamic models of movement" (Gallagher, 2005, p. 239). In short, Gallagher is addressing questions I raised in my keynote address, and addressing neuroscientific questions as well.

The discussion concerning body image and body schema is thus hardly closed, as the reviewer implied in his reference to Gallagher and Cole's 1995 article. For one thing, dynamic systems theory supports phenomenological findings, as this essay shows, and that relationship cannot be ignored. That the discussion in fact continues and centers on dynamics is apparent not only from the title of Gallagher's conference article but from the way in which he begins his concluding remarks in the article: "I want to reject the specific conclusion reached by Sheets-Johnstone [concerning neuroscientist Alexander Luria's notion of 'kinetic melodies'], and at the same time embrace the general tenor that motivates her critique ... I am tempted to say that both Sheets-Johnstone and Marc Jeannerod's suggestions are at best terminological and not conceptual points, since there are clear ways to think of body schematic processes and even the body image as dynamical processes" (*ibid.*, pp. 246–7).

Terminological and conceptual 'points' obviously relate to the specific questions posed at the very beginning of this essay. What Gallagher is addressing with respect to these 'points' concerns precisely the semantic liability of terms and concepts that are essentially static: 'body schema' and 'body image' do not inherently suggest much less capture the dynamics of the phenomena they are attempting to specify. It is not just a matter of retentions and protentions, as Gallagher suggests in his conference article (*ibid.*, pp. 241–2), that is, of imbuing 'body schema' and 'body image' with temporal dimensions. It is rather a matter of acknowledging lived-through qualitative dynamics, and even further, a matter of acknowledging *the familiarity* of lived-through qualitative dynamics, a topic outside the bounds of the present essay but one of clearly fundamental significance. Such familiarity allows the formation of all well as corporeal capacity. The basic claim thus has substantive intersubjective meanings and implications. It affirms that to understand or to explain how we do what we do, we must necessarily turn our attention both to the ways in which movement grounds our practical ways of being in the world and to the ways in which movement grounds our ways of being with others. Given the scope of the subject, these latter ways will be touched on only marginally and in passing.

I begin by substantiating aspects of the claim from several perspectives, laying out empirical grounds for its validation in the process.

1

Infants and young children live in a world of movement. Well-known researchers in infant/child development regularly highlight the centrality of movement. Psychologist Colwyn Trevarthen, for example, writes that in two-month-old infants, "movements of the whole body... accompany vocalizations and movements of the lips and tongue, and that "[v]igorous calls or shouts are generally combined with longer movements including waving of the hand ..." (Trevarthen, 1977, pp. 251–2; see also Trevarthen, 1979); psychiatrist Daniel Stern points out that "intensity, timing, and shape" "of a person's behavior ... form the basis of attunement" (Stern, 1985, p. 146), i.e., intersubjective "sharing of affective states" (*ibid.*, p. 138), intensity, timing, and shape being instantiated in and through movement in each exemplification; psychologist Jerome Bruner states that the principal linguistic interest of young children "centers on *human action and its out-comes*, particularly, *human interaction* (Bruner, 1990, p. 78); psychologist Philippe Rochat affirms that among the experiences that an infant has of itself in the course of moving its limbs, touching itself, or hearing its own voice, "Proprioception is indeed the sensory modality of the self 'par excellence'" (Rochat, 2002, p. 91). In short, empirical findings underscore the fact that infants are kinesthetically alive and kinetically attuned. Clearly, they are doing something and/or learning something in and through movement.

But what exactly are they doing or learning? Certainly we can answer—and with strong empirical backing—that they are learning their bodies and learning to move themselves (Sheets-Johnstone, 1999a). To flesh out this learning, however, requires what physiological psychologist

those everyday habits that inform our lives. Indeed, such familiarity undergirds the very formation of habits as readily carried through complexes of movement to begin with: brushing our teeth, writing our name, sweeping the floor, stepping off a curb and walking across the street. In short, everyday habitual movements are readily, smoothly, and efficiently carried out because they are dynamically familiar corporeal-kinetic intentionalities and patternings. (For a full phenomenological investigation of the relationship between qualitative dynamics and familiarity and habit, see Sheets-Johnstone, 2006.)

Hans Teuber (Teuber, 1966, p. 441) described as a "different way of looking." Indeed, when we ask what they are doing or learning with the combined acuity and puzzlement of the autistic child who remarked, "People
talk to each other with their eyes. What is it that they are saying" (Frith,
1993, p. 113), we step back from a ready-made wisdom and have the possibility not only of uncovering much of what we take for granted about
movement, but of uncovering assumptions underlying our natural attitude toward movement, assumptions that quite precisely lie in the way of
understanding or explaining 'how we do what we do'. For example, we
might readily find the common assumption that movement is a change of
position; or the common assumption that our awareness of our own movement consists of sensations of movement; or the common assumption that
movement is nothing more or other than behavior, and that behavior more
aptly and properly describes kinetic phenomena, as the terms eating,
standing up, grasping, and chasing clearly indicate. With such assumptions intact, an appreciation of movement, particularly an appreciation of
the fact that any movement creates its own qualitative dynamics (Sheets-
Johnstone, 1966 [1979/1980], 1999a, 1999b), is straightaway diminished if
not obliterated. The assumptions blind us in each instance and are obstacles to an accurate, veridical account of 'how we do what we do'.

In the context of discussing volitional movement, for instance, people
often give the example of raising one's arm overhead.[2] They in turn commonly speak of the sensation of movement. Yet movement is never experienced as a sensation, either a single sensation or a group of sensations.
Consider actual experience. When you walk, do you have *sensations* of
movement or are you aware of an unfolding spatio-temporal-energic
dynamic? When you hammer a nail or tie a shoelace or reach for a glass of
water, do you have *sensations* of movement or are you aware of a felt,
ongoing, and familiar dynamic? Freud rightly observed that there are both
sensations and feelings "from within" (Freud, 1955, p. 19). The difference
bears thinking about. Movement is not sensational. To say that someone
has sensations of movement is a contradiction in terms. Movement is not
punctual: it is quite unlike the proverbial touching hand and the proverbial touched hand, both of which may be spoken of as yielding sensations
of touch. Everyday self-movement is in contrast a dynamically felt temporal phenomenon. Any time we care to pay attention to ourselves in everyday movement, we find, in the words of Alexandr Luria ("a founding
father of neuropsychology" [Goldberg, 1990]), a kinetic melody (Luria,

---

2   For philosophers, at least, the example may well have its origins in the writings of A. I. Melden.
    See Melden, 1966.

1973, 1966).[3] While sensations might be appropriate descriptions for a *corps morcelé* (Lacan, 1977a, 1977b) that feels twinges here, tensions there, cramps here, pains there, and so on—a *corps*, we might note, that is not at all the preserve of infancy, but in many ways constitutes the frequently distant, third-person bodies of adult humans—sensations are not appropriate descriptions for a *corps engagé*, not only one that is reflectively attentive to its own movement in the course of being *engagé*, but one that is pre-reflectively attentive as well, and that, in fact, in being pre-reflectively attentive, is necessarily aware if "something goes wrong."

The assumption that we have sensations of movement distorts the reality of self-movement and has far-reaching consequences. To illustrate these, consider that the difference in use of the terms sensation and perception often rests on a distinction between inner and outer: whatever the modality of objects sensed out there in the world, we have *perceptions* of them; whatever the modality of objects sensed in our bodies, we have *sensations* of them. The perceptual/sensational distinction, however, does not hold when it comes to self-movement. This is not simply because, as shown above, self-movement is not sensational like pains, itches, a scratchy throat, and so on. It is because, in addition, self-movement is at once both a tactile-kinesthetic and kinetic happening: it is perceivable from both within and without; it is a perceptual experience for both mover and any observer of movement.[4] Its double mode of presence has sizable

---

3 Luria speaks in fact of "*kinaesthetic melodies* (Luria, 1973, p. 253).

4 While it is true that we do not have sensations of movement, it is only partially true that we have *perceptions* of movement "from both within and without." We have *perceptions* of movement only when we experience movement—our own or that of others—as a three-dimensional phenomenon, a happening *in* space (and *in* time). In other words, kinesthetic experience is first and foremost not a perceptual but a *felt* experience, a matter of feeling a certain dynamic flow. One need only consider infant and early childhood experiences, experiences that ground our very capacity for movement.

Movement may thus certainly be a perceptual experience for a mover, but it is not necessarily nor indeed from the beginning a perceptual experience. As adults, we typically have *perceptions* of movement when we are practicing a golf swing, for example, or a tennis serve, or when we are getting a sliver out of a child's thumb. Our experience is not of a qualitative kinetic dynamic, an immediate and direct experience of movement. It is an experience that has a quasi-reflective or monitoring component, precisely as in discriminating too much force, a spatial waywardness that falls short of the mark, a too hasty twist, and so on.

A sizable and absolutely fundamental error in the phenomenological elucidation of the experience of self-movement lies precisely in the failure of not specifying the essentially *felt* nature of kinesthesia. When we move, we *feel* a certain qualitative kinetic flow. Our movement has certain qualitative contours that might be described as rushed, hesitant, expansive, cringing, or explosive. It has, in short, a certain qualitative dynamic created by the movement itself and felt directly by the mover. It should be noted that the felt dynamic may be experienced anywhere along a gradient of awareness: at stage center by a gymnast or dancer; at the margins by a person walking down a corridor to a meeting and deep in thought about the agenda.

implications for Husserl's notion of pairing in relation to intersubjectivity, as philosopher Soren Overgaard deftly shows in a recent article (Overgaard, 2003). Overgaard's findings are based on detailed consultations of Husserl's three-volume analyses of intersubjectivity, in which Husserl calls attention to "the exteriority" of movement as well as to the kinestheses of movement. The intersubjective significance of the double mode of presence can be spelled out beyond Overgaard's insightful article, namely, along the lines of the qualitative dynamics that any movement creates (for a fuller discussion of the significance and its experiential foundations, see Sheets-Johnstone, 2003b, 2008).

To appreciate the double perceptual character of movement and the possibility of its further intersubjective elaboration is in essential ways to heed the earlier cited words of Hans Teuber. Teuber (Teuber, 1966, pp. 440–1) was agreeing with physiologist Ernest von Holst that we ought to change our habitual point of departure in perception and begin instead with movement when he stated that such a shift in perspective "requires some different way of looking". Indeed it does. The "different way of looking" readily challenges the terms and concepts 'body image' and 'body schema', as we will presently see. The more general point here is twofold. First, neuroscientific studies anchored in perception tend not to entertain or to investigate the fundamental ways in which self-movement anchors our cognitive/affective lives. On the contrary, self-movement not infrequently appears merely an afterthought in these studies, something that has no significance in and of itself but simply trails along after 'input'. The work of Giacomo Rizzolatti, Vittorio Gallese, and colleagues (e.g., Rizzolatti et al., 1996; Rizzolatti and Gallese, 1997; Gallese, 2000) reflects the possibility of changing the favored neuroscientific point of departure and the insights that can come of it.

The second point concerns the fact that life in the animal kingdom starts with movement, self-movement, certainly not in the absence of a perceived world, but just as certainly a phenomenon—an experiential phenomenon—in its own right. More finely stated, it starts with an intrinsic dynamics by which animate movement organizes itself and does so on the basis of the immediate kinetic possibilities of the moving organism itself. J.A. Scott Kelso, Director of the Center for Complex Systems and Brain Sciences at Florida Atlantic University, has consistently shown in his research how, through an intrinsic dynamics, different patterns of movement arise, depending upon changes in a control parameter within the particular system investigated (e.g., Kelso, Scholz, and Schöner, 1988; Kelso, 1995; Kelso

---

For phenomenological elucidations of the distinction between sensations and perceptions, and between perceptions and feelings of movement, see Sheets-Johnstone, 2003b, 2006, 2008.

and Zanone, 2002; Zanone and Kelso, 1992). In other words, in a biological system, as in any purely physical or chemical system, change is not brought about only by *circonstances*, that is, by something external; it is brought about equally by the self-organizing dynamics of the system itself, a dynamic *tendance intérieur*, we might say, to follow through with a remarkably applicable Lamarckian vocabulary. Given this fact of nature, we would do well to pay attention to movement and to probe nature's dynamic strategies through experimental and experiential methodologies. In fact, Kelso has strongly criticized any neuroscience that, rather than probing nature's dynamic strategies, postulates entities and in consequence comes up with "switches", or "schema", or "traces" as explanatory mechanisms, completely overlooking self-organizing coordinative patterns. He states forthrightly, for example, that one of his motivations for working out basic laws of coordination was "to counter the then dominant notion of motor programs, which tries to explain switching (an abrupt shift in spatiotemporal order) by a device or a mechanism that contains 'switches'" (Kelso, 1995, p. 57). In his discussion of research on the dynamics of learning, he points out with equal candidness that "[u]sually, some hypothetical construct located inside the head, such as a *schema* or a *trace*, is said to be built up or strengthened as a result of the learning process" (*ibid.*, p. 161), a formulation that reduces to the simple truism that through practice, "[a] subject's performance improves and becomes less variable" — something, he adds, "your grandmother could have told you" (*ibid.*).[5]

Surely if, as Kelso and other dynamic systems theorists have shown, the tendency of nature is to self-organize, then attention to the self-organizing strategies of nature should predominate over any attempts to organize nature from without by creating structures along a cerebral mall: cognitive maps, feature analyzers, a "corollary discharge of attention module" (Taylor, 2002), an "internal, innately specified vocal-tract synthesizer" (Liberman and Mattingly, 1985, p. 26), an "intentionality detector" (Baron-Cohen, 1995), body image, body schema, and so on, all of them hypothetical entities conjured to do the trick of explaining how we do

---

5   It is not only Kelso who decries the practice of explaining something by conjuring an entity in the head. Lecours, Nespoulous, and Desaulniers do the same in their discussion of the deficient heuristic value of psychological and psychopathological typologies of apraxia: "[U]nless one considers, for example, that it is an explanation to say, after observing ideatory apraxia, that this behavior testifies to the existence of a programming mechanism, and that dysfunction of this programming mechanism will lead to ideatory apraxia," the typologies are useless (Lecours, Nespoulous, and Desaulniers, 1986, p. 240). Their earlier observation is similarly to the point. After reviewing standard teachings on apraxia and declaring that "Standard teaching on apraxia is no doubt coherent," they write, "To what extent... it correspond[s] to reality is another question" (*ibid.*).

what we do. Clearly, Kelso's understandings and explanations of 'how we do what we do' "[require] some different way of looking." They require an open mind-set oriented to the dynamic rather than to the mechanical, and to what I would suggest is thereby properly oriented to the sensory-kinetic rather than to the sensory-motor (Sheets-Johnstone, 1999a; see also Sheets-Johnstone, 1990, 1994). They thereby require that we cease looking for or designating some *thing* that will answer to a capacity or function, giving the thing the status of an object by spatializing it, locating it in the brain, thereby putting it on the map, however hypothetical the map (e.g., brain modules) or the thing itself (e.g., body image, body schema). It is of more than passing historical interest to note that Aristotle would agree. That nature must be understood dynamically because dynamics are at the heart of nature was a principle readily recognized by Aristotle in his observation that "Nature is a principle of motion and change ... " and in his conclusion that "We must therefore see that we understand what motion is; for if it were unknown, nature too would be unknown" (Aristotle *Physics* 200b12–14).

2

To sum up the basic claim, its ready validation in ontogenetical studies, and the waywardness and far-reaching consequences of unexamined assumptions—in reality, *misconceptions*—about movement, we can conclude that to find out what is going on in and through movement—and not only in infancy, I might add, but in the course of human lifetimes and in the course of lifetimes across the animal kingdom—we must turn attention to the thing itself, or more accurately, to the dynamic process itself, hewing to the truths of experience and jettisoning assumptions that shroud movement in something either less or other than movement.

The conclusion brings us directly to the question, what are we naming?—or, following the thrust of the previous line of discussion, what are we *trying* to name by 'body image' and 'body schema'? In answer, we might observe first that to language experience in more than colloquial ways—"I'm on my way to the store"; "I visited my friend this morning"—is challenging. Everyday speech rarely includes a fine-grained descriptive account of experience—whether something as brief as the experience of a hot stove or as extended as the experience of traveling from Yachats, Oregon to Ghent. In ways similar to everyday speech—and concomitantly dissimilar from the challenge of descriptively languaging lived-through experiences—observations from a third-person perspective commonly tend to be given a generic name, a ready label by which one can conveniently refer to the phenomenon, something as simple as 'hot stove' or as complex as 'travel'. The point is that languaging experience takes reflective thought and effort beyond the easy flow of everyday speech. Such reflective thought and effort can result in an accurate descriptive analysis and taxonomy of experience, much in the manner of Darwin's keenly detailed descriptive analyses and taxonomies of animate life prior to his formulation of the theory of evolution. Just such accurate *descriptive* analyses and taxonomies are wanted in advance of third-person namings that attempt to capture fundamental aspects of life. A name may otherwise be unanchored in the very reality of life being investigated, and thus be not only an ongoing source of schisms between first-person experience and third-person observational labellings, but an obstacle in the path of truth. In short, attention to the name we give things is of critical importance. The term 'image' in the label 'body image' is a classic example.

The term is unequivocally misleading. In everyday speech, an image refers primarily to something visual. Equally significant, it refers primarily to something not actually perceived. How, then, to begin with, can the term 'body image' be the proper term for "*perceptions* ... pertaining to one's own body" (Gallagher, 2000, p. 4), most prominently, kinesthesia and proprioception, modalities that are definitely not only *not* visual, but modalities that are definitely *not* absent but, on the contrary, livingly present. The dictionary leaves no doubt about the disparity. The first Oxford English Dictionary definition of 'image' reads: "a physical likeness or representation of a person, animal, or thing, photographed, painted, sculptured, or otherwise made visible." The second definition begins: "an optical counterpart or appearance of an object ... "; the third definition begins "a mental representation ... "; the fourth definition, identified as psychological, reads: "a mental representation of something previously perceived, in the absence of the original stimulus"; and so on. Clearly, the word refers to something visual, something absent, and, equally critical, to 'some-*thing*', i.e., an object of some kind. No sense of animation whatsoever attaches to the word. Yet if the quest is to name something that refers to what Gallagher identifies as the "intentionality" (*ibid.*) of "embodied experience" (*ibid.*, p. 2), and if the first "intentional element" of "embodied experience" is "the subject's *perceptual* experience of his/her own body" (*ibid.*, p. 4), then the word 'image' not only fails to capture "embodied experience"; it leads us far, far astray, for the first and foremost perceptual aspect of one's own body—and in fact any living body—is its animation: in the beginning and straight through to the end, the quintessential perceptual experience of one's body—and in fact any living body—is its movement.

I respectfully suggest that we need to start from scratch. By this I mean starting with Gallagher's first intentional element of 'body image', for the first intentional element is the ground of the other two intentional elements of 'body image' specified by Gallagher, i.e., "the subject's *conceptual* understanding ...of the body in general; and the subject's *emotional* attitude toward his/her own body" (*ibid.*, pp. 4–5). Perceptions of one's own body are, in other words, the *sine qua non* of both conceptual understandings of, and emotional attitudes toward, one's body. If one did not *perceive* one's body, one would have no grounds for building or having such conceptual understandings or emotional attitudes. Starting from scratch in this way directs us to the possibility of identifying a *corporeal-kinetic intentionality*, of spelling out the foundations and dimensions of this intentionality, of thus doing justice to our primal animation (Sheets-Johnstone, 1999a), and correlatively, to what I would term not "*embodied* experience," but *bodily-kinetic* experience. Other facets of corporeal-kinetic intentionalities could be added to those Gallagher lists, in particular, affective intentionalities, that is, emotional experiences of one's own body or experiences of one's own bodily felt emotions, but consideration of these is not to the point here. Let me also add incidentally that the term "embodied experience," though popular, is problematic in its own right. What is it that is embodied? Our minds? Our "cognitive functions"? Our sex and gender? Our perceptions? Our emotions? Our selves? As I have elsewhere suggested, our minds, sex, gender, selves, and more, are conveniently packaged like frozen orange juice and TV dinners — all thanks to the packaging magic of 'embodiment'" and its variations (Sheets-Johnstone, 1999a, p. 359). The all-purpose packaging offers a solid and perdurable container that can hold a variety of precious goods. The packaging, however, solidifies experience in ways counter to the animated ways in which we ordinarily live our bodies. Contrary to a fixed and constant *container sense of experience*, bodily experience is basically neither static nor receptacle-like. Life is precisely not a series of stills. It is no surprise, then, that living bodies do not experience themselves as embodying minds, cognitions, perceptions, and so on, and certainly do not experience themselves as embodied. They experience themselves first and foremost as animate and animated, precisely because they are. Our terminology should reflect this fact; it should be true to the truths of experience.

Corporeal-kinetic intentionality puts us rightfully on the path toward such truths, beginning with both felt and perceptual experiences of our own bodies and building from there both to emotional attitudes toward our bodies and to conceptual understandings of bodies in general. In a strongly phenomenological/developmental/evolutionary sense, it puts us on the path toward understanding and explaining the origins and progressive histories of how we do what we do, from learning our bodies and learning to move ourselves to progressively subtle and complex corporeal-kinetic learnings that inform and structure our practical and social lives, and our individual self-cultivations. In a deeply psychological sense, *corporeal-kinetic intentionality* puts us on the further path of understanding and explaining the origins and progressive histories of *why* we do what we do and have done what we have done. Still further, it leaves intact the term 'body image' to refer in its proper sense; that is, corporeal-kinetic intentionality preserves the lexical meaning of 'body image' as something preeminently visual, imagined, and objectified, subsuming that meaning within its corporeal-kinetic compass as one species among many within its genus. It thus leaves intact the visual picture one has of one's body, the imaginative consciousness of what one's body looks like together with one's emotional attitudes toward it, and this not only within a normal range but as in anorexia and as in the various transformations of one's body that occur in schizophrenia.

In sum, we should not rest content with present use of the term 'body image'. It is inapt, and misleads us because it is conceptually wayward. The kinetic dynamics that in the most fundamental sense constitute bodily experience cannot be captured by an essentially static, visually anchored, and thing- or object-tethered terminology.

The fundamental dynamic oversight is actually evident early on in the history of neurology, specifically, in the context of neurologist Henry Head's original formulation of the parallel notion 'body schema'. "By means of perpetual alterations in position," Head states, "we are always building up a postural model of ourselves, which constantly changes" (quoted in Schilder, 1950, p. 12). Clearly, "perpetual alterations in position" and "a postural model of ourselves, which constantly changes" testify to the fact that the term 'body schema' attempts to name something animate and animated. The term, however, gives no sense of the kinetic dynamics that constitute "perpetual alterations in position," nor is it anywhere clear how a body schema that "constantly changes" can do so short of being itself constantly animated and thus being not a vague structure, mental diagram, organizing framework, or whatever, *but a dynamic patterning of some kind*. Earlier, we saw how assumptions about movement can skew understandings of movement. "Perpetual alterations in position" and a postural model that "constantly changes" do just that by reducing movement to a *change of position*, and then subsequently trying verbally to accommodate the existential fact of animation. Its attempt to explain movement — how we do what we do — amounts to nothing more than verbal magic. Clearly, Head's use of the term 'body schema' generates positional rather than kinetic understandings and does not penetrate to the core phenomenon — movement; hence, it does not and cannot do justice to a kinetic dynamics.

Gallagher's keen and explorative research has done much to correct the earlier situation, and in fact Gallagher all but specifies a kinetic dynamics in his discussion of body schema as "a system of processes that constantly regulate posture and movement .... [and] that function without reflective awareness or the necessity of perceptual monitoring" (Gallagher, 2000, p. 4). For example, in his discussion of aplasic phantoms — limbs that are congenitally absent but are taken in various ways as present by the person so afflicted — Gallagher comes close to affirming outright the kinetic origins of body schemas. Pointing out that "The actual development of embryonic neural tissue depends, in part, on fetal movement," and the fact that "Ultrasonic scanning of fetuses shows that movement of the hand to the mouth occurs between 50 to 100 times an hour from 12 to 15 weeks gestational age," he goes on to suggest that "This kind of prenatal movement may in fact be precisely the movement that helps to generate or facilitate the development of body schemas." He points out that this suggestion is "quite consistent with the traditional hypothesis" concerning the acquisition of a body schema over time, the only difference being that "this movement occurs much earlier, and by implication, body schemas develop much earlier than the traditional account permits" (*ibid.*, p. 20).

That body schemas are movement generated and movement dependent, and are in fact themselves kinetic phenomena, means that we should not be content merely to invoke the term *body schema* as an explanation and have done with it, whether in neuroscience, psychiatry, neuropsychiatry, phenomenology, or neurophenomenology. We must first explain a body schema itself. To do this, we must take self-movement and the self-organization of movement seriously, starting with the development of embryonic neural tissue and proceeding to the development of coordinated movement. In the process, we can hardly fail to realize the necessity of choosing a more appropriate term, one that duly captures the true nature of the phenomenon that the words 'body schema' attempt unsuccessfully to capture, namely, *corporeal-kinetic patterning*. Such a term properly identifies the hand-mouth coordination that arises early in fetal life and that Gallagher discusses. Similarly, it properly identifies "perpetual alterations" and "constant changes" that arise and unfold in the course of self-movement. In brief, the term *corporeal-kinetic patterning* does justice to neurological and neurologically-based kinetic dynamics. The term 'body schema' — like the term 'motor programs' — fails to capture these dynamics. It cannot capture them because the dynamics, while structurally played out, are not themselves objects — specifiable "things" — in the brain. They are transitory spatio-temporal phenomena, corporeal-kinetic patternings that, properly identified, are the neurological complement of corporeal-kinetic intentionalities.

Evolutionary and related methodological implications follow from the preceding diagnosis of failings in the term 'body schema', the former implications having to do with a broad pan-animate perspective, the latter with reification and reductionism. How, we might ask with reference to the former, do nonhuman animals navigate or locomote in the world? Do they have body schemas? Is there something equivalent in nonhuman animals to having a feather in your hat and climbing into a car? How about deftly navigating the climbing of a tree with a caught prey in your mouth? *Corporeal-kinetic patterning* goes a long way toward establishing a credible neurological foundation of how we do what we do because the term is ultimately tethered to evolutionary life and to the manifold and diverse kinetic dynamics that sustain that life in all of its forms. Second, corporeal-kinetic patternings do not reduce evolutionary life — *animate* forms — to motor programs and such, but identify the neurological, or better, neurophysiological, dynamics of corporeal-kinetic intentionalities. They are thus not amenable to reification and in turn to reductionism; as indicated above, a corporeal-kinetic pattern is not a posited structure or conjured entity in the brain or any place else. In this respect, it is quite unlike a *body schema*, a term invented to create a structure to explain a function. Corporeal-kinetic patternings identify the neurology, or again, better, the neurophysiology of coordinative dynamics as they are played out in the lives of animate forms. By recognizing the kinetic dynamics — and correlatively, by not mechanizing life — there is virtually no possibility of reification and, in turn, virtually no possibility of reductionism because no fixed spatial entity is created on which to hang the kinetic dynamics. Moreover there is virtually no possibility of making experiential ascriptions to brains or things in brains because no "thing" exists or is theorized to exist on which to pin verbal predicates, predicates such as "ascertains" (Zeki, 1992, p. 69), "asserts" (Rizzolatti and Gallese, 1997, p. 222), "infers" (Crick and Koch, 1992, p. 153), etc. This is as it should be, and for an even further reason. If we say that the brain or its neurons assert, ascertain, infer, detect, and so on, where do we draw the line? Are the brain or its neurons overjoyed at seeing an old friend? Are they gripped with fear in face of the oncoming car? Do they excuse themselves to go to the toilet? Are they indifferent to whether red wine or white is served with the fish? Experiential ascriptions to brains or to neurons constitute a pernicious linguistic practice that runs hard against the truths of experience. Its reductionistic efforts are, ironically, a form a brain-washing.

3

The above observations on reification and reductionism point us toward the fundamental conceptual deficiency of 'body image' and 'body schema'. Reification concretizes the concepts 'body image' and 'body schema', making each not just a spatial entity, but a spatial entity with no inherent temporal dimensions. Spatialization through reification indeed conveniently evades the temporal, and happily so for reductionists, because the temporal destroys their cultivated ontology of perdurable objects or structures. Temporal dimensions would "kineticize" body image and body schema, forcing recognition of their foundational *impermanence*, and eliminate the possibility of conceiving them as fixed and durable material entities in the brain. As currently conceived, body image and body schema do indeed *pin things down*. They provide a localization of kinetic function; they give 'how we do what we do' a structural home, a place along the cerebral mall to explain intelligent, effective, and efficient movement.[6] They are indeed "embodied" structures, and being "embodied," easily lend themselves to talk of body positions, body sensations, and body behaviors, and in turn, to the essentially static and/or mechanical rather than the animated and dynamic.

Kinetic melodies challenge this spatialization; so also does a coordination dynamics. By their very nature, kinetic melodies and coordination dynamics recognize changing, qualitatively modulated kinetic processes that are played out in ways that defy modular—"a place-for-'everything'-and-'every-thing'-in-its-place"—explanations. Changing, qualitatively modulated kinetic dynamics exceed essentially *spatial*, i.e., localized, explanations, exceed them in the sense of a temporal dynamics. Luria's studies of complex sequential activity, and his emphasis on muscle innervations and denervations in the course of complex sequential activity (Luria, 1973, 1966), attest to these dynamics. Kelso's analyses of coordination dynamics attest to them equally. Complex sequential activity is a spatio-*temporal*-energic phenomenon, whether in the form of articulatory gestures, coherent narratives, calculations of mathematical sums, skilled whole body movement, fluctuating facial expressions, or whatever. Self-organizing kinetic patterns undergirding coordinations are similarly temporal in character, from the macroscopic to the microscopic, that is, from first-person experiences of everyday movement and learning to the

---

6   Thus, with respect to mirror neurons, grasping happens here; holding happens here; and so on.

kinetic dynamics of brain processes and of the neuromuscular system as a whole. What we see in pathologies is in part precisely the loss of a temporal dynamic, a temporal dynamic that exists not in the absence of a spatial kinetic dimension, but a dynamic that is not either reducible to that dimension. What we see in the course of gained proficiencies is the reverse: the acquirement of complex spatio-temporal-energic dynamic patternings, all the way from the mastery of walking and speaking to the mastery of performing surgical techniques and playing the violin.

The fact that self-movement is always co-articulated (see Sheets-Johnstone, 1999a) and is anatomically and physiologically defined in terms of degrees of freedom (Bernstein, 1984) testifies in further ways to the necessity of recognizing a temporal dynamic, of eschewing the practice of creating structures to explain functions, and of creating a proper terminology and arriving at proper conceptualizations of life. We might note in this regard that it is not just articulatory gestures that are co-articulated, but any and all movement of our bodies. Any everyday act such as reaching or grasping is a whole body movement, the coordination of which is differentially played out according to context and the specific bodily posture from which movement originates. Even gymnasts and dancers, for example, never kinetically depart from the exact same place twice, nor perform the exact same sequence of movement twice. Everyday movements such as reaching, grasping, getting into a car, and writing one's name are thus aptly described as variations on a theme, a theme whose major contours describe a kinetic melody or coordination dynamic that is differentially instantiated in the corporeal-kinetic temporal flow of a particular patterning of neuromuscular innervations and denervations, precisely as Luria describes. From both a behavioral and brain perspective, kinetic melodies, coordination dynamics, co-articulations, kinetically-defined degrees of freedom are not written in stone — in the brain or anywhere else — but are differentially played out in and through corporeal-kinetic intentionalities and corporeal-kinetic patternings. They are played out in a dynamic that is through and through temporal in nature.

It bears notice that the term *kinetic melody* may sound frou-frou, unscientific, even "arty" to ears accustomed to the hard, rock-solid entities that populate specified regions of our brains in present-day neurology. But then we must face the fact that what is kinetic is not a hard, rock-solid entity, and in turn face the task of describing what is transitory. When proprioceptive awareness is ecologically defined simply in terms of "a spatial presence and a set of capabilities" (Gallagher and Marcel, 1999, p. 290), for example, the transitory kinetic realities of self-movement are ignored. These realities are something sizably more than an ecological sense of oneself as being in a particular spatial setting, i.e., a sense of one-self as being *in* space and as having certain movement possibilities.[7] The living dynamic reality of movement itself and the actual experience of moving that goes with it, i.e., the lived-through experience of a distinctive kinetic melody or coordination dynamic, is not equivalent to being *in* space and as having certain movement possibilities any more than it is equivalent to being *in* time and as having certain movement possibilities. Proprioceptive awareness is not either simply a matter of *whethers*— "whether I am moving or staying still, whether I am sitting or standing, whether I am reaching or grasping or pointing, whether I am speaking or maintaining silence" (Gallagher and Marcel, 1999, p. 290) and so on—but again, a matter of a particular *dynamics*, a kinetic dynamics that, in virtue of its spatio-temporal-energic kinetic patterning, is distinctive and thereby familiar, precisely as the experience of running, turning, reaching, throw-ing, picking up, putting down, and so on, indicates. In short, proprioception, like kinesthesia, centers on the experience of movement itself. We must therefore indeed heed Aristotle and "see that we under-stand what motion is." From an evolutionary perspective, our challenge could hardly be otherwise. As the categorization 'kingdom Animalia' incontestably indicates, living forms are animate and animated.

4

In conclusion, and to suggest in broad terms possible directions for future research, I would like briefly to adduce two final reasons—one psychoana-lytic, one neuroscientific—in support of my critique of the terms and con-cepts 'body image' and 'body schema' and my recommendation of their

---

7   In a subsequent section of their article, Gallagher and Marcel attempt to provide the "ecological self" with "temporal extension," and thus temporalize its essential spatial character. They state, for example, "But proprioceptive and ecological awareness also must include a sense of self over time, a sense of self as temporally extended" (Gallagher and Marcel, 1999, p. 23). The problem is that they nowhere recognize nor spell out how temporality is inherent in movement, hence inherent in proprioceptive and kinesthetic awareness. Indeed, the problem is indigenous to their point of departure, which upholds the following received wisdom: "Ecological self-awareness is normally considered to be momentary, providing a sense of posture or movement at any particular instant" (*ibid.*). It is equally indigenous to their reliance on an "implicit" sense of time with respect to capabilities and to past learnings (*ibid.*, pp. 23–4). Foundational understandings of self-movement and its kinetic dynamics are obscured in both instances. In fact, they are obscured from the start by a "momentary" conception of proprioceptive awareness, as is evident not only in the above citation, but in the following statement concerning capabilities: "the very doing of an action brings into the momentary proprioceptive awareness of the actor the sense that he knows how to do *x*" (*ibid.*, p. 24). "Momentary" proprioceptive awarenesses are closely connected with sensational conceptions of self-movement discussed earlier in the text of this paper.

replacement by corporeal-kinetic intentionality and corporeal-kinetic patterning.

Conclusions reached by psychiatrist Giovanni Stanghellini in his clinical work with schizophrenics are topical to the critique and to the recommendations. Quotations from his interviews with patients document his twofold diagnostic of schizophrenia and his explanatory thesis of its emergence: a morbid bodily self and a complementary morbid sociality are undergirded by "*the same objectifying attitude*" (Stanghellini, 2003, p. 24]; see also Stanghellini, 2000). More precisely, the anchor post of each component is what Stanghellini terms a "de-animated body," a body that is lived at a distance from itself and that lacks spontaneity, and correlatively, that lives among others in the same distanced and non-spontaneous manner. As Stanghellini writes, "If one feels his self as a de-animated body, then the others' bodies are to him lifeless too. The disintegration of one's own sensory self-awareness implies the impossibility of attunement and without attunement the others are meaningless things — *Körper*" (Stanghelllini, 2003, p. 24). That attunement disintegrates along with "one's own sensory self-awareness" is no wonder since a de-animated body is a de-temporalized one, one in which the flow of life stops dead in its tracks. *Körper* are indeed objects, spatial entities. A living body that is present only as a spatial entity is one incapable of a fluidity of movement and of a shared dynamics. An objective form — a *Körper* — is there, in other words, but the preeminent spark of life — spontaneous animation — is missing. The fundamental deficiency is not a deficiency in body image or body schema, but something far more basic: a sense of aliveness and the spontaneous animation that goes with it.

We see this sense of aliveness and the spontaneous animation that goes with it in non-pathological animate bodies, animate bodies that, from the beginning and across the animal kingdom, are kinetically motivated. In human terms, they are kinetically motivated to suck, to cry, to kick, to grasp, to reach, to smile. The ego is indeed "first and foremost a bodily ego" (Freud, 1955, p. 26), a bodily-*kinetic* ego. It is kinetically motivated not only to suck, to cry, and so on, but to turn toward and to attend — to movement, touch, sound, light, smell, and to others. It is kinetically motivated to develop coordinated kinetic dynamics in relation its surrounding world. In effect, corporeal-kinetic intentionalities and patternings develop on the basis of kinetic motivations into a kinetic repertoire that is at once both personal and social, a repertoire of temporally constituted coordinated patterns of movement and possibilities of movement, and of ever more complex sequential activities.

Kinetic motivations that are fundamental to life find no home in what Stanghellini terms de-animated bodies. From this perspective, schizophrenia might be described as a kinesthetic/kinetic illness, that is, *a corporeal-kinetic illness;*[8] not that something is amiss with Golgi tendon organs, muscle fibers, or the like, but that there is a break in the dynamic flow of aliveness, of one's own aliveness and one's aliveness in concert with others. Objectified bodies — mere spatial presences — are either no longer naturally kinetically motivated or no longer find a natural attunement in whatever kinetic motivations they might have. They may indeed be kinetically motivated in self-damaging ways, as Stanghellini points out.

The neuroscientific research studies of philosopher Dan Lloyd are similarly topical to my critique and recommendations. Lloyd's fine-grained and highly original reanalyses of functional magnetic resonance imaging data recently won the $5,000 award offered by the fMRI Institute in New Hampshire for the most innovative use of its data (see Bower, 2002 for report). What is of moment for us here, among the many significant aspects of Lloyd's re-analyses,[9] is his finding that, in the course of a variety of tasks performed by subjects in experimental situations, brain activity not only consistently changes, but does not come to an end on completion of the task. Brain activity is ongoing and inherently temporal (Lloyd, 2002). Lloyd's re-analyses furthermore document that changes in brain activity are formally distinct: images temporally closer to one another resemble one another, while those farther away do not. At any particular moment, brain activity thus engenders aspects of its past and future activity (*ibid.*). Lloyd ties the temporal dimensions of fMRI recorded brain activity to Husserl's analysis of internal time consciousness, that is, to the foundational *flow* of consciousness and to the temporally constituting nature of consciousness (*ibid.*; see also Lloyd, 2000). His remarkable

8   Subsequent to the writing this paper, I chanced upon discussions of the work of psychiatrist Andras Angyal in Harry Hunt's *On the Nature of Consciousness*. Hunt quotes from one of several of Angyal's papers on "the phenomenology and cognitive bases of somatic hallucinations in schizophrenia" (Hunt 1995, p. 200), and speaks of "Angyal"s model of the kinesthetic bases of somatic hallucinations in schizophrenia" (*ibid.*p. 205).

9   Specific mention should be made of Lloyd's extraordinarily novel and meticulous methodology, which distinguishes itself from the subtractive methodology of fMRI researchers. The latter commonly calculate the average blood-flow in the brains of experimental subjects, then measure brain blood-flow in the subjects during a different activity. The latter measurement is then subtracted from the former, the former being taken as a measurement of brain activity in the subjects during the experimental procedure alone. Lloyd proceeds not by subtraction but by taking the experimental data, i.e., measured brain blood-flow during experimental procedure, as a whole into account. In particular, he considers blood flow changes as they are reflected in all of the digitized dots on an fMRI recording of experimental subjects while they are engaged in the task set them. He then performs a multivariate analysis of all of the thousands of dots generated in each subject's data, specifying volume patternings and relationships.

findings concerning the temporal nature of brain activity clearly document not hypothetical spatial entities or structures in the brain, and not dedicated modules of brain activity, but ever-changing corporeal-kinetic patternings.

Lloyd's remarkable findings furthermore drive home the importance of Teuber's observation, for the temporal has conceptual links to the kinetic. Since the two are conceptually intertwined, it is not surprising that each "requires some different way of looking." Lloyd's different way of looking at already analyzed fMRI data discloses a dimension of brain activity hidden by the ontological commitments, even metaphysical baggage, that present-day neuroscientists typically bring with them. Their entity-oriented commitments precipitate attitudes akin to those of real estate enthusiasts who claim that "location is everything." Hence, in their zeal to pin things down, they typically overlook the fact that, as Aristotle long ago pointed out, "Matter will surely not move itself" (*Metaphysics* 1071b30). Documenting the temporal nature of brain activity and opening us to a proper temporal conception of brain activity, Lloyd's findings affirm that studies of nature cannot rest secure on purely material foundations. The brain's inherent and coherent dynamics document the fact that neither time nor movement can be localized in the brain in the way that specific neurons, lobes, and myriad other brain structures can be; time and movement lack the solidity and permanence of objects and thus cannot be object-ified. Corporeal-kinetic intentionalities and corporeal-kinetic patternings accommodate this fact. They accommodate the moving nature of time and the fleeting nature of movement. In a word, they accommodate the animate.

References

Aristotle *Physics*. In *The Complete Works of Aristotle*, vol. 1, ed. Jonathan Barnes. Princeton: Princeton University Press.

Aristotle *Metaphysics*. In *The Complete Works of Aristotle*, vol. 2, ed. Jonathan Barnes. Princeton: Princeton University Press.

Baron-Cohen, S. 1995. *Mindblindness : An Essay on Autism and Theory of Mind*. Cambridge: MIT Press.

Bernstein, Nicolas. 1984. *Human Motor Actions: Bernstein Reassessed*, ed. H.T.A. Whiting. New York: Elsevier Science Publishing Co.

Bower, Bruce. 2002. "Spreading Consciousness: Awareness Goes Global in the Brain," *Science News* 162/16, pp. 251–2.

Bruner, Jerome. 1990. *Acts of Meaning*. Cambridge, MA: Harvard University Press.

Cole, Jonathan, Shaun Gallagher, and David McNeill. 2002. "Gesture following Deafferentation: A Phenomenologically Informed Experimental Study," *Phenomenology and the Cognitive Sciences* 1, pp. 49–67.

Crick, Francis and Christof Koch. 1992. "The Problem of Consciousness," *Scientific American* 267/3, pp. 153–9.

Freud, Sigmund. 1955. "The Ego and the Id," *Standard Edition XIX*, trans. James Strachey. London: Hogarth Press, pp. 19–27.

Frith, Uta. 1993. "Autism," *Scientific American* 268(6), pp. 108–14.

Gallagher, Shaun. 1986. "Body Image and Body Schema: A Conceptual Clarification", *Journal of Mind and Behavior* 7, pp. 541–54.

Gallagher, Shaun. 1995. "Body schema and Intentionality." In *The Body and the Self*, ed. J.L. Bermúdez, A. Marcel, N. Eilan. Cambridge: Bradford/MIT Press, pp. 225–44.

Gallagher, Shaun. December 2000. "Phenomenological and Experimental Research on Embodied Experience." Paper presented at *Atelier phénomenolgie et cognition, Phénomenologie et Cognition Research Group*, CREA, Paris.

Gallagher, Shaun. 2005. "Dynamic Models of Body Schematic Processes." In *Body Image and Body Schema: Interdisciplinary Perspectives on the Body*, ed. Helena De Preester and Veroniek Knockaert. Amsterdam/Philadelphia: John Benjamins, pp. 233–50.

Gallagher, Shaun and Jonathan Cole. 1995. "Body Image and Body Schema in a Deafferented Subject," *Journal of Mind and Behavior* 16, pp. 369–90.

Gallagher, Shaun and Anthony J. Marcel. 1999. "The Self in Contextualized Action." In *Models of the Self*, ed. Shaun Gallagher and Jonathan Shear. Exeter, UK: Imprint Academic, pp. 273–99.

Gallese, Vittorio. 2000. "The Acting Subject: Towards the Neural Basis of Social Cognition." In *Neural Correlates of Consciousness*, ed. T. Metzinger. Cambridge: MIT Press, pp. 325–33.

Goldberg, E. 1990. "Tribute to A. R. Luria." In *Contemporary Neuropsychology and the Legacy of Luria*, ed. E. Goldberg. Hillsdale, NJ: Lawrence Erlbaum, 1–9.

Hunt, Harry T. 1995. *On the Nature of Consciousness: Cognitive, Phenomenological, and Transpersonal Perspectives*. New Haven: Yale University Press.

Kelso, J.A. Scott. 1995. *Dynamic Patterns*. Cambridge: MIT Press.

Kelso, J.A. Scott, J. P. Scholz, and G. Schöner. 1988. "Dynamics Governs Switching among Patterns of Coordination in Biological Movement," *Physics Letters A* 134 (1), pp. 8–12.

Kelso, J.A. Scott and P.-G. Zanone. 2002. "Coordination Dynamics of Learning and Transfer across Different Effector Systems," *Journal of Experimental Psychology: Human Perception and Performance* 28 (4), pp. 776–97.

Lacan, Jacques. 1977a. "The Mirror Stage as Formative of the Function of the I as Revealed in Psychoanalytic Experience." In *Écrits: A Selection*, trans. Alan Sheridan. New York: W.W. Norton, pp. 2–7.

Lacan, Jacques. 1977b. "Aggressivity in Psychoanalysis." In *Écrits: A Selection*, trans. Alan Sheridan. New York: W. W. Norton, pp. 8–29.

Lecours, André Roch, Jean-Luc Nespoulous, and Pierre Desaulniers. 1986. "Standard Teaching on Apraxia." In *The Biological Foundations of Gestures: Motor and Semiotic Aspects*, ed. Jean-Luc Nespoulous, Paul Perron, André Roch Lecours. Hillsdale, NJ: Lawrence Erlbaum Associates, pp. 231–42.

Liberman, Alvin M. and Ignatius G. Mattingly. 1985. "The Motor Theory of Speech Perception Revised," *Cognition* 21/1, pp. 1–36.

Lloyd, Dan. 2000. "Beyond 'the Fringe': A Cautionary Critique of William James," *Consciousness and Cognition* 9, pp. 629–37.

Lloyd, Dan. 2002. "Functional MRI and the Study of Human Consciousness," *Journal of Cognitive Neuroscience* 14/6, pp. 818–31.

Luria, A.R. 1966. *Human Brain and Psychological Processes*, trans. Basil Haigh. New York: Harper & Row.

Luria, A.R. 1973. *The Working Brain*, trans. Basil Haigh. Harmondsworth, Middlesex, England: Penguin Books.

Melden. A.I. 1966. *Free Action*. New York: Humanities Press, Inc.

Overgaard, Soren. 2003. "The Importance of Bodily Movement to Husserl's Theory of *Fremderfahrung*," *Recherches Husserliennes* 19, pp. 55–65.

Rizzolatti, Giacomo, Luciano Fadiga, Vittorio Gallese, Leonardo Fogassi. 1996. "Premotor Cortex and the Recognition of Motor Actions," *Cognitive Brain Research* 3, pp. 131–41.

Rizzolatti, Giacomo and Vittorio Gallese. 1997. "From Action to Meaning: A Neurophysiological Perspective." In *Les neurosciences et la philosophie de l'action*, ed. Jean-Luc Petit. Paris: Librairie Philosophique, pp. 217–29.

Rochat, Philipe. 2002. "Ego Function and Early Imitation." In *The Imitative Mind*, ed. Andrew N. Meltzoff and Wolfgang Prinz. Cambridge: Cambridge University Press, pp. 85–97.

Schilder, Paul. 1950. *The Image and Appearance of the Human Body*. New York: International Universities Press.

Sheets-Johnstone, Maxine. 1966 [1979/1980]. *The Phenomenology of Dance* Madison, WI: University of Wisconsin Press; 2nd editions: London: Dance Books Ltd.; New York: Arno Press.

Sheets-Johnstone, Maxine. 1990. *The Roots of Thinking*. Philadelphia: Temple University Press.

Sheets-Johnstone, Maxine. 1994. *The Roots of Power: Animate Form and Gendered Bodies*. Chicago: Open Court Publishing.

Sheets-Johnstone, Maxine. 1999a. *The Primacy of Movement*. Amsterdam/ Philadelphia: John Benjamins.

Sheets-Johnstone, Maxine. 1999b. "Emotions and Movement: A Beginning Empirical-Phenomenological Analysis of Their Relationship", *Journal of Consciousness Studies* 6, No. 11, pp. 259–77.

Sheets-Johnstone, Maxine. 2003a. "Kinesthetic Memory", *Theoria et Historia Scientarium International Journal for Interdisciplinary Studies* (Special issue on Phenomenology and Cognitive Science, ed. N. Depraz and S. Gallagher) 7, No. 1, pp. 69–92.

Sheets-Johnstone, Maxine. 2003b. "Further Steps toward a Phenomenological Analysis of Empathy," Conference on Intersubjectivity and Embodiment. Leuven, Belgium.

Sheets-Johnstone, Maxine. 2006. "Essential Clarifications of 'Self-Affection' and Husserl's 'Sphere of Ownness': First Steps toward A Pure Phenomenology of (Human) Nature." *Continental Philosophy Review* 39: 361–91.

Sheets-Johnstone, Maxine. 2008. *The Roots of Morality*. University Park, PA: Pennsylvania State University Press.

Stanghellini, Giovanni. 2000. "Vulnerability to Schizophrenia and Lack of Common Sense." *Schizophrenia Bulletin* 26/4, pp. 775–87.

Stanghellini, Giovanni. 2003. "Schizophrenia and the Sixth Sense." In *The Philosophical Understanding of Schizophrenia*, ed. Man Chung, George Graham, Bill Fulford. Oxford: Oxford University Press.

Stern, Daniel N. 1985. *The Interpersonal World of the Infant*. New York: Basic Books.

Taylor, John G. 2002. "From Matter to Mind," *Journal of Consciousness Studies* 9/4, pp. 3–22.

Teuber, H. L. 1966. "Discussion" of "Cerebral Organization and the Conscious Control of Action", by D.M. MacKay. In *Brain and Conscious Experience*, ed. J.C. Eccles. New York: Springer-Verlag, pp. 442–5.

Trevarthen, Colwyn. 1977. "Descriptive Analyses of Infant Communicative Behaviour." In *Studies in Mother-Infant Interaction*, ed. H.R. Schaffer. London: Academic Press, pp. 227–70.

Trevarthen, Colwyn. 1979. "Communication and Cooperation in Early Infancy: A Description of Primary Intersubjectivity." In *Before Speech*, ed. Margaret Bullowa. Cambridge: Cambridge University Press, pp. 321–47.

Zanone, P.G. and J.A.S. Kelso. 1992. "Evolution of Behavioral Attractors with Learning: Nonequilibrium Phase Transitions", *Journal of Experimental Psychology: Human Perception and Performance* 18 (2), pp. 403–20.

Zeki, Semir. 1992. "The Visual Image in Mind and Brain", *Scientific American* 267/3, pp. 69–76.

Chapter XIV

The Kinetic Basis of the Biological Disposition to Sense-Making

Further Steps Toward an Evolutionary Semantics

1

As documented from a different perspective in an earlier article on evolutionary semantics, living creatures are animate forms geared in bodily meaningful ways to the world about them. They are geared according to the body they are. In the most basic sense, this is what natural selection is all about: those creatures who are most congenially attuned to the particular world in which they find themselves—those who are able actively to make sense of that world in continuously life-enhancing ways—are the creatures who survive and reproduce. But animate forms may also be semantically exploratory and creative; that is, they may create meanings as well as find them ready-made in an already existing world. They may thus affect the course of their evolution by new behaviors that maximize survival and reproductive capacities. Thus, to account for the origins of sense-making, one must account for "signs of meaning in the universe"— to use biologist Jesper Hoffmeyer's apt phrase (Hoffmeyer, 1996)— not only as those meanings are found embedded in myriad ways in the world, but as those meanings are newly minted by animate forms themselves in the course of their evolution. In a word, one must account for sense-making in a double sense.

Within the kingdom Animalia, many animate organisms make sense of other creatures, at minimum those that are edible and those that are harmful. In some instances, they make sense of their own bodies prior to and/or coincident with these sense-makings (Sheets-Johnstone, 1999a). In and through such sense-makings, meanings are constituted. An appreciation of the ways in which they are constituted can lead to understandings of how sense-making itself has evolved in the course of evolution and of the diverse ways in which it is fundamental to life. The constitution of meaning is thus of central importance. One aspect of its importance—the aspect on which I shall focus—is capsulated in primatologist Thelma Rowell's statement that "Once an intention movement has acquired meaning . . . *and this is a matter of the evolution of the receiver rather than the animal making the movements*, it may presumably come under selection pressure as a signal" (Rowell, 1972, p. 94; italics added). The question of how a displayed-to animal comes to validate the movements or gestures of another as meaningful, how it acquiesces to meaning and thus officially instantiates a particular meaning in the repertoire of the species, is a constitutional question fundamental to the origin of sense-making. It is indeed a basic question within the larger framework of an evolutionary semantics (Sheets- Johnstone, 1990, 1999a,b). As formatively realized over the course of evolution, new interanimate meanings have been realized on the basis of new corporeal acts, and as such, require understandings of the living organisms that define natural history, in particular, understandings of the diverse ways in which they both move about in and experience the world. A particularly graphic example of a newly-minted meaning, though one that has not entered into the repertoire of the species, comes from a recent book titled *Primate Cognition*:

> [T]he initiation of play often takes place in chimpanzees by one juvenile raising its arm above its head and then descending on another, play-hitting in the process. This then becomes ritualized ontogenetically into an 'arm-raise' gesture in which the initiator simply raises its arm and, rather than actually following through with the hitting, stays back and waits for the other to initiate the play, monitoring its response all the while ... If the desired response is not forthcoming, sometimes the gesture will be repeated, but quite often another gesture will be used. In other situations a juvenile was observed to actually alternate its gaze between the recipient of the gestural signal and one of its own body parts; for example, one individual learned to initiate play by presenting a limp leg to another individual as it passed by (an invitation to grab it and so initiate a game of chase), looking back and forth between the recipient and its leg in the process" (Tomasello and Call, 1997, p. 244).

How, we may ask, does any so-designated "recipient" know that the gesturing individual wants to initiate a game of chase? A quite sophisticated meaning is intended, after all, by the combined gesture and look. Two captioned pictorial examples provide additional perspectives on the question and underscore in further ways the complexities and challenges of elucidating sense-making, the gestures in these instances being gestures in the species' repertoires. The first instance is striking in that we might think of the gesture as a uniquely human one. The caption reads—"Gorilla using hand clapping as auditory attention-getting gesture" (*ibid.*, p. 248). That hand-clapping has human affinities is of considerable significance for an evolutionary semantics, and particularly from the viewpoint of origins. To clap one's hands to get attention is to have a sense of oneself as a sound-maker, hence to have not only a sense of oneself as an individual but a sense of oneself as an agent within a social group or communal setting, someone who can make things happen, and happen precisely by way of movement, exactly as a human does when he or she claps his or her hands to get people's attention at a gathering. Clearly, interanimate meanings are tied to movement possibilities and movement possibilities for any particular individual are tied to its being the body it is. In broader terms, movement possibilities are the ground on which a repertoire of 'I cans' is generated, 'I cans' that define not only individual but species-specific and species-overlapping repertoires.

The second pictorial example includes two pictures and is tantalizingly under-explained. The pictures show two hamadryas baboons and the caption simply reads: "The young adult male gives his one-year-old female a gestural invitation to climb on his back; he then carries her across a difficult passage in the sleeping-cliff" (Kummer, 1968, p. 302). However deficient its description, the gestural invitation testifies to at least three distinct awarenesses on the part of both male and female baboon: an awareness that the expanse or jaggedness of the cliff is too difficult for the young female to manage; an awareness that the male can cross the passage himself; an awareness that the male can transport the female on his back across the passage. Because the male's backward-turning of his head is not described, one wonders: does he jerk his head slightly toward his back, pointing as it were with his head — in the same way that a human might when he or she specifies "over there" with a head gesture? Does he look directly at the female at the same time that he gestures with his head? If so, there is a basic similarity between the baboon's gesture and look and the chimpanzee's gesture and look, the difference being that the baboon looks and gestures simultaneously and the chimpanzee alternates his gaze between his limp leg and the passing individual with whom he wants to play.

An important aspect of gesturing — of *kinetically instantiating intercorporeal meanings* — warrants mention in this context. Primatologist Emil Menzel (1973; see also Lieberman, 1983) observed that chimpanzees do not point dexically but use their whole bodies in a deictic manner as when, by bodily orientation, they point in the direction they will go and want others to go.[1] Looking back and forth between one's limp leg and a

---

1   "[O]ne good reason that chimpanzees very seldom point manually is that they do not have to; rising to a quadrupedal position, glancing at a follower, and orienting 'out there' conveys all the directional information one could ask for" (Menzel, 1973, p. 218).

passing individual does exactly this: the back and forth look is a way of pointing with one's body. In effect, what a human finger does and does effectively is what other parts of the body or the body as a whole can do and do effectively. Moreover there is an iconic aspect to what we may call corporeal pointing with one's body, just as there is an iconic aspect to dexical pointing. Primate psychologists Michael Tomasello and Josep Call virtually dismiss the possibility of nonhuman iconic relationships. With respect to a report that a bonobo male's gestures to a female are iconically-based sexual invitations, they state that "the 'iconic' relation-ship of the gestures to the desired action may be from the human point of view only, as for the bonobo they may just signal the desired action in the same way as other ritualized signals, that is, based on the mutual shaping of behavior in previous interactive sequences" (Tomasello and Call, 1997, p. 247). Their explanation clearly sidesteps the question of how the ges-tures originated, that is, how the recipient comes to authenticate the mean-ing of the gestures, literally solidifying the gesturing individual's intended meaning. Moreover to suggest ritualization rather than iconicity and in turn clothe the answer in talk of "mutual shaping" and "previous interactive sequences" merely poses the question anew. Such talk, while ostensibly taking one step forward, in truth takes two steps back.

In all three examples, there is no doubt but that the gesturing individual intends a meaning, but why should hand-clapping make others turn in the direction of the clapper?; why should a backward turn of the head and backward glance toward another individual constitute for that individual an invitation to climb on the other's back?; why should the offering of a limp leg and a direct gaze at a passing individual constitute for that indi-vidual an invitation to play chase? To describe interanimate meaning con-sistently in terms of what is commonly termed 'the displaying' rather than 'the displayed-to' individual, and in fact to put interanimate meaning in the perspective of movement possibilities and 'I cans', appears to preclude any answers by inverting the question, focusing on the "sender" instead of the "recipient." Indeed, rather than shedding light on how one individual knows what another intends and in turn how it comes to respond in a har-monious way,[2] the examples seem to specify how one individual might go

---

2 The term 'harmonious' should not be taken as an always pacific mode of relating to another. After all, anger and fear, jealousy and resentment, to name perhaps the most outstanding non-pacific emotions, are also ways of relating to another. 'Harmonious' thus refers to the fullest possible spectrum of affective-cognitive understandings of another, and includes, for example, understandings of another's motivations and intent to insult (prompting anger), or to menace (prompting fear), or to possess (prompting jealousy) or to flaunt (prompting resentment). In other words, anger, fear, jealousy, resentment, and other such emotions are the motivating force for a *response* to an analogically-based understanding: they move an individual to move.

about motivating or encouraging another individual to do something. To
see the examples in this inverted way, however, misses the point. What the
examples show is not just that movement is used by an individual as an
attractor in an attention-getting sense; they show that *movement is known to
be a social attractor, a semantically rich social attractor, and that being so, it will
generate a response*.[3] From the viewpoint of certifying meaning, then, the
question is not *why*, but *how*: how is it that the individual to whom the gestures and looks or gestures and sounds are addressed grasps the meaning?

The answer to the question—in essence, the answer to the question of
interanimate sense-making—is rooted in *animate* understandings, specifically, in deepened *animate* understandings of what primatologist Stuart
Altmann terms 'comsigns' (Altmann, 1967). Acknowledgement of the
kinetic underpinnings of comsigns—acknowledgement of species-specific
kinetic capacities, dispositions, and possibilities—is at the core of understanding interanimate sense-making. The kinetic underpinnings are structured in species-specific kinetic/tactile-kinesthetic invariants. Short of
species-specific kinetic/tactile-kinesthetic invariants,[4] there would
be—and could be—no species-specific interanimate communication. The
claim is validated not only by the hand-clapping gorilla, the gesturing and
visually-oriented male hamadryas baboon, and the gesturing and visually-oriented chimpanzee. All forms of intended kinetically enacted
interanimate meanings are contingent on a common body of experience,
hence on species-specific kinetic capacities, dispositions, and possibilities
and their corresponding tactile-kinesthetic invariants. A honey bee's
dance, a human's speech, a wolf's submissive signalling behavior, and so
on, would be meaningless in the absence of tactile-kinesthetic invariants.
They would be meaningless because short of these invariants, there would
be no common point of departure, no common body of reference, on the
basis of which the individual to whom the intended semantically-laden
kinetics was addressed could make sense.[5] This is precisely the
phenomenological import of Altmann's concept of *comsigns* (*ibid.*). What
the term *comsign* pinpoints is the fact that most primate signals are part of
the repertoire of *all* members of the species or particular group in question,

3   The hand-clapping example shows further that making sounds by way of movement can
     enhance the semantic power of movement, even to the point of specifying what is or was
     moving, precisely as *hands* clapping.
4   For a detailed treatment of tactile-kinesthetic invariants, see Sheets-Johnstone, 1990, ch. 15.
5   Kinetic/tactile-kinesthetic invariants similarly anchor Bertenthal and Pinto's basic notion of
     complementary processes undergirding the perception and production of human movement
     (Bertenthal and Pinto 1993), and Liberman and Mattingly's earlier idea that complementary
     processes anchor speech perception and speech production (Liberman and Mattingly, 1985).

at the very least for some period in each animal's life.[6] What is true of primates is equally true of wolves, ravens, bees, humans, and other social animals. Kinetic/tactile-kinesthetic invariants anchor *interchangeability*:[7] they anchor the possibility of a perceiving animal being the acting animal and the acting animal being the perceiving animal; they anchor the possibility of comsigns — common signs. In the most fundamental sense, one body understands another body to the degree it not only *resembles* that body, but moves and gestures or has the possibility of moving and gesturing in ways similar to the ways in which that body moves and gestures, and in moving and gesturing or in having the possibility of moving and gesturing in ways similar to the ways in which that body moves and gestures, has perceptual experiences similar to that body, perceptual experiences that consistently combine certain tactile-kinesthetic/affective feelings with certain contextually situated kinetic-visual (or kinetic-auditory as in human speech or kinetic-tactile as in the honey bee dance) awarenesses.[8] Meaning is thus in the most fundamental sense dynamically structured; it is articulated along the lines of moving bodies.[9]

When we take seriously the question of how new interanimate meanings are minted, in particular, how it is that one individual knows what another individual means when the latter individual does something the

---

6   Altmann points out that some comsigns (which he conceives as *behaviors* rather than as dynamic patterns of movement) are peculiar to the males or the females of a species and mentions among other examples the roar of an adult male gorilla and "intromission", stating that "intromission (but not mounting) by females will be impossible in all [primate] species" (Altmann, 1967, p. 336).

7   See linguist Charles Hockett's identification of interchangeability as a "design feature" of human language in his article "The Origin of Speech" (Hockett, 1960).

8   For a comparative analysis of primordial/present-day human language and the Tanzsprache (the honeybee dance), see Sheets-Johnstone, 1990.

9   That primordial language was structured analogically along the lines of the body should give pause for thought. Received wisdom urges us to think that language is made up of vocal sounds that are arbitrarily formed and arbitrarily linked to objects in the world, and that naming things and naming them by way of arbitrary sounds is the crowning mark of human achievement (see, for example, Hockett, 1960 and his specification "duality of patterning" a preeminent "design feature" of human language). However brief, the foregoing evolutionary perspective — from precambrian semiosis to morphological and kinetic corporeal representation — challenges the wisdom of that view. More than that, it challenges the empirical evidence — or in truth, lack of evidence — for that view. Indeed, taking a cue from biologists Stephen Jay Gould and Richard Lewontin's critique of adaptationist stories with its cautionary emphasis against taking present-day utility of a trait or behavior as reason for its origin (Gould and Lewontin 1979), we may similarly issue a cautionary note against taking the arbitrary counters of present-day human languages as the defining feature present at the origin of human language. Linguist Mary LeCron Foster's comprehensive studies of languages worldwide point us in an exactly opposite direction and present us with a formidable array of evidence supporting the conclusion that the symbolic structure of primordial language was through and through analogical; particular meanings followed along the lines of the bodily dynamics constituted by particular articulations of the supralaryngeal tract. See Foster 1978, 1990, 1992, 1996.

former individual has not seen done before or heard before, we come to realize the importance of a common body of movement, a species-specific (and possibly species-overlapping) kinetic repertoire. But we realize something further too, namely, that it is necessarily the perceiving rather than acting individual who solidifies meaning. An individual can, after all, move or gesticulate endlessly, and make all kinds of sounds or all kinds of scribbles in the process, but unless and until the individual on the perceiving end responds, and responds in a way coincident with the intended meaning of the movements or gestures, the intended meaning goes unrecognized. The earlier-cited passage from Rowell makes this very point: unless and until the receiver certifies meaning, the movement will not enter the communicative repertoire of the species or group in question. In Altmann's terms, the movement will not become a comsign. The question of how a displayed-to animal comes to validate the movement of another as meaningful is thus of critical importance. Darwin did not consider the question in his rich and pioneering work, *The Expression of the Emotions in Man and Animals*, but he presented three principles[10] in explanation of how "movement or changes in any part of the body — as the *wagging* of a dog's tail, the *drawing back* of a horse's ears, the *shrugging* of a man's shoulders ... may all equally well serve for expression" (Darwin, 1965, p. 28; italics added). In his clear recognition of the *kinetics* of emotional expression, Darwin implicitly affirms the species-specific kinetic foundation of comsigns.

We might note that in his discussion of ritualization, i.e., how "certain movement patterns lose, in the course of phylogeny, their original specific function and become purely 'symbolic' ceremonies" (Lorenz, 1966, pp. 54–5), ethologist Konrad Lorenz speaks of the "reactor", the one to whom a gesture or movement pattern is addressed, as having "an innate understanding" of the gesture or pattern (*ibid.*, p. 63). He later specifies that "The direct cause of changes in behavior [that is, the direct cause of ritualization] "is to be sought in the selection pressure exerted by the limitations of the 'receiving set' which must respond correctly and selectively to the signal emanating from the 'sender,' if the system of communication is to function properly" (*ibid.*, p. 73). Again, the individual on the receiving end is highlighted, but without specification as to *how* the "'receiving set'" comes to "respond correctly." Yet on what could the understanding of a "'receiving set'" rest if not on species-specific kinetic/tactile-kinesthetic

---

10   The first principle is termed "the principle of serviceable associated Habits"; the second, "the principle of Antithesis"; the third, "the principle of actions due to the constitution of the Nervous System" (Darwin, 1965, pp. 28–9). All three principles are spelled out in terms of movement.

bodies and invariants? In other words, on what could a receiver's correct and selective response rest if not on species-specific movement with its common kinetic/kinesthetic dynamics, and hence its foundational possibility of "sender" and "receiver" interchangeability? In short, Lorenz's observations coincide with Rowell's and support the same explanation of how interanimate meanings are forged, namely, through species-specific kinetic/tactile-kinesthetic invariants that underpin the invention of comsigns and the interchangeability of "sender" and "receiver."

Species-specific tactile-kinesthetic invariants go a long way toward answering the question of how interanimate meanings are constituted precisely because they signify a body of common experiences: they are the product of a common body and a common body of movement. In other words, from the viewpoint of an evolutionary semantics, animate bodies move in ways congenial to the bodies they are, and it is on the basis of this kinetic congeniality that they constitute interanimate meanings. The study of the origin of sense-making from an evolutionary perspective thus necessarily involves the study of organic form, for organic forms are sources of meaning. Indeed, a study of the origin of sense-makings should eventuate in a descriptive account of how it is that organisms first came to read the environment in meaningful ways and how they first came to read each other in meaningful ways. The verb "read" is used in only a partially metaphoric sense. The etymology of *read* includes both the sense "to discern" and the sense "to discover the meaning or significance [of something]."[11]

2

Given this evolutionary background of sense-making, the question is how interanimate meanings—specifically, *new* interanimate meanings—pertain to human language, and even more specifically, how they pertain to understandings of what Doug Whalen, Director of Haskins Laboratories at Yale University, described as "[o]ne of the most compelling results we have had at this laboratory", namely, "the discovery that phonemic awareness (the degree to which children can make speech sounds consciously

---

11 Surface recognition sensitivity and morphological corporeal representation are semiotic markers in this respect. They are both ways of reading, the former a matter of reading the world, including the world of others, by touch, the latter a matter of reading the world of others by vision. Surface recognition sensitivity is a primary mode of recognition for soft-bodied invertebrates such as annelids and molluscs, for example, and for human infants as well insofar as their first explorations of the world are through touch and movement. Similarly, the broad range of morphological corporeal representation across the animal kingdom is exemplified by the periodic skin swellings of nonhuman female primates, for example, and by the shell-less gastropod snail *Tethys*, whose sizeable cephalic lobes dramatically differentiate its head end from the rest of its body (Portmann, 1967, pp. 102–3).

available) is the best single predictor of reading success" (pers. comm.). In what follows, I will attempt to answer the question.

To learn to read is to master new interanimate meanings. If we take a cue from the preceding evolutionary semantics to explain how phonemic awareness is the best single predictor of reading success, we see that the key to the new meanings lies in movement: that is, articulatory gestures are their foundation. The gestures are sedimented in a bodily felt sense; that is, they are already experienced elements of sound-making generally, and of speaking in particular, many years before a child learns to read. In phenomenological terms, sound-making generally and speech sounds in particular are already part of a child's "I cans". To elucidate their sedimented nature requires taking infancy and early childhood seriously, duly accrediting early and ongoing experiences of oneself as a sound-maker, and, in effect, taking sound-making experience seriously. It furthermore requires understanding how language — any language — is structured in the bisociation of a sense modality with the common sensible that is movement. Let me briefly detail both necessities a bit further in the context of learning to read.

Making speech sounds "consciously available" already points us in the direction of taking experience seriously, for making speech sounds "consciously available" means *experiencing* articulatory gestures. Merely making sound "consciously available" means experiencing oneself as a sound-maker, and clearly, infants experience themselves as sound-makers. Thus, to begin with, experience cannot be trivialized or bypassed. It cannot be left out of the equation precisely because it structures the equation, structures it fundamentally and unequivocally. Infants are conscious of their own labial/lingual/pharyngeal movements, just as they are conscious of their own leg, arm, head, and torso movements. They experience their own bodies. Their thinking is tied to these experiences, which are essentially kinetic experiences. Indeed, from the viewpoint of an infant, i.e., from a non-adultist perspective, sound-making is not pre-linguistic. On the contrary, language is *post-kinetic*. In effect, if phonemic awareness is the best single predictor of reading success, then sound-making experiences, experiences that begin in infancy with babbling, lip-smacking, cooing, gurgling, and all other labial/lingual/pharyngeal movements, are foundational to reading. They are its experiential backbone. Sound-making and the development of articulatory gestures anchor reading by giving an experiential bodily resonance to an arbitrarily structured visual world, grounding that arbitrarily structured world in kinetic experience.

Lest one think that infants, precisely because they lack language, are experientially deficient (e.g., Dennett, 1983, p. 384) and know not what they do, one has only to update one's acquaintance with ontogenetical research over the past 30 to 35 years, or observe and interact with infants oneself. As psychiatrist Daniel Stern indicates through his criteria of affect attunement (Stern, 1985), and as psychologists Andrew Meltzoff and M. Keith Moore show in their studies of neonates' ability to imitate adult mouth gestures (Meltzoff and Moore, 1977, 1983), human infants are sense-making individuals. In both attunement and imitation, they ratify the meanings of adults, showing that they understand adult movements and gestures. Indeed, movement is their matchpoint. Their sense-making is based on their native disposition to turn toward movement in the double sense of being attentive to movement and being kinetically responsive to movement — in dynamic systems language, to turn toward movement as an *attractor* in the same double sense.

Learning to read has similar kinetic experiential underpinnings. It is anchored in experiences of movement, specifically in speech-making movements whose intricacy and complexity are defined by co-articulations. The difference between "br" and "be", for example, is a matter of co-articulation before it is a matter of written word recognition as in "branch" and "between". A child learning to read reawakens these co-articulations, animating otherwise static, separately drawn linear figures and endowing them with meaning. Kinetic dynamics experienced prior to learning to read bridge the passage from the aural to the visual. In effect, it is not just experience of the moment that must be taken into account in understanding how a child best learns to read, but experience in a developmental and ongoing sense. Indeed, just as, in continuation of its experiences in the womb, an infant learns its body and learns to move itself, building a kinetic repertoire in the process, so, in continuation of its experiences in a spoken linguistic world, a child learns to read.

To answer the question of *how* movement structures the learning of any language — whatever its form — requires insight into how the honey bee dance is a tactile-kinetic phenomenon, how a gorilla's or human's hand-clapping is an aural-kinetic phenomenon, how a baboon's invitational movements are a visual-kinetic phenomenon, how human speech is an aural-kinetic phenomenon, how reading human languages is a visual-kinetic phenomenon, and so on. Movement is a common sensible, precisely as Aristotle long ago observed. It undergirds the tactile, visual, and aural modalities of interanimate sense-making, and, in effect, is the *sine qua non* of the interanimate communicatory powers of those modalities. In short, the bisociation of movement with a sense modality is the foundation of interanimate communication. Moreover the *sensu communis* that is movement is a dynamic phenomenon that can be replicated across sense modalities. A particularly clear instance of this possibility is apparent in affect attunement as described by psychiatrist Daniel Stern. Infant and mother alike experience the same spatio-temporal-energic dynamic, but in a different sensory modality, the mother having sensorily transduced from the kinesthetic to the visual or from the kinesthetic to the auditory in her response to the infant. Something similar happens in learning to read, even if the passage from one sensory modality to the other is confined to the experience of a single person. Just as what is made "consciously available" in learning to read are the sedimented articulatory gestures of speech, so the kinetic dynamics of an aural world animate the visual world of the text; that is, the kinetic dynamics of speech animate in analogously dynamic ways the linear figures the child sees on the pages of a book. In effect, as a child learns to read, the visual forms it sees awaken a lingual kinetic dynamics, the kinetic dynamics of the sound-making that is speech. In the process, otherwise strange and alien visual shapes that have been artificially matched to living bodily realities—to the fluencies of a spoken world—become meaningful. Learning to read is from this experiential perspective a process of bringing the unknown into the world of the known by way of movement.

The common sensible that is movement clearly makes common conceptions of translation across sense modalities unnecessary. That is, in reading, as in attunement, imitation, and speech, interanimate meanings are precisely *not* translated by some algorithmic machinations or some hypothesized brain entity or module. As noted earlier, interanimate meanings are dynamically replicable across different sense modalities. When experienced dynamically as the interanimate phenomena they are, i.e., kinetically and kinesthetically, and in turn conceived in terms of a movement dynamics, one finds no foreign language relationship to obtain among the senses.[12] In each instance, interanimate meaning is dynamically transduced in and through movement. This very dynamic obtains in learning to read: arbitrary visual figures call up articulatory gestures, and in the process, instantiate words.

By way of conclusion, I would like to note that when a concern with behavior eclipses movement and in turn the experiential dynamics of movement, it bypasses the very phenomenon that is of moment. Behavior approximates neither to the spatio-temporal-energic dynamic that constitutes movement nor to the particular unfolding spatio-temporal-energic phenomenon that movement constitutes and that we experience. Ironi-

---

12   Berkeley (1929) wrote of the incommensurate difference between the visual and tactile in a highly object-tethered sense; that is, he did not consider movement and its kinetic dynamics as a common sensible, nor did he consider self-movement.

cally, a textbook titled *The Scientific Basis of Movement* effectively if inadvertently calls attention to the complex spatio-temporal-energic dynamics that constitutes the experience of movement. In a chapter on proprioceptors, the authors write, "The voluntary contribution to movement is almost entirely limited to initiation, regulation of speed, force, range, and direction, and termination of the movement" (Gowitzke and Milner, 1988, p. 193). While the authors are patently and understandably concerned with physiology, not with experience, their stark statement about the seemingly impoverished constituents of voluntary movement highlights in the most striking way the complex spatio-temporal-energic dynamics that constitutes movement and that movement constitutes. Any time we care to notice movement, there it is, its dynamics — its speed, force, range, and direction, and its initiation and termination — in full evidence and entirely under our control. From this vantage point, it is no wonder that movement is our original and abiding matchpoint with the world, as it is the matchpoint of all animate forms that move themselves. It is the basis of our concept of space, time, and force, and is the primary mode of sense-making, basic even to the world of written language.

References

Altmann, Stuart A. 1967. "The Structure of Primate Social Communication." In *Social Communication among Primates*, ed. Stuart A. Altmann. Chicago: University of Chicago Press, pp. 325–62.

Berkeley, Bishop George. 1929 [1709]. *Essay Toward a New Theory of Vision*. In *Berkeley Selections*, ed. Mary W. Calkins. New York: Charles Scribner's Sons.

Bertenthal, Bennett I. and Jeanine Pinto. 1993. "Complementary Processes in the Perception and Production of Human Movements." In *A Dynamic Systems Approach to Development: Applications*, ed. Linda B. Smith and Esther Thelen. Cambridge, MA: Bradford books/MIT Press, pp. 209–39.

Darwin, Charles. 1965 [1872]. *The Expression of the Emotions in Man and Animals*. Chicago: University of Chicago Press.

Dennett, Daniel. 1983. "Intentional Systems in Cognitive Ethology: The 'Panglossian' Paradigm Defended." *The Behavioral and Brain Sciences* 6: 343–90.

Foster, Mary LeCron. 1978. "The Symbolic Structure of Primordial Language." In *Human Evolution: Biosocial Perspectives*, ed. Sherwood L. Washburn and Elizabeth R. McCown. Menlo Park, CA: Benjamin/Cummings, pp. 77–121.

Foster, Mary LeCron. 1990. "Symbolic Origins and Transitions in the Palaeolithic." In *The Emergence of Modern Humans: An Archaeological Perspective*, ed. Paul Mellars. Edinburgh: Edinburgh University Press, pp. 517–29.

Foster, Mary LeCron. 1992. "Body Process in the Evolution of Language." In *Giving the Body Its Due*, ed. Maxine Sheets-Johnstone. Albany, NY: State University of New York Press, pp. 208–30.

Foster, Mary LeCron. 1996. "Reconstruction of the Evolution of Human Spoken Language." In *Handbook of Symbolic Evolution*, ed. Andrew Lock and Charles Peters. Oxford: Oxford University Press, pp. 747–72.

Gould, Stephen Jay and Richard Lewontin. 1979. "The Spandrels of San Marco and the Panglossian Paradigm: A Critique of the Adaptationist Programme." *Proceedings of the Royal Society of London*, Series B, Biological Science 205: 581–98.

Gowitzke, B. A. and M. Milner. 1988. *Scientific Bases of Human Movement*, 3rd ed. Baltimore: Williams and Wilkins.

Hockett, Charles. 1960. "The Origin of Speech." *Scientific American* 203: 89–96.

Hoffmeyer, Jesper. 1996. *Signs of Meaning in the Universe*, trans. Barbara J. Haveland. Bloomington: Indiana University Press.

Kummer, Hans. 1968. "Two Variations in the Social Organization of Baboons." In *Primates: Studies in Adaptation and Variability*, ed. Phyllis C. Jay. New York: Holt, Rinehart and Winston, pp. 293–312.

Liberman, Alvin and Ignatius G. Mattingly. 1985. "The Motor Theory of Speech Perception Revised." *Cognition* 21/1: 1–36.

Lieberman, Philip. 1983. "On the Nature and Evolution of the Biological Bases of Language." In *Glossogenetics*, ed. E. de Grolier. New York: Harwood, pp. 91–114.

Lorenz, Konrad. 1966. *On Aggression*, trans. Marjorie Kerr Wilson. New York: Bantam Books.

Meltzoff, Andrew N. and M. Keith Moore. 1977. "Imitation of Facial and Manual Gestures by Human Neonates." *Science* 198: 75–8.

Meltzoff, Andrew N. and M. Keith Moore. 1983. "Newborn Infants Imitate Adult Facial Gestures." *Child Development* 54: 702–9.

Menzel, Emil W. 1973. "Leadership and Communication in Young Chimpanzees." In *Precultural Primate Behavior*, ed. Emil W. Menzel. Basel: Karger, pp. 192–225.

Portmann, Adolph. 1967. *Animal Forms and Patterns*, trans. Hella Czech. New York: Schocken Books.

Rowell, Thelma. 1972. *The Social Behaviour of Monkeys*. Harmondsworth, Middlesex, England: Penguin Books.

Sheets-Johnstone, Maxine. 1990. *The Roots of Thinking*. Philadelphia: Temple University Press.

Sheets-Johnstone, Maxine. 1999a. *The Primacy of Movement*. Amsterdam/ Philadelphia: John Benjamins Publishing.

Sheets-Johnstone, Maxine. 1999b. "Sensory-Kinetic Understandings of Language: An Inquiry into Origins." *Evolution of Communication* 3/2: 149–83.

Stern, Daniel N. 1985. *The Interpersonal World of the Infant*. New York: Basic Books.

Tomasello, Michael and Josep Call. 1997. *Primate Cognition*. New York: Oxford University Press.

Chapter XV

On the Challenge of Languaging Experience

1. Introduction

Everyday language is clumsy and inadequate when it comes to dynamics. It essentially names things and tags a verb to the name: the waves are rolling; the wind is blowing; the baby is crying; the mailman is coming. Its concern is with *objects* and with what objects *do*, not with dynamics. Even when an adverb is added—the wind is blowing hard, the baby is crying loudly—dynamics are hardly captured. Two liabilities warrant attention in this context, each of them tied to the idea of language as a synchronic ready-made, and each testifying to the challenge of languaging experience.

In a broad sense the first liability centers on the sensuous. Bodily feelings are not easily or readily describable, especially when it comes to affectivity and movement. Neither can be adequately or properly described in static terms, which may indeed be why affectivity is commonly thought to be the province of poets and movement the province of the merely practical and thus rightly specified in purely objective terms. The idea that language names things and that its function is to name things gives precedence to stable items in the world, not to dynamic events experienced in a directly felt sense by sentient living bodies. Given this idea, language rightly preserves its function by adhering to things that are reified or reifiable and that consequently stay in place, and that moreover continue to stay in place or remain the integral 'things' they are even as they move, as waves rolling or wind blowing. In truth, what is being aimed at in such instances is a propositional statement about an object, not a descriptive rendering of the dynamic phenomenon itself. Language as a synchronic ready-made clearly falters in face of the latter task. It cannot give a name to something dynamic and be done with it in the sense of having done justice to the phenomenon, much less to one's knowledge of the phenomenon. The same is all the more true at a personal level, hence a second liability is evident. What is experientially felt both in an affective sense and in a kinesthetic sense clearly poses a challenge to language not only because such experiences are dynamic, but because language is not experience in the first place. Indeed, we experience the world and ourselves in wordless ways before we come to language our experience, whether for own benefit or communicatively for others.

Infant psychiatrist and clinical psychologist Daniel Stern gives a sterling description of these wordless ways of experience in his qualitatively rich description of an infant's "hunger storm" (Stern 1990). As the descriptive label indicates, 'hunger storms' go beyond everyday language. Had Stern written simply on the basis of his observations, "The infant is hungry", or "The infant is saying 'I'm hungry'", he would indeed have fallen radically short of the experiential mark. To describe 'hunger storms' from the inside requires particular and fine-tuned attention to the affective and movement dynamics of infants and to their audible cry patterns, and to one's own felt dynamic experiences of hunger as well; that is, it requires both meticulous observations of infants in the throes of their pangs of hunger and phenomenologically-informed observations of oneself in the felt dynamic throes of hunger. What is remarkable is that Stern not only offers a metaphoric rendering of the dynamics of hunger, but proceeds to anchor the metaphors in concrete bodily feelings of an infant he calls "Joey." For example, at one point in his metaphoric rendering of the dynamics, he says, "The wind and its sound have separated. Each chases after its lost partner in fits and starts" (ibid., p. 31). He ties the separation and chasing not only to Joey's discoordination between breathing and crying but to Joey's total bodily distress. He notes that "Joey's sputtering sounds and jerky motions also make up this discoordinated phase of his distress" (ibid., p. 33). He points out that Joey's "arm and leg movements are not synchronized either with each other or with his crying and breathing", and that, "For Joey ... [there is] a profound disruption of ease, a diffuse feeling with no focus" (ibid.).

Clearly, Joey's experiences are real, and Stern, by capturing their dynamics, makes them real for us. More broadly, by bringing insides to life, Stern gives us an excellent point of departure for questioning received ideas about language and for reflecting on experience itself and its relation to everyday language, that is, for examining a range of human experiences to demonstrate the oftentimes ineffable, oftentimes overlooked centrality of our experiences of insides and the challenge of finding words that do justice to them.

The idea that there are no concepts outside language strikingly illustrates a basic waywardness in received wisdom about language. The commonly used metaphor of our being on a raft, stuck with the concepts we have, not only implicitly denies the possibility of inventing anew, or if inventing anew, denies anything conceptual in the new offering, but implicitly passes over the advent and progressive development of language as both an evolutionary and ontogenetic phenomenon. The idea and its metaphoric illustration basically reject both histories and are thus specieist on the one hand, and adultist on the other. Moreover, in the first instance, not only can they not account for the very invention of a verbal language since the very invention of a verbal language requires first of all a concept of oneself as a sound-maker, but they cannot account for the evolution of language, the multiple and complex changes human languages have undergone in the course of their history since such changes require a concept of language to begin with. In the second instance, they ignore the fact that fundamental linguistic concepts are grounded in elemental corporeal concepts forged in the course of infancy. For example, elemental spatial concepts such as near, far, open, close, inside, and outside, are contingent on kinetic/kinesthetic experience; elemental qualitative concepts such as smooth, sudden, intense, attenuated, and soft, are embodied in affective experience. Affective/tactile-kinesthetic concepts are clearly not lexical creations but the result of affective/tactile-kinesthetic experience; they are clearly tied not to static phenomena but to dynamic happenings and experience. Indeed, when concepts are regarded as strictly lexical creations — coming pre-packaged with the language one speaks and reads — the challenge of languaging affective/tactile-kinesthetic experiences never surfaces and the very possibility of the challenge is denied.

If we are to rise to the challenge, we need to experience it in person, turning attention to experience itself, acknowledging and in turn examining what is there. For example, the standard spatial coordinates of the body — up/down, right/left, front/back — are objective coordinates deriving from bodily experience. The spatiality of the body, however, is actually four dimensional, not with respect to the commonly added temporal dimension, but with respect to a further spatial dimension that is rarely recognized or included in discussions of the spatiality of the body, namely, inside/outside. This fourth coordinate is directly experienced by living bodies and in significantly basic ways not only in terms of the experiential difference between attending to the felt dynamics of one's movement and attending to its perceived three-dimensionality,[1] but in terms of the body itself. At the most obvious level, heart flutterings, a gripping

---

1   Compare, for example, the difference between waving one's arm overhead and feeling the particular rhythm and changing directions of the movement, and waving one's arm overhead and perceiving the movement as a three-dimensional spatial happening.

overall tension, stomach rumblings and churnings, head poundings and pressures, back pains, and so on, attest to experiences of "insides" and to their quintessential import. As neonates, our lives were strongly focused on insides, insides not as opposed to outsides, but as the felt center of dramas such as "hunger storms."

To rise to the challenge, we furthermore need to move ourselves to the end that we catch ourselves in the act of being the animate selves we are. In the experience of self-movement, the mind/body 'problem' disappears; we are all of a piece in the experience, whether we are feeling the qualitative dynamics of the movement as it unfolds or concentrating on learning or perfecting a particular movement, focusing attention on its directional changes, for example, or its speed, or its degree of extension, thus attending objectively to some particular aspect of the movement. While we regularly attribute qualities to objects, self-movement — like any movement — is not an object unless we make it so, precisely by observing it in its particulars as it unfolds. In either instance, being totally engaged in our movement, there is no vehicle and no pilot, only an experienced kinetic dynamic or prominenced aspect of movement. In feeling a kinetic dynamic in the very process of moving, we experience a dynamic form-in-the-making, a qualitative and harmoniously unfolding whole. We meet the challenge face to face when we realize that the qualitative nature of that harmoniously unfolding whole is difficult to describe, more difficult than the qualitative nature of particular aspects of our movement such as its speed, its degree of extension, or its directional changes. This is because the experience of a qualitative dynamic engenders not just one or another quality of movement but the multiple qualities of movement combined — tensional, linear, areal, and projectional qualities, all in one complex whole.[2] The qualities in fact constitute the movement itself; they are the *sine qua non* of its being the movement it is, and in turn, the particular kinesthetic experience it is. Qualities of movement are thus not attributes of movement the way qualities are attributes of objects. A particular apple, for example, could be on the way to ripening or past prime, yellow instead of red, mealy instead of crisp. Though changing qualities over time, we commonly regard the apple as being the same apple throughout. In contrast, though we can speed up a movement or make it larger, the movement is not experienced as the same movement, "only larger" or "speeded up." "Making larger" or "speeding up" are linguistically-aided objectifications of movement. As actually experienced, the movement is a different movement because it creates a different qualitative dynamic. To describe its qualita-

---

2   For an in-depth analysis of the separate qualities and the overall dynamic possibilities they create, see Sheets-Johnstone, 1966 [1979,1980], 1999.

tive dynamic is challenging precisely because the dynamic is qualitatively nonobjective: it does not simply take place in space and in time but creates its own distinctive time, space, and force. To see movement as taking place *in* space and *in* time is in actuality to see not movement but an object in motion. If one is attentive to the spluttering of a blown-up but untied balloon as it is released, for example, that is, if one is attentive to its movement dynamics, one clearly experiences not a balloon *in* space and *in* time, but an erratic and unpredictable spatio-temporal-energic dynamics. As a naming device, the word 'spluttering' falls short of doing full justice to that dynamics. Only if the word resonates in some bodily felt ways, whether evoking incipient movement responses or kinetic/kinesthetic imagery does it rise to the challenge of languaging experience.

To spell out the challenge more fully and thereby answer to the liabilities, an extended case study of a particular experience — the experience of inside(s) — will be presented and analyzed from a diversity of perspectives. As prelude to the examination and analysis, it will be helpful to exemplify the experience of insides further, this time by way of an adult language that is *not* an everyday language. We can do this by consulting how a classic playwright rises to the challenge of languaging experience, precisely eschewing conventional expressions in order to bring to life for others the immediate affective felt sense of a character's aliveness. As will be evident, it is not a matter of specifying bodily churnings, tensions, poundings, contractions, and so on; it is a matter of entering into the felt qualitative aspects of a character's feelings. Shakespeare does just this when he puts us inside suffering, that is, into the dark equivocations and dark despair that respectively clothe Hamlet's and Macbeth's thoughts of death:

> To be, or not to be, — that is the question: —
> Whether 'tis nobler in the mind to suffer
> The slings and arrows of outrageous fortune,
> Or to take arms against a sea of troubles,
> And by opposing end them? — To die, — to sleep; —
> No more; and by a sleep to say we end
> The heart-ache and the thousand natural shocks
> That flesh is heir to, — 'tis a consummation
> Devoutly to be wish'd. To die, to sleep;
> To sleep! perchance to dream: ay, there's the rub;
> For in that sleep of death what dreams may come
> When we have shuffled off this mortal coil,
> ... For who would bear the whips and scorns of time,
> ... But that the dread of something after death,
> ... makes us rather bear those ills we have
> Than fly to others that we know not of?

(*Hamlet*, Act III, Scene 1).

Tomorrow, and tomorrow, and tomorrow,
Creeps in this petty pace from day to day,
To the last syllable of recorded time;
And all our yesterdays have lighted fools
The way to dusty death. Out, out, brief candle!
Life's but a walking shadow; a poor player,
That struts and frets his hour upon the stage,
And then is heard no more: it is a tale
Told by an idiot, full of sound and fury,
Signifying nothing.

(*Macbeth*, Act V, Scene V).

Compare the above soliloquies with everyday language: "I don't know what to do — I feel depressed by all that's going on and like possibly killing myself. But maybe what will happen to me after death is worse than life"; "I feel totally down and gloomy and like wanting to end it all: life is so meaningless." In Shakespeare's plays, first-person bodies are speaking, but clearly not in an everyday idiom. Dire sufferings envelop them and are articulated in ponderous thoughts. Insides are exposed; they are languaged.

2. Inside(s): Ontogenetical Experience

In *The Child's Conception of Space*, Jean Piaget and Bärbel Inhelder write that in contrast to a surface where "one element may be perceived as surrounded by others", in a three-dimensional framework, "enclosure takes the form of the relation of 'insideness', as in the case of an object in a closed box", and that in fact, "'enclosure' undergoes a complex process of evolution, particularly as regards three dimensions" (Piaget and Inhelder, 1967, p. 8). They do not specify the complex process, but their initial observation with respect to 'insideness' is borne out by one of Piaget's observations, which in truth reveals more than he intends. In *La naissance de l'intelligence*, he describes a sixteen-month-old infant opening and closing her mouth several times in prelude to her attempt to open a matchbox. Rather than be intrigued or even puzzled by the lingual acts, Piaget interprets them as a *faute de mieux*: "Lacking the power to think in words or clear visual images, the infant uses, as 'signifier' or symbol, a simple motor indication" (Piaget, 1968, p. 294). He in consequence misses the extraordinary conceptual reality; infants think in bodily terms. They think in nonlinguistic concepts, not in words but in movement, knowing through their own experiences that openings lead to insides. In effect, bodily experiences testify to the fact that the concept of insides exists prior to language.

Experimental studies of infants and young children validate the point along further experiential lines. The studies attest to an infant's fascination for putting—or pouring—one thing inside another, including its own thumb inside the opening that is its mouth. Psychologist T.G.R. Bower writes of his daughter's spending the better part of a night opening his hand, putting something inside it, closing his hand and moving it to a new location, then opening his hand to see if the object was still there (Bower, 1974, p. 238). Piaget himself documents instances in which children put keys inside dishes and watch chains inside boxes (Piaget, 1968). That infants and young children are fascinated by insides should not be surprising given basic facts of human life: bodies go inside clothes; food goes inside mouths; sounds come from insides, breath come from insides, excretory products come from insides, sneezes and coughs come from insides, and so on, not to mention birth itself, an event not remembered, but not thereby not experienced. Insides are fascinating because they are the locus of a multitude of ever-changing experiences; they are the site of untold dynamic happenings. Moreover corporeal insides have the power to transform one thing into another: a voice transforms silence into sound; saliva transforms what is otherwise relatively dry into something juicier; phosphenes transform darkness into patterns of light; insides transform inspired cold air into a warm outward breath. Such powers are matched by the fact that bodily insides are themselves transformable as well as transforming. In nursing or eating, for example, a feeling of emptiness is transformed into a feeling of fullness and satisfaction; the felt character of the body changes in virtue of changing insides. It is not surprising then that the transforming and transformable powers of insides are fascinating and in turn provoke wonder. They provoke astonishment and awe in equal measure because they are complex, unexpected, and not readily or easily explainable or understandable phenomena.

That inside and insideness are corporeal concepts deriving from bodily experience from the beginning of our lives, and that, not being directly explorable like concrete worldly objects, they are mysterious in unfathomable ways can hardly be denied. The literature on language-learning by infants and young children supports this conclusion by providing still further evidence of the significance of insides as a nonlinguistic spatial concept deriving from bodily experience. In particular, numerous studies have shown the prepositional primacy of *in* as both locative state and locative act; that is, the first preposition that a child learns has to do with one thing being inside another or with putting one thing inside another. Psychologist Eve Clark, for example, writes that when a one-and-a-half year old child is given a box and a small toy mouse to play with, the child will put the mouse *in* the box, regardless of whether the box is lying on its side or has its opening facing up." If the child is given a toy table instead of a box, he or she will put the mouse *on* the table (Clark, 1979, p. 159). On the basis of this data, Clark identifies two rules on which "children of this age appear to base their selections", that is, choose what to do with the objects they are given. Rule 1 states, "If B is a container, A belongs inside it"; Rule 2 states, "If B has a supporting surface, A belongs on it" (*ibid.*). The primacy of *in* is implicit in the rule order, a primacy that might be surprising given the fact that the concept of three-dimensional *insides* is the more sophisticated concept. Surprise vanishes, however, in light of everyday bodily experiences. That the concept in fact takes precedence as well over the spatial concept of *under*, a fact noted by many researchers (e.g., Clark, 1973; Grieve, Hoogenraad, Murray, 1977; Cook, 1978), indirectly supports the origin of the concept in bodily experience. Oddly enough, no researcher pinpoints bodily experience as the conceptual source. The most that is suggested with respect to the primacy of *in* in infants' and young children's language-learning is that "the general rule in lexical development may be concept first, then word, the reverse being "exceptional" (Cook, 1978, p. 55); and that "nonlinguistic strategies probably form the basis for [children's] hypotheses about the meanings of new words (Clark, 1973, p. 181).

3. Insides: Caves

A perspicuous and provocative descriptive account of experience by Leonardo da Vinci captures the fascination of insides from an altogether different perspective: that of an ordinary adult human coming upon a cave. Da Vinci writes,

> Urged on by my eagerness to see the many varied and strange forms shaped by artful nature, I wandered for some time among the shady rocks and finally came to the entrance of a great cavern. At first I stood before it dumbfounded, knowing nothing of such a thing; then I bent over with my left hand braced against my knee and my right shading my squinting, deep-searching eyes; again and again I bent over, peering here and there to discern something inside; but the all-embracing darkness revealed nothing.
>
> Standing there, I was suddenly struck by two things, fear and longing: fear of the dark ominous cavern; longing to see if inside there was something wonderful (da Vinci, 1959, p. 19).

Da Vinci's account testifies to the fact that the fundamental fascination with insides is not just of moment in infancy and early childhood and of linguistic significance in that period of human life, but a marker of experiences and a conceptual invariant whose power does not wane. Where a sense of the extraordinary attaches itself spontaneously to experiences of insides, it does so because the phenomenon is experienced as being beyond one's immediate ken and powers of understanding—precisely something *wonderful*. Caves are just such phenomena. While *wonderful* describes the general aura and allure of their insides, however, it does not describe the richness and complexity of the experience of insides themselves or what one might find in actually 'being inside'. The challenge of languaging the experience of 'being inside' remains.

Paleolithic cave art provides an apt example. Several facts and aspects of paleolithic cave art are in fact enlightening. To begin with, it is striking that researchers who have written about the drawings never mention anything about caves themselves. In particular, our humans ancestors who lived twenty to forty thousand years ago and who painted on the walls of caves knew nothing of the geology of caves, of the geology of the earth generally, or of the earth as a planet. In contrast, contemporary art historians, anthropologists, paleoanthropologists, and archaeologists consistently approach the *cave* aspect of paleolithic cave drawings as a geological given of the planet earth. In taking caves for granted, they pass over the original experience of caves. It is worthwhile spelling out their omission in some detail, for it leads directly to the challenge of languaging experience and to a methodology that allows one to rise to the challenge.

I elsewhere showed how in taking caves as a geological given, contemporary researchers take for granted that to enter into a cave is to go *inside*. As a result of taking insides for granted in this way, they take other knowledge for granted as well:

> [T]hey take for granted a radically different earthly landscape and its radically different sensory and spatial qualities — the underfoot terrain, the silence, the natural formations, and so on. Moreover, they take for granted their ready-made — and readily-accessible — knowledge as to how the particular speleological features they see and feel are formed, indeed, how caves themselves are formed and what kind of life — floral and faunal — to expect within them. In consequence, when they go into a cave to explore it and examine its artworks, in fact when anyone conversant with twentieth-century geology goes into any cave to explore or examine it, they are not surprised at the physical features — visual, audible, tactile — of a cave. In proceeding deeper and deeper inside they anticipate finding passages that are tight, that twist and turn, and that seem interminable; findings caverns that are expansive and areas that seem like 'rooms'; finding stalagmites and stalactites; finding moisture, water drippage, water flows; and so on. In short, because they have a twentieth-century concept of *caves* prior to entering into any one cave, they find the experience of *being inside* neither remarkable in itself nor remarkable with respect to perceived features. Even associations such as feeling oneself to be inside the bowels of the earth, for example, are not remarkable but bear testimony to a certain logic of resemblance, what [philosopher Susanne] Langer would term a 'logical congruity of form': animal bowels also twist and turn, are seemingly endless, are moist, and so on (Sheets-Johnstone, 1990, p. 235).

If we ask what it was like to enter a cave with no such geological — or anatomical — knowledge, we come to the challenge of reconstructing an experience we never had and never will have, and the likes of which we never had and never will have. To rise to the challenge, we need indeed to eschew the knowledge we actually have of caves and enter them as if for the first time. To do this, we need a methodology that allows us to uncover what, in the normal course of our everyday lives, we take for granted. In this respect, a phenomenological methodology is without peer. Through the procedure of bracketing, we distance ourselves from what philosopher Edmund Husserl — the founder of phenomenology — termed 'the natural attitude', that is, the attitude that allows us to take whatever comes our way unquestioningly as a known item in the world — a rock, a breeze, a bird — or if something unknown — a new sight, sound, or smell — as something unquestioningly knowable (see, for example, Husserl, 1983, 1970). The natural attitude allows us to go along with our judgments, beliefs, and expectations and to get on with our lives in the world in an unquestioning way. If we ask how we came to the knowledge we have, we are commonly at a loss to trace out its developmental path. What we need is precisely a method by which we can recover the complex of experiences that define our knowledge. When we reverse the natural attitude, we do just this. We make the familiar strange, and thereby come to understand how the familiar came to be familiar, that is, how we came to make what was once new and unfamiliar, familiar. In the process of doing so, we are challenged to language experience, challenged to describe in exacting ways that complex of experiences that defines our knowledge, or in other words, how we have come to the meanings and values we have. We can exemplify the challenge in the context of paleolithic cave art by singling out significant aspects of the natural attitude.

To begin with, in our everyday lives, we regularly find and expect to find that it gets dark and stays dark over certain regular period of time, and that during that time, we sleep; we find and expect to find that we can stand on the earth as a surface, that that surface will support us; we find and expect to find that while we can dig into the earth and uproot vegetables and tubers, the earth has no *insides* as such; we find and expect to find that when we pick up a pen, pencil, or crayon, that we can readily write or draw on paper and other surfaces. In short, we take periods of light and darkness, functional aspects of the earth, writing and drawing, for granted. To enter into a cave as paleolithic humans entered into a cave is to enter into a world that precisely cannot be taken for granted in such ways, not only because that world is different, but because it is extraordinarily different. At minimum, we feel our way into strange and eerie insides; we are surrounded by queer and unknown forms; we are enveloped in a space opaque to everyday visions and sounds. All those aspects of experience that contemporary researchers find and expect to find in the caves them-selves are totally new. "Being inside" is an entirely different experience, precisely an *extra*-ordinary experience. The power to transform insides is part of that *extra*-ordinary experience. By *drawing* on the walls of caves, one can bring forms from the outside world inside—bison, mammoths, horses, oxen, for example—and thereby populate an unfamiliar world with the familiar. Drawing on the walls of caves is from this bracketed perspective not interpreted as "hunting-magic" (Lommel, 1966, p. 29), for example, or as an "antagonism between male and female values" —a "fer-tility cult" (Leroi-Gourhan, 1982, p. 173)—or as "a free play of signifiers" equivalent to meaningless "art-for-art's sake" (Halverson, 1987, p. 69), but is experienced as a way of fathoming insides in the experience of 'being inside'. In fathoming caves, our ancestors brought them within their ken of experience by painting on their walls, inscribing them with forms of life they found and knew outside. In this understanding of paleolithic cave art, the concept of "insides" is preserved as the foundational, spatially reso-nant experiential concept it is—and from the very beginning of life: from the advent of birth itself.

4. Insides: Breath, Pneuma, and Spiritus

Insides have the power of life and death over us. They are normally rela-tively quiet and certainly we prefer it that way, for when they call attention to themselves, especially out of the blue, interrupting the normal flow of our lives, it commonly means something is wrong. Calling attention to themselves in this way, our bodies — or parts of our bodies — easily become objectified; while still part of us, they become distant, something we pos-sess but a wayward possession: "Is it my liver, doctor?" we might ask; "Do I have pneumonia?" "Do I have cancer?" In such situations, a fear of the body may set in: we do not know what it will do to us. Indeed, "fear of the dark ominous cavern" finely pinpoints the fear of what might be lurking in our own insides. The feeling is not only unsettling, but the actual situa-tion may be a possible harbinger of death, an eventuality that not we but our insides control, just as they control spiritus, pneuma, and breath.

At rest or in meditative experiences, insides are commonly present only in the form of breath and the silence that rings in our ears. All is quiet. But all is also warm and alive. *Pneuma*—what classics scholar Arthur Peck characterizes as the 'connate heat' of the body—is directly related to life and to the breath. Following up his thesis that the word cannot actually be adequately translated, Peck writes that "*Pneuma* is certainly corporeal; it is, as we should say, a kind of matter; and it is connate, congenital, present in an animal from the moment of conception and so long as the animal remains alive. It is, in fact, the primary vehicle of life and of the processes peculiar to living organisms" (Peck, 1953, p. 111). While he goes on to emphasize that *pneuma* is not the breath, that is, not the air an animal inhales, since respiration, warmth, and life are connected, and non-respiration, coldness, and death are connected, *pneuma* is intimately related to breath. Both are present as long as a creature is alive. Moreover like the natural connate heat of the body, there is something wondrous about the physiognomy of breath. When one pays attention to the sheer experience of breathing, remarkable aspects are immediately apparent. Its consistent two-phased rhythm is remarkable; its seemingly unsuppressible persistence is remarkable; its extraordinary warmth is remarkable. The warmth of the breath in particular appears quite incredible. The air breathed in can be cold as ice, but lo and behold! when breathed out, it is all warm and toasty. The seemingly unsuppressible persistence of the breath, however, is equally incredible in that one cannot commit suicide by holding one's breath. Perceived in this way, one can readily understand why the breath is regarded in many non-Western traditions, and was regarded in the early history of Western scientific thought itself, as something wondrous and quintessential to life. Breathing, warmth, and aliveness form a natural trinity. Moreover Latin as well as ancient Greek confirms their linkage. *Spiritus*—meaning not just breath, but soul, mind, life—and its English derivatives—not just inspiration and expiration, but inspire and expire—testifies to an integral relationship.

The trinity dissolves and necessarily loses its wondrousness when breathing is explained as a mechanism for oxidizing tissues and warmth is explained by the process of oxidation. Indeed, where direct experiences of our bodies recede and functional explanations take their place, warmth and breath lose their immediately felt living significance. Not that we are regularly aware of ourselves in breathing and of our natural warmth or that we must initiate or keep close watch on our breath. On the contrary, breathing takes place by itself; it happens naturally without our doing anything. That breath comes and goes without any help from us makes its all the more wondrous. *Pneuma* suggests as much. Peck's detachment of *pneuma* from breath notwithstanding, the meaning of *pneuma* derives etymologically from "breath, blow", and the word's basic meaning is "'air in motion'" (Oxford Classical Dictionary, 3rd ed. 1996). We rarely put or keep 'air in motion'. The self-propelling dynamics of breath, like the generation of warmth and the autopoesis of life itself are part of the wonder of insides. We thus see from this perspective too that insides are not an object but akin to fluids, shifting and fluctuating on their own, precisely dynamic rather than static. We can see further that the concept of breath as 'air in motion' is tied to our own animation as living bodies, that is, to first-person spatial experiences of ourselves in motion. It is thus tied not to a mechanics of life discovered after the fact, but to life itself as it is lived.

The full power of insides is commonly muted, but when it appears on the horizon and its full import comes to be experienced, not only do we realize that no object is being named in the experience of insides and that the concept of insides is a corporeal concept, precisely as Peck suggests of *Pneuma* when he says it "is certainly corporeal", but we realize further why languaging the experience of insides is the challenge it is. Like bodily feelings, "air in motion", the spontaneous generation of warmth from insides, and the animation of life itself are through and through dynamic phenomena.

V: Insides: The Shadow

Psychologically inflected probings into insides disclose a further dimension that, though named, is not formally an object, and though dynamic, is not straightforwardly so. That a shadow side of ourselves exists is evident in feelings of guilt, remorse, envy, shame, and so on, feelings that are uncomfortable and tend to be suppressed. Jung's concept of the shadow falls between object and dynamic in that while *shadow* names some-*thing* inside ourselves, the something it names embraces feelings, proclivities, and attitudes that are under cover and that remain under cover unless we open ourselves to them, exploring our psychic inside like the "dark ominous cavern" it is. The shadow, in other words, comprises all those aspects of ourselves we in some way disown or do not want to admit or acknowledge — feelings of fear, a wish that another were dead or out of our way, a desire for revenge, a disposition toward greed, and so on. Were we to admit these inside facets of ourselves, we would be other than the person we want to be and want to show ourselves to be. In short, the shadow is an unwanted dimension of ourselves that we find when we look penetratingly and honestly *inside*.

Jung delineates the shadow as one side of our insides. He describes psychic processes as "behav[ing] like a scale along which consciousness 'slides'", resulting in a "psychic one-sidedness which is typical of the normal man of today" (Jung, 1969, p. 117). The sliding may be now in the direction of instinct, now in the direction of spirit, for example, that is, toward now one, now another antithetical pole of an oppositional pairing. Psychic one-sidedness, Jung states, "can be removed by what I have called the 'realization of the shadow'" (*ibid.*, p. 118). His subsequent if brief comments on the process necessary to removal are provocative. They document from a psychological perspective the dynamic nature of the shadow and merit full quotation.

> A less 'poetic' and more scientific-looking Greco-Latin neologism could easily have been coined for this operation [i.e., 'realization of the shadow']. In psychology, however, one is to be dissuaded from ventures of this sort, at least when dealing with eminently practical problems. Among these is the 'realization of the shadow', the growing awareness of the inferior part of the personality, which should not be twisted into an intellectual activity, for *it has far more the meaning of a suffering and a passion that implicate the whole man*. The essence of that which has to be realized and assimilated has been expressed so trenchantly and so plastically in poetic language by the word 'shadow' that it would be almost presumptuous not to avail oneself of this linguistic heritage. Even the term 'inferior part of the personality' is inadequate and misleading, whereas 'shadow' presumes nothing *that would rigidly fix its content*. The 'man without a shadow' is statistically the commonest human type, one who imagines he actually *is* only what he cares to know about himself. Unfortunately neither the so-called religious man nor the man of scientific pretensions forms any exception to this rule (*ibid.*; italics added).

As Jung shows in his psychoanalytic writings, the shadow weaves its way silently into seemingly unperturbed areas of a person's life, precisely insofar as the person "imagines he actually *is* only what he cares to know about himself." Moreover sufferings and passions of a person's shadow side can wax in intensity when exacerbated by circumstances that bring them close to the surface. The shadow is indeed a plastic 'entity' at the same time that it is a dynamic phenomenon, a matter of feelings, proclivities, and attitudes that attest to a 'content' that is not rigidly fixed, and that, though unacknowledged, "implicate[s] the whole man". Jung describes and in fact emphasizes how, in default of acknowledging shadow aspects of oneself, one projects one's shadow onto others, seeing in another one's own cupidity, for example, or one's own fears, foisting onto others the dark interiority that is in actuality a part of oneself. It is not surprising, then, that Jung recognizes the shadow as a moral problem. He writes,

> The shadow is a moral problem that challenges the whole ego-personality, for no one can become conscious of the shadow without considerable moral effort. To become conscious of it involves recognizing the dark aspects of the personality as present and real. This act is the essential condition for any kind of self-knowledge, and it therefore, as a rule, meets with considerable resistance (Jung, 1968, p. 8).

The point here is not to pursue Jung's psychoanalytic, but to highlight the challenge of acknowledging the shadow side of ourselves and the challenge of languaging it in ways that justly illuminates it. Such illuminations are dramatically in evidence in the soliloquies of many of Shakespeare's ill-fated heroes whose introspective ruminations, as we have already seen, expose insides. The shadow side appears in some of these soliloquies, not only in relatively brief self-deriding moments, as in Hamlet's "O! what a rogue and peasant slave am I!" but in the more nefarious soliloquized plottings of Gloucester, for example, in his resolute intention to become Richard III. Musing on his physical deformities and his inability to "prove a lover", he affirms his determination "to prove a villain" by setting his brother and his father (King Edward) "[i]n deadly hate the one against the other", and this in order that he himself will be crowned king. His plan will work, he says, "if King Edward be as true and just/As I am subtle, false, and treacherous" (King Richard III, Act 1, Scene 1). In this and other such soliloquies, it is not just that insides are exposed, but that the shadow side of those insides — not just one's fears and self-doubts, for example, but one's cunning and deceit — are exposed and languaged. It is critical to note that what is languaged is not itself language-dependent; Richard's plan to do away with his brother, for example, is not contingent on language any more than his desire to be king or his physical deformities are dependent on language. Moreover what is languaged is not some *thing* — the words 'treacherous' and 'villain', for example, do not name any-*thing* but descriptively pinpoint a nonlinguistic way of being toward others.

Shakespeare's soliloquies are indeed testimonials to the full range of insides; they give voice to the flow of a character's feelings and thoughts in a language that does full justice to the complexities and subtleties of those feelings and thoughts, their self-recriminations, anxieties, memories, questions, hesitations, desires, and so on. To write comprehendingly about a character's shadow side, one must be aware of and have reflected on one's own inner processes. In his book, *Will in the World: How Shakespeare Became Shakespeare*, literature scholar Stephen Greenblatt stresses what we might designate Shakespeare's 'languaging of interiority'. In the character of Hamlet, for example, he shows how Shakespeare presents us with "an intense representation of inwardness" (Greenblatt, 2004, p. 323); how, in the character of Richard III, he presents us with a less intense representation, a soliloquy that "has a staccato vigor … as a way of sketching inner conflict" (*ibid.*, p. 299); how, in the character of Richard II, he presents us with "a kind of inner theater, akin to that already found in Richard III's soliloquy but with a vastly increased complexity, subtlety, and above all, self-consciousness", an inner theater in which Richard "watches himself think, struggling to forge a metaphoric link between his prison and the world, reaching a dead end, and then forcing his imagination to renew the effort: 'Yet I'll hammer it out'" (*ibid.*, p. 300). Greenblatt's point is that Shakespeare had "[a] growing interest in the hidden processes of interiority" (*ibid.*), and that characters involved in those hidden processes are "suspended, for virtually the whole length of a play" in what he terms a "strange interim" (*ibid.*, p. 302). Clearly that 'strange interim' is a particular unfolding inward dynamic that is progressively acknowledged and languaged. Illuminating "hidden processes of interiority", Shakespeare's soliloquies are indeed existential soundings, not from the shallows, but from the deep. His plays would hardly resound as deeply as they do in us or be valued as the enduring classics they are for us if the inwardness of his characters' profound ruminations did not touch something equally profound within us.

In sum, psychological probings disclose a shadow side of insides that is alive with feelings and thoughts normally disowned and unarticulated. Shakespeare's ill-fated characters are emblematic of this dark but dynamic side of the human psyche. They not only meet the challenge of languaging experience, but by the depth of their soundings and powers of evocation, transcend it, bringing what is below the surface to brilliant light.

6. Conclusion

Multiple perspectives on the experience of insides show no objects to be named but rather a complex diversity of feelings and thoughts that exceed the bounds of everyday language precisely because they are experienced dynamically and are in fact dynamic. The perspectives show further that the concept of insides derives from just such dynamic experiences. To meet the challenge of languaging these dynamics is to be true to the truths of experience. As indicated by Shakespeare's soliloquies, by "hunger storms" and infant experience generally, by paleolithic cave drawings, by breath, pneuma, and spiritus, and by the shadow side of our insides, the truths clearly require a methodology proper to the task, i.e., a methodology that follows along phenomenological lines. Such a methodology demands our drawing back from an easy, ready-made everyday language and our turning attention first of all to experience itself. In phenomenological terms, it demands that we *bracket* our natural attitude toward the world and thereby meet an experience as if for the first time. By bracketing, we make the familiar strange: we put aside everyday beliefs, reactions, judgments, *and* everyday habits of languaging experience. We are thereby able to foreground experience itself and listen to its interior dynamics. In doing so, we actually become aware of how everyday beliefs, reactions, judgments, *and* everyday language habitually color over the dynamics, hiding them behind an easy and ready manner of living in the world.[3] A keen literary imagination involves a similar backward step away from everyday language and a turning of attention first of all to experience itself. The credibility of a character, after all, is contingent on an author's ability to describe in livingly resonant ways the interior dynamics of the character's experiences — his or her motivations, plans, recollections, grievances, cravings, and so on. However closely tied to the author, the character is not the author in person, but a person in his or her own right. Accordingly, the author enters into and inhabits the character's world, a world of values, feelings, actions, and beliefs that are not his or her own. In effect, what the author describes are experiences not within an autobiography, but within a fiction so real as to be convincing. A keen literary imagination rings dynamically true to the truths of human experience. The challenge of languaging experience is thus no mere "subjective" enterprise. On the contrary, for a literary imagination as for a phenomenologist, the challenge catapults one into languaging foundational aspects of animate experience. While humans talk and read daily, they do not start in this foundational way, from linguistic scratch as it were. They do not make the familiar strange, but draw on what is already habitually and conventionally there for them. Further, not only is a ready-made language at their command, but their everyday point of interest commonly lies not in perspicuous and meticulous descriptions of an experience, particularly descriptions of its dynamics, but in labels that succinctly capture the general flavor of the experience — it was "scary", "fun", "awesome", "nice", "okeh", and so on. Even the ready-made language by which one describes the composition and placement of muscle tissue or the pathways of cranial nerves, for example, and the ready-made language that one draws on to name hypothetical structures in the brain — "feature analyzers", "cognitive maps", and "dedicated brain modules", for example — is not up to the foundational task.[4] As emphasized above, to describe the dynamics, one

3   The challenge might be likened to the challenge of a scientific comprehension of the body as a singular living organism rather than as a series of discrete systems — physiological, genetic, anatomical, neurological, immunological, circulatory, excretory, and so on. A number of years ago, the idea in scientific circles was in fact to connect psychological, neurological, and immunological systems into a singular whole, into a psycho-neuro-immunology. Certainly multiple facets of bodily experience attest to the scientific challenge of interrelating discretely considered objective systems of the body. The challenge of languaging experience, however, is more directly akin to the challenges Charles Darwin met in the course of his five-year travels on the Beagle. New and alien worlds appeared over the entire course of his travels, worlds demanding finely detailed descriptions not only of the animate forms inhabiting those worlds, but the actual lives of those animate forms. For more on the confluence of evolutionary, phenomenological, and literary approaches to the challenge of languaging experience, see Sheets-Johnstone, 2002.

4   Even when a new species is discovered, it is readily languageable within a ready-made nomenclature system.

must first actually experience them. In actually experiencing them, one readily finds that "For all this, names are lacking." The phrase comes from Husserl[5] and is apt beyond words, one might say. *Names* are indeed lacking not only because everyday language is basically deficient with respect to dynamics but because *names* cannot do justice to dynamics. The situation might be compared to those instances in which we are at a loss for words, so stunned by something that we cannot speak. In such instances, we are in thrall to the felt sense of an event. It is emotionally laden in the double sense of permeating us to the bone and animating — or not animating — us to the bone. Indeed, emotions move through us in distinctive ways and move us to move in distinctive ways. Their double dynamic is as experientially evident in feelings of determination, conviction, hesitancy, doubt, and curiosity, that is, in what are sometimes referred to as 'cognitive emotions' — as it is in feelings of fear, sadness, and delight. In each instance, a felt dynamic moves through our bodies and moves us to move — or not move — in an affectively unique manner.[6] A dynamic congruity obtains between affect and movement, feelings and action. The challenge of languaging experience, of distilling experienced "hidden processes of interiority" and languaging their basically nonlinguistic dynamics is clearly illuminated, even crystallized, in experience itself.

References

Bower, T.G.R. 1974. *Development in Infancy*. San Francisco: W. H. Freeman and Co.

Clark, Eve V. 1973. "Non-Linguistic Stragegies and the Acquisition of Word Meanings," *Cognition* 2: 161–82.

Clark, Eve V. 1979. "Building a Vocabulary: Words for Objects, Actions and Relations." In *Language Acquisition*, ed. Paul Fletcher and Michael Garman. Cambridge: Cambridge University Press, pp. 149–60.

Cook, Nancy. 1978. "In, On and Under Revisited Again." In *Papers and Reports on Child Language Development* 15. Stanford: Stanford University Press, pp. 38–45.

---

5   Husserl uses the phrase in the context of trying to describe what he calls "the temporally constitutive flux" of internal time consciousness (Husserl, 1964, p. 100). Though he makes no mention of dynamics, his point that "For all this, names are lacking", is implicitly insightful with respect to dynamic phenomena; that is, to say that "For all this, names are lacking" is not simply to point to a deficiency in language, but to call attention to a phenomenon that cannot be named to begin with. Indeed, he writes, "We can only say that this flux is something which we name in conformity with what is constituted, but it is nothing temporally "Objective" (*ibid.*).

6   Moreover particular emotional experiences — of anger, irritation, frustration, dismay, alarm, apprehension, relief, calm, and so on — move through our bodies and move us to move — or not move — in affectively unique ways. Any named emotion is, in effect, not one thing, one state of affairs. On the contrary, any named emotion has a gamut of possible variations, variations that themselves can wax and wane, and in so doing can shade off into another emotion: anger into dismay, for example, dismay into apprehension, apprehension into relief, and so on.

da Vinci, Leonardo. 1959. *Philosophical Diary*, trans. Wade Baskin. New York: Wisdom Library.

Greenblatt, Stephen. 2004. *Will in the World: How Shakespeare Became Shakespeare*. New York: W.W. Norton and Co.

Grieve, Robert, Robert Hoogenraad, and Diarmid Murray. 1977. "On the Young Child's Use of Lexis and Syntax in Understanding Locative Instructions." *Cognition* 5: 235–50.

Halverson, John. 1987. "Art for Art's Sake in the Paleolithic." *Current Anthropology* 28/1: 63–89.

Husserl, Edmund. 1966. *The Phenomenology of Internal Time-Consciousness*, ed. Martin Heidegger, trans. James S. Churchill. Bloomington: Indiana University Press.

Husserl, Edmund. 1970. *The Crisis of European Sciences and Transcendental Phenomenology*, trans. David Carr. Evanston: Northwestern University Press.

Husserl, Edmund. 1983. *Ideas Pertaining to a Pure Phenomenology and to a Phenomenological Philosophy (Ideas I)*, trans. Fred Kersten. The Hague: Martinus Nijhoff Publishers.

Jung, Carl G. 1968. *Aion: Researches into the Phenomenology of the Self*, 2nd ed., trans. R.F.C. Hull. Princeton: Princeton University Press.

Jung, Carl G. 1969. *On the Nature of the Psyche*, trans. R.F.C. Hull. Princeton: Princeton University Press.

Leroi-Gourhan, André. 1982. *The Dawn of European Art*, trans. Sara Champion. Cambridge: Cambridge University Press.

Lommel, Andreas. 1966. *Prehistoric and Primitive Man*. New York: McGraw-Hill.

Peck, Arthur. 1975. "The Connate Pneuma." In *Science Medicine and History*, ed. E. Ashworth Underwood, vol. 1. New York: Arno Press (reprint edition), pp. 111–21.

Piaget, Jean. 1968. *La naissance de l'intelligence chez l'enfant*, 6th ed. Neuchatel, Switzerland: Delachaux et Niestlé.

Piaget, Jean and Bärbel Inhelder. 1967. *The Child's Conception of Space*, trans. F.J. Langdon and J.L. Lunzer. New York: W. W. Norton & Co.

Sheets-Johnstone, Maxine. 1966 [1979/1980]. *The Phenomenology of Dance* Madison, WI: University of Wisconsin Press; 2nd editions: London: Dance Books Ltd.; New York: Arno Press.

Sheets-Johnstone, Maxine. 1979; New York: Arno Press, 1980].

Sheets-Johnstone, Maxine. 1999. *The Primacy of Movement*. Amsterdam/ Philadelphia: John Benjamins.

Sheets-Johnstone, Maxine. 2002. "Descriptive Foundations," *Interdisciplinary Studies in Literature and Environment* 9/1: 165–79.

Stern, Daniel N. 1990. *Diary of a Baby*. New York: Basic Books.

Subject Index

Name Index